Defending young people

in the criminal justice system

third edition

D1514188

Mark Ashford is a solicitor with Taylor Nichol, a criminal defence practice in north London, where he specialises in representing young people. He regularly trains lawyers, social workers and mental health professionals on the youth justice system as well as speaking on subjects related to youth crime. Mark Ashford has been a member of the Barrow Cadbury Trust Commission on Young Adults in the Criminal Justice System (report published in 2005) and a Royal College of Psychiatrists working party on child defendants (report published in 2006).

Alex Chard is Director of YCTCS ltd, a company which provides consultancy services on the management and delivery of services for young offenders and other socially excluded children and young people. He has a background in direct work with young offenders and currently works closely with managers and staff in youth offending teams as well as in other children's service settings. He recently completed a masters dissertation into the impact of inspection on a youth offending team.

Naomi Redhouse is a freelance solicitor advocate with Central Booking, specialising in trial advocacy and in the youth court. She is an experienced trainer in both of these fields, having trained extensively for a number of organisations. Naomi has been a freelance advocate for 17 years, having previously worked in criminal specialist firms. Since 2003 she has been involved in developing and delivering training in the work of the defence lawyer in the youth court in collaboration with the Youth Justice Board and the Law Society. Naomi used to be a youth worker.

The Legal Action Group is a national, independent charity which campaigns for equal access to justice for all members of society. Legal Action Group:
- provides support to the practice of lawyers and advisers
- inspires developments in that practice
- campaigns for improvements in the law and the administration of justice
- stimulates debate on how services should be delivered.

Defending young people
in the criminal justice system

THIRD EDITION

Mark Ashford, Alex Chard and
Naomi Redhouse

 Legal Action Group
2006

Third edition published in Great Britain 2006
by LAG Education and Service Trust Limited
242 Pentonville Road, London N1 9UN
www.lag.org.uk

First published 1997 (© Mark Ashford and Alex Chard)
Second edition 2000 (© Mark Ashford and Alex Chard)

British Library Cataloguing in Publication Data
a CIP catalogue record for this book is available from the British Library.

ISBN 10: 1 903307 34 1
ISBN 13: 978 1 903307 34 1

Typeset by Regent Typesetting, London
Printed by Hobbs the Printers, Totton, Hampshire

Preface

It is six years since the publication of the second edition. In the intervening years the torrent of new legislation and policy initiatives has continued unchecked. The changes introduced by eight criminal justice statutes have been covered as well as other significant legislation such as the Children (Leaving Care) Act 2000, Children Act 2004 and the Courts Act 2003. As a result of these changes this edition is half as long again as the previous edition.

Readers familiar with the previous edition will note a number of significant changes. Firstly, there is the welcome arrival of Naomi Redhouse as a third author. Secondly, in response to the landmark judgment of the European Court of Human Rights in *T v United Kingdom, V v United Kingdom* we have substantially revised the trial chapter as well as including new chapters on the adolescent client and effective participation in the trial process. Thirdly, we have greatly expanded the treatment of mentally disordered young people as well as local authority duties under the Children Act 1989 and prisoner's rights. Fourthly, the statutory extracts previously reproduced in the appendices have been largely removed. This was necessary to limit the increase in cost (and weight) of this edition.

Thanks are owed to a number of people who provided information or ideas for this edition. Tim Bateman of Nacro Youth Crime provided a wealth of information and helpful comments on chapter 1. Chris Callender, legal director of the Howard League for Penal Reform, provided the benefit of his experience in the areas of the Children Act 1989 and the rights of juvenile prisoners and made many useful comments on chapters 3 and 26. A number of mental health professionals also provided valuable comments on the adolescent development section in chapter 4. These include Professor Philip Graham, Dr Philippa Hyman, Hannah Kanter, Dr Peter Misch and David Morgan. Other people who provided useful information or comments were Kate Aubrey-Johnson, Richard Chown, Mary Duff JP, Elizabeth Hogben and Peter Minchin. We have to thank the staff of Legal Action Group, and particularly Esther Pilger, who has patiently waited for the text of the book to be delivered. Thanks are also due to our families, friends and work colleagues who have been helpful and patient in the face of a seemingly never-ending task. In particular, Mark wishes to thank Carolyn Taylor and Jim Nichol for agreeing to a sabbatical and Naomi wishes to thank Esther and Gus for being so patient.

As with previous editions, we cannot claim the credit for all the ideas contained in this book. We do, however, have to accept the responsibility for any mistakes.

We have endeavoured to state the law in England and Wales as at 1 July 2006. We have however made reference to the Criminal Defence Service Act 2006 which is due to be implemented on 2 October 2006.

At the time of writing the Home Office is reviewing its plans to implement Schedule 3 of the Criminal Justice Act 2003 in November 2006. It is possible that the planned implementation date will be postponed. As Schedule 3 constitutes a radical overhaul of the mode of trial provisions in relation to young defendants we have chosen to include, at appendix 13, a version of the mode of trial chapter covering the law that will apply upon full implementation, even though the implementation date is currently uncertain.

Mark Ashford
Alex Chard
Naomi Redhouse
July 2006

Note to readers

Consolidated Criminal Practice Direction – first issued on 8 July 2002, since when there have been a number of significant amendments. The original version of the Practice Direction was published in a number of law reports. As the text of these printed versions is now out of date, we have chosen not refer to printed versions of the Practice Direction. Instead the reader is referred to the up-to-date electronic version on the website of the Department for Constitutional Affairs (see appendix 14 for contact details).

Criminal Procedure Rules 2005 – made under powers conferred by Courts Act 2003 s69 and originally issued as the Criminal Procedure Rules 2005 SI No 384. Since implementation the rules have been amended by the Criminal Procedure (Amendment) Rules 2006 SI No 353. For an up-to-date version of the Rules, as subsequently amended, the reader is referred to the electronic version of the Rules available on the Department for Constitutional Affairs website (see appendix 14 for contact details)

Neutral citations – since 11 January 2001 every judgment delivered by the House of Lords, Court of Appeal and the Administrative Court has been issued with a neutral citation. Since 14 January 2002 neutral citations have also been issued to every judgment of the remaining divisions of the High Court. For an explanation of the neutral citation system the reader is referred to *Consolidated Criminal Practice Direction*, Part I paras 12.1 – 12.6. Where available the neutral citation has been given as the first reference for a case.

Youth Justice Board – from 3 April 2006 the Youth Justice Board will refer to itself as YJB. This change has not been reflected in the text of this book as, in the absence of amendments to the Crime and Disorder Act 1998, the legal title is still the Youth Justice Board for England and Wales.

Contents

(ii) Custodial remands
Children and Young Persons Act 1969

Table of cases

Table of statutes

References in **bold** indicate where an Act is set out in part or in full.

Table of statutory instruments

References in **bold** indicate where an SI is set out in part or in full.

Table of European and international conventions, rules, treaties and charters and directives

References in **bold** indicate where material is set out in part or in full

List of tables

Young people and crime

Introduction

1.1   Above the main entrance of the Central Criminal Court at the Old Bailey are carved the words 'Protect the children of the poor and punish the wrongdoer'. This apparently straightforward injunction has proved extraordinarily difficult to carry out because in the juvenile courts of England and Wales the wrongdoers are also the children of the poor.

Pitts (1988)

1.2   Since the publication of the first edition of this book in 1997 there have been major changes in the law as it relates to young offenders and the way that official bodies deal with them. Much of this change has been prompted by the widespread public concern regarding the perceived problem of youth crime.

1.3   To explain the thinking behind these changes, this chapter seeks to give the defence lawyer an introduction to the criminological issues involved in defending young people in the criminal justice system. The first section aims to provide an overview of what is known about the extent and nature of offending by young people. This section is reproduced with kind permission of Nacro Youth Crime from their *Youth crime briefing: some facts about children and young people who offend – 2004.* The second section gives the defence lawyer a summary of research into the characteristics of young people involved in the criminal justice system. The third section looks at features of adolescent offending which have an importance for the way the criminal justice system deals with young people. The final section provides some statistical information regarding the operation of the youth justice system.

1.4   During the course of the chapter a number of issues will be discussed which provoke considerable academic controversy. As this chapter aims to be a practical introduction for defence lawyers, no attempt has been made to discuss the opposing views or to offer an opinion on their merits. Readers who wish to consider the issues in more depth are referred to the suggested further reading at the end of this chapter.

The extent of youth crime

Self reported offending

1.5   Youth crime and disorder continue to provoke widespread public concern. For instance, during 2004/2005 almost one in three adults (31%) reported that teenagers hanging around on street corners was a very, or fairly, big problem in their locality, a significantly higher figure than the 27% recorded for the previous year (Bhimjiyani and Allen, 2005). At the same time, public rating of the ability of the criminal justice system to deal effectively with young people accused of offending, while still relatively low, appears to be rising. In the same year, 27% of those interviewed indicated that they were fairly, or very, confident in this aspect of the system's performance, compared with 24% 12 months earlier and 21% during 2002/2003 (Bhimiyani and Allen, 2005).

1.6　　Self-report surveys confirm that a minority of young people do behave, on occasion, in ways which might be considered anti-social. Thus during 2004, a quarter of 10- to 25-year-olds surveyed admitted that they had engaged in at least one of four types of such behaviour in the past year. The most common form of anti-social behaviour was being noisy or rude in a public place (16%), followed by behaving in a way that led to a neighbour complaining (12%). Involvement in graffiti or religiously or racially motivated abuse was significantly rarer at 3% and 2% respectively (Budd et al, 2005). At the same time, it is important to note that three-quarters of young people had not engaged in any form of anti-social behaviour within the relevant period. Moreover, of those who admitted such behaviour, 72% had been involved in just one sort and the large majority had done so just once or twice.

1.7　　Indeed, self-reported offending appears to be more common than anti-social behaviour – perhaps because of the wider range of behaviours considered in the survey. So 35% of boys and 22% of girls, aged 10–17 years, admitted having committed at least one of 20 core offences during the past year. Almost one in five males indicated that they had committed one of six more serious offences and 11% admitted offending on at least six occasions during that same 12-month period (Budd et al, 2005).

1.8　　But it is important to place this information in context. In the first place, most of the incidents recorded are of a relatively minor nature. Thus, while assault was the most frequently cited offence, half of these involved no injury to the victim. Moreover, given that one in four boys and one in five girls aged 12–13 years admitted a violent offence, it seems likely that a considerable proportion involved playground fights or similar disputes among children of the same age. Indeed, more than half of assaults resulting in injury were described as 'grabbing, pushing or pulling'. By contrast, robbery was very rare: only 1% of those surveyed reported that they had committed an offence of that nature in the past year (Budd et al, 2005).

1.9　　Second, it is clear that such findings are not new. The *Youth Lifestyles* Survey, for instance, conducted prior to the implementation of the youth justice reforms, reported that 33% of males aged 15–17 years admitted at least one offence in the previous 12 months (Flood-Page et al, 2000). More than 20 years earlier, Belson's 1977 study produced a rate of lifetime theft from shops of 70%.[1] Moreover, such levels of youth offending are not unique to England and Wales. While there are inevitably difficulties of comparison, recent research has suggested that self-reported delinquency among 14- to 21-year-olds in England and Wales is no higher than that in either the Netherlands or Spain, the other two jurisdictions included in the study. Property crime, violence, vandalism and traffic offences were each found to be lower in England and Wales, although the researchers suggest that the finding for the former category might be explained by the differences in the questionnaires administered. Cannabis use was similar across each of the three countries studied, but use of 'hard drugs' was highest in England and Wales (Barbaret et al, 2004).

1　Cited in Pitts and Bateman (2005).

Detected crime

1.10   Only a small proportion of those children who admit offending come into contact with the youth justice system as a consequence. So while 28% of 10- to 17-year-olds had committed an offence within the past year, just 6% of these had been arrested and only 2% had been taken to court (Budd et al). In part, this wide differential can be explained in terms of continuing low detection rates, which during 2004/2005 stood at 26%, a modest increase of 3% over the previous year (Thomas and Feist, 2005). (Offences of violence, it should be noted, have much higher than average clear-up rates since the victim is more frequently able to identify his/her assailant.) It seems probable too that many of the offences admitted by children in the survey were considered insufficiently serious to be reported to the police.

1.11   In terms of detected crime, it is true that young people are more likely than adults to offend. During 2004, the peak age of offending was 17 years for boys and 15 years for girls. Nonetheless, because 10- to 17-year-olds make up a relatively small proportion of the total population, offences committed by adults account for the large majority. During 2004, children and young people aged 17 years or under accounted for just 11% of all detected crime, as indicated in the following table.[2]

Table 1: Detected offending by age

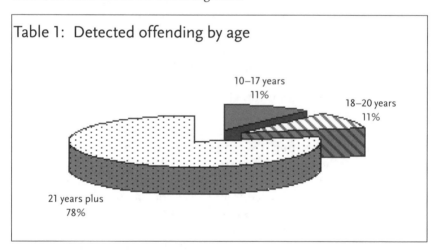

10–17 years
11%

18–20 years
11%

21 years plus
78%

Trends in youth crime

1.12   Finally, it is also important to consider the relatively high levels of self-reported crime in the context of what appears to have been a significant fall in youth crime over the past 12 years. Sixty-one per cent of the public believes that crime in England and Wales is rising, but this perception is not borne out by official data (Bhimjiyani and Allen, 2005). While the number of young people who were reprimanded, warned or convicted for an indictable offence during 2004 shows a 7.8% increase over the previous year, the longer-term trend is one of declining youth offending. The latest rise notwithstanding, the number of indictable offences committed by young people under 18 has fallen from 143,600 in 1992 to 112,900 – as indicated in the following table – a drop of 21%.

2   The figures include both summary and indictable offences.

Table 2: Children and young people cautioned, reprimanded, warned or sentenced for indictable offences 1992–2004

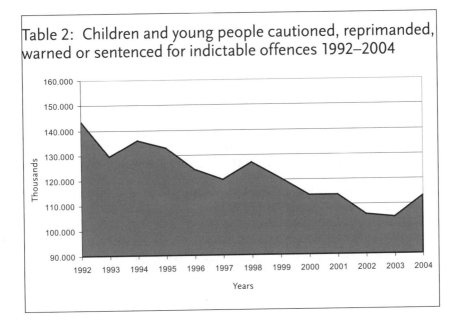

1.13   Moreover, the fall in youth crime appears equally as significant when demographic change is taken into account. It cannot, in other words, be explained by reductions in the youth population. Offending by young people has also declined – indeed the fall appears sharper – when expressed as a proportion of the youth population. For instance, the number of 15- to 17-year-old males cautioned, reprimanded or warned for an indictable offence was 7,065 for every 100,000 of the population in that age group in 1992, compared with 5,479 in 2004.

1.14   As noted earlier, recorded crime figures do not give a full account of offending, in part because of the relatively low rate of detection. This raises the possibility that falls in detected youth offending do not necessarily represent the underlying trends in youth crime. Clear-up rates, for instance, declined during the early part of the 1990s and it might be argued therefore that this accounted for some of the recorded fall in offending by children and young people during that period. However, from 1995 onwards, there was an upturn in rates of detection, which has more recently remained relatively stable (Thomas and Feist, 2005). From the mid-1990s, therefore, shifts in detection could not have contributed to the continued downward trend in recorded youth crime.

1.15   In any event, it seems unlikely that a 'gap' between offences committed and those brought to justice, could account for the pattern of youth crime captured by official statistics, even during the earlier period. Other sources of information appear to paint a picture which is consistent with a real decline in youth offending since at least 1992. The number of crimes recorded by the police fell during the first part of the 1990s, and the Home Office suggests that much of the subsequent increase is attributable to changes in the counting rules introduced in 1999, and the subsequent adoption by the police of the National Crime Recording Standard, which encourages formal recording of a greater proportion of incidents reported by the public (Bhimjiyani and Allen, 2005).

1.16   The annual British Crime Survey measures trends in self-reported victimisations, and is generally considered to provide a more accurate indication of levels of crime, since it is not susceptible, in the same way as recorded crime, to changes in police practice or recording. During 2004/2005, the survey registered a fall of 7% in overall crime over the previous year, continuing a downward trend which began in 1995. The risk of victimisation has accordingly fallen by 40% in the past ten years and is currently at the lowest level recorded since the survey was first conducted in 1981 (Bhimjiyani and Allen, 2005).

1.17   Thus other measures of trends in offending – although they provide a picture of overall crime rather than that which can be attributed to young people alone – are consistent with the data for recorded youth crime. They might therefore be thought to add weight to the suggestion that the decline recorded in *Criminal Statistics* represents a genuine fall.

1.18   In this light, it is also worth considering the possibility that the rise in detected youth offending over the past year might be influenced by recent changes in practice. The government has set a target for all agencies working within the criminal justice system to narrow the 'justice gap' between offences recorded and those brought to justice by increasing the number that result in a recognised sanction detection,[3] to 1.25 million by 2007/2008, as compared with 1.025 million offences in the year ending March 2002 (Office for Criminal Justice Reform, 2004). One possible consequence of this target is that offences which would previously have been dealt with informally (and go unrecorded) might attract a formal response, reflected in the recorded figures for youth crime.

The nature of youth offending

1.19   Much of the public concern in relation to young people's behaviour tends to focus on 'street crime' and other offences of violence. Such offending frequently has serious consequences for the victim and the concentration on incidents of this nature is understandable. It should be acknowledged too that violent offences and robbery have increased, in recent years, as a proportion of all youth crime. Nonetheless, much of this apparent rise is due to a relative fall in the incidence of less serious offences such as theft and handling stolen goods: the rise in absolute numbers of violent incidents is accordingly much smaller than the percentage figures might suggest. At the same time, the focus on more serious offences tends to obscure the fact that the majority of youth crime continues to be directed against property despite the relative fall in such offences. In 2004, theft, handling stolen goods, burglary, fraud or forgery and criminal damage, accounted for 63% of indictable offences committed by young people. Indeed, theft and handling offences alone represent more than four out of every ten. Violence, robbery and sexual assault remain relatively rare.

1.20   Violent offending against the person, for instance, constitutes less than 17% of indictable offences leading to reprimand, final warning or conviction, a rise from 12% since 1993. A significant proportion of such offences

---

3   Recognised sanction detections are: cautions, reprimands, final warnings, fixed penalty notices, convictions and offences taken into consideration.

are, moreover, relatively minor. In 2004, for instance, 63% resulted in a reprimand or a warning, suggesting that they arose out of incidents of a less serious nature. (This does not necessarily imply that cases resulting in a conviction are always serious. Relatively minor offences of violence will lead to prosecution if the young person does not make a full admission at the police station, or if s/he has previously received a final warning or conviction.)

1.21 Robbery is another offence which generates the highest levels of public concern. The figures for 2004 show a slight increase in the number of robberies after a fall over the previous two years. Overall, such offences continue to be relatively rare, accounting for 2.8% of indictable matters.

1.22 Sexual offences too make up a very small proportion, less than 1%, of youth crime. Furthermore, offences of a sexual nature have fallen, both in terms of absolute numbers and as a proportion of all indictable offences, since the early 1990s. During 2004, half of sexual offences committed by children under the age of 18 years, resulted in a pre-court disposal rather than prosecution.

1.23 The table below provides a comparative breakdown of indictable offences resulting in caution, reprimand, warning or conviction by offence type, for the years 1993, 2003 and 2004. Other than those categories already discussed, the major point of significance is a large increase in drugs offences since the early 1990s, most of which involve possession of cannabis, now a class C drug. Since the figures exclude summary offences, the picture displayed somewhat overstates the general gravity of youth offending. (Were summary offences included, for instance, robbery would constitute less than 2% of recorded crime.)

1.24 But if a focus on serious youth offending tends to obscure the general nature of the majority of crime committed by young people, it also detracts attention from the fact that the large preponderance of serious offences are committed by adults. During 2004, persons over the age of 18 years were

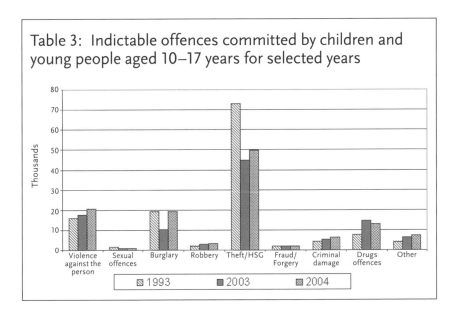

Table 3: Indictable offences committed by children and young people aged 10–17 years for selected years

responsible for more than three-and-a-half times as many violent offences and more than six times as many sexual offences as children and young people. Robbery is frequently portrayed as a 'young person's offence', but even here, adults accounted for 57% of the total.

Profile of young people involved in the criminal justice system

Age

1.25   The peak age of detected offending for males was 17 years in 2004, whereas the peak age for females in the same year was 15 years (Nacro, 2006). Official statistics indicate that involvement in crime increases rapidly through the age range of the youth court. This phenomenon, and the fact that the younger offenders are more likely to benefit from pre-court diversion, mean that the concentration at the upper ages is more pronounced for those young people who attend court (Youth Justice Board, 2006).

Age	All young offenders	Sentenced at court
10–11 years	2.6%	1%
12–14 years	25.7%	21%
15 years	19.5%	20%
16 years	24.9%	28%
17 years	27.3%	30%

Gender

1.26   Self-report studies indicate that young women commit less crime than young men. Official statistics not only confirm this, but also point to other significant differences. According to Rutter et al (1998) findings from official statistics may be summarised as follows:

- more males than females are convicted (currently a ratio of 4:1);
- the preponderance of males is greatest for sex crimes, drug offences and crimes involving force against persons or property;
- the male excess among offenders is least evident in early adolescence and most marked in early adult life; female offenders commit fewer crimes than male offenders, they are less likely to be recidivist, and they are less likely to commit very serious crimes; and
- young women's offending careers tend to be shorter.

1.27   As well as differences in the offending patterns, there is evidence that young female offenders are treated differently within the present youth justice system. For instance, in a survey of 17,000 cases in eight youth offending team areas, Feilzer and Hood (2004) noted a number of differences based on gender, including:

- a much lower proportion of females than males in all ethnic categories had a criminal record and a higher proportion admitted guilt;
- police were more likely to divert from the court process a female offender than a male offender;
- slightly more females received a more restrictive community penalty than would have been expected from their case characteristics (the chances of a male receiving a more restrictive community penalty was 20% lower than that of a female); and
- male young offenders were twice as likely to be sentenced to custody as their female equivalents.

1.28 Feilzer and Hood concluded that there was evidence consistent with differential treatment of male and females both at the pre-court and the sentencing stages. Similar findings of differential treatment have been made for many years (Gelsthorpe, 2004). Various explanations have been offered for this differential treatment. It has been argued that social attitudes to women can lead to more punitive or restrictive disposals. Taking a feminist perspective, Hudson (1989) has argued that girls who appear before the youth court are subject to a 'double penalty', in that they are punished both for the offence and for the 'social' crime of contravening normative expectations of 'appropriate' female conduct. She also argues that a common response to delinquent behaviour by girls is to be concerned that they are beyond control and/or at risk morally. The differential approach to girls who offend could therefore lead to a more punitive penalty, for example where a girl is convicted of a violent offence (seen as unfeminine behaviour); or a more intrusive sentence than is proportionate for the seriousness of the offence (because of concern for the girl's welfare). Ironically, the recent move towards a more risk-oriented youth justice system may have contributed to an abandonment of such welfare models in favour of more punitive responses, leading to an increased criminalisation of young women (Gelsthorpe, 2004).

Race

1.29 The disproportionate representation of black and minority ethnic young people in the criminal justice system remains a significant concern.

1.30 In their study of self-reported offending, Graham and Bowling (1995) found that there was no difference in the overall rates of offending reported by white and black young people, though young people of Pakistani, Indian or Bangladeshi origin reported substantially lower rates of offending. A wide range of variation in the types of offences committed was also reported. Other self-report studies have found similar results, both in relation to the levels of offending and the variation in the types of offences committed (eg Flood-Page et al, 2000).

1.31 Official statistics showing the ethnic background of defendants reveal discriminatory responses from first contact with the police to the end of the criminal justice process. Police records indicate that in 2004, black

people were 6.4 times more likely, and Asian people twice as likely, to be
stopped and searched as white people (Home Office, 2005). In the court
system itself, differential treatment is most noticeable for black young
people. Official statistics for the financial year 2004/2005 (Youth Justice
Board, 2006) indicate that, whereas they only make up 2.7% of the general
population aged 10 to 17 years, young people classified as black or black
British make up:

- 6% of those convicted of an offence;
- 17.3% of secure remands and remands to custody;
- 11.6% of custodial sentences; and
- 24.5% of those sentenced to long-term detention under Powers of
  Criminal Courts (Sentencing) Act 2000 ss90 and 91.

1.32   The statistics also reveal differential outcomes for young people of both
Asian and mixed ethnicity, although the figures are not so disproportionately poor (Youth Justice Board, 2006).

1.33   Explanations for the disproportionate representation of black and
minority ethnic young people in the criminal justice system have included
differences in the seriousness of convictions, as well as social factors such
as demographics (the black and minority ethnic population is comparatively young and will therefore make up a greater proportion of the peak
offending age) and greater social exclusion (higher rates of school exclusion, homelessness and unemployment will have a negative impact on
bail and sentencing decisions (Bowling and Phillips, 2002)). Nevertheless, there is also evidence to indicate that the potential for discriminatory
decision-making exists at every stage of the criminal justice process:

- *Policing.* Black and ethnic minority people in general are less likely to
  have confidence in the fairness of the police and the criminal justice
  system in general (Home Office, 2003). Black young people have a lack
  of trust in policing generally and report conflict in their day-to-day dealings with the police (Sharp, 2005). This conflict will increase the likelihood of arrests for public order offences.

- *Prosecution.* Black and mixed origin boys are more likely to be prosecuted than white boys, even taking into account variables such as
  seriousness of allegation (Feilzer and Hood, 2004). Whilst black and
  minority ethnic defendants are more likely to plead not guilty than
  white defendants, they still have a higher acquittal rate (Barclay and
  Mhlanga, 2000), leading the Denman Report (2001) to conclude that
  the Crown Prosecution Service appeared to be discriminating against
  ethnic minority defendants by failing to correct the bias in police charging decisions and allowing a disproportionate number of weak cases
  against ethnic minority defendants to go to trial.

- *Remands.* The Denman Report (2001) raised a concern that some ethnic minority prosecutors cited some decisions to oppose bail for a black
  or minority ethnic defendant as discriminatory. The Inquiry concluded
  that it is essential that the possibility of unwitting discrimination is not
  underestimated.

- *Sentencing.* There is a slightly greater use of more restrictive community sentences for all young people of ethnic minority origin, with this

most pronounced for young people aged between 12 and 15 (Feilzer and Hood, 2004). Not only will the more onerous requirements of the order increase the likelihood of the young person breaching the order (thereby risking a custodial sentence on re-sentence) but it also means that a subsequent offence is more likely to receive a custodial sentence as the young person has been placed higher on the sentencing tariff. There is also a greater chance than an ethnic minority young person will be committed to the Crown Court, where the chance of a custodial sentence in much greater (Feilzer and Hood, 2004).

1.34 There are clearly a wide range of complex and interrelated factors that lead to the markedly poorer outcomes for some groups of black and ethnic minority young people. It may be argued that this is rarely explained by a single act of overt discrimination but rather by the accumulation of social and criminal justice factors, the 'multiplier effect' (Goldson and Chigwada-Bailey, 1999), which acts to discriminate against black and ethnic minority defendants (Muncie, 2002).

Family background

1.35 The home circumstances of a significant number of young offenders are characterised by instability. Baker et al (2003) found that only 30% of the sample of young people attending youth offending teams lived with both biological parents. In another survey (Youth Justice Trust, 2003) of 1,000 young people supervised by youth offending teams it was found that 92% had experienced at least one of the following:

- bereavement;
- separation;
- rejection;
- impermanence of home; or
- loss due to illness.

1.36 As well as experiencing instability and loss, young people involved in the youth justice system have experienced high levels of abuse. For instance, one London youth offending team found that between 40% and 64% under its supervision in any one year had previously been on the child protection register as a result of neglect or violent or sexual abuse (Jones and Pitts, 2001, cited in Pitts, 2004). High levels of abuse have also been reported by young offenders in long-term detention (Boswell, 1995).

1.37 In the light of these domestic backgrounds, it is perhaps not surprising that a large proportion of the young people involved in the youth justice system have had contact with the care system. Baker et al (2003) found that 18% of young people attending youth offending teams were currently or had previously been accommodated by a local authority with the agreement of parents and 7% were or had in the past been the subject of a care order. Many of these young people will have experienced a lack of continuity of carers. For example, Jones and Pitts (2001) found that children on the child protection register who subsequently became involved in the criminal justice system often had an extremely unstable care history with 40% of this group having experienced ten or more residential or foster placements between the ages of one and 15.

Schooling and learning difficulties

1.38   Young people involved in the youth justice system often have negative experiences of school, leading to disaffection and failure in the academic system. In a survey in 2000 of over 3,000 standardised assessments of young people carried out by youth offending team staff, Baker et al (2003) noted that of those currently receiving any kind of educational provision, only 59% were in mainstream school, 15% of the young people in the sample were currently excluded from school, 27% had previous permanent exclusions and 32% had experienced fixed term exclusions in the last year; 40% of those receiving statutory education were regularly truanting and over one-third were assessed to have a poor relationship with teachers.

1.39   Studies also reveal low levels of educational attainment. Harrington and Bailey (2005) assessed the literacy levels of 301 young people who were either attending youth offending teams or in a secure institution. The vast majority had a reading age and reading comprehension age below their chronological age (mean reading age was 11.3 years, reading comprehension 10 years; mean chronological was age 16 years). Such levels of literacy may be as a result of lack of schooling or specific learning difficulties, or a combination of both (severe learning problems being found greatly to increase the likelihood of truancy (Maughan et al, 1996, cited in Rutter et al, 1998)).

1.40   It should also be noted that there appears to be a much greater incidence of learning disability (that is, an IQ below 70) among young offenders. Whilst a learning disability would be expected in about 2% of the general population, studies among young offenders have shown proportions generally between 7% and 15% (Kazdin, 2000). Two recent studies have, however, found even higher incidence of disability. Kroll et al (2002) carried out a survey of mental disorder involving 97 boys detained in secure units: 27% were assessed as having an IQ below 70 and a further 43% were assessed as having an IQ between 70 and 85. Harrington and Bailey (2005) carried out a larger survey of 301 young people, half of whom were attending youth offending teams and the other half detained in secure children's homes or young offender institutions. This survey found that 23% had an IQ of less than 70 and 36% had an IQ between 70 and 79 (borderline learning disability). Harrington and Bailey do warn that psychometric testing cannot easily differentiate those with intrinsic learning difficulties from those with a low IQ score secondary to a lack of education, nevertheless their findings raise serious concerns regarding the ability of young people to cope with the intellectual demands of the criminal justice process (see chapters 10 and 15).

Social deprivation

1.41   Young people in Britain experience high levels of deprivation with an estimated 25% living in neighbourhoods characterised by poverty, unemployment and poor health with a very transient population and high crime rates (Burroughs, 1998, cited in Pitts, 2004) and a higher proportion living in households where no adult is in work than in any other member country of the Organisation for Economic Co-operation and Development (OECD) (Social Exclusion Unit, 2000).

1.42 Young people involved in the criminal justice system are likely to live in areas of social deprivation. Baker et al (2003) found that of the young people supervised by youth offending teams in their survey, there were problems in accommodation and the neighbourhoods where the young people lived. The survey found that 8% of 15- to 18-year-olds had no fixed abode and 25% of 10- to 14-year-olds were considered to live in deprived households. It also found that 24% of the young people lived in an area with obvious signs of drug dealing, 36% in areas with a lack of age-appropriate facilities and 6% in areas with racial or ethnic tensions. Young people of black or mixed ethnicity were found to be significantly more likely to live in areas with obvious signs of drug dealing and young people of Asian ethnicity were found to be more likely to live in areas with racial or ethnic tensions.

Victimisation

1.43 When outside the home environment, young people are more likely to be victims of crime than other age groups. This phenomenon has been noted for some time (Smith and Gray, 1985; Aye Maung, 1995) but has only recently been the subject of much attention by academics or policy makers. Recent official surveys have all questioned young people about their experiences being victims of crime and all have found similar results (MORI, 2004; Wood, 2005; Baker et al, 2005). Analysing the results of the Home Office's 2003 Crime and Justice Survey, Wood (2003) found that:

- about a third of young people aged 10 to 17 had experienced at least one personal crime in the last 12 months;
- the types of crime that young people experienced changed with age (for, example, robbery and thefts from the person were less common experiences for 10- and 11-year-olds than for 16- or 17-year-olds);
- the degree of repeat victimisation for violent offences was particularly high for young people, with 19% of 10- to 15-year-olds experiencing five or more incidents in the last 12 months.

1.44 Self-report surveys of young people also reveal:

- most assaults happened at or near school and most perpetrators were the same age and sex as their victims (Aye Maung, 1995);
- school-age children are particularly vulnerable to victimisation when travelling to and from school on public transport (Pitts and Smith, 1995, cited in Pitts, 2004);
- a majority of young people do not report the crime to either parents or the police (Aye Maung, 1995).

1.45 Studies have noted that offending by young people was the factor most strongly associated with the chances of being victims themselves (Smith, 2004; Wood, 2005). Explanations for this correlation have included victims and perpetrators sharing similar lifestyles and personality traits (Smith, 2004), victims of crime being prompted to target others to re-establish their status (Sanders, 2003, cited in Pitts, 2004) and the overlap of risk factors for being a victim of a crime and its perpetrator. This last factor is particularly true in relation to young people in deprived neighbourhoods with high crime rates (Pitts, 2004).

1.46   The high levels of victimisation have a marked effect on the ways that young people live their lives. The Social Exclusion Unit (2000) noted:

> A recurrent theme among surveys of young people is the fear of bullying and crime, particularly violent crime. In some places these concerns are expressed through a fear of travel, and increased 'territoriality'. In others, there is the additional factor of a very real fear of racial harassment and violence.

Alcohol use

1.47   Alcohol use by young people in the United Kingdom is higher than in any other of the 14 countries in the pre-2004 European Union (Social Exclusion Unit, 2000). Matthews et al (2006) examined responses to questions regarding alcohol use in the 2004 Offending, Crime and Justice Survey and found:

- just over half of all 10- to 17-year-olds reported having an alcoholic drink in the previous 12 months; the figure is highest for 16- to 17-year-olds (88%) and lowest for 10- to 12-year-olds (29%); and
- one-third of young people who reported drinking at least once during the lest 12 months reported feeling very drunk once a month or more in the last 12 months.

1.48   Matthews et al also noted a significant correlation between the frequency of alcohol use and offending. Those young people who reported drinking at least once a week admitted committing considerably more crime than those young people who said they never drank. There was also some evidence for a direct link between drinking alcohol and crime and disorderly behaviour. For instance, of 10- to 17-year-olds who drank at least once a month, 28% reported that they had got into an argument during or after drinking in the past 12 months and 12% reported getting into a fight.

Substance misuse

1.49   Experimentation with substances is widespread among young people. In 2005, 11% of secondary school children reported using drugs in the month prior to interview, while 19% reported using drugs within the previous 12 months (National Statistics, 2006). The most common drug used is cannabis, used by 11% of all 10- to 17-year-olds in the previous 12 months (Budd et al, 2005). This average hides the fact that much higher proportions of the older end of the age range use cannabis (16% of 14- and 15-year-olds and 27% of 16- and 17-year-olds reported using it at least once in the previous 12 months (Budd et al, 2005)).

1.50   Young people identified as vulnerable (defined as those who have ever been in care, the homeless, truants, those who have ever been excluded from school and serious or persistent offenders) reported significantly higher levels of drug use (43.7%), class A drugs use (18.1%) and were more likely to be frequent drug users (26.2%) compared with those not identified as vulnerable (13%, 3.2% and 4.8% respectively) (National Statistics, 2006).

1.51   Another survey found that that 15% of young offenders were rated as at high risk of substance abuse problems (10 times the proportion identified in a survey of the general school population) (Hammersley et al, 2003). Among the custodial population a significant number of young people reported a daily use of heroin and crack cocaine (10.5% and 6.6% respectively) before their entry to the institution (Youth Justice Board, 2004).

1.52   The age at which young people report the first use of a drug varies depending on the drug. Among the general population the median age for the first use of solvents and cannabis is reported to be 14 years and 16 years respectively, whereas the median age for first use of cocaine is 19 years (only 5% of respondents saying that their first use was between the age of 10 and 15 years) (National Statistics, 2006). Pudney (2002) found little evidence for a 'gateway effect' for drugs use into crime. Analysing responses from 3,900 young people in the 1998/1999 Youth Lifestyles Survey, he noted that the average age of onset for truancy and crime were 13.8 years and 14.5 years respectively, compared for 16.2 years for drugs generally and 19.9 years for class A drugs. Rather than drugs causing offending, it therefore seems more likely that young offenders and drug users share similar characteristics.

Physical health

1.53   Young people involved in the criminal justice system have been found to have many unmet health needs. One survey of young people attending youth offending teams in Manchester found that two-thirds who were given health checks were malnourished and half considered to be in some sort of medical distress. Many had missed routine health checks and inoculations as a consequence of missed schooling (Youth Justice Trust, 2001, cited in Pitcher et al, 2004).

1.54   There is a high correlation between offending by young people and other types of risky behaviour, such as heavy drug use, dangerous activities such as driving stolen motor vehicles and unprotected sex. A significant minority will be putting their physical health at risk. Baker et al (2003) noted that 11% of young people attending youth offending teams in their survey were considered to be putting their health at risk through their own behaviour.

Mental health

1.55   Since the end of the Second World War there has been a significant rise in the incidence of mental disorders among young people (Rutter at al, 1998). A recent survey of 11- to-15-year-olds in England and Wales estimated that 13% of girls and 10% of boys had a mental health problem (Meltzer et al, 1999). The most common disorders identified were emotional disorders (6%), conduct disorders (6%) and hyperkinetic disorders (1.5%). Hagell (2002) found that studies involving young people involved in the criminal justice system consistently reveal a significantly higher prevalence of psychiatric diagnosis – estimates ranging from 46% to 81% for young people in custody and 25% to 77% for those in the criminal justice system but not in custody. She concluded:

> A conservative estimate based on these figures would suggest that the rate of mental health problems are at least three times as high for those within the criminal justice system as within the general population, if not higher.

1.56   Young offenders have been found to suffer from a wide range of mental health problems, many of which are likely to have a significant impact upon their lives and, more specifically, their ability to cope with the demands of the criminal justice process. For instance, an assessment of mental health needs of young offenders commissioned by the Youth Justice Board (Harrington and Bailey, 2005) found that 31% of the sample were identified with mental health problems. Using a fully validated mental health screening tool, the study found that of the 301 young offenders interviewed:

- 18% had problems with depression;
- 9% reported harming themselves in the last month;
- 10% were suffering from anxiety;
- 9% had post-traumatic stress disorder;
- 7% had a hyperactivity disorder; and
- 5% displayed psychotic-like symptoms.

Custodial population

1.57   Various reports have noted that young people held in custody have suffered from exceptionally high levels of deprivation and are some of the neediest young people in the youth justice system (HM Inspector of Prisons, 1997; Moore and Peters, 2003). The extent of that need may be illustrated by the summary of recent research findings contained in a report regarding provision for those leaving custody (Youth Justice Board, 2005):

- 40% to 49% have been in local authority care at some point and about 18% are still subject to care orders;
- half the population in young offender institutions were functioning educationally below the level of the average 11-year-old on entry to the institution (more than a third of those of compulsory school age had a reading age of 7 of less);
- 31% had mental health problems;
- 44.8% used more than one type of drug;
- 45.4% had been dependent on a substance prior to entry;
- 40% of girls and 25% of boys reported suffering violence at home; and
- 33% of girls and 5% of boys reported previous sexual abuse.

Features of adolescent offending

Risk and protective factors

1.58   The focus of much criminological research is to attempt to identify the factors which prompt some individuals to commit crime and others not to do so. One of the main research tools is the longitudinal study of large groups of young people over many years, sometimes decades. The lives of the subjects will be followed in an attempt to identify personal and social factors which have a correlation with offending. The most famous British study is a study of South London males known as the Cambridge Study in Delinquent Development which started in 1961 (Farrington, 1995).[4] A number of studies have analysed the information from such longitudinal studies to identify what are usually called 'risk' and 'protective' factors. A risk factor is an individual, family or social factor in the young person's life which has been found to have a statistical correlation with offending. However, the existence of one or more of these factors does not in itself mean that a young person will commit a crime. A protective factor may be more than just the absence of a risk factor. Research has shown that there are some factors which seem to moderate the effects of exposure to risk; it is these identified factors which are most properly termed protective factors.

1.59   In Youth Justice Board (2001, 2005) the risk factors identified by research studies were summarised as follows:

Family risk factors	*Individual risk factors*
Poor parental supervision and discipline	Hyperactivity and impulsivity
Family conflict	Low intelligence and cognitive impairment
Family history of criminal activity	Alienation and lack of social commitment
Parental attitudes that condone anti-social and criminal behaviour	Attitudes that condone offending and drug misuse
Low income	Early involvement in crime and drug misuse
Poor housing	
Large family size	Peers involved in crime and drug misuse
School risk factors	*Community risk factors*
Low achievement	Living in a disadvantaged neighbourhood
Aggressive behaviour (including bullying)	Community disorganisation and neglect
Lack of commitment to school (truancy)	Availability of drugs
School disorganisation	Availability of guns
	High turnover and lack of neighbourhood attachment

4   Other important longitudinal studies in the English-speaking world have been running for many years in Pittsburgh in the United States and Dunedin in New Zealand. In 2002 a study involving approximately 4,000 school children in Edinburgh was started by researchers at the University of Edinburgh. Some of the findings from the Edinburgh Study of Youth Transitions and Crime will be mentioned below.

1.60   In the same survey, significant protective factors were identified as including:

- a resilient temperament;
- a positive outgoing disposition (a quality which elicits positive responses from adults and peers);
- high intelligence;
- a repertoire of social problem-solving skills and belief in their own self-efficacy;
- a strong bond of attachment with one or both parents characterised by a stable, warm, affectionate relationship; and
- the young person bonding to a school and, later, to the community in which s/he lives.

1.61   A number of commentators have warned of the dangers of a simplistic or mechanistic approach to the question of risk of offending. For example, Rutter et al (1998) warn:

- different risk factors and outcomes are associated with different types of anti-social behaviour;
- young people's experiences continue to be important, and nothing is cast in stone; life events, turning points and transition periods can all play a part in whether anti-social behaviour continues or ceases (for which see paras 1.63 and 1.64 below).

1.62   The youth justice system has reacted to the research findings on risk and protective factors by adopting a standardised assessment tool which is intended to aid the collection of information about the young person, including the risk factors associated with their offending. The standardised assessment tool developed on behalf of the Youth Justice Board is called *Asset* (see paras 2.23–2.27). With the information gained from completing the standardised assessment, the youth offending team should plan a programme aimed at reducing the identified risk factors (sometimes termed, meeting the young person's 'criminogenic needs'). The interventions which might be planned by youth offending teams could include:

- cognitive-behavioural work to address anti-social attitudes, increase victim empathy, self-management or problem-solving;
- help to get the young person into education or training;
- referring the young person to organised leisure activities such as youth clubs or youth sports teams; and
- arranging a mentor for the young person to have a positive adult role model.

Desistance

1.63   Involvement in criminal activity for most young people appears to decline rapidly after the age of peak offending. This phenomenon has been described as 'growing out of crime' (Rutherford, 1988). Graham and Bowling (1995) carried out a series of detailed interviews with people who had offended during adolescence. An analysis of the information provided by those who had desisted from offending led them to identify four principal mechanisms or processes which influence desistance:

- disassociation from offenders;
- forming stable relationships and having children;
- acquiring a sense of direction;
- realising in time or learning the hard way.

1.64 Linked to the phenomenon of desistance is more recent identification of sub-groups of young offenders. Moffitt (1993) identifies two important sub-groups which she terms 'life-course-persistent' and 'adolescent-limited' offenders. Life-course-persistent offenders are said to display anti-social behaviour from as early as 3 years. Their offending generally starts at a relatively early age and continues into adulthood. In contrast, adolescence-limited offenders commence offending around puberty. Whilst they may be prolific in their offending for a short period, they desist relatively quickly. There is evidence that the risk factors for these two sub-groups are not the same (Rutter et al, 1998). It should also be noted that, even with those who display the features associated with being life-course-persistent offenders, their situation is not fixed and they can be diverted from criminality by protective factors (Sutton et al, 2004).

Group offending

1.65 Young people, particularly those aged 14 to 17 years, tend to socialise in groups. This socialising in groups is more likely to be unstructured 'hanging around' without any adult involvement in the case of young people of poorer socio-economic status (Coleman and Hendry, 1999). This social phenomenon is inevitably going to have an effect on the pattern of offending by young people. Steinberg and Schwartz (2000) have commented:

> Adolescents are, for the most part, pack animals, and their activities – whether harmless or worrisome – are typically pursued in group settings ... Understanding the importance of the peer group during adolescence is fundamental to understanding juvenile offending because the dynamic of the group may play a crucial role in drawing some youngsters into antisocial activities.

1.66 Self-report studies have found that a majority of young people report committing offences with others (MORI, 2004). Research in the United States also indicates that group offending is more common among teenagers than it is among adults (Zimring, 1998, cited in Steinberg and Schwartz, 2000). Such research evidence has relevance in the youth justice system as offending by a group is treated as an aggravating factor on sentence (see para 17.7 and table 19).

1.67 Group offending by most adolescents should be distinguished from a much smaller group of teenagers who are involved in delinquent youth groups. Sharp et al (2006) defined a delinquent youth group as a group of young people who spend time in groups of three or more (including themselves) where the group spends a lot of time in public places, has existed for three months or more, has engaged in delinquent or criminal behaviour together in the last 12 months and has at least one structural feature (either a name, an area, a leader or rules). Using this definition Sharp et al analysed responses from a series of specially designed questions contained in the Home Office's 2004 Offending, Crime and Justice Survey. The study found that:

- overall, an estimated 6% of young people aged 10 to 17 were classified as belonging to a delinquent youth group;
- involvement in such groups was highest among those aged 14 to 15 (12%) and 16 to 17 (9%);
- male involvement was highest in 14- to 17-year-olds, whilst female involvement was highest in 14- or 15-year-olds;
- the factors most strongly associated with group membership were: having friends in trouble with the police; having run away from home; commitment to deviant peers; having been expelled or suspended from school; and being drunk on a frequent basis.

1.68   Both Sharp et al (2006) and Smith and Bradshaw (2005) have found that involvement in a delinquent youth group significantly increases the likelihood of a young person offending.

Frequent offending

1.69   As seen at paras 1.7–1.9, a significant proportion of young people commit a crime at some time during their adolescence. There is, however, considerable evidence that a much smaller group of young people commit a substantially greater proportion of offences than their age peers. For instance, Graham and Bowling (1995) found that about 3% of offenders aged between 14 and 25 accounted for approximately a quarter of all self-reported offences. Similar examples of disproportionate offending have been found by Hagell and Newburn (1994) and Arnull et al (2005), amongst others.

1.70   Terminology used to describe this phenomenon varies depending on the context and the professional background of the person discussing the issue. Mental health professionals will often refer to such young people as 'chronic' offenders, whereas youth justice professionals (following the lead of the Home Office and Youth Justice Board) will usually use the term 'persistent' offenders. Whichever term is used, there is no consistency of definition of the term in relation to number of qualifying offences and the qualifying timescale.

1.71   Reviewing the research on the characteristics of young people who offend frequently, Rutter et al (1998) note that studies suggest that they are broadly similar to other offenders but 'show their characteristics to a greater degree'. In particular, they are more likely to be male and to have started offending at an early age.

1.72   In their study Hagell and Newburn (1994) commented:

> The majority of the interviewed sample reported that they had left school and were not doing anything structured with their time. Few were on employment or training schemes. Rates of childbirth for the girls seemed very high, but the numbers were too small to be conclusive. Approximately half of the children lived in households where the heads were not working or unemployed, and this reinforced the general picture of disadvantage that appeared to characterise the lives of these young reoffenders.

1.73 Those young people who offend frequently have a high nuisance factor in the communities in which they live (Arnull et al, 2005) and consequently attract considerable media attention (Hagell and Newburn, 1994). As a result, there are a number of initiatives in the youth justice system designed to target the problems of frequent offenders. These include:

- fast-tracking certain young offenders through the youth justice system (see paras 2.104–2.106);
- providing high levels of supervision and surveillance to some young offenders while they are on bail, serving a community order or serving the community part of a custodial sentence (see paras 2.28–2.33); or
- programmes which target frequent offenders with a combination of intense supervision and social support designed to prevent offending (see paras 2.34–2.41).

The youth justice system

1.74 In 2004/2005 the youth justice system dealt with 287,013 offences committed by young people (Youth Justice Board, 2006). When summary-only motoring offences are excluded, children and young persons comprise almost a fifth of those who receive a pre-court disposal or are convicted at court (Home Office, 2005).

Diversion

1.75 Diverting offenders from the court system by the police administering cautions in place of prosecution dates back to the 1920s. Cautioning was a non-statutory response to minor offending which was initially at the discretion of individual police forces. During the 1990s official guidance began to regulate the practice.[5] Since 2000 there has been a statutory scheme for pre-court diversion which involves the police administering reprimands or warnings to young offenders (see chapter 9).

Trends

1.76 The practice of diverting young people from the criminal courts has been declining steadily since the early 1990s (Bateman, 2002). In 1992 the diversion rate was 73% (Bateman, 2002) whereas in the financial year 2004/05 it was 44% (Youth Justice Board, 2006).

Geographical variation

1.77 Under the previous non-statutory cautioning scheme, there was concern about the marked variation in the use of diversion for young offenders (Wilkinson and Evans, 1990). Unfortunately, even with the introduction of statutory criteria, there is still a huge variation in the proportion of young offenders diverted from court. In 2004 the rate of diversion for 15- to 17-year-old males ranged from 71% in Surrey to 34% in Durham and Greater Manchester (Nacro, 2006, analysing Home Office, 2004).

5 Home Office Circulars 59/1990 and 18/1994.

Court remands

1.78   Official statistics (Youth Justice Board, 2006) reveal that in the financial year 2004/05 there were 128,875 court remands. The type of remand was recorded as follows:

Unconditional bail	58.5%
Conditional bail without intervention	30%
Conditional bail with intervention (eg tag, bail supervision and support or bail ISSP)	5%
Remand to local authority accommodation	1.5%
Remand to secure accommodation	0.5%
Remand to custody (YOI)	4.5%

Court disposals

1.79   Since the youth justice reforms of the late 1990s, there has been a trend towards a greater use of higher tariff community sentences and a lesser use of fines and discharges (Audit Commission, 2004). Youth Justice Board (2006) indicates that during 2004/05 disposals in all courts comprised fines and discharges 23%, community sentences 31% and custodial sentences 6%. The most common sentence was the referral order which comprised 24% of total sentences. The most common community sentence was the supervision order which comprised 8% of sentences (Youth Justice Board, 2006).

Custodial sentencing

1.80   The current rate of incarceration for young people aged 10 to 17 years in England and Wales is one of the highest among the member states of the Council of Europe.

Trends in sentencing

1.81   Throughout the 1980s the use of custody for young people fell sharply (7,900 sentences in 1981 falling to 1,700 sentences in 1990) (Allen, 1991, cited in Goldson, 2006). This changed during the period 1992 to 1997 when there was a 40% increase in the numbers in custody (Audit Commission, 2004). Since then the number of people under 18 detained at any one time has remained relatively stable. A particularly worrying feature of this increased use of custody was the higher proportion of young people under 15 years receiving custodial sentences. The proportion receiving a custodial sentence in this age group went from about 3% in the early 1990s to more than 6% a decade later (Audit Commission, 2004). During that same period, the proportion of 15- to 17-year-olds receiving a custodial has remained relatively steady at 14% to 15% (Audit Commission, 2004).

Detention within juvenile secure estate

1.82 In March 2005 just under 2,700 young people (both on remand and sentenced) were in the juvenile secure estate, of which 82% were detained in young offender institutions and 9% in both secure children's homes and secure training centres (figures derived from Youth Justice Board, 2006).

Geographical differences

1.83 The proportion of custodial sentences given to young people varies substantially across youth offending team areas, ranging from less than 2% to more than 18% (Audit Commission, 2004). Local variations are loosely related to the seriousness of offending in the local area, but there is also considerable variation in custody rates among areas with similar gravity of offending (Audit Commission, 2004).

1.84 Nacro (2002) examined sentencing patterns in 20 youth offending team areas with the aim of identifying factors which explained the high use of custody. The study noted that in low custody areas the courts made greater use of low tariff sentences (such as discharges and fines), lower use of 'adult-type' community sentences (community rehabilitation order, community punishment order etc) and more use of reparation orders. The study also concluded that custody rates are related to magistrates' levels of confidence in the local youth offending team, the quality of the information they supply and their delivery of community sentences.

Anti-social behaviour orders

1.85 The anti-social behaviour order was introduced in April 1999. Home Office statistics indicate that since its implementation there has been a rapid increase in its use. In 2001 only 133 orders were made, whereas in 2004 (the last year for which complete figures exist) 2,668 orders were made. A significant proportion of the orders have been made in relation to young people aged 10 to 17 (43% of all orders made between May 2000 and September 2005).[6]

Re-offending rates

1.86 Official statistics for re-offending rates for young people look at the proportion who re-offended during a one year follow-up period and subsequently received a pre-court disposal or were convicted in court. The latest figures available are for young offenders who received pre-court disposals, non-custodial disposals and those who were released from custody in the first quarter of 2004. Whiting and Cuppleditch (2006) found that in the 2004 cohort the actual one-year re-offending rate was 43.3%. They also found that there was a clear pattern between re-offending rates and age, with older offenders in the sample considerably more likely to re-offend than the youngest offenders.

6 Figures obtained from the Home Office website: www.crimereduction.gov.uk (accessed 3 June 2006).

1.87   The average re-offending rate hides considerable variation in the re-offending rate for different types of disposal. In the 2004 cohort there were the following actual re-offending rates:

Reprimand/warning	28%
First tier penalty (discharge/fine/reparation/ referral order)	52%
Community sentence	71%
Custodial sentence	78%

Costs

1.88   A decade ago the Audit Commission (1996) estimated that the total cost to public bodies of dealing with the detection and processing of offending by young people under the age of 18 totalled £1 billion a year (two-thirds of that cost being the cost to the police of identifying the young people dealt with by the youth justice system). The court process costs were estimated to average £2,500 for each young person sentenced. More recently, Byford and Barrett (2004), cited in Harrington and Bailey (2005), have attempted to calculate the cost of youth crime by considering the contact with health, education, social, voluntary, private and criminal justice sector resources. It was estimated that the average cost per year of a young person in the youth justice system was £39,120 (costs were considerably higher for those in custody at £55,674 per year). The main cost was found to be accommodation (both within the juvenile secure estate and in the community with placements in foster care or children's homes). The individual characteristics of the young offenders which increased the cost included: younger age, history of violent offence and depressed mood.

1.89   The most expensive part of the youth justice system is the juvenile secure estate. The National Audit Office (2004) estimated that the annual cost of a bed in each type of institution was as follows:

Secure training centre	£165,000
Secure children's home	£185,000
Young offender institution	£51,000

1.90   In comparison, a six-month intensive supervision and surveillance programme (see para 2.28) has been estimated to cost £8,500 (Audit Commission, 2004).

References

Allen, R. Out of Jail: The Reduction in the Use of Penal Custody for Male Juveniles 1981-1988. *The Howard Journal of Criminal Justice*, 30(1): 30-52, 1991.

Arnull, E, Eagle, S, Gammampila, A, Archer, D, Johnston, V, Miller, K and Pitcher, J, *Persistent young offenders: a retrospective study*, London: Youth Justice Board, 2005.

Audit Commission, *Misspent youth: young people and crime*, London: Audit Commission, 1996.

Audit Commission, *Youth Justice 2004*, London: Audit Commission, 2004.

Aye Maung, N, *Young people, victimisation and the police: British Crime Survey findings on experiences and attitudes of 12 to 15 year olds*, Home Office Research Study No 140 London: Home Office, 1995.

Baker, K, Jones, S, Roberts, C and Merrington, S, *Asset: the evaluation of the validity and reliability of the Youth Justice Board's assessment for young offenders*, London: Youth Justice Board, 2003.

Barbaret, R, Bowling, B, Junger-Tas, J, Rechea-Alberola, C, van Kesteren, J, Zurawan, A, *Self reported juvenile delinquency in England and Wales, the Netherlands and Spain*, European Institute for Crime Prevention and Control, 2004.

Barclay, G and Mhlanga, B, *Ethnic differences in decisions on young defendants dealt with by the Crown Prosecution Service*, Section 95 Findings No 1, London: Home Office, 2000.

Bateman, T, 'Living with final warnings: making the best of a bad job?' *Youth Justice* 2(3), 2002, pp131–140.

Bhimjiyani, H and Allen, J, 'Extent and trends' in Nicholas, S, Povey, D, Walker, A and Kershaw, C (eds), *Crime in England and Wales, 2004/2005*, Home Office Statistical Bulletin 11/05, London: Home Office, 2005.

Boswell, G, *Violent victims: the prevalence of abuse and loss in the lives of section 53 offenders*, London: The Prince's Trust, 1995.

Bowling, B and Phillips, C, *Racism, crime and justice*, London: Longman, 2002.

Budd, T, Sharp, C, Weir, G, Wilson, D and Owen, N, *Young people and crime: findings from the 2004 Offending, Crime and Justice Survey*, Home Office Statistical Bulletin 20/05, London: Home Office, 2005.

Burroughs, D, *Contemporary patterns of residential mobility in social housing in England*, York: University of York, 1998.

Byford, S and Barrett, B, *The cost of youth crime: study of young people in custody and in the community*, London: Centre for the Economics of Mental Health, Institute of Psychiatry, 2004.

Coleman, J and Hendry, L, *The nature of adolescence*, 3rd edn, London: Routledge, 1999.

Farrington, D., The Twelfth Jack Tizard Memorial Lecture: The development of offending and antisocial behaviour from childhood: Key findings from the Cambridge Study in Delinquent Development. *Journal of Child Psychology and Psychiatry*, 36, 929-964, 1995.

Feilzer, M and Hood, R, *Differences or discrimination?*, London: Youth Justice Board, 2004.

Flood-Page, C, Campbell, S, Harrington, V and Miller, J, *Youth crime: findings from the 1998/1999 youth lifestyles survey*, Home Office Research Study 209, London: Home Office, 2000.

Gelsthorpe, L, 'Girls in the youth justice system' in Bateman, T and Pitts, J (eds), *The RHP companion to youth justice*, Lyme Regis: Russell House Publishing, 2004.

Goldson, B, Penal Custody: Intolerance, Irrationality and Indifference. Goldson, B and Muncie, J (eds), *Youth Crime and Justice*. London: Sage, 2006.

Goldson, B and Chigwada-Bailey, R, '(What) justice for black children and young people?' in Goldson, B (ed), *Youth justice: contemporary policy and practice*, Aldershot: Ashgate, 1999.

Graham, J and Bowling, B, *Young people and crime,* Home Office Research Study No 145, London: Home Office, 1995.

Gray, E, Taylor, E, Roberts, C, Merrington, S, Fernandez, R and Moore, R, *ISSP: the final report,* London: Youth Justice Board, 2005.

Hagell, A and Newburn, T, *Persistent young offenders,* London: Policy Studies Institute Publishing, 1994.

Hagell, A, *The mental health of young offenders,* London: Mental Health Foundation, 2002.

Hammersley, R, Maynard, L and Reid, M, *Substance use by young offenders: the impact of normalization of drug use in the early years of the 21st century,* Home Office Research Study No 261, London: Home Office, 2003.

Harrington, R and Bailey, S, *Mental health needs and effectiveness of provision for young offenders in custody and in the community,* London: Youth Justice Board, 2005.

HM Inspector of Prisons, *Young prisoners: a thematic review,* London: Home Office, 1997.

Home Office, *Criminal statistics, England and Wales – 2001,* London: The Stationery Office, 2002.

Home Office, *Race and the criminal justice system: an overview to the complete statistics 2002–2003,* London: Home Office, 2003.

Home Office, *Criminal Statistics 2004 England and Wales.* Home Office Statistical Bulletin 19/05 2nd Edition. London: Home Office, 2005.

Home Office, *Statistics on race and the criminal justice system – 2004,* London: Home Office, 2005.

Hudson, A, '"Troublesome girls": towards alternative definitions and policies', 1989; reproduced in abridged form in Muncie, J, Hughes, G and McLaughlin, E (eds), *Youth justice: critical readings,* London: Sage, 2002.

Jones, K, and Pitts, J, *Early childhood child protection registration and subsequent involvement with a youth justice team/youth offending team in a London borough,* Luton: Vauxhall Centre for the Study of Crime, University of Luton, 2001.

Kazdin, A, 'Adolescent Development, Mental Disorders, and Decision Making of Delinquent Youths' in Grisso, T and Schwartz, R (eds), *Youth on trial: a developmental perspective on juvenile justice,* Chicago: University of Chicago Press, 2000.

Kroll, L, Rothwell, J, Bradley, D, Shah, P, Bailey, S and Harrington, RC, 'Mental health needs of boys in secure care for serious or persistent offending: a prospective, Longitudinal Study' *The Lancet,* 359, 2002, pp1,975–1,979.

Maughan, B, Pickles, A, Hagell, A Rutter, M & Yale, W, Reading Problems and antisocial behaviour: Developmental trends in comorbidity. *Journal of Child Psychology and Psychiatry,* 37, 405-418, 1996

Meltzer, H, Gatwood, R, Goodman, R and Ford, T, *The mental health of children and adolescents in Great Britain,* Office of National Statistics, London: The Stationery Office, 1999.

Moffitt, TE, 'Adolescence-limited and life-course-persistent antisocial behavior: a developmental taxonomy' *Psychological Review,* 100, 1993, 674–701.

Moore, S and Peters, *A beacon of hope: children and young people on remand – final report of the national remand review initiative,* London: The Children's Society, 2003.

MORI, *Youth Survey 2004,* London: Youth Justice Board, 2004.

Muncie, J, *Youth and crime* 2nd edn, London: Sage, 2004.

Nacro, *Differential patterns of custodial sentencing,* London: Youth Justice Board, 2002.

Nacro, *Youth crime briefing: some facts about children and young people who offend – 2004,* London: NACRO, 2006.

National Audit Office, *Youth Offending: the delivery of community and custodial sentences,* London: National Audit Office, 2004.

National Statistics, *Statistics on young people and drug misuse: England 2006,* London: NHS Information Centre, 2006.

Office for Criminal Justice Reform, *Strategic plan for criminal justice 2004*, London: Home Office, 2004.

Pitcher, J, Bateman, T, Johnston, V and Cadman, S, *Health, Education and substance misuse services: the provision of health, education and substance misuse workers in youth offending teams and the health/education needs of young people supervised by youth offending teams*, London: Youth Justice Board, 2004.

Pitts, J, *The politics of juvenile crime*, London: Sage, 1988.

Pitts, J, 'The Criminal Victimisation of Children and Young People' in Bateman, T and Pitts, J (eds), *The RHP companion to youth Justice*, Lyme Regis: Russell House Publishing, 2004.

Pitts, J and Bateman, T, 'Youth crime in England and Wales' in Bateman, T and Pitts, J (eds), *The RHP companion to youth justice*, Lyme Regis: Russell House Publishing, 2004.

Pudney, S, *The road to ruin? Sequences of initiation into drug use and offending by young people in Britain*, Home Office Research Study No 253, London: Home Office, 2002.

Rutherford, A, *Growing out of crime*, London: Penguin, 1988.

Rutter, M, Giller, H and Hagell, A, *Anti-social behaviour by young people*, Cambridge: Cambridge University Press, 1998.

Sanders, W, *Our Manor: Youth crime and youth culture in the inner city*, unpublished PhD Thesis, London: Goldsmith College, 2003.

Sharp, D, *Serve and protect? Black young people's experiences of policy in the community*, London: The Children's Society, 2005.

Sharp, C, Aldridge, J and Medina, J, *Delinquent youth groups and offending behaviour: findings from the 2004 Offending, Crime and Justice Survey*, Home Office Online Report 14/06, 2006.

Smith, D, *The links between victimization and offending*, The Edinburgh Study of Youth Transitions and Crime, No 5, Edinburgh: University of Edinburgh, 2004.

Smith, D and Bradshaw, P, *Gang membership and teenage offending*, The Edinburgh Study of Youth Transitions and Crime, No 8, Edinburgh: University of Edinburgh, 2005.

Smith, D and Gray, J, *Police and People in London*. Aldershot: Gower, 1985.

Social Exclusion Unit, *National strategy for neighbourhood renewal – report of Policy Action Team 12: young people*, London: Social Exclusion Unit, 2000.

Steinberg, L, and Schwartz, R, 'Developmental psychology' in Grisso, T and Schwartz, R (eds), *Youth on trial: a developmental perspective on juvenile justice*, Chicago: University of Chicago Press, 2000.

Sutton, C, Utting, D and Farrington, D (eds), *Support from the start: working with young children and their families to reduce the risks of crime and anti-social behaviour*, Department for Education and Skills Research Report No 524, London: Department for Education and Skills, 2000.

Thomas, N and Feist, A, 'Detection of crime' in Nicholas, S, Povey, D, Walker, A and Kershaw, C (eds), *Crime in England and Wales, 2004/2005*, Home Office Statistical Bulletin, London: Home Office, 2005.

Whiting, E and Cuppleditch, L, *Re-offending of juveniles: results from the 2004 cohort*, Home Office Statistical Bulletin 10/06, London: Home Office, 2006.

Wilkinson, C and Evans, R, 'Police Cautioning of Juveniles: The Impact of Home Office Circular 14/1985', [1990] Crim LR 165.

Wood, M, *The victimization of young people: findings from the Crime and Justice Survey 2003*, Home Office Findings No 245, London: Home Office, 2005.

Youth Justice Board, *Risk and protective factors associated with youth crime and effective interventions to prevent it*, London: Youth Justice Board, 2001, 2005.

Youth Justice Board, *Substance misuse and the juvenile secure estate*, London: Youth Justice Board, 2004.

Youth Justice Board, *Youth resettlement: a framework for action*, London: Youth Justice Board, 2005.

Youth Justice Board, *Youth Justice Annual Statistics 2004/05,* London: Youth Justice Board, 2006.

Youth Justice Trust, *Health needs,* Manchester: Youth Justice Trust, 2001.

Youth Justice Trust, *On the case: a survey of over 1,000 children and young people under supervision by youth offending teams in Greater Manchester and West Yorkshire,* Manchester: Youth Justice Trust, 2003.

Zimring, F, *The challenge of youth violence,* New York: Cambridge University Press, 1998.

Further reading

For a general overview of the issues touched upon in this chapter see:

- Bateman, T and Pitts, J (eds), *The RHP companion to youth justice,* Lyme Regis: Russell House Publishing, 2004; or

- Fionda, J, *Devils and angels: youth policy and crime,* Oxford: Hart Publishing, 2005; or

- Muncie, J, *Youth and crime* 2nd edn, London: Sage, 2004.

For a comprehensive and authoritative review of the research evidence (up to 1998) see:

- Rutter, M, Giller, H, and Hagell, A, *Anti-social behaviour by young people,* Cambridge: Cambridge University Press, 1998.

For a brief treatment of the issues which also allows young people to speak for themselves, see:

- Neuberger, A, *Locked in, locked out: the experience of young offenders out of society and in prison,* London: Calouste Gulbenkian Foundation, 2002.

CHAPTER 2

The youth justice system

Introduction

2.1   The youth justice system is the system of criminal justice insofar as it relates to children and young people.[1]

2.2   During the 1990s the system came under considerable criticism for its management deficiencies as well as its perceived failure to tackle youth offending. In 1996 the Audit Commission carried out a comprehensive survey of the youth justice system.[2] Their report identified a lack of co-ordination amongst the various agencies involved in the system which resulted in inefficient working practices and enormous delays.

2.3   In 1997 the Labour government published a white paper, *No More Excuses – A New Approach to Tackling Youth Crime In England and Wales* (Cm 3809). In the preface, the then Home Secretary, Jack Straw, explained why he considered that reform was necessary:

> An excuse culture has developed within the youth justice system. It excuses itself for its inefficiency, and too often excuses the young offenders before it, implying that they cannot help their behaviour because of their social circumstances. Rarely are they confronted with their behaviour and helped to take more personal responsibility for their actions. The system allows them to go on wrecking their own lives as well as disrupting their families and communities.

2.4   In response to these perceived faults substantial reforms were instituted in the late 1990s. The white paper indicated that the reform programme aimed to provide:

- a clear strategy to prevent offending and re-offending;
- that offenders, and their parents, face up to their offending behaviour and take responsibility for it;
- earlier and more effective intervention when young people first offend;
- faster, more efficient procedures from arrest to sentence; and
- partnership between all youth justice agencies to deliver a better, faster system.

2.5   To effect these changes there was a complete overhaul of the management structure of the agencies involved in the youth justice system. The Youth Justice Board was established to ensure national co-ordination and at the local level the various agencies are now required to work together to establish multi-agency teams called youth offending teams, which provide relevant services to the courts and young offenders.

2.6   The Home Office has proposed further changes to the youth justice system in its policy document *Youth Justice – The Next Steps* (September 2003).[3] Among other proposals, this paper suggests simplifying the range of sentences available for young offenders. At the time of writing, it is understood that a bill to introduce the proposals contained in the policy document has been drafted but it has not been introduced to parliament because of a lack of legislative time.

---

1   Crime and Disorder Act 1998 s42(1).
2   *Misspent Youth* (Audit Commission, 1996).
3   Available on the Youth Justice Board website – see appendix 14 for contact details.

Youth Justice Board for England and Wales

2.7   The Youth Justice Board was established on 30 September 1998 by the Crime and Disorder Act 1998 s41. The Board is an executive non-departmental public body, which is accountable to the Home Secretary. The Board consists of between 10 and 12 members appointed by the Home Secretary, including people who have extensive recent experience of the youth justice system. The functions of the Board include:

- monitoring the operation of the youth justice system and the provision of youth justice services;
- advising the Home Secretary on this and the setting of national standards for the provision of youth justice services and custodial accommodation;
- advising on how the principal aim of the youth justice system might most effectively be pursued; and
- identifying and promoting, and making grants for the development of, good practice in the operation of the youth justice system and the preventing of youth offending.[4]

2.8   Since April 2000 the Board has also had responsibility for the commissioning and purchasing of secure facilities for juveniles on remand and under sentence. Through its Secure Estate Clearing House it allocates juvenile prisoners within the secure estate.

2.9   In order to perform its function of monitoring the operation of the youth justice system, the Board has powers to require local authorities, police authorities, local probation boards and health authorities to provide information.[5] The Board regularly issues National Standards for all areas of work within the youth justice system from the police station to the custodial institution where a young offender may serve his/her sentence.[6]

2.10   In the financial year 2004/05 the budget of the Board was £377 million. It directly employs a range of staff, however most of its budget £246 million was allocated to purchasing places or improvements in the secure estate. Youth offending teams (which are principally locally funded) received £40 million in funding from the Board, a further £32 million was spent on the Intensive Supervision and Surveillance Programme and a combined total of £13 million on preventative and community intervention schemes. Just under £1.8 million was spent on research and evaluation.[7]

Youth justice provision in Wales

2.11   Since the implementation of the Government of Wales Act 1998, the Welsh Assembly has had responsibility for social services and education provision. The Assembly determines policy by issuing guidance and by passing secondary legislation. As a result, some of the relevant guidance and

---

4   Crime and Disorder Act 1998 s41(5).
5   Ibid, s41(5)(d).
6   See para 2.20 below.
7   Youth Justice Board, *Annual Accounts 2004/05*.

regulations discussed in this book will be found in a different form in Wales. Where possible, the reference to the relevant Welsh provision will be made in the text. Where the Youth Justice Board issues guidance for the whole of England and Wales it will be done in consultation with the Welsh Assembly.

2.12   It should also be noted that the Welsh Language Act 1993 establishes the principle that in the conduct of public business and the administration of justice in Wales the English and Welsh languages should be treated on a basis of equality. Every public body providing services in Wales is required to prepare a scheme specifying the measures which it proposes to take as to the use of the Welsh language in connection with the provision of such services.[8]

Provision of youth justice services

2.13   Youth justice services are defined as:

- appropriate adult services;
- assessment and intervention work in support of a final warning;
- bail support;
- the placement in local authority accommodation of children and young people remanded or committed to such accommodation;
- reports and other information required by the courts;
- the implementation of referral orders;
- providing responsible officers in relation to parenting orders, child safety orders, reparation and action plan orders;
- supervision of children and young persons under supervision orders and detention and training orders;
- supervision of young persons under community rehabilitation orders, community punishment orders or community punishment and rehabilitation orders; and
- post-release supervision of children and young persons released from custody.[9]

2.14   By the Crime and Disorder Act 1998 s38(1) every local authority with responsibility for education and social services has a duty to secure that, to such an extent as is appropriate for their area, all the youth justice services listed above are available in their area. A duty to co-operate with the local authority in the discharge of this obligation is placed on:

- every chief officer of police or police authority any part of whose area lies within the local authority's area;
- every probation committee or health authority any part of whose area lies within the local authority's area.[10]

---

8   The provision of services for Welsh speakers in the juvenile secure estate has been criticised – see C Hughes and H Madoc-Jones, 'Meeting the needs of Welsh speaking young people in custody', *The Howard Journal*, Vol 44 No 4, September 2005, pp374–386.

9   Crime and Disorder Act 1998 s38(4).

10   Ibid, s38(2).

Youth offending teams

2.15   Every local authority with responsibility for education and social services is under a duty to establish for their area one or more youth offending teams.[11] It is possible for neighbouring local authorities to establish a joint youth offending team.[12] A duty is placed on the relevant police service, local probation board and health authority to co-operate in the discharge of the local authority's duty to establish youth offending teams.[13]

2.16   A youth offending team must consist of at least one of each of the following:

- a probation officer;
- a social worker of a local authority social services department;
- a police officer;
- a person nominated by a health authority; and
- a person nominated by the chief education officer.[14]

2.17   In many youth offending teams there will also be staff from other organisations, such as local authority housing departments and Connexions.

Youth justice plans

2.18   Following consultation with the relevant police service, probation committee and health authority, every local authority with responsibility for education and social services must formulate and implement an annual youth justice plan. The plan must detail:

- how youth justice services are to be provided and funded;
- how the youth offending team is to be composed and funded, how it is to operate and what functions it is to carry out.

2.19   Youth justice plans must be submitted to the Youth Justice Board each year and published as directed by the secretary of state.[15]

National Standards for Youth Justice Services

2.20   The Home Secretary has delegated his power to issue national standards for the operation of the youth justice system and the provision of youth justice services to the Youth Justice Board.[16] Under this delegated power the Youth Justice Board publishes from time to time *National Standards for Youth Justice Services*. At the time of writing, the most recent edition was published in April 2004.

2.21   In carrying out any of their duties under Part 1 of the Crime and Disorder Act 1998 a local authority, a police authority, a probation committee,

11 Crime and Disorder Act 1998 s39(1).
12 Ibid, s39(2).
13 Ibid, s39(3).
14 Ibid, s39(5).
15 Ibid, s40(4).
16 Ibid, s41(5)(b)(iii).

a health authority or a Primary Care Trust shall act in accordance with the *National Standards for Youth Justice Services.*[17]

2.22   The defence lawyer would be well advised to obtain a copy of the current *National Standards for Youth Justice Services.*[18]

Standardised assessment

2.23   The Centre for Criminological Research at the University of Oxford has developed, on behalf of the Youth Justice Board, a standardised assessment tool to be used with children and young persons. This is commonly referred to as *Asset.* The Youth Justice Board website describes the purpose of *Asset* as follows:

> *Asset* is a structured assessment tool to be used by YOTs [youth offending teams] in England and Wales on all young offenders who come into contact with the criminal justice system. It aims to look at the young person's offence or offences and identify a multitude of factors or circumstances – ranging from lack of educational attainment to mental health problems – which may have contributed to such behaviour. The information gathered from *Asset* can be used to inform court reports so that appropriate intervention programmes can be drawn up. It will also highlight any particular needs or difficulties the young person has, so that these may also be addressed. *Asset* will also help to measure changes in needs and risk of reoffending over time.

2.24   *Asset* must be completed for all children and young persons subject to:

- bail supervision and support;
- a request for a pre-sentence or specific sentence report;
- community disposals (final warnings, referral orders, reparation orders and community orders) at the start, quarterly review and closure stages; and
- custodial sentences at the assessment, transfer to the community and closure stages.[19]

2.25   The *Asset* assessment must be informed by:

- at least one interview with the young person;
- an interview with parent(s) or carers(s) unless the young person is aged 16 or over and/or estranged from his/her parents; and
- existing reports including any previous *Asset* or other assessments, pre-sentence reports, list of previous convictions, statement of special educational needs and any other information relevant to the offending.[20]

2.26   *Asset* comprises the following:

- *Core profile* completed by a youth offending team worker;
- *What do you think?* – a self-completion questionnaire for the young offender; and
- *Risk of serious harm* (only completed if the core profile indicates that

17 Crime and Disorder Act 1998 s42(3).
18 Copies may be downloaded from the Youth Justice Board website – see appendix 12.
19 Youth Justice Board: *National Standards for Youth Justice Services* (2004) para 4.1.
20 Ibid, para 4.4.

there is a risk of the child or young person committing serious harm to him/herself or others).

2.27 There are also shorter versions of the profile to be used when working with a young offender on a final warning or when conducting an assessment for bail supervision and support.[21]

Programmes designed to reduce offending

Intensive Supervision and Surveillance Programmes

2.28 The Youth Justice Board website explains the purpose of Intensive Supervision and Surveillance Programmes (often referred to as ISSPs) as follows:

> ISSP was devised following evidence that suggested 3% of young offenders were responsible for 25% of all youth crime. In response to this, since 2001, the YJB has invested approximately £80 million to establish ISSP across England and Wales as the most robust alternative to custody for prolific and serious young offenders.
>
> ISSP is a mixture of punishment and positive opportunities, available 365 days a year. It is designed to:
> * ensure that the young person makes recompense for his or her offences
> * address the underlying causes of the offending
> * put in place structures that will allow the young person to avoid offending in future
> * manage the risks posed by the young person to the community
> * stabilise what is often a very chaotic lifestyle
> * reintegrate the young person into the community, particularly through activities that can be continued when supervision by the scheme has ended
> * help the young person to lead an independent life free of offending.
>
> ISSP can be a condition of bail, a Supervision Order, Community Rehabilitation Order, or the community portion of a custodial sentence (Detention and Training Order or Section 90/91). It is not a court order.

Supervision

2.29 For those on six-month programmes, the first three months should involve a structured programme of at least five hours a day during the week, with access to support during the evenings and weekends. After three months, a less intensive period of supervision will normally follow and will include at least one hour each weekday, with evening and weekend support still available.[22]

2.30 The programme must include elements which address:

* education and training (especially basic literacy and numeracy) and employment;
* interventions to tackle offending behaviour;
* reparation to victims or the community;
* assistance in developing interpersonal skills and support.[23]

---

21 *Asset* Bail is considered in more detail at para 13.4A
22 Youth Justice Board: *National Standards for Youth Justice Services* (2004), para 9.2.
23 Ibid, para 9.9.

2.31   In addition, programmes should include access to support for individual problems – for example homelessness, drug misuse or mental health problems.[24]

Surveillance

2.32   There should be a minimum of two surveillance contacts a day and 24-hour cover seven days a week. The child or young person must be monitored by a least one of the following:

- **tracking** – staff who track the whereabouts of the children or young people throughout the week, reinforcing participation in their supervision programme by accompanying them to appointments, providing support and advice and following up any non-attendance;
- **tagging** – electronic monitoring of the child or young person;
- **voice verification** – to confirm that the child or young person is where s/he is supposed to be (for example, at school);
- **intelligence-led policing** – the police will overtly monitor the movements of the child or young person at key times to reinforce the programme as well as sharing information with the programme staff.[25]

Eligibility

2.33   Intensive Supervision and Surveillance Programmes are very expensive to operate, therefore it is not surprising that there are strict criteria for deciding whether a child or young person should be considered. The current criteria are set out in table 4 below.

Prolific and priority offender strategy

2.34   The prolific and priority offender strategy is targeted at a relatively small number of offenders (both adult and youth) who are thought to cause a disproportionate amount of crime and disorder. It has been in operation nationally since November 2004.

2.35   The strategy has three parts:

- **prevent and deter** – to stop people engaging in offending behaviour and graduating into prolific offenders;
- **catch and convict** – actively tackling those who are already prolific offenders;
- **rehabilitate and resettle** – working with identified prolific offenders to stop their offending by offering a range of supportive interventions – offenders will be offered the opportunity of rehabilitation or face a very swift return to the courts.

2.36   Young people identified as being at risk of becoming prolific and priority offenders will be offered various services intended to prevent offending in the future. Such services may include referral to:

- a referral to a youth inclusion project;
- Connexions; or
- drugs counselling.

---

24   Youth Justice Board: *National Standards for Youth Justice Services* (2004), para 9.9.
25   Ibid, para 9.10.

Table 4: Criteria for Intensive Supervision and Surveillance Programme

A child or young person is eligible if s/he meets any of the following criteria:

1. Prolific offender

A young person must have (sic) four or more previous imprisonable offences in the last 12 months and be appearing in court for a fifth (at least) offence. The young person must have at least one previous community or custodial penalty.

2. Serious crime short cuts

(i) The young person is charged with an offence for which an adult could receive 10 years or more in custody; or

(ii) Any young person initially charged with s18(GBH) who subsequently has the charge reduced to s20; or

(iii) Any young person charged with aggravated vehicle-taking

3. Bail short cut

The young person must be at risk of a secure remand under Children and Young Persons Act 1969 s23(5).

4. Previous custodial sentence short cut

The young person must have previously had a detention and training order and – within a year of leaving custody – is facing custody again.

Source: Youth Justice Board, *ISSP Management Guidance* (2005) as amended by email notification from Mary Wyman, Head of Service Development, Youth Justice Board (3 January 2006).

2.37 Young offenders identified as prolific and priority offenders may be the subject of:

- higher levels of police monitoring, whether by way of stop and search or checking on bail curfews;
- fast track decision-making by the Crown Prosecution Service; or
- bail supervision and support programmes or bail Intensive Supervision and Surveillance Programmes.

2.38 Unlike the persistent young offender categorisation, being deemed a prolific and priority offender should not have any significance in court hearings, nor should it be referred to in pre-sentence reports.[26]

2.39 Where a community penalty is being recommended, the writer of the pre-sentence report is advised to consider intensive programmes including an Intensive Supervision and Surveillance Programme. Consideration of curfew orders is also encouraged.[27]

---

26 Youth Justice Board *Prolific and Other Priority Offenders Strategy: Guidance for Youth Offending Teams* (November 2004), para 65.

27 Ibid, para 69.

2.40   Where a young person deemed to be a prolific and priority offender receives a custodial sentence, the youth offending team is advised to arrange intensive and robust supervision packages for the period of supervision in the community. Where the criteria for an Intensive Supervision and Surveillance Programme are met, this should be made a requirement of the post-release supervision or licence.[28] Youth offending teams and custodial institutions should ensure that comprehensive resettlement plans are in place pre-release for all youth persistent and prolific offenders to ensure that they leave custody to suitable accommodation, training, and, where appropriate, support to address substance misuse or mental health problems.[29]

2.41   In the case of young people deemed to be prolific and priority offenders, alleged breaches of bail conditions, community order or post-release supervision/licence requirements should be fast tracked through the courts.[30]

Sources of law and principles

2.42   The law and guiding principles applicable to the youth justice system may be found in both domestic law and in international standards.

Domestic legislation

Statutes

2.43   Despite the existence of a specialist criminal court to deal with defendants under the age of 18, the law relating to children and young persons is not to be found solely in one statute. Instead, relevant statutory provisions are scattered through a series of statutes spanning more than 70 years. It is perhaps inevitable that the relevant law is not wholly consistent in content or purpose.

2.44   Even following the major reforms of the management of the youth justice system introduced by the Crime and Disorder Act 1998, it is still best to think of the law relating to children and young persons in the criminal justice system as an adaptation of the rules applying to adults. The main pieces of legislation which alter those rules are:

- Children and Young Persons Act 1933;
- Children and Young Persons Act 1963;
- Children and Young Persons Act 1969;
- Bail Act 1976;
- Magistrates' Courts Act 1980;
- Crime and Disorder Act 1998;
- Powers of Criminal Courts (Sentencing) Act 2000;
- Anti-social Behaviour Act 2003; and
- Criminal Justice Act 2003.

28 Youth Justice Board *Prolific and Other Priority Offenders Strategy: Guidance for Youth Offending Teams* (November 2004), paras 72 and 73.

29 Ibid, para 74.

30 Ibid, para 76.

2.45 It is still the opinion of the authors that there is much to be said for a consolidating statute which would contain all relevant statutory provisions relating to children and young persons.

Procedural rules

2.46 The Criminal Procedure Rules 2005[31] established for the first time an overriding objective of the criminal justice process. Rule 1 provides:

1.1 The overriding objective
(1) The overriding objective of this new code is that criminal cases be dealt with justly.
(2) Dealing with a criminal case justly includes—
  (a) acquitting the innocent and convicting the guilty;
  (b) dealing with the prosecution and the defence fairly;
  (c) recognising the rights of a defendant, particularly those under Article 6 of the European Convention on Human Rights;
  (d) respecting the interests of witnesses, victims and jurors and keeping them informed of the progress of the case;
  (e) dealing with the case efficiently and expeditiously;
  (f) ensuring that appropriate information is available to the court when bail and sentence are considered; and
  (g) dealing with the case in ways that take into account—
    (i) the gravity of the offence alleged,
    (ii) the complexity of what is in issue,
    (iii) the severity of the consequences for the defendant and others affected, and
    (iv) the needs of other cases.

1.2 The duty of the participants in a criminal case
(1) Each participant, in the conduct of each case, must—
  (a) prepare and conduct the case in accordance with the overriding objective;
  (b) comply with these Rules, practice directions and directions made by the court; and
  (c) at once inform the court and all parties of any significant failure (whether or not that participant is responsible for that failure) to take any procedural step required by these Rules, any practice direction or any direction of the court. A failure is significant if it might hinder the court in furthering the overriding objective.
(2) Anyone involved in any way with a criminal case is a participant in its conduct for the purposes of this rule.

1.3 The application by the court of the overriding objective
The court must further the overriding objective in particular when—
  (a) exercising any power given to it by legislation (including these Rules);
  (b) applying any practice direction; or
  (c) interpreting any rule or practice direction.

European Convention on Human Rights

2.47 The European Convention for the Protection of Human Rights and Fundamental Freedoms (1950) (Cmd 8969) was adopted by the member states of the council of Europe in 1950. It was ratified by the United Kingdom in 1951. It is usually referred to as the European Convention on Human

31 SI No 384.

Rights. Under the Human Rights Act 1998 it is unlawful for any public authority, including a court, to act in a manner which is incompatible with a convention right. Even in the case of primary legislation, every court has to strive to interpret the statute to ensure compatibility with convention rights. If this proves impossible, the higher courts (High Court, Court of Appeal and House of Lords) may issue declarations of incompatibility which could lead to early amendment of the relevant legislation.

2.48   Relevant principles applicable to the youth justice system are:

- Article 3: protection from inhuman and degrading treatment;
- Article 5: guarantee of the right to liberty and the security of the person;
- Article 6: guarantee of due process (fair trial, impartial and independent tribunal etc);
- Article 8: right to privacy and family life;
- Article 14: non-discrimination in the application of rights guaranteed by the convention.

2.49   The convention does not specifically address the rights of children, but the European Court of Human Rights has demonstrated a willingness to use other international conventions and standards to inform their decision-making when considering the rights of a child.[32]

Inhuman and degrading treatment or punishment

2.50   Article 3 provides:

> No one shall be subjected to torture or to inhuman or degrading treatment or punishment.

2.51   Article 3 is an absolute right, which means that contracting states cannot use any grounds for breaching this guarantee. In *T v United Kingdom, V v United Kingdom*[33] the European Court of Human Rights has provided a succinct survey of the criteria for determining what would constitute inhuman or degrading treatment or punishment:

> Ill-treatment must attain a minimum level of severity if it is to fall within the scope of Article 3. The assessment of this minimum is, in the nature of things, relative; it depends on all the circumstances of the case, such as the nature and context of the treatment or punishment, the manner and method of its execution, its duration, its physical or mental effects and, in some instances, the sex, age and state of health of the victim (see, amongst many other examples, the *Soering v. the United Kingdom* judgment of 7 July 1989, Series A no. 161, p. 39, § 100).

> Treatment has been held by the Court to be "inhuman" because, inter alia, it was premeditated, was applied for hours at a stretch and caused either actual bodily injury or intense physical and mental suffering, and also "degrading" because it was such as to arouse in its victims feelings of fear, anguish and inferiority capable of humiliating and debasing them. In order for a punishment or treatment associated with it to be "inhuman" or "degrading", the suffering

---

32   See *A v United Kingdom* (1998) 27 EHRR 611; [1998] 2 FLR 959 sub nom *A v United Kingdom (Human Rights: Punishment of Child)* and *T v United Kingdom, V v United Kingdom* [2000] 2 All ER 1024 (Note); (2000) 30 EHRR 121; 7 BHRC 659, ECtHR.

33   *T v United Kingdom, V v United Kingdom* [2000] 2 All ER 1024 (Note); (2000) 30 EHRR 121; 7 BHRC 659, ECtHR.

or humiliation involved must in any event go beyond that inevitable element of suffering or humiliation connected with a given form of legitimate treatment or punishment (ibid.). The question whether the purpose of the treatment was to humiliate or debase the victim is a further factor to be taken into account (see, for example, the *Raninen v. Finland* judgment of 16 December 1997, *Reports* 1997-VIII, pp. 2821-22, § 55), but the absence of any such purpose cannot conclusively rule out a finding of a violation of Article 3.

2.52 The mere attribution of criminal responsibility to a child aged 10 years is not in itself a breach of Article 3.[34] Exposing an 11-year old boy accused of murder to a jury trial in the public and formal environment of a Crown Court could not be said to be a breach of Article 3, despite psychiatric evidence that at least one of the defendants was traumatised by the experience.[35]

2.53 The existence of Article 3 places positive duties upon contracting states. In *Z v United Kingdom*[36] the court declared:

> The obligation on High Contracting Parties under Article 1 of the Convention to secure everyone within their jurisdiction the rights and freedoms defined in the Convention, taken together with Article 3, requires States to take measures designed to ensure that individuals within their jurisdiction are not subjected to torture or inhuman or degrading treatment, including such ill-treatment administered by private individuals. These measures should provide effective protection, in particular, of children and other vulnerable persons and include reasonable steps to prevent ill-treatment of which the authorities had or ought to have had knowledge.

2.54 The practical implications of this duty in relation to young people detained in the juvenile secure estate are considered at para 26.124.

Right to liberty

2.55 Article 5(1) provides:

> Everyone has the right to liberty and security of person. No one shall be deprived of his liberty save in the following cases and in accordance with a procedure prescribed by law:
> (a) the lawful detention of a person after conviction by a competent court;
> (b) the lawful arrest or detention of a person for non-compliance with the lawful order of a court or in order to secure the fulfilment of any obligation prescribed by law;
> (c) the lawful arrest or detention of a person effected for the purpose of bringing him before the competent legal authority on reasonable suspicion of having committed an offence or when it is reasonably considered necessary to prevent his committing an offence or fleeing after having done so;
> (d) the detention of a minor by lawful order for the purpose of educational supervision or his lawful detention for the purpose of bringing him before the competent legal authority;
> (e) the lawful detention of persons for the prevention of the spreading of infectious diseases, of persons of unsound mind, alcoholics or drug addicts or vagrants;
> (f) the lawful arrest or detention of a person to prevent his effecting an unauthorised entry into the country or of a person against whom action is being taken with a view to deportation or extradition.

---

34 *T v United Kingdom, V v United Kingdom* [2000] 2 All ER 1024 (Note); (2000) 30 EHRR 121; 7 BHRC 659, ECtHR, for further discussion see para 6.8.
35 Ibid.
36 (2001) 34 EHRR 97.

2.56   The right to liberty will be relevant when considering bail, secure accommodation orders and custodial sentences. The exception to the right to
liberty for the purpose of educational supervision was invoked to justify
the lawfulness of a secure accommodation order.[37]

Right to a fair trial

2.57   Article 6 provides:

1. In the determination of his civil rights and obligations or of any criminal
charge against him, everyone is entitled to a fair and public hearing within
a reasonable time by an independent and impartial tribunal established by
law. Judgment shall be pronounced publicly but the press and public may be
excluded from all or part of the trial in the interest of morals, public order or
national security in a democratic society, where the interests of juveniles or the
protection of the private life of the parties so require, or to the extent strictly
necessary in the opinion of the court in special circumstances where publicity
would prejudice the interests of justice.

2. Everyone charged with a criminal offence shall be presumed innocent until
proved guilty according to law.

3. Everyone charged with a criminal offence has the following minimum
rights:
(a) to be informed promptly, in a language which he understands and in detail,
    of the nature and cause of the accusation against him;
(b) to have adequate time and facilities for the preparation of his defence;
(c) to defend himself in person or through legal assistance of his own choosing
    or, if he has not sufficient means to pay for legal assistance, to be given it
    free when the interests of justice so require;
(d) to examine or have examined witnesses against him and to obtain the attend-
    ance and examination of witnesses on his behalf under the same conditions
    as witnesses against him;
(e) to have the free assistance of an interpreter if he cannot understand or speak
    the language used in court.

2.58   In *Nortier v Netherlands*[38] Judge Walsh in his Commission decision stated
that the due process guarantees of Article 6 apply with equal force to juveniles as they do to adults:

Juveniles facing criminal charges are as fully entitled as adults to benefit from
all the Convention requirements for a fair trial. Great care must always be taken
to ensure that this entitlement is not diluted by considerations of rehabilitation
or reform. These are considerations which should be in addition to all the procedural protections available. Fair trial and proper proof of guilt are absolute
conditions precedent.

2.59   This statement has been quoted with approval by the full court.[39]

2.60   As well as being entitled to the full protection of due process, it was also
suggested that children and young persons should receive extra protection
as a result of their youth:

---

37 *Re K (a child) (secure accommodation order: right to liberty)* [2001] 2 All ER 719; [2001]
    2 WLR 1141; [2001] 1 FCR 249, CA.

38 (1993) 17 EHRR 273.

39 Eg *T v United Kingdom, V v United Kingdom* [2000] 2 All ER 1024 (Note); (2000) 30
    EHRR 121; 7 BHRC 659, ECtHR.

[M]inors are as entitled to the same protection of their fundamental rights as adults ... but the developing state of their personality – and consequently their limited social responsibility – should be taken into account in applying Article 6 of the Convention.[40]

2.61 The European Court of Human Rights has held that the guarantees of Article 6, when taken together, amount to a right to participate effectively in any criminal trial. The application of this principle to a young defendant was considered in *T v United Kingdom, V v United Kingdom*[41] where the court stated (at para 86 of judgment in relation to V):

[I]t is essential that a child charged with an offence is dealt with in a manner which takes full account of his age, level of maturity and intellectual and emotional capacities, and that steps are taken to promote his ability to understand and participate in the proceedings.

2.62 The practical implications of this principle are considered in detail in chapter 10.

Right to respect for private and family life

2.63 Article 8 provides:

1. Everyone has the right to respect for his private and family life, his home and his correspondence.

2. There shall be no interference by a public authority with the exercise of this right except such as is in accordance with the law and is necessary in a democratic society in the interests of national security, public safety or the economic well-being of the country, for the prevention of disorder or crime, for the protection of health or morals, or for the protection of the rights and freedoms of others.

2.64 Article 8 is a qualified right, which means that interference may be justified provided that the interference is necessary to meet one of the legitimate aims specified in Article 8(2). In the context of the youth justice system, that legitimate aim will nearly always be the prevention of disorder or crime, although the aim of protection of health and morals could be invoked in certain case involving young offenders.

2.65 In determining whether a limitation on a fundamental right is arbitrary or excessive, the courts will apply the 'proportionality' test – that is, the court will ask itself whether:

- the legislative objective is sufficiently important to justify limiting a fundamental right;
- the measures designed to meet the legislative objective are rationally connected to it; and
- the means used to impair the right or freedom are not more than is necessary to accomplish the objective.[42]

---

40 *Nortier v Netherlands* (1993) 17 EHRR 273, per Judge Morenilla at p291.
41 *T v United Kingdom, V v United Kingdom* [2000] 2 All ER 1024 (Note); (2000) 30 EHRR 121; 7 BHRC 659, ECtHR.
42 Formulated by Lord Clyde in *de Freitas v Permanent Secretary of Ministry of Agriculture, Fisheries, Lands and Housing* [1999] 1 AC 69 and expressly adopted by Lord Steyn in *R v A* [2001] UKHL 25, [38]; [2002] 1 AC 45.

2.66   Tackling the problem of youth crime has been described as a pressing social need which would be a sufficiently important objective to meet the first of the three questions.[43]

2.67   In the context of the youth justice system, Article 8 has been held to be engaged in the following circumstances:

- the requirements contained in parenting orders;[44]
- the use of custodial remands;[45] and
- detaining young offenders in the juvenile secure estate.[46]

Prohibition of discrimination

2.68   Article 14 provides:

> The enjoyment of the rights and freedoms set forth in this Convention shall be secured without discrimination on any ground such as sex, race, colour, language, religion, political or other opinion, national or social origin, association with a national minority, property, birth or other status.

2.69   As yet there is no guidance from the European court to indicate whether 'other status' could include children as a status group.

2.70   When considering the application of Article 14 to qualified rights such as Article 8, the European Court of Human Rights in *Inze v Austria*[47] stated:

> For the purpose of Article 14, a difference of treatment is discriminatory if it 'has no objective and reasonable justification', that is, if it does not pursue a 'legitimate aim' or if there is not a 'reasonable relationship of proportionality' between the means employed and the aim sought to be realised.

2.71   In the youth justice context the application of Article 14 has been considered by the administrative court in *R(SR) v Nottingham Magistrates' Court*.[48] In this case the provisions for secure remands introduced by the Criminal Justice and Police Act 2001 s98 were said to breach the prohibition against discrimination as most 15- and 16-year-old boys were remanded to Prison Service establishments, whereas all girls of that age were remanded to secure training centres or local authority secure children's homes. Having heard evidence regarding the limited resources available within the juvenile secure estate, Brooke LJ held that the admitted discrimination on the basis of gender was in pursuit of a legitimate purpose and was a proportionate response to the problem.

---

43   Per Laws LJ in *R (on the application of M) v Inner London Crown Court* [2003] EWHC 301 (Admin), [58].

44   *R (on the appication of M) v Inner London Crown Court* [2003] EWHC 30; [2003] 1 FLR 944.

45   *R (SR) v Nottingham Magistrates' Court* [2001] EWHC 802 (Admin).

46   *R (Howard League for Penal Reform) v Secretary of State for the Home Department* [2002] EWHC 2497 (Admin).

47   (1987) 10 EHRR 344.

48   [2001] EWHC 802 (Admin).

Charter of Fundamental Rights of the European Union

2.72 The charter is designed to be a summary of human rights already applicable to citizens of the European Union. It was proclaimed in December 2000 and incorporated as Part Two of the Treaty establishing a Constitution for Europe on 18 June 2004. Until the adoption of the constitution by member states, the charter has no legal force but has persuasive force within the European Union.

2.73 Article 24 provides:

> 1. Children shall have the right to protection and care as is necessary for their well-being. They may express their views freely. Such views shall be taken into consideration on matters which concern them in accordance with their age and maturity.
>
> 2. In all actions relating to children, whether taken by public authorities or private institutions, the child's best interests must be a primary consideration.
>
> 3. Every child shall have the right to maintain on a regular basis a personal relationship and direct contact with both his or her parents, unless that is contrary to his or her interests.

UN Convention on the Rights of the Child

2.74 Although not part of domestic law, it is relevant, when considering the welfare of the child or young person, to note that the United Kingdom is a signatory to the United Nations Convention on the Rights of the Child (1989). Accordingly, government departments are obliged to ensure that relevant legislation and practice in the criminal justice system conforms to the principles set out in the convention. To this end, the *National Standards for Youth Justice Services* (2004) make specific reference to its principles.[49]

2.75 The following articles are relevant to the youth justice system:

- Article 3: the best interests of the child to be the primary consideration in any proceedings before a court of law;
- Article 37(b): the deprivation of liberty through detention shall be used as a measure of last resort and for the shortest appropriate period of time;
- Article 40(1): a youth justice system should treat a child in a manner consistent with his/her age and the desirability of promoting the child's reintegration and the child's assuming a constructive role in society;
- Article 40(2): specific guarantees of due process in the youth justice system.[50]

2.76 Although not directly enforceable before domestic courts, the standards established in the convention are being increasingly accepted as relevant to decisions regarding the rights of children and young persons under the European Convention on Human Rights.[51]

---

49 Introduction, para 3.
50 For a detailed discussion of these provisions see G van Bueren, *The international law on the rights of the child* (Nijhoff, 1998) chs 7 and 8.
51 Eg *T v United Kingdom, V v United Kingdom* [2000] 2 All ER 1024 (Note); (2000) 30 EHRR 121; 7 BHRC 659, ECtHR and *McKerry v Tyne and Wear Valley Justices* (2000) 164 JP 355; [2000] Crim LR 594, DC.

2.77   The United Nations has adopted detailed standards for children and young persons involved in the youth justice system. These are contained in the:

- UN Standard Minimum Rules for the Administration of Juvenile Justice (1985) ('the Beijing Rules');
- UN Rules for the Protection of Juveniles Deprived of their Liberty (1990) ('the Havana Rules');
- UN Guidelines for the Administration of Juvenile Delinquency (1990) ('the Riyadh Guidelines').

Terminology

2.78   Various terms are used to describe persons of particular ages. Unfortunately the relevant statutes do not use the terms consistently. The following terms are used.

Child

2.79   'Child' is defined as a person aged between 10 and 13 inclusive.[52] However, it should be noted that for the purposes of the Children Act 1989 the term refers to a person under the age of 18.[53]

Young person

2.80   In general 'young person' is defined as a person who has attained the age of 14 and is under the age of 18.[54] However, it should be noted that for the purposes of Children and Young Persons Act 1969 s23 (remand to local authority accommodation) and the Police and Criminal Evidence Act 1984, the term refers to persons who are under the age of 17.[55]

Juvenile

2.81   In the context of the police station, a 'juvenile' is defined as a person under the age of 17.[56] To confuse matters, the term is also used in Magistrates' Courts Act 1980 s29 to mean a person under the age of 18.

Young offender

2.82   This term has no statutory definition but it used in sentencing law to refer to offenders under the age of 21 to whom the sentence of imprisonment is not available.

---

52   Children and Young Persons Act 1933 s107(1).
53   Children Act 1989 s105(1).
54   Children and Young Persons Act 1933 s107(1).
55   Children and Young Persons Act 1969 s23(12) and Police and Criminal Evidence Act 1984 s37(15).
56   Police and Criminal Evidence Act 1984 s37(15) and PACE Code C para 1.5.

Terminology in the book

2.83 No generic term exists which covers the full age range of 10 years to 17 years – the jurisdiction of the youth court. Some lawyers, particularly when in the magistrates' court, refer loosely to the defendant being a 'youth'. However, this term has no legal status. Because of the word's negative connotations, the authors have decided not to adopt it as a generic term. Instead it has been decided to use the following terms:

- child: ages 10–13 years;
- young person: ages 14–17 years;
- juvenile: ages 10–16 years (in the context of the police station and bail hearings only).

Principles of the youth justice system

2.84 Domestic law establishes five principles which are relevant to the youth justice system. These are as follows:

- preventing offending by children and young persons;
- having regard to the welfare of children and young persons;
- avoiding delay;
- proportionality in sentencing; and
- the prevention of discrimination.

2.85 Each of these principles will be considered in more detail below.

Preventing offending

2.86 Crime and Disorder Act 1998 s37 provides:

(1) The principal aim of the youth justice system shall be to prevent offending by children and young persons.

(2) In addition to any other duty to which they are subject, it shall be the duty of all persons and bodies carrying out functions in relation to the youth justice system to have regard to that aim.

2.87 The government has issued guidance on the implementation of Crime and Disorder Act 1998 s37 (*Youth Justice: the statutory principal aim of preventing offending by children and young people*). The need for a principal aim is explained as follows:

The new statutory aim of preventing offending ... provides a new guiding principle to which all agencies and individuals can relate their work and responsibilities. There has been conflict within the youth justice system between the interests of the victim and the public and the interests of the child or young person who has offended or is alleged to have offended. There has been conflict between promoting the welfare of the child or young person and taking firm action to deal with his or her offending behaviour. These conflicts have affected the operation of the youth justice system ... An effective youth justice system must ensure that justice is delivered for *all* concerned and that the best interests of *all* are served. There must be consideration, by all agencies and individuals, of the welfare of the child or young person: this is required by the

UN Convention on the Rights of the Child to which the UK is a signatory. But there must also be a balance between the interests of the child or young person who has offended and the interests of the victim, or potential victim.[57]

2.88   The government has suggested that this aim may be achieved by the following objectives:

(i)   the swift administration of justice so that every young person accused of breaking the law has the matter resolved without delay;

(ii)   confronting young offenders with the consequences of their offending, for themselves and their families, victims and the community;

(iii)   intervention which tackles the particular factors (personal, family, social, educational or health) that puts the young person at risk of offending and which strengthens 'protective factors';

(iv)   punishment proportionate to the seriousness and persistency of the offending behaviour;

(v)   encouraging reparation by young offenders for victims; and

(vi)   reinforcing parental responsibility.

2.89   The guidance also emphasises the importance of developing strategies which will have a long-term effect upon the behaviour of the child or young person who has contact with the youth justice system.

> Achieving the aim of preventing offending children and young people means that interventions following a police final warning or as part of a sentence should seek to prevent offending beyond the formal response as well as during it. The objective should be to re-integrate the young person into the community. This means planning ahead; maintaining links with the community where a young person is serving a custodial sentence; putting in place longer term action to tackle education, employment, health issues or homelessness; and encouraging young people to become involved in sporting or other constructive leisure activities which can provide structure and support for young people beyond their sentence or final warning intervention.[58]

2.90   The role the defence lawyer has to play in relation to this statutory aim is considered at paras 5.23–5.25.

Welfare of the child or young person

2.91   Children and Young Persons Act 1933 s44 provides:

> Every court in dealing with a child or young person who is brought before it, either as an offender or otherwise, shall have regard to the welfare of the child or young person, and shall in proper cases take steps for removing him from undesirable surroundings, and for securing that proper provision is made for his education and training.

2.92   There is no statutory definition of 'welfare', nor has the concept received any judicial attention. Individual courts have been left to apply the principle as seems appropriate in the circumstances. When considering Children and Young Persons Act 1933 s44, a court must interpret it in the context of subsequent legislation. For example, the court is required in proper cases to take steps to remove a child or young person from undesirable surround-

---

57   Inter-departmental Framework document, *Youth justice: the statutory principal aim of preventing offending by children and young people*, para 1.

58   Ibid, para 18.3.

ings. Many courts may wish to interpret this to mean removal from the care of parents who are not deemed to be appropriate carers. Such a decision could run counter to the philosophy of the Children Act 1989, which is based on the belief that children are best looked after within the family while aiming to protect children both from the harm which can arise from failures of abuse within the family and from the harm which can be caused by unwarranted intervention in their family life.[59] Perhaps even more significantly, the Criminal Justice Act 1991 (now substantially re-enacted in the Criminal Justice Act 2003) established a statutory framework for sentencing offenders which emphasises proportionality and protection of the public. It is difficult to reconcile these sentencing principles with that of the welfare of the child or young person.

2.93　A court dealing with a child or young person must, therefore, balance competing factors before reaching a decision. In such circumstances, section 44 only requires the court to 'have regard' to the welfare of the child or young person. The weight given to the principle in practice will depend on the seriousness of the offence and the stage of the proceedings.

Scope

2.94　The youth court, with its near exclusive remit to deal with children and young persons, will usually have a particular ethos which gives prominence to the welfare principle. This will be reinforced by the special training justices on the youth court panel receive.[60] It is, however, important to note that the principle applies in 'every court', a fact often overlooked by adult magistrates' courts and the Crown Court. The defence lawyer may have to ensure that these courts have regard to the principle.

2.95　It should be noted that the duty imposed by section 44 applies not only to the defendant but to any child or young person brought before it as a witness. It has been held that the court can only have regard to the welfare of a witness who is a child or young person when that person appears before the court to testify.[61] It would seem, therefore, that only the welfare of the defendant can be taken into account until that stage.

Parental involvement

2.96　All courts have a power to require the attendance of parents or guardians at hearings. In cases where the child or young person is estranged from the parent, the defence lawyer may wish to raise the welfare of the child or young person as an opposing factor to the presumption that a parent should attend. Similarly, when the court is considering imposing a financial penalty upon a parent, the defence lawyer may wish to draw to the court's attention the effect that the consequent loss of income will have upon a family reliant on welfare benefits or a low wage. If the family will have to forgo basics, this will clearly have an impact upon the young offender's welfare.

59　Department of Health, *The Children Act 1989 Guidance and Regulations* (HMSO, 1991), Introduction.

60　See *Youth Court Bench Book* (Judicial Studies Board, 2005).

61　*R v Highbury Corner Magistrates' Court ex p Deering* [1997] Crim LR 59, QBD.

Bail and remands

2.97   The welfare of a child or young person is referred to in the Bail Act 1976 but only as a ground for refusing bail. Instead the Act establishes the importance of preventing further offences, ensuring the defendant's attendance at court and avoiding interference with the administration of justice. With such concerns prominent in the bail decision-making process, it may be difficult to ensure that the court considers the defendant's welfare. Nevertheless, the defence lawyer should draw to the court's attention the consequences of any bail conditions which, for example, prevent parental contact or interfere with schooling. If a custodial remand is contemplated, s/he will also want to highlight any concerns concerning the ability of the young person to cope in a remand centre or prison.

Background

2.98   Any court will only be able to have proper regard of the welfare of the child or young person if it has available to it sufficient information regarding the background of the defendant. Accordingly social services and education departments are under an obligation to provide background information to the court.[62] Where such information is not available, youth courts are required to consider the desirability of adjourning the proceedings to allow the necessary enquiries to be made.[63] Furthermore, when dealing with a young offender the court must obtain and consider a pre-sentence report (either a new one or one written for a previous sentencing hearing) before imposing either a community or custodial order.[64]

Sentencing

2.99   It has already been noted that it is difficult to reconcile the welfare principle with the conflicting principles of proportionality and protection of the public contained in the Criminal Justice Act 2003. The practical implications of this conflict are explored in more detail at paras 17.28–17.30.

Other agencies

2.100   Children and Young Persons Act 1933 s44 only applies to the courts, nevertheless the Crown Prosecution Service has accepted that it should have regard to the welfare principle when deciding whether it is in the public interest to prosecute a child or young person.[65]

Avoiding delay

2.101   In family proceedings involving children there is a statutory presumption that delay is prejudicial to the welfare of the child.[66] No such statutory presumption exists in relation to the youth justice system. Nevertheless,

---

62 Children and Young Persons Act 1969 s9.
63 Magistrates' Courts (Children and Young Persons) Rules 1992 SI No 2071 r10(2)(c).
64 Criminal Justice Act 2003 s156.
65 Crown Prosecution Service, *Code for Crown Prosecutors* (2004), para 8.8.
66 Compare the position in family proceedings: Children Act 1989 s1(2).

there is strong official encouragement for an assumption that it is desirable that any case involving a child or young person should be dealt with expeditiously.

> Speedy procedures avoid the uncertainty and stress of a long wait for trial for the child or young person accused of an offence and for the victim of the alleged offence; minimise the risks of offending while awaiting trial; ensure that, if found guilty, the sentence is meaningful and understood by the young person as a consequence of his or her behaviour; and ensure that early action can be taken to help prevent further offending. Dealing with cases quickly, so that action can be taken to prevent further offending if the young person is found guilty, is particularly important where the child or young person has a history of offending or is alleged to have committed several offences.[67]

2.102   In order to reduce delay, the Labour government has introduced the following:

- targets to ensure a more efficient management of cases;
- encouraging the establishment fast track schemes for some young offenders; and
- the introduction of statutory time limits.

Efficient management of cases

2.103   Following the election of a Labour government in May 1997 there has been a much greater emphasis on the efficient management of the youth justice system. One of the key aims has been to reduce the time that it takes to deal with a young offender from arrest to sentence. The election pledge was to reduce this from a national average of 142 days to 71 days. During 1997 all agencies were encouraged to do everything possible to reduce delays (Lord Chancellor's letter dated 21 May 1997 addressed to youth court chairmen and an inter-departmental circular dated 15 October 1997). As well as encouraging inter-agency working, this guidance suggested that courts should:

- scrutinise the need for adjournments;
- consider whether reports are needed before sentencing;
- sentence for offences before the court without waiting for other matters to be disposed of.

Fast tracking persistent young offenders

2.104   A further election pledge of the Labour government was to ensure that those young offenders who offend frequently (commonly referred to as 'persistent young offenders') should be processed through the youth justice system more quickly than other defendants.

2.105   The Home Office has adopted the following definition for a persistent young offender:

> A child or young person sentenced by any court on three or more separate occasions for one or more recordable offences, and within three years of the last sentencing occasion is subsequently arrested or has an information laid against him/her for a further recordable offence.

---

67 Inter-departmental framework document, *Youth Justice: the statutory principal aim of preventing offending by children and young persons*, para 11.1.

2.106   Where a child or young person satisfies this definition the joint Home Office/Lord Chancellor's Circular *Measuring performance to reduce delays on the youth justice system* (issued 15 September 1998) gives the following guidelines on the length of time each stage of the youth justice process should take in a straightforward case:

Cases dealt with in youth court		Cases committed to Crown Court	
Arrest to charge	2 days	Arrest to charge	2 days
Charge to first appearance	7 days	Charge to first appearance	7 days
First appearance to start of trial	28 days	First appearance to committal for trial	28 days
Verdict to sentence	14 days	Committal to PDH	14 days
		PDH to start of Crown Court trial	28 days
		Verdict to sentence	14 days

Statutory time limits

2.107   Crime and Disorder Act 1998 ss43–45 introduce statutory time limits for all stages of the criminal justice process from arrest to sentence. Some of these time limits were piloted from 1999 to 2003. Since the expiry of the pilots, no statutory time limit has been in force in any part of the country.

Proportionality

2.108   The Criminal Justice Act 2003 establishes the sentencing principle that punishment must be proportionate to the seriousness of the offence(s) before the court. This principle applies to both the choice of sentence and also the length of that sentence.[68]

2.109   When sentencing a young offender, the question of proportionality is the first consideration, but preventing offending and the welfare of the child or young person are important in deciding which type of sentence to impose.

Non-discrimination

2.110   Equality of treatment within the youth justice system is a fundamental right. There is a range of domestic legislation designed to prevent discrimination including the Race Relations Act 1976, the Sex Discrimination Act 1975 and the Disability Discrimination Act 1995.

2.111   Criminal Justice Act 1991 s95(1) requires the secretary of state to publish each year such information as s/he considers expedient for the pur-

---

68   Criminal Justice Act 2003 ss148 and 152.

pose of facilitating the performance by such persons of their duty to avoid discrimination against any persons on the grounds of race or sex or any other improper ground.

2.112   Government guidance has emphasised the importance of the principle of non-discrimination within the youth justice system.

> In delivering all [the objectives of the youth justice system], and in all other work with children and young people in the youth justice system, agencies and individuals must carry out their responsibilities fairly and without discrimination on grounds of race, sex or any other irrelevant factor. Section 95 of the Criminal Justice Act 1991 makes clear the responsibility of all those in the administration of justice to avoid unfair discrimination.[69]

---

69 Inter-departmental Framework document, *Youth justice: the statutory principal aim of preventing offending by children and young people*, para 12.

CHAPTER 3

Local authority duties under the Children Act 1989

Introduction

3.1   In addition to work focussed on prevention of offending, local authorities have significant duties to those involved in the youth justice system under the Children Act 1989. Those duties may be summarised as:

- the provision of services to safeguard and promote the welfare of a child;
- the provision of accommodation;
- the maintenance of children in the care system and ongoing support for care leavers; and
- the investigation of child protection concerns.

3.2   This chapter provides an introduction to the most important duties owed to children by the local authority. It aims to give the defence lawyer a basic understanding of a young client's rights and the duties owed to him/her. With such an understanding, the defence lawyer should be able to identify occasions when the Children Act 1989 can be used to meet a young client's immediate needs for support or accommodation while involved in the youth justice system. It is also important to be alert to the possibility that children's broader needs may not have been identified and, where necessary, a referral for assessment should be made. On occasions, the defence lawyer may be forced into the role of advocate for the child so that appropriate services can be provided. Where the defence lawyer is not able to take on this role, a referral to a specialist community care lawyer should be made.[1]

Legal framework

Statutes

3.3   The law relating to a local authority's duties to children is mainly set out in Part III of the Children Act 1989. Since implementation, the 1989 Act has been amended on a number of occasions, most significantly by the Children (Leaving) Care Act 2000. The provisions of the 1989 Act will have the most practical relevance for the defence practitioner. The 1989 Act also imposes general duties upon local authorities to reduce the need for criminal proceedings[2] and to encourage children not to commit crime.[3]

3.4   The law relating to the management and delivery of children's services in England and Wales is contained in the Children Act 2004. The 2004 Act makes separate provision for the delivery of services in England and the delivery of services in Wales. In England, the 2004 Act establishes a statutory post of Director of Children's Services which will have responsibility for both social services functions as far as they relate to children, as well

---

1   Details of lawyers who have contracts to do work in the Community Care Law Class may be obtained from the Legal Services Commission. In the case of detained children, the Howard League for Penal Reform operates a children's advice line and takes on individual cases with a view to initiating court proceedings – for contact details see appendix 14.

2   Children Act 1989 Sch 2 Part I para 7(a)(ii).

3   Ibid, Sch 2 Part I para 7(b).

as the functions of the local education authority.[4] In the majority of local authorities, youth offending teams will be the managerial responsibility of the Director of Children's Services.

3.5 In England, Children Act 2004 Act s10 establishes a broad duty on many public bodies including local authorities, the police, youth offending teams, local probation boards to co-operate to improve the well-being of children.[5] Children Act 2004 s11 also requires those public bodies, as well as the governors of young offender institutions or secure training centres, to make arrangements for ensuring that their functions are discharged having regard to the need to safeguard and promote the welfare of children.[6]

Regulations

3.6 Detailed regulations covering the exercise of almost every duty under the Children Act 1989 have been issued as delegated legislation. Since devolution in Wales, the applicable regulations may be different in England and Wales. For reasons of space, where the regulations are different, the text will consider the regulations applicable in England but the relevant Welsh regulations will also be cited for readers in Wales to refer to.

Guidance

3.7 Until June 2003 the government department responsible for overseeing the provision of social services to children was the Department of Health. In England that responsibility has now passed to the Department for Education and Skills. In Wales the responsibility is with the Welsh Assembly.

3.8 The relevant government department may issue guidance to local authorities. That guidance may be issued under Local Authority Social Services Act 1970 s7 which requires local authorities to perform their duties under the general guidance of the secretary of state. Where policy guidance has been issued under section 7, local authorities are required to follow the path charted by the guidance, with liberty to deviate from it where the local authority judges on admissible grounds that there is good reason to do so, but without freedom to take a substantially different course.[7] A local authority which does not follow policy guidance will need to give reasons for departing from the guidance. In the absence of clear and adequate reasons, the authority may be in breach of the law and the subject of judicial review.[8]

Essential definitions

3.9 Below are definitions of a number of important terms used in the Children Act 1989. For a more extensive list of terms used in the provision of children's services, the reader is referred to appendix 1.

---

4 Children Act 2004 s18.
5 In Wales, the relevant provision is Children Act 2004 s25.
6 In Wales, the relevant provision is Children Act 2004 s28.
7 *R v Islington LBC ex p Rixon* (1997) 1 CCLR 119, per Sedley J at p123.
8 Ibid.

Child

3.10   For the purposes of the Children Act 1989, 'child' is defined as a person under the age of 18.[9] In this chapter the term 'child' will be used throughout with this meaning.

Care order

3.11   Children are made the subject of care orders under Children Act 1989 s31(1) following family proceedings. Upon the making of the order the local authority acquires parental responsibility and has the power to determine the extent to which a parent or guardian of the child may meet his/her parental responsibility for the child.[10] The local authority is under a duty to accommodate and maintain any child for whom a care order is held.[11]

'Looked after' child

3.12   A 'looked after' child is defined by Children Act 1989 s22(1) and (2) as any child who:

- is in the care of a local authority; or
- provided with accommodation for a continuous period of more than 24 hours by the local authority in the exercise of any functions which are social services functions within the meaning of the Local Authority Social Services Act 1970, apart from functions under Children Act 1989 ss17, 23B and 24B (duties to children in need or relevant children or to provide advice and assistance).

3.13   The majority of looked after children are not the subject of care orders. These children are sometimes said to be in 'voluntary care', although this term has no statutory basis.

Parental responsibility

3.14   Defined as 'all the rights, duties, powers, responsibilities and authority which, by law, a parent has in relation to a child and his property'.[12] Where parents are married at the time of the child's birth, both have parental responsibility automatically; otherwise, the mother alone has it. A father who does not have parental responsibility may acquire it by making a parental responsibility agreement with the mother or by applying to a court for an order.[13] People, other than parents, may only acquire parental responsibility by the private appointment of a guardian or by order of a court.

3.15   A local authority only acquires parental responsibility as the result of the making of one of the following orders:

9   Children Act 1989 s105(1).
10   Ibid, s33(3).
11   Ibid, s23(1).
12   Ibid, s3(1).
13   Ibid, s4(1).

- a care order;[14] and
- an emergency protection order.[15]

Principles of the Children Act 1989

3.16   The principles underlying the Children Act 1989 include:

- the overriding purpose is to promote and safeguard the welfare of children;
- children are best looked after within the family with both parents playing a full part without recourse to legal proceedings;
- where parents are unable to care for a child properly, any help should be provided, if possible, on a voluntary basis with the local authority working in partnership with the parents;
- whilst caring for a child, a local authority must promote contact with the child's parents;
- in caring for a child, a local authority must take into account a child's racial origin and cultural and linguistic background;
- children should be protected both from the harm which can arise from failures or abuse within the family and from the harm which can be caused by unwarranted intervention in their family life.

3.17   When considering their duties under the 1989 Act, local authorities will seek to implement these principles.

Involving children in decision-making

3.18   Most of the statutory duties owed to children discussed below include provision for the child to be involved in the process of assessment and deciding what services to provide.[16] These provisions reflect the obligation imposed on the United Kingdom by Article 12 of the United Nations Convention on the Rights of the Child to allow a child capable of forming his/her own views the right to express those views freely and to give due weight to the views expressed in accordance with the child's age and maturity.[17]

3.19   Excluding the child from the decision-making process and merely sharing the decision with him/her is a practice which has received strong judicial criticism.[18] Such an approach may well involve breach of the child's rights under Article 8 (right to respect for private and family life) of the European Convention on Human Rights to be properly involved in the decision-making process.[19]

14   Children Act 1989 s33(3).
15   Ibid, s44(4)(c).
16   See Children Act 1989 ss17(8), 20(6) and 22(5). A similar requirement is also included in many of the applicable regulations issued under the Act.
17   For more on the United Nations Convention see paras 2.74–2.77.
18   Eg *R (on the application of J) v Caerphilly County Borough Council* [2005] EWHC 586 (Admin), at [34].
19   See *CF v Secretary of State for the Home Department* [2004] EWHC 111 Fam; [2004] 2 FLR 517, at [158], [167], [173].

Child in need

3.20   The duty to children in need is of great importance in the context of the youth justice system. As seen in chapter 1, children involved in the youth justice system have high levels of personal and social need and meeting those needs is likely to have a significant impact on the risk of offending. More specifically, the availability of services for a child in need will be relevant to whether:

- the public interest requires a prosecution;
- bail to the home address is suitable;
- a community order is an appropriate sentencing disposal;
- early release or release on licence is appropriate; and
- an anti-social behaviour order is necessary.

Statutory duty

3.21   Children Act 1989 s17(1) provides:

> It shall be the general duty of every local authority ... −
> (a) to safeguard and promote the welfare of children within their area who are in need; and
> (b) so far as is consistent with that duty, to promote the upbringing of such children by their families,
> by providing a range and level of services appropriate to those children's needs.

3.22   A child is defined as being in need if:

- s/he is unlikely to achieve or maintain, or have the opportunity of achieving or maintaining, a reasonable standard of health or development without the provision of services by the local authority; or
- his/her health or development is likely to be significantly impaired, or further impaired, without the provision of local authority services; or
- s/he is disabled.[20]

3.23   Before determining what (if any) services to provide for a particular child in need in the exercise of functions conferred on them by this section, a local authority shall, so far as is reasonably practicable and consistent with the child's welfare:

- ascertain the child's wishes and feelings regarding the provision of those services; and
- give due consideration (having regard to his age and understanding) to such wishes and feelings of the child as they have been able to ascertain.[21]

3.24   Every local authority is required to take reasonable steps to identify the extent to which there are children in need within their area.[22] Information regarding their services must be provided and steps must be taken to ensure that those who might benefit receive information about services.[23]

---

20 Children Act 1989 s17(10).
21 Ibid, s17(4A) inserted by Children Act 2004 s53.
22 Ibid, Sch 2 Part I para 1.
23 Ibid, Sch 2 Part I para 2.

Within most local authorities the provision of services to young offenders is primarily through the youth offending team. The extent to which the needs of young offenders are recognised and met by other departments of the local authority will depend on local variations in service structure. Although clearly a very needy group, young offenders compete with other groups for scarce resources.

3.25 If a child is not already being treated as a child in need, a referral will need to be made to the local authority department dealing with children's services. A referral could be made through a youth offending team, but there is no reason why the referral could not be made by a defence lawyer, for example, when the youth offending team is not currently working with the young client.

Statutory guidance

3.26 The way that local authorities should approach an assessment of a child in need is considered in detail in *Framework for the assessment of children in need and their families* (2000) policy guidance jointly issued by the Department of Health, Department for Education and Employment (as it then was) and the Home Office under Local Authority Social Services Act 1970 s7.[24] The scheme of the guidance has been summarised as follows:

> The intended procedure is as follows: first, assess the needs of a ... child and, where appropriate, the carers and other members of the family; second, produce a care plan; third, provide the identified services.[25]

Assessment

3.27 The policy guidance sets out the timetable and structure of an assessment of need:

> 3.8 There is an expectation that within one working day of a referral being received or new information coming to or from within a social services department about an open case, there will be a decision about what response is required. A referral is defined as a request for services to be provided by the social services department. The response may include no action, but that is itself a decision and should be made promptly and recorded. The referrer should be informed of the decision and its rationale, as well as the parents or caregivers and the child, if appropriate.
>
> 3.9 A decision to gather more information constitutes an initial assessment. An initial assessment is defined as a brief assessment of each child referred to social services with a request for services to be provided. This should be undertaken within a maximum of 7 working days but could be very brief depending on the child's circumstances. It should address the dimensions of the Assessment Framework, determining whether the child is in need, the nature of any services required, from where and within what timescales, and whether a further, more detailed core assessment should be undertaken. An initial assessment is deemed to have commenced at the point of referral to the social services department or when new information on an open case indicates

24 The guidance is available on the Department of Health website.
25 *R v Lambeth LBC ex p K* (2000) 3 CCLR 141 at 144H, per Nigel Pleming QC (sitting as Deputy High Court Judge, quoted with approval by Richards J in *AB and SB v Nottingham City Council* [2001] EWHC Admin 235, at [8]).

an initial assessment should be repeated. All staff responding to referrals and undertaking initial assessments should address the dimensions which constitute the Assessment Framework. ...

3.10   Depending on the child's circumstances, an initial assessment may include some or all of the following:

- interviews with child and family members, as appropriate;
- involvement of other agencies in gathering and providing information, as appropriate;
- consultation with supervisor/manager;
- record of initial analysis;
- decisions on further action/no action;
- record of decisions/rationale with family/agencies;
- informing other agencies of the decisions;
- statement to the family of decisions made and, if a child is in need, the plan for providing support.

As part of any initial assessment, the child should be seen. This includes observation and talking with the child in an age appropriate manner ...

3.11   A core assessment is defined as an in-depth assessment which addresses the central or most important aspects of the needs of a child and the capacity of his or her parents or caregivers to respond appropriately to these needs within the wider family and community context. While this assessment is led by social services, it will invariably involve other agencies or independent professionals, who will either provide information they hold about the child or parents, contribute specialist knowledge or advice to social services or undertake specialist assessments. Specific assessments of the child and/or family members may have already been undertaken prior to referral to the social services department. The findings from these should inform this assessment. At the conclusion of this phase of assessment, there should be an analysis of the findings which will provide an understanding of the child's circumstances and inform planning, case objectives and the nature of service provision. The timescale for completion of the core assessment is a maximum of 35 working days. A core assessment is deemed to have commenced at the point the initial assessment ended, or a strategy discussion decided to initiate enquiries under s47, or new information obtained on an open case indicates a core assessment should be undertaken. Where specialist assessments have been commissioned by social services from other agencies or independent professionals, it is recognised that they will not necessarily be completed within the 35 working day period. Appropriate services should be provided whilst awaiting the completion of the specialist assessment.[26]

3.28   Where a core assessment reveals that the child is at risk of significant harm, an investigation under Children Act 1989 s47 may have to be instituted.[27]

3.29   An inadequate assessment of need may result in judicial review of the local authority and a mandatory order to carry out a core assessment.[28]

Child in need plan

3.30   At the conclusion of the core assessment there should be a child in need plan which will involve the child and family members, as appropriate, and

26 Department of Health, Department for Education and Employment, Home Office, *Framework for the assessment of children in need and their families* (2000).

27 Ibid, paras 3.15 onwards.

28 *AB and SB v Nottingham City Council* [2001] EWHC Admin 235.

the contributions of the local authority and other agencies.[29] A child in need plan should not be merely a descriptive document. It should provide a clear identification of needs and state what is to be done about them, by whom and when.[30]

Provision of services

3.31 The local authority may chose to make use of its own services or it may facilitate the provision of services by others, such as the Connexions Service, local mental health or drugs services, or voluntary organisations.[31] The services provided under Children Act 1989 s17 may include providing accommodation, giving assistance in kind or, in exceptional circumstances, in cash.[32]

Services to children involved in the youth justice system

3.32 There can be difficulties in accessing services for children who do not already have contact with children's services. Writing in 2004, the Audit Commission commented:

> Local authority social service departments provide by far the largest proportion of local [youth offending team] funding ... and social work is the largest single professional group within [youth offending teams] ... Social services departments also provide resources in kind, such as premises, human resources and finance functions. Despite this close relationship, young offenders and their families in some areas are not receiving the social services support they need. The demand for social services support is so great in many areas that its threshold for accepting referrals is very high. This means that [youth offending teams] often have to fill the gap; many [youth offending teams] staff and managers said they had to respond to problems, such as family support, for which they felt other agencies should be taking responsibility. About a third of [youth offending teams] are rarely or never able to access social services and a further third are only sometimes able to do so ...[33]

3.33 The Children Act 2004 is intended to ensure closer cooperation to safeguard and promote the welfare of children, therefore it is hoped that the position described by the Audit Commission will not be encountered in the future. Nevertheless, the defence lawyer will need to be alert to the possibility of 'service gaps' as described in the above quotation existing.

3.34 The types of services which would be relevant to the youth justice system include:

- financial support for a family;
- respite care for children in the family;
- outreach workers to be allocated to the family to work with the child or young person;
- resources to keep a child living within the family including the provision of resources to supplement any bail support.

---

29 Where the leaving care provisions apply the plan may be a pathway plan (see paras 3.84–3.88 below).

30 *AB and SB v Nottingham City Council* [2001] EWHC Admin 235, at [43].

31 Children Act 1989 s17(5).

32 Ibid, s17(6).

33 Audit Commission, *Youth Justice 2004* (2004), para 148.

Provision of accommodation

3.35   The fact that a child involved in the youth justice system does not have suit-able stable accommodation will be a risk factor for offending. It will also affect the child's position in relation to the following:

- grant of bail by the police or the courts;
- appropriateness of a community order;
- early release from a custodial sentence;
- release on licence.

3.36   The defence lawyer may therefore need an understanding of the various obligations to accommodate a child. Where the youth offending team is involved with the child, a request for accommodation is likely to be made through the team. The defence lawyer should, however, be alert to a client's need for accommodation and be prepared to argue for the most appropriate provision.

General duty

3.37   Children Act 1989 s20 provides:

> Every local authority shall provide accommodation for any child in need within their area who appears to them to require accommodation as a result of –
> (a) there is no person who has parental responsibility;
> (b) the child is lost or abandoned;
> (c) the person caring for him being prevent (whether or not permanently, and for whatever reason) from providing him with suitable accommoda-tion or care.
>
> ...
>
> (3) Every local authority shall provide accommodation for any child in need within their area who has reached the age of sixteen and whose welfare the authority consider is likely to be seriously prejudiced if they do not provide him with accommodation.
>
> ...
>
> (6) Before providing accommodation under this section, a local authority shall, so far as it is reasonably practicable and consistent with the child's welfare–
> (a) ascertain the child's wishes and feelings regarding the provision of accommodation; and
> (b) give due consideration (having regard to his age and understand-ing) to such wishes and feelings of the child as they have been able to ascertain.

3.38   In accordance with the principles of the Children Act 1989 (see para 3.16 above), a local authority will always wish to explore the possibility of a placement back at home (perhaps with extra support provided under sec-tion 17), or with a member of the extended family. If feasible, such options may very well be the most appropriate for the child.

3.39   Providing accommodation to a child under section 20 will make him/ her a looked after child and the local authority will then have a number of specific duties to the child (see paras 3.53–3.67 below).

Provision of accommodation under section 17 (child in need)

3.40   The Adoption and Children Act 2002 amended Children Act 1989 s17(6) to confirm that a local authority could provide accommodation to a child in need. Since that amendment came into force in November 2002, some local authorities have been making use of the amendment to provide accommodation without treating the child as a looked after child. This practice was discouraged in Local Authority Circular LAC (2003) 13 *Guidance on accommodating children in need and their families* which states:

> The amendment to section 17 did not affect the duties and powers of local authorities to provide accommodation for lone children under section 20 of the Children Act 1989, or under a care order. Accordingly, the power to provide accommodation under section 17 will almost always concern children needing to be accommodated with their families. However, there may be cases where a lone child who needs help with accommodation, but does not need to be looked after, might appropriately be assisted under section 17.
>
> Before deciding which section of the Children Act 1989 provides the appropriate legal basis for provision of help or support to a child in need, a local authority should undertake an assessment in accordance with the statutory guidance set out in the Framework for the Assessment of Children in Need and their Families, published by the Government in April 2000. It should then use the findings of that assessment, which will include taking account of the wishes and feelings of the child (as required by section 20(6) of the Children Act), as the basis for any decision about whether he should be provided with accommodation under section 20 (and therefore become looked after) or whether other types of services provided under section 17 of the Act are better suited to his circumstances.
>
> The assessment should first determine whether the child meets the criteria set out in section 20(1) ... [see para 3.37 above]. For example, where a child has no parent or guardian in this country, perhaps because he has arrived alone seeking asylum, the presumption should be that he would fall within the scope of section 20 and become looked after, unless the needs assessment reveals particular factors which would suggest that an alternative response would be more appropriate. While the needs assessment is being carried out, he should be cared for under section 20.
>
> Local authorities have reported cases where older asylum seeking children have refused to become looked after, but where because of their immigration status the Children Act provides their only lawful means of support in this country. In such cases the child's being without a family or responsible adult in this country would appear to trigger a duty under section 20(1), However, after taking account of the child's wishes as required by section 20(6), the local authority might judge that the child is competent to look after himself. In such circumstances it would not need to assume the whole responsibility for accommodating him under section 20 (and thereby taking him into the looked after system). In such cases section 17 may be used for support, including help with accommodation, without making the child a looked after child.

3.41   A child accommodated under section 20 will not also benefit in the short term from the duties owed to a looked after child (see paras 3.53–3.67 below) but will also acquire important rights to leaving care provision (see paras 3.68–3.97 below). Where the local authority is requested to provide accommodation, it is important to argue for the child to be accommodated under section 20 rather than under any other statutory provision.

Referral to housing department

3.42   Homeless 16- and 17-year-olds are often referred to the relevant housing department for them to be considered for housing under Part VII of the Housing Act 1996 and the Homeless Act 2002.[34] This approach risks inappropriate housing provision being made and a failure to assess the young person as a child in need. It is also unlikely to be a practicable solution where the details of the accommodation are required before a decision to release a child on bail or on early release can be made.

3.43   It should also be noted that any accommodation provided under housing legislation will not necessarily make the young person a looked after child with all the consequent benefits that this brings (see paras 3.53–3.67 below). Wherever possible, therefore, the request for accommodation should be directed to the local authority department providing children's services and it should specify that the request is to accommodate under Children Act 1989 s20.

3.44   Where a local authority is carrying out a child in need assessment, it has been held:

> It is the responsibility of the social services authority to meet the identified housing need. It can seek the assistance of the housing authority, but cannot simply wash its hands of the matter by referring those in need to the housing authority.[35]

3.44A   The interaction of the Children Act 1989 and the Housing Act 1996 was recently considered by the Court of Appeal in *R (on the application of M) v London Borough of Hammersmith and Fulham*.[36] Whilst upholding a decision to provide accommodation to a 17-year-old under the Housing Act 1996, Wall LJ emphasised that local authorities had a duty to investigate the circumstances of those under 18 who may be in need, and, where appropriate, to make provision for them under the Children Act 1989 Part III. He added that the onus is not upon the child to identify and request the services required. Furthermore, he warned that if a local authority failed inappropriately to identify a child in need, that failure is amendable to judicial review.

Duty to accommodate detained and remanded children

3.45   There are a number of specific duties which are relevant to the youth justice system.

3.46   Children Act 1989 s21(2) provides:

> Every local authority shall receive, and provide accommodation for, children—
> (a) ...
> (b) whom they are requested to receive under section 38(6) of the Police and Criminal Evidence Act 1984;
> (c) who are—
>   (i) on remand under paragraph 7(5) of Schedule 7 to the Powers of Criminal Courts (Sentencing) Act 2000 or section 23(1) of the Children and Young Persons Act 1969;

---

34   Consideration of these provisions is beyond the scope of this book. The reader is referred to Arden and Hunter, *Homelessness and allocations* 7th edn, LAG, 2006.

35   *AB and SB v Nottingham City Council* [201] EWHC Admin 235, per Richards J at [46].

36   [2006] EWCA Civ 917.

(ii) the subject of a supervision order imposing a local authority residence requirement under paragraph 5 of Schedule 6 of that Act of 2000 or a foster parent residence requirement under paragraph 5A of that Schedule, and with respect to whom they are the designated authority.

Children in police detention

3.47 The duty to receive and provide accommodation to children under Children Act 1989 s21(2)(b) has been reviewed by the Court of Appeal in *R (on the application of M) v Gateshead Council.*[37] Dyson LJ held that:

- the duty to provide accommodation in response to the custody officer's request falls on the authority which receives the request;
- the custody officer is not required to approach first the local authority in which area the police station is situated (eg it may be more sensible to approach another authority which is already accommodating the child);
- section 21(1)(b) creates an absolute duty to provide accommodation but not an absolute duty to provide secure accommodation;
- subject to section 25 of the Children Act 1989 (for which see chapter 14) local authorities have a discretion to provide secure accommodation which may be exercised generally and which should be exercised when they receive requests for secure accommodation from a custody officer insofar as it is practicable for them to do so to further the policy objective of preventing children being detained in police cells.

Children remanded to local authority accommodation

3.48 The duty to receive the child and provide accommodation falls upon the authority specified by the court as the designated local authority. In the case of a defendant already being looked after by a local authority, it shall be that authority. In all other cases it may be either:

- the authority in whose area it appears to the court that the defendant resides; or
- the authority in whose area the offence or one of the offences was committed.[38]

3.49 The type of accommodation chosen by the local authority is completely in their discretion, however, the Department of Health has given the following guidance:

> While a remand to 'local authority accommodation' continues to leave the authority with discretion about the most appropriate placement for the juvenile on remand, full account should be taken of the fact that:
> (a) The court has already been required to consider why the juvenile should not be bailed and allowed to return home, and has determined that this would not be appropriate;
> (b) The local authority has a responsibility to ensure that the juvenile is produced in court at the date, place and time specified, and to take all reasonable steps to protect the public from the risk of the juvenile committing further offences during the remand period. (The nature of the steps

---

37 [2006] EWCA Civ 221.
38 Children and Young Persons Act 1969 s23(2).

required to protect the public will depend on the juvenile concerned and on the alleged offence.)[39]

3.50   Even where a child has been remanded into custody, the designated local authority should keep the question of alternative local authority accommodation under active review.

> On each occasion that a juvenile is returned to the court for the remand to be reviewed, careful consideration should be given to advising the court whether alternative arrangements might be considered. For example, where a juvenile has been remanded to a penal establishment [under section 23(5)], the court may be willing to consider a remand to local authority accommodation if they are presented with a clear statement of how the juvenile would be accommodated within the care system in such a way that the public would be protected from the risk of further offending and that he would be produced in court when required.[40]

3.51   A defendant remanded to local authority accommodation is a looked after child for the purposes of the Act. The local authority, therefore, has the same obligations to him/her that apply to any other looked after child and will have to arrange regular reviews of the child's case. The Department of Health guidance states:

> [I]n considering how they exercise their general powers in relation to [remanded children] under section 22, local authorities may have regard to the need to protect members of the public from serious injury (section 22(6)). Because of the transitory nature of the status of remanded alleged juvenile offenders it is not practicable to make long-term plans for such children, but interim contingency plans might be formulated to take account of the sentencing options available to the court if convicted.[41]

3.52   Even an interim plan could be extremely useful when presenting mitigation to the sentencing court and it is important to ensure that such planning does in fact take place.

Duties to looked after children

3.53   Local authority duties to looked after child apply equally to those already in the care system as they do to those children remanded to local authority accommodation by the criminal courts.

General duty

3.54   Children Act 1989 s22(3) provides that it shall be the duty of a local authority looking after any child:

- to safeguard and promote his/her welfare; and
- to make such use of services available for children cared for by their own parents as appears to the authority reasonable in his/her case.

---

39   *The Children Act 1989 Guidance and Regulations* (HMSO, 1991), Vol 1, Court Orders, para 6.37.
40   Ibid, para 6.39.
41   Ibid, para 6.36.

3.55   Before making any decision with respect to a child whom they are looking after, a local authority shall, so far as is reasonably practicable, ascertain the wishes and feelings of:

- the child;
- his/her parents;
- any person who is not a parent but who is has parental responsibility for him/her; and
- any other person whose wishes and feelings the authority considers to be relevant.[42]

3.56   In making any such decision, a local authority shall give due consideration:

- having regard to his/her age and understanding, to such wishes and feelings of the child as they have been able to ascertain;
- to such wishes and feelings of any person mentioned in para 3.55 above as they have been able to ascertain; and
- to the child's religious persuasion, racial origin and cultural and linguistic background.[43]

Duty to provide accommodation and maintain the child

3.57   Children Act 1989 s23(1) provides that it shall be the duty of any local authority looking after a child:

- when s/he is in their care, to provide accommodation for him/her; and
- to maintain him/her in other respects apart from providing accommodation for him/her.

3.58   Placement may be with the child's family, a relative, a foster parent, any other suitable person or in a children's home.[44] Where a local authority provides accommodation, they shall, so far as is reasonably practicable and consistent with the child's welfare, secure that:

- the accommodation is near his/her home; and
- where the authority are also providing accommodation for a sibling, they are accommodated together.[45]

Obligation to protect public from serious injury

3.59   Children Act 1989 s22(6) provides that, if it appears to a local authority that that it is necessary, for the purposes of protecting members of the public from serious injury, to exercise their powers with respect to a child whom they are looking after in a manner which may not be consistent with their

---

42   Children Act 1989 s22(4).

43   Ibid, s22(5).

44   Children Act 1989 s23(2). For England see Arrangements for Placement of Children (General) Regulations 1991 SI No 890 (as amended), Placement of Children with Parents Regulations 1991 SI No 893 (as amended) and Fostering Services Regulations 2002 SI No 57 (as amended). For Wales see Arrangements for Placement of Children (General) Regulations 1991 SI No 890 (as amended), Placement of Children with Parents Regulations 1991 SI No 893 (as amended).

45   Children Act 1989 s23(7).

duties under section 22, they may do so. This provision has been held to allow for the use of secure accommodation by the local authority to protect the public.[46] If the Secretary of State considers it necessary, for the purposes of protecting members of the public from serious injury, s/he may give directions to a local authority with respect to the exercise of the powers with respect to a child whom they are looking after.[47] Where such directions are given by the Secretary of State, the local authority must comply with them even though doing so is inconsistent with the other duties under section 22.[48]

Review of looked after child's case

3.60   Each child looked after or provided accommodation by a local authority must have his/her case reviewed by the authority on a regular basis. The first review must take place within four weeks of the date upon which the child begins to be looked after or provided with accommodation.[49] The second review shall be carried out not more than three months after the first, and thereafter subsequent reviews shall be carried out not more than six months after the date of the previous review.[50] The obligation to review the child's case will apply to children remanded to local authority accommodation including those subject to a security requirement and placed in secure children's home or secure training centres.

3.61   Before conducting any review, the responsible authority shall, unless it is not reasonably practicable to do so, seek and take into account the views of:

- the child;
- his/her parents;
- any person who is not a parent of the child but who has parental responsibility for the child; and
- any other person whose views the authority consider to be relevant, including, in particular, the views of those persons in relation to any particular matter which is to be considered in the course of the review.[51]

3.62   Where the child is remanded to local authority accommodation, a social worker in the youth offending team may sometimes act as the local authority social worker for the child's case. Where this does not happen, a youth offending team remand worker should clearly be consulted as part of the review process. It is also submitted that the defence lawyer should be consulted.

3.63   During the course of a review the local authority shall have regard to the considerations contained in Schedules 2 and 3 of the Review of Children's Cases Regulations 1991.[52] These considerations include:

46   *Re M (secure accommodation order)* [1995] 1 FLR 418, CA
47   Children Act 1989 s22(7).
48   Ibid, s22(8).
49   Review of Children's Cases Regulations 1991 SI No 895 reg 3(1).
50   Ibid, reg 3(2).
51   Ibid, reg 7(1).
52   SI 1991 No 895.

- whether the local authority should apply for a care order;
- arrangements for contact, and whether there is any need for changes in the arrangements in order to promote contact with the child's family and others so far as is consistent with his welfare.
- any special arrangements that have been made or need to be made for the child, including the carrying out of assessments either by a local authority or other persons, such as those in respect of special educational need;
- the state of the child's physical, emotional and mental health, current arrangements for the child's medical and dental care, as well as the possible need for preventative measures such as vaccination or screening for vision and hearing;
- the authority's immediate and long-term arrangements for looking after the child or providing the child with accommodation, whether a change in those arrangements is needed and consideration of alternative courses of action;
- whether an independent visitor should be appointed if one has not already been appointed;
- the child's educational needs, progress and development;
- whether arrangements need to be made for the time when the child will no longer be looked after or provided with accommodation by the responsible authority.
- whether plans need to be made to find a permanent substitute family for the child.

3.64 The local authority should, so far as is reasonably practicable, involve the child and the other persons mentioned in para 3.61 including, where the authority considers appropriate, the attendance of those persons at part or all of any review meeting which is to consider the child's case.[53]

3.65 The local authority must appoint a registered social worker (not employed by the authority) to be an independent reviewing officer to participate in the review of the child's case and to monitor the performance of the authority's functions in respect of the review.[54]

3.66 The local authority shall, so far as is reasonably practicable, notify details of the result of the review and of any decision taken by them in consequence of the review to:

- the child;
- his/her parents;
- any person who is not a parent of the child but who has parental responsibility for the child; and
- any other person whom they consider ought to be notified.[55]

3.67 The local authority shall make arrangements themselves or with other persons to implement any decision which the authority propose to make in the course, or as a result, of the review of a child's case.[56]

---

53 Review of Children's Cases Regulations 1991 SI No 895 reg 7(2)
54 Children Act 1989 s26 and Review of Children's Cases Regulations 1991 SI No 895 reg 2A.
55 Review of Children's Cases Regulations 1991 SI No 895 reg 7(3).
56 Ibid, reg 8.

Duties to care leavers

3.68   Local authorities owe specific duties to care leavers up to the age of 21 (and in certain cases, up to the age of 24). These provisions were introduced by the Children (Leaving Care) Act 2000, which added new sections 23A–23E and 24A–24D to the Children Act 1989.

3.69   Detailed provisions for how local authorities are to discharge their duties to care leavers are contained in the Children (Leaving Care) (England) Regulations 2001.[57] In Wales, the Children (Leaving Care) (Wales) Regulations 2001[58] apply.

3.70   Policy guidance in the form of *Children (Leaving Care) Act 2000: Regulations and guidance* has been issued by the Department of Health under section 7 of the Local Authority Social Services Act 1970.[59]

3.71   The defence lawyer will need to be familiar with the leaving care provisions both to understand what support a young client may already be receiving but also to identify other clients who qualify for services but who may have been overlooked. Receiving support under these provisions could make a substantial difference to a young client's life and be a significant factor in decisions within the youth justice system, such as release from custody.

Definitions

3.72   Local authorities must provide leaving care services to children who meet the definition of eligible or relevant children.

Eligible child

3.73   Defined as a child who:

- is aged 16 or 17; and
- has been looked after by a local authority for a period of 13 weeks (or periods amounting in all to a total of 13 weeks) which began after s/he reached the age of 14 and ended after s/he reached the age of 16.[60]

3.74   A child is not an eligible child if s/he has been looked after by a local authority in circumstances where:

- the local authority has arranged to place him/her in a pre-planned series of short-term placements, none of which individually exceeds four weeks (even though they may amount in all to a total of 13 weeks); and
- at the end of each such placement the child returns to the care of his/her parent, or a person who is not a parent but who has parental responsibility for the child.[61]

---

57   SI No 2874.
58   SI No 2189.
59   The Welsh Assembly has issued separate guidance.
60   Children Act 1989 Sch 2 para 19B(2) and Children (Leaving Care) (England) Regulations 2001 SI No 2874 amended by SI 2002 No 546.
61   Children (Leaving Care) (England) Regulations 2001 reg 3(3).

Relevant child

3.75   Children Act 1989 s23A(2) defines a relevant child as a child who:

- is not being looked after by any local authority;
- was, before ceasing to be looked after, an eligible child; and
- is aged 16 or 17.

3.76   Any person aged 16 or 17 may also be a relevant child if:

- s/he is not subject to a care order; and
- at the time when s/he attained the age of 16 s/he was detained or in hospital and immediately before s/he was detained or admitted to hospital s/he had been looked after by a local authority for a period of, or periods amounting in all to, at least 13 weeks, which began after s/he reached the age of 14.[62]

3.77   In calculating the period of 13 weeks, no account is to be taken of any period in which the child was looked after by a local authority in any of a pre-planned series of short-term placements, none of which individually exceeded four weeks, where at the end of each such placement the child returned to the care of his/her parent, or a person who is not a parent but who has parental responsibility for the child.[63]

3.78   'Detained' means detained in a remand centre, a young offenders institution or a secure training centre or any other institution pursuant to an order of a court.[64]

'Responsible local authority'

3.79   The responsible local authority is the one which last looked after an eligible or relevant child or young person.[65] The responsible local authority will retain the responsibility for a care leaver wherever the young person may be living in England or Wales.

Assessment of needs

3.80   For each eligible child, the local authority shall carry out an assessment of his/her needs with a view determining what advice, assistance or support it would be appropriate for them to provide:

- while they are still looking after him/her; and
- after they cease to look after him/her.[66]

3.81   It is also the duty of each local authority in relation to any relevant child who does already have a pathway plan to carry out an assessment of his/her needs with a view to determining what advice, assistance and support it would be appropriate for them to provide to him/her.[67]

---

62 Children (Leaving Care) (England) Regulations 2001 reg 4(2).
63 Ibid, reg 4(3).
64 Ibid, reg 4(4)(a).
65 Children Act 1989 s23A(4).
66 Ibid, Sch 2 para 19B(2).
67 Ibid, s23B(3).

3.82   The assessment is to be completed:

- in the case of an eligible child, not more than three months after the date s/he reaches the age of 16 or becomes an eligible child after that age; and
- in the case of a relevant child who does not already have a pathway plan, not more than three months after the date s/he becomes a relevant child.[68]

3.83   In carrying out an assessment, the responsible authority shall take account of the following considerations:

- the child's health and development;
- the child's need for education, training or employment;
- the support available to the child from members of his/her family and other persons;
- the child's financial needs;
- the extent to which the child possesses the practical and other skills necessary for independent living; and
- the child's needs for care, support and accommodation.[69]

Pathway plan

3.84   Having carried out an assessment of the needs of an eligible or relevant child's needs, the local authority must prepare a pathway plan for him/her.[70] The pathway plan must be prepared as soon as possible after the assessment.[71] The plan must be recorded in writing.[72]

3.85   A pathway plan must cover the following:

- the nature and level of contact and personal support to be provided, and by whom, to the child or young person;
- details of the accommodation the child or young person is to occupy;
- a detailed plan for the education or training of the child or young person;
- how the responsible authority will assist the child or young person in relation to employment or other purposeful activity or occupation;
- the support to be provided to enable the child or young person to develop and sustain appropriate family and social relationships;
- a programme to develop the practical and other skills necessary for the child or young person to live independently;
- the financial support to be provided to the child or young person, in particular where it is to be provided to meet his/her accommodation and maintenance needs;
- the health needs, including any mental health needs, of the child or young person, and how they are to be met;

---

68 Children (Leaving Care) (England) Regulations 2001 reg 7(2).
69 Ibid, reg 7(4).
70 Children Act 1989 Sch 2 para 19B(4) and s23B(3)(b) respectively.
71 Children (Leaving Care) (England) Regulations 2001 reg 8(1).
72 Ibid, reg 8(3).

- contingency plans for action to be taken by the responsible authority should the pathway plan for any reason cease to be effective.[73]

3.86   The pathway plan must, in relation to each of the above matters, set out:

- the manner in which the responsible authority proposes to meet the needs of the child; and
- the date by which, and by whom, any action required to implement any aspect of the plan will be carried out.[74]

Involvement of the child

3.87   The responsible authority, in carrying out an assessment and in preparing or reviewing a pathway plan, shall, unless it is not reasonably practicable:

- seek and have regard to the views of the child or young person to whom it relates; and
- take all reasonable steps to enable him/her to attend and participate in any meetings at which his/her case is to be considered.[75]

Review of pathway plan

3.88   The responsible authority shall arrange a review:

- if requested to do so by the child or young person;
- if it, or the personal adviser, considers a review necessary; and
- in any other case, at intervals of not more than six months.[76]

Personal adviser

3.89   A local authority shall arrange for each child whom they are looking after who is an eligible child to have a personal adviser.[77] It is also the duty of each local authority to appoint a personal adviser for each relevant child (if they have not already done so whilst the child was an eligible child).[78]

3.90   A personal adviser has the following functions:

- to provide advice (including practical advice) and support;
- where applicable, to participate in his assessment and the preparation of his/her pathway plan;
- to participate in reviews of the pathway plan;
- to liaise with the responsible authority in the implementation of the pathway plan;
- to co-ordinate the provision of services, and to take reasonable steps to ensure that s/he makes use of such services;
- to keep informed about the child's progress and wellbeing; and
- to keep written records of contact with the child.[79]

73 Children (Leaving Care) (England) Regulations 2001 reg 8(1) and Schedule.
74 Ibid, reg 8(2).
75 Ibid, reg 6(1).
76 Ibid, reg 9(2).
77 Children Act 1989 Sch 2 para 19C.
78 Ibid, s23B(2).
79 Children (Leaving Care) (England) Regulations 2001 reg 12.

3.91 In *R (on the application of J) v Caerphilly County Borough Council*[80] Munby J described the role of the personal adviser as follows:

> It is not part of the personal adviser's functions to undertake the statutory assessment or the preparation of the pathway plan, nor should he do so. The Regulations, in my judgement, show that it is not permissible for him to do so. It is in any event undesirable that he should do so. Part of the personal adviser's role is, in a sense, to be the advocate or representative of the child in the course of the child's dealings with the local authority. As the *Children (Leaving Care) Act Guidance* puts it, the personal adviser plays a 'negotiating role on behalf of the child'. He is, in a sense, a 'go-between' between the child and the local authority. His vital role and function are apt to be compromised if he is, at one and the same time, both the author of the local authority's pathway plan and the person charged with important duties owed to the child in respect of its preparation and implementation.

Accommodation and support for relevant children

3.92 The responsible local authority must safeguard and promote a relevant child's welfare and, unless satisfied that his/her welfare does not require it, support him/her by:

- maintaining him/her;
- providing him/her or maintaining him/her in suitable accommodation; and
- providing support of such other description as may be prescribed.[81]

3.93 'Suitable accommodation' means accommodation:

- which, so far as reasonably practicable, is suitable for the child in the light of his/her needs, including his/her health needs and any needs arising from any disability;
- in respect of which the responsible authority has satisfied itself as to the character and suitability of the landlord or other provider; and
- in respect of which the responsible authority has, so far as reasonably practicable, taken into account the child's:
  (a) wishes and feelings; and
  (b) education, training or employment needs.[82]

Uncooperative children

3.94 Not all children will keep all appointments arranged or co-operate with every assessment planned as part of the leaving care provisions. In *R (on the application of J) v Caerphilly County Borough Council*[83] Munby J warned local authorities such behaviour is not an excuse to do nothing:

> The fact that a child is uncooperative and unwilling to engage, or even refuses to engage, is not reason for the local authority not to carry out its obligations under the Act and the Regulations. After all, a disturbed child's unwillingness to engage with those who are trying to help is often merely a part of the overall problems which justified the local authority's statutory intervention in the first place. The local authority must do its best.

80 [2005] EWHC 586 Admin, at [30].
81 Children Act 1989 s23B(8).
82 Children (Leaving Care) (England) Regulations 2001 reg 11(2).
83 [2005] EWHC 586 Admin, at [55].

Duties to former relevant children

3.95 A local authority has continuing duties to young adults who meet the definition of 'former relevant child'. These duties will be of significance for a young person who attains 18 during the time of a community order or custodial sentence.

3.96 'Former relevant child' is defined as:

- a person who has been a relevant child (and would be one if s/he were under 18); and
- a person who was being looked after when s/h e attained the age of 18, and immediately before ceasing to be looked after was an eligible child.[84]

3.97 The duties owed to a former relevant child fall on the last responsible authority. The various duties are set out in Children Act 1989 23C. In summary these include:

- taking reasonable steps to keep in touch whether the young adult is in their area or not, and if they lose touch to re-establish contact;
- to continue the appointment of a personal adviser;
- to continue to keep the pathway plan under regular review;
- to give assistance, to the extent that the young adult's welfare requires it, by contributing to expenses incurred in living near the place where s/he is or, or will be, in employment or where s/he is, or will be, in education or training.

Duty to investigate alleged abuse against children

3.98 Children Act 1989 s47 provides:

Where a local authority–
(a) are informed that a child who lives, or is found, in their area–
  (i)   is the subject of an emergency protection order; or
  (ii) is in police protection; or
  (iii) has contravened a ban imposed by a curfew notice within the meaning of Chapter I of Part I of the Crime and Disorder Act 1998;
(b) have reasonable cause to suspect that a child who lives, or is found, in their area is suffering, or is likely to suffer, significant harm,
the authority shall make, or cause to be made, such enquiries, as they consider necessary to enable them to decide whether they should take any action to safeguard or promote the child's welfare.

3.99 When construing the meaning of serious harm, the following definitions are to be used:

- 'harm' means ill-treatment or the impairment of health or development;
- 'development' means physical, intellectual, emotional, social or behavioural development;
- 'health' means physical or mental health;
- 'ill-treatment' includes sexual abuse and forms of abuse which are not physical.[85]

---

84 Children Act 1989 s23C(1).
85 Ibid, ss31(9) and 105(1).

3.100   Where the question of whether harm suffered by a child is significant turns on the child's health or development, his/her health or development shall be compared with that which could be reasonably expected of a similar child.[86]

3.101   For the purposes of making a determination under this section as to the action to be taken with respect to a child, a local authority shall, so far as is reasonably practicable and consistent with the child's welfare:

• ascertain the child's wishes and feelings regarding the action to be taken with respect to him/her; and
• give due consideration (having regard to his/her age and understanding) to such wishes and feelings of the child as they have been able to ascertain.[87]

Child protection referral

3.102   The government has issued *Working together to safeguard children* (April 2006).[88] Chapter 5 of the guidance sets out the procedure following a child protection referral. In summary, the guidance states:

• the local authority should decide and record next steps within one working day;
• initial consideration of the case should consider whether there are concerns about either the child's health and development or actual and/ or potential harm which justifies an initial assessment to establish ,whether the child is a child in need;
• any initial assessment should be undertaken in accordance with the Framework for the assessment of children in need and their families (Department of Health et al, 2000);
• in the course of an initial assessment, the local authority should ascertain whether the child is a child in need or is suffering, or is likely to suffer, significant harm;
• where there is a risk to life or a likelihood of serious immediate harm, an agency with statutory child protection powers should act quickly to secure the immediate safety of the child;
• if there is reason to suspect that a child is suffering or is likely to suffer significant harm, there should be a strategy discussion involving local authority children's social care, the police and any other bodies as appropriate (eg school and health);
• the strategy meeting will agree a plan for how a core assessment will be carried out;
• a core assessment is the means by which a section 47 enquiry is carried out; it should be completed with 35 days;
• where the agencies most involved judge that a child may continue to suffer, or be at risk of suffering, significant harm, the local authority's children's social care should convene a child protection conference;

---

86   Ibid, ss31(10) and 105(1).
87   Ibid, s47(5A) inserted by Children Act 2004 s53.
88   Available as download from Department for Education and Skills website – see appendix 14. In Wales separate guidance is in force.

- all initial child protection conferences should be within 15 days of the initial strategy discussion;
- the purpose of an initial child protection conference is to analyse the information gathered, consider the evidence to determine the likelihood of the child suffering significant harm in the future and to decide the future action required to safeguard and promote the welfare of the child;
- where the conference considers that the child is at continuing risk of significant harm, it may decide to draw up a child protection plan;
- a child protection plan should specify which category of abuse or neglect the child has suffered or is at risk of suffering (categories may be physical, emotional, sexual abuse or neglect);
- even if it is decided that the child is not at risk of significant harm, s/he may still be a child in need and it may therefore be appropriate to carry out a more detailed assessment of his/her needs as a child in need (see paras 3.21–3.34 above).

Child protection considerations with suspected sexually abusive children

3.103 *Working together to safeguard children* gives non-statutory guidance regarding the proper response to an allegation of sexual abuse. The guidance states that work with children who abuse others should recognise that such children are likely to have considerable needs themselves, and also that they may pose a significant risk of harm to other children.[89]

3.104 The guidance continues (at para 11.35):

> Three key principles should guide work with children and young people who abuse others:
> - there should be a co-ordinated approach on the part of youth justice, children's social care, education (including educational psychology) and health (including child and adolescent mental health) agencies;
> - the needs of children and young people who abuse others should be considered separately from the needs of their victims; and
> - an assessment should be carried out in each case, appreciating that these children may have considerable unmet developmental needs, as well as specific needs arising from their behaviour.

3.105 Consideration should be given to convening a child protection conference for the suspected perpetrator. The guidance suggests (at para 11.39):

> A young abuser should be the subject of a child protection conference if he or she is considered personally to be at risk of continuing significant harm. Where there is no reason to hold a child protection conference, there may still be a need for a multi-agency approach if the young abuser's needs are complex. Issues regarding suitable educational and accommodation arrangements often require skilled and careful consideration.

Children in custody

3.106 The duty to investigate abuse of children in custody is considered below at para 3.115.

---

89 Para 11.34.

Duties to children in custody

3.107   It was long considered that the Children Act 1989 had no application to children detained in Prison Service establishments. This belief was proved wrong in *R (Howard League for Penal Reform) v Secretary of State for the Home Department*[90] where Munby J held that, although the Act did not confer any functions or powers or impose any duties, responsibilities or obligations upon the Home Office or the Prison Service, it did apply to children in Prison Service establishments subject to the necessary requirements of imprisonment.

3.108   The practical implication of the judgment is that local authorities, in whose area a young offender institution is situated, have the statutory responsibility for:

- assessing children in need in the institution under Children Act 1989 s17; and
- conducting children protection investigations at the institution under Children Act 1989 s47.

3.109   At the time of writing, the Youth Justice Board is providing funding for the placement of local authority staff in young offender institutions to undertake these duties under the Children Act 1989.[91]

3.110   In response to the judgment of Munby J in the *Howard League* case, the Department for Education and Skills issued Local Authority Circular LAC (2004) 26 *Safeguarding and promoting the welfare of children and young people in custody*. This circular reviews the services that that should be provided to children in custody by local authorities. The main provisions are considered below.

Assessment and service provision for children in need

3.111   LAC 2004(26) notes that, although very large numbers of children in custody will be children in desperate need, it does not follow that they are children whose needs will not be properly met without the provision of services by the local authority.[92] However, the guidance does state:

> Where a child or young person has been receiving services under Part III of the Children Act 1989 immediately prior to entering custody, from the local authority in whose area he was living, then as part of his responsibility for sentence and discharge planning, the youth offending team worker for the area where the child was living should request relevant information from the local authority children's social services. This information may include, for example, the results of any assessments under the 'Framework for the Assessment of Children in Need and Their Families'. He or she will then need to discuss with the local authority in whose area the child will be living, as part of planning for the child's discharge, what services the local authority will provide to the child when he is discharged

---

90 [2002] EWHC 2497 (Admin).

91 *Strategy for the secure estate for children and young people: plans for 2005/06 to 2007/08*, Youth Justice Board (2005).

92 A point made by Munby J in *R (Howard League for Penal Reform) v Secretary of State for the Home Department* [2002] EWHC 2497 (Admin).

Where a child has not been receiving services from a local authority immediately prior to entering custody, the local authority in whose area the YOI is located will need to make a judgement about whether the child is likely to be a child in need on release, and will therefore need services provided by the local authority in whose area he will be living, on discharge. Where this is so, then they should make a referral to the relevant YOT worker or local authority.

There may be occasions, for example, for a disabled child or young person, or a child with unmet mental health needs, where a child or young person in custody requires an assessment using the 'Framework for the Assessment of Children in Need and their Families' and services provided to meet those needs while in custody: this will be the responsibility of the local authority in whose area the [young offender institution or secure training centre] is located.

Children in care prior to their entry to custody

3.112 A substantial proportion of the children or young persons who enter custody each year are looked after children immediately before their incarceration.[93] In LAC 2004 (26) the Department for Education and Skills clarified which local authority has a duty to promote the welfare of those children. The guidance distinguishes between those children subject to full care orders and those who were in voluntary care.

3.113 In the case of children subject to full care orders LAC 2004 (26) states:

Where a looked after child who is the subject of a court order placing parental responsibility on a council enters a [young offender institution or secure training centre], or is placed there on remand, the *responsible authority* i.e. the one that looks after him, has continuing responsibilities towards his or her welfare, as a corporate parent. Where these children are 16+ they would be 'eligible' children and entitled to leaving care services.

It is therefore expected that the responsible authority will make arrangements for regular contact with any child who is looked after under a care order while they are in custody, whether by visiting themselves or by making arrangements with the local authority in whose area the [young offender institution or secure training centre] is located. The responsible authority should arrange to maintain regular contact with the child and reviews of his care plan or pathway plan should continue. The responsible authority should also ensure that ongoing contact with siblings, where that is part of the care plan, is facilitated. When considering where the young person should live on release from custody, it will be necessary to make appropriate plans in advance of the end of the sentence. It will be important to assess the parental capacity to resume care of the young person or to plan for their move to a placement that is appropriate to meeting the needs identified in the care or pathway plan.

3.114 In the case of children in voluntary care before their incarceration, LAC 2004 (26) states:

Where a child who has previously been an 'accommodated' child under Section 20 of the Children Act enters custody, he does not remain a looked after child. The local authority where he is to live on release must establish arrangements for his care on release, including carrying out an assessment of his needs and arranging for services, including accommodation if necessary. The local

---

93 Association of Directors of Social Services, the Local Government Association and the Youth Justice Board, *The application of the Children Act (1989) to children in young offender institutions* (September 2003).

...y in whose area the [young offender institution or secure training cen-
.._ is located will need to identify where the young person is to live on release
and contact the relevant authority. The young person may need to resume his
'accommodated' status or, depending on his age, he may be a 'relevant' care
leaver as defined in the Children Act 1989 s23 and s24. Where a local authority
will resume responsibility for the care of a child on discharge from custody, it is
important that contact with him is maintained by that local authority.

Child protection in custodial institutions

3.115   A joint report by the Association of Directors of Social Services, the Local
Government Association and the Youth Justice Board identified that in a
custodial institution the main risks of significant harm were from:

- self-harm and suicide;
- other detained young people (bullying or worse); and
- adults (staff, volunteers, visitors and others).

3.116   These risks are very real. Since April 2000 when the Youth Justice Board
took over the running of the juvenile secure estate, 12 children have died
in custody (11 were self-inflicted deaths and one 15-year-old died after
being restrained by staff).[94] In 2002 there were 393 recorded incidents of
self-harm by children held in young offender institutions, of which 53%
involved cutting or scratching and 23% involved hanging, strangulation or
suffocation.[95] In one survey of children detained in young offender institutions just over a third reported feeling unsafe at some time whilst detained
in the institution.[96] In the light of such high levels of risk, the defence
lawyer will need to be alert to any warning signs indicating a risk of significant harm.

3.117   In relation to the duty to be discharged by the local authority, Local
Authority Circular LAC 2003 (26) states:

> It is ... the authority in whose area the custodial establishment is located which
> is responsible for carrying out section 47 enquiries in relation to any child in
> custody who they have reasonable cause to suspect is suffering, or likely to suf-
> fer, significant harm.

> If a child in custody makes allegations about abuse that happened before they
> entered the custodial establishment, or it becomes clear that they may be at risk
> of significant harm on leaving the establishment, the local authority in whose
> area the custodial establishment is located will need to initiate s47 enquiries,
> and negotiate transfer to the local authority in whose area the child was liv-
> ing or will be living, or where the abuse is alleged to have taken place, where
> appropriate.

---

94 Information provided by the Howard League for Penal Reform.

95 Association of Directors of Social Services, the Local Government Association and
the Youth Justice Board, *The application of the Children Act (1989) to children in young
offender institutions* (September 2003). ♪

96 HM Inspector of Prisons, *Juveniles in custody: a unique insight into the perceptions of
young people held in Prison Service* (2004).

Remedies

3.118 When the defence lawyer wishes to secure particular local authority services for his/her client during the course of criminal proceedings, time will usually be of the essence. The quickest way to resolve any problem will always be to negotiate with the social services department. If necessary, attempts may have to be made to contact senior management. If such representations are not successful, the following may have to be considered.

Complaints procedure

3.119 Every local authority must establish a procedure for considering representations and complaints by (or on behalf of) a child regarding the provision of services under Part III of the Act.[97] Part III covers the duties to provide services to children in need as well as the duties to provide accommodation and the use of secure accommodation orders.[98] This complaints procedure should be advertised by the authority.[99]

3.120 The procedure should ensure that at least one person who is not a member of the local authority takes part in the consideration of any representations or complaints and any discussions which are held by the authority about the action (if any) to be taken in relation to the child.[100] The authority is required to provide a written response within 28 days of receiving the complaint.[101]

Local government ombudsman

3.121 A complaint may be made to the local government ombudsman.[102] The ombudsman will investigate the complaint to establish whether there has been maladministration on the part of the local authority which has led to injustice. If the ombudsman establishes that this is the case, s/he may order remedies such as:

- the making of an apology;
- ordering the local authority to take action to make a decision which should have been made before; and
- the payment of compensation.

3.122 The ombudsman may not investigate a complaint before a local authority has had an reasonable opportunity to respond to it. This is generally taken to be a period of 12 weeks. An investigation may not be initiated if the complainant has already started court proceedings against the local authority.

---

97 Children Act 1989 s26(3).
98 Complaints regarding other local authority services and decisions may be made under Local Authority Services Act 1970 s7B.
99 Children Act 1989 s26(8).
100 Ibid, s26(4).
101 Representations Procedure (Children) Regulations 1991 SI No 894 reg 6(1).
102 There are separate ombudsmen for England and Wales – for contact details see appendix 14.

Judicial review

3.123   Judicial review is a discretionary remedy. It is a general principle that relief will not generally be granted unless all other remedies have been exhausted. The complaints procedure is designed to be the main remedy for persons aggrieved by the services (or lack of them) provided by a local authority. As a result, the Administrative Court will be reluctant to entertain an application for judicial review.[103] It has, however, demonstrated that it will interfere where it can be demonstrated that the local authority has failed to have regard to the recommendations of a complaints panel.[104]

3.124   Where the services of the local authority are required urgently and the complaints procedure is, therefore, not an effective remedy, the Administrative Court has demonstrated a willingness to grant relief where the local authority has failed to carry out an adequate child in need assessment[105] or leaving care assessment.[106]

Default powers of the Secretary of State

3.125   If the Secretary of State for Education and Skills is satisfied that any local authority has failed without reasonable excuse to comply with any duty imposed on them by the Children Act, s/he may make an order declaring that authority to be in default with respect to that duty.[107] An order may be issued giving such directions as appear necessary to ensure that the duty is complied with.[108] These directions are enforceable by the secretary of state by means of an application for judicial review to the divisional court.[109]

3.126   There seems to be little evidence that this power is being used. It is not clear whether it would be an effective remedy where a local authority has refused to allocate resources in a particular case or whether its main use is where an authority does not have a service envisaged under the Act.[110]

103   See, for example, *R v Birmingham City Council ex p A (a minor)* (1997) *Times* 19 February, FD.
104   See *Re T (Accommodation by Local Authority)* [1995] 1 FLR 159 and *R v Avon County Council ex p M (a minor)* [1994] 2 FCR 259.
105   *AB and SB v Nottingham City Council* [2001] EWHC 235 Admin.
106   *R (on the application of J) v Caerphilly County Borough Council* [2005] EWHC 586 Admin.
107   Children Act 1989 s84(1).
108   Ibid, s84(3).
109   Ibid, s84(4).
110   For example, in *R v Barnet London Borough Council ex p B* [1994] 1 FLR 592 where it was alleged the authority had no day care service.

The adolescent client

4.1 The moral, legal, political, and practical concerns that one brings to the table for a discussion of juvenile crime may be different from those that are raised in a discussion of adult crime simply because of the developmental status of the offender. A fair punishment for an adult may seem unfair when applied to a child who may not have understood the consequences of his or her actions. The way we interpret and apply laws may rightfully vary when the specific case at hand involves a defendant whose understanding of the law is limited by immaturity. The practical and political implications of treating offenders in a particular fashion may be different when the offender is young than when he is an adult. Reasonable people may differ in their views of the extent to which, and the ways in which, an offender's age and developmental status should be taken into account in discussions of juvenile crime, but ignoring this factor entirely is like trying to ignore a very large elephant that has wandered into the room.

Lawrence Steinberg and Robert G Schwartz, *Developmental psychology goes to court*[1]

[I]t is essential that a child charged with an offence is dealt with in a manner which takes full account of his age, level of maturity and intellectual and emotional capability and that steps are taken to promote his ability to understand and participate in the proceedings.

European Court of Human Rights, *V v UK*[2]

4.2 The developmental status of a young client is an important issue for the defence lawyer to bear in mind. It will affect culpability, understanding of the legal system, decision-making, ability to express remorse and ability to change for the better.

4.3 This chapter provides a brief overview of the normative changes experienced by young people as they develop from childhood to adulthood, a period of development normally termed adolescence. It should be noted, however, that there is considerable variation in the way that children develop into adults. This process is affected by family environment, culture and life experience. Mental disorders which may also have an impact on an adolescent's development are outlined in appendix 2. After considering how the young client may be developing, the chapter goes on to offer some practical advice on how to work with the young client.

The changes of adolescence

4.4 Adolescence is the period of change from childhood to adulthood, which spans the ages of approximately 10 years to 20 years. It may be further subdivided as follows:

- early adolescence (ages 10–13 years);
- middle adolescence (ages 14–17 years); and
- late adolescence (ages 18–20 years).

4.5 In relation to the youth justice system, the changes of early and middle adolescence are obviously the most relevant. During those stages the following changes may be noted:

1 Chapter 1 in T Grisso and R Schwartz (eds), *Youth on trial: a developmental perspective on juvenile justice*, University of Chicago Press, 2000.
2 (1999) 30 EHRR 131.

- physical development;
- intellectual (cognitive) development;
- emotional development;
- moral development.

Physical development

4.6　The changes most obvious to those around the adolescent are the physical changes which occur. These are referred to as puberty. The physical changes include:

- a growth spurt;
- growth of pubic hair;
- development of sexual organs;
- in girls, onset of menstruation and development of breasts;
- in boys, deepening of the voice, development of facial hair and increase in muscle mass and definition; and
- changes in the structure of the brain.

4.7　There is considerable variation in the onset of the physical changes of puberty, for example the average age for the start of the growth spurt in boys is around 12–13 years but it can start as young as 9 years or as late as 15 years; in girls the average age is about 10–11 years but it can start as young as 8 years or as late as 14 years.[3]

4.8　There is no direct correlation between the physical changes of puberty and the intellectual and emotional development of the adolescent. It is, therefore, important that the defence lawyer does not treat a young client on the basis of his/her physical maturity alone.

Intellectual (cognitive) development

4.9　Important intellectual developments will normally be noted during adolescence in the following areas:

- abstract thinking;
- reflection;
- balancing and weighing decisions;
- relativity;
- attention;
- memory;
- information processing; and
- communication.

Abstract and hypothetical thinking

4.10　Younger children need to see or manipulate objects in order to learn about them. Adolescents develop a greater ability to deal with intangible concepts. This means that they acquire a greater ability to estimate distance, mass and the passage of time, as well as a greater ability to think about situations they have not experienced before.

3　Coleman and Hendry, *The nature of adolescence*, 3rd edn, Routledge, 1999.

Reflection

4.11   As they move into their teenage years, adolescents acquire greater ability to think about their thought processes and to explain their motivation and behaviour. They also become more aware of and able to explain their emotions.

Balancing and weighing decisions

4.12   A child will only be able to approach a problem from one dimension at a time. An adolescent develops an increasing ability to deal with several dimensions at the same time to reach a decision.

Relativity

4.13   Adolescents develop a greater ability to see things in relative terms, rather than 'black and white' terms. They are also more able to question statements made by other people rather than accepting them at face value.

Attention

4.14   During the teenage years adolescents generally show improvements in both selective attention (knowing which cues to focus on) and divided attention (being able to deal with more than one cue at a time).

Memory

4.15   During early to mid-adolescence there is usually an improvement in both short-term and long-term memory. The young client's short- and long-term memory will be important to his/her ability to recall details of an incident and to his/her ability to retain information about the legal process.

Information processing

4.16   Research evidence indicates that young people in late adolescence are able to process information at a faster rate and have improved organisational strategies.

Communication

4.17   There is a close relationship between vocabulary, abstract thought and reasoning. The broader an individual's vocabulary, the larger is their range of choice in descriptive language and the greater the potential for accuracy in communication, comparison and differentiation.

4.18   During the secondary school years (ages 11–16) a pupil would normally gain:

- greater comprehension of the spoken and written word through an increase in the understanding of a wider range of words used by others and a greater ability to understand complex sentence structure; and
- improved oral expression through the use of a wider range of words and more sophisticated manipulation of sentence structure and grammar.

4.19   Although some of these communication skills will improve without formal education, the progress will be significantly slower if there is no planned input from teachers. Teenagers who miss lengthy periods of schooling (from exclusion, truancy or illness) are likely to have poorer communication skills.

Other features of adolescent thinking

4.20 Even where adolescents are able to employ logical, abstract thought processes they may not be able to apply these advanced skills to their own personal lives. Their thinking may also be influenced by features of behaviour prominent during adolescence, such as:

- a tendency to be attracted to risky behaviour (even if the negative outcome is foreseen);
- a desire to experience a new experience (sensation-seeking);
- a tendency to think in the present (choosing short-term gain despite long-term negative consequences – for example, an adolescent confessing to a crime so that s/he can leave the police station more quickly);
- being extremely self-conscious and self-absorbed (ego-centric), leading in extreme cases to a belief that the adolescent is always being observed or judged or that his/her experiences are unique and therefore no one can understand what s/he is going through;
- a belief in the adolescent's own invulnerability (linked to risk-taking and also to an unrealistic belief in not being apprehended for committing a crime); and
- wishful thinking – that is, avoiding a difficult problem by producing an unrealistic excuse for bad behaviour or producing an obviously unrealistic solution to a problem.

4.21 Adolescents with a learning disability are more likely to display concrete thinking, poor information processing skills and poor problem-solving skills. These cognitive deficits may not be immediately apparent as the adolescents may be functioning socially in an apparently normal manner.

4.22 All of these features of adolescent thinking have obvious relevance both when analysing a young person's decision-making at the time of an offence and when asking him/her to make decisions within the legal proceedings.

Emotional development

4.23 Adolescence is a time of important psychological changes which affect:

- the way the adolescent feels about him/herself (identity);
- the adolescent's ability to function independently (autonomy);
- romantic relationships; and
- sexual feelings (sexuality).

Identity

4.24 It is an important developmental goal of adolescence to develop a stable sense of identity. During adolescence the various physical and cognitive changes prompt a greater self-awareness. Adolescents begin to think more about their own personality and how other people perceive them. They also acquire an increasing ability to reflect on their own personality. When asked to describe themselves, young children will normally describe physical features only, whereas adolescents will increasingly describe personality traits or aptitude for a particular activity.

4.25   As a normal part of adolescence there will be an element of 'trying on' a new personality or behaviour. This process will be most successful where the adolescent benefits from a safe, nurturing family environment; it will be much less successful where there is an abusive or neglectful family background.

4.26   An adolescent's peers also play an important role in the development of identity, principally by giving the adolescent a sense of belonging. The influence of the peer group is strongest in early adolescence and particularly in boys. Peer influence and the strong wish to be 'part of the crowd' will be of significance in the many occasions when a group of young people has offended together. It may also affect the behaviour and decision-making of a young defendant who is concerned about the way his/her delinquent peers will react to his/her conduct during the trial process.

4.27   The development of an ethnic identity will also be an important developmental goal for young people from an ethnic minority culture. This process will involve finding a personal compromise between retaining the young person's own culture and assimilating the dominant culture. The competing demands will be all the more marked when English is not the young person's first language.

Autonomy

4.28   During adolescence there is a move from dependence on parents or carers to emotional and social independence. This is an essential developmental task for any person to reach adulthood. The physical changes of puberty allow adolescents to act more independently and adults respond to increasing physical maturity by giving more scope for independent action.

4.29   Developing autonomy can be a difficult process in the context of the family. It may be a time of conflict within the family as the adolescent tests the boundaries, for example by breaking curfew or refusing to perform household chores.

Interpersonal and intimate relationships

4.30   As a person moves through adolescence s/he can be expected to:
- develop close friendships with persons of a similar age;
- have greater contact with friends of the opposite sex; and
- become involved in romantic relationships.

Sexuality

4.31   Developing a sexual identity is an important developmental goal of adolescence. Along with the physical changes of puberty, adolescents will experience new feelings which require negotiating issues such as the choice of sexual partner, how to relate to a partner and the limits (if any) of sexual experimentation.

Moral development

4.32 Most adolescents will develop a more sophisticated moral reasoning during their teenage years.

4.33 In childhood the concept of right and wrong is generally based on external punishment and rewards. 'Good' and 'bad' are determined by obedience to rules and authority, particularly those of the parent.

4.34 By early adolescence the young person is generally more concerned with how s/he will be judged by others if s/he behaves in a particular way. The concept of 'being good' is based more on pleasing and helping others. Increasingly the concept of morality expands to include society as a whole rather than just family and friends.

4.35 An adolescent's moral values may be derived from family, relationships, religious beliefs and popular culture. A tight-knit group of delinquent peers may provide a simple, and therefore easy, moral code for an adolescent, which includes rigid rules such as never revealing friends' bad behaviour and always being willing to fight to help a friend.

4.36 When considering an adolescent's moral reasoning it is important to remember that his/her reasoning will be affected by intellectual ability and social experience.

Working with an adolescent client

4.37 The developmental status of an adolescent client means that the defence lawyer must:

- assess the young client's level of development;
- establish a rapport;
- ensure the young client understands the role of a defence lawyer;
- ensure the young client understands the concept of a legal right;
- ensure the young client understands legal procedure;
- interview in a way that obtains reliable factual information; and
- help the young person to make informed decisions.

Assessing level of development

4.38 The defence lawyer will always need to consider the developmental status of a young client. It is not suggested that this should be a formal process, but it should be built into a defence lawyer's agenda for any contact with a young client.

4.39 The assessment should include:

- considering the effectiveness of communication between client and lawyer (eg do questions have to be repeated several times? is the young person struggling to express him/herself? does the young person appear distractible or inattentive?);
- observing the interaction between the young client and any parent or carer (how autonomous does the young client appear?);

- questioning the young client about schools (mainstream or special needs?), academic attainment and any identified special education needs;
- asking the young client about general interests (are they age appropriate?); and
- asking any parent or carer to describe the young client's behaviour and personality, as well as to provide any relevant information about the young person.

4.40   Factors adversely affecting intellectual functioning will include a learning disability, past trauma and mental disorder. The defence lawyer will also need to take account of cultural differences, or the fact that English may be the adolescent's second language.

4.41   During the course of a criminal case, the defence lawyer should also collect as much information about the young person's level of development as possible. This could involve:

- interviewing a parent or carer;
- obtaining school records;
- obtaining any statement of special educational needs;
- interviewing a school teacher;
- reviewing records held by social services or health professionals;
- obtaining copies of any previous assessments of the young person (medical, psychological or psychiatric);
- commissioning a psychological or psychiatric assessment of the young person.

4.42   The right to access personal records is considered in appendix 3. Instructing experts to assess the client is discussed at paras 10.30–10.38.

Establishing a rapport

4.43   No matter how pressured the defence lawyer is, it is essential to spend some time establishing a rapport with a young client. Many adolescents involved in the youth justice system will have suffered abuse at the hands of adults or have unhappy experiences of schooling. It is perhaps not surprising that they may be suspicious of adults and have no expectation that an adult will pay attention to their views.

Understanding the role of a defence lawyer

4.44   A defence lawyer should never assume that a young client understands the role of a lawyer. There may be considerable confusion among young clients about the role of the lawyer and even whether the lawyer is on the young person's side. Furthermore, research indicates that young clients also have difficulty distinguishing between the function of the defence lawyer and the authority of the court.[4]

4.45   As a minimum the lawyer should explain or confirm the young client's understanding of a lawyer's:

---

4   T Grisso 'Juvenile competency to stand trial: questions in an era of punitive reform', Criminal Justice Vol 12(3) Fall 1997.

- duty to protect the client's legal interests;
- duty to act on the client's instructions; and
- duty of confidentiality.

Duty to protect the client's legal interests

4.45A The defence lawyer may need to explain that the duty to protect the client's interests exists even if the young client has done something wrong.

Duty to act on client's instructions

4.46 Adolescent clients, particularly those in early adolescence, may have no experience of making decisions for adults to follow. It is therefore important that the duty is explained in a practical way that the young client will understand.

Duty of confidentiality

4.47 Adolescents may not have experienced a situation where an adult promises to keep what the adolescent tells the adult secret. Instead they may be used to teachers and other professionals insisting that information about them must be passed on to a parent. The defence lawyer needs to state explicitly that the duty of confidentiality applies to a parent or carer just as much as to any other person. It has also been argued that the defence lawyer representing a young client should go out of his/her way to demonstrate the rule in action by excluding a parent or guardian from part or all of an interview with the client and taking every opportunity to assert the duty of confidentiality in the young client's presence.[5]

Understanding the concept of a right

4.48 The concept of a legal right as an entitlement belonging to the child or young person may not be fully understood. Children and many adolescents only have experience of being told what to do by adults (parents, teachers, etc). Research in the United States carried out by the psychologist Thomas Grisso found that it is only around ages 13 or 14 that adolescents develop the capacity to think of rights as 'belonging' to them. In a review of his research findings Dr Grisso commented:

> Even at ages 14 to 16, only about one-fourth of delinquent youths, as compared to about one-half of adults offenders, described a 'right' in a way that connotes an entitlement. Thus, when asked what is meant when police said, 'You do not have to make a statement and have the right to remain silent,' many youths indicated a conditional view of legal rights, such as 'You can be silent unless you are told to talk,' or 'You have to be quiet unless you are spoken to.' Even though youths may develop the capacity for understanding rights early in adolescence, it often takes additional time and life experiences before their capacity influences their actual understanding.[6]

5 E Buss 'The role of lawyers', chapter 9 in Grisso and Schwartz (eds), *Youth on trial: a developmental perspective on juvenile justice*, University of Chicago Press, 2000.

6 T Grisso 'Juvenile competency to stand trial: questions in an era of punitive reform' *Criminal Justice*, vol 12(3) Fall 1997 – available at www.abanet.org/crimjust/juvjus/12-3gris.html.

4.49   Faced with such research evidence, it is clear that the defence lawyer should always check that the young client understands the concept of legal rights.

Understanding legal procedure

4.50   The defence lawyer needs to ensure that even the most basic elements of court procedure are explained fully to the young client.

4.51   The use of legal jargon should be avoided when talking to the young client and where important legal terms will be mentioned during a court hearing, they should be explained beforehand. During a Home Office study of youth court procedure, the researchers noted a number of terms used in the court hearings observed which were taken for granted by the professionals in court, but which were questioned by the young defendants or their parents. This list (reproduced at table 5) and the suggested alternative ways of expressing the same idea may be of use to the defence lawyer.

4.52   When explaining court procedure, the defence lawyer may find it may helpful to do this in a concrete way by drawing a basic diagram showing the layout of the courtroom and marking on it the positions of the respective professionals. While doing this, their roles can be explained. When in the court building, the lawyer could also show the young client, and any parent, the courtroom before the court starts sitting.

4.53   The defence lawyer should not assume that explaining legal words and procedure on one occasion only will be sufficient. With young clients the lawyer should be prepared to explain important words and concepts more than once. Research conducted in the United States also suggests that it would be unwise to assume that young offenders with previous convictions understand the legal process any better than those young people experiencing their first contact with the youth justice system.[7]

Obtaining reliable factual information

4.54   A young person accused of a crime will need to give reliable information about:

- past events relevant to the allegation;
- his/her thoughts and feelings at the time; and
- his/her background.

4.55   The developmental status of the young client will affect the taking of factual instructions because of potentially:

- greater distrust of the lawyer;
- poorer cognitive skills; and
- increased suggestibility.

7   T Grisso, 'What we know about Youths' Capacities as Trial Defendants' in T Grisso and R Swartz (eds), *Youth on Trial: a developmental perspective on juvenile justice,* Chicago University Press (2000).

Table 5: Court language

Community penalty – A sentence that you have to complete in the community.

Compliance – Go along with.

Concurrent – At the same time.

Consecutive – One after another.

Consolidate fines – Put all the fines that you have together into one sum.

Custody – Locked up (in a Young Offender Institution).

Date of birth – Birthday.

Do you have any means? – Are you receiving any money that you can use to pay a fine?

Dis-served – Not served.

If you fail to surrender then you render yourself liable to another offence of absconding – If you do not come back to court at the time that we have arranged, this is an offence and you may be charged with it.

Incommoded – Unavailable.

In drink at the time – Drunk at the time.

Just received AO – You have just been given an attendance centre order.

Live witnesses – Witnesses who come to court to give evidence.

Lose your liberty – You may be locked up.

NFA – No further action.

Peer group – Friends.

Remorse – Feel sorry.

Remit – The case will not be dealt with here – we will send it to 'X' court and they will deal with it from now on.

Retail premises – Shops.

Retire – We will leave the courtroom to consider what to do.

Stand down – This case will be put off for the moment, and we will call you back into court later.

The bench will ... – The magistrates will ...

The magistrates may decline jurisdiction today – The magistrates may decide that they cannot deal with the case today, as it is so serious that it will have to go to Crown Court.

We like juveniles to see the duty solicitor – We like people who appear at the Youth Court to see the 'duty solicitor', who is a solicitor here at the court that you can speak to for free.

Your licence will be endorsed – A record of these offences will be put on your driving licence.

You will be dealt with by the 'X' bench – The magistrates in 'X' will deal with this case.

(To witness): You may be released – As you have given your evidence, you may leave the courtroom.

Source: Appendix F of Home Office Research Study No 214 *Evaluation of the Youth Court Demonstration Project*, Home Office, 2000

Distrust of the lawyer

4.56   To trust a lawyer a young client will need to understand the role of the law-yer (see paras 4.44–4.47 above) and have sufficient trust in the individual lawyer to disclose information which may reveal reprehensible behaviour or distressing personal information. In the case of young people who have suffered physical or sexual abuse in the past or who are suffering from depression, the defence lawyer may be faced with resistance if the young person believes there is no point in talking as they will not believed or their lives are of no consequence to adults.

4.57   To foster trust the defence lawyer needs to demonstrate to the young client that his/her views are important. To do this the defence lawyer should:

- give the client his/her undivided attention during any interview;
- demonstrate an attentive attitude by both verbal prompts and body language;
- avoid judgmental reactions (whether verbal or physical) to information divulged by the young client;
- avoid questions which may be taken by the young client as judgmental or accusatory (eg rather than 'why didn't you ...?' ask 'what stopped you ...?').

Poorer cognitive skills

4.58   As discussed earlier, the young client may:

- have problems thinking in an abstract way;
- have a poor grasp of the duration of events, distance etc;
- have limited powers of self-expression; or
- have a poor memory.

4.59   To facilitate the recall of important information, the defence lawyer should:

- invite the young client initially to explain an incident in his/her own words;
- seek further detail by asking simple questions (such as 'what happened?', 'who said that?', 'who did that?', 'what did you feel when that happened?');
- give the young client time to answer questions, without letting any period of silence become uncomfortable;
- make use of visual prompts, such as photographs of the scene, plans or street maps;
- invite the young client to draw a picture or plan to explain what happened;
- invite the young client to demonstrate distances by reference to furniture in the room or by pacing out distances;
- demonstrate an event such as a struggle with another person by acting it out.

Suggestibility

4.60   Suggestibility is the tendency to provide false information whilst under pressure from a figure of authority in the interrogative setting. Research indicates that adolescents are more suggestible than adults.[8] Learning disability among adults has been found to result in increased suggestibility.[9] It is likely, therefore, that learning disabled adolescents will be abnormally suggestible.

4.61 The defence lawyer needs to be aware that s/he will be perceived as a figure of authority by most young clients, simply by virtue of being an adult. Consequently the problem of suggestion and false information being inadvertently provided during an interview is always present. To minimise the risk, particularly with clients in early adolescence, the defence lawyer needs to avoid:

- telling the client what the lawyer thinks happened during an incident;
- verbal prompts or body language which may give the client the mistaken impression that a certain answer is expected;
- leading questions where the client may assume s/he is expected to agree with the question.

Decision-making

4.62 The defence lawyer should aim to ensure that the young client's decisions are:

- voluntary;
- informed; and
- rational.

Voluntary

4.63 The defence lawyer must establish that any decision made by the young client is really that of the client rather than the decision of a parent, carer or other significant adult in the young person's life. At the very least, the decision and the reasons for it must be confirmed with the client in the absence of any other adult.

Informed

4.64 For a young client to make an informed decision about a choice presented in the youth justice system s/he must understand:

- the concept of a legal right;
- relevant legal procedure;
- his/her factual options; and
- the consequences of each option.

Rational

4.65 Even if an adolescent client is capable of abstract and hypothetical thought, there are many developmental factors which may adversely affect an adolescent's judgment. These factors include:

8 G Gudjonssen and K Singh 'Interrogative suggestibility and delinquent boys: an empirical validation study' *Personality and Individual Differences* 5, pp425–430; and G Gudjonssen, *The Psychology of Interrogations and Confessions: a handbook*, Wiley, 2003.

9 Ibid.

- a lack of life experience, leading to his/her failing to foresee problems;
- thinking which is orientated in the present;
- wishful thinking which leads to unrealistic options being favoured;
- being concerned about the attitude of peers even when it is contrary to the adolescent's best interests (eg refusing to plead guilty because it is not 'cool').

4.66   A defence lawyer cannot substitute his/her views for those of the young client, but the lawyer should endeavour to provide the missing perspective and life experience to the young client's decision-making.

Table 6: Interviewing an adolescent client: good practice points

To build rapport and trust

- Plan to spend some time at the start of the interview breaking the ice
- Invite the young client to discuss a topic in which s/he has a particular interest or aptitude
- Empower the young client by seeking permission before seeking sensitive information, eg 'Do you mind if I ask you about ...?'
- Avoid questions which may be taken as judgemental or accusatory, eg. 'why didn't you ...?' or 'how could you ...?'

To facilitate communication

- Avoid complex language
- Avoid long questions
- Avoid asking for abstract thinking, eg 'What if ...?'

To facilitate recall

- Ask open-ended questions
- Avoid closed questions, that is questions which can be answered by a simple 'yes' or 'no' answer
- Use visual props or ask client to demonstrate what happened

To avoid the risk of unreliable information

- Don't ask leading questions
- Be aware of tone of voice and body language – don't let either suggest a preferred answer to a question

To manage an interview with a volatile adolescent

- Consider personal safety in every interview situation – position yourself between the client and the exit
- Don't take difficult behaviour or 'attitude' personally

The defence lawyer

5.1   Work in the [youth] court has traditionally been seen as the 'kids' stuff' of the legal profession. This must be challenged. It will not be done by merely providing the facilities for more legal representation. However, the presence of a representative can be a precursor to providing justice. The legal profession must become as concerned with the substance of [youth] justice as with its form if it wish to be more than a passive participant in the rhetoric of due process.

Allison Morris, *Legal representation and justice*[1]

5.2   Advocacy on behalf of young clients is a specialist area undervalued by many criminal defence lawyers. As a result of this attitude, representation in the youth court is often delegated to the most junior lawyers. In practice the youth of the client, the frequent chaos of their lives and the complexity of the procedural rules applicable to children and young persons make this an extremely challenging area of defence practice. As well as a detailed knowledge of the law applicable to children and young persons, the defence lawyer needs:

- an ability to communicate effectively with the young client;
- a knowledge of the role of the various agencies involved in the youth justice system as well as an ability to interact effectively with those agencies on behalf of the young client;
- knowledge of other local services relevant to the young client; and
- an advocacy style appropriate to the more informal environment of the youth court.

5.3   This chapter considers some of the professional challenges that may arise when representing children and young persons.

Professional and ethical issues

5.4   Very little attention has been paid to the professional or ethical implications of representing a child or young person in the criminal justice system.[2] There is no guidance in statute or procedural rules, as found in family proceedings. What follows is an attempt to consider the issues which may arise and to offer practical solutions. If there is ever any doubt a solicitor should consult Professional Ethics at the Law Society and a barrister should consult the Bar Council.

General duties owed by a solicitor to a client in criminal proceedings

5.5   A solicitor's professional conduct is governed by the *Solicitors Practice Rules 1990* (last amended in 2004) and *The Guide to the Professional Conduct of Solicitors*.[3]

1   Morris and Giller (eds) *Providing criminal justice for children* (Edward Arnold, 1983).
2   The notable exception is the very brief Law Society's Criminal Law Committee publication *Youth Court Cases – Defence Good Practice* (April 2002).
3   The last printed version of the Guide was the 8th edition published by the Law Society in 1999. This version of the text is out-of-date and the reader is referred to the up-to-date electronic version of the Guide at www.guide.lawsociety.org.uk. This website also provides links to the current version of the Solicitors Practice Rules

5.6   The solicitor has a professional duty to act in the best interests of his/her client.[4] A solicitor acting as an advocate in criminal proceedings must at all times follow the *Law Society's Code for Advocates*.[5] The Code at para 2.3(a) states:

> Advocates must promote and protect fearlessly and by all proper and lawful means the clients' best interests and do so without regard to their own interests or to any consequences to themselves or to any other person (including professional clients or fellow advocates or members of the legal profession).

5.7   *The Guide to the Professional Conduct of Solicitors* para 21.20 states:

> A solicitor who appears in court for the defence in a criminal case is under a duty to say on behalf of the client what the client should properly say for himself or herself if the client possessed the requisite skill and knowledge. The solicitor has a concurrent duty to ensure that the prosecution discharges the onus placed upon it to prove the guilt of the accused.

Who is the client?

5.8   Unlike civil proceedings, where a person under the age of 18 is presumed incapable of looking after his/her own affairs, a child or young person may be prosecuted in his/her own name and no adult will be appointed to act as a litigation friend. This will apply to any child who has attained the age of 10, the current age of criminal responsibility.

5.9   In family proceedings the lawyer is expected to determine whether the young client is competent to give instructions. If the minor is considered competent, s/he should be represented in accordance with those instructions; if s/he is not considered to be so, the lawyer should act in the child's best interests.[6] This notion sits uneasily with the criminal defence lawyer's duty towards a client. It is the opinion of the authors that a defence lawyer should always act on the instructions of the young defendant. A rare exception would be where s/he is clearly incapable of giving any instructions, in which case serious consideration should be given to arguing that the accused is not able to participate effectively in the proceedings.[7]

5.10   In addition to the general duties owed to a client, it may be helpful to quote two of the general principles given in guidance by the Solicitors Family Law Association to solicitors acting for children in family proceedings:

> The lawyer should retain a professional and objective relationship with the client and not allow his/her own emotional response to either the child or any issue in the case to interfere with that professional relationship.

> A child [or young person] as client should always be given the same respect afforded to an adult as client.[8]

---

and the Law Society's Code for Advocates. In the text which follows, references are to the current version rather than that found in the 1999 printed 8th edition. Note that since 1999 there has been significant reorganisation of the text including the alteration of paragraph numbers.

4   Law Society, Solicitors' Practice Rules 1990 rule 1.
5   Ibid, rule 16A.
6   Family Proceedings Courts (Children Act 1989) Rules 1991 SI No 1395 r12(1).
7   See paras 10.43 onwards.
8   *Guide to Good Practice for Solicitors Acting for Children* (6th edn).

Confidentiality

General duty

5.11   The Solicitors' Practice Rules 1990 rule 16E(1) requires a solicitor to keep the affairs of clients and former clients confidential except where disclosure is required or permitted by law or by the client.

Exceptions to the duty of confidentiality

5.12   A solicitor may reveal confidential information to the extent that he or she believes necessary to prevent the client or a third party committing a criminal act that the solicitor reasonably believes is likely to result in serious bodily harm.[9]

5.13   There may be exceptional circumstances involving children where a solicitor should consider revealing confidential information to an appropriate authority. This may be where the child is the client and the child reveals information which indicates continuing sexual or other physical abuse but refuses to allow disclosure of such information. The solicitor must consider whether the threat to the child's life or health, both mental and physical, is sufficiently serious to justify a breach of the duty of confidentiality.[10]

Explaining the duty of confidentiality to the young client

5.14   A duty of confidentiality is owed by a lawyer to a child or young person in the same way as it is owed to adult clients. It is important to explain to a child or young person how this duty of confidentiality works in practice. The concept should be explained at the first meeting in terms appropriate for the age and understanding of the client (see para 4.47).

Withholding information from a young client

5.15   The Solicitors' Practice Rules 1990 rule 16E(3) establishes the general rule that a solicitor must disclose to a client all information of which s/he is aware which is material to that client's matter regardless of the source of the information. Accordingly s/he should not agree to accept information on the basis that it will not be disclosed to the young client.

5.16   The Solicitors' Practice Rules 1990 rule 1 6E(3)(ii)(C) does allow non-disclosure if the solicitor reasonably believes that serious physical or mental injury will be caused to any person if the information is disclosed to a client. The current guidance on rule 16E does not provide any further comment on this exception, however previous guidance did provide the example where a medical report received by the solicitor discloses that the client has a terminal illness.[11]

5.17   The solicitor would seem to be under a duty to withhold information contained in a court report from a young client if the court so directs.[12]

---

9 Law Society, *Confidentiality and Disclosure Guidance* (May 2006), para 13.
10 Ibid, para 14.
11 *The Guide to the Professional Conduct of Solicitors* (Law Society Publishing, 8th edn, 1999), para 16.06.04.
12 Criminal Procedure Rules 2005 r44.1(3)(c). See para 20.65.

Duty not to discriminate

5.18 The Solicitors' Anti-discrimination Rules 2004 rule 1 states:

Solicitors must comply with all anti-discrimination legislation from time to time in force and must, at all times, in their professional dealings with staff, partners, other solicitors, barristers, clients or third parties;

(a) not discriminate against any person, directly or indirectly, nor victimise or harass them on the grounds of their sex (including their marital status); on racial grounds; or on grounds of their racial group; ethnic or national origins; colour; nationality; religion or belief; or sexual orientation

(b) not discriminate against any person on grounds of disability except where, in relation to legislation, there is a specific exception or limitation preventing such discrimination from being unlawful.

Involvement of parents or guardians

5.19 The parent may wish to play a role in the process of taking instructions. When acting for a child or young person, the defence lawyer is under a duty to take instructions from the young client and not from any adult on his/her behalf. This applies even if the adult is the young client's parent. This may cause difficulties where the child is very young or where the parent believes that s/he has the right to make decisions on the child's behalf. The defence lawyer should explain the role of the solicitor to the parent and child or young person at the outset, including confirmation of the duty to take instructions from the child or young person and to act on those instructions.

5.20 It is perfectly proper for the defence lawyer to see the child or young person in the absence of the parent to take instructions. This should be done, where possible, with the agreement of all parties as the exclusion of an aggrieved parent from an interview may be problematic, especially if the client gives instructions which the parent believes are against the interests of the child or young person. Where a parent does object to a private interview matters may be resolved by taking instructions from the child or young person in the presence of the parent but ensuring that there is ample opportunity for him/her to talk privately with the lawyer and to speak freely. In any event should the wishes or instructions of the child or young person conflict with the opinions of the parent, it is the young client's instructions which must prevail.

5.21 The defence lawyer should always ensure that any parent (or guardian) who attends a police station or court with the child or young person understands what will happen and what may be expected of him/her. In the case of parent who does not speak English, this could involve asking the police or the court to arrange for an interpreter to be present.

5.22 When at court it may be necessary to remind the court that the lawyer's professional duties are solely owed to the young defendant. This is particularly important when the court is considering exercising its power to hold the parent responsible for any financial penalty or to impose a bindover or parenting order. Courts frequently invite submissions from the defence lawyer on behalf of the parent. If it is apparent that any such submissions would involve supplying the court with information detrimental to the interests of the defendant, the lawyer should decline to do so.

It is advisable to canvass the possibility of this happening with the parent before the hearing. The parent should be advised to seek the advice of the court duty solicitor.

Working within the youth justice system

A role in preventing offending?

5.23   As discussed above, the professional obligation of the defence lawyer is to protect the legal interests of the defendant. This will involve putting the prosecution to proof and presenting to the court all favourable information relevant to mitigation. The defence lawyer has no professional obligation to do otherwise.

5.24   Crime and Disorder Act 1998 s37 establishes a duty to prevent offending which applies to all participants in the court process.[13] How can a defence lawyer help to prevent offending whilst still fulfilling his/her professional obligations to his/her client? The government view as expressed in its guidance *Youth justice: the statutory principal aim of preventing offending by children and young people* is that the lawyer can further the aim by doing the following:

- acting quickly and efficiently to reduce delay;
- ensuring that the decisions of the court are understood by the young client and any parent or guardian;
- encouraging parents or guardians to attend court; and
- giving an opportunity for the defendant to participate in youth court proceedings.

5.25   This list focuses on the court process itself. The defence lawyer has an equally important role to ensure that the young client receives services from statutory and voluntary agencies to help remove factors which mean there is a risk of further offending. This broader advocacy role could involve ensuring:

- social services provide support to the client's family where needed;[14]
- appropriate education provision is provided;[15] and
- welfare benefits advice is given or a referral to a specialist agency is made.[16]

---

13 See para 2.86.

14 See the local authority's duty to provide services to a child in need under the Children Act 1989 s17 – see paras 3.20–3.34.

15 For detailed treatment of education law see J Ford, M Hughes and D Ruebain, *Education Law and Practice*, 2nd edn, Jordans, 2005. If referral to a specialist education lawyer is necessary contact the Education Law Association (see appendix 14) or visit www.clsdirect.org.uk.

16 Welfare benefits provision for 16- and 17-year-olds involves complex rules. A useful handbook which explains the rules is L Britton (ed), *The Young Persons Handbook: financial support and learning routes for 16- to 19-year-olds*, Centre for Economic and Social Inclusion, 3rd edn, 2006.

Giving meaning to the welfare principle

5.26   In an increasingly punitive justice system which emphasises children and young persons taking responsibility for their wrong-doing, the challenge for the defence lawyer is to ensure that the welfare principle is given real meaning in practice.[17]

Office management

5.27   For the defence lawyer to be able to prepare cases quickly and efficiently maximum use will need to be made of case management systems in the office so that all cases for a client in both courts and police stations can be co-ordinated. In particular, with the introduction of fast tracking, priority will need to be given to the preparation of cases for clients treated as persistent young offenders.

5.28   The developmental immaturity of young clients mean that they will find it particularly difficult to establish a collaborative relationship with the defence lawyer.[18] It is, therefore, important that every effort is made to ensure that the same lawyer represents the young client at every hearing and deals with the client at appointments in the office or in a secure institution.

Getting to know local services

5.29   To operate effectively in the youth court, the defence lawyer needs to be familiar with the services provided in the local area for young people.

Youth justice services

5.30   The defence lawyer should obtain a copy of the youth justice plans for all local authorities covered by his/her local courts. S/he would also be well advised to familiarise him/herself with local diversion, bail support or community sentence programmes. Many such projects will have publicity material and some will organise open days for criminal justice professionals or the general public. Being familiar with local projects will allow the defence lawyer to explain how the projects work to his/her client as well as being able to explain their operation to a court.

Local authority children's services

5.31   Although not directly involved in the criminal justice process, the services provided by the local authority social services department (or, increasingly the children's trust) to children and families is of considerable importance. The defence lawyer should obtain the children services plan produced by all the local authorities covered by his/her local courts.

---

17   See paras 2.91–2.100.
18   See chapter 4.

Education provision

5.32 Research reveals that a significant proportion of young defendants have truanted from school or have been excluded from mainstream education. The defence lawyer can expect, therefore, to deal with many defendants who have had contact with the education welfare service and who have attended special schools or pupil referral units. The defence lawyer would again be well advised to become familiar with local provision.

Public funding for legal representation

5.33 Article 6(3)(c) of the European Convention on Human Rights establishes the right of every person charged with a criminal offence to legal assistance at public expense when the interests of justice require it.[19] This right is of particular importance for children and young persons as they are unlikely to have the financial means to pay a lawyer privately.

5.34 Public funding of legal assistance in England and Wales is currently provided under the Access to Justice Act 1999. Under the Act, legal aid has been replaced by public funding from the Criminal Defence Service, part of the Legal Services Commission. The funding is provided to firms of solicitors who have been granted a contract to provide legal advice in criminal cases and, in a small number of cases, to salaried public defenders.

5.35 The rules regarding the scope of public funding for legal advice are contained in the Criminal Defence Service (General) (No 2) Regulations 2001[20] and the *General Criminal Contract* issued by the Criminal Defence Service to all firms of solicitors on the criminal panel. Important guidance will also be found in the *Criminal Bills Assessment Manual.*[21]

The investigation stage

5.36 Advice and Assistance (see below) is available to any person who:

- is arrested and held in custody in a police station or other premises;
- is being interviewed in connection with a serious service offence; or
- is a volunteer.[22]

5.37 A 'volunteer' is defined as:

> a person who, for the purposes of assisting with an investigation, attends voluntarily at a police station or a customs house, or at any other place where a constable or customs officer is present, or accompanies a constable or customs officer to a police station or a customs office or any other such place, without having been arrested.[23]

---

19 A similar right is recognised by Article 40(2)(b)(iii) of the United Nations Convention on the Rights of the Child.

20 SI No 1437.

21 All of these documents may be downloaded from the Law Services Commission website – see appendix 14.

22 Criminal Defence Service (General) (No 2) Regulations 2001 SI No 1437 reg 4.

23 Ibid, reg 2.

5.38 This definition arguably includes a child or young person who is interviewed by a police officer either at home or on school premises.

5.39 A solicitor may accept instructions directly from a suspect under the age of 16.[24] A solicitor may also accept an application from the parent/guardian or carer on behalf of a person under the age of 16. It is also arguable that an appropriate adult is entitled to apply for Advice and Assistance from a solicitor as the adult would satisfy the definition of a volunteer discussed above.

5.40 In general, a solicitor may provide only telephone advice to:

(a) a client detained in relation to a non-imprisonable offence;

(b) a client arrested on a bench warrant for failing to appear and being held for production before the court, except where the solicitor has clear documentary evidence available that would result in the client being released from custody, in which case attendance may be allowed provided that the reason is justified on file;

(c) a client arrested on suspicion of:
  (i) driving with excess alcohol, who is taken to the police station to give a specimen (Road Traffic Act 1988 s5);
  (ii) failure to provide a specimen (Road Traffic Act 1988 ss6, 7 and 7A);
  (iii) driving whilst unfit/drunk in charge of a motor vehicle (Road Traffic Act 1988 s4);

(d) a client detained in relation to breach of police or court bail conditions.[25]

5.41 It should be noted that one of the exceptions to the prohibition on attending the police station is where the client is eligible for assistance from an appropriate adult.[26]

5.42 Advocacy Assistance may be provided to a client in a magistrates' court or before a judicial authority in connection with an application for a warrant of further detention, or for an extension of such a warrant, under Police and Criminal Evidence Act 1984 s43 or s44 or Terrorism Act 2000 Sch 8 para 29 or para 36.[27]

Advice and Assistance

5.43 Advice and Assistance prior to the accused being charged or summonsed may be provided outside the police station under the Criminal Defence Service (General) (No 2) Regulations 2001.

5.44 In normal circumstances a solicitor is not permitted to accept an application for Advice and Assistance from a person under the age of 16. This may, however, be done if the prospective client would be entitled to begin, prosecute or defend proceedings without a litigation friend.[28] This

24 Criminal Defence Service, *General Criminal Contract* Contract Specification Part B rule 1.2.
25 Ibid, Part B rule 3.7.7.
26 Ibid, Part B rule 3.7.8.
27 Ibid, Part B rule 2.2.1(d).
28 Ibid, Part B rule 1.2(a).

exception would cover all criminal proceedings except an application to state a case or for judicial review. Where an application for Advice and Assistance is accepted from a client aged under 16, the client will still sign the application form (form CDS2).[29]

5.45   The solicitor may only provide Advice and Assistance if the client meets the financial eligibility criteria. Details of the income and savings of the prospective client must be taken. When providing Advice and Assistance to a client under 16, the solicitor will need to consider whether it is just and equitable not to aggregate the young client's means with those of the person liable to maintain him/her. There is a presumption that there should be aggregation, but the solicitor may decide not to aggregate (and assess only the young client's means) if, having regard to all the circumstances, including the age and resources of the child and to any conflict of interest, it appears just and equitable to do so. Not aggregating an adult's resources is likely to be justified where there is a conflict of interest or the young client is a nondependent.[30]

Court duty solicitor

5.46   Every court will have a duty solicitor who is available to provide free advice to defendants at court. The court duty solicitor may provide Advice and Assistance and Advocacy Assistance.

5.47   The service requirements of the court duty solicitor are set out in the *General Criminal Contract* Part B, para 8.3:

1. A Duty Solicitor at a magistrates' court shall provide the following services to any defendant who wishes to receive Advice and Assistance or Advocacy Assistance:
    (a) advice to a Client who is in custody;
    (b) the making of a bail application unless the Client has received such assistance on a previous occasion.

2. The Duty Solicitor may subject to paragraph 8.3.3 below also provide:
    (a) Advice and Assistance (including Advocacy Assistance) to a Client who is in custody on a plea of guilty where the Client wishes the case to be concluded at that appearance in court, unless the Duty Solicitor considers that the case should be adjourned in the interests of justice or of the Client;
    (b) [not applicable to children or young persons]
    (c) Advice and Assistance and, where appropriate, Advocacy Assistance to any other Client who is not in custody provided it is in connection with an imprisonable offence where, in the opinion of the Duty Solicitor, such a Client requires Advice and Assistance or Advocacy Assistance;
    (d) help to a Client who is eligible for assistance from the court Duty Solicitor to make an application for a Representation Order in respect of any subsequent appearance of the Client before the court. Where such an application is made the Duty Solicitor shall enquire whether the Client wishes to instruct another Solicitor to act for him or her. If the Client does so wish, the Duty Solicitor shall insert the name of that Solicitor in the application form;
    (e) Advice and Assistance and, where appropriate, Advocacy Assistance to a parent or guardian in connection with a proposal by the court to bind over

29 Criminal Defence Service, *General Criminal Contract* Contract Specification Part B rule 1.2 note 2.

30 Ibid.

the parent or guardian under section 150 of the Powers of Criminal Courts (Sentencing) Act 2000 or in breach of such an order;

(f) Advice and Assistance and, where appropriate, Advocacy Assistance to a respondent in proceedings under sections 1 or 1D (anti-social behaviour order), 2 or 2A (sex offender order) or 8(1)(b), (c) or (d) (parenting order) of the Crime and Disorder Act 1998 or of an applicant or respondent in proceedings to vary or discharge an order made against that person;

(g) Advice and Assistance and, where appropriate, Advocacy Assistance to a respondent in proceedings under sections 2 and 5 of the Anti-social Behaviour Act 2003 relating to the making or extension of a closure order;

(h) Advice and Assistance and, where appropriate, Advocacy Assistance, to a respondent in proceedings under section 14B (banning orders made on complaint), an applicant in proceedings under section 14G (variation of a banning order) or section 14H (termination of a banning order) and a recipient of a notice under section 21B(2) of the Football Spectators Act 1989.

(i) Advice and Assistance and, where appropriate, Advocacy Assistance to an individual to apply to vary bail conditions imposed by police under Section 47 (1E) of the Police and Criminal Evidence Act 1984, as amended by the Criminal Justice Act 2003.

3. A Duty Solicitor shall not under paragraph 8.3.2 above provide Advocacy Assistance in committal proceedings or at a not guilty trial, nor subject to paragraphs 8.3.2(e) to (g), Advice and Assistance or Advocacy Assistance to a Client in connection with a non-imprisonable offence.

4. On any adjourned hearing, a Duty Solicitor shall not, as Duty Solicitor, provide Advice and Assistance or Advocacy Assistance to a defendant to whom he or she or any other Duty Solicitor has provided services in the same Case except in connection with defendants coming within paragraph 8.3.2(b) above.

5.48 It should be noted that a court duty solicitor may not provide either Advice and Assistance or Advocacy Assistance to a young defendant charged with a non-imprisonable offence, if the defendant is on bail. This restriction applies even if the duty solicitor is asked to do so by the youth court magistrates. If the youth court considers that the young defendant is in need of legal representation in such circumstances, a representation order should be granted.

Advocacy Assistance by own solicitor

5.49 Advocacy Assistance by an own solicitor may only be provided in the following circumstances:

- in proceedings under Crime and Disorder Act 1998 ss1, 1D, 2 or 2A relating to an anti-social behaviour order (including an application to vary or discharge such an order);
- to a parent in proceedings under Crime and Disorder Act 1998 s8(1)(b) relating to a parenting order made where an anti-social behaviour order or a sex offender order is made in respect of a child or young person (including an application to vary or discharge such an order);
- to a parent in proceedings under Crime and Disorder Act 1998 s8(1)(c) relating to a parenting order made on the conviction of a child or young person (including an application to vary or discharge such an order);
- in proceedings under Football Spectators Act 1989 s14B (banning orders made on complaint), an applicant in proceedings under s14G (variation of a banning order) or s14H (termination of a banning order).

5.50   The solicitor must complete form CDS3 and certify that providing the assistance will meets the sufficient benefits test. Costs of more than £1,500 may not be incurred without the prior authority of the Criminal Defence Service.

Representation order

5.51   The main way that funding is provided for court proceedings is through a representation order granted to a defendant. The order is issued in favour of a named firm of solicitors. Applications for a representation order are made to the court before which the defendant is due to appear and the grant of an order is not subject to any means testing.

5.52   The Criminal Defence Service Act 2006 will re-introduce means testing for representation orders from 2 October 2006. At the time of writing the Criminal Defence Service (Financial Eligibility) Regulations 2006 have been issued in draft. Defendants who at the date of application are under the age of 16 or under the age of 18 and in full-time education are exempt from means testing (reg 5(2)). An applicant will also qualify automatically if s/he is in receipt of a qualifying benefit, which includes income support and income-based job seeker's allowance (reg 5(3)). In all other cases a young defendant will have to complete a means form and provide documentary evidence in support of the application (reg 6). Regulation 7(2) allows the representation authority (normally a court officer acting under delegated powers from the Legal Services Commission) to take into account the resources of any other person who appears to be substantially maintaining the applicant. In the absence of guidance from the Legal Services Commission, it is not clear whether this would mean that young defendants living at home with their parents will have to provide details of their parents' financial resources. Where an applicant fails to comply with a requirement to provide documentary proof of his/her financial resources and a representation order has been granted, the representation authority must withdraw the order unless it is satisfied that there are good reasons why it should not do so (reg 15).

Interests of justice

5.53   The criteria for deciding whether it is in the interests of justice to grant representation are the same for a child or young person as for an adult. When considering whether it is in the interests of justice to grant a representation order, Access to Justice Act 1999 Sch 3 para 5 requires that the following factors be taken into account:

- whether the individual would, if any matter arising in the proceedings is decided against him/her, be likely to lose his/her liberty or livelihood or suffer serious damage to his/her reputation;
- whether the determination of any matter arising in the proceedings may involve consideration of a substantial question of law;
- whether the individual may be unable to understand the proceedings or to state his/her own case;
- whether the proceedings may involve the tracing and interviewing of

witnesses or expert cross-examination of witnesses on behalf of the individual;[31] and

- whether it is in the interests of another person that the individual be represented for the prosecution.

5.54   When completing a representation order application form on behalf of a child or young person, the defence lawyer will always wish to draw the court's attention to the age of the defendant. The youth of the accused will usually mean that a court is more likely to grant a representation order.

Choice of solicitor

5.55   In normal circumstances the representation order would be granted in favour of the firm of solicitors nominated by the applicant. This freedom of choice has been limited since 2004 by the Criminal Defence Service (General) (No 2) Regulations 2001 reg 16A which provides:

> Where an individual who is granted a right to representation is one of two or more co-defendants whose cases are to be heard together, that individual must select the same representative as a co-defendant unless there is, or is likely to be, a conflict of interest.

5.56   In response to the introduction of regulation 16A, the Standards Board and Criminal Law Committee of the Law Society issued guidance to help criminal practitioners identify conflicts of interest.[32] The guidance provides advice on the dangers of representing two clients where there is a significant age difference:

> When considering whether there is an actual conflict there are obvious indicators such as whether the clients have differing accounts of the important relevant circumstances of the alleged crime or where one seems likely to change his or her plea. There are also less obvious indicators. These would include situations where there is some clear inequality between the co-defendants which might, for example, suggest that one client is acting under the influence of the other rather than on his own initiative. If you are acting for both this may make it difficult for you to raise and discuss these issues equally with them. In trying to help one, you might be undermining the other. If you believe you are going to be unable to do your best for one without worrying about whether this might prejudice the other you should only accept instructions from one.

> The risk of future conflict can be an even more difficult issue to assess. It may be that you have two clients who are pleading not guilty and who are apparently in total agreement on the factual evidence. Should they both be found guilty, you need to consider at the outset whether you would be able to mitigate fully and freely on behalf of one client without in so doing harming the interests of the other. It may be that one has a long list of convictions and is considerably older than the other. If so, it may be that the younger client with a comparatively clean record was led astray or pressurised into committing the crime and would want you to emphasise this in mitigation. If there is a significant risk of this happening you should not accept instructions from both.[33]

---

31   Refusal to grant legal aid to a defendant aged 16 who wishes to challenge whether a police officer has acted in the execution of his duty is irrational as the expertise required to cross-examine police witness and find, select and proof defence witnesses is beyond that of a defendant aged 16: *R v Scunthorpe Justices ex p S (a minor)* (1998) *Times* 5 March, QBD.

32   Law Society, *Conflicts of interest when acting for co-defendants* (March 2005). This guidance has now been incorporated into Law Society, *Conflict Guidance* (May 2006).

33   Law Society, *Conflict Guidance* (May 2006), paras 31 and 32.

5.57   Regulation 16A unfortunately does not give the court any discretion to grant a representation order to the solicitor nominated by a child or young person, even where that solicitor has built up a relationship with the young defendant or is already dealing with other cases.

Work reasonably done when representing a young client

5.58   The developmental status of the client is likely to mean that the defence lawyer will have to spend more time than usual explaining court procedure, taking factual instructions and helping the client to make decisions during the proceedings. This may need to be explained in a file note or covering note to the determining officer in Crown Court cases.

5.59   The fact that the client is a child or young person is a factor likely to justify attendance at:

- a formal remand hearing;[34]
- a distant court instead of using a local agent;[35]
- an institution in the juvenile secure estate which is a considerable distance from the solicitor's office.[36]

Enhanced payment for representing a young client

5.60   Enhanced rates may be paid where, taking into account all the relevant circumstances of the case, it appears that:

- the work was done with exceptional competence, skill or expertise; or
- the work was done with exceptional dispatch; or
- the case involved exceptional circumstances or complexity.[37]

5.61   An enhanced rate may be claimed where it can be demonstrated that the character of the client substantially increased the burden upon the solicitor.[38] In the opinion of the authors this could be demonstrated in some cases where the client is particularly young or developmentally immature.

Payment for involving a parent or carer

5.62   The *Criminal Bills Assessment Manual* paras 2.9.4 and 2.9.5 provide the following advice:

> When representing young offenders, i.e. those under 18, it will normally be necessary for the solicitor to spend some time in attending and advising parents, guardians or other relatives. The assessor should consider the age and capacity of the client and allow such time as is reasonable.

> The assessor should ensure that time has not been claimed in respect of unreasonable attendances on parents or other relatives. There is a distinction between attendances on parents or relatives which advance the case in a material manner and attendances which are, in essence, non-legal in nature e.g. counselling and other support.

---

34 *Criminal Bills Assessment Manual* para 3.1.2.
35 Ibid, para 2.13.6.
36 Ibid, para 2.9.11.
37 *General Criminal Contract,* Contract Specification Part E rule 3.5.18.
38 *Criminal Bills Assessment Manual* para 7.1.4.

5.63 It is also accepted that it is permissible to claim for the cost of sending a further copy of a letter addressed to a child or young person to his/her parent or guardian.[39]

Representation by both solicitor and advocate in the youth court

5.64 A representation order for proceedings in the youth court will normally only cover representation for solicitor. On written application, the court may extend the order to cover representation by both solicitor and advocate (ie barrister or solicitor with higher courts rights) if:

- the defendant is charged with an indictable offence; and
- the court is of the opinion that, because of circumstances which make the proceedings unusually grave or difficult, representation by both a solicitor and an advocate would be desirable.[40]

5.65 Where there is an order for representation for both solicitor and advocate, the attendance of both a solicitor and advocate at a hearing must still be justified. Attendance of both may be reasonable where the defendant is a child or young person.[41]

5.66 The different mode of trial rules for children and young persons inevitably mean that the youth court deals with more serious and complex allegations than would normally be dealt with in the adult magistrates' court. Accordingly, consideration should be given to when it would be appropriate to apply for an order allowing representation by an assigned advocate.

Attendance of solicitors at Crown Court hearings

5.67 Where the defendant was under the age of 18 on the time when the Crown Court acquired jurisdiction in the case (by committal, notice of transfer or otherwise), a solicitor may claim for attendance on the advocate in any of the following hearings:

- trials;
- hearings of cases listed for pleas of guilty following a plea and case management hearing;
- sentence hearings following a committal for sentence; and
- appeals against conviction or sentence.[42]

5.68 There is therefore no need to apply for a litigation certificate for a trial in the Crown Court when the client is a child or young person.

Prison law

5.69 Solicitors on the Crime Panel or firms which hold a Prison Law Contract may provide both Advice and Assistance and Advocacy Assistance.

5.70 Advice and Assistance may be provided to:

- prisoners (either post conviction or on remand) on legal issues arising from their treatment or discipline within the prison system; or

---

39 *Criminal Bills Assessment Manual* para 2.8.28 and CRIMLA2.
40 Criminal Defence Service (General) (No 2) Regulations 2001 SI No 1437 reg 12(1).
41 Criminal Defence Service, *Criminal Bills Assessment Manual* para 9.6.2.
42 Criminal Defence Service (Funding) Order 2001 SI No 855 reg 12(7) and (8).

- prisoners regarding their sentences (including where released under continuing conditions, for example on licence or parole).

5.71   Advocacy Assistance may be provided for representation at:

- hearings before a governor or other prison authority; or
- hearings before the Parole Board.

5.72   To provide Advocacy Assistance the solicitor must complete form CDS3. Again, costs of more than £1,500 may not be incurred without the prior authority of the Criminal Defence Service.

Associated Community Legal Service Work

5.73   Work for actual or proposed proceedings concerning public law challenges by way of judicial review (including under the Human Rights Act 1998) or habeas corpus applications the defence lawyer will be funded by the Community Legal Service. The General Criminal Contract allows such work to be done without any restriction on the number of matter starts. The work will be governed by the General Civil Contract.

Age and the criminal law

Introduction

6.1   There is surprisingly little in the criminal law that deals directly with age. Children and young people do not have many concessions made to them for their lack of developmental maturity, intellectually or emotionally, within statute or common law. This chapter deals with the relevance of age within the criminal law and highlights the areas where chronological age and developmental maturity may be relevant issues. This chapter does not deal with how the courts determine age (covered at para 11.17) or the relevance of age in sentencing (covered at paras 19.1–19.7).

Age of criminal responsibility

6.2   Children and Young Persons Act 1933 s50 provides:

> It is conclusively presumed that persons under the age of 10 cannot be guilty of any offence.

Practical implications

6.3   The presumption means that the police may not arrest a person known to be under that age and a person under that age also may not be prosecuted. It follows that a person who causes a person under the age of 10 to commit a criminal act is a principal, and not a secondary, party to the offence. The child is treated as an innocent agent. A further consequence of the presumption is illustrated by the case of *Walters v Lunt*[1] where the parents of a 7-year-old child were held to be not guilty of dishonestly receiving a tricycle from their child even though they knew that it was stolen. As the child could not steal, the court ruled that in law the tricycle was not stolen.

6.4   Children under the age of 10 who come to the attention of the police for behaviour which would constitute a criminal offence if the child had been over 10, may be the subject of an application for a child safety order. Such an application is made by the relevant local authority to the family proceedings court.[2]

International standards

6.5   United Nations Convention on the Rights of the Child Article 40(3)(a) requires each signatory state to establish a minimum age below which children shall be presumed to have the capacity to infringe the penal law. In addition, Beijing Rules (see para 2.77) rule 4.1 provides:

> In those legal systems recognising the concept of the age of criminal responsibility for juveniles, the beginning of that age shall not be fixed at too low an age level, bearing in mind the facts of emotional, mental and intellectual maturity.

6.6   The fact that England and Wales has a low minimum age of criminal responsibility has been the subject of much criticism by child welfare and

---

1   [1951] 2 All ER 645.
2   Crime and Disorder Act 1998 ss11–13. See para 29.158.

penal reform organisations.[3] It has also been the subject of specific criticism by the United Nations Committee on the Rights of the Child which, in its October 2002 report on the United Kingdom's compliance with the Convention on the Rights of the Child, stated:

> The Committee ... note with serious concern that the situation of children in conflict with the law has worsened since the consideration of the initial report [in 1995]. The Committee is particularly concerned that the age at which children enter the criminal justice system is low with age of criminal responsibility still at 8 years in Scotland and at 10 years in [England and Wales], and the abolition of the principle of doli incapax.[4]

6.7   Despite the widespread criticism of the minimum age, there appears to be little or no government consideration of the issue as far as the law in England and Wales is concerned. Speaking in the House of Lords in July 2002, the Lord Chancellor, Lord Falconer, confirmed that the government was not considering changing the age of criminal responsibility.[5] Giving evidence to the Home Affairs Select Committee in December 2002, the then Chair of the Youth Justice Board, Lord Warner, admitted that he was not even sure what was the Board's view on the age of criminal responsibility.[6]

6.8   The European Court of Human Rights has held that an age of criminal responsibility set at the age of 10 years is not a breach of the European Convention on Human Rights. In *T v United Kingdom, V v United Kingdom*[7] it was argued that the criminal trial of two boys accused of a murder committed when they were 10 years old was inhuman and degrading treatment in breach of Article 3 of the European Convention. In rejecting this argument the court stated:

> The Court has considered first whether the attribution to the applicant of criminal responsibility in respect of acts committed when he was ten years old could, in itself, give rise to a violation of Article 3. In doing so, it has regard to the principle, well established in its case-law that, since the Convention is a living instrument, it is legitimate when deciding whether a certain measure is acceptable under one of its provisions to take account of the standards prevailing amongst the member States of the Council of Europe (see the *Soering* judgment cited above, p. 40, § 102; and also the *Dudgeon v. the United Kingdom* judgment of 22 October 1981, Series A no. 45, and the *X, Y and Z v. the United Kingdom* judgment of 22 April 1997, *Reports* 1997-II).

> In this connection, the Court observes that, at the present time, there is not yet a commonly accepted minimum age for the attribution of criminal responsibility in Europe. While most of the Contracting States have adopted an age limit which is higher than that in force in England and Wales, other States, such as Cyprus, Ireland, Liechtenstein and Switzerland, attribute criminal responsibility from a younger age. Moreover, no clear tendency can be ascertained from examination of the relevant international texts and instruments ... Rule 4 of the Beijing Rules which, although not legally binding, might provide some indication of the existence of an international consensus, does not specify the age at

---

3   See, for example, *Restoring youth justice: new directions in domestic and international law and practice*, Justice (2000), available via their website – see appendix 14.

4   United Nations, *Concluding Observations of the United Nations Committee on the Rights of the Child*, 31st session, 9 October 2002, para 59.

5   Hansard, Col 953.

6   Hansard, Select Committee on Home Affairs, Minutes of Evidence (3 December 2002) Questions 80–87.

7   [2000] 2 All ER 1024 (Note); (1999) 30 EHRR 131; 7 BHRC 659, ECtHR.

which criminal responsibility should be fixed but merely invites States not to fix it too low, and Article 40 § 3 (a) of the UN Convention requires States Parties to establish a minimum age below which children shall be presumed not to have the capacity to infringe the criminal law, but contains no provision as to what that age should be.

The Court does not consider that there is at this stage any clear common standard amongst the member States of the Council of Europe as to the minimum age of criminal responsibility. Even if England and Wales is among the few European jurisdictions to retain a low age of criminal responsibility, the age of ten cannot be said to be so young as to differ disproportionately from the age-limit followed by other European States. The Court concludes that the attribution of criminal responsibility to the applicant does not in itself give rise to a breach of Article 3 of the Convention.

6.9   Since the decision of the European Court was delivered in December 1999, there have been a number of moves to raise the age of criminal responsibility in other European jurisdictions. In Scotland in 2001 the Scottish Law Commission recommended raising the minimum age in Scotland from 8 years to 12 years.[8] To date this recommendation has not been implemented but it is also contained in the *Draft Penal Code for Scotland* issued in 2003.[9] In 2001 Ireland passed legislation to raise its minimum age of criminal responsibility from 7 years to 12 years but this has not yet been implemented.[10] Also in 2001 Denmark implemented legislation raising its minimum age from 12 years to 14 years.[11] If the proposed changes in Scotland and Ireland are in fact implemented, it may be that the European Court will be willing to reconsider its decision that a minimum age of 10 years is compatible with Article 3 of the Convention.

Abolition of common law presumptions

Boy physically incapable of rape

6.10   The irrebuttable common law presumption that a boy aged under 14 was physically incapable of committing rape was abolished by Sexual Offences Act 1993 s1.

Doli incapax

6.11   The common law presumed that children aged under the age of 14 were incapable of committing crime. This presumption (often referred to as 'doli incapax') could be rebutted by the prosecution proving beyond reasonable doubt that the child defendant know what s/he had done was seriously

8   Scottish Law Commission, *Report on Age of Criminal Responsibility* – Report no 185 (January 2002). The report may be downloaded from www.scotlawcom.gov.uk.
9   The Draft Code may be downloaded from www.scotlawcom.gov.uk.
10 Children Act 2001 – according to *The Irish Times* the change was not implemented because of a government fear that social services departments would be overwhelmed by referrals of children below the new age of criminal responsibility. There is now consideration being given to raising the minimum age to 10 years (*The Irish Times* (2005) 16 June, www.ireland.com – accessed 1 July 2006).
11 J Muncie, 'Repenalisation and Rights: Explorations in Comparative Youth Criminology', *Howard League Journal* Vol 45 No 1, February 2006.

wrong rather than merely a naughty act. This presumption has been abolished by the Crime and Disorder Act 1998 for any offence committed on or after 30 September 1998.

Relevance of chronological age to offences

6.12 The criminal law in England and Wales has very few offences which can only be committed by a person under a certain age. Such offences which do exist include:

- offences relating to possession of various types of firearm (Firearms Act 1968 s22);
- offences relating to the improper use of an air weapon (Firearms Act 1968 s23);
- possession of an adult firework by a person under the age of 18 years (Fireworks Act 2003 s11 and Fireworks Regulations 2003 SI No 3085 reg 3);
- purchasing alcohol under the age of 18 (Licensing Act 2003 s149(1));
- consuming alcohol on relevant premises when under 18 (Licensing Act 2003 s150).

The mental element of criminal offences

6.13 The criminal law makes few concessions to the youth of an accused. This may produce very harsh results, especially after the abolition of the presumption of doli incapax for those aged 10 to 14 years. However, recent decisions in relation to some aspects of the mental element of criminal acts do indicate a recognition of the relevance of the circumstances of the individual.

6.14 Smith and Hogan, *Criminal Law* (11th edn)[12] defines mens rea as:

> Intention, knowledge or recklessness with respect to all the elements of an offence together with any ulterior intent which the definition of the crime requires.

6.15 Some offences, statutory or at common law, include particular requirements as to the mental state of the defendant, eg 'wilfully' in the case of obstruction of an officer in the execution of his duty (Police Act 1996 s89) or 'maliciously' in the case of unlawful wounding (Offences Against the Persons Act 1861 s20).

Intent

6.16 Intention relates to the consequences of the actions of a person, whether the consequences are desired ('direct' intent) or not desired but known to be virtually certain to follow ('indirect' intent). The degree of intention required to found guilt in relation to particular offences may vary, but the difficulties of demonstrating the intent of a defendant remain a constant.

12 Oxford University Press, 2005.

6.17   It is for the prosecution to prove the presence of the relevant mens rea beyond reasonable doubt. This will often involve the court being asked to infer the intention of the defendant from the actions and circumstances surrounding the actus reus of the offence charged. It will involve the examination of the individual charged: what s/he did or did not say; did or did not do and possibly the effect of his/her actions or inaction. These will be considered at the time of and after the alleged offence.

6.18   Where the prosecution seek to prove that the defendant intended or foresaw something, the provisions of Criminal Justice Act 1967 s8 apply:

> A court or jury, in determining whether a person has committed an offence,
> (a) shall not be bound in law to infer that he intended or foresaw a result of his actions by reason only of its being a natural and probable result of those actions; but
> (b) shall decide whether he did intend or foresee that result by reference to all the evidence drawing such inferences from the evidence as appears proper in the circumstances.

6.19   Therefore the age and stage of developmental maturity of the defendant may be a relevant factor in assessing whether he/she did in fact foresee what might seem to an adult to be the obvious consequences of his/her actions or whether he/she was aware of the relevant circumstances[13].

6.20   The defence practitioner is always concerned to ensure that where it has been decided that their client will answer questions in interview with the police, or provide a prepared statement, they give a full account of themselves. Similar considerations apply to a young defendant giving evidence in court. It may be necessary to emphasise the age and understanding of the defendant in relation to the formation of intention, direct or indirect.

Recklessness

6.21   The test for recklessness in relation to offences under the Criminal Damage Act 1971 is set out in *R v G and R*.[14] Lord Bingham in the House of Lords stated:

> A person acts recklessly ... with respect to—
> • a circumstance when he/she is aware of a risk that it exists or will exist;
> • a result when he/she is aware of a risk that it will occur;
> and it is, in the circumstances known to him/her, unreasonable to take the risk.[15]

6.22   In some circumstances to run a very high risk may not be reckless, eg attempting a life-saving operation; whilst in others to run any risk at all, even a relatively low one, may be reckless, eg throwing an object over a railway bridge late at night. Previously the objective test using the yardstick of the ordinary prudent adult person, was applied to children and young persons sometimes with harsh results.[16] Since the decision in *R v G and R* it is no longer relevant and the emphasis is now on the degree of risk of

---

13   See chapter 4.
14   [2003] UKHL 50.
15   Ibid, para 41.
16   *Metropolitan Police Commissioner v Caldwell* [1982] AC 341.

which the defendant is aware or has actually foreseen, so an element of subjectivity is introduced.

6.23   In *R v G and R* the defendants were 11 and 12 years old at the time the alleged arson. They entered the back yard of a shop where they found bundles of newspapers. The boys then lit some of the newspapers with a lighter they had with them. Each of them threw some burning newspaper under a large plastic wheelie-bin which was positioned beside another wheelie-bin which was adjacent to the wall of the shop. The boys left the yard without extinguishing the burning paper. The newspapers set fire to the first wheelie-bin and the fire spread from it to the wheelie-bin next to the shop wall. From the second bin the fire spread up the shop resulting in £1 million worth of damage. The case at trial was that the boys expected the newspaper fires to extinguish themselves on the concrete floor of the yard. It was accepted that neither of them appreciated that there was any risk whatsoever of the fire spreading in the way that it eventually did.

6.24   In the young client, lack of foresight may arise because of developmental immaturity or simply because of less extensive experience of life and its everyday risks.

Maliciously

6.25   The same test applies to offences under the Offences Against the Person Act 1861 which require malice. Such offences require an actual intention to cause the harm alleged or foresight of the risk of causing the harm. The test was defined in *R v Cunningham*[17] where it was said:

> ... malice must be taken ... as requiring either
> (1) an actual intention to do the ... harm ...; or
> (2) recklessness as to whether such harm should occur or not (i.e., the accused has foreseen that the particular type of harm might be done and yet has gone on to take the risk of it).

6.26   In *W (a minor) v Dolbey*[18] a young person was charged with malicious wounding after he fired an air rifle at his friend. The justices found that he had not foreseen that any harm would come to the victim as he did not believe that the air rifle was loaded, nevertheless they convicted him. The conviction was quashed by the Divisional Court.

Dishonesty

6.27   The criteria for a jury considering whether a defendant was acting dishonestly were set out by the Court of Appeal in *R v Ghosh*:[19]

> [1] ... a jury must first of all decide whether according to the ordinary standards of reasonable and honest people what was being done was dishonest. If it was not ... the prosecution fails.
>
> If it was dishonest by those standards, then the jury must consider:
>
> [2] ... Whether the defendant himself must have realised that what he was doing was by [the standards of reasonable and honest people] dishonest.

17   [1957] 2 QBD 396.
18   (1983) 88 Cr App R 1, QBD.
19   [1982] QB 1053.

6.28 The courts will also consider the actions and circumstances of the defendant in relation to the offence in deciding whether a dishonest intent exists in cases such as theft and handling stolen goods, which require the prosecution to prove the existence of such intent to found a conviction. The guidance on the approach to dishonesty contained in *Ghosh* confirms the need to consider the individual and their state of mind, allowing for the age and developmental immaturity of the defendant to be a consideration. The 'standards of reasonable and honest people' are not always the standards held by the child or young person accused of an offence involving dishonesty. The question of whether that young person was aware that others might not share his/her view of his/her own actions will depend to a large extent on the young defendant's stage of moral development.[20]

Defences to criminal offences

Duress

6.29 When a person commits a criminal offence under the threat of violence from another, s/he may be able to rely on the defence of duress. The threat involved must be of death or grievous bodily harm. The fact that the defendant took the threat seriously is not enough if a person of reasonable firmness sharing the characteristics of the defendant would not have given way to the threats.[21] It has been held that the youth of the accused is a relevant characteristic, which should be taken into account when considering the reasonableness of the behaviour.[22] It has been held that in most cases it is probably only the age and sex of the defendant that is capable of being relevant.[23] However, post-traumatic stress disorder has been accepted as a relevant characteristic.[24]

6.30 The questions of the immediacy of the threat and any opportunity to render it ineffective will also be relevant to the court's consideration of this defence. In *R v Hudson*[25] the Court of Appeal indicated that in deciding whether the threat could reasonably be rendered ineffective, for example by obtaining police protection, the jury should have regard to the age, circumstances and any risks to the defendant. However, in *R v Hasan*[26] Lord Bingham warned against 'the weakening of the requirement that execution of a threat must be reasonably believed to be imminent and immediate' and confirmed that belief in the threat must be 'reasonable as well as genuine'.

6.31 There will be many occasions when children or young persons have committed crimes out of a fear of others. The fear may be understandable in the light of the defendant's age but not be sufficient to constitute duress. In such circumstances the defence lawyer should consider making

---

20 See paras 4.32–4.36.
21 *R v Howe* [1987] AC 417, HL.
22 *R v Hudson* [1971] 2 QB 202, CA.
23 *R v Bowen* [1997] 1 WLR 372, CA.
24 *R v Sewell* [2004] EWCA Crim 2322.
25 See n22 above.
26 [2005] UKHL 22; [2005] 2 WLR 709.

representations to the Crown Prosecution Service regarding discontinuance, arguing that the prosecution is not in the public interest.[27]

Self-defence

6.32 'The test to be applied for self-defence is that a person may use such force as is reasonable in the circumstances as he honestly believes them to be in the defence of himself or another.'[28] The personal characteristics of the defendant may well be relevant as to his/her honest belief as to the circumstances existing at the time of the allegation. To have available a defence of self-defence, the accused must have used reasonable force. The test as to whether the degree of force used was reasonable has both an objective and subjective element. In *R v Shannon*[29] Ormrod LJ stated that the court or jury has to apply a test which is somewhere between:

- an objective test – that is what is reasonable judged from the viewpoint of an outsider looking at the situation quite dispassionately; and
- a subjective test – that is the viewpoint of the accused him/herself with the intellectual capabilities of which s/he may be possessed and with all the emotional strains and stresses to which at the moment he may be subjected.

6.33 The second subjective element would allow the court to take into account the age of a defendant and other matters relevant to his/her particular circumstances at the time of the offence.

6.34 Once self-defence is properly raised before a court, it is for the prosecution to disprove beyond reasonable doubt.

Provocation

6.35 Provocation is a defence to a charge of murder only. It has been defined as some act, or series of acts, done by the dead person to the accused which would cause in any reasonable person, and actually causes in the accused, a sudden and temporary loss of control, rendering the accused so subject to passion as to make him/her for the moment not the master of his/her mind.[30] Homicide Act 1957 s3 provides:

> Where ... there is evidence on which a jury can find that the person charged was provoked (whether by things done or by things said or by both together) to lose his self-control, the question whether the provocation was enough to make a reasonable man do as he did shall be left to de determined by the jury; and in determining that question the jury shall take into account everything both done and said according to the effect which, in their opinion, it would have on a reasonable man.

6.36 In *R v Camplin*[31] Lord Diplock stated that 'to require old heads upon young shoulders is inconsistent with the law's compassion to human infirmity'. It

---

27 See chapter 8.
28 *Beckford v The Queen* [1988] AC 130.
29 (1980) 71 Cr App R 192.
30 *R v Duffy* [1949] 1 All ER 932.
31 [1978] AC 707, HL.

was held that the age of the accused at the time of the killing was a relevant characteristic to be taken into account by the jury when assessing the reasonableness of the accused's conduct. The extent to which the characteristics of the defendant should be applied to the 'reasonable man' in applying the test set out in the Homicide Act 1957 has recently been resolved by the adoption by the Court of Appeal in the case of *R v James*[32] of the Privy Council decision in the case of *Attorney-General for Jersey v Holley*.[33] In *James*, the Court of Appeal approved the formulation of:

> Taking into account the age and sex of a defendant, as mentioned in *Camplin*, is not an exception ... The powers of self-control possessed by ordinary people vary according to their age and, more doubtfully, their sex. These features are to be contrasted with abnormalities, that is, features not found in a person having ordinary powers of self-control. The former are relevant when identifying and applying the objective standard of self-control, the latter are not.[34]

32   [2006] EWCA Crim 14.
33   [2005] UKPC 23.
34   *Attorney-General for Jersey v Holley* [2005] UKPC 23 [13].

Police powers

Stop and search powers

7.1   The police possess a number of stop and search powers. The most significant are those granted by the following statutory provisions:

- Police and Criminal Evidence Act 1984 s1;
- Misuse of Drugs Act 1971 s23;
- Criminal Justice and Public Order Act 1994 s60; and
- Terrorism Act 2000 ss43 and 44.

Police and Criminal Evidence Act 1984 s1

7.2   A police constable in a public place may search any person or motor vehicle if the constable has reasonable grounds to believe that s/he will find any of the following:

- stolen articles;
- an article made or adapted for use in the course of or in connection with an offence of:
  (a) burglary;
  (b) theft;
  (c) taking without consent;
  (d) obtaining property by deception; or
  (e) criminal damage (including arson);
- offensive weapons (ie articles made or adapted for use for causing injury to persons, intended by the person having it with him/her for such use by him/her or by some other person);
- any bladed article prohibited by Criminal Justice Act 1988 s139;
- any firework which a person possesses in contravention of a prohibition imposed by fireworks regulations.[1]

7.3   'Public place' is defined as:

- any place to which at the time of the proposed search the public or any section of the public has access, on payment or otherwise as of right or by virtue of express or implied permission; or
- any other place to which people have ready access at the time of the proposed search but which is not a dwelling.[2]

7.4   If the person whom the constable intends to search is in a garden or yard occupied with or used for the purposes of a dwelling, or on other land so occupied and used, a constable may not search that person unless the constable has reasonable grounds for believing:

- that the person does not reside in the dwelling; and
- that the person is not in the place in question with the express or implied permission of a person who resides in the dwelling.[3]

---

1   Police and Criminal Evidence Act 1984 s1(2), (3), (7)–(9) as amended by Criminal Justice Act 2003 s1 and Serious Organised Crime and Police Act 2005 s115.
2   Ibid, s1(1).
3   Ibid, s1(4).

Misuse of Drugs Act 1971 s23

7.5   Where a police constable has reasonable grounds to suspect that any person is in possession of a controlled drug, the constable may:

- search that person and detain that person for the purpose of the search; and
- search any vehicle in which the constable suspects that the drug may be found and for that purpose require the person in control of the vehicle to stop it.[4]

Criminal Justice and Public Order Act 1994 s60

7.6   Authorisation under section 60 may be given by a police officer of or above the rank of inspector who reasonably believes that:

- incidents involving serious violence may take place in any locality in his/her area and it is expedient to do so to prevent their occurrence; or
- persons are carrying dangerous instruments or offensive weapons without good reason in any locality in the officer's police area.[5]

7.7   Authority may only be given in the first instance for a maximum of 24 hours, though there is provision for a extension of the authority for a further six hours.[6]

7.8   Authority under section 60 confers on a constable in uniform power:

- to stop any pedestrian and search him/her or anything carried by him/her for offensive weapons or dangerous instruments; or
- to stop any vehicle and search the vehicle, its driver and any passenger for offensive weapons or dangerous instruments.[7]

7.9   A constable may, in the exercise of those these powers, stop any person or vehicle and make any search s/he thinks fit whether or not s/he has any grounds for suspecting that the person or vehicle is carrying weapons or articles of that kind.[8]

7.10   A person who fails to stop or when required to do so by a constable in the exercise of a power under section 60 commits a criminal offence.[9]

Powers under the Terrorism Act 2000

7.11   The Act creates two separate stop and search powers.

Stop and search on reasonable suspicion

7.12   A police constable may stop and search a person whom s/he reasonably suspects to be a terrorist to discover whether s/he has in his/her possession anything which may constitute evidence that s/he is a terrorist.[10]

---

4   Misuse of Drugs Act 1971 s23(2).
5   Criminal Justice and Public Order Act 1994 s60(1).
6   Ibid, s60(1) and (3).
7   Ibid, s60(4).
8   Ibid, s60(5).
9   Ibid, s60(8). On summary conviction the maximum penalty for an adult is one month's imprisonment. A child or young person cannot therefore receive a detention and training order if convicted of the offence – see paras 24.33–24.35.
10   Terrorism Act 2000 s43(1).

7.13   A search of a person under this section must be carried out by someone of the same sex.[11] A constable may seize and retain anything which s/he discovers in the course of a search of the person.[12]

Stop and search powers under section 44

7.14   Authorisation under section 44 may only be given:

- by a police officer of at least the rank of assistant chief constable (commander in the Metropolitan Police);[13] and
- if the person giving it considers it expedient for the prevention of acts of terrorism.[14]

7.15   An authorisation gives a police constable in uniform the power to stop a vehicle in an area or at a place specified in the authorisation and search:

- the vehicle;
- the driver of the vehicle;
- a passenger in the vehicle;
- anything in or on the vehicle or carried by the driver or a passenger.[15]

7.16   An authorisation gives a police constable in uniform to stop a pedestrian in an area or at a place specified in the authorisation and to search:

- the pedestrian; and
- anything carried by him.[16]

7.17   The stop and search powers granted under an authorisation:

- may be exercised only for the purpose of searching for articles of a kind which could be used in connection with terrorism; and
- may be exercised whether or not the constable has grounds for suspecting the presence of articles of that kind.[17]

7.18   A constable may seize and retain an article which he discovers in the course of a search and which he reasonably suspects is intended to be used in connection with terrorism.[18]

7.19   A constable exercising the power conferred by an authorisation may not require a person to remove any clothing in public except for headgear, footwear, an outer coat, a jacket or gloves.[19]

7.20   Where a constable proposes to search a person or vehicle, s/he may detain the person or vehicle for such time as is reasonably required to permit the search to be carried out at or near the place where the person or vehicle is stopped.[20]

---

11 Terrorism Act 2000 s43(3).
12 Ibid, s43(4).
13 Ibid, s44(4).
14 Ibid, s44(3).
15 Ibid, s44(1).
16 Ibid, s44(2).
17 Ibid, s45(1).
18 Ibid, s45(2).
19 Ibid, s45(3).
20 Ibid, s45(4).

Reasonable grounds

7.21   Reasonable grounds for the for the search is a pre-condition for the exercise of a power under the following provisions:

- Police and Criminal Evidence Act 1984 s1;
- Misuse of Drugs Act 1971 s23; and
- Terrorism Act 2000 s43.

7.22   The Police and Criminal Evidence Act 1984 Codes of Practice, Code A paras 2.2–2.6 give the following guidance:

> Reasonable grounds for suspicion depend on the circumstances in each case. There must be an objective basis for that suspicion based on facts, information, and/or intelligence which are relevant to the likelihood of finding an article of a certain kind or, in the case of searches under section 43 of the Terrorism Act 2000, to the likelihood that the person is a terrorist. Reasonable suspicion can never be supported on the basis of personal factors alone without reliable supporting intelligence or information or some specific behaviour by the person concerned. For example, a person's race, age, appearance, or the fact that the person is known to have a previous conviction, cannot be used alone or in combination with each other as the reason for searching that person. Reasonable suspicion cannot be based on generalisations or stereotypical images of certain groups or categories of people as more likely to be involved in criminal activity. A person's religion cannot be considered as reasonable grounds for suspicion and should never be considered as a reason to stop or stop and search an individual.

> Reasonable suspicion can sometimes exist without specific information or intelligence and on the basis of some level of generalisation stemming from the behaviour of a person. For example, if an officer encounters someone on the street at night who is obviously trying to hide something, the officer may (depending on the other surrounding circumstances) base such suspicion on the fact that this kind of behaviour is often linked to stolen or prohibited articles being carried. Similarly, for the purposes of section 43 of the Terrorism Act 2000, suspicion that a person is a terrorist may arise from the person's behaviour at or near a location which has been identified as a potential target for terrorists.

> However, reasonable suspicion should normally be linked to accurate and current intelligence or information, such as information describing an article being carried, a suspected offender, or a person who has been seen carrying a type of article known to have been stolen recently from premises in the area. Searches based on accurate and current intelligence or information are more likely to be effective. Targeting searches in a particular area at specified crime problems increases their effectiveness and minimises inconvenience to law-abiding members of the public. It also helps in justifying the use of searches both to those who are searched and to the public. This does not however prevent stop and search powers being exercised in other locations where such powers may be exercised and reasonable suspicion exists.

> Searches are more likely to be effective, legitimate, and secure public confidence when reasonable suspicion is based on a range of factors. The overall use of these powers is more likely to be effective when up to date and accurate intelligence or information is communicated to officers and they are well-informed about local crime patterns.

> Where there is reliable information or intelligence that members of a group or gang habitually carry knives unlawfully or weapons or controlled drugs, and wear a distinctive item of clothing or other means of identification to indicate their membership of the group or gang, that distinctive item of clothing

or other means of identification may provide reasonable grounds to stop and search a person.

Conduct of search

7.23   Before any search of a detained person or attended vehicle takes place the officer must take reasonable steps to give the person to be searched or in charge of the vehicle the following information:

(a) that they are being detained for the purposes of a search;

(b) the officer's name (except in the case of enquiries linked to the investigation of terrorism, or otherwise where the officer reasonably believes that giving his or her name might put him or her in danger, in which case a warrant or other identification number shall be given) and the name of the police station to which the officer is attached;

(c) the legal search power which is being exercised; and

(d) a clear explanation of:

- the purpose of the search in terms of the article or articles for which there is a power to search; and
- in the case of powers requiring reasonable suspicion, the grounds for that suspicion; or
- in the case of powers which do not require reasonable suspicion, the nature of the power and of any necessary authorisation and the fact that it has been given.[21]

7.24   All stops and searches must be carried out with courtesy, consideration and respect for the person concerned.[22] Every reasonable effort must be made to minimise the embarrassment that a person being searched may experience. The co-operation of the person to be searched must be sought in every case, even if the person initially objects to the search. A forcible search may be made only if it has been established that the person is unwilling to co-operate or resists. Reasonable force may be used as a last resort if necessary to conduct a search or to detain a person or vehicle for the purposes of a search.[23]

7.25   The length of time for which a person or vehicle may be detained must be reasonable and kept to a minimum. Where the exercise of the power requires reasonable suspicion, the thoroughness and extent of a search must depend on what is suspected of being carried, and by whom. If the suspicion relates to a particular article which is seen to be slipped into a person's pocket, then, in the absence of other grounds for suspicion or an opportunity for the article to be moved elsewhere, the search must be confined to that pocket. In the case of a small article which can readily be concealed, such as a drug, and which might be concealed anywhere on the person, a more extensive search may be necessary.[24]

7.26   The search must be carried out at or near the place where the person or vehicle was first detained.[25]

21 Code A para 3.8.
22 Code A para 3.1.
23 Code A para 3.2.
24 Code A para 3.3.
25 Code A para 3.4.

7.27 A search in public of a person's clothing which has not been removed must be restricted to superficial examination of outer garments. This does not, however, prevent an officer from placing his or her hand inside the pockets of the outer clothing, or feeling round the inside of collars, socks and shoes if this is reasonably necessary in the circumstances to look for the object of the search or to remove and examine any item reasonably suspected to be the object of the search. For the same reasons, subject to the restrictions on the removal of headgear, a person's hair may also be searched in public.[26]

7.28 Where on reasonable grounds it is considered necessary to conduct a more thorough search (eg by requiring a person to take off a T-shirt), this must be done out of public view, for example, in a police van, or police station if there is one nearby. Any search involving the removal of more than an outer coat, jacket, gloves, headgear or footwear, or any other item concealing identity, may only be made by an officer of the same sex as the person searched and may not be made in the presence of anyone of the opposite sex unless the person being searched specifically requests it.[27]

7.29 Searches involving exposure of intimate parts of the body must not be conducted as a routine extension of a less thorough search, simply because nothing is found in the course of the initial search. Searches involving exposure of intimate parts of the body may be carried out only at a nearby police station or other nearby location which is out of public view (but not a police vehicle). Such searches must be carried out in the same way as a strip search in the police station (see paras 7.140–7.143).[28]

7.30 All stops and searches must be carried out with courtesy, consideration and respect for the person concerned. The co-operation of the person to be searched must be sought in every case, even if the person initially objects to the search. A forcible search may be made only if it has been established that the person is unwilling to co-operate or resists. Reasonable force may be used as a last resort if necessary to conduct a search or to detain a person or vehicle for the purposes of the search.[29]

Documentation to be supplied to person stopped or searched

7.31 An officer who has carried out a search must make a record of it at the time, unless there are exceptional circumstances which would make this wholly impracticable (eg in situations involving public disorder or when the officer's presence is urgently required elsewhere). If a record is not made at the time, the officer must do so as soon as practicable afterwards.[30]

7.32 A copy of a record made at the time must be given immediately to the person who has been searched. The officer must ask for the name, address and date of birth of the person searched, but there is no obligation on a person to provide these details and no power of detention if the person is unwilling to do so.[31]

26 Code A para 3.5.
27 Code A para 3.6.
28 Code A para 3.7.
29 Code A para 3.8.
30 Code A para 4.1.
31 Code A para 4.2.

Power of arrest

7.33   The same police powers of arrest exist for children and young persons as exist for adult suspects. In addition, there are some powers specific to children and young persons.

Arrest under warrant

7.34   A police constable may arrest a child or young person against whom a court has issued an arrest warrant. This will usually be after the child or young person has failed to attend a court hearing, although it is possible to initiate court proceedings by means of a warrant. The court may endorse the warrant as with or without bail.

7.35   When arrested on warrant, a juvenile must not be released unless his/her parent or guardian enters into a recognisance for such amount as the custody officer at the police station where s/he is detained considers will secure the juvenile's attendance at the hearing of the charge. Any recognisance entered into may, if the custody officer thinks fit, be conditioned for the attendance of the parent or guardian at the hearing in addition to the juvenile.[32]

Arrest without warrant: police constables

7.36   A police constable may arrest without warrant:

- anyone who is about to commit an offence;
- anyone who is in the act of committing and offence;
- anyone whom s/he has reasonable grounds for suspecting to be about to commit an offence; and
- anyone whom s/he has reasonable grounds for suspecting to be committing an offence.[33]

7.37   If a constable has reasonable grounds for suspecting that an offence has been committed, s/he may arrest without a warrant anyone whom s/he has reasonable grounds to suspect of being guilty of it.[34]

7.38   If an offence has been committed, a constable may arrest without a warrant:

- anyone who is guilty of the offence; or
- anyone who s/he has reasonable grounds for suspecting to be guilty of it.[35]

7.39   The above powers of summary arrest may only be exercised if the police constable has reasonable grounds for believing that it is necessary to arrest the person for any of the following reasons:

(a) to enable the name of the person in question to be ascertained (in the case where the constable does not know, and cannot readily ascertain,

---

32   Children and Young Persons Act 1969 s29(1).
33   Police and Criminal Evidence Act 1984 s24(1).
34   Ibid, s24(2).
35   Ibid, s24(3).

the person's name, or has reasonable grounds for doubting whether a name given by the person as his name is his real name);

(b) correspondingly as regards the person's address;

(c) to prevent the person in question:
   (i) causing physical injury to himself or any other person;
   (ii) suffering physical injury;
   (iii) causing loss of or damage to property;
   (iv) committing an offence against public decency (only where members of the public going about their normal business cannot be reasonably expected to avoid the person in question); or
   (v) causing an unlawful obstruction of the highway;

(d) to protect a child or other vulnerable person from the person in question;

(e) to allow the prompt and effective investigation of the offence or of the conduct of the person in question;

(f) to prevent any prosecution for the offence from being hindered by the disappearance of the person in question.[36]

7.40   In considering the individual circumstances, the police constable must take into account the situation of the victim, the nature of the offence, the circumstances of the suspect and the needs of the investigative process.[37]

7.41   Factors relevant to the prompt and effective investigation of the offence may include cases such as:

(i) where there are reasonable grounds to believe that the person:
   • has made false statements;
   • has made statements which cannot be readily verified;
   • has presented false evidence;
   • may steal or destroy evidence;
   • may make contact with co-suspects or conspirators;
   • may intimidate or threaten or make contact with witnesses;
   • where it is necessary to obtain evidence by questioning; or

(ii) when considering arrest in connection with an indictable offence, there is a need to:
   • enter and search any premises occupied or controlled by a person;
   • search the person;
   • prevent contact with others; or
   • take fingerprints, footwear impressions, samples or photographs of the suspect; and

(iii) ensuring compliance with statutory drug testing requirements.[38]

7.42   There may be a risk that a criminal prosecution could be hindered by the disappearance of the suspect, if there are reasonable grounds for believing that:

• if the person is not arrested he or she will fail to attend court;
• street bail after arrest would be insufficient to deter the suspect from trying to evade prosecution.[39]

---

36   Ibid, s24(4) and (5).
37   Code G para 2.8.
38   Code G para 2.9.
39   Code G ibid.

Arrest without warrant: community support officers and other civilians

7.43   A person other than a constable may arrest without warrant:

- anyone who is in the act of committing an indictable offence;
- anyone whom s/he has reasonable grounds for suspecting to be committing an indictable offence.[40]

7.44   Where an indictable offence has been committed, a person other than a constable may arrest without a warrant:

- anyone who is guilty of the offence;
- anyone whom s/he has reasonable grounds for suspecting to be guilty of it.[41]

7.45   The power of summary arrest is exercisable only if:

(a) the person making the arrest has reasonable grounds for believing that the arrest is necessary to prevent the suspect:

- causing physical injury to himself or any other person;
- suffering physical injury;
- causing loss of or damage to property; or
- making off before a constable can assume responsibility for him/her; and

(b) it appears to the person making the arrest that it is not practicable for a constable to make the arrest instead.[42]

Relevance of age

7.46   There is no statutory restriction on the exercise of a power of arrest in relation to a child or young person. In practice most police forces will make very few concessions to the youth of a suspect when exercising the power of arrest.

Suspects under 10

7.47   Such suspects are under the age of criminal responsibility and as such are conclusively deemed to be incapable of committing a criminal offence.[43] A police officer will not, therefore, be able to arrest a child who is known to be under the age of 10 as there will be no power of arrest derived from the suspicion that a criminal offence has been committed.[44]

7.48   A constable may have a power to detain a child under the age of 10 if s/he is considered to be in breach of a local child curfew order or a truant from school in a designated area. For both of these powers see chapter 29.

---

40 Police and Criminal Evidence Act 1984 s24A(1).
41 Ibid, s24A(2).
42 Ibid, s24A(3) and (4).
43 Children and Young Persons Act 1933 s50.
44 A police officer faced with such a situation may wish to exercise the power to take a child into police protection under Children Act 1989 s46.

Arresting juveniles at their place of education

7.49 The PACE Codes of Practice give the following guidance:

> It is preferable that a juvenile is not arrested at his place of education unless this is unavoidable. Where a juvenile is arrested at his place of education, the principal or his nominee must be informed.[45]

Wards of court

7.50 Where the suspect is a ward of court, the procedure is governed by the *Consolidated Criminal Practice Direction*. The general rule is that where the police wish to interview a child who is a ward of court, application must, save in exceptional circumstances, must be made to the wardship court for leave for the police to do so.[46] Leave need not be sought where the ward is suspected by the police of having committed a criminal act and the police wish to interview him/her about it.[47]

7.51 Where a ward of court is arrested, the police should notify the parent or foster parent with whom the ward is living so that s/he has the opportunity of being present when the police interview the ward. In addition, if practicable, the reporting officer (if one has been appointed) should be notified and invited to attend the police interview or to nominate a third party to attend on his/her behalf. A record of the interview or a copy of any statement made by the ward should be supplied to the reporting officer. Where the ward has been interviewed without the reporting officer's knowledge, s/he should be informed at the earliest opportunity.[48]

7.52 The wardship court should be apprised of the situation at the earliest possible opportunity thereafter by the reporting officer, the parent, foster parent (through the local authority) or other responsible adult.[49]

7.53 No evidence or documents in the wardship proceedings or information about the proceedings should be disclosed in the criminal proceedings without the leave of the wardship court.[50]

Street bail

7.54 Instead of taking an arrested person to a police station immediately, the arresting officer may grant 'street bail' to an arrested person, requiring him/her to attend a police station at a future date.[51] There is no power to impose conditions as part of the street bail.[52]

---

45 Code C Note for Guidance 11C.
46 *Consolidated Criminal Practice Direction* I.5.1.
47 Ibid, I.5.3.
48 Ibid.
49 Ibid.
50 Ibid, I.5.4.
51 Police and Criminal Evidence Act 1984 s30A(1)–(3).
52 Ibid, s30A(4).

7.55   Before granting street bail, the officer must give the arrested person a written notice stating:

- the offence for which s/he was arrested;
- the ground on which s/he was arrested; and
- that s/he is required to attend a police station.[53]

7.56   The notice may also specify the police station and the date and time when the arrested person is required to attend to answer bail.[54] If the notice does not so specify, the arrested person must subsequently be given a further notice in writing which gives that information.[55]

7.57   The arrested person may be required to answer bail at a different police station or at a different time.[56] S/he must be given written notice of any such changes.[57]

7.58   Home Office Circular 61/2003 *Criminal Justice Act 2003: Bail Elsewhere Than At A Police Station* provides guidance to police officers on the exercise of their discretion to grant street bail. There are four key considerations:

(i)   the nature of the offence;
(ii) the ability to progress the investigation at the station;
(iii) confidence in the suspect answering bail;
(iv) the level of awareness and understanding of the procedure by the suspect.[58]

7.59   In the case of a juvenile, the arresting officer must assess the level of risk to the safety and welfare of the juvenile. Telephone contact should be made as soon as practicable with the parent/guardian or other carer. The purpose of the contact is to inform that person at the earliest possible stage of the arrest and issuing of bail to the juvenile. In making this contact, the parent/guardian or other carer should be informed:

- that the juvenile has been arrested;
- of the offence;
- that bail has been granted;
- that the offender has a copy of the bail notice; and
- that a further copy of the bail notice will be forwarded to them setting out the reporting requirements.[59]

7.60   Save in exceptional circumstances, the date for attendance at the police station should normally be no more than six weeks from the date of arrest.[60]

---

53   Police and Criminal Evidence Act 1984 s30B(1)–(3).
54   Ibid, s30B(4).
55   Ibid, s30B(5).
56   Ibid, s30B(6).
57   Ibid, s30B(7).
58   Home Office, *Street Bail Guidance,* Part A.3.
59   Ibid, Part B.3.
60   Ibid, Part B.3(c).

Authorising detention at the police station

7.61 Unless street bail has been granted, a suspect should be taken to a police station as soon as practicable.[61]

Initial authorisation

7.62 A custody officer may authorise the detention of a suspect at a police station. The custody officer must first determine if there is sufficient evidence to charge the suspect for the offence for which s/he has been arrested. If the custody officer considers there is not sufficient evidence, the suspect *must* be released on bail or without bail, unless the custody officer has reasonable grounds for believing that the suspect's detention without being charged is *necessary*:

- to secure or preserve evidence relating to an offence for which s/he is under arrest;
- to obtain such evidence by questioning him/her.[62]

Detention reviews

7.63 A detention review must be conducted by a police officer of the rank of at least inspector;

- not later than six hours after detention is first authorised;
- not later than nine hours after the first review; and
- at nine-hourly intervals thereafter.[63]

7.64 The review officer must be a police officer of at least the rank of inspector who is not involved in the investigation of the offence. To authorise further detention the review officer must be satisfied that there are still grounds for the detention of the suspect. S/he has to be satisfied, therefore, that detention is necessary:

- to charge the suspect;
- to secure or preserve evidence; or
- to obtain evidence by questioning the suspect.

7.65 Reviews can be conducted in person or by telephone. The benefits of carrying out a review in person should always be considered, based on the individual circumstances of each case with specific additional consideration if the detainee is (among other factors) a juvenile.[64]

7.66 Before authorising such detention the officer must give the suspect, any appropriate adult and his/her solicitor, if available at the time of the review, the opportunity to make representations.[65] The suspect should be informed of the grounds for his/her continued detention and they should be recorded in the custody record.[66]

---

61 Police and Criminal Evidence Act 1984 s30(1A).
62 Ibid, s37(1).
63 Ibid, s40.
64 Code C para 15.3C.
65 Police and Criminal Evidence Act 1984 s40(12) and Code C para 15.3.
66 Code C para 15.6.

Limit of detention without charge

7.67   In general no suspect may be detained without charge for more than 24 hours from the time of arrival at the police station.[67] This time limit applies equally to juveniles.

Extension of detention up to 36 hours

7.68   Before the expiry of the initial 24-hour detention period, a police officer of the rank of at least superintendent may authorise further detention up to a maximum of 36 hours.[68] This may only be done if s/he has reasonable grounds for believing:

- the offence for which the suspect is under arrest is an indictable offence;
- the detention of the suspect without charge is necessary to secure or preserve evidence relating to an offence for which s/he is under arrest or to obtain such evidence by questioning him/her; and
- the investigation is being conducted diligently and expeditiously.[69]

7.69   Before authorising such detention the officer must give the suspect, any appropriate adult and his/her solicitor, if available at the time of the review, the opportunity to make representations.[70] The suspect should be informed of the grounds for his/her continued detention and they should be recorded in the custody record.[71]

7.70   Detaining a juvenile or mentally vulnerable person for longer than 24 hours will be dependent on the circumstances of the case and with regard to the person's:

- special vulnerability;
- the legal obligation to provide an opportunity for representations to be made prior to a decision about extending detention;
- the need to consult and consider the views of any appropriate adult; and
- any alternatives to police custody.[72]

Warrants of further detention

7.71   A magistrates' court, on an application on oath made by a police constable and supported by an information, may issue a warrant of further detention, if the court is satisfied that there are reasonable grounds for believing:

- the detention without charge of the suspect is necessary to secure or preserve evidence relating to an offence for which s/he is under arrest or to obtain such evidence by questioning him/her;

---

67   Police and Criminal Evidence Act 1984 s41.
68   Ibid, s42.
69   Ibid, s43.
70   Ibid, s42(6) and Code C para 15.3.
71   Code C para 15.6.
72   Code C para 15.2A.

- an offence for which s/he is under arrest is an indictable offence; and
- the investigation is being conducted diligently and expeditiously.[73]

7.72 The court may issue a warrant authorising further detention for up to 36 hours. Further applications may be made but detention may not be authorised for more than a total of 96 hours. The suspect has the right to be legally represented at the hearing.

7.73 In the case of a child or young person, it would seem that an adult magistrates' court bench may still hear the application as such warrants of further detention are not matters specifically assigned to the youth court under Children and Young Persons Act 1933 s46.[74]

A juvenile

7.74 A juvenile is a person who has not attained the age of 17. For the purposes of the Codes of Practice:

> If anyone appears to be under the age of 17, they shall be treated as a juvenile for the purposes of this Code in the absence of clear evidence that they are older.[75]

7.75 The police are, therefore, required to treat a suspect as a juvenile if his/her physical appearance suggests that s/he is under the age of 17 and they have no clear evidence to the contrary. Equally, if the suspect lies about his/her age and s/he looks mature enough to be 17 years old, the police are entitled to treat the suspect as an adult. Obviously as soon as the error is discovered the police must treat the suspect as a juvenile.

7.76 A juvenile is considered as a vulnerable suspect by the Codes of Practice, and consequently a number of protective measures have been imposed to protect the juvenile suspect. None of these protective measures apply to 17-year-old suspects.

Duty to notify

7.77 When a juvenile arrives at the police station, the custody officer has a duty to notify various persons of the arrest.

Person responsible for a juvenile's welfare

7.78 The custody officer shall take such steps as are practicable to ascertain the identity of the person responsible for his/her welfare.[76] This may be:

- the juvenile's parent or guardian;[77] or
- any other person who has for the time being assumed responsibility for his/her welfare.[78]

---

73 Police and Criminal Evidence Act 1984 s43.
74 See para 11.22ff.
75 Code C para 1.5.
76 Children and Young Persons Act 1933 s34(2).
77 'Guardian' includes a local authority if the child is in care: Police and Criminal Evidence Act 1984 s118.
78 Children and Young Persons Act 1933 s34(5).

7.79   If it is practicable to ascertain the identity of a person responsible for the juvenile's welfare, that person shall be informed unless it is not practicable to do so:

- that the juvenile has been arrested;
- why s/he has been arrested; and
- where s/he is being detained.[79]

7.80   If it is practicable to contact a person responsible for the welfare of the juvenile, the above information shall be given. The obligation exists whether or not the juvenile wishes to inform anyone of his/her arrest and cannot be delayed for any reason.

7.81   If the juvenile is in the care of the local authority or voluntary organisation but is living with his/her parents or other adults responsible for his/her welfare, the police should normally notify that person as well as the care organisation, unless the person is suspected of involvement in the offence. Even if a juvenile in care is not living with his/her parent, consideration should be given to informing them as well.[80]

Juvenile subject to a court order

7.82   If a juvenile is known to be subject to a court order under which a person or organisation is given any degree of statutory responsibility to supervise or otherwise monitor him/her, reasonable steps must be taken to notify the responsible officer, who will normally be a member of a youth offending team, except in the case of a curfew order when the contractor providing the monitoring will normally be the responsible officer.[81]

The rights of a person detained

7.83   A person in police custody has three rights:

- to have a person informed of his/her arrest;
- to obtain legal advice; and
- to consult a copy of the Codes of Practice.

7.84   The custody officer is obliged to inform the prisoner of these rights when a person is brought to the police station under arrest or when a volunteer is arrested at the police station. The prisoner should also be informed that these rights are continuing and may be exercised at any time while under arrest. A written copy of the rights should be handed to the prisoner.

7.85   In the case of a juvenile, the rights must be confirmed at some point in the presence of the appropriate adult. In normal circumstances the appropriate adult will not be present when the juvenile is brought into the police station. The custody officer should inform the juvenile of his/her rights and allow him/her to exercise any of them immediately without waiting for an appropriate adult to be contacted.[82] However, when the appropriate

---

79 Children and Young Persons Act 1933 s34(3).
80 Code C Note for Guidance 3C.
81 Code C para 3.14.
82 Code C Note for Guidance 3G.

adult attends the station the juvenile should be informed of his/her rights again in the presence of the appropriate adult. If an appropriate adult attends the station with the juvenile, the rights will be read in the presence of the appropriate adult.

Right to inform another of arrest

7.86   A suspect under arrest and held in a police station or other premises, may have one friend or relative or other person who is known to him/her or who is likely to take an interest in his/her welfare informed of the arrest. This right may be exercised as soon as is practicable.[83] If the person nominated to be informed cannot be contacted, the suspect may choose up to two alternatives. If they cannot be contacted, the person in charge of detention or the person in charge of the investigation has discretion to allow further attempts until the information has been conveyed.[84]

7.87   It may only be delayed in the case of a indictable offence and on the authority of an officer of at least the rank of inspector. This officer may only authorise delay if s/he has reasonable grounds for believing that telling the named person of the arrest will:

- lead to interference with or harm to evidence connected with an indictable offence or interference with or physical injury to other persons; or
- lead to the alerting of other persons suspected of having committed such an offence but not yet arrested for it; or
- hinder the recovery of any property obtained as a result of such an offence.[85]

7.88   The delay may only be authorised for a maximum of 36 hours. The duty to inform the parent or guardian of a juvenile's arrest is unaffected by this power. In any event, the custody officer must make arrangements for an appropriate adult to attend the police station.

7.89   In addition to the right to have someone informed of the arrest, a detained person shall be supplied with writing materials on request and allowed to speak on the telephone for a reasonable time to one person. This right may only be delayed or denied by an officer of the rank of inspector or above:

- if the person is detained in relation to an indictable offence; and
- the officer considers that the sending or a letter or the making of a telephone call will lead to any of the consequences listed above at para 7.87 above.[86]

Legal advice

7.90   A person arrested and held in custody in a police station or other premises shall be entitled, if s/he so requests, to consult a solicitor privately at any

---

83 Police and Criminal Evidence Act 1984 s56(1).
84 Code C para 5.1.
85 Police and Criminal Evidence Act 1984 s56(5). Note the right may also be delayed in drug trafficking cases where notification will hinder the recovery of the proceeds of trafficking: s56(5A).
86 Code C para 5.6 and Annex B paras 1 and 2.

time.[87] If s/he makes such a request, it should be recorded in the custody record and s/he should be permitted to consult with the solicitor as soon as is practicable.

7.91　A suspect may nominate a solicitor of his/her choice. If the suspect does not know of a solicitor, s/he may ask to speak to the duty solicitor. If the suspect does not want to consult the duty solicitor s/he should be provided with a list of solicitors willing to provide advice. All legal advice in the police station is free of charge.

7.92　This right may only be delayed in the case of an indictable offence on the authority of a police officer of at least the rank of superintendent who has reasonable grounds for believing that the exercise of the right to legal advice at the time when the suspect wishes to exercise it will:

- lead to interference with or harm to evidence connected with a indictable offence or interference with or physical injury to other persons; or
- lead to the alerting of other persons suspected of having committed such an offence but not yet arrested for it; or
- will hinder the recovery of any property obtained as a result of such an offence.[88]

7.93　Access to a solicitor may only be delayed for a maximum of 36 hours.[89] The superintendent may only authorise delay in access to a specific solicitor if s/he has reasonable grounds for believing that specific solicitor will, inadvertently or otherwise, pass on a message from the detained person or act in some other way which will lead to any of the three results listed above. In such circumstances the detainee must be allowed to choose another solicitor.[90]

7.94　The duty to inform the parent or guardian of a juvenile's arrest is unaffected by this power. In any event the custody officer must make arrangements for an appropriate adult to attend the police station.[91]

The appropriate adult

The role of the appropriate adult

7.95　The custody officer is required to inform the juvenile that:

- the appropriate adult's duties include giving advice and assistance to the juvenile; and
- that the juvenile may consult privately with the appropriate adult at any time.[92]

7.96　The appropriate adult must be present while the juvenile:

(a) is informed of his/her rights by the custody officer (Code C para 3.17);
(b) is strip searched (Code C Annex A para 11(c));

87　Police and Criminal Evidence Act 1984 s58(1).
88　Ibid, s58(8).
89　Ibid, s58(5).
90　Code C Annex B para 3; see also *R v Samuels* (1987) 87 Cr App R 232, CA.
91　Code C Annex B Note for Guidance B1.
92　Code C para 3.18.

(c) is required to submit to an intimate search (Code C Annex A para 5);
(d) is cautioned (Code C para 10.12);
(e) is interviewed (Code C para 11.14);
(f) takes part in any identification procedure (Code D para 1.14).

Who may act?

7.97 The Codes of Practice gives the police the following guidance as to who to select as the appropriate adult (Code C para 1.7):

(i) the parent or guardian or, if the juvenile is in local authority or voluntary organisation care, or is otherwise being looked after under the Children Act 1989, a person representing that authority or organisation

(ii) a social worker of a local authority social services department;

(iii) failing these, some other responsible adult aged 18 or over who is not a police officer or employed by the police.

7.98 The Codes of Practice can be seen to establish a clear order of preference. The police should therefore attempt to arrange for a parent/guardian or social worker to act before approaching any other responsible adult. A solicitor acting in a professional capacity or an independent custody visitor (formerly a lay visitor) should never act as the appropriate adult.[93]

7.99 In general only one person should be designated to act as the appropriate adult, but there may be occasions when it would be proper for more than one adult to be present in the interview, for example when both parents wish to perform the role.[94]

Parent or guardian

7.100 In the vast majority of cases it will be the parent or guardian who attends the police station to act as the appropriate adult. The police should take all reasonable steps to secure the attendance of the parent or carer before requesting an appropriate adult service.[95] If the parent or carer is not available for practical reasons, such as commitments to care for younger children, the youth offending team should explore ways of supporting the parent or carer to attend the police station.[96]

7.101 There are occasions when it is unsuitable for the parent/guardian to act in this capacity.

Estrangement from the juvenile

7.102 Code C Note for Guidance 1B states:

> If a juvenile's parent is estranged from the juvenile, they should not be asked to act as the appropriate adult if the juvenile expressly and specifically objects to his presence.[97]

---

93 Code C Note for Guidance 1F.
94 *H and M v DPP* [1998] Crim LR 653, QBD.
95 Youth Justice Board, *National Standards for Youth Justice Services* (2004), para 2.7.
96 Ibid, para 2.8.
97 Code C Note for Guidance 1C.

7.103   This guidance is intended to reflect the decision of the Court of Appeal in *DPP v Blake*.[98]

7.104   In many cases where the juvenile is estranged from his/her parent(s), the question of objecting to the police's choice of appropriate adult will not arise, as the parent will refuse to attend the police station. If the parent has attended, the issue of estrangement will call for professional judgment. There will often be a tense relationship between a parent and his/her child in the police station. However, if the relationship is noticeably worse than this, the defence lawyer should consider whether the parent should be excluded from acting as the appropriate adult. This will obviously be a difficult decision for the juvenile to make as it may provoke further repercussions after the juvenile's release from custody, nevertheless, the defence lawyer should always tactfully enquire in a private consultation in the absence of the appropriate adult whether the parent's presence at the police station will be a problem for the juvenile. If it will be, the juvenile should be advised of his/her right to object to the parent's presence.

Physical disability

7.105   A parent who has a disability for which special provision is made in the Codes of Practice is probably not a suitable person to act as an appropriate adult. This would include a person who was blind or deaf. However, if the police arranged for a sign interpreter for a deaf parent, the role could be performed effectively.

Mental disorder/disability

7.106   A parent who would require an appropriate adult him/herself is clearly not an appropriate adult and if the mental condition of the parent becomes apparent to the police or the lawyer then another adult should be sought.

7.107   The courts have had to consider on a number of occasions whether to exclude evidence obtained from a juvenile in the presence of a mentally disordered parent. It has been held that the test as to whether a particular adult may fulfil the role is an objective one. An interview may be excluded if the court is satisfied that a parent was of too low intelligence to perform the role adequately, even if the police were unaware of the father's condition and there was no suggestion of impropriety.[99] However, an interview was not excluded when a court was satisfied that a parent with significant impairment of intelligence and social function could nevertheless perform the role of appropriate adult.[100]

Unable to speak English

7.108   If the parent or guardian cannot communicate in English, s/he will not be able to safeguard the juvenile's interests. In certain cases the police may be willing to arrange for an interpreter to attend to translate for the parent. Although cumbersome, this would allow the parent to fulfil the role effectively.

---

98 [1989] 1 WLR 432.

99 *R v Morse* [1991] Crim LR 195, Wisbech Crown Court.

100 *R v W* [1994] Crim LR 130, CA.

Suspected of involvement in the crime

7.109   Code C Note for Guidance 1B states:

> A person, including a parent or guardian, should not be an appropriate adult if they ... are suspected of involvement in the offence.

7.110   The police are likely to object not only to a parent or guardian who is suspected of involvement in the crime but also where the parent or guardian is suspected of attempting to dispose of evidence or otherwise obstruct the investigation. The defence lawyer also needs to keep the situation under review, in case information is forthcoming from the young client which indicates the involvement of the parent or guardian in the offence. In such circumstances it would be inappropriate for that person to continue in the role of appropriate adult as s/he cannot be seen to be impartial.

Complainant or witness to the offence

7.111   Code C Note for Guidance 1B states:

> A person, including a parent or guardian, should not be an appropriate adult if they ... are:
> - the victim;
> - a witness; or
> - involved in the investigation of the offence.

7.112   The rationale for this rule is that none of the above can be expected to be independent or impartial. Although the police will usually identify people who fall into the above categories, the defence lawyer still needs to consider whether an adult should perform the role. For example, it may become apparent after talking to the young client that the parent or guardian is an alibi witness. This fact may not be known to the police at the time. Clearly arrangements should be made for another adult to perform the role of appropriate adult. A parent may also not be a suitable person to perform the role if the alleged victim is another family member.

Received an admission from the juvenile

7.113   Code C Note for Guidance 1C states:

> A person, including a parent or guardian, should not be an appropriate adult if they ... received admissions prior to attending to act as the appropriate adult.

Social worker

7.114   This could include a generic social worker, a member of a youth offending team, a residential care worker or a member of an emergency out-of-hours team. Inevitably the level of experience and familiarity with police stations will vary enormously.

7.115   In certain circumstances it may be inappropriate for certain individuals from a social services department to act as the appropriate adult. Such circumstances would include:

- when s/he is the complainant or a witness to the offence;
- when s/he has received an admission of guilt from the juvenile.

Complainant or witness to the offence

7.116   As with parents (see above), the Codes prohibit a person acting as the appropriate adult in such circumstances. This most frequently arises when an incident occurs in a children's home and a member of staff calls the police who subsequently arrest the juvenile. In those circumstances the juvenile will inevitably see all members of the staff at the home as being against him/her. In such circumstances it is advisable that someone other than a care worker is asked to act as the appropriate adult. In practice this may have to be local authority's duty social worker.

Received admissions of guilt

7.117   Code C Note for Guidance 1C states:

> If a juvenile admits an offence to, or in the presence of, a social worker or member of a youth offending team other than during the time that person is acting as the juvenile's appropriate adult, another appropriate adult should be appointed in the interest of fairness.

7.118   When an admission to a social worker, particularly a residential care worker, results in the police being informed, it is again advisable that a person wholly unconnected with the children's home should be asked to act as the appropriate adult as there is a significant danger that the juvenile will not regard the care worker as impartial.

Another responsible person

7.119   In the experience of the authors this has included other members of the family, friends, volunteers from local authority schemes, local shopkeepers, the Salvation Army and even members of the public passing the police station.

7.120   Code C para 1.7 simply stipulates that the person performing the role should be over the age of 18. It has been suggested that there should be a sufficient age gap between the responsible person and the juvenile so that the adult is able to exercise some degree of authority over the juvenile.[101]

Elder brother or sister

7.121   Older siblings may often be very effective appropriate adults as they are well known to the juvenile and are not so likely to wish to punish the juvenile for being arrested. However, the police may seek to object to the suitability of a sibling especially if s/he is recognised by a police officer as having been arrested on a number of occasions in the past. No such objection is usually raised to a parent who is known to have a criminal record. It is submitted that if there is a sufficient gap between the ages of the sibling and the juvenile, rather than extend further the juvenile's detention, the lawyer should seek to dissuade the custody officer from objecting.

---

101 *Palmer v R* September 1991 *Legal Action* 21, CC.

Teacher

7.122 There will be occasions when a teacher is asked to act as the appropriate adult especially if an interview is to take place at school. The Codes of Practice state that a teacher should not act as the appropriate adult at an interview at school if the juvenile is suspected of an offence against the educational establishment.[102] By extension it is submitted that a teacher is not a suitable adult if a member of the school staff called in the police. In such circumstances the teacher cannot be seen as impartial by the juvenile.

Appropriate adult schemes

7.123 Youth offending teams are required to provide appropriate adults to safeguard the interests of children and young persons detained or questioned by police officers in their local authority area.[103] Appropriate adult services may be provided directly by the youth offending team, or by accredited volunteers.[104] An appropriate adult service must be provided within two hours of the initial request from the police.[105]

Duty in relation to the appropriate adult

7.124 Code C para 3.15 requires the custody officer, as soon as practicable:

- to inform the appropriate adult of the grounds for the juvenile's detention and his/her whereabouts; and
- to ask the adult to come to the police station to see the juvenile.

7.125 This requirement to contact an appropriate adult does not mean that a breathalyser procedure in road traffic cases need be delayed.[106]

Rights of the appropriate adult

7.126 The appropriate adult may do the following while performing the role:

- read the custody record as soon as practicable after arrival at the police station (Code C para 2.4);
- consult with the juvenile in private at any time (Code C para 3.18);
- instruct a solicitor at any time on behalf of the juvenile *or* instruct a solicitor to advise him/her while performing the role of appropriate adult (Code C para 3.19 and 6.5A).

7.127 Code C para 6.5A states:

> In the case of a juvenile, an appropriate adult should consider whether legal advice from a solicitor is required. If the juvenile indicates that they do not want legal advice, the appropriate adult has the right to ask for a solicitor to attend if this would be in the best interests of the person. However, the detained person

---

102 Code C para 11.15.
103 Crime and Disorder Act 1998 s38(1) and (4)(a).
104 Youth Justice Board, *National Standards for Youth Justice Services* (2004), para 2.4.
105 Ibid, para 2.6.
106 *R (DPP) v Evans* [2002] EWHC 2976 Admin.

cannot be forced to see the solicitor if he is adamant that he does not wish to do so.

Confidentiality

7.128   The presence of the appropriate adult in the police station can cause problems in relation to the disclosure of information. This could arise after s/he has received information directly from the juvenile or by being present during a consultation between the juvenile and the defence lawyer.

Disclosure of information

7.129   There is no specific duty of confidentiality imposed upon a person acting as an appropriate adult and Code C Note for Guidance 1E states that appropriate adults are not subject to legal privilege. As a consequence, the defence lawyer should be alert at all times to the danger of disclosure. A parent or guardian may be confused and upset to learn of their child's arrest and s/he may volunteer information or disclose it if approached by a police officer. A social worker will subscribe to the general principle that information received from a client should not be disclosed. There are, however, exceptions to this and disclosure may take place if the social worker considers that the juvenile suspect presents a danger to another person or the public in general.[107] Even if the particular social worker at the police station does not wish to disclose information, s/he may be directed to do so by a line manager.

7.130   When a social worker does disclose an incriminating remark made by a juvenile whilst in the police station, there is a real risk that the information obtained may be admitted as evidence at any subsequent trial. In *R v Marcus Brown*[108] a 16-year-old was arrested on suspicion of attempted murder. He was interviewed in the presence of a solicitor and a social worker from the local youth justice team. This social worker was also the juvenile's supervising officer for a current supervision order. No admissions were made during the police interview. After the interview the juvenile was left for a short while in the presence of the social worker only. The social worker initiated a conversation with the juvenile in which she indicated that she thought the juvenile knew about the assault. The juvenile indicated that he had been involved in the serious assault. The social worker later disclosed this information to the police. At the trial the judge refused to exclude the admission even though he ruled as a matter of fact that the juvenile had only responded to the social worker's comment because he did not think his reply would be disclosed by her. On appeal it was held that the admission had been properly admitted as evidence in the trial.

7.131   As a result of concerns regarding disclosure, the Criminal Law Committee of the Law Society has issued guidance to solicitors.[109] This advises that a solicitor should give initial advice to the juvenile suspect in the absence of the appropriate adult. In this initial consultation the juvenile

---

107 The Department of Health has issued guidance to social services departments, which contemplates disclosure in such circumstances: see LAC(88) 17.

108 98/7320/Y2, (1999) 21 May, CA, unreported.

109 (1993) LS Gaz 19 May.

should be advised of the danger of disclosure. The advice continues that the question of whether the appropriate adult's presence is desirable or not during any further consultation can then be considered in consultation with the appropriate adult, taking into account any risk of disclosure and the wishes of the juvenile who may find reassurance in the presence of an appropriate adult whom s/he knows. In addition, many social services departments have issued guidance to their staff. This usually advises a social worker acting as appropriate adult to see the juvenile on his/her own and to explain both the role of the appropriate adult and that it is not possible to guarantee that any information would remain confidential. It is the opinion of the authors that such a procedure would be good practice.

Searches

Search of the person

General search

7.132 A police constable may search an arrested person:

- in any case where the person has been arrested at a place other than a police station, if the constable has reasonable grounds for believing that the arrested person may present a danger to himself or others;
- to search for anything which the arrested person might use to escape from lawful custody; or
- to search for anything which might be evidence to an offence.[110]

7.133 The power to search for articles to assist escape or for evidence only exists to the extent that it is reasonably required for the purpose of discovering any such thing or any such evidence. The power does not authorise a constable to require a person to remove any of his/her clothing in public other than an outer coat, jacket or gloves, but does authorise a search of a person's mouth.

7.134 In practical terms this power of search will normally involve no more than the arrested person being required to empty their pockets and to be subject to a body rub down. The search may take place at the point of arrest or on arrival at the police station. In the case of a juvenile, the presence of an appropriate adult is not required.

Power of seizure

7.135 On searching a person, a police constable may seize and retain anything which the constable has reasonable grounds for believing:

- the suspect might use to cause physical injury to him/herself or to another; or
- the suspect might use to assist him/her to escape from lawful custody;
- it is evidence of an offence or has been obtained in the consequence of the commission of an offence.[111]

---

110 Police and Criminal Evidence Act 1984 s32(1).
111 Ibid, s32(8) and (9).

7.136   Items subject to legal privilege may not be seized or retained under this power.

Searches and examination to ascertain identity

7.137   A person who is detained in a police station may be searched or examined, or both:

- for the purpose of ascertaining whether s/he has any mark that would tend to identify him/her as a person involved in the commission of the offence; or
- for the purpose of facilitating the ascertainment of his identity.[112]

7.138   A search and/or examination *to find marks* may be carried out without the detainee's appropriate consent, only if authorised by an officer of at least the rank of inspector when consent has been withheld or it is not practicable to obtain consent.[113] A search or examination *to establish a suspect's identity* may be carried out without the detainee's appropriate consent only if authorised by an officer of at least the rank of inspector when the detainee has refused to reveal his/her identity or the authorising officer has reasonable grounds for suspecting that the detainee is not who s/he claims to be.[114]

7.139   The search or examination must only be carried out by a person of the same sex as the suspect.[115] Any identifying mark found on a search found on a search or examination may be photographed.[116] There is no requirement for an appropriate adult to be present before a juvenile detainee may be search or examined.

Strip search

7.140   A strip search is defined as 'a search involving the removal of more than outer clothing'.[117] The following guidance is given for the use of strip searches:

> A strip search may take place only if it is considered necessary to remove an article which a person would not be allowed to keep, and the officer reasonably considers that the person might have concealed such an article. Strip searches shall not routinely be carried out if there is no reason to consider that articles have been concealed.[118]

7.141   The police officer carrying out a strip search must be of the same sex as the person searched. The search must take place in an area where the person being searched cannot be seen by anyone who does not need to be present, nor by a member of the opposite sex (except an appropriate adult who has been specifically requested by the person being searched). Except in cases of urgency, where there is a risk of serious harm to the person detained or to others, wherever a strip search involves exposure of intimate parts of

---

112 Police and Criminal Evidence Act 1984 s54A(1).
113 Ibid, s54A(1) and (2).
114 Ibid, s54A(1) and (3).
115 Ibid, s54A(7).
116 Ibid, s54A(5).
117 Code C Annex A para 9.
118 Code C Annex A para 10.

the body, there must be at least two people present other than the person searched.[119]

7.142   Except in cases of urgency (ie where there is a risk of serious harm to the person detained or to others) a juvenile should only be strip searched in the presence of an appropriate adult. The presence of the appropriate adult may only be dispensed with if the juvenile signifies in the presence of the appropriate adult that s/he prefers the search to be done in his/her absence and the appropriate adult agrees. A record must be made of the juvenile's decision and this record should be signed by the appropriate adult.[120]

7.143   The search shall be conducted with proper regard to the sensitivity and vulnerability of the person in these circumstances and every reasonable effort shall be made to secure the person's co-operation and minimise embarrassment. People who are searched should not normally be required to have all their clothes removed at the same time. The Codes of Practice suggest that a man should be allowed to put on his shirt before removing his trousers and a woman should be allowed to put on her blouse and upper garments before further clothing is removed. Where necessary to assist the search, the person may be required to hold his/her arms in the air or to stand with his/her legs apart and to bend forward so that a visual examination may be made of the genital and anal areas, provided that no physical contact is made with any body orifice.[121]

Intimate search

7.144   This is defined by the Codes of Practice as follows:

> An 'intimate search' is a search which consists of the physical examination of a person's body orifices other than the mouth.[122]

7.145   An intimate search may only be authorised by a police officer of at least the rank of inspector who has reasonable grounds for believing;

- that an article which could cause physical injury to a detained person or others at the police station has been concealed; or
- that the person has concealed a Class A drug which s/he intended to supply to another or export; and
- in either case, an intimate search is the only practicable means of removing it.[123]

7.146   A drug offence search shall not be carried out unless appropriate consent has been given in writing.[124] Where the appropriate consent is refused without good cause, in any proceedings against the accused, the court may draw such inferences from the refusal as appear proper.[125]

7.147   An intimate search may not be authorised to search for evidence.

7.148   An intimate search may only be carried out by a registered medical practitioner or registered nurse, unless an officer of at least the rank of

---

119 Code C Annex A para 11.
120 Code C Annex A para 11.
121 Ibid.
122 Ibid, para 1.
123 Police and Criminal Evidence Act 1984 s55(1).
124 Ibid, s55(3A). For the definition of 'appropriate consent' see para 7.229 below.
125 Ibid, s55(13A).

inspector considers that it is not practicable and the search is for an article which could cause physical injury.[126] The intimate search may take place at a hospital, doctor's surgery or other medical premises but an intimate search which is only a drug offence search may not be carried out at a police station.[127]

7.149   An intimate search for an article likely to cause injury which is carried out by a police officer must be carried out by an officer of the same sex as the suspect. Subject to the requirement for an appropriate adult, no person of the opposite sex who is not a medical practitioner or nurse shall be present, nor shall anyone whose presence is unnecessary. A minimum of two people, other than the person being searched, must be present during the search. The search shall be conducted with proper regard to the sensitivity and vulnerability of the person in these circumstances.[128]

7.150   An intimate search of a juvenile must be carried out in the presence of an appropriate adult of the same sex (unless the juvenile specifically requests the presence of a particular adult of the opposite sex who is readily available). The search may take place in the absence of the appropriate adult only if the juvenile signifies in the presence of the appropriate adult that s/he prefers the search to be done in his/her absence and the appropriate adult agrees. A record shall be made of the juvenile's decision and signed by the appropriate adult.[129]

X-rays and ultrasound scans

7.151   An officer of at least the rank of inspector may authorise that an x-ray be taken of the suspect or an ultrasound be carried out of the suspect if:

- the suspect is under arrest for an offence and in police detention; and
- the officer has reasonable grounds for believing that the suspect:
  (a) may have swallowed a class A drug; and
  (b) was in possession of it with the appropriate criminal intent (eg supplying or importing) before his/her arrest.[130]

7.152   An x-ray must not be taken of a suspect and an ultrasound scan must not be carried out unless the appropriate consent has been given in writing.[131]

7.153   If it is proposed to take an x-ray of a suspect or to carry out an ultrasound scan of the suspect, s/he must be informed:

- that authorisation for the x-ray or ultrasound scan has been given; and
- the grounds for the authorisation.[132]

7.154   An x-ray may be taken or an ultrasound scan carried out only by a registered medical practitioner or a registered nurse and only at:

- a hospital;

---

126 Police and Criminal Evidence Act 1984 s55(5).
127 Ibid, s55(8) and (9).
128 Code C Annex A para 6.
129 Ibid.
130 Police and Criminal Evidence Act 1984 s55A(1) inserted by Drugs Act 2005 s5.
131 Ibid, s55A(2). For the definition of 'appropriate consent' see para 7.229 below.
132 Ibid, s55A(3).

- a registered medical practitioner's surgery; or
- some other place used for medical purposes.[133]

Search of premises

7.155   Having arrested a person a police officer may enter and search:

- the premises where the suspect is arrested or where s/he was immediately before arrest (Police and Criminal Evidence Act 1984 s32);
- any premises controlled by the suspect (Police and Criminal Evidence Act 1984 s18).

Section 32 search

7.156   A police constable has a power to enter and search any premises in which a suspect was when arrested or immediately before s/he was arrested for evidence relating to the offence for which s/he has been arrested.[134]

7.157   This power only extends to a search which is reasonably required for the purpose of discovering any such thing or any such evidence.[135]

Section 18 search

7.158   A police constable may enter and search any premises occupied or controlled by a person who is under arrest for an indictable offence, if the constable has reasonable grounds for suspecting that there is on the premises evidence other than items subject to legal privilege that relates to that offence or to some other indictable offence which is connected with or similar to that offence.

7.159   The power to search is only a power to search to the extent that is reasonably required for the purpose of discovering such evidence. A constable may seize and retain anything which s/he reasonably believes may be evidence relating to the offence for which the suspect is under arrest or some other indictable offence connected with or similar to that offence.[136]

Premises occupied or controlled by the suspect

7.160   This will normally be the place where the young suspect is living. Where a young suspect lives in the parental home, the police will often restrict their search to the young suspect's bedroom, but in law there is no requirement to restrict the search in this way. Depending on the circumstances of the case, the investigating officers may wish to search other parts of the house, for example to find blood-stained clothing which may be awaiting washing.

Authorisation

7.161   A section 18 search should only be carried out with the written authority of a police officer of at least the rank of inspector unless the search is carried

133   Police and Criminal Evidence Act 1984 s55A(4).
134   Ibid, s32(2)(b).
135   Ibid, s32(3).
136   Ibid, s18(2).

out before the suspect is taken to the police station and his/her presence is necessary for the effective investigation of the offence.[137]

Conditions of detention

7.162   The Codes of Practice provide detailed guidance as to how the police should treat a suspect while in custody.

Property

7.163   The custody officer at a police station shall ascertain everything which a person has with him/her when s/he is either brought to the police station or arrested at the station.[138] The custody officer may record or cause to be recorded all or any of the things which the detained person has with him/her. Whenever a record is made, the detainee must be allowed to check and sign the record of property as correct.[139]

Cell

7.164   As far as practicable, only one prisoner should be held in a cell at any one time.[140] The cells should be adequately heated, cleaned and ventilated. They must also be adequately lit.[141] Blankets, mattresses, pillows and other bedding should be provided and should be of a reasonable standard and in a clean and sanitary condition.[142] Access to toilet and washing facilities must be provided.[143]

7.165   A juvenile should not be placed in a police cell unless no other secure accommodation is available and the custody officer considers that it is not practicable to supervise him/her if s/he is not placed in a cell or the custody officer considers that a cell provides more comfortable accommodation than other secure accommodation in the police station. If a juvenile is placed in a cell, the reason must be recorded on the custody record. A juvenile must never be placed in a cell with a detained adult.[144]

7.166   Some police stations have detention rooms where juveniles will normally be detained. From the inside the difference between a detention room and a cell is not immediately obvious. While the appropriate adult is at the station it may be possible to persuade the custody officer to allow the juvenile to sit with the appropriate adult in an interview or other room in the custody area.

---

137 Police and Criminal Evidence Act 1984 s18(2).
138 Ibid, s54(1) as amended by Criminal Justice Act 2003 s8.
139 Code C para 4.4.
140 Code C para 8.1.
141 Code C para 8.2.
142 Code C para 8.3.
143 Code C para 8.4.
144 Code C para 8.8.

Supervision

7.167 People detained should be visited every hour.[145] Whenever possible, juveniles and mentally vulnerable detainee should be visited more frequently.[146]

7.168   Those suspected of being intoxicated through drink or drugs or whose level of consciousness causes concern must, subject to any clinical directions given by a health care professional, be visited and roused at least every half hour, have their condition assessed and clinical treatment arranged if appropriate.[147]

Food

7.169 At least two light meals and one main meal shall be offered on any period of 24 hours. Drinks should be provided at meal times and upon reasonable request between meal times. As far as practicable, meals provided shall offer a varied diet and meet any special dietary needs or religious beliefs that the person may have. A detained person may also, at the custody officer's discretion, have meals supplied by his/her family or friends at their expense.[148]

Clothing

7.170 If it is necessary to remove a person's clothes for the purposes of investigation, for hygiene or health reasons or for cleaning, replacement clothing of a reasonable standard of comfort and cleanliness shall be provided. A person may not be interviewed unless adequate clothing has been offered to him/her.[149]

7.171   The alternative clothing the police normally offer is a paper suit and plimsolls. There is no reason why alternative clothing may not be brought from the suspect's home.

Exercise

7.172 Brief outdoor exercise shall be offered daily if practicable.[150]

Medical

7.173 Every police station has a GP or rota of GPs who attend police stations to meet the medical needs of prisoners and also to examine injuries with a view to gathering evidence. This GP may be referred to as the police doctor, the divisional surgeon or the forensic medical examiner (FME). Some police stations now employ registered nurses to work in the custody suite full-time. The codes of practice makes use of the generic term 'appropriate health care professional'.

---

145 Code C para 9.3.
146 Code C Note for Guidance 9B.
147 Code C para 9.3.
148 Code C para 8.6.
149 Code C para 8.5.
150 Code C para 8.7.

7.174   The custody officer must ensure that a detainee receives appropriate clinical attention as soon as reasonably practicable if the person:
- appears to be suffering from physical illness; or
- is injured; or
- appears to be suffering from a mental disorder; or
- appears to need clinical attention.[151]

7.175   If a detainee requests a clinical examination, an appropriate health care professional must be called as soon as practicable to assess the detainee's clinical needs. If a safe and appropriate care plan cannot be provided, the police surgeon's advice must be sought. The detainee may in addition be examined by a medical practitioner of his/her own choice at his/her own expense.[152]

Reasonable force

7.176   Reasonable force may be used if necessary for the following purposes:
- to secure compliance with reasonable instructions, including instructions given in pursuance of the provisions of a Code of Practice; or
- to prevent escape, injury, damage to property or the destruction of evidence.[153]

7.177   No additional restraints shall be used within a locked cell unless absolutely necessary, and then only restraint equipment, approved for use in that force by the chief officer, which is reasonable and necessary in the circumstances having regard to the detainee's demeanour and with a view to ensuring their safety and the safety of others. If a detainee is deaf, mentally disordered or otherwise mentally vulnerable, particular care must be taken when deciding whether to use any form of approved restraints.[154]

The police interview

Definition

7.178   Code C para 11.1A of the Codes of Practice defines an 'interview' as follows:

> An interview is the questioning of a person regarding their involvement or suspected involvement in a criminal offence or offences which, under paragraph 10.1, must be carried out under caution.

7.179   Code C para 10.1 states:

> A person whom there are grounds to suspect of an offence ... must be cautioned before any questions about an offence, or further questions if the answers provide the grounds for suspicion are put to them if either the suspect's answer or silence, (i.e. failure or refusal to answer satisfactorily) may be given in evidence

---

151   Code C para 9.5.
152   Code C para 9.8.
153   Code C para 8.9.
154   Code C para 8.2.

to a court in a prosecution. A person need not be cautioned if questions are for other necessary purposes, e.g.:

(a) solely to establish their identity or ownership of any vehicle;

(b) to obtain information in accordance with any relevant statutory requirement;

(c) in furtherance of the proper and effective conduct of a search, e.g. to determine the need to search in the exercise of powers of stop and search or to seek co-operation while carrying out a search;

(d) to seek verification of a written record;

...

7.180 It is clear that the term 'interview' is not restricted to a formal taped interview in the police station.

Caution

7.181 The caution should be in the following terms:

You do not have to say anything. But it may harm your defence if you do not mention when questioned something which you later rely on in court. Anything you do say may be given in evidence.[155]

7.182 Minor deviations from this wording do not constitute a breach of the requirement that a caution must be administered before questioning a suspect provided that the sense of the caution is preserved.[156]

7.183 If a juvenile is cautioned in the absence of the appropriate adult, the caution must be repeated in the adult's presence.[157]

Interview records

7.184 An accurate record must be made of each interview with a person suspected of an offence, whether or not the interview takes place at a police station. The record must state the place of the interview, the time it begins and ends, the time the record was made (if different), any breaks in the interview and the names of all those present. The record must be made during the course of the interview, unless in the investigating officer's view this would not be practicable or would interfere with the conduct of the interview.[158] If the interview record is not made during the course of the interview it must be made as soon as practicable after its completion.[159]

Verification by suspect

7.185 Unless it is impracticable, the person interviewed shall be given the opportunity to read the interview record and to sign it as correct or to indicate the respects in which s/he considers it inaccurate.[160] If the suspect agrees to sign the interview record, s/he should be asked to endorse the record with words such as 'I agree that this is a correct record of what was said.'[161]

---

155 Code C para 10.5.
156 Code C para 10.7.
157 Code C para 10.12.
158 Code C para 11.7.
159 Code C para 11.8.
160 Code C para 11.11.
161 Code C Note for Guidance 11E.

Verification by appropriate adult or solicitor

7.186 If the appropriate adult or the suspect's solicitor is present during the interview s/he should also be given an opportunity to read and sign the interview record.[162]

Interviewing a juvenile at their place of education

7.187 Code C para 11.16 states:

> Juveniles may only be interviewed at their place of education in exceptional circumstances and only when the principal or their nominee agrees. Every effort should be made to notify the parent(s) or other person responsible for the juvenile's welfare and the appropriate adult, if this a different person, that the police want to interview the juvenile and reasonable time should be allowed to enable the appropriate adult to be present at the interview. If awaiting the appropriate adult would cause unreasonable delay and unless the juvenile is suspected of an offence against the educational establishment, the principal or their nominee can act as the appropriate adult for the purposes of the interview.

Presence of the appropriate adult

7.188 A juvenile must not be interviewed by the police in the absence of an appropriate adult.[163] There are two exceptions to this rule:

- if an urgent interview is necessary before the juvenile arrives at the police station; or
- if an urgent interview is necessary at a police station.

Prior to arrival at the police station

7.189 Following a decision to arrest, the suspect should not be interviewed about the offence except at a police station unless the consequent delay would be likely to:

- lead to interference with, or harm to, evidence connected with an offence, or interference with, or physical harm, to other people, serious loss of, or damage to, property; or
- lead to the alerting of other people suspected of having committed an offence but not yet arrested for it; or
- hinder the recovery of property obtained in consequence of the commission of an offence.[164]

7.190 Interviewing in any of these circumstances must cease once the relevant risk has been averted or the necessary questions have been put in order to attempt to avert the risk.[165]

At the police station

7.191 An officer of the rank of superintendent or above may authorise that a juvenile be interviewed at a police station in the absence of an appropriate adult

---

162 Code C para 11.12.
163 Code C para 11.14.
164 Code C para 11.1.
165 Ibid.

if s/he considers that delay will lead to any of the consequences outlined in para 7.189 and s/he is satisfied the interview would not significantly harm the juvenile's physical or mental state.[166] An interview may not continue once sufficient information has been obtained to avert the consequences outlined in para 7.189.[167] A record shall be made of the grounds for any decision to interview a juvenile in such circumstances.[168]

Admissibility of an interview conducted in the absence of the appropriate adult

7.192 The admissibility of such an interview with a juvenile is considered at paras 15.23–15.32.

Right to silence

7.193 The provisions of the Criminal Justice and Public Order Act 1994 notwithstanding, a suspect may still refuse to answer questions put to him/her by a police officer. To that extent the right to silence may be considered to have been preserved. However, the right has been curtailed in a significant respect in that a court may be invited to draw adverse inference from a suspect's failure to answer questions.

7.194   The relevant provisions are set out in Criminal Justice and Public Order Act 1994 ss34, 36 and 37. When a suspect who is interviewed after arrest or fails to answer certain questions, or to answer them satisfactorily, after due warning, court or jury may draw such inference as appears proper under the following provisions

Section 34

7.195 At any time before s/he was charged with the offence, when questioned under caution by a constable trying to discover whether or by whom the offence was committed, the suspect failed to mention any fact relied on in his/her defence in those proceedings.

Section 36

7.196 Having been arrested by a constable or officer of Customs and Excise, on his/her person, in or on his/her clothing or footwear or otherwise in his/her possession or in any place in which s/he is at the time of his/her arrest, there is any object or mark on any such object and the suspect fails to or refuses to account for the objects, marks or substances found.

Section 37

7.197 The suspect is arrested by a constable or officer of Customs and Excise and s/he was found by the arresting officer at a place at or about the time the offence was for which s/he was arrested is alleged to have been committed

---

166 Code C para 11.18.
167 Code C para 11.19.
168 Code C para 11.20.

and the suspect fails to or refuses to account for his/her presence at that place.

Special warnings

7.198 No inference may be drawn under sections 36 and 37 unless the interviewing officer gives the suspect a 'special warning'. The interviewing officer must tell the suspect in ordinary language:

- what offence s/he is investigating;
- what fact s/he is asking the suspect to account for;
- that s/he believes this fact may be due to the suspect's taking part in the commission of the offence in question;
- that a court may draw a proper inference if the suspect fails or refuses to account for the fact about which s/he is being questioned; and
- that a record is being made of the interview and that it may be given in evidence is s/he is brought to trial.[169]

Advising a young suspect

Attending the police station

7.199 By reason of their age alone, suspects under the age of 18 are vulnerable. Some lawyers consider attendance not to be important either because it is a petty offence which will have no serious consequences for the young suspect or the suspect is a regular client and 'knows what to do'. In the first category, there is still a need for advice and assistance because the person is likely to be unfamiliar with police procedures and susceptible to pressure, and may not have very effective support from the appropriate adult. In the case of regular young suspects the attendance of a lawyer is still important as the young person's familiarity with police custody may lead them to underestimate the seriousness of the situation.

Establishing a rapport with a young suspect

7.200 Children and many adolescents have little experience of dealing with adults outside the immediate family, except for professionals such as teachers, who may not be seen as being on the young person's side. Frequent offenders, in particular, may have very negative experiences of dealing with adults and may be extremely suspicious of an adult stranger even if s/he is supposedly there to help.

7.201   If the lawyer is to represent a young suspect effectively, s/he should make every effort to establish a rapport with him/her. Spending some time at the beginning of the consultation to break the ice usually pays dividends. Care should be taken, too, to grade the language used so that it is comprehensible to the young suspect.

Appropriate adults

7.202 Although intended as a safeguard for juveniles, it is all too common that the presence of the appropriate adult, particularly if s/he is the parent of

169 Code C para 10.11.

the juvenile, can undermine the other legal protection for the young suspect. It is very difficult for a lawyer to step between a parent and his/her child at a very stressful time and try to ensure that the parent's anger at the juvenile's perceived wrongdoing does not affect the juvenile's legal rights. Although the lawyer must at all times keep in mind that the juvenile is the client, it is vital that every effort is made to win over a parent acting as the appropriate adult.

7.203   Because of concerns regarding confidentiality, the defence lawyer should always see the juvenile initially in the absence of the appropriate adult.[170] Parents acting as appropriate adults will often object to this and it is common for custody officers to disapprove too. The lawyer should explain to the appropriate adult that s/he is required to have such a consultation by professional rules and s/he should refer the custody officer to Code C Note for Guidance 1E which states:

> A detainee person should always be given an opportunity, when an appropriate adult is called to the police station, to consult privately with a solicitor in the appropriate adult's absence if they want.

7.204   In this initial consultation the lawyer should introduce him/herself and establish whether there will be any problems with the appropriate adult who has been called to the station. The juvenile should also be given the option of having the appropriate adult present during the rest of the consultation or of continuing with a private consultation in private with the lawyer. In any event, it should be explained to the juvenile that the lawyer has a duty of confidentiality to his/her client which may not extend to anything overheard by the appropriate adult and therefore if the juvenile wishes something to remain confidential s/he should discuss it with the lawyer when they are alone.

7.205   Once the danger of disclosure has been explained to the juvenile, the defence lawyer should discuss whether the juvenile whether s/he wants the appropriate adult to be present for the rest of the consultation. It may be preferable to delay inviting the adult to join the consultation until any discussion about the allegation has been completed. This does need to be balanced against the age of the juvenile and any reassurance to be derived from having a familiar adult present. In any event, it is wise to make a point of speaking to the appropriate adult after any consultation, both to explain what decisions have been made regarding the conduct of the interview and to ensure that the adult understands his/her role in the interview.

Explaining the elements of the offence

7.206   Having explained the allegation to the young suspect and described the evidence the police have, it is important that it is made clear to him/her what are the legal elements of the offence alleged. Young people may not have reached a level of understanding to distinguish between criminal offences and behaviour contrary to parental or school rules.

7.207   Frequently, young suspects will be worried about what their parents may say. Even if the young suspect has not committed a criminal offence, s/he may fear retribution from parents because s/he broke a parental

170 See para 7.131.

curfew, went to an area of town prohibited by parents or was arrested with another young person of whom his/her parents disapprove.

Explaining police procedures

7.208   Explaining what will happen next and giving some idea of the time scale will both take away the sense of uncertainty and in most cases reassure the young suspect that s/he will be released shortly. Making reference to the popular television programme *The Bill* will often provide an easy way to explain basic police procedures.

7.209   Warning suspects that the police may seize trainers or wish to take fingerprints or DNA samples also removes the shock of being told bluntly by the custody officer that such procedures will take place.

Advising on the exercise of the right to silence

7.210   When explaining about the right to silence, it is important that the lawyer explains that a police interview is a unique type of conversation for which the normal social conventions do not apply. The young suspect may need to be reassured that s/he will not be accused of being rude if s/he refuses to answer police questions. It may be helpful to specifically state that the interview is not the same as would be expected if a parent or teacher were questioning the young person when rule-breaking is suspected.

7.211   When considering whether to advise that the right to silence should be exercised, Cape, *Defending Suspects in the Police Station*[171] identifies the following criteria:

- knowledge of the police case;
- apparent strength of the police evidence;
- admissibility of the police evidence;
- prior comments and/or 'significant silences' of the client;
- likely fairness of the interview;
- apparent intelligence of the client;
- apparent mental condition of the client;
- strength of the client's defence;
- any reason for early statement of the client's defence;
- specific reasons for remaining silent (eg to protect others);
- possible advantages of early admission of the offence(s);
- whether a statement at charge would be more appropriate.

7.212   All of these criteria are equally valid when dealing with a young suspect. It is proposed only to highlight considerations which are of particular relevance to young suspects.

Youth of suspect

7.213   Interviewing a child or young person is not necessarily unfair, but the extreme youth of the suspect makes the chance of unfairness much more likely. If a lawyer is concerned that a young suspect does not have the maturity to cope with a police interview then the exercise of the right to silence should be considered for that reason alone.

171 5th edn, LAG, 2006.

Preparing for the interview

7.214 If the right to silence is to be exercised, the young suspect will need as much support as possible before the interview and during the interview. One easy way to boost the young suspect's confidence is to practice the interview. The lawyer should take the role of the police officer and should both ask the anticipated questions and include likely strategies the police may employ to induce a suspect to talk. In the context of young suspects, these could include:

- asking seemingly innocent questions about school or leisure interests;
- inviting the parent acting as appropriate adult to express his/her disapproval of the juvenile's alleged conduct;
- informing the suspect that friends have already admitted the offence and have implicated the suspect; and
- emphasising the potential for a court to draw adverse inference from the exercise of the right to silence.

7.215 Practising an interview with an appropriate adult present also has the advantage of giving him/her the opportunity to see how an interview is conducted and this may help to reassure the adult who has never been in a police custody area before.

Possibility of a reprimand or warning

7.216 Where the young client has no previous convictions, the defence lawyer will need to keep in mind the possibility of a reprimand or warning.[172] In *R v Crown Prosecution Service and Chief Constable of Merseyside* [173] Rose LJ gave the following advice:

> The final warning scheme ... is designed to benefit both young offenders and the public. Its expressed purpose is to divert children and young people from offending behaviour before they enter the court system. The scheme is structured and progressive, providing the police with three options: reprimand, final warning, or charge.

> Two features of the scheme are of particular present relevance. First: the consequences of offending behaviour should be brought home to the young person without delay and short timetables to that end are prescribed by the scheme. Secondly: an admission of guilt is essential before a reprimand or final warning can be given.

> It follows, in my judgment, that it is in the interests of offenders and the public that the sooner a young person who has committed an offence admits his guilt to the police, the better. If such a person, in interview, denies guilt or declines to answer questions, he or she cannot, at that stage, be the beneficiary of a reprimand or final warning.

> The necessary consequence of such a course is that the possibility of a reprimand or final warning being the ultimate outcome will be substantially reduced. Once a young person has been charged it is likely to be only in exceptional circumstances that a reprimand or final warning will be given.

> These considerations, as it seems to me, ought to be in the forefront of the mind of those advising young persons at the time at which they are interviewed.

---

172 See chapter 9.
173 [2003] EWHC 3266 (Admin).

The conduct of the interview

7.217 Code C Note for Guidance 11C gives the following general advice:

> Although juveniles ... are often capable of providing reliable evidence, they may, without knowing or wishing to do so, be particularly prone in certain circumstances to provide information which is unreliable, misleading or self-incriminating. Special care should therefore always be exercised when questioning such a person, and the appropriate adult should be involved, if there is any doubt about a person's age, mental state or capacity. Because of the risk of unreliable evidence it is also important to obtain corroboration of any facts admitted whenever possible.

Role of the appropriate adult

7.218 The interviewing officer is required to advise the appropriate adult at the start of the interview that:

- s/he is not expected simply to act as an observer; and
- the purpose of his/her presence is:
  (i) to advise the juvenile being questioned;
  (ii) to observe whether the interview is being conducted properly and fairly; and
  (iii) to facilitate communication with the juvenile being interviewed.[174]

7.219 Failure to give this notice to the appropriate adult is a breach of the codes of practice. Whether it is a substantial breach requiring the exclusion of the interview depends on the circumstances of each individual case.[175]

Role of the lawyer

7.220 Cape, *Defending Suspects in the Police Station*[176] summarises the objectives of the lawyer in the interview as follows:

- ensuring that the suspect does his/her best in the interview whether or not s/he is answering questions;
- keeping an accurate record of the interview;
- ensuring the police act fairly and in accordance with the Police and Criminal Evidence Act 1984 and the Codes of Practice; and
- protecting the suspect from unnecessary pressure and distress.

Ensuring the young suspect does his/her best

7.221 Building up a rapport in the private consultation and preparing thoroughly for the interview will go a long way to ensuring that the young suspect performs to his/her best in the interview. Most importantly, it will ensure that s/he has confidence in his/her lawyer and it will prove much more difficult for the police to undermine that confidence.

7.222 The lawyer should also be aware of the physical conditions in the interview room. The Codes of Practice require that, as far as practicable, the interview room should be adequately heated, lit and ventilated.[177] The

---

174 Code C para 11.17.
175 *H and M v DPP* [1998] Crim LR 653, QBD.
176 5th edn, LAG, 2006.
177 Code C para 12.4.

lawyer should pay attention to the seating arrangements and ensure that the young suspect has somebody sitting next to him/her who will provide moral support. In normal circumstances this will be the appropriate adult in the case of a juvenile; however, if the current relationship appears frosty, the lawyer should consider sitting next to the juvenile. In any event, the lawyer should sit in a position which is visible to the young suspect and preferably where eye contact is possible.

Ensuring the police act fairly

7.223   If the lawyer has advised the young suspect to answer police questions in the interview, the questioning should be monitored with particular attention paid to the complexity of the language and the use of such ploys as multiple questions, leading questions and hypothetical questions, especially regarding intent.

7.224   The lawyer must also be vigilant for any signs that a young suspect may be susceptible to any veiled threat by the police which may not be immediately obvious. A young suspect being interviewed in the absence of parents may be desperate for his/her parents not to find out about the arrest and any mention by the police of telling the parents if the matter is not resolved in the interview could induce a false confession. Even seemingly bizarre considerations may affect a young suspect's willingness to confess – for example, the police making it clear that in the absence of a confession a young suspect's trainers will have to be seized for laboratory analysis.

Protecting the young suspect from pressure or distress

7.225   A lawyer must always ensure that the interview is not conducted in an oppressive manner. In the case of a young suspect, s/he must be particularly sensitive to factors which may put undue pressure on the interviewee. The officers raising their voices or demanding that a young suspect looks at them when they are talking can put enormous pressure on someone so young and also reinforces associations with parental disciplining. Similar considerations apply to an officer rebuking a young suspect for smiling or giggling out of nervousness.

7.226   It is also very easy to demoralise a juvenile whose parents have not attended the police station to act as appropriate adults by suggesting that the juvenile has been deserted by the parents.

Tape recording

7.227   Most interviews carried out in a police station should be tape-recorded.[178] The standard police interview room has a double tape recorder. Blank tapes should be opened in the presence of the suspect.[179] At the start of the interview the interviewing officers will introduce themselves and ask all other people to introduce themselves.

7.228   At the end of the interview one of the two tapes will be selected by the suspect and sealed in his/her presence. Both the suspect and any

---

178 Code E para 3.1.
179 Code E para 4.3.

appropriate adult will be asked to sign the seal.[180] If the suspect is charged s/he has a right to a copy of the interview tape as soon as practicable.[181]

Taking fingerprints, photographs and samples

Consent

7.229   When considering identification procedures, Police and Criminal Evidence Act 1984 s65 states that references to 'appropriate consent' shall be construed as follows:

- in relation to a person who has attained the age of 17 years, the consent of that person;
- in relation to a person who has not attained that age but has attained the age of 14 years, the consent of that person and his/her parent or guardian; and
- in relation to a person who has not attained the age of 14 years, the consent of his/her parent or guardian.

7.230   Where a juvenile is in care to a local authority, 'parent or guardian' means that authority.[182] This would mean that a representative of the authority could give consent in relation to a looked after child.

7.231   It should be noted that the definition of 'appropriate consent' prevents an appropriate adult, who does not satisfy the definition of parent or guardian, from giving valid consent.

7.232   The parent or guardian is not required to be present to give his/her consent, but it is important that a parent or guardian not present is fully informed before being asked to consent. The parent or guardian must be allowed to speak to the juvenile and the appropriate adult if s/he wishes. Provided the consent is fully informed and is not withdrawn, it may be obtained at any time before the taking of a sample.[183]

Fingerprints

7.233   The fingerprints of a person detained at a police station may be taken without the appropriate consent if:

- s/he is detained in consequence of his/her arrest for a recordable offence; or
- s/he has been charged with a recordable offence or informed that s/he will be reported for such an offence.[184]

7.234   In either case, fingerprints can only be taken if the suspect has not had his/her fingerprints taken in the course of the investigation of the offence by the police.[185]

---

180 Code E para 4.18.
181 Code E para 4.19.
182 Police and Criminal Evidence Act 1984 s118(1).
183 Code D Note for Guidance 2A.
184 Police and Criminal Evidence Act 1984 s61(3), (4) as amended by Criminal Justice Act 2003 s9.
185 Ibid.

7.235   With the introduction of electronic means of taking fingerprints, many police forces are now routinely taking fingerprints after arrival at the police station to establish whether the suspect has given a false name.

7.236   Fingerprints may be taken without the appropriate consent prior to a person's arrest and away from the police station if a police constable:

- reasonably suspects that the person is committing or attempting to commit an offence, or has committed or attempted to commit an offence; and
- either:
  (a) the name of the person is unknown to, and cannot be readily ascertained by the constable; or
  (b) the constable has reasonable ground for doubting whether a name furnished by the person as his/her name is his/her real name.[186]

7.237   This new power is likely to be used in conjunction with the granting of street bail.

Photographs

7.238   A person who is detained at a police station may be photographed:

- with the appropriate consent; or
- if the appropriate consent is withheld or it is not practicable to obtain it, without it.

7.239   A police officer proposing to take a photograph may require the removal of any item or substance worn over the whole or any part of the head or face of the person to be photographed.

7.240   Again it is now common in some police forces for the suspect to be photographed shortly after arrival at the custody suite.

7.241   A person may now be photographed or videoed away from a police station without appropriate consent if the person has been:

- arrested by a constable for an offence;
- taken into custody by a constable after being arrested for an offence by a person other than a constable;
- made subject to a requirement to wait with a community support officer; or
- given a penalty notice.[187]

Impressions of footwear

7.242   Where a person is detained at a police station, an impression of his/her footwear may be taken without the appropriate consent if:

- s/he is under arrest for a recordable offence, has been charged with such an offence, or informed that s/he will be reported for such an offence; and

---

186 Police and Criminal Evidence Act 1984 s61(6A) as inserted by Serious Organised Crime and Police Act 2005 s117.
187 Ibid, s64A(1A) and (1B) as inserted by Serious Organised Crime and Police Act 2005 s116.

- s/he has not had an impression taken of his/her footwear in the course of the investigation of the offence by the police.[188]

Non-intimate samples

7.243   A 'non-intimate sample' means:

- a sample of hair other than pubic hair;
- a sample taken from a nail or from under a nail;
- a swab taken from any part of a person's body including the mouth but not any other body orifice;
- saliva; or
- a skin impression.[189]

7.244   A non-intimate sample may be taken from a person without the appropriate consent if the person:

- is in police detention in consequence of his/her arrest for a recordable offence; and s/he has not had a non-intimate sample of the same type and from the same part of the body taken in the course of the investigation of the offence by the police, or s/he has had such a sample taken but it proved insufficient;[190] or
- is being held by the police on the authority of a court and an officer of at least the rank of inspector authorises it to be taken;[191] or
- has been convicted of a recordable offence.[192]

7.245   In practice the most common non-intimate sample is a mouth swab to allow DNA analysis. A DNA sample is frequently taken shortly after arrival at the police station, if the suspect's profile is not already present on the national database.

7.246   When a non-intimate sample is being taken from a juvenile, an appropriate adult should be present.[193] Where clothing needs to be removed in circumstances likely to cause embarrassment to the suspect, no person of the opposite sex who is not a medical practitioner or nurse shall be present, unless the presence of an appropriate adult of the opposite sex is specifically requested and is readily available.[194] However, in the case of a juvenile, this is subject to the overriding proviso that such a removal of clothing may take place in the absence of the appropriate adult only if the juvenile signifies in the appropriate adult's presence that the juvenile prefers the adult's absence and the adult agrees.[195]

---

188 Police and Criminal Evidence Act 1984 s61A(3) as inserted by Serious Organised Crime and Police Act 2005 s118.
189 Ibid, s65(1).
190 Ibid, s63(2) as amended by Criminal Justice Act 2003 s10.
191 Ibid, s63(3) as amended by Criminal Justice Act 2003 s10.
192 Ibid, s63(3B).
193 Code D para 2.15.
194 Code D para 5.12.
195 Code D para 6.9.

Intimate samples

7.247 An 'intimate sample' means:

- a sample of blood, semen or any other tissue fluid, urine or pubic hair;
- a dental impression;
- a swab taken from any part of a person's genitals (including pubic hair) or from a person's body orifice other than the mouth.[196]

7.248 An intimate sample may only be taken from a person in police detention if:

- a police officer of at least the rank of inspector authorises it, and
- the appropriate consent is given.[197]

7.249 Authorisation may only be given if the officer has reasonable grounds for:

- suspecting the involvement of the person from whom the sample is to be taken in a recordable offence; and
- believing that the sample will tend to confirm or disprove his/her involvement.[198]

7.250 Where the appropriate consent to the taking of an intimate sample from a person was refused without good cause, a court or jury may draw such adverse inferences from the refusal as appear proper.[199] It is questionable whether it would be proper to draw an adverse inference when the appropriate consent is not given because of the non-cooperation of the parent or guardian of a juvenile.

7.251 After the authority of an officer of the rank of superintendent or above has been obtained, the suspect must be informed that authorisation has been given and the grounds for giving it.[200] The suspect must be asked whether s/he consents to the taking of the intimate sample. The suspect must be warned that an adverse inference may be drawn from the refusal to consent to a sample being taken.[201] This information and any request for consent must take place in the presence of the appropriate adult.[202] The appropriate consent must be in writing.[203]

7.252 Except for a sample of urine, intimate samples or dental impressions may only be taken by a registered medical or dental practitioner as appropriate. When an intimate sample is being taken from a juvenile, an appropriate adult should be present.[204] Where clothing needs to be removed in circumstances likely to cause embarrassment to the suspect, no person of the opposite sex who is not a medical practitioner or nurse shall be present, unless the presence of an appropriate adult of the opposite sex is specifically requested and is readily available.[205] However, in the case of a juvenile, this is subject to the overriding proviso that such a removal of clothing

---

196 Police and Criminal Evidence Act 1984 s65(1).
197 Ibid, s62(1).
198 Ibid s62(2).
199 Ibid, s62(10).
200 Ibid, s62(5).
201 Code D para 6.3.
202 Code D para 2.14.
203 Code D para 6.10.
204 Code D para 2.15.
205 Code D para 5.12.

may take place in the absence of the appropriate adult only if the juvenile signifies in the appropriate adult's presence that the juvenile prefers the adult's absence and the adult agrees.[206]

Identification by witnesses

7.253   If the identity of the perpetrator of a crime is in doubt, the police have a number of ways of seeking identification evidence. If the identity of the suspect is not known, the police may seek a street identification or an identification by photographs. If the suspect's identity is known, the police have the following options:

- video identification;
- identification parade;
- group identification; or
- confrontation;

7.254   Provided it is practicable to do so, an identification procedure should be held whenever:

- a witness has identified a suspect or purported to have identified them prior to any formal identification procedure having been held; or
- there is a witness available, who expresses an ability to identify the suspect, or where there is a reasonable chance of the witness being able to do so, and they have not been given an opportunity to identify the suspect in a formal identification procedure; and
- the suspect disputes being the person the witness claims to have seen.[207]

7.255   An identification procedure need not be held if it would serve no useful purpose in proving or disproving whether the suspect was involved in committing the offence – for example, when it is not disputed that the suspect is already well known to the witness who claims to have seen him/her commit the crime.[208]

7.256   An identification procedure may also be held if the officer in charge of the investigation considers it would be useful.[209]

7.257   Where the identification procedure involves the participation of a juvenile, the procedure must take place in the presence of an appropriate adult.[210]

7.258   Before any identification procedure, the suspect or the defence lawyer must be provided with the first description of the suspect given by any witness who is to attend the identification procedure.[211]

7.259   If an identification procedure is to be held, the suspect shall initially be offered a video identification unless:

206 Code D para 6.9.
207 Code D para 3.12.
208 Ibid.
209 Code D para 3.13.
210 Code D para 2.15.
211 Code D Annex A para 8, Annex B para 3, Annex C para 11 and Annex D para 2.

- a video identification is not practicable; or
- an identification parade is both practicable and more suitable than a video identification.[212]

7.260 A group identification may initially be offered if the officer in charge of the investigation considers it more suitable than a video identification or an identification parade and the identification officer considers it practicable to arrange.[213]

Consent

7.261 The consent of the suspect should be sought before a video identification, identification parade or a group identification takes place. In the case of a juvenile, this consent is only valid if the consent of the parent or guardian is also obtained unless the juvenile is under 14, when the consent of the parent or guardian is sufficient in its own right.[214] Where a juvenile is in the care of a local authority or voluntary organisation, consent may be provided by a representative of that organisation.[215]

7.262 The parent or guardian is not required to be present to give his/her consent, but it is important that a parent or guardian not present is fully informed before being asked to consent. The parent or guardian must be allowed to speak to the juvenile and the appropriate adult if s/he wishes. Provided the consent is fully informed and is not withdrawn, it may be obtained at any time before the identification procedure takes place.[216]

7.263 If the only obstacle to an identification procedure is that a juvenile's parent or guardian refuses consent or reasonable efforts to obtain it have failed, the identification officer may follow the video identification procedure but using still images.[217]

Video identification

7.264 A video consisting of clips of the suspect and at least eight volunteers will be compiled for viewing by any witnesses. The volunteers should resemble the suspect in age, height, general appearance and position in life.[218] The suspect and other people shall, as far as possible, be filmed in the same positions or carrying out the same activity and under identical conditions, unless the identification officer reasonably believes:

- because of the suspect's failure or refusal to co-operate or other reasons, it is not practicable for the conditions to be identical; or
- any difference in the conditions would not direct a witness's attention to any individual image.[219]

---

212 Code D para 3.14.
213 Code D para 3.16.
214 Code D para 2.12.
215 Code D Note for Guidance 2A.
216 Ibid.
217 Code D para 3.21.
218 Code D Annex A para 2.
219 Code D Annex A para 3.

7.265　In the case of a juvenile, the filming and the selection of volunteers' images must take place in the presence of an appropriate adult.[220] The suspect and his/her solicitor, friend or appropriate adult must be given a reasonable opportunity to see the complete film before it is shown to witnesses. If there is a reasonable objection to the video film or any of its participants, steps shall, if practicable, be taken to remove the grounds for objection.[221]

7.266　The suspect or any lawyer must be given reasonable notification of the time and place that it is intended to conduct a video identification in order that a representative may attend on behalf of the suspect. The suspect may not attend the showing.[222]

Identification parade

7.267　A parade may take place in a normal room or a special identification suite with a two-way mirror. A suspect must be given a reasonable opportunity to have a solicitor or friend present.[223] In the case of a juvenile the parade must take place in the presence of an appropriate adult.[224]

7.268　The parade shall consist of at least eight volunteers who so far as is possible resemble the suspect in age, height, general appearance and position in life. In normal circumstances, only one suspect may stand on a parade at any one time. However, if there are two suspects of roughly similar appearance, they may be paraded together but in that case there must be at least 12 volunteers.[225]

7.269　The suspect may choose his/her place in the line-up and if there is more than one witness the suspect may change position between witnesses.[226] Witnesses must view the parade one at a time.[227] A video recording must normally be taken of the identification parade. If that is impracticable, a colour photograph must be taken.[228]

Group identification

7.270　A group identification should take place in a place where other people are either passing by or waiting around informally, in groups such that the suspect is able to join them and be capable of being seen by the witness at the same time as others in the group.[229] They are usually held at train, bus or underground stations or in busy shopping areas. In selecting the venue, the identification officer must reasonably expect that over the period the witness observes the group, s/he will be able to see from time to time, a number of other members of the public who are broadly similar to the suspect.[230]

220 Code D para 2.15.
221 Code D Annex A para 7.
222 Code D Annex A para 9.
223 Code D Annex B para 1.
224 Code D para 2.15.
225 Code D Annex B para 9.
226 Code D Annex B para 13.
227 Code D Annex B para 16.
228 Code D Annex B para 23.
229 Code D Annex C para 4.
230 Code D Annex C para 6.

7.271   With a young suspect it is particularly important to consider whether a busy place will have many young people at the time of the parade. For example, a commuter station at rush hour will be crowded but it is unlikely to have many teenagers walking around.

7.272   A group identification may be carried out with the suspect's consent or covertly (if it is practicable for the police to do so). If it is carried out by consent, the suspect must be given a reasonable opportunity to have a solicitor or friend present.[231] In the case of a juvenile, the group identification procedure must take place in the presence of an appropriate adult.[232]

Confrontation

7.273   Confrontations may take place without the suspect's consent but force may not be used to make the suspect's face visible to the witness.[233] Confrontations should normally take place in a police station.[234]

7.274   The confrontation should take place in the presence of the suspect's solicitor or friend, unless this would cause unreasonable delay.[235] In any event, in the case of a juvenile, an appropriate adult must be present.[236] The suspect must be confronted independently by each witness, who shall be asked: 'Is this the person?'[237]

Possible disposals

7.275   The fact that there appears to be sufficient evidence for a successful prosecution does not mean that court proceedings will automatically follow. The following options are available to the custody officer:

- take no further action;
- give an informal warning;
- issue a penalty notice;
- administer a reprimand or warning;
- report for summons; and
- charge.

No further action

7.276   Even if there is sufficient evidence to secure a conviction, a decision may be taken to take no further action, if it is considered not to be in the public interest to take the matter any further.

---

231 Code D Annex C para 13.
232 Code D para 2.15.
233 Code D Annex D para 3.
234 Code D Annex D para 6.
235 Code D Annex D para 4.
236 Code D para 2.15.
237 Code D Annex D para 5.

Informal warning

7.277 Even with the existence of reprimands and warnings, there is still the possibility of an informal warning. This is expressly acknowledged by the Association of Chief Police Officers whose publication *Youth Offender Case Disposal Gravity Factor System* gives the following guidance:

> An 'informal warning' which falls outside the parameters of [the normal gravity score response – see para 9.20 and appendix 5], should only be given in exceptional circumstances where a minimal response is appropriate and usually when anti-social behaviour falls short of a substantive criminal offence. It may be administered instantly by the officer in the case, or by letter if the decision is made by a police decision-maker, when the case against the young person is unlikely to be proceeded with in the Youth Court.

Penalty notice

7.278 A constable who has reason to believe that a person aged 10 or over has committed a penalty offence may give him/her a penalty notice in respect of the offence.[238]

7.279   A penalty notice may be given in the street without the need for the person to be arrested. Unless the penalty notice is given in a police station, the constable giving it must be in uniform.[239] The giving of a penalty notice is not a criminal conviction.

Penalty offence

7.280 The various penalty offences are set out in table 7.

Notification of parent or guardian

7.281 Where a person under the age of 16 has received a penalty notice, the police must notify the parent or guardian in writing of the giving of the penalty notice. The written notice must have a copy of the penalty notice attached and may be served in person or by first class post.[240]

Payment of the penalty

7.282 If the person receiving the penalty notice decides to pay the penalty, it should be paid to the magistrates' court specified in the notice within 21 days.[241]

7.283   If payment is not made within that period nor is any challenge is made to the notice, the penalty will increase by 50 per cent and will be enforced as a fine.[242]

---

238 Criminal Justice and Police Act 2001 s2(1) as amended by the Penalties for Disorderly Behaviour (Amendment of Minimum Age) Order 2004 SI No 3166.

239 Ibid, s2(2).

240 Penalties for Disorderly Behaviour (Amendment of Minimum Age) Order 2004 SI No 3166 article 3.

241 Criminal Justice and Police Act 2001 s5(1) and (2).

242 Ibid, s4(5).

Table 7: Offences for which a penalty notice may be issued

Offences attracting penalty of £80 for persons 16 and over, or £40 for persons under 16

- Knowingly giving a false alarm to a fire brigade (Fire Services Act 1947 s31)
- Wasting police time or giving false report (Criminal Law Act 1967 s5(2))
- Nuisance telephone calls (Telecommunications Act 1984 s43(1)(b))
- Disorderly behaviour (Public Order Act 1986 s5)
- Theft (Theft Act 1968 s1) – maximum value £200
- Criminal damage (Criminal Damage Act 1971) – maximum value £500
- Throwing fireworks in a public thoroughfare (Explosives Act 1875 s80)

Offences attracting penalty of £50 for persons 16 and over, or £30 for persons under 16

- Being drunk in a highway, other public place or licensed premises (Licensing Act 1872 s12)
- Trespassing on a railway (British Transport Commission Act 1949 s55)
- Throwing stones etc or other things on railways (British Transport Commission Act 1949 s56)
- Buying or attempting to buy alcohol for consumption in a bar in licensed premises by a person under 18 (Licensing Act 1964 s169C(3))
- Disorderly behaviour while drunk in a public place (Criminal Justice Act 1967 s91)
- Consumption of alcohol in designated public place (Criminal Justice and Police Act 2001 s12)

Penalties for Disorderly Behaviour (Amount of Penalty) Order 2002 SI No 1837 as amended by Penalties for Disorderly Behaviour (Amount of Penalty) (Amendment No 4) Order 2004 SI No 3371

Liability of parent or guardian to pay penalty

7.284 Where a parent or guardian of a person under the age of 16 is notified in writing of the giving of a penalty notice, s/he is liable to pay the penalty under the notice.[243] The parent or guardian must pay the notice within 21 days of receipt of the notice.[244] If payment is not made, enforcement will be against the parent or guardian rather than the child or young person.[245]

Challenging the penalty notice

7.285 To dispute the penalty notice written notice must be sent to the magistrates' court specified in the notice stating that the child or young person

---

243 Penalties for Disorderly Behaviour (Amendment of Minimum Age) Order 2004 SI No 3166 article 5.

244 Ibid.

245 Criminal Justice and Police Act 2001 s4(5) as amended by the Penalties for Disorderly Behaviour (Amendment of Minimum Age) Order 2004 SI No 3166 article 6.

wishes to be tried for the offence.²⁴⁶ This must be done within 21 days of receiving the notice.²⁴⁷ Such a notice is termed a 'request to be tried'.²⁴⁸

Reprimands and warnings

7.286   When considering how to dispose of a case, the custody officer must take account of the existence of reprimands and warnings as an alternative to prosecution.²⁴⁹ The law and guidance on reprimands and warnings is considered in chapter 9.

Charge

7.287   The new statutory procedure for deciding whether to charge a suspect is considered in chapter 8.

Bail prior to charge

Bail to allow further investigation by police

7.288   Where there is no longer a need for the suspect to be detained whilst the investigation continues, the custody officer may release the suspect on bail with a duty to surrender to the police station at a specified time while further enquiries are made.²⁵⁰ The bail period will be used to take further witness statements, arrange identification procedures or submit evidence for laboratory analysis.

7.289   When the bail to return is for the purpose of gathering further evidence, the custody officer has no power to impose bail conditions.

7.290   During the period of bail, essential witness statements will be taken or investigations into the suspect's explanation of events.

Bail to determine disposal

7.291   Where the custody officer considers that there is sufficient evidence to charge the person arrested with an offence, s/he may, rather than charging the suspect, release the suspect on bail:

- for a prosecutor to determine the disposal;²⁵¹ or
- to refer to a youth offending team to assess the young suspect with a view to a reprimand or warning being administered; or
- to allow a reprimand or warning to be administered by a trained officer or as part of a restorative process.²⁵²

---

246 Criminal Justice and Police Act 2001 s4(2) and (3).
247 Ibid.
248 Ibid, s4(4).
249 Code C Note for Guidance 16A.
250 Police and Criminal Evidence Act 1984 s47(2).
251 Ibid, s37(7)(a).
252 Ibid, s34(5)(b).

7.292 Where bail is granted to refer the case to a prosecutor to determine disposal, the custody sergeant has the power to impose conditions on the bail.[253] In the other circumstances there is no such power.

Failure to answer police bail

7.293 If the suspect fails to answer his/her bail, s/he commits an offence under Bail Act 1976 s6. The power to prosecute the offence is subject to time limits.

7.294 A constable may arrest without a warrant any person who fails to return on bail to a police station at the appointed place and time.[254] The suspect must be taken to the police station appointed as the place at which to surrender to custody as soon as practicable after the arrest.[255]

Charge

Procedure

7.295 When a detainee is charged with, or informed they may be prosecuted for, an offence, s/he shall be cautioned as follows:

> You do not have to say anything, but it may harm your defence if you do not mention now something which you later rely on in court. Anything you do say may be given in evidence.[256]

7.296 A record must be made of anything said upon charge.[257] A court may draw an inference from the fact that a suspect does not mention when charged a fact, which in the circumstances existing at the time s/he could reasonably have been expected to mention, and which s/he subsequently relies upon in his/her defence.[258]

7.297 When a detainee is charged, he/she shall be given a written notice showing particulars of the offence. As far as possible, the particulars of the charge shall be stated in simple terms, but they shall also show the precise offence in law with which the detainee is charged.[259]

Presence of appropriate adult

7.298 If the appropriate adult is present at the police station when a juvenile is to be charged:

- the charging procedure should be carried out in his/her presence;[260] and
- a copy of the charge sheet should be given to him/her.[261]

253 Police and Criminal Evidence Act 1984 s47(1A).
254 Ibid, s46A(1).
255 Ibid, s46A(2).
256 Code C para 16.2.
257 Code C para 16.8.
258 Criminal Justice and Public Order Act 1994 s34(1)(b).
259 Code C para 16.3.
260 Code C para 16.1.
261 Code C para 16.3.

7.299   Code C Note for Guidance 16C states that there is no power to detain a person and delay charge solely to await the arrival of the appropriate adult.

Choice of court for first appearance

7.300   In general, a child or young person will appear before a youth court unless an adult co-defendant is involved.[262] Custody officers sometimes overlook this rule, particularly with 17-year-olds, therefore it is advisable for the defence lawyer to check that the correct court has been chosen.

Bail granted

7.301   Where a custody officer grants bail after charge, s/he shall appoint for the first court appearance:

- a date which is not later than the first sitting of the local court after the accused is charged with an offence; or
- where the custody officer is informed by the clerk to the justices for the relevant local justice area that the appearance cannot be accommodated until a later date, that later date.[263]

Bail refused

7.302   If a child or young person has been refused bail and either kept in police custody or transferred to local authority accommodation, s/he must be produced at the next available court sitting.[264] If no youth court is due to sit the next day, special arrangements may be made to convene a youth bench or, more frequently, the accused will be sent to the adult court.[265]

Drug testing after charge

7.303   A sample of urine or a non-intimate sample may be taken from a person in police detention for the purpose ascertaining whether s/he has heroin or cocaine in his/her body. A person who fails without good cause to give a sample shall be guilty of an offence.[266]

Pre-conditions

7.304   Drug testing may only take place if the suspect has attained the age of 14 and has been charged with:

- a trigger offence; or
- any offence but only if a police officer of at least the rank of inspector,

262 Children and Young Persons Act 1933 s46(1): For the various exceptions to this rule see para 11.86ff.

263 Police and Criminal Evidence Act 1984 s47(3A) as inserted by Crime and Disorder Act 1998 s46.

264 Ibid, s47(2).

265 Children and Young Persons Act s46(2).

266 Police and Criminal Evidence Act 1984 s63B(8). The maximum penalty in the case of an adult is three months' imprisonment, therefore a detention and training order could not be imposed upon a child or young person.

who has reasonable grounds for suspecting the misuse by the suspect of heroin or cocaine caused or contributed to the offence, has authorised the sample to be taken.[267]

7.305 A 'trigger offence' is an offence specified in Criminal Justice and Court Services Act 2000 Sch 6 (for which see appendix 8).[268]

Procedure

7.306 Before requesting the suspect to give a sample, a police officer must:
- warn the suspect that he commits a criminal offence if s/he refuses to supply sample when requested to do so;
- (if relevant) inform him/her that specific authorisation has been granted by an inspector and the reasons for that authorisation.[269]

7.307 In the case of a juvenile, an appropriate adult must be present for:
- the request for a sample;
- the giving of the warning regarding refusal to provide a sample and any explanation for specific authorisation; and
- the taking of the sample.[270]

7.308 A custody officer may authorise continued detention for up to six hours from the time of charge to enable a sample to be taken.[271]

Use of the drug test result

7.309 Information obtained from a sample may be disclosed for any of the following purposes:
- to inform any decision about granting bail in criminal proceedings;
- where the young suspect is in police detention or remanded in custody by a court, to help determine the nature of his/her supervision in custody;
- where the young suspect has been granted bail, to help determine the nature of his/her supervision by the youth offending team;
- where a suspect is convicted of an offence, to help a court decide on the appropriate sentence;
- to inform the decision about a convicted offender's supervision or release.[272]

7.310 Drug testing samples and the information derived from them may not be subsequently used in the investigation of any offence or in evidence against the detained person.[273]

---

267 Police and Criminal Evidence Act 1984 s63B(2).
268 Ibid, s63B(6).
269 Ibid, s63B(5).
270 Code C para 17.5.
271 Police and Criminal Evidence Act 1984 s38(1)(iiia), (2).
272 Ibid, s63B(7).
273 Code C Note for Guidance 17D.

Bail after charge

7.311　Following charge, Police and Criminal Evidence Act 1984 s38 requires the custody officer (subject to Criminal Justice and Public Order Act 1994 s25[274]) to order the release of the detainee on bail unless:

- the detainee's name or address cannot be ascertained or the custody officer has reasonable grounds for doubting whether a name or address furnished by the detainee as his/her name or address is his/her real name or address;
- the custody officer has reasonable grounds for believing that the person arrested will fail to appear in court to answer bail;
- (in the case of a person arrested for an imprisonable offence) the custody officer has reasonable grounds for believing that the detention of the person is necessary to prevent him/her from committing an offence;
- (in the case of a person arrested for a non-imprisonable offence) the custody officer has reasonable grounds for believing that the detention of the person is necessary to prevent him/her from causing physical injury to any other person or from causing loss or damage to property;
- the custody officer has reasonable grounds for believing that the detention of the person is necessary to prevent him/her from interfering with the administration of justice or with the investigation of offences or a particular offence;
- the custody officer has reasonable grounds for believing that the detention of the person is necessary for his/her own protection;
- in the case of a juvenile, the custody officer has reasonable grounds for believing that s/he ought to be detained in his/her own interests.[275]

7.312　There is no definition of a juvenile's 'own interests', but the fact that it exists as a separate grounds for detention must mean that it has a wider meaning than the juvenile's physical safety which would be covered by the penultimate exception. It has been invoked by custody officers who are concerned about the juvenile's health or moral well-being – for example, when the juvenile is known to misuse solvents or to be involved in prostitution. It should be noted that even if bail has been refused in the juvenile's interests, there will still be an obligation to transfer to local authority accommodation.[276]

7.313　Code C Note for Guidance 16C makes it very clear that after charge, bail cannot be refused, or release on bail delayed, simply because an appropriate adult is not available, unless the absence of that adult provides the custody officer with the necessary grounds to authorise detention after charge under Police and Criminal Evidence Act 1984 s38.

274　See para 13.32.
275　Police and Criminal Evidence Act 1984 s38(1).
276　See para 7.319 below.

Conditional bail

7.314 The custody officer has the power to impose conditions on bail granted under the following provisions of the Police and Criminal Evidence Act 1984:

- section 37(7)(a) (bail to seek prosecutor's advice on disposal);
- section 38 (bail after charge).[277]

7.315 The accused has a right to unconditional bail unless the custody officer is satisfied that conditions are necessary:

(a) for the purposes of preventing the accused from:
- failing to surrender;
- committing an offence while on bail;
- interfering with witnesses;
- otherwise obstructing the course of justice whether in relation to him/herself or any other person; or

(b) for the accused's own protection; or

(c) in the case of a juvenile, for his/her own welfare or in his/her own interests.[278]

7.316 The custody officer may impose any condition available to a court,[279] except a condition of residence in a probation hostel.[280]

7.317 In the case of bail after charge, there seems no reason in principle why a youth offending team could not offer a bail supervision and support package for a child or young person in serious risk of being refused bail by a custody officer. In practice this is extremely rare.

7.318 Application may be made to a custody officer or a court for variation of the bail conditions (see paras 13.105 onwards).

Transfer to local authority accommodation

Duty to transfer

7.319 In the case of a juvenile refused bail under Police and Criminal Evidence Act 1984 s38(1), the custody officer shall secure that the detained juvenile is moved to local authority accommodation unless:

- it is impracticable for the custody officer to do so; or
- in the case of a juvenile aged 12 to 16, no secure accommodation is available and keeping him/her in other local authority accommodation would not be adequate to protect the public from serious harm from him/her.[281]

The custody officer has a wide discretion in deciding which local authority to approach.[282] This means that a local authority which already has a

277 Police and Criminal Evidence Act 1984 s47(1A).
278 Bail Act 1976 s3A(5).
279 The practical considerations of bail conditions imposed upon children and young persons are considered in detail in chapter 13.
280 Bail Act 1976 s3A(2).
281 Police and Criminal Evidence Act 1984 s38(6).
282 *R (on the application of M) v Gateshead Council* [2006] EWCA Civ 221.

connection with a juvenile may be approached if the custody officer considers it appropriate, even if the juvenile is not currently detained in that authority's area.

After charge

7.320   The duty to transfer applies when the custody officer has refused bail under section 38(1), that is 'where a person arrested for an offence otherwise than under a warrant endorsed for bail is charged with an offence'. There is therefore no obligation upon the custody officer to secure a juvenile's move to local authority accommodation in the following circumstances:

- when a juvenile is arrested on a court warrant not backed for bail; or
- when a juvenile is arrested for breach of bail conditions under Bail Act 1976 s7 or for breach of remand conditions under Children and Young Persons Act 1969 s23A.

Local authority accommodation

7.321   This is defined as 'accommodation provided by or on behalf of a local authority (within the meaning of the Children Act 1989)'.[283] The choice of accommodation remains in the discretion of the local authority. It could include a placement back with parents, a remand foster placement, a residential children's home or secure accommodation. When exercising this discretion, the Department of Health has advised local authorities 'to have regard to the fact that the police custody officer has not ordered the juvenile's release from police detention, either on bail or without bail'.[284]

Secure accommodation

7.322   'Secure accommodation' means accommodation provided for the purpose of restricting liberty.[285] Upon receiving a child or young person from police detention, the local authority may only place him/her in secure accommodation if it appears that any accommodation other than that provided for the purpose of restricting liberty is inappropriate because:

(a) the child is likely to abscond from such other accommodation; or

(b) the child is likely to injure him/herself or other people if he is kept in any such other accommodation.[286]

7.323   The local authority may only keep a child or young person in secure accommodation without the authority of a court for a maximum of 72 hours.[287]

Custody officer to produce certificate

7.324   If a juvenile is not transferred to local authority accommodation, the custody officer must certify which exception applied. If no transfer took place

---

283   Police and Criminal Evidence Act 1984 s38(6A).
284   *The Children Act 1989 Guidance and Regulations* (HMSO, 1991), Vol 1, Court Orders, para 6.40.
285   Police and Criminal Evidence Act 1984 s38(6A).
286   Children (Secure Accommodation) Regulations 1991 SI No 1505 reg 6.
287   Ibid, reg 10.

because it was impracticable to do so, the certificate should specify the circumstances which resulted in this.[288]

7.325　The certificate signed by the custody officer must be produced to the court before which the juvenile is first brought.[289] In the experience of the authors, the contents of the certificate are never considered in any court hearing.

Exceptions to the duty to transfer

Transfer is impracticable

7.326　It is suggested that this should be interpreted narrowly, applying only if it is physically impossible to secure a move to local authority accommodation. This interpretation is supported by Home Office Circular No 78/1992 *Criminal Justice Act 1991: Detention etc of Juveniles* which states:

> The circumstances in which a transfer would be impracticable are those, and only those, in which it is physically impossible to place the juvenile in local authority accommodation. These might include extreme weather conditions (e.g. floods or blizzards), or the impossibility of contacting the local authority.

7.327　A wider definition of impracticable was contemplated by the Divisional Court in *R v Chief Constable of Cambridgeshire ex p Michel*.[290] Here it was held that it would be impracticable to transfer to local authority accommodation if no secure accommodation was available and in the custody officer's opinion secure accommodation is the only type of accommodation suitable to avoid the consequences which led to the decision to refuse bail. This decision would seem to have been overruled by the Criminal Justice Act 1991 which created the separate exception of protection of the public.[291] This point is made clear by the Codes of Practice:

> ... neither a juvenile's behaviour nor the nature of the offence provides grounds for the custody officer to decide that it is impracticable to seek to arrange for juvenile's transfer to local authority care. Similarly, the lack of secure local authority accommodation does not make it impracticable to transfer the juvenile. The availability of secure accommodation is only a factor in relation to a juvenile aged 12 or over when the local authority accommodation would not be adequate to protect the public from serious harm from the juvenile. The obligation to transfer a juvenile to local authority accommodation applies as much to a juvenile charged during the daytime as it does to a juvenile to be held overnight ...[292]

Protection of public from serious harm

7.328　This exception applies to both males and females. The custody officer must first determine whether the juvenile presents a risk of serious harm to the public. It is only if a risk of serious harm is identified can the custody officer refuse to transfer to local authority accommodation.

288　Police and Criminal Evidence Act 1984 s38(6).
289　Ibid, s38(7).
290　(1990) 91 Cr App R 325; [1991] Crim LR 382, QBD.
291　This view is endorsed by Home Office Circular No 78/1992.
292　Code C Note for Guidance 16D.

7.329   'Serious harm' is defined as follows:

> any reference, in relation to an arrested juvenile charged with a violent or sexual offence, to protecting the public from serious harm from him shall be construed as a reference to protecting members of the public from death or serious personal injury, whether physical or psychological, occasioned by further such offences committed by him.[293]

7.330   A 'violent offence' is defined as murder or an offence specified in Criminal Justice Act 2003 Sch 15 Part 1 (see appendix 7).[294]

7.331   A 'sexual offence' is defined as an offence specified in Criminal Justice Act 2003 Sch 15 Part 2 (see appendix 7).[295]

7.332   There is no statutory definition of 'serious harm' in relation to other offences. The Home Office Circular 78/1992 does, however, offer the following guidance:

> 'Serious harm' is not defined in relation to other offences. However, the definition for sexual or violent offences suggests the gravity of the harm to which the public would have to be exposed from a juvenile charged with any other offence before the test is likely to be satisfied.

Arguing for a transfer

7.333   In the authors' experience it is extremely rare that a juvenile is transferred from police detention to local authority accommodation, even where there are no grounds for asserting that the juvenile presents a risk of serious harm to the public. This is partly explained by considerable police resistance to the requirement coupled with unwarranted demands for secure accommodation to be provided. Another major problem is the failure of local authorities to provide accommodation to allow the transfer to take place, particularly if the juvenile refused bail is not already a looked after child.

7.334   Despite the practical difficulties, it is important for the defence lawyer to challenge any decision not to transfer, if at all possible. Having a juvenile produced from local authority accommodation rather than police detention can have a significant impact upon the choice of remand placement made by the court before which the juvenile is first produced. The fact that the juvenile has been accommodated overnight by the local authority and produced at court can demonstrate to the court that s/he can be successfully supervised in the community.

7.335   Where a defence lawyer is told by the custody officer that a transfer will not take place because no accommodation is available, the defence lawyer should contact the local authority directly. In office hours this may involve contacting the local youth offending team or the local social services department; out of office hours it is likely to involve contacting the emergency duty team social worker. The person who is spoken to may not be familiar with the local authority's legal obligations and s/he will need to be referred to:

- the statutory duty under Children Act 1989 s21(2)(b) to receive and provide accommodation for children refused police bail; and

---

293   Police and Criminal Evidence Act 1984 s38(6A).
294   Ibid.
295   Ibid.

- the requirement under para 2.10 of the *National Standards for Youth Justice Services* (2004) for local authorities to ensure that beds are available to comply with this statutory duty.

7.336   If it proves possible to persuade the local authority to provide a bed, the defence lawyer will then need to return to the custody officer. If reference to the relevant law and guidance still does not produce the desired result, the defence lawyer will need to consider lodging a complaint with the relevant duty officer that the custody officer is not fulfilling his/her legal duties (see below).

7.337   Where the defence solicitor experiences frequent problems with the lack of local authority accommodation, s/he should consider lodging a complaint that the local authority is not providing a particular service to children in its area as required by the Children Act 1989 (see para 3.119).

Complaints

7.338   The Police Reform Act 2002 established the Independent Police Complaints Authority and a new statutory framework for the making of complaints about police conduct.[296]

Who can make a complaint?

7.339   The statutory framework applies to complaints about the conduct of a person serving with the police which is made (whether in writing or otherwise) by:

- a member of the public in relation to whom the conduct took place;
- a member of the public who was adversely affected by the conduct;
- a member of the public who witnessed the conduct; or
- a person acting on behalf of any of the above.[297]

7.340   A complaint may be made by a child or young person in his/her own right. The Independent Police Complaints Commission provides the following advice to police services:

> Where a young person under the age of 16 wishes to make a complaint, the IPCC encourages the police to have regard to the principle in the Gillick Competency Guidelines that children under the age of 16 years are able, under Common Law, to give valid consent provided they have sufficient understanding and intelligence to enable them to understand fully what is involved. Applying this to the complaints system means that as long as the child under 16 understands fully what is involved in making a complaint they should be able to do so. However the police service, and the IPCC, have a responsibility to ensure a young person making a complaint does understand the process and potential outcomes and where necessary is provided with appropriate support in making the complaint. The IPCC will work with the police and with young people's organisations on this issue.
>
> ...

296 For a more detailed treatment of the law relating to the making of a complaint regarding police conduct, see Harrison et al, *Police Misconduct: legal remedies*, Legal Action Group, 2005, 4th edition.

297 Police Reform Act 2002 s12(1).

A complaint can be made on behalf of a child or young person by a parent or guardian or a third party.[298]

7.341   It is clear from this guidance that a complaint from a child or young person who is deemed to be of sufficient age and understanding does not need the permission of a parent or guardian.

Recording a complaint

7.342   When a complaint is made, it is the duty of the police to record it.[299] Code C para 9.2 gives the following guidance when a complaint is made while in police custody:

> If a complaint is made by, or on behalf of, a detainee about their treatment since their arrest, or it comes to notice that a detainee may have been treated improperly, a report must be made as soon as practicable to an officer of inspector rank or above not connected with the investigation. If the matter concerns a possible assault or the possibility of the unnecessary or unreasonable use of force, an appropriate health care professional must also be called as soon as practicable.

7.343   It is usual for the duty inspector to take brief details of the complaint and then to pass the complaint onto the relevant complaints unit who will later contact the complainant to take a full statement and identify any potential witnesses to the incident.

Responses to a complaint

7.344   Once a complaint has been recorded it may be the subject of:

- local resolution;
- local investigation; or
- in certain cases specified cases, referral to the Independent Police Complaints Commission.

Local resolution

7.345   This is intended to be a relatively quick and straightforward process involving the station inspector or police staff manager or at Basic Command Unit level. The complainant must give consent to the complaint being dealt with in this way.[300] This consent must be based on sound information and a clear understanding of what will and will not happen before consent is given.[301] Local resolution of the complaint may result in an apology by the officer concerned or a manager or by an oral or written explanation for the police conduct. The Independent Police Complaints Commission encourages police forces to work to wards an average of 28 days for dealing with complaints by way of local resolution.[302]

---

298 Independent Police Complaints Commission, *Making the new police complaints system work better: Statutory guidance* (December 2005), para 5.1.9.

299 Police Reform Act 2002 Sch 3 para 2(6).

300 Ibid, Sch 3 para 6(2), (6) and (7).

301 Independent Police Complaints Commission, *Making the new police complaints system work better: Statutory guidance* (December 2005), para 5.3.1.

302 Ibid, para 5.3.8.

Local investigation

7.346 An investigation will involve the appointment of a single person serving with the police, referred to as the investigating officer. S/he will investigate the complaint and prepare a written report which will be submitted to the appropriate authority. The level of an investigation should be proportionate both to the seriousness of the allegation or incident being investigated and to the likelihood of a criminal or disciplinary outcome.[303] The complainant should be kept informed of the progress of the investigation at least every 28 days.[304]

Referral to Independent Police Complaints Commission

7.347 The police must refer to the Commission any incidents where persons have died or been seriously injured following some form of direct or indirect contact with the police and there is reason to believe that the contact may have caused or contributed to the death or serious injury.[305]

7.348 The police must also refer to the Commission complaints which include the following allegations:

- serious assault by a member of the police service;
- serious sexual assault by a member of the police service;
- serious corruption;
- criminal offence or behaviour aggravated by discriminatory behaviour; or
- serious arrestable offences.[306]

7.349 Depending on the seriousness of the case, the Commission may determine to investigate the complaint by way of:

- an independent investigation by a commission staff;
- a managed investigation conducted by the police under the direction and control of the Commission;
- a supervised investigation where a Commission commissioner approves the choice of investigating officer and the terms of reference for the investigation; or
- referral back to the relevant police service for local investigation.

Appeals to the Independent Police Complaints Commission

7.350 A complainant who is not satisfied with the outcome of a local or supervised investigation may appeal to the Commission within 28 days of notification of the outcome of the investigation.

---

303 Independent Police Complaints Commission, *Making the new police complaints system work better: Statutory guidance* (December 2005), para 5.4.2.
304 Police (Complaints and Misconduct) Regulations 2004 SI No 643 reg 11.
305 Police Reform Act 2002 Sch 3 paras 4(1)(a) and 13(1)(a).
306 Police (Complaints and Misconduct) Regulations 2004 SI No 643 regs 2(2) and 5(1).

The decision to prosecute

The statutory charging scheme

8.1　The new statutory charging system was introduced by the Criminal Justice Act 2003. Its application is governed by guidance issued by the Director of Public Prosecutions under Police and Criminal Evidence Act 1984 s37A.

Charging by prosecutors

8.2　Prosecutors are responsible for the decision to charge and the specifying or drafting of the charges in all indictable-only, either-way or summary offences where the custody officer determines that there is sufficient evidence to secure a conviction.[1]

8.3　To facilitate the referral of charging decisions, duty prosecutors are now based in police stations during office hours. When there is no prosecutor available in the police station, the charging decision is referred to CPS Direct.

Charging by prosecutors – transitional arrangements

8.4　Implementation of the above principle will be achieved incrementally. Until implementation has been effected, the police may determine the charge in any either-way or summary offence (except for those offences listed in table 8 below) where it appears to the custody sergeant that:

- a guilty plea is likely; and
- the case is suitable for sentencing in the magistrates' court.[2]

Charging by the police

8.5　The police retain the power to determine the charge in some cases, including:

- any offence under the Road Traffic Acts except where:
  (a) the circumstances have resulted in the death of any person;
  (b) there is an allegation of dangerous driving;
  (c) the allegation is one of driving whilst disqualified and the has been no admission in a police interview to both driving and disqualification; or
  (d) the statutory defence of being in charge of a motor vehicle may be raised; or
  (e) there is an allegation of the unlawful taking of a motor vehicle or the aggravated taking of a motor vehicle (unless the case is suitable for disposal as an early guilty plea);
- an offence of failing to answer bail under Bail Act 1976 s6;
- an offence of disorderly behaviour contrary to Public Order Act 1986 s5; and
- any summary offence punishable on conviction with a term of imprisonment of three months or less except where guidance requires the offence to be dealt with by a prosecutor).[3]

1　*The Director's Guidance on Charging* (January 2005), para 3.1.
2　Ibid, para 3.2(ii).
3　Ibid, para 3.3.

Table 8: Offences or circumstances which must always be referred to a Crown prosecutor for early consultation and charging decision – whether admitted or not

- Offences requiring the consent of the Attorney-General or Director of Public Prosecution
- Any indictable-only offence
- Any either-way offence triable only on indictment due to the surrounding circumstances of the commission of the offence or the previous convictions of the offender

Insofar as not covered by the above:

- Offences under the Terrorism Act 2000 or any other offence linked with terrorist activity
- Offences under the Anti-terrorism, Crime and Security Act 2001
- Offences under the Explosive Substances Act 1883
- Offences under any of the Official Secrets Acts
- Offences involving any racial, religious or homophobic aggravation
- Offences under the Sexual Offences Act 2003 committed by or upon persons under the age of 18 years
- The following specific offences:
  - Wounding or inflicting grievous bodily harm, contrary to Offences Against the Person Act 1861 s20
  - Assault occasioning actual bodily harm, contrary to Offences Against the Person Act 1861 s47
  - Violent Disorder contrary to Public Order Act 1986 s2
  - Affray, contrary to Public Order Act 1986 s3
  - Offences involving deception, contrary to the Theft Acts 1968 and 1978
  - Handling stolen goods, contrary to Theft Act 1968 s22

Police discretion to administer a reprimand or caution

8.6 The police retain the discretion to administer a reprimand or warning without reference to a prosecutor, except in the case of indictable-only offences.

Directing the administration of a reprimand or warning

8.7 When the police refer a child or young person's case to a prosecutor for pre-charge advice, the prosecutor has the power to direct that s/he be given a reprimand or warning.[4]

8.8 If the prosecutor's decision is that the child or young person should be given a reprimand or warning in respect of the offence and it proves not to be possible to administer the reprimand or warning, s/he shall instead be charged with the offence.[5]

4 Police and Criminal Evidence Act 1984 s37B(6).
5 Ibid, s37B(7).

Code for Crown Prosecutors

8.9 The Code is issued under Prosecution of Offenders Act 1985 s10. The current version of the Code was issued in 2004.[6] Applying the Code, the prosecutor must determine whether:

- there is sufficient admissible evidence to secure a conviction; and
- a prosecution is the public interest.

Full Code test

8.10 Prosecutors must be satisfied that there is enough evidence to provide a 'realistic prospect of conviction' against each defendant on each charge.[7] A realistic prospect of conviction is an objective test. It means that a jury or bench of magistrates, properly directed in accordance with the law, is more likely than not to convict the defendant of the charge alleged.[8] In considering whether there is enough evidence to convict, the prosecutor must consider whether the evidence is admissible and reliable.[9]

Threshold test

8.11 In cases where the accused is not considered suitable for release on bail, the prosecutor may decide to charge even though there is not at present sufficient evidence to secure a conviction. In such circumstances, the prosecutor must consider if the evidence meets the threshold test – that is, whether there is at least a reasonable suspicion against the person of having committed an offence and that at that stage it is in the public interest to proceed.[10]

Public interest

8.12 Even if the Crown Prosecutor is satisfied that there is sufficient evidence to secure a conviction, it does not automatically follow that the prosecution will proceed.[11] The Code states:

> The public interest must be considered in each case where there is enough evidence to provide a realistic prospect of conviction. Although there may be public interest factors against prosecution in a particular case, often the prosecution should go ahead and those factors should be put to the court for consideration when sentence is being passed. A prosecution will usually take place unless there are public interest factors tending against prosecution which clearly outweigh those tending in favour, or it appears more appropriate in all the circumstances of the case to divert the person from prosecution.

8.13 The various factors for and against a prosecution listed in the Code are listed at table 9 below. Where the prosecutor is applying the threshold test,

---

6 Copies of the Code in English and a number of other languages may be obtained from CPS Headquarters or downloaded from the CPS website.

7 Crown Prosecution Service, *Code for Crown Prosecutors* (2004), para 5.2.

8 Ibid, para 5.3.

9 Ibid, para 5.4.

10 Ibid, paras 6.1 and 6.2.

11 Ibid, para 5.6.

Table 9: Code for Crown Prosecutors: public interest factors

Some common public interest factors in favour of prosecution

A prosecution is likely to be needed if:

(a)   a conviction is likely to result in a significant sentence;

(b)   a conviction is likely to result in a confiscation or any other order;

(c)   a weapon was used or violence was threatened during the commission of the offence;

(d)   the offence was committed against a person serving the public (for example, a police or prison officer, or a nurse);

(e)   the defendant was in a position of authority or trust;

(f)   the evidence shows that the defendant was a ringleader or an organiser of the offence;

(g)   there is evidence that the offence was premeditated;

(h)   there is evidence that the offence was carried out by a group;

(i)   the victim of the offence was vulnerable, has been put in considerable fear, or suffered personal attack, damage or disturbance;

(j)   the offence was committed in the presence of, or in close proximity to, a child;

(k)   the offence was motivated by any form of discrimination against the victim's ethnic or national origin, disability, sex, religious beliefs, political views or sexual orientation, or the suspect demonstrated hostility towards the victim based on any of those characteristics;

(l)   there is a marked difference between the actual or mental ages of the defendant and the victim, or if there is any element of corruption;

(m) the defendant's previous convictions or cautions are relevant to the present offence;

(n)   the defendant is alleged to have committed the offence while under an order of the court;

(o)   there are grounds for believing that the offence is likely to be continued or repeated , for example, by a history of recurring conduct;

(p)   the offence, although not serious in itself, is widespread in the area where it was committed; or

(q)   a prosecution would have a significant positive impact on maintaining community confidence.

Some common public interest factors against prosecution

A prosecution is less likely to be needed if:

(a)   the court is likely to impose a nominal penalty;

(b)   the defendant has already been made the subject of a sentence and any further conviction would be unlikely to result in the imposition of an additional sentence or order, unless the nature of the particular offence requires a prosecution or the defendant withdraws consent to have an offence taken into consideration during sentencing;

(c)   the offence was committed as a result of a genuine mistake or misunderstanding (these factors must be balanced against the seriousness of the offence);

(d)   the loss or harm can be described as minor and was the result of a single incident, particularly if it was caused by a misjudgment;

(e)   there has been a long delay between the offence taking place and the date of the trial, unless:

- the offence is serious;
- the delay has been caused in part by the defendant;
- the offence has only recently come to light; or
- the complexity of the offence has meant that there has been a long investigation;

(f)   a prosecution is likely to have a bad effect on the victim's physical or mental health, always bearing in mind the seriousness of the offence;

(g)   the defendant is elderly or is, or was at the time of the offence, suffering from significant mental or physical ill health, unless the offence is serious or there is real possibility that it may be repeated;

(h)   the defendant has put right the loss or harm that was caused (but defendants must not avoid prosecution or diversion solely because they pay compensation); or

(i)   details may be made public that could harm sources of information, international relations or national security.

s/he will still have to consider the public interest on the information available at the time, which may very well be limited.[12] The public interest test will need to be considered again when the full Code test is applied.

Views of the victim

8.14   Although the victim's views regarding a prosecution are important, the Code makes it clear that those views cannot override a proper consideration of public interest factors:

> The Crown Prosecution Service does not act for victims or the families of victims in the same way as solicitors act for their clients. Crown Prosecutors act on behalf of the public and not just in the interests of any particular individual. However, when considering the public interest, Crown Prosecutors should always take into account the consequences for the victim of whether or not to prosecute, and any views expressed by the victim or the victim's family.[13]

Diversion from prosecution

8.15   When considering whether to divert a child or young person from the criminal courts, the Code states:

> Crown Prosecutors must consider the interests of a youth when deciding whether it is in the public interest to prosecute. However Crown Prosecutors

12   Crown Prosecution Service, *Code for Crown Prosecutors* (2004), para 6.5.
13   Ibid, para 5.12.

should not avoid prosecuting simply because of the defendant's age. The seriousness of the offence or the youth's past behaviour is very important.

Cases involving youths are usually only referred to the Crown Prosecution Service for prosecution if the youth has already received a reprimand and final warning, unless the offence is so serious that neither of these were appropriate or the youth does not admit committing the offence. Reprimands and final warnings are intended to prevent re-offending and the fact that a further offence has occurred indicates that attempts to divert the youth from the court system have not been effective. So the public interest will usually require a prosecution in such cases, unless there are clear public interest factors against prosecution.[14]

Duty to keep prosecution under review

8.16   Once a person has been charged, there is an ongoing duty upon the prosecutor to keep the decision to prosecute under active review, particularly when there has been a change of circumstances.[15]

Specific considerations for children and young persons

8.17   As well as the general principles contained in the Code for Crown Prosecutors, there are also a number of sources of specific guidance in relation to charging children or young persons with certain offences. This guidance is considered below.

Youth offender specialists

8.18   A youth offender specialist is a designated prosecutor who has undertaken the Crown Prosecution Service youth offender course. Youth offender specialists will be expected to appear regularly in the youth court. A youth offender specialist should undertake the major reviews of files involving children and young persons and take all major decisions in relation to those files.[16]

School bullying

8.19   The Legal Guidance issued by the Crown Prosecution Service states:

Prosecution may not be necessary because of other available alternatives, but there will be cases in which a prosecution is needed in the public interest.

In cases of serious or persistent bullying, prosecutions must be carefully considered. Such cases usually involve one pupil or a group of pupils using their strength or power to induce fear in the victimised pupil, whether or not for a particular purpose such as extortion of money or valuables. They may involve verbal persecution and abuse, physical assault or the threat of it, or even the degradation or humiliation of the victim. Such attacks tend to be systematic and persistent leading to the oppression of a fellow pupil and his or her virtual isolation from the support and friendship of others.

14   Crown Prosecution Service, *Code for Crown Prosecutors* (2004), paras 8.8 and 8.9.
15   Ibid, para 4.2.
16   Crown Prosecution Service, *Legal Guidance: Youth Offenders*.

It is important to differentiate occasional jibes from systematic bullying of children because of ethnic origin, religion, gender, sexual orientation or disability.

In all cases relevant considerations will include:

- any background to the incident in question including any history of bullying of the same victim by the offender or generally;
- the attitude and behaviour of the offender and the offender's parent(s) or guardian(s);
- the effect of the behaviour on the victim;
- any internal remedies already taken by the school whether in connection with the incident or in the past, such as, where the victim and offender no longer attend the same school.

It is important to ensure that the seriousness of the conduct is accurately and appropriately reflected in the seriousness of the charge.

If school bullying incidents are regularly referred for prosecution (particularly if they are often appropriate for reprimands or final warning), it may well be necessary for the AYJC/local CPS to contact the local police department and the YOT responsible for youth offender cases with a view to them examining the policies of the local schools and the police.

All schools should have internal procedures and strategies for dealing with these incidents. It may be necessary to explore with the police and the YOT whether certain schools are in fact accepting their responsibility in this area fully.

In such cases the file should include information on the background of the incident, any previous incident and any disciplinary measures taken by the school.

If the incident has taken place outside school but is connected to conduct occurring at school the same information described above is relevant. Schools often feel unable to act in these circumstances.

Offences committed within the family home

8.20   The government definition of domestic violence is:

> ... any incident of threatening behaviour, violence or abuse (psychological, physical, sexual, financial or emotional) between adults who are or have been intimate partners or family members, regardless of gender or sexuality.[17]

8.21   The Crown Prosecution Service has issued a guidance document *Policy for Prosecuting Cases of Domestic Violence* (2005) which makes it clear that a wider definition of domestic violence will be applied:

> Because victims' and children's safety issues and defendant accountability are so important to us, we will also apply our domestic violence policy when dealing with criminal offences that occur in a domestic context involving victims and abusers whatever their age.

8.22   This wider definition would encompass violence and other behaviour by a child or young person directed towards a parent or other carer, as well as towards siblings.

---

17   Quoted in Crown Prosecutuion Service, *Policy for Prosecuting Cases of Domestic Violence*, para 2.2.

8.23   Where there is sufficient evidence to prosecute in a case of domestic violence and the victim is willing to testify, the Policy states that a prosecution will go forward even if the injury suffered by the victim was minor or the parties have reconciled.[18]

8.24   Where the victim indicates that s/he no longer supports the prosecution, the case will not be automatically dropped. The Policy requires the prosecutor to consider the wider public interest in preventing domestic violence, and where a prosecution is still in the public interest the victim may be summonsed to give evidence at a trial.

8.25   Factors for the prosecutor to consider include:

- the seriousness of the offence;
- the victim's injuries – whether physical or psychological;
- if the defendant used a weapon;
- if the defendant has made any threats before or after the attack;
- if the defendant planned the attack;
- if there are any other children living in the household;
- if the offence was committed in the presence of, or near, a child;
- the chances of the defendant offending again;
- the continuing threat to the health and safety of the victim or anyone else who is, or may become, involved;
- the current state of the victim's relationship with the defendant;
- the history of the relationship, particularly if there has been any violence in the past;
- the defendant's criminal history, particularly any previous violence.[19]

8.26   The Policy suggests that the prosecutor will ask the police to provide information about family circumstances and the likely effect of prosecuting on the victim and any other children in the household.[20] In the case of a young accused, it is submitted that information should also be sought from the youth offending team or a social worker, where there has already been any contact with the family.

Offences committed within a children's home

8.27   The Legal Guidance issued by the Crown Prosecution Service provides the following general advice:

> A criminal justice disposal, whether a prosecution, reprimand or warning, should not be regarded as an automatic response to offending behaviour by a looked after child, irrespective of their criminal history. This applies equally to Persistent Young Offenders and adolescents of good character. A criminal justice disposal will only be appropriate where it is clearly required by the public interest.
>
> Informal disposals such as restorative justice conferencing, reparation, acceptable behaviour contracts and disciplinary measures by the home may be sufficient to satisfy the public interest and to reduce the risk of future offending.

---

18 Crown Prosecutuion Service, *Policy for Prosecuting Cases of Domestic Violence*, para 6.5.
19 Ibid, para 6.4.
20 Ibid, para 6.6.

8.28   The Guidance also provides advice on individual cases:

Factors that should be considered include:
- The disciplinary policy of the Home.
- An explanation from the Home regarding their decision to involve the police, which should refer to the procedures and guidance on police involvement.
- Information from the Home about the recent behaviour of the youth, including similar behaviour and any incidents in the youth's life that could have affected their behaviour, any history between the youth and the victim, any apology or reparation by the youth, history of the incident and any action under the disciplinary policy of the Home.
- The views of the victim, including their willingness to attend court to give evidence and/or participate in a restorative justice or other diversionary programme.
- The views of the key worker, social worker, counsellor or CAHMS worker on the effect of criminal justice intervention on the youth, particularly where the youth suffers from an illness or disorder.
- Any explanation or information about the offence from the looked after child.
- If the looked after child wishes it to be considered, information about the local authority's assessment of his/her needs and how the placement provided by the Home is intended to address them. The local authority should be able to provide this information as it should be an integral part of the Care Plan for the looked after child.

[Prosecutors who are youth offender specialists] should consider all of the aggravating and mitigating features when deciding on the appropriate outcome.

Aggravating features include:
- The offence is violent or induces the genuine fear of violence in the victim.
- The offence is sexual.
- The offence is motivated by hostility based on the gender, sexuality, disability, race, religion or ethnicity of the victim.
- The victim is vulnerable.
- The damage or harm caused is deliberate and cannot be described as minor.
- The offence forms part of a series of offences.
- Informal measures have been ineffective in preventing offending behaviour.

Mitigating features include:
- The damage or harm caused is at the lower end of the scale and has been put right.
- Appropriate action has already been taken under the disciplinary procedure or other informal disposal.
- Genuine remorse and apology to the victim.
- The behaviour is a symptom of a disorder or illness that cannot be controlled by medication or diet .... Care should be taken where it appears that the youth has deliberately refused medication or deliberately consumed a substance knowing that his or her behaviour will be affected.
- Isolated incident or out of character.
- The young person is under extreme stress or appears to have been provoked and has overreacted.

The reasons for the charging/diversion decision should be clearly recorded and show the factors that have been considered by a youth specialist to determine how the public interest is satisfied.

Sexual offences

8.29 Particular care should be taken before deciding how to deal with a child or young person who committed a sexual offence. The decision to prosecute should always be referred to a prosecutor who is a youth offender specialist.[21]

8.30 The Legal Guidance issued by the Crown Prosecution Service gives the following general advice:

> If an allegation of any sexual abuse committed by a youth offender has been fully investigated and there is sufficient evidence to justify instituting proceedings, the balance of the public interest must always be carefully considered before any prosecution is commenced. Positive action may need to be taken at an early stage of offending of this type. Although a reprimand or final warning may provide an acceptable alternative in some cases, in reaching any decision, the police and the CPS will have to take into account fully the view of other agencies involved in the case, in particular the Social Services. The consequences for the victim of the decision whether or not to prosecute, and any views expressed by the victim or the victim's family should also be taken into account.

> In child abuse cases, it will be important to have the views of the Social Services on file if at all possible, as well as any background or history of similar conduct, information about the relationship between the two and the effect a prosecution might have on the victim.

> Any case referred to the CPS for advice, or in which a prosecution does proceed, must be dealt with as quickly as possible to minimise the delay before the case comes to court.

Offences committed against children under 13 (Sexual Offences Act 2003 ss5–8)

8.31 The public interest does not automatically require prosecution when a young person commits an offence in relation to a child under the age of 13. The Legal Guidance issued by the Crown Prosecution Service gives the following advice to prosecutors:

> When reviewing a case, in which a youth under 18 is alleged to have committed an offence contrary to sections 5 to 8, careful regard should be paid to the following factors:
> - the relative ages of both parties and;
> - the existence of and nature of any relationship;
> - the sexual and emotional maturity of both parties and any emotional or physical effects as a result of the conduct;
> - whether the child under 13 in fact freely consented (even though in law this is not a defence) or a genuine mistake as to her age was in fact made;
> - whether any element of seduction, breach of any duty of responsibility to the girl or other exploitation is disclosed by the evidence.

> If the sexual act or activity was in fact genuinely consensual and the youth and the child under 13 concerned are fairly close in age and development, a prosecution contrary to sections 5 to 8 is unlikely to be appropriate. Action falling short of prosecution may be appropriate. In such cases, the parents and/or welfare agencies may be able to deal with the situation informally.

---

21 Crown Prosecution Service, *Legal Guidance: Young Offenders.*

However, if a very young child has been seduced by a youth, or a baby-sitter in a position of responsibility has taken advantage of a child under 13 in his/her care, prosecution is likely to be in the public interest. Where a child under 13 has not given ostensible consent to the activity, then a prosecution contrary to sections 5 to 8 is likely to be the appropriate course of action.

Child sex offences (Sexual Offences Act 2003 s13)

8.32   During the passage of the Sexual Offences Act 2003 through parliament there were concerns raised about the wide scope of the clause which eventually became section 13 of the Act. In response to this concern, government ministers confirmed on several occasions that underage sexual activity would not automatically be prosecuted and undertakings were given to issue guidance on the appropriate use of section 13.[22] In fulfilment of those undertakings, Home Office Circular 20/2004 *Guidance on Part 1 of the Sexual Offences Act 2003* was issued. In addition, the Legal Guidance issued by the Crown Prosecution Service was revised to give the following advice to prosecutors:

> It should be noted that where both parties to sexual activity are under 16, then they may both have committed a sexual offence. However, the overriding purpose of the legislation is to protect children and it was not Parliament's intention to punish children unnecessarily or for the criminal law to intervene where it was wholly inappropriate. Consensual sexual activity between, for example, a 14 or 15 year-old and a teenage partner would not normally require criminal proceedings in the absence of aggravating features. The relevant considerations include:
> * the respective ages of the parties;
> * the existence and nature of any relationship;
> * their level of maturity;
> * whether any duty of care existed;
> * whether there was a serious element of exploitation.[23]

8.33   The Legal Guidance also states that a reprimand or warning should not be issued where the sexual activity was entirely mutually agreed and non-exploitative.[24]

Familial sexual offences

8.34   The Legal Guidance issued by the Crown Prosecution Service states:

> In cases of sexual activity between siblings, care should be taken to balance the public interest in prosecuting such conduct with the interests and welfare of the victim and the family unit. As a general rule, alternatives to prosecution should be sought where the sexual activity was wholly consensual. The welfare agencies will normally intervene.
>
> Prosecution should be considered where there is evidence of:
> * seduction;
> * coercion;

---

22 Eg Baroness Scotland, Hansard Debates col 689, 17 June 2003.
23 Crown Prosecution Service Legal Guidance: Youth Offenders.
24 Crown Prosecution Service Legal Guidance: Sexual Offences and Child Abuse (Sexual Offences Act 2001).

- exploitation or violence;
- a significant disparity in age;

In all cases the effect of prosecution on a victim and family should be taken into account and if the views of the welfare agencies are not included with the file they should be sought.

Young people involved in prostitution

8.35 When considering whether to prosecute a child or young person for prostitution, the Legal Guidance issued by the Crown Prosecution Service states that it is essential for the prosecutor to be familiar with the inter-agency guidance *Safeguarding Children Involved in Prostitution* issued in 2000.[25] This guidance states:

> The vast majority of children do not freely and willingly become involved in prostitution. The entire emphasis of the Guidance is on diversion using a welfare based approach to children and that it should be adopted in all cases. However, it would be wrong to say that a boy or girl under 18 never freely chooses to continue to solicit, loiter or importune in a public place for the purposes of prostitution, and does not knowingly and willingly break the law. In such cases, the police should only start to consider whether criminal justice action is required, following a strategy discussion when all diversion work has failed over a period of time and a judgement is made that it will not prove effective in the foreseeable future. What constitutes 'a period of time' and 'the foreseeable future' will vary in each case.

> The criminal justice process should only be considered if the child persistently and voluntarily continues to solicit, loiter or importune in a public place for the purposes of prostitution. Police and colleagues in other agencies, who will be involved in considering whether there is a genuine choice, must be aware of the high degree of coercion and malign influence that can be exercised by abusers and be fully alive to the possibility that what is claimed as a voluntary activity simply masks threats or coercion.

> Persistence is generally understood in law to require a determined repetition of an activity. It is not appropriate to define persistence more closely as each case should be looked at in the round. A determined and regular return to soliciting, loitering or importuning over a period of time would, however, be regarded as persistent. In practice, any child who is being sold for sex is likely to meet the criterion of persistence, as is a child who is dependent on drugs. In such cases the relationship between the coercer, prostitution and drug misuse requires careful analysis and consideration. It should be borne in mind that it may be very difficult to break the control of the abuser established though a high level of physical violence and fear. In these situations consideration should be given to initiating proceedings for care and supervision under section 31 of the Children Act 1989 in order to ensure the child's welfare.

> The initial presumption should always be that a boy or girl is not soliciting voluntarily. What seems to be a persistent and voluntary return to soliciting by a child, should never be taken at face value. There must be a thorough investigation of all aspects of a case to ensure that there is no evidence of an abusive relationship that could involve physical, mental or emotional coercion. There should also be a shared conviction of those involved in the inter-agency discussion that an individual's return to prostitution is genuinely of their own volition.

25 The guidance may be downloaded from the Department of Health website – see appendix 14.

The decision on whether to initiate criminal justice action is for the police, and at a later stage, the Crown Prosecution Service. In the context of this inter-agency approach, unilateral action by the police would not be appropriate. If police officers think that it would be appropriate to consider criminal justice options, then inter-agency discussion should take place within the ACPC guidelines.

Police would not normally take criminal justice action unless there had been inter-agency discussion to consider the full circumstances of each case and it was agreed that all other avenues had been explored. Particular attention should be given to the following factors:

- the age and vulnerability of the child;
- the needs of the child;
- any drug misuse by the child;
- that the return is genuinely voluntary and that there is no evidence of physical, mental or emotional coercion; and
- that the child understands that criminal proceedings may follow, and the effect these may have in later life.

As with other parts of the diversion process, it is important that a record should be kept of any conversation with the child concerning possible prosecution. Once this stage has been reached, if the child is found breaking the law, the criminal justice response will depend on whether the child admits the offence or not - although attempts at diversion should continue in either event.

Mentally disordered young offenders

8.36   Guidance on diverting mentally disordered offenders from the criminal justice process is contained in Home Office Circular HOC 66/1990 *Provision for Mentally Disordered Offenders* and the Crown Prosecution Service's Legal Guidance. This guidance is considered in detail at paras 30.13–30.15.

Influencing the decision whether to prosecute

8.37   Before making representations to the prosecution, it is important to bear in mind that the civil concept of 'without prejudice' negotiations during litigation does not apply to criminal proceedings. The defence lawyer needs to consider what factual information regarding the circumstances of the allegation should be disclosed in any representations. Specific instructions will need to be taken from the client regarding this and the potential adverse use of the information in a subsequent trial must be pointed out.

Prior to charge

8.38   Where the police refer the charging decision to the duty prosecutor while the child or young person is still in police detention, it may be impracticable to speak directly to the prosecutor considering the police file. Alternatively, the defence lawyer could write out representations to give to the custody officer with a request that the representations be passed onto the duty prosecutor.

8.39   Where the child or young person has been bailed for the advice of a prosecutor, the defence lawyer could submit written representations. Here the practical problem will be identifying the prosecutor who will be responsible for making the charging decision. Preparing such written representations regarding the charging decision would be claimed as Advice and Assistance in the investigation stage.[26]

After charge

8.40   As the prosecutor must keep the decision to prosecute under active review, it is open to the defence lawyer to make representations to the Crown Prosecution Service seeking a review of the decision to prosecute. The power to discontinue proceedings under Prosecution of Offences Act 1985 s23 may be exercised on public policy grounds as well as evidential grounds.

8.41   To allow representations to be considered, the defence lawyer may need to apply to the court for the proceedings to be adjourned prior to the taking of a plea. There may be resistance to such an application, therefore the defence lawyer will need to be prepared to outline the substance of the representations to justify their merits to the court.

8.42   When making the representations it is important to be clear what the prosecutor is being asked to do as part of the review of the prosecution. A decision to discontinue court proceedings could be made:

- with no alternative disposal;
- with a request for the court to bind over the young defendant; or
- a direction to the police to administer a reprimand or warning.

No alternative disposal

8.43   Where a decision to charge has ignored public policy guidance, such as that relating to offences committed in children's homes (see para 8.27 above) or consensual sexual activity (see para 8.32 above), it would be reasonable to argue that no criminal justice action is appropriate.

Bindover

8.44   In cases involving minor public disturbances, it may be appropriate to suggest a bindover (see para 22.65). A bindover is not a criminal conviction, so it does not preclude a reprimand or warning in the future, but it does preclude the making of a referral order.

Reprimand or warning

8.45   Where the young client is eligible for a reprimand or warning and there was an admission to the offence prior to charge, the prosecutor could be asked to direct the police to administer the reprimand or warning.

---

26 See paras 5.43–5.45.

Judicial review of the decision to charge

8.46　A decision to prosecute an adult is not amenable to judicial review in the absence of dishonesty, mala fides or an exceptional circumstance.[27] The grounds for reviewing the decision to charge a child or young person, however, would seem to be wider. In *R v Chief Constable of Kent ex p L*,[28] a case decided before reprimands and warnings replaced cautions, Watkins LJ suggested that children and young persons were in a special position and he stated:

> I have come to the conclusion that, in respect of juveniles, the discretion of the CPS to continue or to discontinue criminal proceedings is reviewable by this court but only where it can be demonstrated that the decision was made regardless of or clearly contrary to a settled policy of the DPP evolved in the public interest, for example the policy of cautioning [children and young persons], a policy which the CPS are bound to apply, where appropriate, to the exercise of their discretion to continue or discontinue criminal proceedings. But I envisage that it will be only rarely that a defendant could succeed in showing that a decision was fatally flawed in such a manner as that.

8.47　He went on to say:

> I find it very difficult to envisage, with regard to that policy, a circumstance, fraud or dishonesty apart possibly, which would allow of a challenge to a decision to prosecute or continue proceedings unless it could be demonstrated, in the case of a [child or young person], that there had been either a total disregard of the policy or, contrary to it, a lack of enquiry into the circumstances and background of that person, previous offences and general character and so on, by the prosecutor and later by the CPS. But here too I envisage the possibility of showing such disregard had happened as unlikely. Therefore, although the CPS may in principle be reviewed, in practice it is rarely likely to be successful.

8.48　In *R (F) v Crown Prosecution Service and Chief Constable of Merseyside*[29] Jackson J stated that the principles outlined by Watkins LJ were still valid even after the introduction of the statutory system of reprimands and warnings. Introduction of the statutory charging scheme would not seem to change the position either.

27　*R (Pepushi) v Crown Prosecution Service* [2004] EWHC 798 following *R v Director of Public Prosecutions ex p Kebilene* [2002] 2 AC 326.

28　[1991] 1 All ER 756; (1991) 93 Cr App R 414, QBD.

29　[2003] EWHC 3266 (Admin).

Reprimands and warnings

9.1   It is good for children to learn to take responsibility for their actions: that is part of growing up to be responsible members of society. It is therefore good for children to 'own up' when they have done wrong. But it is absolutely vital that children's admissions, like adults', should be voluntary and reliable. Corners should not be cut just because the offender is a child. They must not be under any pressure to 'admit it and we'll let you off with a caution'.

Baroness Hale of Richmond in *R (on the application of R) v Durham*
Constabulary[1]

9.2   Police forces have been diverting young people from the criminal courts for many years by way of cautions.[2] For the first time, the Crime and Disorder Act 1998 introduced a statutory framework for diverting offenders from the criminal courts. This framework only applies to offenders under the age of 18. No child or young person may any longer receive a caution.[3]

9.3   Under the statutory scheme, a first offence may result in a reprimand, warning or a prosecution. A warning rather than a reprimand will be given where the first offence is considered too serious to justify a reprimand. Following a reprimand, a subsequent offence may only be dealt with by a warning or charge. Any further offence will normally lead to a prosecution, however, a second warning may be administered but only where the offence is not serious and more than two years have passed since the first warning was given. No person may receive more than two warnings.

9.4   The Home Office is required to issue guidance on the use of reprimands and final warnings.[4] The current guidance, issued jointly with the Youth Justice Board, is contained in *Final Warning Scheme: Guidance for the Police and Youth Offending Teams* issued in November 2002 and supplemented by Home Office Circular HOC 14/2006: *The Final Warning Scheme*. The Association of Chief Police Officers (ACPO) has also issued guidance to police officers in the form of the *ACPO Youth Offender Case Disposal Gravity Factor System*.

9.5   When considering how to dispose of a case, the custody officer must take account of the existence of reprimands and warnings as an alternative to prosecution.[5]

Statutory requirements

9.6   Crime and Disorder Act 1998 s65(1) provides that a reprimand or warning may only be administered if:

- a police constable has evidence that a child or young person has committed an offence;
- the constable considers that the evidence is such that, if prosecuted for the offence, there would be a realistic prospect of the child or young person being convicted;

1   [2005] UKHL 21.
2   For a brief history of diversion for juveniles see Baroness Hale's judgment in *R (on the application of R) v Durham Constabulary* [2005] UKHL 21 [30]–[38].
3   Crime and Disorder Act s65(8).
4   Ibid, s65(6).
5   PACE Code C Note for Guidance 16A.

- the child or young person admits to the constable that s/he committed the offence;
- the child or young person has not previously been convicted of an offence; and
- the constable is satisfied that it would not be in the public interest for the child or young person to be prosecuted.

9.7 A reprimand may be administered if the young offender has not previously been reprimanded or warned.[6]

9.8 A warning may be administered if:

- the offender has not previously been warned; or
- where the offender has previously been warned, the offence was committed more than two years after the date of the previous warning and the offence is not so serious as to require a charge to be brought.[7]

9.9 A young offender may not receive more than two warnings in any circumstances.[8]

9.10 Any caution given to a child or young person before the introduction of reprimands and warnings shall be treated as a reprimand. Any second or subsequent caution shall be treated as a warning.[9]

Realistic prospect of a conviction

9.11 At the time of administering a reprimand or warning, the police officer must consider that the evidence against the child or young person is such that, if s/he were prosecuted for the offence, there would be a realistic prospect of a conviction.[10] A realistic prospect of a conviction in the Code for Crown Prosecutors (2004) para 5.2 is taken to mean 'more likely than not'.

9.12 Rather surprisingly, *The Director's Guidance on Charging* (January 2005) para 9.1 contemplates police officers deciding to administer a reprimand or warning on the basis of the much lower evidential test of there being reasonable suspicion that the suspect committed the offence (termed the 'threshold test' in the Code). The threshold test is supposed to be applied to the charging decision where the suspect is not suitable for bail and therefore it is undesirable to wait for sufficient evidence to provide a reasonable prospect of a conviction. It should only be applied where there is a reasonable expectation that the required extra evidence will be forthcoming.[11]

9.13 In most cases the difference between the two tests will have no practical relevance, as the decision-making process is carried out after the child or young person has made an admission to the offence, which in itself is likely to provide the means to secure a conviction. The question does remain whether a police officer should proceed to administer a reprimand or warning if, the admission apart, there is no admissible evidence – for example, where a crucial witness refuses to make a witness statement.

6 Crime and Disorder Act 1998 s65(1).
7 Ibid, s65(3).
8 Ibid, s65(3).
9 Ibid, Sch 9 para 5.
10 Ibid, s65(1)(b).
11 Crown Prosecution Service *Code for Crown Prosecutors* (2004), para 6.4.

Admission of guilt

9.14   A reprimand or warning can be given only if the child or young person makes a clear and reliable admission to all elements of the offence. This should include an admission of dishonesty and intent, where applicable.[12] Case law in relation to the non-statutory cautioning system suggests that the admission does not necessarily need to have been made in a formal taped interview,[13] but it should be made before a decision to administer a reprimand or warning is taken.[14]

9.15   An admission would be vitiated if it were obtained by oppression or an unlawful inducement.[15] A police officer telling an adult suspect in police custody on suspicion of disorderly behaviour that he could be cautioned if he admitted the offence, has been held to be an unlawful inducement.[16]

No previous convictions

9.16   By virtue of Powers of Criminal Courts (Sentencing) Act 2000 s14(1) an absolute or conditional discharge shall be deemed not to be a conviction for any purpose other than the proceedings in which the order is made. It would, therefore, follow that a child or young person who has previously been absolutely or conditionally discharged by a court could still receive a reprimand or warning.[17]

9.17   A fixed penalty notice is also not a criminal conviction and would not prohibit the administering of a reprimand or a warning.

Consent

9.18   There is no statutory requirement that either the child or young person or his/her parent or guardian need consent to the administering of the reprimand or warning. In *R v Durham Constabulary ex p R*[18] the House of Lords held that this omission is not in breach of the European Convention on Human Rights. Lord Bingham in his judgment noted that reprimands and warnings were an alternative to court proceedings which involved no element of punishment. He concluded that neither the administration of a warning nor the decision to warn a child or young person involved the determination of a criminal charge, and as such the fair trial guarantees of Article 6 of the convention were not engaged. Consequently there was no issue of the child or young person waiving any convention right.

12 Home Office/Youth Justice Board Final Warning Scheme: Guidance for Youth Offending Teams (November 2002), para 4.12.
13 *R v Chief Constable of Lancashire Constabulary ex p Atkinson* CO/3775/96 (1998) 5 February, unreported.
14 *R v Metropolitan Police Commissioner ex p Thompson* [1997] 1 WLR 1519, QBD.
15 Ibid.
16 Ibid.
17 A point now expressly accepted in Home Office Circular 14/2006, para 7.
18 [2005] UKHL 21.

Determining the seriousness of the offence

9.19 To help police officers determine the seriousness of the offence, the Association of Chief Police Officers (ACPO) formulated the *Youth Offender Case Disposal Gravity Factor System*. This gives individual offences a gravity score between 1 for the most minor and 4 for the most serious.

9.20   The appropriate police response is as follows:

Gravity score	Police action
1	Always the minimum response applicable to the individual offender, ie reprimand, warning or charge.
2	Normally reprimand for a first offence. If offender does not qualify for a reprimand but qualifies for a warning, then give warning. If offender does not qualify for a warning, then charge.
3	Normally warn for a first offence. If offender does not qualify for a warning, then charge. Only in exceptional circumstances should a reprimand be given. Decision-maker needs to justify reprimand.
4	Always charge.

9.21 Having identified the offence committed and its gravity score, the police officer should consider any aggravating or mitigating features which may increase or decrease the seriousness of the offence. The guidance is reproduced in full in appendix 5.

Police decision-making

9.22 In an attempt to ensure consistency in decision-making by different police forces, the Home Office has given the following advice in Home Office Circular HOC 14/2006 para 8:

> It is apparent that there is some inconsistency between forces about the circumstances in which they consider it appropriate to administer a reprimand or a warning. *The guidance states that the final warning scheme **aims** to divert children and young people from offending behaviour before they enter the court system.* This means that where possible they should be warned, as opposed to prosecuted, if it is appropriate to do so within the terms of the Final Warning Scheme Guidance. However, the proper use of discretion requires that the decision must be reasonable, made on the basis of relevant factors and the questions set out below should be asked in each case .... We expect a view to be formed by the police in conjunction with the Crown Prosecution Service (CPS) as necessary:
>
> – Is there evidence that the young person has committed an offence?
> – Is the evidence such that, if prosecuted for the offence, there would be a realistic prospect of a conviction?

- Does the young person make a clear and reliable admission to all elements of the offence?
- Has the young person previously been convicted of any offence recordable or non-recordable? *(Discharges are not to be treated as convictions for the purposes of the Final Warning Scheme).*
- Has the young person previously been reprimanded/warned?
- How serious is the offence according to the ACPO Gravity Factor System? *(This also caters sufficiently for the public interest consideration from the police perspective, but the CPS will apply their own test when consulted.)*

Assessment by the youth offending team

9.23   Where the custody officer considers that there is sufficient evidence to charge the person arrested with an offence, s/he may, rather than charging the suspect, bail the suspect to return to the police station so that a youth offending team may assess the suspect with a view to a reprimand or warning being administered.[19]

9.24   When the police refer a child or young person, the youth offending team must undertake an assessment of the young offender within ten working days. The assessment must be based on *Asset* (see paras 2.23–2.27) and should include a home visit where possible.[20]

Administering a reprimand or warning

9.25   A reprimand or warning may be administered at premises specified in guidance issued by the Home Secretary.[21] If the offender is under the age of 17, the reprimand or warning must be administered in the presence of an appropriate adult.[22]

Venue

9.26   The reprimand or warning may be administered at a police station or other premises. The Home Office/Youth Justice Board guidance states:

> Where the young person is bailed for a Yot assessment of the public interest prior to the decision regarding the final warning, the bail period can be used to give consideration to the selection of the venue most appropriate for the delivery of the warning. Bail can also be given for the purpose of arranging delivery.

> The selection of the right venue may have a restorative effect and help bring home to the young person the consequences of his or her behaviour. For example, if the offence was one of criminal damage to a school or youth club, the warning could be delivered on the premises. The local community centre may also be a more accessible and less threatening venue for victims attending a restorative conference than the police station.

---

19   Police and Criminal Evidence Act 1984 s34(5)(b).
20   Youth Justice Board *National Standards for Youth Justice Services* (2004), para 6.6.
21   Crime and Disorder Act 1998 s65(6)(aa).
22   Ibid, s65(5)(a).

All venues should be assessed for suitability; they must be easily accessible to all participants (in particular the victim); and secure. It would not be appropriate for reprimands or final warnings to be delivered on the street. Nor would it normally be appropriate for them to be delivered in an individual's home.

Local police services and Yots should give particular consideration to using Yot premises for the delivery of warnings, especially in cases where the young person has been bailed for a Yot assessment. This will provide greater continuity in the final warning process (as the Yot will already have engaged with the young person), and it can also facilitate the involvement of the victim in the delivery of the warning (as the Yot will normally already have been in contact with the victim). This should increase the likelihood both of the young person engaging with the intervention programme after the warning, and of the young person and the victim participating in a restorative process as part of the intervention programme. However, some victims may not wish to attend at Yot premises and it is important that victims' preferences are taken into account.[23]

Appropriate adult

9.27 For the purposes of administering a reprimand or caution, 'appropriate adult' is defined as:

(a) the juvenile offender's parent or guardian or, if s/he is in the care of a local authority or voluntary organisation, a person representing that authority or organisation;
(b) a social worker of a local authority social services department;
(c) if no person falling within (a) or (b) above is available, any responsible person aged 18 or over who is not a police officer or a person employed by the police.[24]

9.28 If a youth offending team worker is present at the administering of the reprimand or warning, s/he may not also act as the appropriate adult.[25]

Explaining the effect of the reprimand/warning

9.29 The constable administering the reprimand or warning must explain to the young offender and, if s/he is under 17, the appropriate adult in ordinary language the effect of a reprimand or warning.[26]

Written records

9.30 Whenever a reprimand or warning is given, the child or young person, the officer and any parent, guardian or appropriate adult present must sign a form to confirm that it was given for the offence indicated.[27]

---

23 Home Office/Youth Justice Board *Final Warning Scheme: Guidance for the Police and Youth Offending Teams* (November 2002) paras 9.18–9.21.
24 Crime and Disorder Act 1998 s65(7).
25 Home Office/Youth Justice Board *Final Warning Scheme: Guidance for the Police and Youth Offending Teams* (November 2002) para 9.15.
26 Crime and Disorder Act 1998 s65(5)(b).
27 Home Office/Youth Justice Board *Final Warning Scheme: Guidance for the Police and Youth Offending Teams* (November 2002) para 9.16.

Rehabilitation programme

9.31   Young offenders given a warning will normally receive a rehabilitation programme delivered by the youth offending team. The Youth Justice Board has
set a target for youth offending teams to deliver a rehabilitation programme
in support of 80 per cent of warnings.[28] A rehabilitation programme will
also be offered on a voluntary basis in some cases of offenders given a reprimand, where the risk of further offending is considered to be high.[29]

Content of programme

9.32   The purpose of a rehabilitation programme is to rehabilitate participants
and to prevent them from re-offending.[30] It may include short-term counselling or group work, reparation to victims, supervised youth activities
or work to improve school attendance. The programme must consist of at
least one post-assessment contact.[31] The level of contact will depend on the
Asset assessment (see paras 2.23–2.27) and could range from one hour to
over ten hours.[32]

Non-compliance

9.33   If a young offender fails to participate in the rehabilitation programme,
s/he cannot be prosecuted, but a report on his/her failure to participate
in the programme may be cited in criminal proceedings in the same circumstances as a conviction.[33] The decision whether there has been non-
compliance rests with the youth offending team, not a court. It should be
noted that the legislation does not incorporate any requirement to assess
the reasonableness of any alleged non-compliance.

9.34   If the rehabilitation programme was offered on a voluntary basis after
the administering of a reprimand or further voluntary contact is offered
after the end of the formal rehabilitation programme, non-compliance
should not be cited in subsequent court proceedings.[34]

Consequences of receiving a reprimand or warning

Effect of a reprimand

9.35   The reprimand will be recorded by the police. It may be cited in subsequent
criminal proceedings in the same circumstances as a conviction may be
cited.[35]

---

28 Home Office/Youth Justice Board *Final Warning Scheme: Guidance for the Police and
Youth Offending Teams* (November 2002), para 10.1.
29 Ibid, para 10.3.
30 Crime and Disorder Act 1998 s66(6).
31 *Final Warning Scheme: Guidance for the Police and Youth Offending Teams*, para 10.8.
32 Ibid, paras 10.11 and 10.14.
33 Crime and Disorder Act 1998 s66(5)(c).
34 *Final Warning Scheme: Guidance for the Police and Youth Offending Teams*, para 10.7.
35 Crime and Disorder Act 1998 s66(5)(a).

Effect of a warning

9.36 When a child or young person is given a warning s/he shall be referred to a youth offending team as soon as practicable.[36] The youth offending team must carry out an assessment of the offender and, unless it considers it inappropriate to do so, it shall arrange for the young offender to participate in a rehabilitation programme.[37]

9.37 The warning will be recorded by the police. It may be cited in subsequent criminal proceedings in the same circumstances as a conviction may be cited.[38]

9.38 If a person is convicted of an offence within two years of receiving a warning, the sentencing court may not conditionally discharge him/her, unless it is of the opinion that there are exceptional circumstances which justify its doing so.[39] There is no such restriction upon a court imposing an absolute discharge.

Notification requirement as a sex offender

9.39 Where a child or young person receives a reprimand or a warning for certain sexual offences s/he will be required to register under Part II of the Sexual Offences Act 2003.[40] The requirement to register lasts for two-and-a-half years from the date of the administering of the reprimand or caution.[41]

9.40 For offences committed on or after 1 May 2004 there is a requirement to register if a reprimand or warning is administered for the following offences :

- rape (Sexual Offences Act 2003 s1);
- assault by penetration (Sexual Offences Act 2003 s2);
- causing sexual activity without consent (Sexual Offences Act 2003 s4);
- rape of a child under 13 (Sexual Offences Act 2003 s5);
- sexual assault of a child under 13 by penetration (Sexual Offences Act 2003 s6);
- offences against persons with mental disorder (Sexual Offences Act 2003 ss31–38); and
- administering a substance with intent (Sexual Offences Act 2003 s61).[42]

9.41 For more information regarding the registration requirements see chapter 28.

---

36 Crime and Disorder Act 1998 s66(1).
37 Ibid, s66(2).
38 Ibid, s66(5)(b).
39 Ibid, s66(4).
40 Sexual Offences Act 2003 ss80(1)(d) and 133(1).
41 Ibid, s82(1) and (2).
42 Ibid, s80(1)(d) and Sch 3.

Retention on police records

9.42　Police records of a reprimand or warning will be retained until the young person attains the age of 18 or for five years, whichever is the longer period.[43]

Rehabilitation of Offenders Act 1974

9.43　Reprimands and warnings are currently not covered by the Rehabilitation of Offenders Act 1974. There is therefore no provision for the reprimand or warning to be spent.

9.44　Reprimands and warnings are not convictions so a young person would not need to disclose their existence on most job application forms which only require details of criminal convictions. If the form specifically requires information about reprimands or warnings, the young person will have no choice but to disclose the information.

Attaining 18

9.45　Offenders who were under 18 at the time of the offence, but who have attained that age by the time that the police are considering disposal, should not be given a reprimand or warning.[44] Instead the police should consider a non-statutory caution or a conditional caution under Part 3 of the Criminal Justice Act 2003.[45]

Judicial review of a reprimand or warning

9.46　It is impossible to appeal against the administering of a reprimand or warning to any criminal court, therefore the only remedy available is judicial review.

9.47　Judicial review will only be appropriate in those exceptional cases where the decision to administer a reprimand or warning was fatally flawed by a clear breach of the statutory requirements or the current guidance issued by or on behalf of the Home Secretary.[46]

9.48　In cases involving cautions, judicial review has been granted quashing the caution, where there was no admission to the offence,[47] and where the admission was vitiated by an unlawful inducement.[48]

43　Home Office/Youth Justice Board *Final Warning Scheme: Guidance for the Police and Youth Offending Teams* (November 2002), para 12.10.
44　Ibid, para 4.33.
45　These disposals are outside the scope of this book. For further information see Home Office Circular HOC 30/2005: Cautioning of Adult Offenders.
46　*R v Commissioner of Police for the Metropolis ex p P (a minor)* (1995) 160 JP 367, QBD.
47　Ibid.
48　*R v Commissioner of Metropolitan Police ex p Thompson* [1997] 1 WLR 1519, QBD.

Effective participation

Effective participation as a pre-condition to a fair trial

10.1   As discussed in chapter 2, the guarantee of a fair trial contained in Article 6 of the European Convention on Human Rights applies to children and young persons just as much as it applies to adults.[1] The substance of that right when proceedings involve a young defendant was first considered by the European Court of Human Rights in the case of *T v United Kingdom, V v United Kingdom*.[2] The case involved the trial of the boys who abducted and killed James Bulger, who were aged 10 at the time of their arrest and 11 at the time of their trial. Their trial took place in a Victorian wood-panelled courtroom in Preston Crown Court, where they sat beside social workers on a raised platform in the dock. The case provoked considerable public emotion, with hostile crowds outside the court buildings on most days and massive national and international press interest. The trial lasted three weeks and on every day the large courtroom was crowded with journalists and members of the public. The formality of court procedure was maintained, with the judge and barristers wearing wigs and gowns, but the court day was reduced to end at 3.30pm with ten-minute breaks every hour. Throughout the trial proceedings there were reporting restrictions in place prohibiting the name or other personal details of the defendants being reported. These restrictions were lifted by the trial judge upon sentence and the following day the defendants' names, photographs and personal histories were reported in detail in newspapers in the UK and abroad. Psychiatric evidence before the European Court indicated that the second applicant had been terrified of being looked at by adult strangers sitting in court and that he had not been able to follow the evidence given in court. A further expert assessment reached the conclusion that it had taken him 12 months to recover from the trauma of the trial itself.

10.2   The applicants argued that the trial process amounted to inhuman and degrading treatment in breach of Article 3 of the convention and that the two boys had not had a fair trial in breach of Article 6. The arguments in relation to Article 3 are considered at paras 2.51 and 6.8. In relation to the fair trial argument, the court stated that Article 6 read as a whole guarantees the right of an accused to participate effectively in his criminal trial.[3] The court went on to say:

> [I]t is essential that a child charged with an offence is dealt with in a manner which takes full account of his age, level of maturity and intellectual and emotional capability and that steps are taken to promote his ability to understand and participate in the proceedings.[4]

> The Court does not consider that it was sufficient for the purposes of Article 6.1 that the applicant was represented by skilled and experienced lawyers ... Although the applicant's legal representatives were seated, as the government put it 'within whispering distance', it is highly unlikely that the applicant would have felt sufficiently uninhibited, in the tense courtroom and under public scrutiny, to have consulted with them during the trial or indeed that, given his immaturity and his disturbed emotional state, he would have been capable

1   *Nortier v Netherlands* (1993) 17 EHRR 273 – see para 2.60.
2   [2000] 2 All ER 1024 (Note); (2000) 30 EHRR 121; 7 BHRC 659, ECtHR.
3   *T v United Kingdom, V v United Kingdom* (1999) 30 EHRR 131, para 85.
4   Ibid, para 86.

outside the courtroom of co-operating with his lawyers and giving them information for the purposes of his defence.[5]

10.3   The court concluded that both applicants had been unable to participate effectively in the criminal proceedings against them and were, in consequence, denied a fair hearing in breach of Article 6(1).

Judicial response

10.4   In response to this decision, the then Lord Chief Justice Lord Bingham issued, on 16 February 2000, a Practice Direction *Trial of Children and Young Persons in the Crown Court*. This Practice Direction has now been incorporated in the *Criminal Consolidated Practice Direction (Criminal)* at Part IV.39. The full text is reproduced at reproduced in table 10 below.

Political response

10.5   The government's response to the decision of the European Court of Human Rights that the two applicants had not had a fair trial was outlined by the then Home Secretary, Jack Straw, to the House of Commons on 13 March 2000. He explained:

> The first issue on which the Court found against the United Kingdom was in respect of article 6(1), on the right to a fair trial. The Court said that, although special arrangements had been made in the Crown Court, the two youths – then aged 11 – were highly unlikely to have felt able to follow the proceedings properly or to pass information to their lawyers.
>
> The European Court did not conclude that young people should not be tried in the Crown Court. For our part, the Government believe that serious crimes with serious penalties continue to need a high-level judicial process, before a judge and jury. Rather, it is necessary to ensure that those trials take account of the particular circumstances of young people, although that must never undermine the seriousness of the proceedings or make it more difficult to convict the guilty.
>
> If justice is not open, it cannot be seen to be fair. Therefore, juvenile trials for serious crimes must be held in open court. However, to avoid an unnecessarily overbearing atmosphere in the courtroom, the Lord Chief Justice's practice direction makes it clear that, although the proceedings must be in open court, judges should be prepared to restrict attendance of the public at the trial to a relatively small number.
>
> On facilities for the press, courts already have discretion to limit the number of press representatives in court, taking account of the public's right to be informed about trials. The Lord Chief Justice has advised that limits on press numbers should, as necessary, be coupled with arrangements for audio and, if possible, closed-circuit television feed to another room in the courthouse.
>
> As to reporting cases in the media, the practice direction also makes it clear that the courts already have powers to order that nothing should be reported that would lead to the identification of juvenile defendants, but, as now, the detail of the case and the arguments made in court should still be fully reported.
>
> Given the Court's judgment, I have considered whether any legislative changes are needed on media attendance and reporting. I have concluded that they are not, although I know that the House will expect me to keep the implementation

5   *T v United Kingdom, V v United Kingdom* (1999) 30 EHRR 131, para 90.

Table 10: Criminal Practice Direction – Part IV.39 (Trial of Children and Young Persons)

IV.39.1. This direction applies to trials of children and young persons in the Crown Court. In it children and young persons are together called 'young defendants'.

IV.39.2. The steps which should be taken to comply with paragraphs IV.39.3 to IV.39.17 should be judged, in any given case, taking account of the age, maturity and development (intellectual and emotional) of the young defendant on trial and all other circumstances of the case.

The overriding principle

IV.39.3. Some young defendants accused of committing serious crimes may be very young and very immature when standing trial in the Crown Court. The purpose of such trial is to determine guilt (if that is in issue) and decide the appropriate sentence if the young defendant pleads guilty or is convicted. The trial process should not itself expose the young defendant to avoidable intimidation, humiliation or distress. All possible steps should be taken to assist the young defendant to understand and participate in the proceedings. The ordinary trial process should, so far as necessary, be adapted to meet those ends. Regard should be had to the welfare of the young defendant as required by section 44 of the Children and Young Persons Act 1933.

Before trial

IV.39.4. If a young defendant is indicted jointly with an adult defendant, the court should consider at the plea and directions hearing whether the young defendant should be tried on his own and should ordinarily so order unless of opinion that a joint trial would be in the interests of justice and would not be unduly prejudicial to the welfare of the young defendant. If a young defendant is tried jointly with an adult the ordinary procedures will apply subject to such modifications (if any) as the court may see fit to order.

IV.39.5. At the plea and directions hearing before trial of a young defendant, the court should consider and so far as practicable give directions on the matters covered in paragraphs IV.39.9-IV.39.15.

IV.39.6. It may be appropriate to arrange that a young defendant should visit, out of court hours and before the trial, the courtroom in which the trial is to be held so that he can familiarise himself with it.

IV.39.7. If any case against a young defendant has attracted or may attract widespread public or media interest, the assistance of the police should be enlisted to try and ensure that a young defendant is not, when attending for the trial, exposed to intimidation, vilification or abuse.

IV.39.8. The court should be ready at this stage (if it has not already done so) to give a direction under section 39 of the 1933 Act or, as the case may be, section 45 of the Youth Justice and Criminal Evidence Act 1999. Any such order, once made, should be reduced to writing and copies should on request be made available to anyone affected or potentially affected by it.

The trial

IV.39.9. The trial should, if practicable, be held in a courtroom in which all the participants are on the same or almost the same level.

IV.39.10. A young defendant should normally, if he wishes, be free to sit with members of his family or others in a like relationship and in a place which permits easy, informal communication with his legal representatives and others with whom he wants or needs to communicate.

IV.39.11. The court should explain the course of proceedings to a young defendant in terms he can understand, should remind those representing a young defendant of their continuing duty to explain each step of the trial to him and should ensure, so far as practicable, that the trial is conducted in language which the young defendant can understand.

IV.39.12. The trial should be conducted according to a timetable which takes full account of a young defendant's inability to concentrate for long periods. Frequent and regular breaks will often be appropriate.

IV.39.13. Robes and wigs should not be worn unless the young defendant asks that they should or the court for good reason orders that they should. Any person responsible for the security of a young defendant who is in custody should not be in uniform. There should be no recognisable police presence in the courtroom save for good reason.

IV.39.14. The court should be prepared to restrict attendance at the trial to a small number, perhaps limited to some of those with an immediate and direct interest in the outcome of the trial. The court should rule on any challenged claim to attend.

IV.39.15. Facilities for reporting the trial (subject to any direction given under section 39 of the 1933 Act or section 45 of the 1999 Act) must be provided. But the court may restrict the number of those attending in the courtroom to report the trial to such number as is judged practicable and desirable. In ruling on any challenged claim to attend the courtroom for the purpose of reporting the trial the court should be mindful of the public's general right to be informed about the administration of justice in the Crown Court. Where access to the courtroom by reporters is restricted, arrangements should be made for the proceedings to be relayed, audibly and if possible visually, to another room in the same court complex to which the media have free access if it appears that there will be a need for such additional facilities.

IV.39.16. Where the court is called upon to exercise its discretion in relation to any procedural matter falling within the scope of this practice direction but not the subject of specific reference, such discretion should be exercised having regard to the principles in paragraph IV.39.3.

Appeal and committals for sentence

IV.39.17. This practice direction does not in terms apply to appeals and committals for sentence, but regard should be paid to the effect of it if the arrangements for hearing any appeal or committal might otherwise be prejudicial to the welfare of a young defendant.

of the practice direction under review, in consultation with the Lord Chief Justice.

The practice direction requires courts to take positive steps to ensure that a juvenile defendant understands court procedure and that, where practicable, all the participants in the courtroom should be on the same level. The Government will be inviting Lord Justice Auld, in his review of the working of the criminal courts, to look in more detail at working of juvenile trials in the Crown Court.[6]

10.6   The Auld Committee reported in 2001 and made the following recommendations in relation to the trial of children and young persons for serious offences:

- all cases involving young defendants who are presently committed to the Crown Court for trial or for sentence should in future be put before the youth court consisting, as appropriate, of a High Court Judge, Circuit Judge or Recorder sitting with at least two experienced magistrates and exercising the full jurisdiction of the present Crown Court for this purpose;
- the only possible exception should be those cases in which the young defendant is charged jointly with an adult and it is considered necessary in the interests of justice for them to be tried together; and
- the youth court so constituted should be entitled, save where it considers that public interest demands otherwise, to hear such cases in private, as in the youth court exercising its present jurisdiction.[7]

10.7   The government has chosen not to implement these proposals, or indeed any other procedural changes, to deal with the criticism of the European Court in the case of *T v United Kingdom, V v United Kingdom*.

Subsequent decisions

10.8   The European Court of Human Rights has returned to the issue of effective participation in the case of *SC v United Kingdom*.[8] The applicant, aged 11, and a 14-year-old boy approached an 87-year-old woman in the street and tried to take her bag. She fell down and fractured her arm. The applicant's defence to attempted robbery was that he had acted under duress from the other boy. The case was committed to the Crown Court as a grave crime. After committal, the defence lawyer obtained a psychological and psychiatric assessment of the applicant. The psychological assessment indicated that the applicant had an IQ of 56 and suggested that his cognitive abilities were more consistent with a child of 8 rather than 11. The psychiatric assessment was hampered by the applicant's unwillingness to engage in the assessment process, but suggested that he had complex needs which would be ideally addressed under the provisions of a care order. The psychiatrist concluded that the applicant was aware of his actions and was aware that they were wrong, but that his understanding of their consequences may have been adversely affected by his learning difficulties and impaired

---

6   Hansard HC Debates col 21, 13 March 2000.

7   *Review of the Criminal Courts of England and Wales by the Right Honourable Lord Justice Auld* (September 2001), Chapter 5, pp214–217. An electronic version of the report is available at www.criminal-courts-review.org.uk.

8   [2004] 40 EHRR 10.

reasoning skills. Nevertheless, she concluded that he was sufficiently capable of entering a plea but that the court process would need to be explained in a manner commensurate with his learning difficulties. In the light of the expert assessments of the applicant, the defence barrister applied to the trial judge for the proceedings to be stayed as an abuse of process. This application was refused, the trial judge holding that the applicant appeared to be a streetwise child, whose intellectual impairment was largely the result of spending two of his critical formative years outside the education system. The trial proceeded in December 1999, lasting a single day. The applicant was not required to sit in the dock and he was accompanied by a social worker. The judge and barristers dispensed with the formality of wearing wigs and gowns and the court took frequent breaks. The prosecution case consisted of the oral testimony of two eye-witnesses and two written statements. The applicant gave evidence that he had acted under duress. He was convicted and sentenced to 30 months' detention. A subsequent appeal against conviction was rejected by the Court of Appeal.[9]

10.9 Before the European Court of Human Rights it was argued that the applicant had not had a fair trial as required by Article 6. As well as the original psychological and psychiatric assessment, the court considered the evidence of the social worker who had accompanied the applicant to the trial. This social worker stated that the applicant had little comprehension of the role of the jury in the proceedings or of the importance of making a good impression on them. He also did not seem to have grasped the fact that he risked a custodial sentence as even after sentence he appeared confused and expected to be able to go home with his foster parent.

10.10 In relation to the meaning of effective participation, the court declared:

> The Court accepts the Government's argument that Article 6 § 1 does not require that a child on trial for a criminal offence should understand or be capable of understanding every point of law or evidential detail. Given the sophistication of modern legal systems, many adults of normal intelligence are unable fully to comprehend all the intricacies and exchanges which take place in the courtroom: this is why the Convention, in Article 6 § 3 (c), emphasises the importance of the right to legal representation. However, 'effective participation' in this context presupposes that the accused has a broad understanding of the nature of the trial process and of what is at stake for him or her, including the significance of any penalty which may be imposed. It means that he or she, if necessary with the assistance of, for example, an interpreter, lawyer, social worker or friend, should be able to understand the general thrust of what is said in court. The defendant should be able to follow what is said by the prosecution witnesses and, if represented, to explain to his own lawyers his version of events, point out any statements with which he disagrees and make them aware of any facts which should be put forward in his defence.

10.11 In the light of the evidence presented, the court concluded that the applicant had not been able to participate effectively in his trial. The court went on to comment:

> The Court considers that, when the decision is taken to deal with a child, such as the applicant, who risks not being able to participate effectively because of his young age and limited intellectual capacity, by way of criminal proceedings

---

9 *R v C(S)* (2000) 19 June, No 990783/21.

rather than some other form of disposal directed primarily at determining the child's best interests and those of the community, it is essential that he be tried in a specialist tribunal which is able to give full consideration to, and make proper allowance for, the handicaps under which he labours, and adapt its procedure accordingly.

10.12　In the opinion of the authors, it is questionable whether the Crown Court in its current form constitutes the specialist tribunal considered essential by the European Court of Human Rights.

10.13　The question of effective participation in youth court proceedings has also been recently considered by the Administrative Court in the case of *R (on the application of TP) v West London Youth Court*.[10] The applicant was a 15-year-old boy charged with robbery and attempted robbery and the trial was due to take place in the youth court. He was assessed by a psychologist as having an IQ of 63 and the intellectual capacity of an 8-year-old child. Prior to the trial hearing, the defence solicitor argued that the applicant's cognitive impairment was such that he could not participate effectively in the proceedings. She therefore argued that the proceedings should be stayed as an abuse of process. A district judge considered testimony from the psychologist and concluded that, notwithstanding his learning disability, he could receive a fair trial bearing in mind the fact that he had the benefit of an experienced youth court advocate and the range of modifications to the trial procedure which could be implemented. The decision not to stay the proceedings was judicially reviewed.

10.14　The Administrative Court reviewed the decisions of the European Court of Human Rights in *T v United Kingdom, V v United Kingdom*[11] and *SC v United Kingdom*[12] and concluded:

> The judge had earlier correctly directed himself that the minimum requirements for a fair trial for the claimant were:
> i)　he had to understand what he is said to have done wrong;
> ii)　the court had to be satisfied that the claimant when he had done wrong by act or omission had the means of knowing that was wrong;
> iii)　he had to understand what, if any, defences were available to him;
> iv)　he had to have a reasonable opportunity to make relevant representations if he wished;
> v)　he had to have the opportunity to consider what representations he wished to make once he had understood the issues involved.
>
> He had therefore to be able to give proper instructions and to participate by way of providing answers to questions and suggesting questions to his lawyers in the circumstances of the trial as they arose.
>
> It was essential to the judge's decision ... that the appellant would be tried in a Youth Court as apposed to a Crown Court and that he would be assisted by specialists and experienced Youth Court representatives. The Youth Court is a specialised court designed and adapted for hearing cases where youngsters are charged with criminal offences. Specialist judges with the requisite training sit in them ... Judges, and the advocates who appear in those courts, have special expertise and experience in dealing with the kind of problems presented by the claimant and other youngsters whose intellectual capacity falls at the lower end of the scale.

10　[2005] EWHC 2583 (Admin).
11　(1999) 30 EHRR 131.
12　[2004] 40 EHRR 10.

10.15   In refusing the application for judicial review, Baker LJ noted:

> The fundamental distinction between *SC* and the present case is that *SC* was tried in the Crown Court; the claimant will be tried in the youth court. The question in our view is this. Taking into account the steps that can be taken in the youth court will the claimant be able effectively to participate in his trial? [The psychologist] did not go so far as to say that effective participation would not be possible.
>
> It is apparent from the judge's judgment and [psychologist's] evidence that there are indeed a number of steps that can be taken during the trial. These include:
> i)   keeping the claimant's level of cognitive functioning in mind;
> ii)   using concise and simple language;
> iii)   having regular breaks;
> iv)   taking additional time to explain court proceedings;
> v)   being proactive in ensuring the claimant has access to support;
> vi)   explaining and ensuring the claimant understands the ingredients of the charge;
> vii)   explaining the possible outcomes and sentences;
> viii) ensuring that cross-examination is carefully controlled so that questions are short and clear and frustration is minimised.
>
> In our judgment neither youth nor limited intellectual capacity necessarily leads to a breach of Article 6.

Ability to testify in own defence

10.16   It is perhaps surprising that none of the decisions discussed above mention the question of the defendant's capacity to testify in his/her own defence. In an adversarial trial process, this is a very important ability, particularly with the possibility of an adverse inference being drawn from a failure to testify.[13] In the opinion of the authors, the ability to testify coherently and reliably should be one of the minimum requirements for a defendant's effective participation.

Ensuring effective participation

10.17   The United States psychologist Thomas Grisso argues that consideration of this issue must include both an understanding of the functional abilities needed by a defendant and their interaction with the situational demands of the particular court proceedings faced by the young defendant.[14] Using this approach, the defence lawyer needs to consider the following questions:

- What are the demands of the proceedings s/he currently faces?
- What is the defendant able to do?
- What is needed to maximise the young defendant's ability to participate?

13   Criminal Justice and Public Order Act 1994 s35.
14   T Grisso, *Forensic evaluation of juveniles*, Professional Resource Press, USA, 1998.

The demands of the court proceedings

10.18   Not every criminal case places the same demands upon a defendant. The most important variables are:

- the seriousness of the charges;
- the complexity and number of the charges;
- the venue for the proceedings;
- the nature of the prosecution evidence;
- the involvement of co-defendants;
- the availability of emotional support from others.[15]

Seriousness of the charges

10.19   The seriousness of the charges will affect the level of resources the police devoted to the investigation. This in turn will affect the number of prosecution witnesses and the volume of unused material in the case. The seriousness of the charges will also have an effect on the emotional pressure of the proceedings.

Complexity and number of charges

10.20   Individual charges may be more difficult for a young defendant to understand where they involve a level of intent. Court cases which involve charges relating to more than one incident will also put greater demands on a young client because of the greater complexity of the information to be processed.

Venue of the proceedings

10.21   As noted by Brooke LJ in *R (on the application of TP) v West London Youth Court* there is a fundamental difference between a youth court trial and a Crown Court trial. Youth court trials are conducted in private, often in purpose-built court rooms. The simplicity of the trial procedure will usually mean that the trial is short, rarely taking more than a day. In contrast, a jury trial in the Crown Court will inevitably be more formal and more intimidating, largely because of the participation of 12 adult jurors and the consequent need for larger court rooms, a more cumbersome procedure and a more expansive style of advocacy.

Nature of the prosecution evidence

10.22   The demands of the court process will be greater where:

- there are a large number of witness statements; and
- the case is circumstantial, requiring the young client to cope with more abstract information.

Involvement of co-defendants

10.23   The existence of co-defendants in a case means that there are likely to be more lawyers questioning witnesses, thereby increasing the length of

15   T Grisso, *Competency to stand trial evaluations: a manual for practice*, Professional Resource Exchange, USA, 1988.

the case as well as the complexity of the testimony heard in court as each lawyer presents a different version of the incident to the witness. Where co-defendants are expected to blame each other during any trial, the young client not only has to cope with conflicting factual versions but also hostile cross-examination from co-defendant lawyers as well as the prosecutor.

Availability of emotional support

10.24 A young defendant who is offered emotional and practical support during court proceedings is much more likely to cope with the stress of court proceedings. Unfortunately not all young clients have the benefit of such support from a parent or other carer. Particularly in lengthy court cases, the defence lawyer needs to assess the ability of adults in the young client's life to provide emotional and practical support.

What is the defendant able to do?

10.25 The young client needs to be able to:

- understand the charges and potential consequences;
- understand the court process;
- participate with the defence lawyer in the defence; and
- participate in the court hearings.

10.26 A more detailed analysis of the required functional abilities has been carried out by Grisso – see table 11 below.

10.27 In a review of research carried out in the United States, Grisso concluded:

(i) For defendants under 14 years, the balance of evidence is that as a group they are at greater risk than adults for deficits in abilities associated with effective participation. Young people of that age who have defendant abilities similar to those of adults represent a significant exception to the norm.

(ii) Among defendants who are 14 to 16, age itself tends to be a poor indicator of abilities required for effective participation. By about 14 or 15 years, some young people appear to have developed legally relevant cognitive abilities that approximate to those of older adolescents. Many other young people do not seem to reach that stage until late adolescence. This developmental delay is seen especially in delinquent populations, which have a greater proportion of adolescents with intellectual deficits, learning disabilities, emotional disorders, and reduced educational and cultural opportunities.

(iii) Even among 14- to 16-year-olds who have achieved adult capacity for understanding and reasoning, some may not have achieved the ability to maintain or use those capacities consistently across situations and under stress in ways that they will achieve on entering their adult years.[16]

16 T Grisso, 'What we know about youths' capacities as trial defendants' in Grisso and Schwartz (eds) *Youth on trial: a developmental perspective on juvenile justice*, University of Chicago Press, 2000.

Table 11: Functional abilities required to participate in the trial process

Understanding of charges and potential consequences

1 Ability to understand and appreciate the charges and their seriousness

2 Ability to understand possible consequences of potential pleas

3 Ability to appraise realistically the likely outcomes

Understanding of the trial process

4 Ability to understand, without significant distortion, the roles of participants in the trial process (eg judge, defence lawyer, prosecutor, witness, jury)

5 Ability to understand the process and potential consequences of pleading

6 Ability to grasp the general sequence of pre-trial/trial events

Capacity to participate with lawyer in a defence

7 Ability to trust adequately or work collaboratively with lawyer

8 Ability to disclose to lawyer reasonably coherent description of facts relating to the charges, as perceived by the defendant

9 Ability to reason about available options by weighing the consequences, without significant distortion

10 Ability to challenge realistically prosecution witnesses and monitor trial events

Potential for court room participation

11 Ability to testify coherently, if testimony is needed

12 Ability to control own behaviour during trial proceedings

13 Ability to manage stress of trial

Adapted from: T Grisso, *Forensic evaluation of juveniles*, Professional Resource Press, Sarasota, USA, 1998.

10.28 From the very start of the case, the defence lawyer needs to assess the young client's ability to understand both court procedure and the actual content of hearings. Part of this assessment will involve noting how difficult it is to explain important information and concepts to the client as well as how well s/he is able to retain this information. It will also be important to consider what problems are faced in explaining the prosecution evidence to the young client, as well as taking factual instructions from him/her.

10.29 An essential part of this ongoing assessment will include obtaining information from other sources such as parents or carers, teachers, social services departments and health professionals.

Assessment by experts

10.30 Where the defence lawyer's own assessment and research reveals significant concerns about the young client's ability to participate effectively in the proceedings, the expert opinion of a psychologist or psychiatrist will need to be sought.

10.31 Bearing in mind the significantly greater demands of a jury trial, it is the opinion of the authors that an assessment should be obtained in all Crown Court cases involving:

- all defendants under the age of 14;
- a defendant who has an identified learning disability or obvious problems with learning;
- a defendant who has missed a significant period of schooling (whether through long-term illness, exclusion or truanting);
- a defendant who has a mental disorder which may significantly impair his/her level of cognitive and emotional functioning.

Choice of expert

10.32 A chartered psychologist should be instructed if the main concern is the defendant's developmental immaturity or any learning ability or mental disorder which will affect cognitive functioning of the client. A psychologist can use psychometric evaluations to provide an objective assessment of the client's:

- intelligence quotient (IQ);
- level of understanding of the spoken word (listening comprehension);
- level of reading;
- level of oral expression;
- degree of suggestibility; and
- degree of acquiescence.

10.33 The defence lawyer should only consider instructing a chartered psychologist who has both forensic experience and experience of assessing adolescents.

10.34 A psychiatrist would be instructed where the concern is regarding a mental disorder which may affect the young client's ability to participate. At least one psychiatrist must be instructed where the statutory fitness to plead procedure is to be used in the Crown Court (see paras 10.44–10.51 below). A psychiatrist will often request that the young person be assessed by a psychologist to establish his level of cognitive functioning before a clinical assessment is carried out.

10.35 The defence lawyer should only consider instructing a child and adolescent psychiatrist with forensic experience. Although adult psychiatrists may be willing to carry out an assessment of a defendant aged 16 years or over, they are unlikely to be sufficiently alert to the relevant developmental issues.

Funding the cost of the assessment

10.36 The cost of an expert assessment may be claimed as a disbursement under the General Criminal Contract or as part of the Crown Court bill. Prior authority for the cost of the report should be obtained from the Criminal Defence Service on Form CDS4. The application will have to explain the purpose of the report and why it is a reasonable and necessary disbursement for the proper conduct of the proceedings.[17] This explanation will

---

17 Criminal Defence Service, *Criminal Bills Assessment Manual*, para 4.3.12 and CRIMLA 3.

need to include a justification for the choice of an expert with experience of assessing adolescents. To provide the necessary developmental information, the expert will often want to interview a parent or carer personally. This will obviously involve extra expense which will need to be specifically justified.

Instructions to the expert

10.37   Having obtained prior authority from the Criminal Defence Service, the defence lawyer should send written instructions to the chosen expert. The relevant personal information and personal records should be obtained prior to the instructions being sent. A checklist of relevant information to provide to the expert is provided in table 12 below.

10.38   Where the defence lawyer arranges for a young client to be assessed by a psychologist or psychiatrist, the client is entitled to assume that what s/he says has the same status as communications with the defence lawyer. It follows that both the interview with the mental health professional and the opinion based on that interview are privileged.[18] Nevertheless, it is recommended that the instructions to the expert do not include any details of the client's factual instructions in relation to the charge(s) and that the expert is specifically prohibited from discussing the details of the allegation with the client during the assessment. This avoids problems later if the report is to be disclosed to the prosecution and court.

The role of the defence lawyer

10.39   In a thoughtful article[19] Emily Buss, an American academic lawyer, argues that lawyers can maximise a young defendant's ability to participate effectively in two basic ways by:

- acting as an instructor; and
- developing a lawyer-client relationship.

Acting as instructor

10.40   Buss suggests that the defence lawyer should make every effort to improve their clients understanding by communicating how legal system works and what is at stake. She argues however that instruction, applied in isolation, is unlikely to be an effective tool on its own to ensure effective participation. Drawing on the work of developmental psychologist Lev Vygotsky, she argues that a young client is more likely to learn about the court process when the instruction occurs in the course of natural interactions with an adult model who plays an important role in his/her life.

Developing a lawyer-client relationship

10.41   Buss goes on to state that this understanding of how children learn leads to the question of building a meaningful relationship with the young

---

18   *R v Davies* 166 JP 243, CA.
19   E Buss, 'The Role of Lawyers' in T Grisso and R Schwartz (eds) *Youth on Trial: A Development Perspective on Juvenile Justice*, University of Chicago Press, 2000.

Table 12: Assessment of ability to participate effectively – checklist for instructing the expert

- **Personal details of client**
  - Name, date of birth and current whereabouts (ie bail address or where detained)
- **Details of court proceedings**
  - Charges
  - Court
  - History of proceedings
  - Date of any trial
- **Demands of the court process faced by the client**
  - Venue
  - Estimated length of any trial
  - Nature of prosecution evidence (include copies of important witness statements)
  - Participation of co-defendants
  - Availability of emotional support
- **Relevant information about defendant**
  - Home circumstances
  - Care history
  - Schooling
  - Previous assessments by professionals (enclose any written reports available)
  - Contact details for parent/carer or any other person who expert should interview as part of assessment
- **Confirmation that the report will be a privileged documents and instruction that the current allegation is not to be discussed during the assessment**
- **Questions to address**
  - Does the client have any relevant cognitive deficits?
  - Does the client have any relevant mental disorder?
  - Are any cognitive deficits or mental disorder of sufficient degree to affect the client's ability to participate effectively in the current proceedings? (Refer to abilities listed in table 11)
  - If yes to above, what modifications to court procedure are recommended to maximise ability to participate effectively in proceedings?
  - Will modifications to court procedure be sufficient to ensure effective participation?
  - Will the client be able to testify coherently and reliably in his/her own defence?
  - Should any modifications be made to normal court procedure to ensure that the client gives best evidence?
- **Arrangements for appointment to assess client**
- **Confirmation of case being publicly funded and limit of prior authority granted**
- **Deadline for preparation of report**

client. She explains that young clients have no expectation of a relationship of trust with a lawyer, partly because the lawyer-client relationship may be completely beyond their experience, but also because many children and young persons involved in the youth justice system have difficulties forming relationships of trust. A proper professional relationship will not develop she argues unless the defence lawyer devotes time and effort to cultivating it. To develop the required relationship Buss suggests the lawyer should:

- involve the client in the case preparation as much as possible; and
- take every opportunity to demonstrate loyalty to the client (for example by asserting confidentiality or demonstrating a willingness to exclude a parent or carer from a discussion about the young client's case).

10.41A   When the young client understands that s/he has the lawyer's undivided loyalty, Buss argues that the client is likely to be more willing to disclose information and seek advice. S/he is also more likely to listen to information provided by the lawyer and to trust advice received.

Modifying court procedure

10.42   Throughout the court proceedings the defence lawyer should consider whether any modifications to the court's usual practices would improve the young defendant's ability to participate effectively in the proceedings. A checklist of possible modifications is in table 13 below. The question of necessary modifications to facilitate the young defendant giving best evidence in his/her own defence is considered at paras 15.64–15.83.

Defendant unable to participate effectively

10.43   In a small number of cases, the assessment of the expert will identify problems which are so great that they prevent a young defendant from participating effectively in the proceedings no matter what modifications to court procedure are made. The procedural means by which the defence lawyer will deal with this, depends on the court which is dealing with the proceedings.

Fitness to plead

10.44   Fitness to plead is relevant only in the Crown Court where the procedure for raising the issue is governed by the Criminal Procedure (Insanity) Act 1964 as amended by Domestic Violence, Crime and Victims Act 2004 s22.

10.45   The test of whether a defendant is fit to plead was set out by Alderson B in *R v Pritchard*[20] more than 150 years ago and is now 'firmly embodied in our law'.[21] In deciding whether the defendant is fit to plead, the court should consider:

> Whether he is of sufficient intellect to comprehend the course of proceedings on the trial, so as to make a proper defence – to know that he might challenge

---

20   (1836) 7 C& P 303.
21   Lord Parker CJ in *R v Podola* [1960] 1 QB 325, CA.

Table 13: Modifications to court procedure

To reduce the formality of the proceedings

- Refer to defendant by his/her first name
- Removal of wigs and gowns by judge and barristers (in Crown Court)
- Allow defendant to leave dock

To facilitate communication between defendant and his/her lawyer

- Allow defendant to sit next to trial advocate
- Encourage young defendant to seek explanations when development in proceedings is not understood
- Adjourn on regular basis to allow the defence lawyer to check his/her client's understanding

To minimise the potential distress and inhibition caused by a hearing in public

- Imposition of reporting restrictions (Children and Young Persons Act 1933 s39)
- Request by court to lawyers, witnesses and members of public concerned with other cases to leave court room

To enable the defendant to follow the testimony of prosecution witnesses

- Ask all witnesses and advocates to avoid as much as possible complex language during the course of evidence
- Help the young defendant to concentrate during the proceedings by adjourning for short breaks regularly

To facilitate the effective testimony of the young defendant

- Use of simple language in examination-in-chief and cross-examination
- Questions to only contain one idea
- Avoid pressure during cross-examination
- Use of screen while defendant testifying
- Clearing court (if public hearing) while defendant testifies in a case involving an offence against, or any conduct contrary to, decency or morality (Children and Young Persons Act 1933 s37)

To ensure adequate social support during the trial

- Presence of a parent or guardian in close proximity to defendant
- Access to parent, guardian or other carer during adjournments in the court day
- Where parent/carer unavailable/unsuitable arrange another adult (eg relative, youth offending team worker, youth worker) to be present
- During long trials ensuring support is provided on regular basis, ideally by same individual each day

[any jurors] to whom he may object – and to comprehend the details of the evidence ... if you think that there is no certain mode of communicating the details of the trial to the prisoner, so that he can clearly understand them, and be able properly to make his defence to the charge; you ought to find that he is not of sane mind. It is not enough, that he may have a general capacity of communicating on ordinary matters.

10.46　Despite Alderson B's reference to finding the accused 'not of sane mind', a defendant may be unfit to plead even if not legally insane.[22]

Procedure

10.47　The question of whether a defendant is fit to plead is determined by a judge sitting without a jury.[23] If, on the evidence of written or oral reports from two or more registered medical practitioners (at least one of whom is registered under Mental Health Act 1983 s12), the judge concludes that the defendant is not fit to plead, a jury shall be empanelled to determine whether the defendant did the act or made the omission charged against him/her.[24]

10.48　　If, after hearing the expert evidence, the judge decides that the defendant is fit to plead, a jury will be empanelled to decide on the defendant's guilt in a normal criminal trial.

10.49　　In *R v H*[25] the House of Lords held that the statutory procedure for determining fitness to plead was compatible with the European Convention on Human Rights. Article 6 was not engaged as the accused who had been found unfit no longer faced a criminal charge or a criminal penalty. In addition, the procedure was thought to be an appropriate balance between the rights of the unfit person and the rights of victims and the general public to be protected.

Burden of proof

10.50　If the issue is raised by the defence, the burden of proof must be discharged by the accused on a balance of probabilities.[26]

Disposals for an unfit accused

10.51　See para 30.28 onwards.

Abuse of process in the Crown Court

General principles

10.54　A court may exercise its common law power to stay proceedings as an abuse of process where the court considers that:

* the defendant cannot receive a fair trial; or
* it would be unfair for the defendant to be tried.[27]

22　*R v Governor of Stafford Prison ex p Emery* [1909] 2 KB 81 (a case involving a deaf defendant who was unable to read, write or communicate with sign language).
23　Criminal Procedure (Insanity) Act 1964 s4(5).
24　Ibid, s4A(2).
25　[2003] UKHL 1, [2003] 1 WLR 411.
26　*R v Robertson* [1968] 1 WLR 1767, CA.
27　*R v Beckford* [1996] 1 Cr App R 94.

10.55   In either case the exercise of the power to stay proceedings ought only to be employed in exceptional circumstances, as in most cases the alleged unfairness could be covered in the trial process itself.[28]

Application to cases of inability to participate effectively

10.56   Where the statutory procedure for determining fitness to plead exists, it seems that abuse of process is not an available remedy. Delivering judgment in the Court of Appeal hearing of *R v M, K and H*,[29] Rose LJ stated that although an abuse of process application to stay proceedings for abuse could be made prior to the determination of the question of fitness to plead, the defendant's disability or matters related to it, cannot in themselves found a successful abuse application. Instead Rose LJ considered that the application should be founded on oppressive behaviour of the Crown or agencies of the state or conduct which would deprive the defendant of a fair trial (such as destruction of vital documents during a long period of delay or an earlier assurance that the defendant would not be prosecuted).[30] This point was not expressly dealt with in any of the opinions delivered in the subsequent appeal to the House of Lords.[31]

Summary trial

10.57   It is clear that there is no statutory procedure by which a person's fitness to plead can be determined in the youth court or adult magistrates' court.[32] Quite what is the appropriate procedure to raise the question of the defendant's inability to participate effectively in the proceedings is less clear.

10.58   In *R (on the application of P) v Barking Youth Court*[33] the 16-year-old defendant was charged with charges under the Protection from Harassment Act 1997 and the Criminal Damage Act 1971. When he was 12 years old, psychometric testing had indicated his IQ was 52, meaning that at that age he had been functioning intellectually at a level bettered by 99.9 per cent of his age peers. Later he was referred to a specialist adolescent psychiatric unit where he was found to be demonstrating some features of an autistic spectrum disorder coupled with severe behavioural problems. A psychological assessment was commissioned by the defence for the purposes of the proceedings, but the applicant's cooperation was limited. At the youth court the defence lawyer indicated that he wished to raise the question of the defendant's fitness to plead as a preliminary issue. The psychologist who had carried out the recent assessment was called to give evidence. He testified that the applicant was suffering an incomplete development of mind to such an extent that he was incapable of understanding the nature of the offence and therefore unable to give any objective or rational instructions. He further offered the opinion that due to his

28 Attorney-General's Reference No 1 of 1990 [1992] QB 630; (1992) 95 Cr App R 296.
29 [2001] EWCA Crim 2024.
30 Ibid, [35]–[36].
31 Sub nom *R v H*, see n25 above.
32 *R v Horseferry Road Magistrates' Court ex p K* [1996] 3 All ER 719, QBD; see also *DPP v H* [1997] 1 WLR 1406, QBD.
33 [2002] EWHC 734 (Admin); [2002] 2 Cr App R 19; [2002] Crim LR 657.

impaired intellect and inattentiveness, the applicant would not be able to follow the course of proceedings or understand the details of evidence. Clearly following the *Pritchard* criteria, the psychologist also gave the opinion that the applicant would not be able to understand or reply rationally to the indictment or to challenge jurors on a rational basis. Having considered the expert testimony, the justices ruled that the applicant was fit to plead, as his behaviour indicated that he was capable of understanding the proceedings. The justices also indicated that they did not think that the *Pritchard* criteria were relevant in the youth court.

10.59   The applicant sought judicial review of the justices' decision, arguing that it was irrational as it ignored expert testimony and substituted the justices' non-expert assessment of the defendant based solely on observing his behaviour during the court hearing. It was further submitted that in the circumstances the proceedings against the applicant should be stayed as an abuse of process.

10.60   In refusing the application, the Administrative Court managed to give their judgment without once referring to the fair trial guarantee of Article 6 of the European Convention on Human Rights. The court ruled that in summary proceedings there was 'a complete statutory framework for the determination by [a summary court] of all the issues which arise in cases of defendants who are or may be mentally ill or suffering from severe mental impairment in the context of offences which are triable summarily only'. This framework involves Powers of Criminal Courts (Sentencing) Act 2000 s11, which permits a court to adjourn a case to enable medical examination to be carried out where the court is satisfied that the accused did the act or omission charged and it is of the opinion that an inquiry ought to be made into the accused's physical or mental condition before the method of dealing with him/her is determined. The second part of this framework is Mental Health Act 1983 s37(3), which permits the making of a hospital order or guardianship order without convicting the accused in cases where it is satisfied that the accused did the act or omission charged.

10.61   In the opinion of the authors, the solution proposed by the Administrative Court in this case raises more questions than it answers. It does not explain how the trial court is to decide whether it is conducting a criminal trial or a hearing to determine only the question of the commission of the act or omission charged without any need to consider a mental element to the offence. It also does not explain what the court should do if the accused does not meet the criteria of a hospital or guardianship order.

10.62   In the subsequent case of *R (on the application of TP) v West London Youth Court* (see paras 10.13–10.15 above),[34] a differently constituted Administrative Court seems to have assumed that there was a power to stay the proceedings as an abuse of process on the basis of an inability on the part of the defendant to participate effectively in the proceedings. In the judgment of the court delivered by Brooke LJ, there is no reference to the *Barking Youth Court* case. It is the opinion of the authors that the approach taken in the *West London Youth Court* case is preferable and should be the way by which a defence lawyer should ask the youth court to consider a young defendant's inability to participate in the proceedings.

34 [2005] EWHC 2583 (Admin).

CHAPTER 11

Court powers and procedure

Introduction

11.1   The youth court is part of the magistrates' court.[1] This chapter will examine the ways in which the procedure of the youth court is different to the adult court, and the different considerations in the Crown Court. The areas of mode of trial and trial procedure are dealt with in separate chapters. In some of the areas dealt with in this chapter there is considerable local variation in court practice. Where this may affect the conduct of the case, it is highlighted.

Commencing proceedings

11.2   There is no restriction upon who may commence proceedings against a child or young person, but in practice it would be very rare for a private prosecution to be brought against a person under the age of 18. The police will bring most prosecutions.

Notification to local authority and probation

11.3   Before proceedings are commenced against a child or young person, notification should be given to the relevant local authority department and probation service.

Local authority

11.4   Children and Young Persons Act 1969 s5 provides:

> (8) It shall be the duty of a person who decides to lay an information in respect of an offence in a case where he has reason to believe the alleged offender is a young person to give notice of the decision to the appropriate local authority unless he is himself that authority.

> (9) In this section–
> 'the appropriate authority', in relation to a young person, means the local authority for the area in which it appears to the informant that the young person resides or , if the informant appears not to reside in the area of a local authority, the local authority in whose area it is alleged that the relevant offence or one of the relevant offences was committed.
> But nothing in this section shall be construed as preventing any council or other body from acting by an agent for the purposes of this section.

11.5   This provision has been considered by the Divisional Court in the case of *DPP v Cottier.*[2] Saville LJ held that notice could be given orally to the relevant social services department and that the section did not require notification to be effected by a particular stage in the proceedings. He further held that the purpose of the section was to allow the local authority to comply with its duty under Children and Young Persons Act 1969 s9 to provide to the court relevant background information regarding the young

---

1   Children and Young Persons Act 1933 s45.
2   [1996] 3 All ER 126; [1996] 1 WLR 826; [1996] Crim LR 804, QBD.

defendant. In practice, notification is generally sent to the youth offending team.

Probation

11.6 Children and Young Persons Act 1969 s34(2) provides:

> In the case of a person who has not attained the age of eighteen but who has attained such lower age as the Secretary of State may by order specify no proceedings for an offence shall be begun in any court unless the person proposing to begin the proceedings has, in addition to any notice to be given to a local authority in pursuance of section 5(8) of this Act, given notice of the proceedings to a probation officer for the area for which the court acts.

Such lower age

11.7 This has been fixed as the age of 10.[3]

11.8 Proceedings have been held to begin when the defendant is first brought before the court.[4] Notice, whether oral or in writing, should be served prior to that date so that the probation service is in a position to provide any possible help to the court by providing information regarding the young defendant.

The effect of failure to notify

11.9 Both of the above provisions have been held to be directory, and if the police fail to make the required notification the validity of the court proceedings are not affected.[5]

Requiring attendance at court

11.10 There are three ways of requiring attendance at court. These are by way of:

(i) charge;
(ii) summons;
(iii) warrant.

Charge

11.11 A child or young person charged by the police must be handed a written notice of the offences with which s/he has been charged. If the accused is a juvenile, the notice should be handed to the appropriate adult.[6]

11.12 There is no power for the police to require a parent or guardian to attend court with the child or young person. Once the child has appeared at court the court has power to issue a summons or warrant to enforce the attendance of a parent or guardian.[7]

---

3 Children and Young Persons Act 1969 (Transitional Modifications of Part I) Order 1970 SI No 1882.
4 *DPP v Cottier* [1996] 1 WLR 826; [1996] 3 All ER 126.
5 Ibid; confirmed in relation to section 34(2) by the Court of Appeal in *R v Marsh* [1997] 1 WLR 649.
6 PACE Code C para 16.3.
7 Children and Young Persons Act 1933 s34A, Criminal Procedure Rules 2005 r7.8.

Summons

11.13   Upon receiving an information, a justice of the peace (or a justice's legal adviser[8]) may issue a summons requiring the attendance at court of any person suspected of having committed a criminal offence.[9]

11.14   A summons issued against a child or young person may also require the attendance of the parent or guardian.[10]

Warrant

11.15   Upon receiving a written information sworn on oath, a justice of the peace may issue a warrant for the arrest of a person suspected of committing a crime. The warrant will direct the police to bring the person arrested before the court.[11]

11.16   It is possible for the justices to endorse a warrant so that upon its execution the person arrested may be released on bail to attend court.[12]

Determining age

11.17   Children and Young Persons Act 1933 s99(1) provides:

> Where a person is brought before a court and it appears to the court that s/he is a child or young person, the court is required to make due inquiry as to his/her age, and for that purpose shall take such evidence as may be forthcoming at the hearing of the case.

11.18   In most cases the court will accept the date of birth given by the defendant as their correct age on their first appearance before the court. If the police or prosecution do not accept the age given as correct, the court will need to make a determination as to age. This will take place immediately, whether the young defendant is appearing in the youth or adult magistrates' court.

11.19   It may be necessary to point out to the court that physical maturity is not a determinant of age.[13] The defence lawyer needs to consider whether any evidence can be called from an adult relative or whether any documentary evidence can be produced.

Effect of discovering the defendant's true age later

11.20   Children and Young Persons Act 1933 s99(1) provides:

> [A]n order or judgment of the court shall not be invalidated by any subsequent proof that the age of that person has not been correctly stated to the court, and the age presumed or declared by the court to be the age of the person so brought before it shall, for the purposes of this Act, be deemed to be the true age of that person.

8   Justices' Clerks Rules 1999 SI No 2784 r2.
9   Magistrates' Courts Act 1980 s1(1)(a).
10   Criminal Procedure Rules 2005 r7.8.
11   Magistrates' Courts Act 1980 s1(1)(b).
12   Ibid, s117.
13   See paras 4.6–4.8.

By virtue of Children and Young Persons Act 1969 s70(3), this applies to the 1969 Act and therefore applies to remands to local authority accommodation.

The youth court

Definition

11.21 The youth court is defined in Children and Young Persons Act 1933 s45(1) (as amended by Courts Act 2003 s50) as:

Magistrates' courts
(a) constituted in accordance with tis section or section 66 of the Courts Act 2003 (judges having powers of District Judges (Magistrates' Courts)), and
(b) sitting for the purpose of –
   (i) hearing any charge against a child or young person, or
   (ii) exercising any other jurisdiction conferred on youth courts by or under this or any other Act,
are to be known as youth courts.

General principle

11.22 Children and Young Persons Act 1933 s46(1) establishes the following principle:

Subject as hereinafter provided, no charge against a child or young person, and no application whereof the hearing is by rules made under this section assigned to youth courts, shall be heard by a court of summary jurisdiction which is not a youth court.

11.23 A youth court is a court of summary jurisdiction assigned a special type of defendant defined by reference to age. It is the opinion of the authors that the above section should, therefore, be read as assigning certain matters to the youth court but not as exclusively defining the jurisdiction of the court.

What matters are assigned?

Charges and summonses

11.24 All informations involving defendants under the age of 18 must first be dealt with by a youth court, unless an adult is also one of the defendants (for which see chapter 12 below). In certain serious cases the case may ultimately be dealt with before a Crown Court.

Applications by rules made under s46

11.25 No rules have been made under this section assigning any applications to the youth court.

Breach of the peace

11.26 The police have a common law power to arrest a person to prevent a breach of the peace. In certain circumstances that person will then be brought before a court to be bound over to keep the peace under Magistrates' Courts Act 1980 s115. Although not expressly assigned to the youth court, it is submitted that a child or young person should be brought before a youth court if one is sitting.

Applications for anti-social behaviour orders

11.27   An application for a stand-alone anti-social behaviour order under Crime and Disorder Act 1998 s1 in relation to a child or young person will be dealt with by the adult magistrates' court. The youth court can only deal with the imposition of an anti-social behaviour order following conviction.[14] Prosecutions for the criminal offence of breach of an anti-social behaviour order will be dealt with by the youth court.

Constitution of a youth court

11.28   The system of commission areas and petty sessional areas, which previously determined where magistrates sat, has now been abolished. All magistrates are now appointed for England and Wales, reflecting the new national jurisdiction. The Courts Act 2003 replaces the local divisions with 'local justice areas' to which magistrates are now assigned.[15]

11.29   It is likely that amendments to the Children and Young Persons Act 1933 will be brought into force in 2006.[16] As a result of these changes a justice of the peace will be qualified to sit as a member of the youth court only if s/he has an authorisation specifically to empower him/her to do so. The authorisation rules will be brought in by statutory instrument and will provide for the selection and training of the youth court bench. Until that time the Youth Courts (Constitution) Rules 1954 apply.[17]

Who can sit in the youth court?

11.30   The specific rules regarding the selection of youth court panels vary between England and Wales in general and Inner London.

England and Wales (except Inner London)

11.31   Each area must appoint magistrates specifically qualified for dealing with juvenile cases to the youth court panel. Any District Judge (Magistrates' Courts) is regarded as a member of the panel. Each youth court bench shall be constituted of not more than three justices and in normal circumstances shall include a man and a woman.[18] Exceptions to this general rule are:

- if at any sitting of the youth court no man or no woman is available owing to unforeseen circumstances when the justices were chosen, the

---

14   Crime and Disorder Act 1998 s1C. See chapter 29.

15   Courts Act 2003 ss8 and 10.

16   Magistrates' Courts Act 1980 s45, as inserted by Courts Act 2003 s50. At the time of writing, draft authorisation rules are in circulation for consultation.

17   SI No 1711.

18   Ibid, r12 (1).

other members of the panel may sit if they consider it inexpedient in the interests of justice to adjourn;[19] or

- a District Judge (Magistrates' Courts) may sit alone.[20]

11.32 These rules are expressly subject to any general rule of law which grants jurisdiction to a single magistrate to act.[21] A single justice of the peace from the youth court panel may still, therefore, hear a bail application or act as an examining magistrate for the purposes of committal.

11.33 The rules in relation to the composition of the bench hearing a trial are mandatory unless the discretion to proceed has been exercised. Such discretion must be exercised publicly with submissions from the parties.[22] The court must canvas the issue with the representatives of all parties and allow them to make any representations.

Inner London

11.34 In Inner London the constitution of the youth court is still governed by Children and Young Persons Act 1933 Sch 2 Part II. The youth court will constitute either a District Judge (Magistrates' Court) sitting alone or a chairman with two other members appointed to the youth panel by the Lord Chancellor. Where it appears that the youth court cannot, without adjournment, be fully constituted and that an adjournment would not be in the interests of justice, a chairman may sit with one other member (whether male or female).

Procedure in the youth court

11.35 Youth courts should sit as often as may be necessary for the purposes of dealing with criminal cases against children or young persons.[23] Local practice varies substantially, depending on the demands of the area. In some areas, a youth court will sit only once a week whereas, particularly in urban areas, there may be a youth court sitting on every weekday. There may even be a youth court sitting on a Saturday.

Separation of children and young persons from adult defendants

11.36 Children and Young Persons Act 1933 s31 imposes an obligation upon the police, secure escort services and court administrators to ensure the separation of juvenile defendants from adult defendants. Arrangements should be made to ensure that no defendant under the age of 17 is allowed to associate with an adult defendant (unless a relative or jointly charged) either while being conveyed to court or while waiting, before or after attendance at court. In addition, a detained female juvenile should be under the care of a woman, while being conveyed to court or waiting at court.

19 Youth Courts (Constitution) Rules 1954 SI No 1711 r12 (2).
20 Ibid, r12(1).
21 Ibid, r12(4).
22 *R v Birmingham Justices ex p F* (2000) 164 JP 523, QBD.
23 Children and Young Persons Act 1933 s47(1).

Access to youth court hearings

11.37   Children and Young Persons Act 1933 s47(2) restricts access to the sittings of the youth court:

> No person shall be present at any sitting of a youth court except–
> (a) members and officers of the court;
> (b) parties to the case before the court, their solicitors and counsel, and witnesses and other persons directly concerned in that case;
> (c) *bona fide* representatives of a news gathering or reporting organisation;
> (d) such other persons as the court may specially authorise to be present.

11.38   In the opinion of the authors, in the context of section 47(2) 'officers of the court' is intended to extend access to court staff. As the lawyers for the parties are dealt with specifically, the practice in some areas of the country of allowing lawyers to be present in court whilst cases other than their own are being dealt with may be unlawful and is certainly undesirable.

11.39   Where a local authority brings criminal proceedings in the youth court for breach of an anti-social behaviour order section 47(2) has effect as if the persons entitled to be present at a sitting include one person authorised to be present by the local authority.[24]

11.40   Guidance on opening up youth court proceedings for more public scrutiny was initially issued by the Lord Chancellor's Department and Home Office in a joint circular.[25] The circular explained the government's view that there should be a presumption that the victim, with a parent or other supporter if appropriate, should be admitted to the courtroom for the trial or earlier hearings, unless there are good and sufficient reasons against this. They should also be encouraged to attend any sentencing hearings. Factors identified as going against this presumption include:

- where the defendant is particularly young or vulnerable;
- where the defendant is charged with a number of offences and allowing a large number of victims to attend would be detrimental to youth court proceedings;
- at the sentencing hearing the court may wish to hear information regarding the young offender which is sensitive or of a personal nature.

11.41   The government's view was that matters such as these are to be balanced by the court in each case against the benefits of opening up the court. It is submitted that it may be difficult to reconcile this guidance, and the assumption of the benefits of openness, with the guarantees of privacy contained in Article 8 of the European Convention of Human Rights and Article 40(2)(b)(vii) of the United Nations Convention on the Rights of the Child.

11.42   In further government guidance issued in 2001, youth courts are encouraged to ensure that victims should have the opportunity to attend a youth court hearing if they want to do so, unless the particular circum-

---

24 Crime and Disorder Act 1998 s1(10A) as inserted by Anti-social Behaviour Act 2003 s85.

25 Home Office and Lord Chancellor's Department *Opening up youth court proceedings* (June 1998).

stances of the case mean it would not be in the interests of justice. In some circumstances reporting restrictions may properly be lifted.[26]

11.43　It is submitted that where a court is considering allowing a victim to be present during the hearing, it should give the defence representative the opportunity to raise any objections before the decision is made.

Informality

11.44　A defendant in a youth court will normally be referred to by his/her first name. In order to ensure that young defendants engage more in the court hearing, government guidance has recommended:

- the development of plain language alternatives for legal and technical words and phrases;
- ensuring that there is a chair in the youth court who receives training to develop oral questioning skills and listening skills; and
- reviewing the physical environment of the courtroom and making changes to foster better communication without compromising the security and authority of the court.[27]

11.45　The importance of ensuring that the young client is able to follow proceedings and the difficulties that may be presented to the defence lawyer are further discussed in other chapters of this work. Bearing in mind the need to ensure effective participation, the defence lawyer needs to maximise ability to communicate and the understanding of the client at every hearing.

Language

11.46　The defence lawyer must ensure that the complexities of the court hearing which is to take place are explained to their client in an accessible way prior to the hearing itself. It is important to use straightforward language without being patronising. The court should also use terms which are easily understood. Unfortunately lawyers often lapse into legal jargon in court and it is essential to use comprehensible terms which are far more effective for the client, the parent or guardian and the court. Most legal terms can be phrased in a simple and accurate way.[28]

Seating arrangements

11.47　Some youth courts are purpose-built with all parties including the magistrates seated at the same level. This is particularly effective where everyone is seated at tables. In many courts there is no dedicated courtroom for the youth court and hearings take place in the more formal arrangement of the adult court.

11.48　The defence lawyer needs to be seated close to his/her client so that the procedure can be confirmed during the proceedings if necessary and the

26 Home Office and Lord Chancellor's Department *Youth Court 2001: The changing culture of the youth court – The Good Practice Guide* (March 2001).

27 Ibid.

28 Examples are shown at table 5 above.

client has access to ask questions if s/he wishes. Where there is a 'secure dock', arrangement it may be desirable to request that the client be permitted to leave the dock to sit near his/her lawyer.

11.49 If there are local difficulties on a regular basis it is a matter that should be raised with the court users committee.

Access to parents

11.50 Parents or guardians are usually seated next to or behind the child or young person. Their proximity is important to reassure the defendant and even where the young person is appearing from custody the parent or guardian should be nearby.

Mode of trial

11.51 This is dealt with in chapter 12.

The oath

11.52 The form of the oath used in the youth court is modified.[29] Instead of starting 'I swear ...' the person taking the oath should say 'I promise ...'. The remainder of the oath is the same as in other courts. This modified wording should also be used by adult witnesses testifying in the youth court.[30]

Terminology

11.53 The words 'conviction' and 'sentence' should not be used in relation to children and young persons dealt with in the youth or magistrates' court. Instead the terms 'finding of guilt' and 'order made upon a finding of guilt' should be used.[31] This is not always observed in practice.

Reporting restrictions

11.54 Children and Young Persons Act 1933 s49 imposes reporting restrictions in relation to proceedings in the youth court. It also imposes such restrictions upon the following:

- proceedings on appeal from a youth court (including proceedings by way of case stated);
- proceedings under Powers of Criminal Courts (Sentencing) Act 2000 Sch 7 (proceedings for varying or revoking supervision orders); and
- proceedings on appeal from a magistrates' court arising out of proceedings under Powers of Criminal Courts (Sentencing) Act 2000 Sch 7 (including proceedings by way of case stated).

11.55 The following prohibitions apply:

- no report shall be published which reveals the name, address or school of any child or young person concerned in the proceedings or includes

29 Children and Young Persons Act 1963 s28(1).
30 Ibid.
31 Children and Young Persons Act 1933 s59.

any particulars likely to lead to the identification of any child or young person concerned in the proceedings; and

- no picture shall be published or included in a programme service as being or including a picture of any child or young person concerned in the proceedings.

11.56 Automatic reporting restrictions under section 49 do not apply to any part of youth court proceedings which relate to the making of an anti-social behaviour order against a defendant following conviction.[32] When a youth court makes an anti-social behaviour order in such circumstances, it still has a discretion to impose reporting restrictions under section 39 of the Children and Young Persons Act 1933.[33]

11.57 The power to lift reporting restrictions may be exercised by a single justice.[34]

11.58 If the defendant attains the age of 18 during the youth court proceedings, the reporting restrictions cease to have effect.[35]

Lifting reporting restrictions

11.59 The court which has proceedings before it may dispense to any specified extent with the requirements of this section if satisfied:

- it is appropriate to do so to avoid injustice to the child or young person; or
- it is necessary to facilitate apprehension of a child or young person unlawfully at large;
- it is in the public interest to do so after conviction.

Avoiding injustice

11.60 The defence lawyer may wish to make an application regarding dispensation of reporting restrictions if it is considered that publicity for the case may prompt potential witnesses to come forward.

Unlawfully at large

11.61 The Crown Prosecution Service may apply to the relevant court if the defendant is charged with or has been convicted of:

- a violent offence;[36]
- a sexual offence;[37] or
- an offence punishable in the case of a person aged 21 or over with imprisonment for 14 years or more.

11.62 Notice of the application must be given by the Crown Prosecution Service to the young person's legal representative.

32 Crime and Disorder Act 1998 s1C(9C) as inserted by Anti-social Behaviour Act 2003 s86.
33 See chapter 29: Measures against youth crime and disorder.
34 Children and Young Persons Act 1933 s49(8).
35 *T v DPP* [2003] EWHC 2408 Admin; 168 JP 194.
36 Defined as an offence listed in Criminal Justice Act 2003 Sch 15 Part 1, listed in appendix 6.
37 Defined as an offence listed in Criminal Justice Act 2003 Sch 15 Part 2, listed in appendix 6.

11.63   Before making an order the court must be satisfied that:

- the child or young person is unlawfully at large; and
- it is necessary to dispense with those requirements for the purpose of apprehending him/her and bringing him/her before a court or returning him/her to the place in which s/he was in custody.[38]

'Public interest'

11.64   The youth court has a power in relation to a child or young person convicted of an offence to dispense to any specified extent with the reporting restrictions where it is in the public interest to do so.[39]

Penalties for breach

11.65   If a report or picture is published or included in a programme service in contravention of section 49 any editor, publisher, newspaper proprietor or broadcast company is liable on summary conviction to a fine not exceeding £5,000.[40]

Accused attaining 18

11.66   When the accused young person attains 18 after arrest it can cause considerable procedural problems. Children and Young Persons Act 1963 s29(1) provides:

> Where proceedings in respect of a young person are begun for an offence and he attains the age of eighteen before the conclusion of the proceedings, the court may deal with the case and make any order which it could have made if he had not attained that age.

11.67   Judicial opinion is divided as to whether this section applies to the whole court process or only the power to sentence. In *R v St Albans Juvenile Court ex p Goodman*[41] Skinner J said obiter that section 29(1) only applied to questions of disposal and not to questions of trial. Unfortunately he reached this view without the benefit of legal argument as both counsel in the case agreed with this view. In *R v Amersham Juvenile Court ex p Wilson*[42] Donaldson LJ took a contrary view:

> In the present case both counsel are equally agreed but in a contrary sense, namely that s29 does relate both to questions of trial and disposal. As they point out, the section in its original unamended form read 'the court may continue to deal', but Parliament when adding the words 'or for an offence' in 1969 deleted the words 'continue to'. This suggests that it now applies to the proceedings ab initio. Furthermore, the words 'deal with the case' stand as a phrase on their own and are used in contradistinction to the words 'make any order', the latter clearly covering all questions of disposal and leaving the earlier words as only really referable to questions of trial.

---

38   Children and Young Persons Act 1933 s49(5)(b).
39   Ibid, s49(4A).
40   Ibid, s49(9).
41   [1981] 2 All ER 311, QBD.
42   [1981] 2 All ER 315, QBD.

11.68　It is submitted that the view of Donaldson LJ, reached after the benefit of legal argument, is the preferable view.[43]

11.69　Children and Young Persons Act 1963 s29(1) does not solve all of the procedural problems that may arise. Some of the problems which may arise are considered below.

To which court should the police bail?

11.70　Donaldson LJ has given the following guidance:

> In our opinion, those who arrest and charge or lay an information against person who are in the juvenile/adult borderline age group should take all reasonable steps to find out exactly when they will attain the age of [18]. If they are to be brought or summoned to appear before a court for the first time on a date when they will have attained the age of [18], the court selected or specified in the summons should be the adult court. If they have not attained the age of [18], it should be a [youth court].[44]

Attaining 18 prior to the first court appearance

11.71　There are occasions when a young person is charged with an offence and bailed to the youth court on a date when s/he will be under 18 years. The young person then fails to surrender to custody on the appointed day. Does the youth court still have jurisdiction to deal with the defendant who has subsequently attained 18, when s/he finally surrenders to court or when brought to court on a warrant?

11.72　The youth court could only retain jurisdiction if the provisions of Children and Young Persons Act 1963 s29(1) could be relied on. The section may only be invoked if the proceedings have already begun. In *R v Billericay Justices ex p Johnson*[45] the Divisional Court held that proceedings had begun against a defendant when a summons was served upon him. In contrast, in *R v Amersham Juvenile Court ex p Wilson*[46] Donaldson LJ stated:

> [Section 29(1)] is wholly consistent with the statutory approach of classifying offenders as adult or [youth] by reference to their age when they first appear or are brought before a magistrates' court, provided that on the true construction of the section proceedings are 'begun' at that time and not at the earlier time when an information is laid or a charge preferred. We have no doubt that it should be so construed ... It is on the defendant first appearing or being brought a court that his age is fixed for the purpose of all of these provisions.

11.73　This latter view was confirmed in *R v Uxbridge Youth Court ex p H*.[47] In this case a 17-year-old had been charged with an offence and had then been bailed to the youth court. He failed to attend court on the day required and a warrant for his arrest was issued. The warrant was not executed until he had attained the age of 18. The youth court then purported to remit him to the adult magistrates' court. The defendant applied for judicial review of that decision. Rose LJ held that as the defendant had attained 18 before the

---

43　See also chapter 17.

44　*R v Amersham Juvenile Court ex p Wilson* [1981] 2 All ER 315 at 320d.

45　(1979) 143 JP 697.

46　[1981] 2 All ER 315.

47　*R v Uxbridge Youth Court ex p Mathew Howard* [1998] EWHC Admin 342.

day when the warrant was executed and the proceedings could be said to have begun, the youth court had no jurisdiction at all. It was also not open to the youth court to remit the case to the adult court as no statutory power existed to do this.[48] Faced with such a situation, the police would have to recharge the accused so that proceedings could be re-commenced in the adult court.

New charges after the first appearance

11.74   It has been held in the case of *R v Chelsea Justices ex p DPP*[49] that any new charges preferred after the defendant has attained 18 must be laid in the adult court even if the new charges arise out of the same facts as the original charges. In this case a 16-year-old was charged with wounding and appeared before the (then) juvenile court. The case was adjourned during which time he attained the age of 17 which at that time would have made him an adult defendant. He was then charged with attempted murder. It was held that the juvenile court had no jurisdiction to hear the new charge and that it should have been laid before an adult magistrates' court.

Attaining 18 and the mode of trial decision

11.75   The age of the defendant on the date on which mode of trial is decided determines the powers of the court and the rights of the defendant.[50]

Remittal to the adult court

11.76   Crime and Disorder Act 1998 s47(1) provides:

> Where a person who appears or is brought before a youth court charged with an offence subsequently attains the age of 18, the youth court may, at any time –
> (a) before the start of the trial;
> ...
> remit the person for trial to a magistrates' court (other than a youth court) acting for the same petty sessions area as the youth court.

11.77   For the above provision, a trial starts when the court begins to hear prosecution evidence.[51] It is not anticipated that the power to remit will be used in every case.

11.78   When a person is remitted under section 47(1) the remitting youth court must adjourn proceedings in relation to the offence.[52] Magistrates' Courts Act 1980 s128 and all other enactments (whenever passed) relating to remands or the granting of bail in criminal proceedings shall have effect in relation to the remitting youth court's power or duty to remand the defendant on the adjournment as if any reference to the court to or

---

48   It would appear that the power to remit to the adult court under Crime and Disorder Act 1998 s47(1) is not available either – see below.

49   [1963] 3 All ER 657; 128 JP 18, QBD.

50   See para 12.119.

51   Crime and Disorder Act 1998 s47(1), adopting the definition in the Prosecution of Offences Act 1985 s22(11B).

52   Ibid, s47(2)(b).

before which the person remanded is to be brought or appear after remand were a reference to the adult court to which s/he is being remitted.[53] There is no right of appeal against the decision to remit.[54]

11.79   Where remittal under section 47(1) takes place, section 47(4) provides:

> The other court may deal with the case in any way in which it would have power to deal with it if all proceedings relating to the offence which took place before the remitting court had taken place before the other court.

11.80   This subsection appears to have the potential to create some bizarre outcomes. For example, if a youth court accepted jurisdiction in relation to a robbery charge prior to the defendant's 18th birthday and s/he was then remitted for trial under section 47(1), the adult magistrates' court would seem to have no option but to try the indictable-only charge.

11.81   Where a defendant has become 18 years of age after the mode of trial decision but before conviction, and the court proposes to remit him/her to the adult court for trial, if the defendant faces a matter which would be indictable-only in the adult court, the defence lawyer will need to consider the analogous situation in the case of *R (Denny) v Acton Youth Court*.[55] It was held in that case that there was no power to remit to the adult court for sentence on an indictable-only matter. In the view of the authors the same principle would apply prior to conviction.[56]

11.82   It should be noted that section 47(1) may only be used where the defendant appeared before the youth court prior to attaining the age of 18. It cannot, therefore, be used to solve the problem of a defendant bailed to the youth court who attains 18 before s/he appears or is brought before that court. In such circumstances the youth court would have no jurisdiction to deal with the defendant and there is no other statutory power to allow for a remittal to the adult magistrates' court.[57]

Adult defendant wrongly before the youth court

11.83   If an adult has lied about his/her age and appears before the youth court, the proceedings may still continue in that court. Children and Young Persons Act 1933 s48(1) provides:

> A youth court sitting for the purpose of hearing a charge against a person who is believed to be a child or young person may, if it thinks fit to do so, proceed with the hearing and determination of the charge, notwithstanding that it is discovered that the person in question is not a child or young person.

11.84   If the court decides not to continue with the proceedings, there would seem to be no statutory mechanism to transfer the case to an adult court.[58] The power to remit a defendant to the adult court in Crime and Disorder Act 1998 s47(1) is of no avail as it only applies to situations where the defendant

---

53 Ibid, s47(2)(c) and (3).
54 Ibid, s47(2)(a).
55 [2004] EWHC 948 (Admin).
56 See para 19.18.
57 *R v Uxbridge Youth Court ex p H* (1998) *Times* 7 April (CO/292/98, 19.3.98).
58 Ibid.

attains the age of 18 after the first appearance. Accordingly, the prosecution would need to discontinue proceedings in the youth court and re-charge the adult.

The adult magistrates' court

11.85   This section deals with the powers of and procedures in an adult magistrates' court where a child or young person appears before it as a defendant, and the circumstances in which this will arise. The question of mode of trial is considered separately in chapter 12.

Power of adult court to deal with a child or young person

11.86   The adult magistrates' court has the power to deal with a child or young person in any of the following circumstances:

- a child or young person in custody;
- the child or young person is jointly charged with an adult; or
- an adult is charged as an aider or abettor to the offence; or
- the child or young person is charged as the aider or abettor of an adult; or
- the child or young person is charged with an offence arising out of the same circumstances as those giving rise to proceedings against an adult.

Child or young person in custody

11.87   In most parts of the country a youth court will only sit once a week or sometimes even less frequently. There will be occasions when the police have to place a child or young person before a court when a youth court is not sitting. This would occur when a child or young person is refused bail by the police after charge or when a warrant not backed for bail has been executed. In such circumstances Children and Young Persons Act 1933 s46(2) provides that any justice or justices may entertain an application for bail or for a remand and may hear such evidence as is necessary for that purpose. The adult court must then remand the child or young person to the youth court for the same area.

Jointly charged with an adult

11.88   Children and Young Persons Act 1933 s46(1)(a) provides:

> [A] charge made jointly against a child or young person and a person who has attained the age of 18 shall be heard by a court of summary jurisdiction other than a youth court, ...

11.89   This provision is mandatory. It follows, therefore, that a youth court has no jurisdiction to deal with the child or young person in these circumstances.

11.90   It is not necessary for the charge to specify that the offence was committed 'jointly' or 'together with' the adult concerned.[59] In the case of taking

---

59   *R v Rowlands* [1972] 1 All ER 306.

without consent or aggravated vehicle-taking, the driver and any passengers charged with allowing to be carried are jointly charged.[60]

Adult charged as aider and abettor

11.91 Children and Young Persons Act 1933 s46(1)(b) provides:

> [W]here a child or young person is charged with an offence, the court may be heard by a court of summary jurisdiction other than a youth court if a person who has attained the age of eighteen years is charged at the same time with aiding, abetting, causing, procuring, allowing or permitting that offence; ...

11.92 This provision is permissive and, therefore, the youth court still retains jurisdiction if a child or young person appears before it.

Charged as an aider and abettor to an adult

11.93 Children and Young Persons Act 1963 s18(1) provides:

> [A] magistrates' court which is not a youth court may hear an information against a child or young person if he is charged–
> (a) with aiding, abetting, causing, procuring, allowing or permitting an offence with which a person who has attained the age of eighteen is charged at the same time ...

11.94 Once again, this provision is permissive and, therefore, the youth court retains jurisdiction and may deal with any child or young person who appears before it.

Charged with an offence arising out of the same circumstances

11.95 Children and Young Persons Act 1963 s18(1) provides:

> [A] magistrates' court which is not a youth court may hear an information against a child or young person if he is charged–
> ...
> (b) with an offence arising out of circumstances which are the same as or connected with those giving rise to an offence with which a person who has attained the age of eighteen is charged at the same time ...

11.96 Once again this provision is permissive and, therefore, the youth court retains jurisdiction and may deal with any child or young person who appears before it.

Remittal to the youth court for trial

11.97 Where a child or young person is brought before an adult magistrates' court jointly charged with an adult, the court may remit him/her for trial in the youth court. This power arises in two circumstances:

- the court proceeds to summary trial and the adult defendant pleads guilty and the child or young person pleads not guilty; or
- the court proceeds to enquire into the information as examining magistrates and either commits the adult for trial or discharges him/her and in the case of the child or young person, proceeds to the summary trial of the information.[61]

---

60 *R v Peterborough Justices ex p Allgood* (1994) 159 JP 627, QBD.
61 Magistrates' Courts Act 1980 s29(2).

11.98   In both cases the plea will be taken before the case is remitted to the youth court. The case may be remitted to a youth court acting for the same place as the remitting court or for the place where the accused habitually resides.

11.99   Where a child or young person is remitted for trial the remitting court may give such directions as appear to be necessary with respect to his/her custody or for his/her release on bail until s/he can be brought before the youth court.[62] There is no right of appeal against the order of remission.[63]

Modifying the usual court procedure

11.100 The considerations raised by earlier chapters of this book in relation to the intellectual and emotional development of the young defendant and his/her ability effectively to participate in the proceedings, have considerable application in the adult magistrates' court. Lawyers representing children or young persons appearing in the adult magistrates' court will need to consider the layout and practice of the adult magistrates' court in which the young defendant is to appear and how that may need to be adapted to assist the individual client. The extent of any necessary modifications may depend on the nature and length of the hearing.[64]

Seating arrangements

11.101 In some courts it is the usual practice to seat the child or young person in front of the dock alongside any parent or guardian accompanying him/her. The defence lawyer may also wish to be seated next to the client to facilitate explanation of the court proceedings. Difficulties may arise in adapting the court's usual practice if the young defendant appears in custody. In the opinion of the authors, in most cases the parents or guardian and defence lawyer should have easy access to the defendant and this may require the removal of the defendant from any secure dock area.

Formality

11.102 Practice varies as to whether the children or young persons will be referred to by their first names.

Language

11.103 The defence lawyer should ensure that the court and the lawyers for the various parties use language which can be understood by the young defendant.

Reporting restrictions

11.104 Unlike in the youth court, when a child or young person appears in the adult courts there is no automatic bar upon reporting. However, the court does have a power to prohibit the publication of details regarding the

---

62 Magistrates' Courts Act 1980 s29(4)(b).

63 Ibid, s29(4)(a).

64 See chapter 10.

defendant or other children or young persons involved in the case. Children and Young Persons Act 1933 s39(1) provides:

> In relation to any proceedings in any court ... the court may direct that–
> (a) no newspaper report of the proceedings shall reveal the name, address or school or include any particulars calculated to lead to the identification of any child or young person concerned in the proceedings, either as being the person by or against or in respect of whom the proceedings are taken, or as being a witness therein;
> (b) no picture shall be published in any newspaper as being or including a picture of any child or young person so concerned in the proceedings as aforesaid; except in so far (if at all) as may be permitted by the direction of the court.

11.105   The provisions of section 39 also apply to the contents of a broadcast service.[65]

11.106   In the adult magistrates' court the defence lawyer should ensure that an order is made at the first hearing. At subsequent hearings it may be desirable to ensure that the existence of the order is confirmed so that all those present in court are aware of it. If such an order is made at the time of committal, the court clerk should forward with the depositions a notice that the order was made by the examining magistrates.[66]

11.107   Publication of material in contravention of an order made under section 39 is a summary offence punishable with a fine of up to £5,000.[67]

Youth defendant wrongly before the court

11.108   Where a child or young person appears before an adult magistrates' court in circumstances where the court would not ordinarily have jurisdiction, the court may continue to determine the case. This situation might arise when an accused gave a false date of birth to the police or simply because the custody sergeant bailed the child or young person in error to an adult court. The Children and Young Persons Act 1933 s46(1)(c) provides:

> [W]here in the course of any proceedings before any court of summary jurisdiction other than a youth court, it appears that the person to whom the proceedings relate is a child or young person, nothing in this subsection shall be construed as preventing the court, if it thinks fit so to do, from proceeding with the hearing and determination of those proceedings.

11.109   Although this section gives the court discretion to proceed with the hearing, it is more common for the court to adjourn the hearing and remand to the next sitting of the youth court under Children and Young Persons Act 1933 s46(2). The power to proceed would still seem to be subject to the provisions of Powers of Criminal Courts (Sentencing Act) 2000 s8, which would require the defendant to be remitted to the youth court for sentence unless a referral order, discharge, fine or a parental bindover was appropriate.

---

65 Broadcasting Act 1990 Sch 20.
66 Home Office Circulars Nos 18/1956 and 14/1965.
67 Children and Young Persons Act 1933 s39(2).

The Crown Court

Modifying the usual court procedure

11.110   Whilst the youth court should be designed to cater for the young defendant, the Crown Court remains a formal setting, the intimidating nature of which can be forgotten by lawyers who attend there regularly. Although the *Consolidated Criminal Practice Direction Part IV.39 – Trial of Children and Young Persons in the Crown Court* strictly only applies to the trial hearing, it is submitted that its spirit should apply, where practicable, to all hearings in the Crown Court.

Seating arrangements

11.111   Practice varies between courts. Some courts allow the child or young person to sit outside the dock beside a parent or other adult, others are extremely reluctant to do so. As there is no fixed practice, the matter should be raised with the judge at the start of every case. To facilitate communication during the hearing, the defence lawyer should also ensure that the young defendant is seated close to him/her.

Language

11.112   The language used on a daily basis in the Crown Court may not be understood by many children and young persons appearing there. There are some legal terms that need to be used. Generally there is a clear and simple way of expressing most words and phrases; lawyers need to ensure that the proceedings are accessible to their clients.[68] It may be decided to refer to the defendant by his/her first name during the proceedings.

Plea and case management hearings

11.113   The defence lawyer should give consideration to any necessary modifications to the usual procedure at preliminary hearings and plea and case management hearings; these can be particularly intimidating for the young defendant who has only previously appeared in the informal, private setting of the youth court. There are likely to be many other cases listed at the same time. In some cases it might be necessary to have the matter listed before or after the rest of the cases in court that day in order to provide a more appropriate setting for the particularly young or particularly vulnerable young defendant.

11.114   The forms to be completed by all parties attending plea and case management hearings make specific mention of young defendants. The parties attending the hearing are asked:

- Does any witness or defendant need an interpreter or have special needs for which arrangements should be made?[69]
- Are any special arrangements needed for a child defendant?[70]

---

68   See chapter 10.
69   Question 18.
70   Ibid.

- Are there any outstanding questions about special measures or live links?[71]

11.115 The *Consolidated Criminal Practice Direction* Part IV.39.5 states that any necessary modifications to the trial process designed to facilitate the understanding and participation of the young defendant should be considered at the plea and directions hearing (now plea and case management hearing). Part IV.39.4 states that severance of the young defendant from any adult defendants should also be considered at the hearing. Adherence to the principles of the Practice Direction varies considerably across the country. The defence lawyer will therefore need to be aware of local practice and be prepared to argue for appropriate modifications as necessary.

11.116 The modifications to the usual court procedure which may be necessary to ensure effective participation of the young defendant should be considered by the defence lawyer from an early stage in the proceedings. Expert evidence may be needed to deal with the modifications appropriate to the needs of the defendant. Any expert evidence relied on in support of a request to modify to the usual trial process should be available to the judge and the prosecution in advance of the hearing.[72]

11.117 The lawyer attending the plea and case management hearing should be prepared to:

- show the defendant around the court room before the hearing starts;
- ask for severance, where appropriate;
- ask for modifications to the usual trial procedure;
- make special measures applications for defence witnesses, where necessary;
- ask for a fixed date for trial; and
- ask for reporting restrictions (see para 11.119 below).

11.118 If the court is unable to deal with these issues immediately, a timetable should be set to ensure that they are dealt with prior to the trial listing. It may be necessary to have the matter brought back to court for mention prior to trial to ensure trial readiness and avoid further delay. Many courts prefer to leave the issue of trial modifications to the trial judge, notwithstanding the clear terms of the Practice Direction and active case management as envisaged by the Criminal Procedure Rules 2005.

Reporting restrictions

11.119 In the Crown Court the judge sitting at the plea and case management hearing should consider whether to make an order restricting the identification of the young defendant.[73] Any such order should be put in writing and copies should be made available to anyone affected or potentially affected by it.[74] The provisions are the same as in the adult magistrates' court.[75] It is important that this order is made at the first hearing in the

---

71 Question 17; see also chapter 16.
72 See chapter 10.
73 Children and Young Persons Act 1933, s39(1).
74 *Consolidated Criminal Practice Direction* IV 39.8.
75 See paras 11.104–11.107.

Crown Court – whether the case originated in the youth or adult magistrates' court. If the order is not made the defendant can be identified in the media. The onus is on the court to make the order and the legal representative for the young defendant should ensure that the issue is raised.

11.120 The factors to be considered by the court in deciding whether to make an order include:

- the stage of the proceedings;[76]
- the age of the defendant;[77]
- the welfare of the child or young person.[78]

11.121 The terms of the order must be clear and unambiguous.[79]

General considerations

Advance information

11.122 Criminal Procedure Rules 2005[80] r21.3 states:

> (1) If, in any proceedings in respect of which this Part applies, either before the magistrates' court considers whether the offence appears to be more suitable for summary trial or trial on indictment or, where the accused has not attained the age of 18 years when he appears or is brought before a magistrates' court, before he is asked whether he pleads guilty or not guilty, the accused or the person representing the accused requests the prosecutor to furnish him with advance information, the prosecutor shall, subject to Rule 21.4, furnish him as soon as practicable with either:
>
> (a) a copy of those parts of every written statement which contain information as to the facts or matters of which the prosecutor proposes to adduce evidence in the proceedings ; or
>
> (b) a summary of the facts or matters of which the prosecutor proposes to adduce evidence in the proceedings.

11.123 These provisions apply both in the youth court and the adult magistrates' court. In the opinion of the authors the effect of this rule for a defendant who is a child or young person is that advance information should be supplied before the court makes any decision in relation to mode of trial. The specific provision that in the case of a person under 18 years of age advance information should be served, if it is requested, prior to plea being entered should mean that advance information is available in every case involving a child or young person.

11.124 The prosecutor will usually have advance information available at the first hearing and this will greatly facilitate the taking of instructions in even the simplest case. Where the first hearing is from custody it is essential that the advance information is requested, if not available at court. Before proceeding to make a decision on jurisdiction or the taking of a plea the court must satisfy itself that the defendant is aware of his/her right to advance information.[81]

---

76 *R v Central Criminal Court ex p S* (1999) 163 JP 776.
77 Ibid.
78 Children and Young Persons Act 1933 s44.
79 *Briffet and Bradshaw v DPP* (2002) 166 JP 841.
80 SI No 384.
81 Ibid, r21.5.

11.125   Where a statement or summary refers to a document on which the prosecutor seeks to rely, the prosecutor shall also supply either a copy of the document or such information as to enable the document or a copy of it to be inspected.[82] The prosecutor may refuse to disclose any particular fact or matter if s/he is of the opinion that the disclosure will lead to the intimidation of any person on whose evidence s/he proposes to rely, or to interference with the course of justice. In these circumstances the prosecutor shall give written notice to the person requesting the advance information indicating that information is being withheld for that reason.[83]

11.126   The extent of disclosure required prior to decisions on jurisdiction and plea may be quite extensive. Video-taped evidence, closed-circuit television evidence, tapes of police interviews or documentary evidence may be needed before full advice can be given. If necessary the defence advocate should request an adjournment for this evidence to be served and considered. The court should grant such adjournment where it is justified.[84] Where the prosecution have not complied with their disclosure duties, the court shall grant a request to adjourn the proceedings to allow the disclosure to take place, unless it is satisfied that the conduct of the case for the accused will not be substantially prejudiced by non-compliance with the requirement of disclosure. If the court refuses an application to adjourn where the prosecution have not complied with a requirement to disclose under the Criminal Procedure Rules, it must record the decision and the reasons why it was satisfied that the conduct of the case for the accused would not be substantially prejudiced by non-compliance on the register.[85]

Taking a plea

11.127   When dealing with a child or young person, a youth or magistrates' court is required to explain the nature of the proceedings and the substance of any charge in simple language suitable to the age and understanding of the young defendant.[86] The court is not required to give a detailed explanation of the charge but it should ensure that the essential elements of the offence are explained.[87]

11.128   Once the court is satisfied that the child or young person understands the charge, it should ask him/her whether s/he pleads guilty or not guilty to the charge.[88] If the defendant pleads not guilty, the court will normally adjourn so that the prosecution will have an opportunity to arrange for its witnesses to attend court. If the defendant pleads guilty the court will proceed to hear the facts of the case from the prosecution, will hear about the defendant and proceed to sentence.[89]

82 SI No 384 r21.3(3).

83 Ibid, r21.4.

84 *R v Calderdale Magistrates' Court ex p Donahue* [2001] Crim LR 141, *R v Southampton Youth Court* [2004] EWHC 2912 (Admin). Also see para 12.64.

85 SI No 384 r21.6.

86 Ibid, r38.3.

87 *R v Blandford Justices ex p G (an infant)* [1966] 1 All ER 1021, QBD.

88 Criminal Procedure Rules 2005 r38.4.

89 See chapters 17 and beyond.

Pleading by post

11.129 Magistrates' Courts Act 1980 s12 allows certain cases to be disposed of without the defendant being required to attend. This procedure only applies to summary-only offences carrying a maximum of three months' imprisonment. In practice it is mainly used in road traffic cases. It only applies to defendants who have attained the age of 16.

11.130   Once issued, the summons will be served by the prosecutor along with:

- an explanatory statement;
- a statement of the facts to be given to the magistrates; and
- any information regarding the accused which will be placed before the court.

11.131 The accused may then choose to attend the court in person or return the form accompanying the summons indicating a guilty plea along with mitigating factors and financial details. In some cases, the court may subsequently require the young person to attend court to 'show cause' why they should not be disqualified from driving.

11.132   It is not uncommon for young persons to be summonsed in error to attend the adult magistrates' court in relation to traffic matters. If a notification that an accused wishes to plead guilty under this provision is received by the clerk of the court, and the court has no reason to believe that the accused is a child or young person, then, if s/he is a child or young person s/he shall be deemed to have attained the age of 18 for the purposes of the proceedings.

11.133   Where a written plea of guilty is entered in respect of an offence involving obligatory or discretionary disqualification details of the date of birth and sex of the accused must be included.[90]

Changing plea

11.134 Any court has a discretion to allow a change of plea any time before sentence is passed, as there is no conviction until sentence has been passed.[91] This inherent jurisdiction still exists after a remit for sentence under Powers of Criminal Courts (Sentencing) Act 2000 s8.[92] This power will be exercised where the plea was equivocal or it is otherwise in the interests of justice that the plea should be reopened.

11.135   The discretion is exercised sparingly. Even where the defendant was unrepresented when he entered his/her guilty plea but subsequently instructs solicitors who advise that there is a defence, the court does not have to exercise its discretion to allow a change of plea.[93] Where the defendant was represented at the time of entering a plea it will be more difficult to persuade the court to exercise its discretion. The age and particular circumstances of the defendant may, in some circumstances, assist in the application.

90 Road Traffic Offenders Act 1988 ss8 and 25.
91 *S (an infant) v Recorder of Manchester* [1971] AC 481, HL.
92 *R v Stratford Youth Court ex p Conde* [1997] 1 WLR 113; (1997) 161 JP 308; [1997] 2 Cr App R 1, QBD.
93 *R v South Thameside Magistrates' Court ex p Rolland* [1983] 3All ER 689.

Live television links

11.136 These provisions apply in the youth court, the adult magistrates' court and the Crown Court.

11.137 In any proceeding for any offence the court may, after hearing representations from the parties, direct that the accused shall be treated as being present in the court for any particular hearing before the start of the trial if:

- s/he is held in a prison or other institution; and
- s/he is able to see and hear the court and be heard and seen by it, whether by means of a live television link or otherwise. [94]

11.138 If a court has the power to make a direction, having been notified by the secretary of state that facilities are available, and it decides not to make a direction, it shall give its reasons.[95]

11.139 In the opinion of the authors, live television links should be used sparingly in the case of young defendants as their use is likely to inhibit effective participation.

---

94 Crime and Disorder Act 1998 s57(1).
95 Ibid, s57(3).

CHAPTER 12

Mode of trial

Introduction

12.1   The law as stated in this chapter is as at publication. It is anticipated that the provisions of Criminal Justice Act 2003 Sch 3 may be implemented in 2006/2007. When these provisions are in force the reader is referred to appendix 13.

12.2   In 2004 4,203 children and young people aged between 10 and 18 years were committed to the Crown Court for trial.[1]

12.3   The majority of children and young people are tried and sentenced in the youth court.

12.4   It is in the area of mode of trial that the law in relation to children and young people differs substantially to that relating to adults. Children and young people do not have the right to elect trial in the Crown Court as adults can for indictable offences. An adult may never be tried summarily for indictable-only matters, whereas the basic rule for a child or young person is that they should be tried summarily for such offences.

12.5   This chapter will examine the exceptions to that rule.

Presumption of summary trial

12.6   The general rule set out in Magistrates' Courts Act 1980 s24 is that a defendant under the age of 18 should be tried summarily, unless s/he:

- is charged with an offence of homicide;[2]
- is charged with possession of a firearm and at the time of the offence s/he had attained the age of 16 years;[3]
- is charged with a grave crime and the court considers that that if s/he is found guilty of the offence it ought to be possible to sentence him/her to detention under Powers of Criminal Courts (Sentencing) Act 2000 s91;[4]
- is jointly charged with an adult and the court considers it necessary in the interests of justice to commit them both for trial;[5]
- is charged with a specified offence and it appears to the court that if she/he is found guilty of the offence the criteria for the imposition of a sentence under Criminal Justice Act 2003 s226(3) or s228(2) would be met (dangerousness provisions).[6]

12.7   Each of these exceptions is examined below.

Homicide

12.8   A child or young person charged with an offence of homicide must be tried in the Crown Court. There will be no mode of trial hearing.

---

1   Home Office *Criminal Statistics for England and Wales*, 2004.
2   Magistrates' Courts Act 1980 s24(1B)(a).
3   Ibid, s24(1B)(b) and Firearms Act 1968 s51A.
4   Magistrates' Courts Act 1980 s24(1)(a).
5   Ibid, s24(1)(b).
6   Crime and Disorder Act 1998 s51A(1), (2) and (3)(d), as inserted by Criminal Justice Act 2003 Sch 3 para 18.

Definition

12.9 There is no statutory definition of 'homicide', but it probably includes:[7]

- murder;
- attempted murder;[8]
- manslaughter;
- infanticide;
- causing or allowing the death of a child or vulnerable adult.[9]

Committal

12.10 The case will proceed to the Crown Court by way of a committal hearing under the Magistrates' Courts Act 1980.

Related offences

12.11 Any other indictable offences with which the defendant is also charged, and which could be joined on the same indictment, may be committed for trial at the same time.[10]

Firearms possession

Criteria

12.12 A young person must be tried at the Crown Court if:

- s/he is charged with an offence under Firearms Act 1968 s5(1)(a), (ab), (aba), (ac), (ad), (ae), (af) or (c) (prohibited weapons); or
- s/he is charged with an offence under Firearms Act 1968 s5(1A)(a); and
- the offence was committed on or after 22 January 2004; and
- at the time of the offence s/he was aged 16 or over.[11]

Committal

12.13 The young persons who meet these criteria will be subject to a mandatory sentence of at least three years' detention. There is no need for a mode of trial hearing and the case will proceed to the Crown Court by way of committal proceedings.

---

7 It is not clear whether 'homicide' extends to: causing death by dangerous driving, causing death by careless driving whilst under the influence of drink or drugs or causing death by aggravated vehicle taking. However, all of these offences are now 'grave crimes' as they carry a maximum sentence of 14 years' imprisonment in the case of an adult and may be tried in the Crown Court if appropriate. The penalties were increased by Criminal Justice Act 2003 s285.
8 Criminal Attempts Act 1981 s2(2)(c).
9 The defendant must be 16 years or above. Domestic Violence, Crime and Victims Act 2004 ss5 and 6(5).
10 Magistrates' Courts Act 1980 s24(1A).
11 Firearms Act 1968 s51A, inserted by Criminal Justice Act 2003 s287.

Related offences

12.14   Any other indictable offences with which the defendant is also charged, and which could be joined on the same indictment, may be committed for trial at the same time.[12]

Dangerous offenders

12.15   The youth court shall send a child or young person for trial at the Crown Court if:

- the offence was committed on or after 4 April 2005; and
- the offence is a specified offence; and
- it appears to the court that if s/he is found guilty of the offence charged the criteria for the imposition of detention for life, detention for public protection or extended detention would be met.[13]

12.16   To impose detention for public protection or extended detention, the court must consider that there is a 'significant risk to members of the public of serious harm occasioned by the commission by the offender of further specified offences'.[14]

12.17   Before addressing a court considering these provisions at the mode of trial stage, the lawyer is advised to familiarise him/herself with the legal provisions to be considered on sentence so as to be in a position to assist the court as to their likely relevance, or otherwise.

12.18   These sentencing provisions are considered in detail in chapter 24.

Criteria

'Specified offence'

12.19   A 'specified offence' is a violent or sexual offence listed in Criminal Justice Act 2003 Sch 15 (see appendix 7).

12.20   There are a number of offences that are 'specified offences' which are not 'grave crimes' – for example, affray, assault occasioning actual bodily harm, racially aggravated public order offences and offences contrary to Offences Against the Person Act 1861 s20.

'Serious offence'

12.21   A 'serious offence' is a specified offence which is punishable in the case of an adult with life imprisonment or imprisonment for ten years or more.[15]

'Serious harm'

12.22   'Serious harm' is defined as 'death or serious personal injury, whether physical or psychological'.[16] See chapter 24.

---

12   Magistrates' Courts Act 1980 s24(1A).
13   Criminal Justice Act 2003 ss226 and 228 and Crime and Disorder Act 1998 s51A(3)(d).
14   Criminal Justice Act 2003 ss226(1) and 228(1).
15   Ibid, s224(2).
16   Ibid, s224(3).

'Significant risk'

12.23   The term 'significant risk' is not defined. The 'significant risk' relates to the risk of serious harm and the risk of re-offending.[17] It is submitted that the court's attention may need to be drawn to this element of the provisions. It will be a matter for the judgment of the sentencing court once it is in possession of all the relevant information about the offence and the offender.

No statutory presumption

12.24   It is important to distinguish the provisions relating to adult dangerous offenders from those relating to children and young persons. The statutory presumption of risk which applies to adult offenders with relevant previous convictions, does not apply to children or young persons.[18]

The assessment of dangerousness

12.25   The court:

- must take into account all such information as is available to it about the nature and circumstances of the offence;
- may take into account any information which is before it about any pattern of behaviour of which the offence forms part; and
- may take into account any information about the offender which is before it.[19]

Applying the provisions

12.26   In *CPS v South East Surrey Youth Court*[20] Rose LJ expressed considerable sympathy with those in the youth court who have to deal with the 'labyrinthine' and 'manifestly inconsistent' provisions as currently enacted. The court sought to give guidance as to how the provisions should be approached.

12.27   The guidance states that the youth court should bear in mind:

- the policy of the legislature is that those who are under 18 should, wherever possible, be tried in a youth court, which is best designed for their specific needs;
- the guidance given by the Court of Appeal (Criminal Division) in the judgment of *R v Lang and others*,[21] particularly in relation to non-serious specified offences;
- the need, in relation to those under 18, to be particularly rigorous before concluding that there is a significant risk of serious harm by the commission of further offences: such a conclusion is unlikely to appropriate in the absence of a pre-sentence report following assessment by a youth offender team;

---

17   *R v Lang and others* [2005] EWCA Crim 2864. See para 24.126.
18   Criminal Justice Act 2003 s229(3).
19   Ibid, s229(2).
20   [2005] EWHC 2929.
21   [2005] EWCA Crim 2864; and see chapter 24.

- in most cases where a non-serious specified offence is charged, an assessment of dangerousness will not be appropriate until after conviction, when, if the dangerousness criteria are met, the defendant can be committed to the Crown Court for sentence.[22]

12.28   In practical terms, where the issue of dangerousness is raised at the mode of trial stage of the proceedings, either by the prosecution or the court, the clear guidance is that, in the majority of cases, the court should consider summary trial wherever possible and apply the 'grave crime' provisions to charges falling within them.[23] For non-serious specified offences, the court should, in most cases, take the view that it does not have sufficient information to make a decision as to dangerousness at this stage, reserving its position in relation to a possible committal for sentence on a plea or finding of guilt.[24] At this later stage the court will have far more information available to it in order to make an assessment of the possible need for the imposition of a sentence under the dangerous offender provisions.

12.29   The case is particularly concerned with an example of a non-serious specified offence. In the view of the authors, the same considerations will arise in many examples of serious specified offences. At an early stage in the proceedings the court will have limited information available in relation to the risks posed by the defendant in the future, in relation to the risk of offending and the risk of serious harm to the public from further offending. The court will be in a position to consider its sentencing powers in relation to 'grave crimes'. If the court decided to retain the matter for trial and sentence, the court would still have the power to send the defendant to the Crown Court for consideration of a sentence under the 'dangerousness' provisions once a pre-sentence report was available to assist the court in the assessment of those risks in relation to that particular defendant.

Co-defendants

12.30   The decision regarding dangerousness is taken separately for each defendant. Where one defendant is to be sent to the Crown Court in accordance with these provisions, there is no provision for the sending, at the same time, of a youth co-defendant who is not deemed dangerous.

Related offences

12.31   Indictable and summary matters which are related to the matter being sent to the Crown Court can be sent for trial at the same time.[25]

Preparing for the dangerousness argument

The court

12.32   When considering the issue of dangerousness in an early stage of the proceeding, the court will have available some details of the allegation and the

---

22 *CPS v South East Surrey Youth Court* [2005] EWHC 2929 para 17.
23 See paras 12.35–12.66.
24 Powers of the Criminal Courts (Sentencing) Act 2000 s3C inserted by Criminal Justice Act 2003 Sch 3 para 23.
25 Crime and Disorder Act 1998 s51A(4).

young offender's previous convictions. Full details of the offence itself and of the offences which led to the earlier convictions (if any) are unlikely to be available. It may be necessary for a defence lawyer to look at further details of previous convictions, which may be contained in previous files for the same defendant, in order to address the court on the issue of 'significant risk to members of the public of serious harm occasioned by the commission of further specified offences'. The lawyer will need to consider sentencing guidelines (if any) for the substantive offence and the factors to be considered in the court's assessment of the offence and the offender. At the early stage of the proceedings the most effective argument may be that there is as yet insufficient information available to enable the court to make the appropriate decision as to whether a longer than usual sentence should be available on the sentencing of the particular offender.

The client

12.33 The court's decision on dangerousness may be alarming for the client and any family member attending court with him/her. It is important that the defence representative takes time to explain to the client, as far as possible, the nature of this part of the proceedings, using language appropriate to his/her age and understanding.

Jointly charged with an adult who has been sent or committed for trial

12.34 There may be occasions where a youth appears in the youth court charged with an offence jointly with an adult who has already been sent or committed to the Crown Court. In these circumstances the youth court will exercise the discretion as outlined in paras 12.82–12.83 and 12.101–12.106.

Grave crimes

Definition of 'grave crime'

12.35 A grave crime is defined by Powers of Criminal Courts (Sentencing) Act 2000 s91. The definition includes:

- an offence punishable in the case of an adult with imprisonment for 14 years or more;
- firearms possession (see para 12.12 above);
- various sexual offences.

Offences punishable with 14 years or more

12.36 The definition would include robbery, residential burglary and handling stolen goods. It does not include non-residential burglary (maximum penalty: ten years) or theft (maximum penalty: seven years). A full list of offences which are grave crimes is produced in appendix 6.

Sexual offences specifically defined as grave crimes

12.37   The following sexual offences may be treated as grave crimes, notwith-standing the fact that the maximum sentence is less than 14 years:

- sexual assault contrary to Sexual Offences Act 2003 s3;
- child sex offences committed by children and young persons contrary to Sexual Offences Act 2003 s13;
- sexual activity with a child family member contrary to Sexual Offences Act 2003 s25; and
- inciting a child family member to engage in sexual activity contrary to Sexual Offences Act 2003 s26.

Fatal driving offences

12.38   Criminal Justice Act 2003 s285 increases to 14 years the maximum penalty for the following offences:

- causing death by dangerous driving contrary to Road Traffic Act 1988 s1;
- causing death by careless driving whilst under influence of drink or drugs contrary to Road Traffic Act 1988 s3A;
- aggravated vehicle-taking resulting in death contrary to Theft Act 1968 s12A(4).

Criteria

12.39   Magistrates Courts Act 1980 s24(1)(a) states that a child or young person charged with a grave crime may be tried on indictment if the court considers that on conviction it ought to be possible to sentence him/her to detention under Powers of Criminal Courts (Sentencing) Act 2000 s91(3). Where a youth court decides to deal with a young offender, on conviction the maximum penalty is a two-year detention and training order. For younger offenders there may be no custodial powers in the event of conviction.[26] The decision being made at this stage involves considering whether an offence may require a greater punishment than the youth court has available. Once the youth court has agreed to deal with a case under these provisions, there is no power to commit the child or young person to the Crown Court for sentence, save under the dangerousness provisions discussed in paras 19.9–19.11 and 24.117–24.142 below.

12.40   In recent years there have been a number of decisions in the Administrative Court regarding mode of trial decisions in the youth court.[27] In an attempt to provide straightforward guidance to magistrates considering the question of jurisdiction under section 24(1)(a) Leveson J in *R (on the application of H, O and A) v Southampton Youth Court*[28] summarised the principles derived from these cases as follows:

---

26   See chapter 24.
27   See, among others, *R (on the application of D) v Manchester City Youth Court* [2001] EWHC 860 Admin; [2002] 1 Cr App R (S) 373; (2001) 166 JP 15, *R (on the application of W) v Thetford Youth Justices* [2002] EWHC 1252 Admin, *R (on the application of W) v Southampton Youth Court* [2002] EWHC 1640 Admin and *R (on the application of C) v Balham Youth Court* [2003] EWHC 1332 Admin; [2004] 1 Cr App R 22; (2003) 167 JP 525; [2003] Crim LR 636.
28   [2004] EWHC 2912 Admin.

1. The general policy of the legislature is that those who are under 18 years of age and in particular children of under 15 years of age should, wherever possible, be tried in the youth court. It is that court which is best designed to meet their specific needs. A trial in the Crown Court with the inevitably greater formality and greatly increased number of people involved (including a jury and the public) should be reserved for the most serious cases.

2. It is a further policy of the legislature that, generally speaking, first-time offenders aged 12 to 14 and all offenders under 12 should not be detained in custody and decisions as to jurisdiction should have regard to the fact that the *exceptional* power to detain for grave offences should not be used to water down the general principle. Those under 15 will rarely attract a period of detention and, even more rarely, those who are under 12.

3. In each case the court should ask itself whether there is a real prospect, having regard to his or her age, that this defendant whose case they are considering might require a sentence of, or in excess of, two years or, alternatively, whether although the sentence might be less than two years, there is some unusual feature of the case which justifies declining jurisdiction, bearing in mind that the absence of a power to impose a detention and training order because the defendant is under 15 is not an unusual feature.

12.41 This guidance has been adopted and repeated in subsequent cases where it has been contended that magistrates have failed properly to exercise their discretion in relation to jurisdiction.[29]

Factors to be taken into consideration

12.42 The Criminal Justice Act 2003 introduced a statutory regime to assist the courts in assessing the seriousness of an offence. In the future, the Sentencing Guidelines Council will produce guidance on the allocation of cases in the youth court. Certain principles may also be extracted from the occasions when the higher courts have considered the question of determining mode of trial in the youth court.

Facts of allegation

12.43 The prosecution version of the allegation should be accepted. It is not appropriate for the court to consider evidence (even by being invited to read prosecution witness statements) to determine seriousness.[30] The facts of the case as alleged, which must be assumed to be true unless manifestly not, should be accurately put before the court. For that reason, the summary of the facts must be scrupulously fair and balanced.[31]

12.44 In offences involving discrimination on the basis of disability or sexual orientation, or involving racial or religious aggravation, these must be regarded as an aggravating factor in sentencing.[32]

---

29 For example: *CPS v South East Surrey Youth Court* [2005] EWHC 2929, *R (on the application of W, S and B) v Brent, Enfield and Richmond Youth Courts* [2006] EWHC 95 (Admin).

30 *R v South Hackney Juvenile Court ex p RB and CB (minors)* (1984) 77 Cr App R 294, QBD.

31 *R (on the application of W, S and B) v Brent, Enfield and Richmond Youth Courts* [2006] EWHC 95 (Admin).

32 Criminal Justice Act 2003 ss145 and 146.

12.45   The Criminal Justice Act 2003 sets out some of the aggravating factors to be taken into account on sentence.[33] The Sentencing Guidelines Council's definitive guidelines, *Overarching Principles: Seriousness*, will be relevant to assist the court in considering the aggravating and mitigating factors to be taken into account in assessing the seriousness of the offence by reference to the culpability of the defendant and the harm caused.[34] The principles of sentencing are further discussed in chapter 17.

Age of the defendant

12.46   When considering the likely sentence the court must have regard to the offender before them and the discount that a sentencing court would allow to the appropriate sentence for an adult to take account of the age of the defendant.

Defendant's previous criminal convictions

12.47   When dealing with a child or young person the court may take into account previous convictions.[35] The court must, in considering the seriousness of an offence, consider previous convictions as an aggravating factor.[36] The defendant's previous record should be accurately described.[37]

Relevant mitigation

12.48   The court should take into account any undisputed facts put forward as mitigation, such as the good character of the accused.[38] In the view of Smith J as expressed in *R (on the application of W, S and B) v Brent, Enfield and Richmond Youth Courts*:

> The court should be told of any undisputed mitigation that will be available to the defendant including, if one has already been made, an indication of an intention to plead guilty.[39]

Age of witnesses

12.49   Although in general a court would take into account the age of the witnesses and the desirability of disposing of the case expeditiously, such considerations could not outweigh the decision as to the proper trial venue.[40]

Age of defendant

12.50   The question of whether the court should have regard to the suitability of the Crown Court as a venue for the trial of a child or young person was

---

33   Criminal Justice Act 2003 s143.
34   Ibid, ss143 and 144, Guideline issued December 2004. The document can be downloaded from www.sentencing-guidelines.gov.uk.
35   *R (T) v Medway Magistrates' Court* [2003] EWHC 2279 (Admin) – reversing *R v Hammersmith Juvenile Court ex p O (a minor)* (1986) 151 JP 740, QBD.
36   Criminal Justice Act 2003 s143.
37   *R (on the application of W, S and B) v Brent, Enfield and Richmond Youth Courts* [2006] EWHC 95 (Admin).
38   *R (on the application of C and D) v Sheffield Youth Court* [2003] EWHC 35 (Admin).
39   [2006] EWHC 95 (Admin) para 6.
40   *R v T and K* [2001] 1 Cr App R 446.

discussed in *R v Devizes Youth Court ex p A*[41] where it was held that the court had no discretion once it formed the view that it ought to be possible to sentence the offender pursuant to section 91. The case must then go to the Crown Court.

Sentencing Guidelines Council

12.51 Guidelines on the allocation of cases and sentencing are issued by the Sentencing Guidelines Council.[42] It is the duty of every court to have regard to those guidelines.[43] At the time of writing there is no allocation guideline for the youth court.

Guidance relating to specific offences

Sentencing Guidelines Council

12.52 The council has not yet published allocation guidelines specific to children and young persons. It has, however, started to issue offence specific guidelines which provide separate guidance on sentencing defendants under the age of 18. The first of these guidelines concerns robbery and is considered below (at para 12.58A).

Sentencing Advisory Panel

12.53 The panel continues to advise the Sentencing Guidelines Council and can make proposals to it.[44] There are conflicting decisions as to whether a court can consider published advice of the panel where it is relevant to sentencing but has not yet been adopted by the Sentencing Guidelines Council.

12.54 Where there is no guidance from the Sentencing Guidelines Council, it may be permissible and helpful for the court to consider any relevant publication of the Sentencing Advisory Panel. In *R (on the application of DPP) v Camberwell Youth Court; R (on the application of H) v Camberwell Youth Court*[45] Kennedy LJ said that:

> ... although the Sentencing Advisory Panel's advice has no legal force, as it is yet to be acted upon, it is helpful as an indication of a considered response to a sentencing problem. In short, providing that the court recognises that the advice does not carry legal force, it is legitimate and helpful to consider such a publication.

12.55 This was followed in *R (on the application of W, S and B) v Brent, Enfield and Richmond Youth Courts*[46] where the court held that a youth court could consider the published advice on sentencing for robbery, allowing it to retain jurisdiction where a previous Court of Appeal guideline case advised a substantial custodial sentence.[47]

---

41 (2000) 164 JP 330.

42 Criminal Justice Act 2003 ss167–173.

43 Ibid, s172.

44 Criminal Justice Act 2003 s171.

45 [2004] EWHC 1805; [2005] 1 WLR 810; [2005] 1 Cr App R 6.

46 [2006] EWHC 95 (Admin).

47 *Attorney-General's Reference Nos 4 and 7 of 2002* [2002] EWCA Crim 127, known as *Lobban and Sawyers*.

12.56   However, in *R v Doidge*[48] the Court of Appeal indicated that it was only the final guidelines of the Council to which the courts had to have regard.

Specific cases

12.57   The court may take account of guidance on the sentencing of specific types of offences where a court has expressly stated that it is giving guidance of general application, but such cases must be treated with caution as the facts and circumstances of offences vary infinitely.[49] The Sentencing Guidelines Council website is linked to a helpful Court of Appeal compendium of relevant cases (see appendix 14).

Burglary (residential)

12.58   The statutory minimum sentence of three years' imprisonment for a third offence of residential burglary does not apply to defendants under 18 years of age.[50] However, in the case of *R v McInerney*[51] the Lord Chief Justice gave the following guidance endorsing the Sentencing Advisory Panel[52] advice:

> 49. As to Juvenile offenders, the Panel stated its advice in the following terms:
> '36. Exceptionally, since domestic burglary is one of the offences which may attract a sentence of long-term detention under s.91 of the Powers of Criminal Courts (Sentencing) Act 2000, a young offender may be committed by the youth court for trial in the Crown Court with a view to such a sentence being passed. A sentence of long-term detention is available in respect of any offender aged 10 to 17 inclusive who is convicted of domestic burglary.
> 37. Where an offender who is now aged 18 or over has two qualifying previous convictions for domestic burglary as a juvenile, a third alleged domestic burglary must be tried in the Crown Court, and the presumptive minimum sentence is a custodial sentence of three years. Although section 111 does not apply until the offender has attained the age of 18, would seem to follow that for an offender who is under 18 but is charged with a third domestic burglary, a custodial sentence in excess of 24 months (the maximum term available for a detention and training order) will be the likely sentence and so the youth court should generally commit the case to Crown Court for trial with a view to sentence under section 91.'
>
> 50. We generally endorse this approach subject to reiterating more strongly in relation to juveniles what we have already said. The Youth Justice Board is spearheading effective punishment in the community and it is important that, where appropriate, juvenile offenders are dealt with in Youth Court and not the Crown Court.

Robbery

12.58A The Sentencing Guidelines Council has issued a definitive guideline on sentencing robbery.[53] The main part of this guideline deals with street

---

48 (2005) *Times* 10 March.
49 *R v Lyon* [2004] EWCA Crim 1365; (2005) *Times* 19 May.
50 Powers of the Criminal Courts (Sentencing) Act 2000 s111.
51 [2002] EWCA Crim 3003.
52 Sentencing Advisory Panel, April 2002.
53 Sentencing Guidelines Council, *Robbery* (July 2006).

robberies and identifies three levels of seriousness. For the first time the guideline provides different starting points for the sentencer when dealing with a child or young person. The guideline is reproduced at appendix 11.

Rape

12.59   In the case of *R v Billam*,[54] subsequently approved in *R v Fareham Youth Court ex p M (a minor)*,[55] rape was said to be an offence which it would not be appropriate to deal with in the youth court. However, at the time of the decision in *Billam* there was a statutory presumption that males under the age of 14 years were not capable of committing this offence. The abolition of the presumption[56] has altered the courts' view. In *R (on the application of W, S and B) v Brent, Enfield and Richmond Youth Courts*[57] at paragraph 44 of her judgment Smith J states:

> I would like to add that it was drawn to our attention that a footnote to Section 24 of the Magistrates' Courts Act 1980 in Stones Justices Manual, the dicta of the court in *R v Billam* [1986] 1 All ER 985 to the effect that a Youth Court should *never* accept jurisdiction in the case of a minor charged with rape … I doubt that there should be such a hard and fast rule in the case of a child aged 12. We were reminded that, at the time of *Billam*, the offence of rape could be committed only by a male of 14 years or over. At that time a boy of 12 or 13 could not be charged with rape. It appears to me that now that a boy of 12 or 13 can be charged with rape, there may well be some cases in which it will not be appropriate to commit such a defendant to the Crown Court. I suggest perhaps that the rule set out in *Billam* and noted in Stone Justices' Manual could now properly be modified so as to indicate that in the case of very young defendants it may be appropriate to accept jurisdiction.

Procedure

12.60   In any case of a grave crime, the issue of mode of trial should be dealt with before any plea is taken from the defendant. It is for the prosecutor and/or legal adviser to draw the court's attention to the fact that mode of trial has to be decided. If a guilty plea is taken without dealing with the question of mode of trial, it is not open to the court to reopen the plea at a later stage.[58] Although the detailed procedural requirements contained in Magistrates' Courts Act 1980 ss18–23 do not apply, it is submitted that as far as possible they should be followed in the interests of fairness to the defendant. First, the prosecutor should present the facts dispassionately. S/he should then make representations as to the court's decision regarding mode of trial. Care should be taken to have regard to existing guidelines.[59] The defence lawyer should then be given the opportunity of making representations.

---

54   [1986] 1 WLR 349.
55   (1998) 163 JP 812.
56   See para 6.10.
57   [2006] EWHC 95 (Admin).
58   *R v Herefordshire Youth Court ex p J (a minor)* (1998) *Times* 4 May (CO/334/97, 23.4.98) QBD.
59   Code for Crown Prosecutors, Crown Prosecution Service. This can be obtained from www.cps.gov.uk.

Co-defendants

12.61   The position of each defendant must be considered separately by the court and an appropriate decision taken for each defendant, even if this results in one defendant being tried in the youth court and the other in the Crown Court. This was confirmed in by Smith J in *R (on the application of W, S and B) v Brent, Enfield and Richmond Youth Courts*:

> Where several defendants are charged together I would stress the need … for the court to consider the position of each defendant separately. Where all the defendants are under the age of 18 there is no power to commit a young person to the Crown Court in the interests of justice, as there is where one defendant is over the age of 18 and must be committed to the Crown Court. If all are under 18, the court must make an appropriate decision for each defendant, even if this results in one defendant being tried in the Youth Court and others in the Crown Court.[60]

Committal of related offences

12.62   Where a child or young person is committed to stand trial for a grave crime, the court may also commit him/her for trial for any other indictable offence with which s/he is charged at the same time if the charges for both offences could be joined in the same indictment.[61] If the grave crime is an either-way offence, the court may commit any summary-only offences punishable by imprisonment or disqualification from driving if the offence arises out of similar circumstances to the either-way offence.[62] A co-defendant charged with a related offence which is not a grave crime cannot be committed to the Crown Court under these provisions.

Preparing for the grave crime decision

The court

12.63   It is essential that the defence lawyer is in a position to assist the court in its consideration of likely sentence and on the factors which will be taken into account. The lawyer will need to consider:

- prosecution disclosure;
- previous convictions;
- instructions, if there may be a guilty plea;
- guidelines on sentencing;
- relevant law on the nature of the decision being taken by the court.

12.64   The advocate should not hesitate to request an adjournment if s/he is not in a position adequately to deal with the issues to be raised. In *R (on the application of H, O and A) v Southampton Youth Court* the mode of trial decision was taken prior to the service of the video-taped evidence of child witnesses. In the subsequent judicial review of the youth court's decision, Leveson J stated:

60   [2006] EWHC 95 (Admin) para 9.
61   Magistrates' Courts Act 1980 s24(1A) as inserted by Crime and Disorder Act 1998 s47(6).
62   Criminal Justice Act 1988 s41(1).

... the very least one would expect is that each solicitor would have taken careful instructions before permitting the court to embark upon the grave crimes procedure. It is said that there is increasing pressure on advocates to make early decisions and rapidly progress all cases, especially those involving serious charges and young people and, rightly or wrongly, the solicitors did not ask for an adjournment, did not obtain further disclosure and did not consider the case in full prior to this hearing. Suffice it to say, it was for the defence representatives to ensure that they knew enough about the case to make an informed judgment about the submissions to be made.[63]

The client

12.65   The court's decision on jurisdiction is a complex one and it is therefore imperative that the defence lawyer takes time to explain to the client, as far as possible, the nature of this part of the proceedings, using language appropriate to his/her age and understanding.

Is the Crown Court a better trial venue?

12.66   Where a choice is available, the Crown Court has traditionally been regarded by defence lawyers as the court of preference for the trial of adults. The Crown Court is seen as having a statistically higher acquittal rate, although this may be due to a number of factors. In the opinion of the authors, this view is not always applicable to children and young persons who may be better dealt with in the more informal atmosphere of the youth court. There has been suggestion that young people are not always sympathetically received by juries or judges. The defence lawyer needs to assist his/her client in understanding and participating in the proceedings and it is submitted that the Crown Court is a more difficult environment for this to take place.[64]

Structured decision-making

12.67   The determination of 'dangerousness' falls to be made under Crime and Disorder Act 1998 s51A(2) and the 'grave crime' decision under Magistrates' Courts Act 1980 s24(1). There are some offences – eg affray, assault occasioning actual bodily harm, racially aggravated offences – which do not fall within the grave crime provisions under the Public Order Act 1986 but are specified offences for the purposes of the dangerousness provisions.

12.68   The legislation, as currently enacted, does not state the order in which decisions are to be made, nor does it state that section 24 is subject to section 51A, or vice versa. The practical approach of the courts has been to regard section 24 as subject to a further implied exception in section 51A.[65]

12.69   It is submitted that in most cases the decision on whether a child or young person should have available a sentence under the dangerousness provisions in the event of conviction, is best made when the court

---

63   [2004] EWHC 2912 (Admin) para 10.
64   See chapter 10.
65   *CPS v South East Surrey Youth Court*, sub nom *R (DPP) v South East Surrey Youth Court* [2005] EWHC 2929; [2006] All ER 444.

has information enabling it to take a full account of the offender and the offence. In cases where the offence is not also a grave crime, the decision can be made following conviction.[66]

12.70   In cases where the offence is also a grave crime, it may be more practical for the court to consider the grave crime provisions following the initial consideration of whether it is clearly a case where detention under the dangerousness provisions should be available on sentence. The court should be encouraged, in all but the clearest of cases, to leave the dangerousness decision until after conviction. The court can be reminded of its powers following conviction to commit to the Crown Court for sentence once full information is obtained.[67]

12.71   A clear exposition by the defence lawyer of the factors being considered by the court and any relevant guidance on sentencing will greatly assist the court in its considerations.

Reviewing the mode of trial decision

12.72   There are limited circumstances in which a court may review its decision, either to reverse a decision to decline jurisdiction or to change from summary trial to commit the defendant. A court may alter its decision as to mode of trial if it appears to the court hearing evidence in a summary trial, at any time before the conclusion of the evidence for the prosecution, that the case is after all one which (under Magistrates' Courts Act 1980 s24(1)) ought not to be tried summarily.[68] 'Evidence for the prosecution' is evidence adduced to prove guilt and therefore it is not open to the court to review its decision regarding jurisdiction after a defendant has pleaded guilty to the offence.[69]

12.73   Where magistrates have commenced committal proceedings by way of examining the evidence under Magistrates' Courts Act 1980 s6(1) in respect of a child or young person, they may revert to summary trial at any time before actually committing the defendant.[70]

12.74   Magistrates' Courts Act 1980 s24 provides for a single decision on the mode of trial decision. It does not permit the question to be revisited, whether or not new material emerges.[71] The court cannot reconsider the question of mode of trial outside the circumstances set out in Magistrates' Courts Act 1980 s25.[72]

12.75   In *R v South Hackney Juvenile Court ex p RB and CB (minors)*[73] McNeill J suggested that at a committal hearing where the sufficiency of evidence is being challenged, it was open to the defence to make representations that

66 *CPS v South East Surrey Youth Court*, sub nom *R (DPP) v South East Surrey Youth Court* [2005] EWHC 2929; [2006] All ER 444.
67 Powers of Criminal Courts (Sentencing) Act 2000 s3C.
68 Magistrates' Courts Act 1980 s25(5)(a).
69 *R v Dudley Justices ex p Gillard* [1986] AC 442.
70 Magistrates' Courts Act 1980 s25(5)(b).
71 *R (DPP) v Camberwell Green Youth Court* [2003] EWHC 3217 (Admin), *R (C) v Grimsby and Cleethorpes Magistrates' Court* [2004] EWHC 224 (Admin).
72 *R (on the application of CPS) v Redbridge Youth Court* [2005] EWHC 1390 (Admin).
73 (1983) 77 Cr App R 294.

the prosecution evidence did not indicate that the case needed to be committed to the Crown Court for trial and to revert to summary trial. This would accord with the provisions of Magistrates' Courts Act 1980 s25.

Committal for trial

12.76 The position is the same as in the adult court. See paras 12.108–12.110.

Transfer for trial

12.77 The position is the same as in the adult court. See paras 12.111–12.118.

The decision in the adult magistrates' court

12.78 The youth defendant appearing in the adult magistrates' court with an adult co-defendant may be tried on indictment when s/he is:
- jointly charged with an adult sent to the Crown Court under Crime and Disorder Act 1998 s51;
- jointly charged with an adult with an either-way offence and the adult is committed for trial;
- charged with homicide;
- charged with firearms possession;
- charged with a 'specified offence' (dangerousness provisions);
- charged with a grave crime.

12.79 In most cases, the child or young person appearing in the adult court will face a joint charge with an adult. There are occasions where the joint charge is summary-only and the child or young person faces a more serious related offence alone. The more serious offence may fall into the four exceptions which have been discussed above. The adult court and the youth court are both the summary court for the purposes of Magistrates' Courts Act 1980 s24 and Crime and Disorder Act 1998 s51A. The adult court can exercise all the powers usually exercised by the youth court under these provisions.

Indictable-only offences

12.80 An adult shall be sent 'forthwith' for trial:
- where s/he faces an indictable-only offence;[74]
- where s/he faces a related either-way offence jointly with a person being sent and s/he appears before the court on the same occasion.[75]

12.81 An adult may be sent for trial where s/he faces a related either-way offence jointly with a person who has been sent and s/he appears before the court on a subsequent occasion.[76]

74 Crime and Disorder Act 1998 s51(1).
75 Ibid, s51(3).
76 Ibid, s51(3).

12.82   If the court considers it to be in the interests of justice to do so, it shall send a child or young person for trial at the Crown Court if:

- it has already decided to send an adult for trial; or
- the child or young person is charged jointly with an adult with an indictable offence for which the adult is sent for trial.[77]

12.83   This applies whether the child or young person appears before the court on the same or a subsequent occasion. This can mean, in practical terms, that a child or young person who is jointly charged with an adult with an indictable offence, can be sent to the Crown Court where the adult is being or has been sent for trial because that adult is linked to another adult who is being or has been sent for trial on indictable-only matters.

Adjournments

12.84   A magistrates' court can adjourn the proceedings prior to sending.[78]

Sending

12.85   The sending is by way of a notice specifying the offences sent for trial and the place at which the trial is to take place. A copy of the notice is served on the accused and given to the Crown Court.[79]

Interests of justice

12.86   This test is discussed at paras 12.101–12.106 in relation to children and young people jointly charged with adults with either-way offences. It is submitted that the same considerations apply in both situations.

Related offences

12.87   An either-way offence is related to an indictable-only offence if they could be joined in the same indictment.[80]

12.88   Where a court sends a child or young person for trial, it may at the same time send him/her to the Crown Court for trial for any either-way or summary only offence with which s/he is charged which:

- appears to the court to be related to the indictable-only offence; or
- in the case of a summary-only offence, it is punishable with imprisonment or carries a power of disqualification from driving.[81]

What about dangerousness?

12.89   Where the court decides that a child or young person should, on conviction, be considered for a sentence under the 'dangerousness' provisions, Crime and Disorder Act 1998 s51A(10) stipulates that the offence shall be

77 Crime and Disorder Act 1998 s51(5).
78 Ibid, s52(5).
79 Ibid, s51(7).
80 Ibid, s51(12).
81 Ibid, s51(6) and (11).

sent to the Crown Court under section 51A(2) and no other provision. It is unclear whether this means that the adult court dealing with a child or young person should consider the dangerousness issue prior to any decision on sending in the interests of justice. The wording of section 51A is designed to relate to a new section 51 which is not yet in force.

12.90   The defence lawyer may wish to argue that the preferable course would be for the court to leave the dangerousness issue for determination on conviction when more information will be available to assist the court.

Either-way offences

12.91   The procedure for deciding the mode of trial for a child or young person jointly charged with an adult is determined by the procedure being employed in relation to the adult co-defendant.

Plea before venue

Where the adult indicates a guilty plea

12.92   The court will normally take a plea from the child or young person. However, if the child or young person is charged with a grave crime, the court should decide whether committal for trial is required under Magistrates' Courts Act 1980 s24(1)(a) before the plea is taken.[82] As the court may not be experienced in youth cases, the defence representative will need to be in a position to assist the court with the decision on mode of trial as set out in paras 12.35–12.66 above.

12.93   If the court accepts jurisdiction for the child or young person and s/he pleads guilty, s/he should be remitted to the youth court for sentence unless the case may be disposed of by way of a discharge, financial order or a parental bindover.[83]

12.94   If the child or young person pleads not guilty, s/he may be tried alone in the adult court or remitted for trial to the youth court.[84] In the opinion of the authors, the latter option is preferable.

Where the adult defendant indicates a not guilty plea or indicates no plea

12.95   The court will proceed to determine mode of trial for the adult pursuant to the principles set out Magistrates' Courts Act 1980 ss18–23. As the child or young person has no right to elect jury trial, s/he would have no right to make representations at this stage but the court could exercise its discretion to allow any representations.

12.96   If the court decides to decline jurisdiction in relation to the adult, or the adult co-defendant elects jury trial, the child or young person may be committed to stand trial along with the adult co-defendant(s), if it is considered 'necessary in the interests of justice to do so'.[85]

82   *R v Tottenham Youth Court ex p Fawzy* [1998] 1 All ER 365, QBD.
83   Powers of Criminal Courts (Sentencing) Act 2000 s8.
84   Magistrates' Courts Act 1980 s29(2).
85   Ibid, s24(1)(b).

12.97   If the court decides not to commit the child or young person for trial, it may take a plea from him/her. If the child or young person pleads not guilty, s/he may be tried in the adult court or remitted for trial to the youth court.[86]

12.98   If s/he pleads guilty, s/he should be remitted to the youth court for sentence, unless the case may be disposed of by way of a discharge, financial order or a parental bindover.[87] In both cases the remittal may be to the youth court acting for the same place as the remitting court or for the place where the child or young person habitually resides.[88]

Aiding and abetting

12.99   Although Magistrates' Courts Act 1980 s24(1)(b) only refers to committing a child or young person to stand trial with an adult when 'jointly charged', the Divisional Court in the case of *R v Coventry City Magistrates' Court ex p M (a minor)*[89] assumed that there was a power to commit a child or young person to stand trial with an adult whom s/he is charged with aiding and abetting. There seems to have been no legal argument on the point during the hearing of the case.

Related offences

12.100   A child or young person may also be committed to stand trial for any other indictable offence for which s/he is charged at the same time (whether jointly with the adult or not) if that other offence arises out of circumstances which are the same as or connected with those giving rise to the joint charge.[90] The court may also commit any summary-only offences punishable by imprisonment or disqualification from driving if the offence arises out of similar circumstances to the either-way offence.[91]

Interests of justice

12.101   When deciding whether it is in the interests of justice to commit or transfer a child or young person for trial along with an adult, the magistrates must act judicially[92] and the court should invite separate representations from the prosecutor and the defence lawyer representing the child or young person.

Sentencing Guidelines Council

12.102   The court must have regard to any guidelines issued on the allocation of cases.[93] At the time of writing, a draft guideline has been published.[94] The

---

86   Magistrates' Courts Act 1980 s29(2).
87   Powers of Criminal Courts (Sentencing) Act 2000 s8.
88   See chapter 19.
89   (1992) 156 JP 809.
90   Magistrates' Courts Act 1980 s24(2).
91   Criminal Justice Act 1988 s41(1).
92   *R v Newham JJ ex p Knight* [1976] Crim LR 323, QBD.
93   Criminal Justice Act 2003 s172.
94   Sentencing Guidelines Council, 16 February 2006 (see appendix 14 for contact details).

relevance of draft guidelines to the deliberations of the court is considered at paras 12.52–12.56.

12.103 In considering whether it is in the interests of justice to send a defendant under the age of 18 years to the Crown Court alongside an adult defendant, the draft guideline states that any presumption that a joint trial would be preferable must be balanced with the general presumption that young people should be tried in the youth court.

12.104 Examples of the factors to be considered include:

- the young age of the defendant, especially where the age gap between the adult and the youth is substantial;
- the immaturity and intellect of the youth;
- the relative culpability of the youth compared with the adult and whether or not the role played by the youth was minor;
- lack of previous convictions on the part of the youth compared with the adult;
- whether or not the trial of the youth and the adult can be severed without inconvenience to witnesses or injustice to the case as a whole.

12.105 The draft guideline is designed to relate to the law as it will be once the remaining parts of Criminal Justice Act 2003 Sch 3 are introduced.[95]

Role of the defence lawyer

12.106 The defence representative needs to be in a position to address the court in relation to these factors. S/he will need to consider the issues raised in chapter 10 (effective participation) and the guidance in relation to mode of trial in the youth court in order to address the court as to the more appropriate venue for trial of a young defendant. It is of note that the Practice Direction[96] urges judges in the Crown Court to consider severing young defendants from adults at an early stage in the proceedings.[97] The adult court may not be familiar with these issues and the defence advocate should be ready to deal with this in some depth in order to assist the court in exercising its discretion.

Reviewing the mode of trial decision

12.107 The position is the same as in the youth court as set out at paras 12.72–12.75.

Committal for trial

12.108 The consideration of evidence is solely on written statements.

12.109 The examining justices will be required to consider whether there is sufficient evidence for a trial if:

- the defendant is not legally represented; or

---

95 Anticipated to be 2006/2007, see chapter appendix 13.
96 *Consolidated Criminal Practice Direction.*
97 See table 10 above.

- the defence lawyer requests that the court considers a submission that there is insufficient evidence to put the accused on trial by jury for the offence.

12.110 Defence lawyers will be familiar with considering whether to challenge the sufficiency of evidence in a committal hearing. An accused under the age of 18 has the same right to challenge the prosecution case at committal as an adult defendant and all the same tactical considerations will apply to an accused who is a child or young person.

Transfer for trial

12.111 In certain circumstances where the alleged victim or a witness is a child, a committal hearing can be dispensed with. In such cases a transfer for trial takes place instead.

12.112 Transfer for trial may take place in relation to the following offences:

- an offence which involves an assault on, or injury or a threat of injury to, a person;
- an offence under Children and Young Persons Act 1933 s1 (cruelty to persons under 16);
- an offence under the Sexual Offences Act 1956, Indecency with Children Act 1960, Sexual Offences Act 1967, Criminal Law Act 1967 s54 or Protection of Children Act 1978; and
- an offence which consists of attempting or conspiring to commit, or of aiding, abetting, counselling, procuring or inciting the commission of, an offence listed above.

Definition of 'child'

12.113 'Child' is defined as follows:

- for a sexual offence it means a person under the age of 17;
- in relation to other offences it means a person under the age of 14.[98]

12.114 If a video recording was made of the witness' evidence when s/he was under the relevant age, then the relevant age is increased by one year to 18 years and 15 years respectively.

Notice of transfer

12.115 To initiate the transfer for trial procedure, the Director of Public Prosecutions must serve a notice of transfer upon the relevant youth court or adult magistrates' court, certifying that s/he is of the opinion:

- that the evidence of the offence would be sufficient for the person charged to be committed for trial;
- that a child who is alleged:
  (i) to be a person against whom the offence was committed; or

98 Criminal Justice Act 1991 s53(6).

(ii) to have witnessed the commission of the offence;

will be called as a witness at the trial; and

- that, for the purposes of avoiding any prejudice to the welfare of the child, the case should be taken over and proceeded with without delay by the Crown Court.[99]

12.116 The notice merely requires the Director of Public Prosecutions to state his/her opinion that the above criteria are satisfied. The decision to serve a notice of transfer shall not be subject to appeal or liable to be questioned in any court.[100]

12.117 A defendant who wishes to argue that there is insufficient evidence justifying a trial may apply to the Crown Court prior to arraignment to have the charge(s) dismissed.[101]

12.118 A notice for transfer may not be served once the justices have begun to inquire into the case as examining justices.[102]

Accused attaining 18

12.119 In the case of a defendant charged with an indictable offence who attains the age of 18 after the first court appearance, the question arises whether s/he should be dealt with under the adult or youth court rules regarding mode of trial. The House of Lords held in the case of *R v Islington North Juvenile Court ex p Daley*[103] that the relevant age is the defendant's age on the day that the mode of trial is determined. If the defendant has attained 18 before that point in the case, s/he has a right to elect jury trial. If the defendant has not attained 18 before the mode of trial is determined, s/he shall be subject to Magistrates' Courts Act 1980 s24. This principle applies equally to indictable-only offences.[104]

12.120 To prevent any doubt arising when dealing with a defendant in the youth court McNeill J in *R v Lewes Juvenile Court ex p Turner*[105] suggested the following practice should be followed:

> [W]here a person under the age of [18] pleads not guilty before a [youth] court, and the circumstances set out in s24 of the Magistrates' Courts Act 1980 do not apply, but when the [youth] court is not there and then able to take evidence in the trial which is to follow, the register of the court should be marked 'remanded for summary trial'. That to my mind, would be decisive and determinative of the date on which, for the purposes of the section, the defendant appeared or was brought before the court.

99 Criminal Justice Act 1991 s53(1).

100 Ibid, s53(4).

101 Ibid, Sch 6 para 5.

102 Ibid, s53(2).

103 [1983] 1 AC 347; (1982) 75 Cr App R 280; [1982] 3 WLR 344.

104 *R v Nottingham Justices ex p Taylor* (1991) 93 Cr App R 365, QBD.

105 (1984) 149 JP 186, QBD.

Jointly charged with an adult with summary-only matters

Where the adult pleads guilty

12.121 A plea will be taken from the young defendant. If the child or young person pleads not guilty, s/he may be tried in the adult court or may be remitted for trial to the youth court.[106] If s/he pleads guilty, s/he should be remitted to the youth court for sentence, unless the case may be disposed of by way of a discharge, financial order or a parental bindover.[107]

Where the adult pleads not guilty

12.122 A plea will be taken from the child or young person. If s/he pleads guilty, s/he should be remitted to the youth court for sentence, unless the case may be disposed of by way of a discharge, financial order or a parental bindover.[108] If the child or young person pleads not guilty s/he must be tried jointly with the adult in the adult magistrates' court.[109]

---

106 Magistrates' Courts Act 1980 s29(2).
107 Powers of the Criminal Courts (Sentencing) Act 2000 s8.
108 Ibid.
109 Children and Young Persons Act 1933 s46(1)(a).

Bail and remands

Introduction

13.1   The rules regarding children and young persons in relation to bail and remands are frequently the source of misunderstanding. This chapter will cover the question of bail and how it affects children and young persons, as well as examining what happens if the court refuses bail.

13.2   It should be emphasised at the outset that the Bail Act 1976 applies in its entirety to children and young people and, as a result, any court is under the same obligation to consider the question of bail as it would be with an adult defendant. It is only if the court refuses bail that the law is substantially different to that applying to an adult. Although the Criminal Justice Act 1991 extended the age range of the renamed youth courts, it created an anomaly in relation to bail by treating 17-year-olds differently to the younger age range of the youth court. In relation to bail and remands, 17-year-olds are treated as though they were adults. In contrast, younger defendants benefit from rules designed to ensure that a remand to custody is always an absolute last resort. In the case of defendants under the age of 17, the Act therefore establishes a three-tier remand system:

- bail with or without conditions;
- remand to local authority accommodation with or without conditions;
- secure remand.

Role of the youth offending team

13.3   When a court is considering bail in relation to a young defendant, the youth offending team may be involved in the following ways:

- assessing the young defendant;
- providing bail information;
- implementing bail supervision and support; and
- providing a bail intensive supervision and surveillance programme ('bail ISSP').

Assessment of the young defendant

13.4   Prior to deciding whether to offer any services to the young defendant, the youth offending team will assess him/her. The *Asset* Bail Profile will be used to assist in the assessment of the particular needs of the young person. The accommodation needs of the young person must be assessed.[1]

13.4A   The *Asset* Bail Profile will be completed by a member of the youth offending team at court, usually in consultation with the child or young person and any family member present at court. It is designed to help youth offending team practitioners to identify and collate relevant information into a detailed picture of the young person's situation, circumstances and history, which can be considered by the court in determining an appropriate bail or remand status.

13.4B   The *Asset* assessment will include:

---

1   Youth Justice Board: *National Standards for Youth Justice Services* (2004), para 2.25.

- details of the current allegations;
- the defendant's bail history;
- details of accommodation;
- family and personal relationships;
- education, training and employment;
- lifestyle;
- physical, emotional and mental health;
- substance misuse;
- attitudes to supervision and support.

13.4C   Where there is a risk of a secure remand for 15-or 16-year-old boys, the *Asset* Bail Profile includes an assessment of vulnerability in terms of the young person's physical or emotional immaturity or propensity to self-harm.[2]

Bail information

13.5   Where there is a risk that bail may be refused, youth offending teams must assess young people on their first appearance before a court in their area, and provide the court with verified factual information about the availability of any appropriate bail address and any other relevant circumstances.[3] Contact may also be made with family members who are not present at court.

13.6   Where a young person from another youth offending team area appears before the court for the first hearing, the youth offending team covering the court area is responsible for liaising with the home area and providing information to the court on the services offered by that area.[4]

Bail supervision and support

13.7   The youth offending team is under a statutory duty to provide support for children and young persons remanded or committed on bail while awaiting trial or sentence.[5] This support is officially called 'bail supervision and support'. It may be provided by the youth offending team directly or contracted out to a voluntary organisation.

13.8   The aims of bail supervision and support are to:

- meet the objections to bail;
- prevent offending on bail;
- ensure the appearance of the young person at court to reduce delays in the court process; and
- ensure remands to custody and secure remands are kept to the essential minimum.[6]

13.9   It is the responsibility of the youth offending team manager to ensure there is a bail supervision and support scheme in operation. The scheme must establish mechanisms to ensure that the scheme providers are aware

2   See paras 13.224–13.235.
3   Youth Justice Board: *National Standards for Youth Justice Services* (2004), para 2.15.
4   Ibid, para 2.16.
5   Crime and Disorder Act 1998 s38(4)(c).
6   Youth Justice Board: *National Standards for Youth Justice Services* (2004), para 2.20.

of and able to deal with any young people appearing at youth courts, adult magistrates' courts and the Crown Court. The service must be available at weekends and bank holidays as well as during the weekdays.[7]

Elements of bail supervision and support

13.10   Most schemes that work with young offenders aim to help the defendants on the programme to comply with their conditions of bail and to provide constructive activities to occupy their time and lessen the risk of further offending. The contents of bail support programmes vary across the country, but may include:

- regular office reporting;
- monitored attendance at youth activities;
- monitoring of school attendance;
- programmes aimed at re-introducing the young defendant to school or arranging specific educational provision;
- assistance with arranging training or finding employment;
- work with families to resolve conflicts and to ensure a continuing home base for the young defendant and to involve the parents in taking more responsibility for their children's behaviour;
- supervision of any curfew imposed by the court;
- placements with volunteers during the evening and weekends; and
- intensive supervision and surveillance programme (see paras 2.28– 2.33).

Liaising with the youth offending team

13.11   The defence lawyer should familiarise him/herself with the local bail information and bail supervision and support provisions. Whenever there is a risk that bail will be refused, it is advisable to make early contact with the bail supervision and support scheme. In some areas, suitability for the intensive supervision and surveillance programme will be assessed by a separate team, but it is necessary to liaise with the bail supervision and support team, so that they can refer the matter on.

The contested bail application

13.12   On the vast majority of occasions when children or young persons appear before a court there will be no problem regarding bail. However, in a significant minority of cases bail will be opposed by the prosecution either because of the seriousness of an individual offence or because of offending while on bail. In such circumstances a bail application can be extremely challenging, as complex rules must be negotiated and an often complicated offending history must be dealt with.

---

7   Ibid, paras 2.21, 2.23 and 2.24.

Preparing the bail application

13.13 Before the hearing the defence lawyer should ensure that s/he speaks to:

- the prosecutor;
- a representative of the youth offending team; and
- the client.

Prosecutor

13.14 As youth courts are private hearings, it is important to arrive before the court sits so that it is possible to speak to the prosecutor. As well as obtaining details of the current allegation, it is also important to establish what other information is held about the young defendant and what the objections are to bail. It is not uncommon to find prosecutors who are unfamiliar with the requirements of Children and Young Persons Act 1969 s23(5) and it may be possible in preliminary negotiations to persuade him/her that there are no grounds to seek a custodial remand or that appropriate conditions would satisfy any objections, particularly once the youth offending team have undertaken their assessment and have a bail support or other package of conditions to suggest to the court.

Representative of the youth offending team

13.15 All too frequently defence lawyers fail to make use of this valuable resource. In many cases the youth offending team will have had previous contact with the young defendant and will know him/her better than the lawyer. The officer will also have access to social services records which may provide useful background information. Most importantly, the officer may be able to provide resources in the form of accommodation or a bail support package. When the prosecution are vigorously opposing bail, a bail application supported by a youth offending team with a well presented bail supervision and support programme has a much greater chance of success.

13.16 If the child or young person is appearing in the adult magistrates' court it is unlikely that a member of the youth offending team will be present at court. The court probation officer should be approached and asked to contact the relevant youth offending team. It may be necessary to persuade a member of the team to attend the court personally, particularly if a bail supervision and support package is to be proposed to magistrates unfamiliar with such programmes.

Instructions from the young defendant

13.17 As well as taking instructions specific to the allegation and the objections to bail, it is usually helpful to attempt to discover some background information about:

- the defendant's family;
- any history of being in care;
- his/her schooling (or lack of it);
- any contact with social services;
- any contact with the youth offending team.

Table 14: Preparing a bail application – checklist

General

1   Full name
2   Current address
3   Date of birth
4   Age
5   Remand rules applicable? juvenile/adult?

Domestic circumstances

6   Live at home?
    If yes:
    – name of parent(s)
    – occupation(s) and hours of work (if applicable)
    – able/willing to supervise bail conditions?
7   In care or looked after by local authority?
    If yes:
    – which local authority?
    – subject of full care order?
    – name of social worker / key worker
    – reasons for being 'in care'

Failure to surrender to custody

8   Does the client have previous conviction(s) for Bail Act offence(s)?
    If yes:
    – when?
    – penalty imposed?
    – what were the circumstances?
    – has s/he been granted bail since the last Bail Act offence?
9   Has the client previously surrendered to custody satisfactorily?
10 Possible conditions
    – a condition of residence? If client has no, or unsuitable, address:
    – local authority willing to accommodate?
    – remand fostering scheme available?
    – (16- and 17-year-olds only) bail hostel available?
    – appropriate police station if reporting condition imposed
    – reporting scheme as part of bail support?
    – where appropriate, the following information in respect of
      possible sureties: name; address; telephone number; occupation;
      relationship to client; any previous convictions; likely financial
      circumstances
    – security?

Fear of further offences

11 Is client currently on bail?

If yes:

– date(s) imposed?

– police or court bail?

– alleged offence(s)

– how long on bail?

– any conditions attached to bail?

12 Does client have previous convictions?

If yes:

– when and where sentence(s) imposed?

– were any of them committed while on bail?

– were any of them for similar offence(s) to offences(s) now charged?

– have client's circumstances changed?

13 Have client's circumstances materially changed since these offence(s) allegedly committed?

14 How does client spend his/her week?

– school

– Youth Training Scheme

– employment

– structured leisure activities, eg, youth club, sports, etc

– times of activities

15 Possible conditions:

– curfew? If so, would curfew be:

- relevant (night time offending / to reinforce parental control)?
- practicable?
- not to go to scene of alleged crime? If so, would condition be:
- relevant?
- practicable?

– availability of bail support?

– parental surety?

– are there other conditions that may be appropriate?

Interference with witnesses

16 Is the identity and address of any witness known to client?

17 Is there any history of threats allegedly made by client against any witness?

18 Possible conditions:

– not to contact witness directly or indirectly? If so, would condition be feasible (eg, do the witness and defendant attend the same school)?

– geographical exclusion? If so, would condition be practicable?

13.18   Such background information may indicate an underlying problem which if addressed is likely to lead to an end to the current offending. By seeking a bail supervision and support package which addresses those issues and problems, the objections to bail can be dealt with much more effectively.

13.19   Magistrates (particularly in adult courts) are sometimes reluctant to listen to lengthy descriptions of a young defendant's background and domestic circumstances. If faced with this response, the court should be reminded of its obligation under Children and Young Persons Act 1933 s44 to have regard to the welfare of the child or young person.

The hearing

Structured decision-making

13.20   There is a real danger in bail hearings for juveniles that the very strict criteria of the Children and Young Persons Act 1969 are not applied because the prosecutor and the magistrates are allowed to turn the hearing into a discussion of why a custodial remand should not be used. It is important for the defence lawyer to insist that the scheme of the legislation is followed. This requires the court to consider the following questions in order:

(a) Are there substantial grounds for believing an objection to bail exists?

(b) Can those objections be met adequately by conditional bail, perhaps with bail support?

(c) If bail is refused, are the criteria of section 23(5) applicable?

(d) If yes, the court should consult with the local authority about possible accommodation and support available?

(e) Is any type of local authority accommodation available which would be adequate to protect the public from serious harm from the defendant?

13.21   As the provisions of Children and Young Persons Act 1969 s23 only apply after a refusal of bail, the hearing may be split into two. First of all there should be a bail application, and only if that is refused should there be further representations regarding a secure remand with the magistrates under a statutory duty to consult social services.

Presentation of the prosecution objections

13.22   The court has a duty to consider whether bail should be granted at each hearing whether or not the defence lawyer makes a bail application. The court will usually start by asking if the prosecutor has any objections to bail being granted. If any objections are raised, the prosecutor will usually start by summarising the allegation made against the defendant. A copy of the list of previous convictions (if any) will be handed to the court and the objections outlined with reference to the offence, previous record of the defendant and his/her current circumstances. Having heard the prosecutor's representations, the court will then hear the defence lawyer's representations regarding bail and any conditions. In many hearings the prosecutor's objections to bail will be followed by his/her representations on the criteria relating to a secure or custodial remand. The defence representative will also need to address the court on all these issues. In some circumstances it may be necessary to ask the court to make a decision on bail and to address the issues relating to the nature of any remand once that decision has been taken.

13.23   In presenting the objections to bail the prosecutor may call a police officer to give evidence, although this will normally only be done in very serious cases. The strict rules of evidence do not apply and the court may consider hearsay evidence.[8] The focus of the court is on the quality of the evidence.[9] The defence may cross-examine any witness called as part of the prosecution presentation of objections to bail.

Procedural requirements

13.24   If, after consulting with the local authority, the court is of the opinion that the criteria of section 23(5) are satisfied, the court must state in open court that it is of that opinion and explain to the defendant in open court and in ordinary language why it is of that opinion.[10] It is submitted that the reasons given should be detailed and address the particular circumstances of the defendant and why the alternative accommodation would not be adequate.[11]

General principles under the European Convention on Human Rights

13.25   The decision regarding bail engages Article 5 (right to liberty) of the European Convention on Human Rights. A person charged with an offence should be released pending trial unless the prosecuting authorities can show that there are 'relevant and sufficient' reasons to justify his/her continued detention.[12] Any court considering bail is to 'examine all the facts arguing for or against the existence of a genuine requirement of public interest justifying ... a departure from the rule of respect for individual liberty and set them out in their decisions on application for relief'.[13] The European court has emphasised that some evidence may be needed before bail is refused, but the nature or extent of the evidence required has not been clarified.[14]

13.26   Article 5(4) of the convention may also require some disclosure before the question of bail is finally determined. The 'equality of arms' principle applies to bail application.[15] This includes:

- the right to disclosure of prosecution evidence for purposes of making a bail application;[16]

---

8   *Moles, Re* [1981] Crim LR 170, QBD.
9   *R (DPP) v Havering Magistrates' Court* [2001] 1 WLR 805.
10 Children and Young Persons Act 1969 s23(6).
11 To the authors' knowledge, on two occasions High Court judges have given leave to move for judicial review on the basis that magistrates had given inadequate reasons. Neither application reached a full hearing.
12 *Letellier v France* (1992) 14 EHRR 83.
13 *Wemhoff v Germany* (1979) 1 EHRR 55.
14 *Lamy v Belgium* (1989) 11 EHRR 529.
15 *Woukam Moudefo v France* (1991) 13 EHRR 549.
16 *Lamy v Belgium* (1989) 11 EHRR 529; and *R v DPP ex p Lee* [1999] 2 Cr App R 304.

- the requirement that the court should give reasons for the refusal of bail;[17]
- the requirement that renewed applications for bail should be permitted at reasonable intervals.[18]

13.27   The grounds accepted by the European Court for withholding bail include:

- the risk that the accused will fail to appear at the trial[19] (the likely sentence is relevant but cannot of itself justify the refusal for bail);[20]
- the risk that the accused will interfere with the course of justice;[21]
- preventing the commission of further offences – there must be good reasons to believe that the accused will commit offences while on bail;[22] and
- the preservation of public order.[23]

The statutory right to bail

General principle

13.28   There is a general right to bail for any person in criminal proceedings.[24] This right applies to the following:

- an accused appearing before a magistrates' or youth court and the Crown Court;[25] or
- a convicted person before any of these courts but only if the court is adjourning the case for the purpose of enabling reports to be prepared before sentence;[26] or
- an offender appearing before the court for alleged breach of a requirement of a probation, community service, combination or curfew order.[27]

13.29   A court must consider bail at every hearing and this obligation exists even if the accused does not apply for bail.

Serious cases

13.30   The generality of the right to bail has been revised in relation to very serious charges.

---

17   *Tomasi v France* (1993) 15 EHRR 1.
18   *Bezicheri v Italy* (1990) 12 EHRR 210.
19   *Stodmuller v Austria* (1979) 1 EHRR 155.
20   *Letellier v France* (1992) 14 EHRR 83.
21   *Clooth v Belgium* (1992) 14 EHRR 717.
22   *Toth v Austria* (1992) 14 EHRR 717.
23   *Letellier v France* (1992) 14 EHRR 83.
24   Bail Act 1976 s4(1).
25   Ibid, s4(2).
26   Ibid, s4(4).
27   Ibid, s4(3).

Homicide, rape and sexual offences

13.31 Special provisions apply to anyone charged with any of the following offences:

- murder;
- attempted murder;
- manslaughter;
- rape;
- attempted rape;
- offences under Sexual Offences Act 2003 ss2, 3, 4, 5, 6, 8, 30 and 31 and an attempt to commit such an offence.

13.32 Criminal Justice and Public Order Act 1994 s25 places restrictions on the granting of bail for a person charged with any of the above offences, if s/he has previously been convicted of one of those offences or convicted in Scotland of culpable homicide. If the previous offence was manslaughter or culpable homicide the person must have been sentenced to long-term detention under the Powers of Criminal Courts (Sentencing) Act 2000 (detention in a young offenders institution or a secure training order will not satisfy this criterion). If these pre-conditions are satisfied, the custody officer or court may only grant bail to the defendant where there are exceptional circumstances which justify so doing. This provision does not rule out a non-custodial remand into local authority accommodation, which would follow a refusal of bail, if the provisions of Children and Young Persons Act 1969 s23(5) were not satisfied (see para 13.155 below).

13.33 The compatibility of these provisions with Article 5 of the European Convention on Human Rights has been questioned by the Law Commission.[28] The creation of a statutory presumption against the grant of bail would conflict with the presumption of liberty with which the Convention starts. However, the courts may regard the provision as placing an evidential burden on the defence to establish matters which can lead the court to consider the existence of 'exceptional circumstances'. The prosecution would then have to satisfy the court that bail should not be granted.[29]

Treason

13.34 Bail may only be granted in a case of treason by a High Court judge or on the direction of the Home Secretary.[30]

Exception to the right to bail

13.35 Where there is a general right to bail, the court may only refuse bail if it can identify one of the prescribed exceptions to that right, which are contained in Bail Act 1976 Sch 1. The exceptions vary depending on whether the offence is imprisonable or non-imprisonable, although there are some grounds which are common to all offences.

---

28 *Bail and the Human Rights Act 1998*, Law Commission No 269.
29 Hooper J in *R (O) v Harrow Crown Court* (2003) *Times* 29 May.
30 Magistrates' Courts Act 1980 s43.

In all cases

13.36   Bail may be refused if:

- the defendant has previously been released on bail and has subsequently been arrested for breach of the conditions of that bail; or
- the defendant is already serving a custodial sentence; or
- the court is satisfied that the defendant should be kept in custody for his/her own protection; or
- in the case of a juvenile, the court is satisfied that the defendant should be refused bail for his/her own welfare.

In cases where the defendant is charged with an imprisonable offence

13.37   Bail may be refused if the court is satisfied that there are *substantial* grounds for believing that if granted bail the defendant would:

- fail to surrender to custody; or
- commit an offence while on bail; or
- interfere with witnesses or otherwise obstruct the course of justice, whether in relation to him/herself or any other person.

13.38   When considering whether there are substantial grounds for fearing one of the above, the court must take into account information available to it regarding the following:

- the nature and seriousness of the offence (and the probable means of dealing with the defendant for it);
- the character, antecedents (eg criminal record), associations and community ties of the defendant;
- the defendant's previous record of complying with the obligation of bail;
- (except in the case of an adjournment for a pre-sentence report) the strength of the evidence against the defendant;
- any other factor which the court considers relevant.[31]

13.39   Bail may also be refused if:

- the defendant is charged with an indictable-only or either-way offence and it appears to the court that s/he was on bail in criminal proceedings on the date of the offence;[32]
- the court is satisfied that it is not practicable to obtain sufficient information for the purposes of a bail decision for want of time since starting proceedings against the defendant;[33]
- the defendant has been convicted of an offence and the court is adjourning the matter for the preparation of a pre-sentence report, but only if it appears to the court that it would be impracticable to complete the enquiries or make the report without keeping the defendant in custody.[34]

---

31   Bail Act 1976 Sch 1 Part I para 9.
32   Ibid, Sch 1 Part I para 2A.
33   Ibid, Sch 1 Part I para 5.
34   Ibid, Sch 1 Part I para 7.

In cases of non-imprisonable offences

13.40 Bail may be refused if the defendant has a previous history of failing to answer to bail and in view of that previous failure the court believes s/he would fail to surrender to custody.[35]

Offence committed whilst on bail

13.41 Adults charged with an offence committed whilst on bail may only be granted bail if the court is satisfied that there is not a significant risk of his/her committing an offence on bail.[36] This reversal of the presumption in favour of bail does not apply to defendants under the age of 18.

13.42 When brought into force, Criminal Justice Act 2003 s14(2) provides that where a defendant is under the age of 18 and it appears to the court that s/he was on bail in criminal proceedings on the date of the offence, the court shall given particular weight to the fact that the defendant was on bail in deciding whether there are substantial grounds for believing that, if admitted to bail, the defendant would commit a further offence whilst on bail.[37]

Bail after positive test for Class A drugs

13.43 There are restrictions on the grant of bail to adult defendants who have tested positive on charge for a Class A drug and who have refused follow-up treatment. These restrictions do not apply to defendants under the age of 18.[38]

Bail after previous absconding in the proceedings

13.44 Adult defendants who have failed to answer bail in the proceedings may not be granted bail again in the same case unless the court is satisfied that there is no significant risk that, if released on bail, s/he would fail to surrender to custody.[39] This restriction does not apply to defendants under the age of 18.[40]

13.45 When brought into force, Criminal Justice Act 2003 s15 provides that where a young person is under the age of 18 and, having been released on bail in connection with the proceedings for the offence, has failed to surrender to custody, in deciding whether there are substantial grounds for believing that, if released on bail, the young person would fail to surrender to custody, the court shall give particular weight to the fact that the defendant has already failed to attend. This only applies where the defendant had no reasonable cause for his/her failure to surrender to custody at the appointed place and time, or as soon as reasonably practicable thereafter.[41]

35 Bail Act 1976 Sch 1 Part II para 2.
36 Ibid, Sch 1 Part I para 2A(1).
37 Ibid, Sch 1 Part I para 9AA.
38 Ibid, Sch 1 Part I para 6A and 6B.
39 Ibid, Sch 1 Part I para 6(1).
40 Ibid, Sch 1 Part I para 6(2)(a).
41 Ibid, Sch 1 Part I para 9AB.

Where bail is refused

13.46 If a court refuses bail to a defendant it must give reasons for the refusal with a view to enabling the defendant make another application for bail to another court.[42] The court is under an obligation to record the reasons for its decision and a magistrates' or youth court must supply a defendant with a copy of the reasons upon request.[43]

13.47 A youth court or an adult magistrates' court must inform an unrepresented defendant of his/her right to apply to the Crown Court for bail.[44]

Where bail is granted

13.48 Any court granting bail to a person to whom Bail Act 1976 s4 applies (see para 13.28 above) where the prosecutor has objected to bail, must give reasons for so doing and have those reasons recorded.[45]

Conditional bail

Power to impose conditions

13.49 Bail Act 1976 s3(6) provides that a person granted bail may be required by the court to comply with conditions both before bail is granted and afterwards. No condition may be imposed unless the court considers it *necessary* to impose conditions for the following reasons:

- to ensure that s/he answers bail;
- to ensure that s/he does not commit an offence while on bail;
- to ensure that s/he does not interfere with witnesses or otherwise obstruct the course of justice;
- for his/her own protection;
- in the case of a defendant under the age of 17, for his/her own welfare or in his/her own interests;
- to ensure that s/he makes him/herself available for the purpose of preparing pre-sentence and other reports;
- to ensure that s/he, before the time appointed for him/her to surrender to custody, attends an interview with a solicitor.

13.50 The court must give reasons for any conditions imposed.[46]

Practical considerations with young defendants

13.51 The defence lawyer should always ensure that when dealing with a child or young person, the court bears in mind the following:

- the obligation to consider the welfare of the child or young person under Children and Young Persons Act 1933 s44;
- the impact on compulsory school attendance;

---

42 Bail Act 1976 s5(3).
43 Ibid, s5(4).
44 Ibid, s5(6).
45 Ibid, s5(2A).
46 Ibid, s5(3).

- that the terms are not onerous in view of the accused's age;
- that no condition requires financial expenditure which neither the accused nor his/her parents will be able to afford;
- that no condition requires the co-operation of another person (eg parent or school teacher) unless they have expressly consented; and
- that the terms of any condition are precise and practicable.

Common conditions

13.52 Some of the more common conditions are as follows:

- residence;
- curfew;
- electronically-monitored curfew;
- exclusion zone;
- non-association;
- not to contact witnesses;
- reporting;
- surety;
- security;
- co-operate with the preparation of reports;
- attend appointment with solicitor;
- compliance with an intensive supervision and surveillance programme (ISSP).

Residence

13.53 A court may impose a condition upon a defendant that s/he is to reside at a particular address whilst on bail. This condition is normally imposed if there are concerns about non-attendance at court. It is also the practice of some courts to impose this condition where it is hoped that imposing a condition to sleep every night at the parental home will ensure closer parental supervision.

13.54 If the condition is to reside at a family address, care should be taken that the condition does not interfere with the reasonable child care arrangements of the family. For example, where parents have separated but continue to share the responsibility of bringing up the defendant, a condition of residence could interfere with access arrangements. The defence lawyer should be alert to such problems and make sure the court is made aware of any problems such a condition would cause.

Reside as directed by local authority

13.55 A significant number of children and young persons who appear before the courts are accommodated by the local authority. In such cases the defence lawyer should attempt to establish how permanent the current accommodation arrangements are. If a court wishes to impose a residence condition, it may be appropriate to suggest that the court bails the defendant 'to live as directed by [specified local authority]'. Such a flexible condition avoids any problems with the care plan and avoids the expense and inconvenience of returning to court for a bail variation application whenever there is a change of child care placement.

13.56   It has been held that when a child or young person is granted bail with a condition of residence to live as directed by a local authority, s/he is accommodated by that local authority within the meaning of Children Act 1989 s20.[47] It is submitted that if the young defendant is not already accommodated by a local authority, the court has no power to order the authority to accommodate the defendant. However, there is nothing to stop the court from consulting with the authority and imposing such a condition if it is indicated that accommodation would be provided under section 20.

Probation hostel

13.57   If a court bails a defendant with a condition that s/he resides at a bail hostel, the court may also impose a condition that the defendant complies with the conditions of the hostel.[48] Although in theory probation hostels accept defendants aged 16 and 17 on bail, in reality it is very difficult to obtain the necessary authorisation for placement.

Curfew

13.58   This is a condition to remain indoors at a particular address after a specified time in the evening until a specified time the following morning. It is imposed when the alleged offences were committed in the late evening or during the hours of darkness and the nature of the offences reveals a risk of similar occurrences if the defendant is at liberty at that time – for example, if the defendant is charged with an office burglary committed at night when the premises were unoccupied, or theft from a car in a quiet residential street at night. Some courts may seek to impose curfew conditions without reference to the nature or time of the alleged offence. The issue of relevance may be raised by the defence lawyer, who should always ensure that they have full instructions on any evening activities which would be prevented by a curfew, eg team sports, youth clubs, other sport training and religious activities. The court may wish to design the curfew hours to allow participation in activities which are regarded as desirable.

Doorstep condition

13.59   The police have no power to enter premises to establish whether a person is observing his/her curfew. It has recently become common for courts to impose a further requirement that the defendant must present him/herself to a police officer who calls at the bail address during the hours of curfew. This requirement is often termed a 'doorstep condition' or 'doorstepping'. Such an ancillary requirement has been held to be lawful, but it remains a question of fact in each case whether it would be appropriate to impose the requirement.[49]

Curfews for defendants accommodated in children's homes

13.60   Children's homes will already operate a curfew, which is usually 10.30 pm or 11 pm. If an earlier curfew is likely to be imposed upon a defendant, the defence lawyer should establish whether the home runs evening activities

47   See chapter 3.
48   Bail Act 1976 s3(6ZA).
49   *R (CPS) v Chorley Justices* [2002] EWHC 2162 Admin; (2002) 166 JP 764.

outside the home. If this is the case and any curfew would prevent the defendant from taking part, it may be possible to persuade the court to vary the proposed curfew to allow the defendant to be outside the home after the curfew hour if accompanied by a member of staff.

24-hour curfew

13.61 An extreme example of this type of condition is where the defendant is not allowed to leave the premises at any time of the day unless accompanied by an adult. This is sometimes loosely referred to as a 24-hour curfew. This should only be considered where a custodial remand is the likely alternative.

Electronically-monitored curfew

13.62 The provisions for electronic monitoring of a bail curfew depend on the age of the defendant.

Defendants under 17 years old

13.63 Bail Act 1976 s3AA creates a statutory framework for the imposition of electronic monitoring of a bail curfew for defendants under the age of 17 years. A court may not impose an electronic monitoring requirement upon a 10- or 11-year-old defendant. In the case of a defendant aged 12–16, the requirement may only be imposed if:

    (i) the defendant is:
      (a) charged with, or has been convicted of, a violent or sexual offence, or an offence punishable in the case of an adult with imprisonment for a term of 14 years or more; or
      (b) charged with, or has been convicted of, one or more imprisonable offences which, together with any other imprisonable offences of which s/he has been convicted in any proceedings, amount to or would, if s/he were convicted of the offence with which s/he is charged, amount to a recent history of repeatedly committing imprisonable offences while remanded on bail or to local authority accommodation;
    (ii) the court has been notified by the secretary of state that electronic monitoring arrangements are available in the court area; and
    (iii) a youth offending team has informed the court that in its opinion the imposition of an electronic monitoring condition will be suitable in the case of the juvenile.

17-year-old defendants

13.64 Although there is no express statutory provision for electronic monitoring of a 17-year-old defendant's curfew, the Home Office is of the opinion that such a condition may still be imposed under the general powers to impose bail conditions conferred by Bail Act 1976 s3(6).

Suitability of address

13.65 It is the responsibility of the youth offending team to determine the suitability of the proposed curfew address. The Home Office has issued guidance suggesting the following:

> At a minimum, contact must be made with a householder (i.e. the person holding the tenancy or the owner/occupier of the proposed bail address), and the parent or carer of the defendant (if different) to ascertain whether s/he consents to the monitoring.

Where the youth offending team has no information about the proposed address, information should be sought from social services departments and other partner agencies. A home visit may be needed before the suitability of an address can be determined. If it is not possible to arrange the home visit on the day of the court hearing then an electronic monitoring requirement may not be used.

For placements in local authority residential accommodation Social Services' consent should be sought for the use of electronic monitoring.

The youth offending team should contact the relevant local authority social services department to ascertain whether there are any current or previous child protection concerns that would indicate that tagging is not advised able in a particular case.[50]

Monitoring compliance

13.66   When a court imposes an electronic monitoring requirement, it shall include provision for making a person responsible for the monitoring. That person shall be shall be from a company specified for the court area by the secretary of state.[51] The monitoring company will install the equipment in the bail address and fit a tag to the defendant's ankle. If the monitoring equipment indicates a breach of the curfew, the monitoring company will inform the local police.

Exclusion zone

13.67   This is a condition imposed either to deal with a fear of further offences or interference with witnesses. If the defendant's record and/or current charges reveal a pattern of offending in a particular area (for example, shoplifting in the city centre), a court may consider forbidding the defendant from entering the area. If the concern is in relation to intimidating a particular witness, the court may consider a condition not to go within a certain distance of the witness's home address or place of work.

13.68   If an exclusion zone is to be a possibility, it is important that the defence lawyer takes instructions on the practical effect of such a condition. Will such a condition interfere, for example, with travelling to school or with constructive leisure activities? It is important that the area covered by any such condition is clear. In some circumstances a map may be used to delineate the area. It is important that care is taken in stipulating distances (eg within 100 yards of a particular address) as some young defendants may not fully understand the distance involved.

Non-association

13.69   This is a condition not to associate with named people. It is usually imposed when the court is concerned that particular defendants have a history of offending together, or it is feared that a concerted effort would be made by defendants to interfere with the administration of justice.

---

50   Home Office Guidance (2002), Criminal Justice and Police Act 2001: electronic monitoring of 12- to 16-year-olds on bail and on remand to local authority accommodation. See appendix 14 for contact details.

51   Bail (Electronic Monitoring of Requirements) (Responsible Officer) Order 2002, SI No 844.

13.70   The defence lawyer should ensure that the court is aware of any practical problems that would arise from the imposition of such a condition – for example, where the named people attend the same school, are neighbours or are part of the same extended family.

Not to contact witnesses

13.71   When the court considers that the defendant may try to intimidate a witness before any trial, it may impose a condition that the defendant is not to contact that witness. The condition is usually phrased in terms of no contact either directly or indirectly, and will obviously cover telephoning, texting or emailing the witness or having a family member or friend contact the witness.

13.72   Care should be taken to ensure that the condition is practicable, particularly if the defendant and witnesses attend the same school.

Reporting

13.73   When the court has good reason to fear that the accused may not surrender to his/her bail, the court may consider a condition of regular reporting to a specified police station. The frequency and times will be specified by the court.

13.74   Careful consideration should be given to the practicability of the condition and how onerous it will be for the accused in view of his/her age. Particular problems may arise with the length of travelling time and the expense of travelling if public transport has to be used.

13.75   If the defendant is accommodated by a local authority in a children's home, it is submitted that a condition of signing at a police station is inappropriate. The police will be informed if the defendant absconds in any event, and the condition will impose a considerable demand on the staff resources of the children's home who will have to accompany the defendant to the local police station.

Reporting as part of a bail support scheme

13.76   If a bail support centre exists in the locality, the defence lawyer may wish to seek to persuade the court to impose a condition of reporting to the scheme as an alternative to reporting to the police. In general it is likely that regular contact with a trained member of the youth offending team will be more beneficial to the young defendant.

Surety

13.77   If the court is concerned about the risk of absconding, one or more sureties may be taken before the defendant is granted bail.[52] A surety is a person who undertakes to guarantee the defendant's attendance at court. This guarantee is supported by the surety offering a sum of money, called the recognizance, which will be forfeited if the defendant fails to surrender to custody. Sureties may be taken in court before the magistrates, by a police inspector or by the governor of the remand centre or prison where the accused is held.

52   Bail Act 1976 s3(4).

13.78   When considering whether a surety is suitable the court may take the following into consideration:

- financial resources;
- character and any previous convictions;
- proximity to the defendant (both in terms of relationship and geography).[53]

13.79   Before a court will accept a surety it will need to be satisfied that the proposed person is able to exercise sufficient influence over the defendant to ensure that s/he attends court. In the case of a child or young person, the court will normally expect a parent or close relative to be the surety.

13.80   The defence lawyer should always ensure that the surety is a suitable person and is prepared for the hearing. The following should be established:

- full name, address and date of birth;
- relationship to defendant;
- what steps would be taken to ensure the defendant's attendance at court;
- amount of money available as recognizance;
- documentary proof of that money, eg building society pass book;
- that the surety understands that all or part of the recognizance can be forfeited if the defendant absconds (and if the surety cannot pay the money as ordered by the court, s/he risks imprisonment);
- whether the surety has any criminal convictions.

13.81   If the surety is taken in court, the surety will be asked to give sworn evidence regarding the above. Once satisfied with the surety's evidence, a court will often indicate that the surety is accepted subject to police checks for criminal convictions. The court may indicate that a surety's obligation lasts only until the next hearing or until the disposal of the case.

13.82   If a surety cannot be taken immediately then the defendant cannot be released. In the case of a 17-year-old youth this would mean that s/he would be held in a remand centre or prison, and in the case of a youth aged 16 years or under s/he would be remanded to local authority accommodation.[54] The defendant will be released on bail once the surety has been taken.

Security

13.83   If the court considers it unlikely that the defendant will surrender to custody, a security can be taken prior to his/her release.[55] A defendant, or someone on the defendant's behalf, would then have to lodge money, travellers' cheques or other valuables with the court to the value of the security required.

Co-operate with the preparation of a pre-sentence report

13.84   This is not a condition which would be imposed routinely following a conviction. However, if the child or young person has failed to attend appoint-

---

53 Bail Act 1976 s8(2).
54 Children and Young Persons Act 1969 s23 (see below).
55 Bail Act 1976 s3(5).

ments with the member of the youth offending team preparing the report, the court may want to adjourn again but this time imposing such a condition. No doubt the court will wish to impress upon the defendant that missing any further appointments will result in the police being informed that s/he is in breach of bail, thus risking arrest.

Attend appointment with solicitor

13.85   The power to impose a condition to attend an appointment with a solicitor was created by Crime and Disorder Act 1998 s54(2). The justification was to avoid unnecessary delays by ensuring that the unrepresented defendant obtained legal advice promptly, thus avoiding the need for further adjournments. The Home Office has confirmed that, in view of a solicitor's duty of confidentiality owed to the client, the court cannot expect the solicitor to report any breach of this condition to the police, instead the breach of the condition will be a factor to consider if a further application for an adjournment is made by the defence.[56]

Comply with requirements of bail supervision and support/bail ISSP

13.86   Bail supervision and support and intensive supervision and surveillance programmes ('bail ISSPs') are services provided by or on behalf of the youth offending team. These are considered above at paras 2.28–2.33 and 13.7–13.10.

Parental surety

13.87   In the case of a defendant under the age of 17 the court may take a surety from a parent or guardian to ensure the defendant's compliance with any condition of bail imposed.[57] The parent or guardian must agree to stand surety and the recognizance must not be greater than £50. Such a surety may not be taken if the defendant will reach the age of 17 before the next hearing date.

13.88   A parental surety is normally sought by the court itself when it considers that there is a lack of parental control which is contributing to the defendant's offending. It is submitted that it is only an appropriate condition when there is clear evidence that the parent is in a position to exercise more supervision over his/her child.

13.89   The defence lawyer should consider carefully whether there is a conflict between the interests of his/her client, the defendant, and the parent if the court raises the possibility of such a surety. In particular the lawyer should consider how to respond to the court's invitation to comment on a proposed surety or to a request for details of a parent's means. Being seen to speak for the parent will inevitably result in the defence lawyer taking on the role of lawyer for the parent. As the parent stands to lose money as a direct result of the defendant's actions, it is doubtful that it is proper to act for both child and parent in such circumstances. Furthermore, there may

---

56   Home Office Circular 34/1998 *New Bail Measures: Sections 54, 55 and 56 of the Crime and Disorder Act 1998*, paras 11 and 12.

57   Bail Act 1976 s3(7).

very well be arguments against such a surety to put to the court. However, presenting such arguments is likely to be detrimental to the interests of the defendant.

Murder cases

13.90   In murder cases, if the court grants bail it shall impose a condition that the defendant undergoes a medical examination by two doctors unless it appears that suitable reports already exist. The court granting bail shall also impose a condition that the defendant attends at a particular place to enable the examinations to take place.[58]

Appeals against bail by the prosecution

Right of appeal

13.91   Where a court grants bail to a person charged with an imprisonable offence, the prosecutor may appeal to the Crown Court against the grant of bail.[59] The right of appeal only exists if the prosecutor made representations against the grant of bail before the magistrates' decision.[60]

Notice of appeal

13.92   Notice of the intention to appeal must be given orally to the magistrates at the conclusion of the proceedings and before the release from custody of the defendant.[61] Written confirmation of the notice of appeal must be served upon the court within two hours of the end of the hearing. If the written notice is not served within that period, the appeal is deemed to have been disposed of.[62]

13.93   Upon receiving oral notice of the intention to appeal, the magistrates shall remand the defendant in custody. In the case of a defendant aged 16 or less this shall mean a remand to local authority accommodation.[63]

Right to representation

13.94   The appeal hearing at the Crown Court is incidental to the criminal proceedings in the youth court or adult magistrates' court and representation at the hearing is therefore covered by the representation order granted for the main proceedings in the youth court or adult magistrates' court.[64]

---

58   Bail Act 1976 s3(6A).
59   Bail (Amendment) Act 1993 s1(1), as amended by Criminal Justice Act 2003 s18.
60   Ibid, s1(3).
61   Ibid, s1(4).
62   Ibid, s1(5) and (7).
63   Ibid, s1(10)(b).
64   Criminal Defence Service, *General Criminal Contract* Part E, para 3.5.3.

Table 15: A structured approach to bail for youth defendants

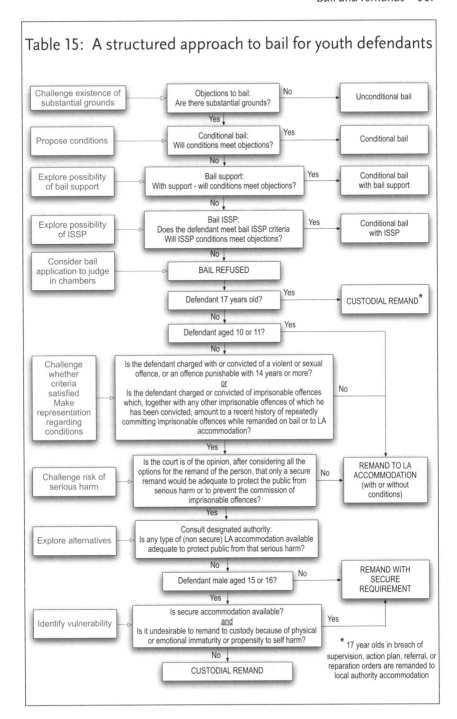

Challenge existence of substantial grounds → Objections to bail: Are there substantial grounds? — No → Unconditional bail

Yes ↓

Propose conditions → Conditional bail: Will conditions meet objections? — Yes → Conditional bail

No ↓

Explore possibility of bail support → Bail support: With support - will conditions meet objections? — Yes → Conditional bail with bail support

No ↓

Explore possibility of ISSP → Bail ISSP: Does the defendant meet bail ISSP criteria Will ISSP conditions meet objections? — Yes → Conditional bail with ISSP

No ↓

Consider bail application to judge in chambers → BAIL REFUSED

Defendant 17 years old? — Yes → CUSTODIAL REMAND*

No ↓

Defendant aged 10 or 11? — Yes

No ↓

Challenge whether criteria satisfied
Make representation regarding conditions
→ Is the defendant charged with or convicted of a violent or sexual offence, or an offence punishable with 14 years or more? or Is the defendant charged or convicted of imprisonable offences which, together with any other imprisonable offences of which he has been convicted, amount to a recent history of repeatedly committing imprisonable offences while remanded on bail or to LA accommodation? — No

Yes ↓

Challenge risk of serious harm → Is the court is of the opinion, after considering all the options for the remand of the person, that only a secure remand would be adequate to protect the public from serious harm or to prevent the commission of imprisonable offences? — No → REMAND TO LA ACCOMMODATION (with or without conditions)

Yes ↓

Explore alternatives → Consult designated authority: Is any type of (non secure) LA accommodation available adequate to protect public from that serious harm?

No ↓

Defendant male aged 15 or 16? — No → REMAND WITH SECURE REQUIREMENT

Yes ↓

Identify vulnerability → Is secure accommodation available? and Is it undesirable to remand to custody because of physical or emotional immaturity or propensity to self harm? — Yes

No ↓

CUSTODIAL REMAND

* 17 year olds in breach of supervision, action plan, referral, or reparation orders are remanded to local authority accommodation

Procedure

13.95   The conduct of the hearing is governed by Criminal Procedure Rules 2005[65] Part 19. Notice of the hearing must be served upon:

- the prosecutor;
- the accused or his/her solicitor; and
- the clerk of the youth or magistrates' court.

13.96   The appeal must be listed before a Crown Court judge with 48 hours of the oral notice of intention to appeal. In calculating this period, Sundays, Christmas day, Good Friday and bank holidays are ignored.[66]

13.97   The appeal is by way of re-hearing and the judge may remand the defendant in custody or grant bail with such conditions (if any) as s/he thinks fit.[67]

Defendant's presence

13.98   The defendant is not entitled to be present at the hearing of the appeal unless s/he is acting in person, or, in any other case of an exceptional nature, a Crown Court judge is of the opinion that the interests of justice require him/her to be present and the judge gives leave.[68]

Refusal of bail

13.99   If a Crown Court judge refuses bail on appeal and the case has not been committed for trial to the Crown Court, the prosecutor should invite the judge to remand the defendant for the same period as the magistrates would have been able to do if they had originally refused bail.[69] This will normally be for eight clear days.

Review of bail granted

13.100 Bail Act 1976 s5B allows the prosecutor to apply to a magistrates' or youth court for a review of court or police bail.

Power to apply

13.101 An application may only be made in relation to bail granted in respect of offences triable on indictment.[70] The application must be based on information not available to the court or custody sergeant who granted bail.[71]

---

65   SI No 384.
66   Bail (Amendment) Act 1993 s1(8).
67   Ibid, s1(9).
68   Criminal Procedure Rules 2005 r19.17(4).
69   *R v Governor of Pentonville Prison ex p Bone* (1994) *Times* 15 November, QBD.
70   Bail Act 1976 s5B(2).
71   Ibid, s5B(3).

Procedure

13.102 The application must be made on notice to the defendant, but the court may proceed to consider the application even if the defendant does not attend.[72]

The court's powers

13.103 On hearing the application the court may:
- refuse to review the defendant's bail;
- vary the conditions of bail;
- impose conditions in respect of bail which has been granted unconditionally; or
- withhold bail.[73]

13.104 If the defendant is before the court s/he may be remanded in custody (subject to the provisions of Children and Young Persons Act 1969 s23) or if absent a warrant for his/her arrest may be issued.[74] When a defendant is arrested on the warrant s/he must be brought before a justice of the peace acting for the area where s/he was arrested within 24 hours. The justice shall then remand the defendant in custody (again subject to the provisions of Children and Young Persons Act 1969 s23).[75]

Applications for variation of conditions

Police bail

13.105 Application for the variation of bail conditions imposed by the police may be made to:
- the custody officer who imposed the conditions or another custody officer serving at the same police station;[76] or
- the magistrates' court or youth court.[77]

13.106 In either case the applicant risks the imposition of more onerous bail conditions and, in the case of an application to a court, the court does have the power to withdraw bail altogether.

Application to a custody officer

13.107 This might be considered where there has been a clear change of circumstances since the original grant of conditional bail, for example a condition of residence at the parental home was imposed and the accused is now estranged from his/her parents and due to be accommodated by the local authority or a curfew was imposed and the accused has now obtained a job

72 Bail Act 1976 s5B(4).
73 Ibid, s5B(1).
74 Ibid, s5B(6).
75 Ibid, s5B(7) and (8).
76 Ibid, s3A(4).
77 Criminal Procedure Rules 2005 r19.1.

which requires him/her to be away from home after the time the curfew comes into force.

13.108   If the accused simply objects to the necessity of particular conditions, it is not expected that a custody officer will overrule a colleague and it is therefore preferable to a make an application direct to court.

Application to a court

13.109 Written notice must be served upon the custody officer at the police station where the accused was bailed and upon the court.[78] From a practical point of view, a copy of the notice should also be sent to the Crown Prosecution Service. The notice must:

- contain a statement of the grounds upon which the application is made;
- specify the offence with which the defendant was charged; and
- specify the reasons given by the custody officer for imposing the bail conditions.[79]

13.110 No minimum period of notice is prescribed, but it is unlikely to be practicable to make the application unless at least 24 hours' notice is given. The time fixed for the hearing shall be not later than 72 hours after receipt of the application (no account being taken of Christmas day, Good Friday, any bank holiday or any Saturday or Sunday).[80]

13.111   There may be problems in obtaining a representation order prior to an attendance at court, as the court will not be in a position to process the application until a charge sheet has been received from the police.

Court bail

13.112 An application may be made to a court which granted conditional bail for the conditions of bail to be varied. The application may be made by the defendant or somebody on the defendant's behalf, as well as the prosecutor.

13.113   The application must be on notice to the court and the prosecution. No minimum period of notice is specified, but in practice the court and prosecutor will need to be given reasonable time to ensure that their files are in court. It is the normal practice of most courts to consider applications before the main business of the day. The defendant or his/her lawyer makes the application explaining why there has been a change of circumstances requiring the change of conditions. The prosecutor will be asked whether there is any objection to the variation and the court will then reach its decision.

13.114   The defendant should be aware that upon an application for variation of bail conditions the court has the power to remove bail altogether. As the application may be made on behalf of the defendant, it is not necessary for him/her to be present in court during the application. It is, however, wise to advise him/her to attend. The court may be reluctant to vary conditions

---

78 Criminal Procedure Rules 2005 r19.1.
79 Ibid.
80 Ibid.

if the defendant is not in court to have the new conditions explained to him/her. Attending court voluntarily (along with any parent or guardian) for the application also demonstrates that the child or young person takes the question of his/her bail conditions seriously.

Bail enlargements

13.115 A youth or adult magistrates' court may remand the defendant in his/her absence in the following circumstances:

- when s/he has failed to attend through reason of illness or accident (applies to a defendant in custody or on bail);[81]
- to enlarge the defendant's bail (that is, appoint a later time for the defendant to surrender to custody).[82]

13.116 A court may also appoint a later time for a defendant to surrender to custody following a grant of bail by the police.[83] All the above powers may be exercised by the court legal advisor under his/her delegated powers.

Failing to answer bail

13.117 Any person bailed by either a custody officer or court is under a duty to surrender to custody.[84] The Bail Act 1976 makes it a criminal offence to fail to answer bail and empowers the court to issue a warrant for the defendant's arrest.

When has a defendant surrendered to his/her bail?

13.118 Surrendering to bail is defined as 'surrendering [him/herself] into the custody of the court or of the constable (according to the requirements of the grant of bail) at the time and place for the time being appointed for [him/her] to do so'.[85] This definition is satisfied if the defendant arrives at the court building at or before the time specified, but only if s/he also reports to the court employee who records the attendance of defendants. This will normally be the court usher or list caller.[86] Once the defendant has reported in this way, s/he has answered bail and if s/he subsequently leaves the court building before the case is called this is not a breach of bail, although it may be a contempt of court. In such circumstances a warrant may still be issued under Bail Act 1976 s7(2).

13.119   It should be noted that bail is granted to a particular time and if the defendant arrives at court after that time the condition to surrender to bail has been breached.

81 Magistrates' Courts Act 1980 s129(1).
82 Ibid, s129(3).
83 Ibid, s43(1).
84 Bail Act 1976 s3(1).
85 Ibid, s2(2).
86 *DPP v Richards* [1988] QB 701; [1988] 3 All ER 406.

Bail Act offences

13.120 Bail Act 1976 s6 creates two criminal offences relating to the failure to surrender to bail. The defendant is guilty of an offence if s/he:

- fails to surrender to custody without reasonable cause: section 6(1);
- having failed to surrender to custody with reasonable cause, fails to surrender to the appointed place as soon after the appointed time as is reasonably practicable: section 6(2).

13.121 The second offence would be committed, for example if a defendant was too ill to come to court on the day appointed but failed to surrender to the court as soon as s/he had recovered.

13.122 If the defendant is convicted of a Bail Act offence in the youth court or an adult magistrates' court, the maximum penalty in the case of an adult is three months' imprisonment.[87] It would not therefore be possible to impose a detention and training order upon a child or young person for this offence. If the defendant is convicted before the Crown Court, the offence is treated as a contempt of court and the maximum penalty for an adult is 12 months' imprisonment.[88] In the case of a child or young person, there is some doubt whether a contempt of court may be punished by a custodial sentence.[89]

13.123 The burden of proving reasonable cause rests upon the defendant.[90] Although it is good practice to give a defendant a copy of the bail date, failure to give written notice of the bail decision cannot constitute reasonable cause.[91] It has also been held that it is not reasonable cause if the defendant mistakenly believes that the hearing date is later and so fails to attend court.[92]

A court's powers on the non-attendance of the defendant

13.124 Faced with the non-appearance of the defendant, the court will first seek confirmation that s/he was properly bailed to that time and place. If satisfied that this was the case, the court may:

- adjourn and enlarge the defendant's bail to a new court date;[93] or
- issue a warrant for the defendant's arrest.[94]

13.125 Many courts will only consider enlarging a defendant's bail if there is information before the court that there is reasonable cause for the non-attendance, for example that s/he is too ill to attend. In the case of a child or young person, it is submitted that a court should be willing to be more flexible and consider the wider circumstances. As a parent or guardian is

---

87 Bail Act 1976 s6(7).
88 Ibid, s6(7).
89 See paras 22.80–22.89.
90 Bail Act 1976 s6(3).
91 Ibid, s6(4).
92 *Laidlaw v Atkinson* (1986) *Times* 2 August.
93 Magistrates' Courts Act 1980 s129.
94 Bail Act 1976 s7(1) (if the defendant surrendered to custody but then left the building, a warrant can still be issued under section 7(2)).

also expected to attend, the court should be asked to consider what responsibility can be reasonably placed upon the defendant. This will depend upon the age of the child or young person. If the defendant is known to be accommodated by a social services department, enquiries should be made through the youth offending team to see whether the reason for non-attendance may be established.

13.126   If the court decides to issue a warrant, it has a choice whether it should be backed for bail. Many courts demonstrate a marked reluctance to consider a warrant backed for bail. Nevertheless, the court's duty to consider the welfare of a child or young person requires a more flexible approach. The defence lawyer may wish to bring to the court's attention:

- the age of the defendant;
- whether, in view of the youth of the defendant, s/he would be expected to travel with a parent;
- the likely penalty (if the offence is minor);
- whether the child or young person has attended the court before and, therefore, whether it is likely s/he knows where it is; and
- if the defendant has previous convictions, whether the list reveals previous Bail Act offences.

13.127   The defence lawyer should also ensure that the court is aware that a warrant not backed for bail which is executed early in the weekend will result in the child or young person spending two nights in a police cell as the warrant gives the custody officer no discretion to transfer to local authority accommodation under Police and Criminal Evidence Act 1984 s38(6).[95]

Execution of a Bail Act warrant

13.128   Where a warrant has been issued, the defendant may come before the court voluntarily, by surrendering to the warrant, or as a result of being arrested by the police. Once before the court, a decision must be taken whether a Bail Act charge will be preferred.

13.129   *The Consolidated Criminal Practice Direction*[96] sets out the procedure to be followed when considering a Bail Act charge. It stresses that the Bail Act offence should be dealt with as soon as practicable and not delayed until the end of the proceedings, unless there is good reason to do so. The detrimental effects of delay to the criminal process caused by the non-appearance of defendants, particularly at trial, are emphasised.

Police bail

13.130   In the case of police bail, the decision as to whether to prefer a Bail Act charge rests with the police or prosecutor. If a decision is made to proceed, the prosecutor will conduct the proceedings. In the case of bail granted by a court, it is more appropriate for the court to initiate the proceedings. The court will invite the prosecutor to conduct the proceedings.

---

95 See para 7.319.
96 Part I 13.

Court bail

13.131 In the case of court bail, the court invites representations from the prosecutor and then has discretion to initiate proceedings if it considers it proper to do so. If proceedings are then initiated, the prosecutor will conduct them and call evidence should the matter be contested. Any trial regarding a Bail Act offence should normally take place immediately after the disposal of the substantive offence, although the need for the matter to be dealt with expeditiously may mean that the Bail Act charge will be determined prior to the conclusion of the substantive matter.

Time limits

13.132 A Bail Act offence in relation to police bail is subject to time limits. A charge may not be tried unless:

(a) an information for the Bail Act offence was laid within six months of the failure to answer bail; or

(b) an information is laid within three months of the earliest of the following events occurring after the failure to surrender to bail:
- the person surrenders to custody at the appointed place;
- the person is arrested, or attends at a police station in connection with the relevant offence or the offence for which s/he was granted bail; or
- the person appears or is brought before a court in connection with the relevant offence or the offence for which s/he was granted bail.[97]

13.133 There is no time limit for initiating proceedings for failure to surrender to custody following a grant of bail by a court.

Procedure

13.134 It is the practice of many courts to invite an explanation for the non-attendance before the decision whether to initiate proceedings is taken. This is good practice, particularly when dealing with a child or young person. The Bail Act offences impose a high standard upon defendants and it could very well be unrealistic to impose that standard on a young defendant. Inviting an explanation before initiating proceedings allows the court to make allowance for explanations which are reasonable in view of the defendant's age but which would not strictly be accepted as 'reasonable cause' within the definition of Bail Act 1976 s6.

13.135   If proceedings are initiated, the matter should be put to the defendant and s/he must give a clear indication of whether the offence is admitted. S/he should then be given an opportunity to put forward any mitigating circumstances.

---

97 Criminal Justice Act 2003 s15(3), revoking Magistrates' Courts Act 1980 s127.

Breach of bail conditions

13.136 The conditions of bail can be enforced by the police but it should be noted that, unlike failing to answer bail, breaching bail conditions is not a criminal offence.

13.137 Bail Act 1976 s7(3) allows a constable to arrest without warrant a person released in criminal proceedings with a duty to surrender to the custody of a court if:

- s/he has reasonable grounds for believing that the accused is not likely to surrender to custody; or
- s/he has reasonable grounds for believing that the accused is likely to break any conditions of bail; or
- s/he has reasonable grounds for suspecting that the accused has broken any of the conditions of bail; or
- in a case where the accused was released on bail with one or more sureties, if a surety notifies the police in writing that the accused is unlikely to surrender to custody and the surety wishes to be relieved of the obligations of a surety.

Procedure on arrest

13.138 On arrest for breach of bail conditions, the custody officer is under an obligation to detain the child or young person at the police station until a court hearing can be arranged. As bail has not been refused by the custody officer following charge, Police and Criminal Evidence Act 1984 s38(6) does not apply and there will not be a transfer to local authority accommodation.

13.139 The police must then bring the accused before a justice of the peace for the local justice area where the accused was arrested as soon as practicable and in any event within 24 hours of the arrest (for the purposes of calculating this time limit, Christmas day, Good Friday and any Sunday are ignored). If the arrest takes place within 24 hours of the time when the accused is due to surrender to custody, then the police should ensure that s/he is taken before the court which originally remanded him/her. If the accused is not brought before a justice of the peace within the specified 24-hour period, then the court has no jurisdiction to deal with the alleged breach.[98]

Court procedure for breach of bail conditions

13.140 When the accused appears, Bail Act 1976 s7(5) requires the court to consider whether the accused is likely to surrender to custody, or whether s/he has broken or is likely to break any of the conditions of bail. If the court is of that opinion, it may:

- refuse bail (in which case a 17-year-old will be remanded in custody and a defendant 16 or under will be remanded to local authority accommodation); or

---

98 *R v Governor of Glen Parva Young Offenders Institution ex p G (a minor)* [1998] 2 Cr App R 349; [1998] QB 877; [1998] 3 WLR 12; sub nom *In re G (a minor)* 162 JP 225, QBD.

- grant bail subject to different conditions; or
- grant bail subject to the same conditions.[99]

13.141   If the court is not of the opinion that one of the factors in section 7(5) is likely, then it must grant the defendant bail on the same conditions as before.

13.142   The way the hearing should be conducted has been examined by the Divisional Court in *R v Liverpool City Justices ex p DPP*.[100] It set out the following principles:

- there is no requirement for evidence to be given on oath and subjected to cross-examination;
- the Bail Act contemplates the constable who has arrested the accused bringing him/her before the court and stating the grounds for believing that the accused has broken the conditions of bail; this may very well involve the giving of hearsay evidence;
- in fairness the court will allow the accused the opportunity to respond to what the constable says;
- the hearing may be before one justice of the peace;
- there is no power to adjourn the proceedings, and therefore the court must reach a decision on the information available to it.

13.143   The above procedure has been held to be compatible with the requirements of Article 5 of the European Convention on Human Rights.[101]

Application for bail to the Crown Court

13.144   Applications for bail are made to a Crown Court judge sitting in chambers. They are governed by Criminal Procedure Rules 2005 Part 19.

Right to representation

13.145   Representation to cover an application for bail to the Crown Court is ancillary to criminal proceedings in the youth court or adult magistrates' court and is consequently covered by a representation order granted by the youth court or adult magistrates' court. The work will form part of the 'case' for the purposes of standard fees.[102]

Notice of application

13.146   Written notice of intention to apply for bail must be served on the Crown Prosecution Service and the relevant Crown Court at least 24 hours before the application. The notice must be in the form prescribed in Schedule 4 to the Criminal Procedure Rules. It will set out:

- the personal details of the applicant;
- the offences with which s/he is charged;

99 Bail Act 1976 s7(5).
100 (1992) 95 Cr App R 222.
101 *R (DPP) v Havering Magistrates' Court* [2001] 1 WLR 805.
102 Criminal Defence Service, *General Criminal Contract* Part A 3.2.1(c).

- details of any previous bail applications either to a court of summary jurisdiction or to a Crown Court;
- the objections to bail; and
- how it is proposed to meet those objections.

13.147 The notice should also be accompanied by:

- details of any surety;
- a list of any convictions recorded against the applicant;
- a certificate of full bail argument issued by the youth or magistrates' court which refused bail.

Presence of applicant

13.148 The Criminal Procedure Rules states that the applicant shall not be entitled to be present on the hearing of his/her application unless the Crown Court gives leave.[103]

Practical considerations

13.149 Before preparing any notice of application to the Crown Court it will be necessary for the defence lawyer to consider whether extra grounds will be needed for a successful application to a higher court. In particular, careful consideration should be given to any bail support package and whether its terms can be improved.

13.150 As the court is hearing a new bail application, the Crown Court judge will be under a statutory duty to consult with the designated local authority before making a decision. It will nearly always be desirable to arrange for a member of the youth offending team to be available at the court for the bail application. This will also allow the judge to ask questions regarding any bail support on offer. It is also helpful if details of any proposed bail support package or intensive supervision and surveillance programme package are available in writing for the court to consider.

13.151 A defence lawyer will always wish to proceed as quickly as possible when making a Crown Court bail application. Nevertheless, there may be delays caused by the Crown Prosecution Service or the Crown Court list office. These delays can be minimised by drawing the court's attention to the fact that the applicant is under 18 years of age. This may be done by sending the formal notice with a covering letter or even by telephoning the list office.

What happens when bail is refused?

13.152 Children and Young Persons Act 1969 s23(1) provides:

> where–
> (a) a court remands a child or young person charged with or convicted of one or more offences or commits him for trial or sentence; and
> (b) he is not released on bail,
> the remand or committal shall be to local authority accommodation.[104]

---

103 Criminal Procedure Rules r19.18.
104 Subject to the provisions of Children and Young Persons Act 1969 s23(5).

13.153 For the purposes of this section, a 'young person' is defined as 'a person who has attained the age of fourteen and is under the age of seventeen'.[105] The situation in relation to accused persons under the age of 18 may be summarised as follows.

17-year-olds

13.154 When a 17-year-old is refused bail, s/he is treated exactly like an adult and will remanded into custody to be held in a prison, or remand centre (if one is available).

16 years and under

13.155 In the case of a defendant aged 16 or under, refusal of bail will normally result in a remand to local authority accommodation. Children and Young Persons Act 1969 s23 has effect subject to Magistrates' Courts Act 1980 s128(7) (remand to police custody for further enquiries).[106] In certain circumstances, when the stringent conditions of Children and Young Persons Act 1969 s23(5) are satisfied, the court may make a secure remand (see paras 13.203–13.242 below).

13.156   It should be noted that a young defendant granted bail with conditions which cannot immediately be met, eg a surety or security, will fall within the provisions of section 23(1) and will be remanded to local authority accommodation until the conditions can be met.

Attaining the age of 17 during the proceedings

13.157 If a defendant attains the age of 17 during a period of remand to local authority accommodation, it is the opinion of the authors that s/he would stay in that accommodation until the next hearing date. Thereafter, if the court refused bail again, s/he would be remanded to custody.

Period of remand after a refusal of bail

General rule

13.158 When a youth or magistrates' court refuses bail, the general rule is that the maximum period of remand is eight clear days.[107] This applies whether or not the defendant is subject to a custodial remand.

Exceptions

13.159 There are two exceptions to this principle. The former rule that these exceptions can only be applied if the defendant has attained the age of 17 has been removed by Criminal Procedure and Investigations Act 1996 s52.

---

105 Children and Young Persons Act 1969 s23(12).
106 Ibid, s23(14).
107 Magistrates' Courts Act 1980 s128(6).

Table 16: Summary of remand outcomes by age

Age / Remand Type	10	11	12	13	14	15	16	17
Unconditional Bail	✓	✓	✓	✓	✓	✓	✓	✓
Conditional Bail	✓	✓	✓	✓	✓	✓	✓	✓
Bail Support	✓	✓	✓	✓	✓	✓	✓	✓
Bail ISSP	✓	✓	✓	✓	✓	✓	✓	✓
Electronic Monitoring			✓	✓	✓	✓	✓	✓
Local Authority Accommodation	✓	✓	✓	✓	✓	✓	✓	breach only
Secure Accommodation	✓	✓	✓	✓	✓	✓	✓	
Court Ordered Secure Remand			✓	✓	✓	✓	✓	
Custodial Remand						M	M	✓

KEY: ✓ – Males and females   M – Males only

13.160 The court may refuse bail and remand a defendant to be produced within 28 days provided the defendant:

- is before the court;
- is legally represented in court; and
- consents not to be produced within eight days.[108]

13.161 A court may remand in custody for up to 28 days without the defendant's consent provided:

- the defendant is before the court;
- s/he has previously been remanded for the same offence; and
- the court has set a date when it expects the next stage of the proceedings, other than a remand, to take place.[109]

13.162 Before making such a remand the court must:

- consider any representations the parties wish to make; and
- have regard to the total length of time which the defendant would spend in custody if it were to exercise the power.[110]

108 Magistrates' Courts Act 1980 s128(1)–(3).
109 Ibid, s128A(2).
110 Ibid.

Remand to police custody

13.163 If a court refuses bail to a defendant it may remand him/her into the custody of the police if such a remand is 'necessary for the purpose of making inquiries into other offences'.[111] If so remanded, s/he should be brought back to court as soon as the need ceases.

13.164 If the defendant is aged 17, the maximum period of such a remand is three days.[112] If the defendant is aged 16 or under, the maximum period is 24 hours.[113] It should be noted that this power to remand is not subject to the provisions of Children and Young Person Act 1969 s23 and therefore a refusal of bail would not mean a remand to local authority accommodation.[114]

13.165 The power is expressly stated to be subject to the right to bail contained in the Bail Act 1976. The court should first consider a full bail application and, only if an exception to the right of bail is established should it then go on to consider whether there are grounds made out for a remand to police custody. If it is considered that there are such grounds, the court should still consider the length of the remand especially in view of the youth of the defendant(s). The defendant could already have spent considerably more than 24 hours in custody and a further remand to a police station to face further lengthy questioning could be oppressive.

13.166 There is power to detain 17-year-olds in police custody for up to 192 hours where they face allegations of possessing or trafficking drugs. This power previously only applied to a remand to customs detention.[115]

Custody time limits

In the youth court or adult magistrates' court

13.167 When a defendant is refused bail in the youth or adult magistrates' court, Prosecution of Offences (Custody Time Limits) Regulations 1987[116] reg 4 stipulates custody time limits. These limits, which apply equally to a juvenile remanded to local authority accommodation, are as follows:

- *Summary only offence:* A maximum of 56 days between the defendant's first appearance and the commencement of the trial.
- *Either-way offences:* A maximum of 70 days between the defendant's first appearance and commencement of the summary trial or committal. If, before the expiry of 56 days, the court decides to proceed to summary trial, the maximum period between the defendant's first appearance and the commencement of the trial is 56 days. It should be noted that in this context 'either way' includes indictable-only offences which by virtue of Magistrates' Courts Act 1980 s24 are triable summarily in the case of a child or young person.[117]

---

111 Magistrates' Courts Act 1980 s128(7) and (8).
112 Ibid, s128(7).
113 Children and Young Persons Act 1969 s23(14)(b).
114 Ibid.
115 Criminal Justice Act 1988 s152(1A) as inserted by Drugs Act 2005 s8.
116 SI No 299.
117 *R v Stratford Youth Court ex p S (a minor)* [1998] 1 WLR 1758; [1999] Crim LR 146, QBD.

- *Indictable-only offences:* A maximum of 70 days between the defendant's first appearance and the date of committal.

In the Crown Court

13.168 In the case of a defendant before the Crown Court, Prosecution of Offences (Custody Time Limits) Regulations 1987 reg 5 stipulates the following custody time limits.

Committed for trial

13.169 112 days from the date of committal to the start of the trial.

Section 51 sending

13.170 182 days from the date of the sending for trial to the start of the trial less any period during which the accused has, since the first appearance for the offence, been in the custody of the youth court or adult magistrates' court.

Extension of the time limits

13.171 The prosecution may apply to the court for an extension to the time limit. This application must be made before the expiry of the time limit.

13.172 The application may be made orally or in writing. Two days' notice must be given to the defence unless:

- the defence waives the requirement; or
- the court is satisfied that it is not practicable in all the circumstances to give such notice.

13.173 The court must be satisfied that:

- there is good and sufficient cause for extending the time limit; and
- the prosecution has acted with all due expedition.

13.174 If no application is made for an extension or an extension is refused, the court must grant bail. The court may impose bail conditions but not a surety, security or other condition to be met before release.

Remand to local authority accommodation

13.175 A remand to local authority accommodation will mean that a social services department will provide accommodation for the juvenile. Whilst remanded, the defendant will be treated for all procedural purposes as though s/he were remanded in custody.

Local authority accommodation

13.176 Local authority accommodation is defined by Children Act 1989 s22.[118] It may include any of the following:

- residential children's homes;
- remand foster placements;
- placement with members of the defendant's family.

118 See paras 3.5–3.58.

13.177   In general the local authority has considerable discretion as to the choice of accommodation, save that the court may stipulate that the defendant is not placed with a named individual (usually a parent).

To which authority?

13.178   The court must designate the local authority social services department which is to accommodate the defendant. In the case of a defendant already being looked after by a local authority, it shall be that authority. In all other cases it may be either:

- the authority in whose area it appears to the court that the defendant resides; or
- the authority in whose area the offence or one of the offences was committed.[119]

Obligations of the authority

13.179   In choosing how to accommodate the juvenile the local authority should bear in mind its obligations both to the court and to the juvenile.

Obligations to the court

13.180   The local authority must:

- ensure the juvenile's attendance at court;
- take all reasonable steps to protect the public from further offending by the juvenile.[120]

Obligations to the juvenile

13.181   A local authority has a duty to provide accommodation for a juvenile remanded to local authority accommodation.[121] While accommodated, the juvenile is deemed to be 'a child who is looked after by a local authority' within the meaning of Children Act 1989 s22(1).[122] The local authority does not, however, acquire parental responsibility.[123]

Conditions on the remand

13.182   Having remanded the juvenile to local authority accommodation, the court may require the juvenile to comply with such conditions as could be imposed under Bail Act 1976 s3(6) if s/he were then being granted bail.[124] Before imposing any conditions upon the remand, the court must consult with the designated authority.

---

119   Children and Young Persons Act 1969 s23(2).
120   See para 3.59.
121   Children Act 1989 s21(2)(c)(i).
122   The local authority will need to implement a care plan and consult with the defendant and his/her parent(s) regarding the placement and plan: see para 3.56.
123   *North Yorkshire County Council v Selby Youth Court Justices* [1994] 2 FLR 169, QBD.
124   Children and Young Persons Act 1969 s23(7).

Consultation

13.183 'Consultation' for the purposes of section 23 is defined as 'such consultation (if any) as is reasonably practicable in all the circumstances of the case'.[125]

Permissible conditions

13.184 Under Bail Act 1976 s3(6) the court may only impose such conditions as it considers necessary:

- to ensure attendance at court;
- to prevent the commission of further offences;
- to avoid interference with witnesses or the obstruction of justice;
- for his/her own protection;
- in the case of a defendant under the age of 17, for his/her own welfare or in his/her own interests;
- to enable reports to be prepared for sentence;
- to ensure that the defendant attends an appointment with his/her solicitor before the next court date.

Specifying the address

13.185 The remanding court may not impose a condition upon the juvenile to reside at a particular address.[126]

Sureties and securities

13.186 A court would be able to require the taking of a surety or the deposit of a security before the accused were released on bail. However, these powers are created by Bail Act 1976 s3(4) and (5) respectively. It is therefore submitted that a court would not be able to impose such conditions upon an accused as part of a remand into local authority accommodation.

Electronically-monitored curfew

13.187 Children and Young Persons Act 1969 s23AA makes provision for the imposition of an electronic monitoring condition as part of the local authority remand. The court may only impose the condition if:

    (i) the juvenile has attained the age of 12 years;
    (ii) the juvenile:
        (a) is charged with, or has been convicted of, a violent or sexual offence, or an offence punishable in the case of an adult with imprisonment for a term of 14 years or more; or
        (b) is charged with, or has been convicted of, one or more imprisonable offences which, together with any other imprisonable offences of which he has been convicted in any proceedings amount to or would, if s/he were convicted of the offence with which s/he is charged, amount to a recent history of repeatedly committing imprisonable offences while remanded on bail or to local authority accommodation;
    (iii) the court has been notified by the secretary of state that electronic monitoring arrangements are available in the court area; and

125 Children and Young Persons Act 1969 s23(13)(b).
126 *Cleveland County Council v DPP* (1994) *Times* 1 December, QBD.

(iv) a youth offending team has informed the court that in its opinion the imposition of an electronic monitoring condition will be suitable in the case of the juvenile.

Reasons for conditions imposed

13.188   When a court has imposed conditions upon a defendant as part of a remand into local authority accommodation, it must explain to him/her *in open court* and in ordinary language why it is imposing those conditions. If the court is a youth or magistrates' court, the stated reasons must be recorded in the court register and in the warrant of remand or commitment.[127]

Requirements on the authority

13.189   After consultation with the designated authority, the court may impose requirements upon the local authority to ensure that the defendant complies with his/her conditions of remand.[128] The court may stipulate that the authority shall not place the defendant with a named person (usually the parent or guardian whom the court considers is unable to exercise any control over the defendant).[129] No other negative requirements can be imposed upon the designated authority.

Breach of conditions of remand to local authority accommodation

13.190   When the accused has been remanded to local authority accommodation with conditions, Children and Young Persons Act 1969 s23A(1) allows a constable to arrest without warrant the accused, but only if the constable has reasonable grounds for suspecting that s/he has broken any of the conditions of the remand. There is no power to arrest because a breach of the conditions is anticipated.

Procedure on arrest

13.191   The custody officer is under an obligation to detain the child or young person at the police station until a court hearing can be arranged. Police and Criminal Evidence Act 1984 s38(6) does not apply, and there will not be a transfer to local authority accommodation.

13.192   The police must then bring the accused before a justice of the peace for the local justice area where the accused was arrested as soon as practicable and in any event within 24 hours of the arrest (for the purposes of calculating this time limit, Christmas day, Good Friday and any Sunday are ignored). If the arrest takes place within 24 hours of the time when the accused is due to surrender to custody, then the police should ensure that s/he is taken before the court which originally remanded him/her.[130] If the

127 Children and Young Persons Act 1969 s23(8).

128 Ibid, s23(9)(a).

129 Ibid, s23(9)(b).

130 Ibid, s23A(2).

accused is not brought before a justice of the peace within the specified 24-hour period, then the court has no jurisdiction to deal with the alleged breach.[131]

Procedure in court

13.193 Children and Young Persons Act 1969 s23A(3) requires a court to determine whether any condition of the remand has been broken. If the court is of the opinion that a condition has been broken, the court must remand the accused. If the court is not of that opinion, then it must remand the accused into local authority accommodation again on the same conditions unless an application for variation is made by the accused or the designated authority. No guidance has been given for the procedure to be followed during such a hearing, but it is submitted that the guidelines set out in *R v Liverpool City Justices ex p DPP*[132] are equally applicable (see para 13.142 above).

13.194 In most circumstances the fact that the conditions of a local authority remand have been breached does not give the court any greater powers to remand in custody. For a custodial remand, the criteria of section 23(5) must still be satisfied and breach of remand conditions is only relevant insofar as it may affect the court's assessment as to the adequacy of local authority accommodation to protect the public from serious harm or to prevent further imprisonable offences.

Failure to attend court after a local authority remand

13.195 When a child or young person is refused bail and remanded to local authority accommodation, no specific legal obligation to attend court is imposed upon the defendant but an implied requirement is imposed upon the local authority to ensure that s/he is produced at the time and place specified by the court. The defendant does not commit an offence under Bail Act 1976 s6 if s/he fails to attend court and a warrant under section 7 of that Act may not be issued.

13.196 The court will normally wish to establish why the local authority has not brought the defendant to court. If it is clear that s/he will not be brought to court that day, the youth or adult magistrates' court should mark the register 'defendant not produced'.[133] The court will then go on to consider whether it should issue a warrant under Magistrates' Courts Act 1980 s13. In the Crown Court there is no comparable statutory power to issue a warrant for the defendant's arrest.

---

131 *R v Governor of Glen Parva Young Offenders Institution ex p G (a minor)* [1998] 2 Cr App R 349; [1998] QB 877; [1998] 3 WLR 12; sub nom *In re G (a minor)* 162 JP 225, QBD.

132 (1992) 95 Cr App R 222.

133 Not 'unlawfully at large' as the period of remand has ended and in any event a magistrates' court has no power to issue declaratory statements of status (see 'Practical Points' (1995) 159 JPN 660).

Absconding during the period of remand

13.197 During the period of remand to local authority accommodation, a defend-ant who has absconded may be arrested without warrant.[134] Once arrested the absconder should be conducted to the local authority accommodation or to such other place as the designated local authority shall direct. Taking the absconder to the accommodation shall be at the authority's expense.

13.198   It is not clear what the police should do if the child or young person is not only an absconder but has also been arrested under Children and Young Persons Act 1969 s23A in breach of a condition of that remand. Do the provisions of section 32(1A) or section 23A of the Children and Young Persons Act 1969 take precedence? The legislation is silent on the point, although in practice it is likely that the custody officer would choose to send the juvenile to court under section 23A.

13.199   In certain circumstances, absconding after a remand from local author-ity accommodation may constitute the offence of escape from lawful cus-tody. In *R (on the application of H) v DPP*[135] the applicant had been refused bail and remanded to local authority accommodation without any condi-tions. He was collected from the court cells by a youth offending team worker and told to wait while a placement was arranged. The applicant absconded from the court building before a placement had been found. The Administrative Court held that there was ample evidence that, at the time the applicant absconded, his immediate freedom of movement was under the direct control of the youth offending team worker, and that by absconding, he was escaping from the worker's custody.

13.200   It is a criminal offence knowingly to compel, persuade, incite or assist another person to become or continue to be absent from local authority accommodation to which s/he has been remanded. The offence is sum-mary only and is punishable by six months' imprisonment or a fine at level five.[136]

Review of remand at request of local authority

13.201 After an accused has been remanded in local authority accommodation with conditions, the accused or the designated authority may apply for the conditions to be varied or revoked.[137] In addition, the designated author-ity may apply for any requirements imposed upon itself to be varied or revoked.[138]

     The application must be made to a relevant court which is defined as 'the court by which [the accused] was so remanded, or any magistrates' court having jurisdiction for in the place where [s/he] is for the time being'.[139]

13.202   A designated local authority may apply to the relevant court for a dec-laration that the criteria for a secure remand apply.[140] Such an application

---

134 Children and Young Persons Act 1969 s32(1A)(b)(ii).
135 [2003] EWHC 878 Admin; (2003) 167 JP 486; [2003] Crim LR 560.
136 Children and Young Persons Act 1969 s32(3).
137 Ibid, s23(11).
138 Ibid.
139 Ibid, s23(12).
140 Ibid, s23(9A).

might be made when the juvenile refused bail behaves in such a way that the local authority considers it can no longer perform its duties to protect the public from injury.

Secure remands

13.203 A secure remand may not be imposed unless the defendant:

- has attained the age of 12;[141] and
- is legally represented.[142]

Criteria for a secure remand

13.204 Children and Young Persons Act 1969 s23(5) provides that no secure remand can be made unless the following criteria are satisfied:

> **SECURE REMAND CRITERIA**
> (1) The defendant:
>   (a) is charged with, or has been convicted of, a violent or sexual offence, or an offence punishable in the case of an adult with imprisonment for a term of 14 years or more,
>   or
>   (b) s/he is charged with, or has been convicted of, one or more imprisonable offences which, together with any other imprisonable offences of which s/he has been convicted in any proceedings amount to or would, if s/he were convicted of the offence with which s/he is charged, amount to a recent history of repeatedly committing imprisonable offences while remanded on bail or to local authority accommodation.
> AND
> (2) The court is of the opinion, after considering all the options for the remand of the person, that only remanding him/her to local authority accommodation with a security requirement would be adequate:
>   (a) to protect the public from serious harm from him/her;
>   or
>   (b) to prevent the commission by him/her of imprisonable offences.

13.205 The criteria for a secure remand are complicated and need to be considered in detail. The criteria may be seen to fall into two parts. Paragraph (1) requires the court to identify facts from the defendant's past; paragraph (2) requires the court to look to the future and attempt to predict the level of risk the defendant poses to the public and whether that risk may be adequately contained in local authority accommodation.

'... has been convicted ...'

13.206 The criterion may be satisfied not just by reference to the offences currently before the court but also by reference to the defendant's previous convictions.[143] This raises practical problems where the court is seeking to rely on a previous conviction but it does not have any details of the offence. As will be seen below, whether an offence satisfies the definition of a violent offence will depend on the circumstances of the offence. The Crown

---

141 Children and Young Persons Act 1969 s23(5A).
142 Ibid, s23(4A).
143 *Re C (a minor)* (1993) unreported, 22 October, per Kennedy LJ.

Prosecution Service may not be able to give the court any details of a previous conviction and the defence lawyer should argue in such circumstances that the conviction may not be relied upon to satisfy the criterion.

'Violent offence'

13.207 This means an offence specified Part 1 of Schedule 15 to the Criminal Justice Act 2003 (see appendix 7).[144]

'Sexual offence'

13.208 This means an offence specified in Part 2 of Schedule 15 to the Criminal Justice Act 2003 (see appendix 7).[145]

Prison term of 14 years or more

13.209 This would include robbery, if not already covered by the definition of a violent offence, as well as domestic burglary and handling stolen goods. It should be noted that the definition does not cover non-residential burglary (maximum sentence of ten years) and theft (maximum seven years). This definition is the same as for grave crimes, and there is a full list of such offences in appendix 6.

Imprisonable offence

13.210 This is defined as an offence punishable in the case of an adult with imprisonment.[146] It is, therefore, irrelevant whether the court would be able to impose a custodial sentence upon the particular defendant in view of his/her age and sentencing restrictions in the youth court.

'While remanded on bail or to local authority accommodation'

13.211 It is a pre-condition that the offence must have occurred during a period when the defendant was remanded on bail or bail had been refused and s/he was remanded to local authority accommodation. Previous offending on bail or whilst remanded to local authority accommodation may also be taken into account. The defence representative may wish to check the accuracy of record of a defendant's convictions that show previous offending to have taken place whilst on bail. Consideration should also be given as to whether any such offending in the past can be regarded as 'recent' or 'repeated'.

'Serious harm'

13.212 This is defined by Children and Young Persons Act 1969 s23(13)(c) as follows:

> Any reference, in relation to a person charged with or convicted of a violent or sexual offence, to protecting the public from serious harm from him shall be

---

144 Children and Young Persons Act 1969 s23(12) as amended by Criminal Justice Act 2003 Sch 32 para 15.
145 Ibid.
146 Ibid.

construed as a reference to protecting members of the public from death or serious personal injury, whether physical or psychological, occasioned by further such offences committed by him.

13.213 In relation to other offences, there is no statutory definition but the defence lawyer may wish to refer the court to the Home Office's *Implementation Guidance: Court-ordered Secure Remands* (para 3.14):

> 'Serious harm' is not defined in relation to other offences. However, the definition for sexual and violent offences gives an indication of the gravity of the harm to which the public would need to be exposed from a young person in other circumstances before the test was likely to be satisfied.

13.214 The meaning of 'serious harm' in relation to offences not covered by the statutory definition has only been the subject of judicial consideration once in *R v Croydon Youth Court ex p G (a minor)*.[147] A 15-year-old had appeared before the court charged with four domestic burglaries, handling stolen goods, criminal damage to a motor car and various motoring offences. These offences were allegedly committed over a three-month period. Since his first appearance at court he had breached the conditions of bail support and been arrested for failing to comply with the conditions of a remand to local authority accommodation. The justices remanded him into custody. The defendant applied for judicial review of that decision. In their affidavit the justices referred to the above statutory definition and said that they considered that any burglary caused psychological harm and that the number of offences allegedly committed by the defendant amounted to serious harm to the public in general. In quashing the remand into custody, Leggatt LJ stated:

> Though it would not be necessary to conclude that there was a risk of death or serious personal injury being caused, the Court would have to be satisfied that the young person whom they were minded to remand was liable to cause harm that could sensibly be described as serious on account of the nature of the offence or offences that might be committed and not merely of the risk of repetition.[148]

'... to protect the public ...'

13.215 Children and Young Persons Act 1969 s23(5) gives no indication of how general a threat the defendant must present to the public. Guidance may perhaps be sought from the judicial authorities on the meaning of the term in similar statutory provisions in Mental Health Act 1983 s43 and Powers of Criminal Courts (Sentencing) Act 2000 s80(2)(b). In relation to both sections it has been decided that it is sufficient for the individual to pose a risk of serious harm to one member of the public.[149] As the wording and purpose of the sections in these Acts are similar to section 23(5), it is likely that the same meaning would be given to the phrase in this context.

---

147 (1995) *Times* 3 May, QBD.
148 Court transcript p5.
149 *R v Birch* (1983) 11 Cr App R (S) 202, CA; and *R v Hashi* (1995) 16 Cr App R (S) 121, CA (decisions on the Mental Health Act 1983 and Criminal Justice Act 1991 respectively).

Identifying serious harm

13.216 The following propositions may be drawn from the judgment of Leggatt LJ in *R v Croydon Youth Court ex p G (a minor)* (see above):

- the fact that a juvenile is charged with a violent or sexual offence or an offence punishable with 14 years or more does not by itself mean that the juvenile presents a risk of serious harm;
- a court may infer from the defendant's record that the public was liable to incur serious harm, having regard to the nature of the offences with which s/he has been charged, or of which s/he has been convicted, or the manner in which s/he had carried them out;
- an apprehended series of offences, which individually could not constitute serious harm, could not be aggregated so as to render serious such harm as might be caused by them.

Satisfying the offence criterion

13.217 Handling stolen goods is an offence punishable with 14 years or more imprisonment, but it will be exceedingly rare when the offence itself will indicate a risk of serious harm to the public. Leggatt LJ declared that domestic burglary would not necessarily satisfy the test and, to illustrate this, he gave the example of an offender who always burgles residential properties during the daytime, having checked that the occupants are out.

Relevance of the defendant's current offence(s) and previous record

13.218 An offender who has a criminal record which shows a pattern of street robberies with significant violence may have demonstrated by his/her record that s/he presents a risk of serious harm to the public. A single very serious offence allegedly committed by a young offender with no previous convictions is more problematic. In itself it may not be an indicator of potential risk.

Frequency of future offending

13.219 The court will often be faced with a young offender who is alleged to, or been found to, offend frequently. The court may have cogent grounds for fearing further multiple offences, but that alone cannot satisfy the criterion of serious harm. The court must have reason to fear that the offender will commit a single offence which in itself will constitute serious harm to the public.

'Consultation'

13.220 This is defined by statute as:

> such consultation (if any) as is reasonably practicable in all the circumstances of the case.[150]

13.221 This may seem a very limited requirement, but the defence lawyer will wish to draw the court's attention to the view taken by Leggatt LJ:

---

150 Children and Young Persons Act 1969 s23(13)(b).

The point is not a formality. Its evident purpose is to inform the Court about the nature and suitability of the available local authority accommodation before it forms the opinion that only a remand centre would be adequate to protect the public from serious harm from a defendant.[151]

Alternative local authority accommodation

13.222 Even if the court is satisfied that the defendant presents a serious risk to the public, the court must still go on to examine what alternative non-secure accommodation options are available. Depending on the resources of the local authority, other local authority accommodation may be available which will provide high levels of supervision for the defendant.

13.223 As soon as the defence lawyer realises that the court may be considering a secure remand, s/he should make contact with the designated local authority to establish what accommodation may be available. Since the reorganisation of social services departments to become service purchasers, it is often a cumbersome process to identify a placement for any child. In many social services departments a placements officer will be involved in finding a placement and senior management will scrutinise the financial implications of any remand. The decision-making process may be even more complicated when the child concerned is accused of a violent or sexual offence where the authority must also assess the potential risk that the defendant poses to other children in a residential setting.

Secure or custodial remands for 15- and 16-year-old boys

13.224 Where the court is satisfied that the criteria of Children and Young Persons Act 1969 s23(5) apply in relation to a 15- or 16-year-old boy, it will normally remand him to a prison or remand centre.

13.225 The court may remand him to local authority accommodation with a security requirement if:

- it is of the opinion that, by reason of his physical or emotional immaturity or a propensity of his to harm himself, it would be undesirable for him to be remanded to a remand centre or prison;
- it is notified that a bed in a secure unit is available.

Vulnerability

13.226 Home Office guidance suggests that it is the responsibility of the designated local authority to draw the court's attention to the potential vulnerability of a young defendant.[152] The defence lawyer should, therefore, ensure that the vulnerability of the young defendant is assessed by the youth offending team. This is usually done in the cells using the *Asset* Bail Profile to enable the easy identification of risk factors.[153] Where the lawyer is already aware of existing documentary evidence, eg educational psychologists reports, these may assist the youth offending team and the court in making their assessment.

---

151 *R v Croydon Youth Court ex p G (a minor)* (1995) *Times* 3 May, court transcript p6.
152 *Implementation Guidance: Court-ordered Secure Remands*, para 3.18.
153 See paras 13.4–13.40.

13.227   The final decision on the vulnerability of a 15- or 16-year-old boy rests with the court and not with the youth offending team. The view of the youth offending team in relation to the young person's vulnerability is likely to be given considerable weight by the court. The physical immaturity of a 15- or 16-year-old boy may be obvious, but it must be remembered that emotional maturity or a propensity to self-harm will not be so obvious. These are matters to which the defence lawyer must be alert. Family members may be more willing to give information than the young person themselves.

Physical or emotional immaturity

13.228   Boys aged 15 and 16 years will be at varying stages in their physical and emotional development. A proper assessment of a young person's maturity cannot be based on physical appearance alone. The Department of Health's maturity assessment objectives applicable to 15-year-olds are set out in table 17 below and may assist in providing a more comprehensive assessment of development.

Risk of self-harm or suicide

13.229   Young prisoners do not cope well with the stresses of custody. Some young people are more vulnerable to self-harm and suicide than others. Some of the main risk factors relevant to young offenders are summarised in table 18 below.

13.230   Research has identified young prisoners as a high risk group,[154] particularly those on remand where the suicide rate is three times the rate in the general prison population.[155] Between 1990 and 1998, 14 boys aged 15 to 17 years committed suicide in Prison Service establishments.[156]

Placement

13.231   Even where a court wishes to determine that a young defendant is vulnerable there may not be a place in a secure unit immediately available. In such circumstances the remand will be to a remand centre or prison, but the defence lawyer should ask the court to remand for the shortest possible period to allow a place in a secure unit to be identified. The duty to have regard to a young person's welfare means that courts should be aware of the need to keep cases involving young people made subject of a secure remand under constant review.[157]

13.232   The placement arrangements whereby 15- and 16-year-old boys are usually placed in custody whereas girls are always placed in a secure unit is not incompatible with Articles 5 and 14 of the European Convention on Human Rights.[158]

---

154 A Liebling, *Risk and prison suicide* in H Kemshall and J Pritchard (eds), *Good practice in risk management*, Jessica Kingsley Publishing, 1997.

155 Grindrod and Black, *Suicides in Leeds Prison: an inquiry into the deaths of five teenagers during 1988/89*, Howard League for Penal Reform, 1989.

156 HM Inspectorate of Prisons, *Suicide is everyone's concern: a thematic review* (Home Office, 1999).

157 *Implementation Guidance: Court-ordered Secure Remands.*

158 *R (SR) v Nottingham Magistrates' Court* [2001] EWHC 802 (Admin); 166 JP 132.

Table 17: Maturity assessment objectives for 15-year-olds

1 Health

The young person is well, weight within normal limits for height.
Ongoing health conditions and disabilities are being dealt with.
The young person does not put their health at risk.

2 Education

The young person's educational attainments match his/her ability.
The young person is acquiring leisure interests and participating in a range of activities.
The young person has developed skills useful to employment.

3 Identity

The young person has a positive view of him/herself and his/her abilities, has an understanding of his/her current situation.
The young person has knowledge of his/her family of origin and can relate to his/her racial and ethnic background.

4 Family and social relationships

The young person has had continuity of care and has positive contact with birth family.
The young person is able to make friendships with others of the same age.

5 Social presentation

The young person's appearance and behaviour are acceptable to young people and adults.
The young person can communicate easily with others.

6 Emotional and behavioural development

The young person is free of serious emotional and behavioural problems or is receiving effective treatment for all problems.

7 Self-care skills

The young person can function independently at a level appropriate to his/her age and ability.

Source: Department of Health, *Looking after children*, 1995. (Developed by the Dartington Social Research Unit.)

Table 18:   Risk factors for suicide or self-harm in custody

- **Development immaturity**

- **Lack of stable background**

  Those who are in care or who have a history of broken placements have a significantly higher incidence of suicide and self-harm.

- **Victims of abuse**

  Victims of abuse, particularly sexual abuse, may have a sense of worthlessness and poor self-image.

- **History of truancy**

  As a result of bullying (as opposed to boredom or peer pressure).

- **The experience of loss**

  Whether by the death of a family member or broken relationship.

- **Social isolation**

  Not having contact with family, friends, social workers or other support networks.

- **Ethnic Minority**

  May suffer racial abuse, which is a factor as it creates extra stress.

- **Gay young people**

  A vulnerable group, not directly as a result of their sexual orientation, but because of the lack of acceptance (and victimisation) they may experience.

- **History of previous self-harm**

  Teenagers who have already made a serious attempt on their lives are particularly likely to commit suicide. There are also risks when a member of the young person's family or friend has attempted or committed suicide.

- **Mental illness**

  Mentally ill young people are at a particular risk; those suffering from depression or schizophrenia are very vulnerable. Sleeping difficulties, self-neglect, helplessness, confusion and cognitive rigidity are common signs of poor mental health.

- **Misuser of drugs, volatile substances or alcohol**

  The use of some illegal drugs increases impulsiveness.

- **No previous experience of custody**

- **Very short periods spent in the community between periods in custody**

Sources: A Liebling, 'Risk and prison suicide' and Lyon, 'Teenage suicide and self-harm' in H Kemshall and J Pritchard (eds), *Good practice in risk assessment and risk management*, Jessica Kingsley Publishing, 1997.

13.233   All placements are dealt with by the Youth Justice Board placements team. On the making of a secure remand, all the details obtained by the youth offending team are forwarded to the placements team who will arrange the bed in a secure institution. Problems may arise over the availability of a place as priority is given to 12-, 13- and 14-year-olds. It can also be difficult to obtain a place near the defendant's home. There may be occasions where the defence lawyer wishes to contact the placements team on behalf of his/her client.

Providing essential information to the secure establishment

13.234   When a secure or custodial remand has been made, an *Asset* Bail Profile (or an *Asset* Core Profile if available) and a completed Post Court Report must be faxed to the Youth Justice Board Placement Team and the secure facility. If *Asset* is not completed before the young defendant is taken to the secure establishment, the establishment must contact the youth offending team within one hour to request that *Asset* be prepared. The secure establishment must treat the young person as vulnerable until *Asset* documentation is received.[159]

13.235   Any concerns regarding the young person's vulnerability will normally be clearly identified on the Post Court Report. If there is particular cause for concern, a telephone call must be made directly to the secure establishment reception unit and to the Youth Justice Board Placement Team, who will send a vulnerability alert to the establishment. Where there is a risk of self-harm or harm to others, the escort contactor must be informed.[160]

Allocation within the Prison Service

13.236   Normally a youth defendant who has been remanded to a Prison Service establishment will be detained at a young offender institution designated for holding juvenile (ie under 18 years of age) prisoners. In cases where the youth defendant has been designated 'provisionally category A',[161] it has been held to be lawful to hold him/her in the hospital wing of an adult prison.[162] Whilst there, s/he should benefit from as full a regime as possible.

Remand management by the youth offending team

13.237   A planning meeting must be organised by the secure establishment within five working days of arrival. The youth offending team worker from the home area (or a youth offending team worker seconded to the secure

159 Youth Justice Board: *National Standards for Youth Justice Services* (2004), para 2.53. For contact details see appendix 14.
160 Ibid, para 2.54.
161 Prisoners whose escape would be highly dangerous to the public, or the police, or the security of the state, no matter how unlikely that escape might be and for whom the aim must be to make escape impossible: see Prison Service Order 900.
162 *R (TB) v Secretary of State for the Home Department* [2004] EWHC 1332 (Admin).

facility, if such arrangements have been agreed) must attend. Parents or carers should be encouraged to attend.[163]

13.238 Before the meeting takes place, youth offending and secure facility staff must collate detailed information from all relevant sources, including the young person and his/her parents or carers about their health, welfare, education, current circumstances and risk to self and others.

13.239 The planning meeting must:

- be informed by the *Asset* assessment;
- determine whether a programme could be offered in support of a bail application at the next court appearance; and
- prepare a remand plan setting out what will be offered to the young person by the secure establishment and the youth offending team, should the remand continue.[164]

13.240 Secure establishment staff must provide the young person remanded to their custody with programmes linked to his/her assessed needs as agreed at the planning meeting.[165] The remand plan must be reviewed monthly by the secure establishment and the youth offending team to review against any targets set, and where there is significant change of circumstances, a further application for bail or an alternative must be considered.[166]

13.241 Where children are remanded to local authority accommodation with a secure requirement, reviews must be carried out in accordance with the Children (Secure Accommodation) Regulations 1991[167] and the Review of Children's Cases Regulations 1991[168] (see paras 3.60–3.67).[169]

13.242 Whilst on remand, the young person must be visited at least monthly by a youth offending team worker, social worker or staff member from a partner agency.[170]

Options after a secure remand

13.243 Once a defendant under the age of 18 has been remanded in custody, the reasons for that remand should be examined. It may, for example, be immediately obvious that a better bail support package would have been decisive. If this is the case, the defence lawyer needs to lobby the youth offending team for more resources to be allocated to the package. It should also be borne in mind that adult courts in general remand young defendants in custody much more frequently than youth courts, and it may be important whether the defendant has now been remanded to the youth court.

13.244 The options available depend on the age of the defendant.

---

163 Youth Justice Board: *National Standards for Youth Justice Services* (2004), para 2.56.
164 Youth Justice Board: *National Standards for Youth Justice Services* (2004), paras 2.57 and 2.58.
165 Ibid, para 2.59.
166 Ibid, para 2.61.
167 SI No 1505.
168 SI No 895.
169 Youth Justice Board: *National Standards for Youth Justice Services* (2004), para 2.62.
170 Ibid, para 2.60.

17-year-olds

13.245 The options available are as follows:

- an immediate application for bail to a judge in chambers in the Crown Court;
- a repeat bail application the following week;
- a secure accommodation application by the local authority.

Applications to judge in chambers

13.246 For a prompt re-hearing of the issues, such applications should be considered.[171]

Repeat bail applications

13.247 A defendant refused bail is always entitled to make one further bail application.[172] Thereafter, s/he may only apply for bail if it can be established that there has been a change of circumstances.[173] Attempts should be made to arrange for a bail support package to be available for any subsequent application, ideally with a bail support officer in court to present the package and to answer any questions and concerns the court may have. It is submitted that the existence of a bail support package or the presentation of a more intensive package is a change of circumstances justifying a fresh bail application.

Secure accommodation applications

13.248 Although 17-year-olds may not be remanded to local authority accommodation, they are still children within the definition of the Children Act 1989. Accordingly, if a 17-year-old was looked after by a local authority before a custodial remand, there would seem to be no reason in principle why a local authority could not make an application under Children Act 1989 s25 for authority to detain in secure accommodation.

13.249 In view of financial restraints, it is likely to be a very rare case where this option would be feasible. Nevertheless, where a 17-year-old has been charged with a very serious offence and the chances of bail are very slim, a secure accommodation application could be considered if there are substantial concerns regarding his/her welfare in custody. Such an application would require the court to grant the defendant bail to live as directed by the local authority. The authority would then need to exercise its power to place in secure accommodation for up to 72 hours while an application is made to the family proceedings court for authority to detain for up to three months.[174]

12- to 16-year-olds

13.250 The options are as follows:

- an immediate application for bail to a judge in chambers in the Crown Court;

---

171 See paras 13.144–13.151.
172 Bail Act 1976 Sch 1 Part IIA para 2.
173 *R v Nottingham Justices ex p Davies* [1981] QB 38; [1980] 2 All ER 775, QBD.
174 See chapter 14.

- a repeat bail application the following week;
- an application for a remand to local authority accommodation rather than a custodial remand;
- a secure accommodation application by the local authority.

Applications to judge in chambers

13.251   Once again, such applications should ensure a prompt re-hearing of the bail application.[175]

Repeat bail application

13.252   As above for 17-year-olds.

Application for placement in local authority accommodation

13.253   It is arguable that, in contrast to applications for bail, there is no limit to the number of times an application can be made to the court for the issue of a custodial remand as opposed to a remand to local authority accommodation to be considered.[176]

13.254   The defence lawyer should ensure that the youth offending team takes an active part in the constant review of a juvenile's place of remand. The Department of Health has given the following advice:

> On each occasion that a juvenile is returned to the court for the remand to be reviewed, careful consideration should be given to advising the court whether alternative arrangements might be considered. For example, where a juvenile has been remanded to a penal establishment ..., the court may be willing to consider a remand to local authority accommodation if they are presented with a clear statement of how the juvenile would be accommodated within the care system in such a way that the public would be protected from the risk of further offending and that he would be produced in court when required.[177]

Reviewing the vulnerability decision

13.255   Where the court has remanded a boy of 15 or 16 years into local authority accommodation with a security requirement and has not found him to be 'vulnerable,'[178] the decision on vulnerability can be revisited at a subsequent hearing if further information becomes available. The youth offending team or the secure establishment may provide information to the court which affects the court's view. The defence lawyer may also be able to provide information from the young person's records with social services or the education authority. There may also be circumstances where a report commissioned by the defence lawyer from a child psychologist or psychiatrist will contain information which may affect the court's decision on vulnerability.

---

175 See paras 13.144–13.151.
176 See 'Does the *Nottingham Justices* rule apply to juveniles?' (1994) 158 JPN 233.
177 *The Children Act 1989 Guidance and Regulations* (HMSO, 1991), Vol 1, Court Orders, para 6.39.
178 See paras 13.224–13.230.

CHAPTER 14

Secure accommodation

Introduction

14.1   This chapter considers the use of secure accommodation in all other con-
texts other than a court-directed remand to local authority accommodation with a security requirement.[1] The use of secure accommodation by
local authorities is controlled by Children Act 1989 s25 and the Children
(Secure Accommodation) Regulations 1991.[2] Within the context of criminal proceedings, secure accommodation may be used for a looked after
child when s/he has been:

- detained by the police and transferred to local authority accommodation;
- remanded to local authority accommodation;
- bailed to reside as directed by a local authority and subsequently placed
  in local authority accommodation;
- made subject to a supervision order with a residence requirement.

14.2   It should be noted that local authorities are subject to a general duty to take
reasonable steps to avoid the need for children in their area to be placed in
secure accommodation.[3]

Application of the European Convention on Human Rights

14.3   In *Re K (a child) (secure accommodation order: right to liberty)* [4] it was held
by the Court of Appeal that whilst a secure accommodation order is a deprivation of liberty within the meaning of Article 5 of the convention, such
orders come within the exception of Article 5(1)(d) as they are lawful orders
made for the purpose of educational supervision.[5]

14.4   Although an application for a secure accommodation order was not to
be characterised as criminal proceedings, the child should be afforded,
as a matter of procedural fairness under the English common law, the
five specific minimum rights described in Article 6(3) (for which, see
para 2.57).[6]

Definition

14.5   The Children Act 1989 defines secure accommodation as 'accommodation provided for the purpose of restricting liberty'.[7] Such accommodation must be registered with the Department of Education and Skills and
at present is run by local authorities, although there is now provision for
secure accommodation to be run by other bodies.[8]

1   For which see chapter 13.
2   SI No 1505.
3   Children Act 1989 Sch 2 Part I para 7(c).
4   [2001] 2 All ER 719; [2001] 2 WLR 1141; [2001] 1 FCR 249, CA.
5   See also *Koniarska v UK*, Application 33670/96, 12 October 2000.
6   Per Thorpe LJ in *Re C (Secure accommodation order: representation)* [2001] EWCA Civ
    458, [2001] 2 FLR 169.
7   Children Act 1989 s25(1).
8   Criminal Justice and Public Order Act 1994 s19.

Placement in secure accommodation

14.6 A child may only be placed in secure accommodation in strictly defined circumstances.

General criteria

14.7 Children Act 1989 s25(1) provides:

> A child who is being looked after by a local authority may not be placed, and, if placed, may not be kept in accommodation provided for the purpose of restricting liberty ('secure accommodation') unless it appears:
> (a) that–
>   (i) he has a history of absconding and is likely to abscond from any other description of accommodation; and
>   (ii) if he absconds he is likely to suffer significant harm; or
> (b) that if he is kept in any other description of accommodation he is likely to injure himself or other persons.

Child

14.8 This means any person under the age of 18.[9]

Looked after

14.9 This obviously includes children subject to full care orders under Children Act 1989 s31 and children looked after by a local authority under section 22(1).[10] A defendant remanded on bail with a condition to reside as directed by a local authority is 'looked after' by that authority and, therefore, may be placed in secure accommodation.[11]

14.10 It should be noted that young people aged 16 or 17 who are accommodated in children's homes under Children Act 1989 s20(5) are not subject to the power to place in secure accommodation.[12]

History of absconding

14.11 One previous instance of absconding is sufficient.[13]

Any other description of accommodation

14.12 As with the criteria for a remand with a security requirement, this is an important consideration.[14] The court must satisfy itself that no other accommodation available is suitable. The local authority should therefore

---

9 Children Act 1989 s105.

10 Note that a 'looked after' child is defined as a child in the care of a local authority or a child provided with accommodation by the authority for a continuous period of 24 hours. It is arguable that this prevents the placement in secure accommodation of a child not previously looked after by the authority.

11 *Re C (a minor) (secure accommodation: bail)* [1994] 2 FCR 1153, FD.

12 Children (Secure Accommodation) Regulations 1991 SI No 1505 (amended by 1992 SI No 2117) reg 5(2)(a).

13 *R v Calder Justices ex p C (a minor)* (1993) 4 May, unreported.

14 See para 13.222.

be in a position to identify what other accommodation has been considered and to explain why the other options are not considered adequate.

14.13   The Department of Health has issued guidance to local authorities considering the exercise of their powers under section 25:

> Restricting the liberty of children is a serious step which must be taken only when there is no appropriate alternative. It must be a 'last resort' in the sense that all else must first have been comprehensively considered and rejected – never because no other placement was available at the relevant time, because of inadequacies in staffing, because the child is simply being a nuisance or runs away from his accommodation and is not likely to significant harm in doing so, and never a form of punishment. It is important, in considering the possibility of a secure placement, that there is a clear view of the aims and objectives of such a placement and those providing the accommodation can fully meet those aims and objectives. Secure placements, once made, should be only for so long as is necessary and unavoidable. Care should be taken to ensure that children are not retained in security simply to complete a pre-determined assessment of 'treatment' programme. [15]

Significant harm

14.14   Children Act 1989 s105 states that the definitions and guidance in section 31 of the Act shall apply.[16]

Modified criteria for detained and remanded children

14.15   Children (Secure Accommodation) Regulations 1991[17] reg 6 modifies the criteria for the use of secure accommodation in the case of:

(a) a detained juvenile transferred to local authority accommodation under Police and Criminal Evidence Act 1984 s38(6); and

(b) a defendant refused bail and remanded to local authority accommodation under Children and Young Persons Act 1969 s23 who is either:

- charged with or convicted of a violent or sexual offence or an offence punishable in the case of an adult with imprisonment for a term of 14 years or more; or
- who has a recent history of absconding while remanded to local authority accommodation, and is charged with or has been convicted of an imprisonable offence alleged or found to have been committed while s/he was so remanded.

14.16   In such cases, the criteria for the use of secure accommodation are reduced to read as follows:

> A child who is being looked after by a local authority may not be placed, and if placed, may not be kept, in accommodation provided for the purposes of restricting liberty ... unless it appears that any accommodation other than that provided for the purpose of restricting liberty is inappropriate because–
> (a) the child is likely to abscond from such other accommodation, or
> (b) the child is likely to injure himself or other people if he is kept in any such other accommodation.

---

15 Department of Health, *The Children Act 1989: Guidance and Regulations* (HMSO, 1991), Vol 4, Residential Care, para 8.5.

16 See paras 3.99–3.100.

17 SI No 1505.

14.17 In *Re G (Secure Accommodation Order)*[18] Munby J held that where a child or young person had been remanded to local authority accommodation, jurisdiction to hear an application for a secure accommodation order lay with the youth court. He went on to say, if the criteria of regulation 6 are not satisfied, the youth court should still consider if the criteria of section 25(1) are satisfied.

Children under the age of 13

14.18 Children (Secure Accommodation) Regulations 1991[19] reg 4 provides:

> A child under the age of 13 years shall not be placed in secure accommodation unless it has been approved by the Secretary of State for such use and approval that is subject to such terms and conditions as he sees fit.

14.19 Where a local authority is considering the use of secure accommodation for a child of this age, contact must be made with the Looked After Children Division of the Department for Education and Skills. After initial contact the Department will discuss the information provided with appropriate inspectors at the Commission for Social Care Inspection. A decision will then be made on behalf of the Secretary of State. This procedure is not necessary if the child is the subject of a court ordered secure remand.

Placement without court authority

14.20 When the criteria are satisfied, a local authority may place a child in secure accommodation for a maximum of 72 hours (in any 28-day period) without seeking the authority of a court.[20] If the authority wishes to keep the child in secure accommodation for a longer period, it must seek the authority of a court.

Role of the court

14.21 The court's duty is to determine whether any relevant criteria for keeping a child in secure accommodation are satisfied.[21] If a court determines that any such criteria are satisfied, the court is required to make an order authorising the child to be kept in secure accommodation and specifying the maximum period for which s/he may be kept.[22]

14.22 The role of the court has been considered by the Court of Appeal in *Re M (Secure Accommodation Application)*.[23] The court held that it was the duty of the court to put itself in the position of a reasonable local authority and consider first, whether the criteria were satisfied, and second, whether it would be in accordance with the local authority's duty under Children Act

18 [2001] 3 FCR 47; [2001] 1 FLR 884, FD.
19 SI No 1505.
20 Ibid, reg 10(1).
21 Children Act 1989 s25(3).
22 Ibid, s25(4).
23 [1995] 2 All ER 407; [1995] 1 FLR 418; [1995] 2 FCR 373.

1989 s22(3) to safeguard and promote the welfare of the child by placing him/her in secure accommodation. Although the welfare of the child was a relevant consideration, it could not be the paramount one as the local authority was permitted to exercise its powers in relation to the child to protect members of the public from serious injury.[24]

Which court?

Remand under Children and Young Persons Act 1969 s23

14.23   Criminal Justice Act 1991 s60(3) provides:

> In the case of a child or young person who has been remanded or committed to local authority accommodation by a youth court or a magistrates' court other than a youth court, any application under section 25 of the Children Act 1989 (use of accommodation for restricting liberty) shall ... be made to that court.

14.24   The application for authority to place in secure accommodation must, therefore be made to a youth court or magistrates' court and not a family proceedings court. The jurisdiction of the youth court is not dependent on the case falling within reg 6(1) of the Children (Secure Accommodation) Regulations 1991[25] (for which see paras 14.15–14.16 above).[26]

14.25   In *Liverpool City Council v B*[27] the question arose whether the application had to be made to the particular court which remanded the defendant. Ewbank J sitting in the Family Division held that the term 'that court' in section 60(3) was a generic term and allowed an application to any court of that type. The section merely required that the application be made be made to a youth court as opposed to a family proceedings court. It has been suggested that a court to which a case has been remitted under Children and Young Persons Act 1933 s56(1) may not consider an application under section 25 until it has remanded the defendant.[28] A similar practical problem may arise when an adult magistrates' court has remanded a child or young person to a youth court under Children and Young Persons Act 1933 s46(2).

14.26   Where a juvenile is committed to stand trial there is no provision for the Crown Court to authorise the use of secure accommodation under Children Act 1989 s25. It is the view of the Home Office that as a result of section 60(3) such authority should be sought from the youth court or adult magistrates' court which committed the juvenile.[29]

Civil

14.27   In other circumstances an application for authority to place in secure accommodation must be made to a family proceedings court.[30] Rather

---

24 See Children Act 1989 s22(6).

25 SI No 1505.

26 See also *Re G (Secure Accommodation Order)* [2001] 3 FCR 47; [2001] 1 FLR 884, Fam D.

27 [1995] 1 WLR 505, [1995] 2 FLR 84.

28 (1992) 156 JPN 208.

29 *Implementation Guidance: Court-ordered Secure Remands*, para 3.10.

30 Children (Allocation of Proceedings) Order 1991 SI No 1677 article 3(1)(a) and Children Act 1989 s92.

confusingly, this also applies to a defendant remanded on bail with a condition of residence as directed by social services.[31]

Legal representation

14.28   No court may authorise the use of secure accommodation for a child who is not legally represented unless, having been informed of the right to apply for legal representation funded by the Legal Services Commission and having had an opportunity to do so, s/he has refused to do so.[32]

14.29   The Department of Health also gives the following guidance:

> Children should be encouraged to appoint a legal representative in such proceedings and given every assistance to make such arrangements ... The child in such circumstances should have details of local solicitors on the Law Society's [Children Panel] made available to him and should be assisted in making contact with the solicitor of his choice.[33]

14.30   Where the application for a secure accommodation order is made to the youth court following a remand to local authority accommodation, it comes within the definition of criminal proceedings contained in section 12(2) of the Access to Justice Act 1999. The existing representation order will therefore cover work relating to the secure accommodation application.[34]

14.31   An application for a secure accommodation order in the family proceedings court is classified as Special Children Act proceedings under the family proceedings heading in the Community Legal Service Funding Code. Accordingly representation may only be provided by a solicitor who has a General Civil Contract which includes licensed work in the Family Category. The solicitor will complete Form CLS APP5 which should be submitted to the Community Legal Service within three working days of receipt of instructions to act. The Community Legal Service will then issue a legal representation certificate.[35]

Powers of the court

Interim orders

14.32   On any adjournment of the hearing of an application for authority to place in secure accommodation, the court may make an interim order permitting the child to be kept during the period of the adjournment in secure accommodation.[36]

Length of authorisation

14.33   This depends on whether the application is made in a remand case or a civil case.

---

31   *Re W (Secure Accommodation Order: Jurisdiction)* [1995] 2 FCR 708, Fam D.
32   Children Act 1989 s25(6).
33   Department of Health, *The Children Act 1989: Guidance and Regulations* (HMSO, 1991) Vol 4, Residential Care, para 8.40.
34   Legal Services Commission Manual, Volume 3, Part C, para 20.25.2.
35   Ibid, para 20.25.12.
36   Children Act 1989 s25(5).

Remand to local authority accommodation under Children and Young Persons Act 1969 s23

14.34   The authorisation may only be for the period of the remand and in any event no longer than 28 days.[37] Authority must therefore be sought at every remand hearing.[38]

Civil

14.35   Authority may be given in the first instance for up to three months.[39] On subsequent applications the court may authorise a child to be kept in secure accommodation for a further period not exceeding six months at any one time.[40]

14.36   For the purposes of calculating the period of authorisation, any interim order must be included.[41]

Procedure

Youth or adult magistrates' court

14.37   The procedure is governed by Magistrates' (Children and Young Persons) Rules 1992[42] Part III (as amended).

Notice of application

14.38   The local authority making the application must send the relevant court a notice:

- specifying the grounds for the application; and
- the name and addresses of the people upon whom notice must be served.

14.39   No minimum period of notice of the application is specified.

14.40   Notice of the application along with the time and date of the hearing must also be given to the following:

- the child who is the subject of the application;
- the parent or guardian[43] of the child, if the whereabouts of such parent or guardian is known to the local authority or can be readily ascertained; and
- where the father and mother of the child were not married to each other at the time of the birth, any person who is known to the local authority to have made an application to acquire parental responsibility which has not yet been determined.[44]

---

37 Children (Secure Accommodation) Regulations 1991 SI No 1505 reg 13.
38 This will cause considerable practical problems during the course of a Crown Court trial.
39 Children (Secure Accommodation) Regulations 1991 SI No 1505 reg 11.
40 Ibid, reg 12.
41 *C (a minor) v Humberside County Council and another* (1994) *Times* 24 May.
42 SI No 2071.
43 For the definition of parent and guardian in these rules see para 31.53.
44 Magistrates' Courts (Children and Young Persons) Rules 1992 SI No 2071 r14(2) and (3).

14.41 Failure to give the requisite notices may render any authority to detain in secure accommodation invalid.[45]

Children's guardian

14.42 There is no provision permitting a court to appoint a children's guardian.

The hearing

14.43 As far as practicable, the court must arrange for copies of any reports in support of the local authority's application to be made available to:

- the defence lawyer;
- the parent or guardian; and
- the child or young person, unless the court considers that it is impracticable to do so having regard to the his/her age and understanding or undesirable to do so having regard to potential serious harm which might thereby be suffered by him/her.[46]

14.44 The court must inform the child or young person of the general nature both of the proceedings and the grounds upon which they are brought. Such an explanation must be in terms suitable for his/her age and understanding.[47] If a child or young person is not legally represented, the court must allow a parent or guardian to conduct the case on the defendant's behalf, unless the child or young person requests otherwise.[48] If it thinks it appropriate, the court may allow another relative or other responsible person to conduct the case on behalf of the child or young person.[49]

14.45 The procedure for the hearing is set out in Magistrates' Courts Rules 1981[50] r14. It should start with the local authority representative addressing the court and thereafter calling any evidence in support of the application. Written statements or reports will have to be adduced in evidence to support the application. At the conclusion of the evidence for the local authority, the lawyer for the child or young person may address the court and thereafter call any evidence. The local authority may call rebuttal evidence. At the conclusion of the evidence, the defence lawyer may address the court if s/he has not already done so. Either party may, with the leave of the court, address the court a second time. If leave is obtained, the address by the defence should precede that of the local authority.

14.46 The child or young person may be excluded from the hearing unless s/he is conducting his/her own case, if the court considers that evidence will be presented which it is not in the interests of the child or young person to hear. Any evidence relating to the character or conduct of the child or young person must be given in his/her presence.

14.47 If a court determines that the criteria for detention in secure accommodation are satisfied, it must then go on to consider the length of the period of authorisation. In reaching this decision it must take into consideration

45 Cf *D v X City Council* [1985] FLR 275.
46 Magistrates' Courts (Children and Young Persons) Rules 1992 SI No 2071 r21(1).
47 Ibid, r17.
48 Ibid, r18(1).
49 Ibid, r18(2).
50 SI No 552.

such information as it considers necessary for the purpose, including such information regarding the background of the child or young person provided by the local authority pursuant to its obligations under Children and Young Persons Act 1969 s9.[51]

Family proceedings court

14.48   An application to the family proceedings court for authorisation to detain in secure accommodation is governed by the Family Proceedings Courts (Children Act 1989) Rules 1991[52] (as amended). An application under section 25 is defined as specified proceedings.[53]

Notice of application

14.49   The local authority must file a notice of application on the prescribed form with the clerk of the justices with sufficient copies for each respondent.[54]

14.50   Notice of the application along with the time and place of the hearing must be served upon the following:

- the child or young person;
- any parent with parental responsibility.

14.51   A minimum period of one day's notice must be given.[55]

Children's guardian

14.52   As the application for authorisation falls within the definition of specified proceedings, a children's guardian should be appointed by the clerk to the court as soon as practicable after the commencement of the proceedings, unless it is considered unnecessary so to do in order to safeguard the interests of the child.[56] Once a guardian has been appointed, the defence solicitor is required to act on the instructions received from the guardian. If the child wishes to give contrary instructions to those of the guardian, the solicitor may act upon the child's instructions if, having taken into account the views of the guardian, the solicitor considers that the child is able, having regard to his/her understanding, to give instructions on his/her own behalf.[57]

The hearing

14.53   The child need not be present during the application. It has been suggested that the court should only allow his/her attendance if it is satisfied that it would be in the interests of the child.[58]

---

51 SI No 552 r21(2): for the duty under section 9 see chapter 17.
52 SI No 1395.
53 Family Proceedings Rules 1991 SI No 1247 (as amended) r4.2(1) and (2)(h).
54 Ibid, r4.4.
55 Family Proceedings Courts (Children Act 1989) Rules 1991, r4(1)(b) and Sch 2 col (ii).
56 Family Proceedings Rules 1991 SI No 1247 (as amended) r4.10(1).
57 Ibid, r4.12(1)(a).
58 *Re W (a minor) (secure accommodation order: attendance at court)* [1994] 2 FLR 1092, Fam D.

14.54 Subject to any directions from the justices' clerk, the various parties to the proceedings should address the court in the following order:

- the representative of the local authority making the application;
- any person with parental responsibility;
- the children's guardian;
- the child, if there is no children's guardian.[59]

14.55 Before the court announces its decision, the justices' clerk must record in writing the names of the justices constituting the bench and the reasons for the court's decision and any finding of fact.[60]

Right of appeal

14.56 The defendant has a right of appeal against the authorisation of detention in secure accommodation. The local authority may also appeal the denial of authorisation. Irrespective of the court which heard the original application, the right of appeal lies to the Family Division of the High Court.[61]

Review of secure placement

14.57 A local authority looking after a child in secure accommodation is required to review the placement in such accommodation within one month of the start of the placement and then at intervals not exceeding three months.[62] This review is separate from the statutory review process required in relation to a looked after child.

14.58 The authority is required to appoint three persons to review the placement. At least one of those persons must be neither a member nor an officer of the authority by or on behalf of which the child is being looked after. Having regard to the welfare of the child in question, the persons appointed to review the placement shall satisfy themselves as to whether or not:

- the criteria for keeping the child in secure accommodation continue to apply;
- the placement continues to be necessary; and
- any other description of accommodation would be appropriate.[63]

14.59 If practicable, the local authority must ascertain the wishes and feelings of:

- the child;
- any parent;
- anyone with parental responsibility;
- persons having had care of the child;
- the independent visitor (if appointed); and
- the authority managing the secure accommodation.[64]

59 Family Proceedings Rules 1991 SI No 1247 (as amended) r4.21(3).
60 Ibid, r4.21(5).
61 Children Act 1989 s94(1).
62 Children (Secure Accommodation) Regulations 1991 SI No 1505 reg 15.
63 Ibid, reg 16(1).
64 Ibid, reg 16(2).

14.60   The authority shall, if practicable, provide information to those it has consulted about what action in intends to take in relation to the child in the light of the review.[65]

---

65   Children (Secure Accommodation) Regulations 1991 SI No 1505 reg 16(3).

The trial

Introduction

15.1   The trial of a child or young person will most commonly take place in the youth court. A smaller number will take place in the Crown Court or in the adult magistrates' court with one or more adults.

15.2   The trial procedure in the youth court is substantially the same as any summary trial in the adult magistrates' court. Where the trial is to take place in the Crown Court, the case will proceed as for an adult standing trial. Consideration should be given to any modifications to the trial process which may be necessary to take account of the age and maturity of the defendant.

15.3   The trial of a child or young person presents particular problems for the defence lawyer. Taking instructions on the facts of the case may be more difficult than in the case of an adult client; the parent may be involved in the trial process and wish to intervene in the solicitor/client relationship; the age of the defendant may have implications for the evidential and procedural requirements in the trial and his/her limited maturity will influence the tactical approach to the trial and the question of whether the juvenile should be advised to give evidence.

Pre-trial preparation

Disclosure of evidence

15.4   Advance disclosure of the prosecution case is required in respect of either-way offences.[1] However, the Criminal Procedure Rules 2005[2] make specific provision that in the case of a person under 18 years of age, advance information should be served, if it is requested, prior to plea being entered.[3]

15.5   Where summary trial is to take place, the prosecution should provide to the defence all the evidence on which the Crown proposes to rely. Sufficient time should be allowed for the evidence to be properly considered by the defendant and his/her advisers before the evidence is called.[4] Failure to comply may raise issues under Article 6 of the European Convention on Human Rights – particularly the right under Article 6(3)(a) 'to be informed promptly ... and in detail, of the nature and cause of the accusation against him' and under Article 6(3)(b) 'to have adequate time and facilities for his defence'.[5]

15.6   Where the evidence of a child witness has been taken in video form, the police often stipulate that a copy must be collected from them by a defence representative. The Legal Services Commission has accepted that this can be taken into account in calculating the costs of a case as an undertaking is required.[6]

---

1   Criminal Procedure Rules 2005 Part 21.
2   SI No 384.
3   Ibid, r21.3(1).
4   *Attorney-General's Guidelines on Disclosure of Information in Criminal Proceedings*, March 2005, para 57.
5   See obiter remarks in *R v Stratford Justices, ex p Imbert* [1999] 2 Cr App R 276.
6   Criminal Defence Service, *Criminal Bills Assessment Manual*, October 2005.

Unused material

15.7 Once a not guilty plea has been entered, the prosecution remain under a duty to make disclosure under Part I of the Criminal Procedure and Investigation Act 1996, as amended by the Criminal Justice Act 2003.

15.8 The prosecutor's duty is to disclose previously undisclosed material to the defence if it might reasonably be considered capable of undermining the case for the prosecution against the accused, or of assisting with the case for the accused.[7] This is an objective test.

15.9 Once the prosecution have complied with their duty of disclosure, the defence may submit a statement of the defence case to the court and the prosecution.[8] This is voluntary in summary proceedings. In the Crown Court it is compulsory and failure to submit the defence case statement within the time limits and in proper form may result in comment and inferences being drawn at trial.

15.10 The required contents of the defence case statement include:

- the nature of the defence;
- any particular defences on which the defendant intends to rely;
- matters of fact with which the defendant takes issue with the prosecution;
- the reasons why issue is taken with particular facts;
- any point of law to be taken including authorities relied on (including points on admissibility of evidence or an abuse of process); and
- particulars of alibi witnesses if relevant.[9]

15.11 The prosecution remain under a continuing duty to review questions of disclosure whether or not a defence case statement is submitted.[10]

Taking instructions

15.12 The main difficulties in taking instructions from a child or young person arise from lack of opportunity and impaired communication. Young clients frequently fail to maintain adequate contact with the defence lawyer before trial, failing to make and/or keep appointments. This may be due to a variety of reasons, eg a chaotic lifestyle, lack of maturity, failure to take the proceedings seriously, fear of the consequences or a parental failure to ensure arrangements are made. As a consequence, lawyers should achieve as much as possible in any contact with the client during the proceedings. There may be only one or two hearings before the trial date but these should be used as fully as possible to take instructions and consider trial preparation. Many youth courts, adult magistrates' courts and Crown Courts have private interview rooms where conditions of confidentiality can be achieved and, as waiting periods at court may be prolonged, instructions may be taken quite fully at the early hearings. Tape players and video recorders are sometimes available to assist in taking full instructions.

---

7 Criminal Procedure and Investigation Act 1996 s3.
8 Ibid, s6.
9 Ibid, s6A as inserted by Criminal Justice Act 2003 s33(2).
10 Ibid, s7A as inserted by Criminal Justice Act 2003 s37.

15.13   The defence lawyer will always need to bear in mind the age and level of understanding of the child or young person when taking instructions. The practical considerations involved in taking instructions from a young client are considered in more detail in chapter 4. The lawyer also needs to consider the issues of effective participation discussed in chapter 10. The position of witnesses in relation to special measures is dealt with in chapter 16.

Defence witnesses

15.14   Children and young people often have witnesses who are of the same or similar age, and this can present a challenge to the defence lawyer. It can be difficult to arrange for witnesses to attend the lawyer's office, although the mobile telephone has made contacting young witnesses easier. It is always desirable to take a statement from any defence witness prior to a trial hearing and to send a copy to him/her to check for accuracy.

15.15   Young defence witnesses may be assisted by a special measures direction.[11] The assistance of the Witness Service[12] is also available for defence witnesses.

15.16   Difficulties can arise when witnesses are contacted without the knowledge of their parents. It is desirable to ensure that a potential witness understands that his/her situation should be explained to a parent or guardian, who may be supportive once they are aware of the circumstances. The Witness Service is willing to deal with young witnesses without a parent or guardian.

15.17   It is good practice for the defence lawyer to explain the court procedure to defence witnesses in advance of the hearing. If possible, and particularly in cases to be heard in the Crown Court, a visit to the court in advance of the trial would be ideal.

15.18   It may also be of assistance to use the video in the Young Witness pack.[13]

15.19   The defence lawyer will need to consider whether a witness summons may be necessary to ensure the attendance of the witness.[14] Where issues of self-incrimination may arise, the witness should be told that he/she is entitled to seek free legal advice from solicitors other than those acting for the defendant and that s/he should do so.[15]

15.20   The Legal Services Commission recognises that it may be essential to take witness statements at an early stage and that, where a case is to be heard in the Crown Court, it may be necessary to take witness statements

---

11 See para 16.12.

12 See para 16.2.

13 See para 16.5.

14 Magistrates' Courts Act 1980 s97 as amended by the Serious Organised Crime and Police Act 2005 s169. The court may now issue a summons if two conditions are met: if a person is likely to be able to give material evidence, or produce any document or thing likely to be material evidence for the purpose of any criminal proceedings before the court; and if the court is satisfied that it is in the interests of justice so to do.

15 Criminal Defence Service, *Criminal Bills Assessment Manual*, October 2005, para 4.19.4.

while the case is still in the magistrates' court to ensure that an accurate record is made of the witness's recollection. In these circumstances, where there is a 'through' representation order, work done whilst the case is still in the magistrates' court which more properly relates to the Crown Court proceedings can be included in the Crown Court bill.[16]

Defence evidence

15.21 In all criminal trials the defence lawyer will need to consider whether the defendant's case will be assisted by practical aids such as plans or photographs. This is particularly so where young people, whether defendants or witnesses, may be better able to explain their evidence by reference to these aids rather than relying on their descriptive abilities. Photographs can bring a case to life and assist a witness and the court in visualising the location where an allegation is said to have taken place. Distances are sometimes difficult to describe and a simple plan may help the defendant and witnesses to give clear evidence.

Fast tracking

15.22 The identification of persistent young offenders[17] who are fast tracked through the court system may lead to some trials taking place very swiftly after charge. The defence lawyer needs to ensure that the preparation of the case for trial is not compromised by the speed in which the case is listed. Vigilance is necessary to ensure that the prosecution have complied with their disclosure duties and, if necessary, the case should be brought to the attention of the Case Progression Officer and listed for mention in court. The defendant's right to a fair trial may lead to an application to adjourn.

Evidential considerations

Exclusion of evidence

15.23 The common law and Police and Criminal Evidence Act 1984 (PACE) ss76 and 78 apply to children and young persons just as much as they apply to adult defendants.

15.24 In addition to the various reasons for excluding evidence applicable to defendants of all ages, the defence lawyer needs to consider whether any comments made by a juvenile in the absence of an appropriate adult are admissible. PACE Code C para 11.15 requires that any interview of a juvenile must be conducted in the presence of an appropriate adult unless it is an emergency covered by Code C paras 11.1,11.18 or 11.20 and Note 11C. It follows that any interview conducted in the absence of an appropriate adult risks being excluded at trial. Code C para 11.16 also provides that interviews with young persons should take place at their educational establishment

---

16 Criminal Defence Service, *Criminal Bills Assessment Manual*, paras 3.3.16–3.3.18.
17 See paras 2.104–2.106.

only in exceptional circumstances. Efforts should be made to contact the parents or other appropriate adult.

Urgent interviews

15.25   If the police claim to have interviewed under one of the exceptions, the defence lawyer should examine whether those grounds existed – and also in the case of an interview in the police station, that the requisite authority was obtained.

Questioning at the time of arrest

15.26   The courts have been willing to exclude admissions made by a juvenile at the time of arrest on the basis that the conversation amounted to an interview[18] but in another case the court ruled that the conversation which followed the arrest was not an interview but 'questions at or near the scene of a suspected crime to elicit an explanation which if true would exculpate the suspect'.[19]

15.27   The question has been considered by the Court of Appeal in the case of *R v Weekes*[20] in which Farquharson LJ stated:

> It is very difficult ... to draw a line between what is an interview for the purposes of the Code and what is not. When a police officer is in the street seeking information and trying to establish whether there are grounds for arresting a suspect, it is absurd to suppose that before questioning a juvenile he has to wait until a parent has been summoned to the scene. Such enquiries are not within the meaning of the word 'interview' as contemplated by the Code.

> But if the police officer persists in his questioning, beyond the point it is necessary for his purposes at the time, it may be that the protection of the Code is invoked, even though the conversation is taking place in the street or in a police car on the way to the police station. Like most of these problems it depends on the judge's assessment of the position in the light of all the circumstances. Is the nature, length, sequence and place where the enquiries takes place such that the person questioned is entitled to the protection of the provisions of the Code concerning interviews?

> The essence of the matter is whether fairness demands that in the circumstances of a particular case the provisions of the Code should be implemented; in other words, one does not construe the word 'interview' as one would in a statute. One looks at what is fair in the light of the provisions of the Code.

15.28   Farquharson LJ obviously takes a very pragmatic view of the question of when an appropriate adult's presence is required. This judgment was delivered before the 1995 edition of the Police and Evidence Act Codes inserted Code C para 11.1A, which clarified the definition of an 'interview'. Although it is probably still correct to say that a police officer may question a juvenile in the street in suspicious circumstances, as soon as the officer suspects the juvenile of a specific offence s/he should caution the juvenile and any further conversation constitutes an interview as defined by Code C para 11.1A.

18   Eg *R v Delroy Fogah* [1989] Crim LR 141, Snaresbrook Crown Court.
19   *R v Maguire (Jason)* (1990) 90 Cr App R 115, CA.
20   (1993) 97 Cr App R 227.

Denial of appropriate adult

15.29   The denial of the right to an appropriate adult might lead to a defendant failing to recognise the need for legal advice, which has a fundamental effect on the fairness of the proceedings.[21]

15.30   The denial of an appropriate adult by the police is relatively unusual. It is more likely that a false date of birth may be given by the person arrested and the police may not then realise that an appropriate adult is necessary.

Suitability of appropriate adult

15.31   This is dealt with in paras 7.100–7.122.

Code breaches

15.32   The courts' powers to exclude evidence under Police and Criminal Evidence Act 1984 s78 relate to the effect on the fairness of the proceedings of the admission of the evidence. Breaches of the Act or the Codes of Practice may have an adverse effect on the fairness of the proceedings and much will depend on the nature and extent of the breach. Whether a breach is significant and substantial will be a question of fact for the court. It is submitted that the age and maturity of a defendant may have an effect on the extent to which it can be said that a breach is significant and may prejudice the defendant.

Failure to mention facts relied on at the trial

15.33   Criminal Justice and Public Order Act 1994 s34 allows a court to draw such inferences as appear proper where at any time before an accused was charged with an offence s/he failed to mention a relevant fact relied on in his/her defence in those proceedings.

15.34   The fact must be one which, in the circumstances existing at the time, the accused could reasonably be expected to mention. When a very young accused failed to mention such facts, there are a number of factors which might be relevant in persuading the court that no inference should be drawn.

Did the accused understand the caution?

15.35   The caution is complicated. A survey carried out with 'A' Level students found that a significant proportion did not understand its meaning. The full implications of any caution given in the absence of a legal adviser may not have been understood by a child or young person, and this must be carefully checked with the young client when taking instructions in preparation for trial.

What facts did the child or young person have while being questioned?

15.36   Section 34 only permits the drawing of inferences where the fact was actually known to the suspect at the time of any questioning under caution.

---

21   *R v Aspinall* [1999] 2 Cr App R 115, a case relating to a mentally disordered defendant.

The actual knowledge of the particular child or young person must be carefully checked. The relevance of facts which might have been obvious to an adult may be less so to a child or young person.

Was it reasonable for the child or young person to have withheld facts?

15.37 Even where the child or young person is aware of the relevant facts, there may be good reason why s/he did not mention them. The test of whether it was reasonable to mention facts is subjective, and therefore the failure should be assessed in the light of the age of the accused. There has been a recognition that a restrictive approach to the range of relevant factors which relate to a defendant and their circumstances is not appropriate. Age, experience, mental capacity, health, tiredness and personality are part of the range of factors to be considered.[22] Circumstances which might carry no weight at the trial of an adult may be highly material in the trial of a child or young person. A young suspect might fail to mention relevant facts because of a fear of parental disapproval or of getting friends into trouble. There may be reasons specific to childhood, such as truanting from school or fear of bullies. The reason for failing to mention facts may be because of the young suspect's acceptance of advice from a lawyer, parent or other appropriate adult. In view of the age difference, the adult will inevitably exercise authority or great influence over the child or young person. It may, therefore, be argued that accepting advice from an adult in such circumstances would be reasonable. The issues arising in relation to accepting legal advice to remain silent are the same as with adults, as are the difficulties in relation to the waiving of privilege.

What was the condition of the accused?

15.38 Where a child or young person is suffering from a condition which justifies failure to mention relevant facts, this must be fully presented to the court. Such conditions may include a learning disability, drug abuse, medical or mental illness. All such conditions might provide adequate reasonable grounds to justify failure to mention facts later relied on at trial.

15.39 It may be necessary to adduce expert medical or psychiatric/psychological evidence or to call a teacher or social worker. If the child or young person has been assessed as requiring special educational needs, the defence lawyer may wish to obtain a copy of the statement as a first step in exploring this issue. The statement will include assessments by teachers, doctors, child therapists and educational psychologists. If no copy of the statement is available at home, a copy may be requested from the relevant education authority.[23]

What happened at the charging procedure?

15.40 Different rules apply to the failure to mention facts at the charging procedure. The court may draw such inferences as appear proper where, on being charged with the offence or officially informed that s/he might be

---

22 *R v Argent* [1997] 2 Cr App R 257, CA.
23 See appendix 3.

prosecuted for it, an accused failed to mention any fact relied on in his/her defence in those proceedings.[24]

15.41 Where an accused child or young person is charged without the benefit of legal advice, it may be argued that it would be unreasonable to expect the significance of this stage to be apparent to him/her. It should, however, be noted that this provision does not depend on the accused understanding the legal implications of silence; the section is based on the assumption that an innocent person (of whatever age) would normally be expected to volunteer facts which tend to show innocence. This assumption should be at its weakest in the case of a child or young person who may have many reasons, including fear of parental reaction, for remaining silent.

15.42 Where failure to mention facts at the charging stage is the result of legal advice, the defence advocate may argue that a child or young person could not be reasonably expected to reject such advice. The issues mentioned above concerning the difficulties of this argument in relation to adults, and in relation to waiver, apply. It is not clear if similar considerations apply if the suspect was advised to remain silent by a parent or other appropriate adult.

Failure to account for marks etc or presence at the scene

15.43 No inference may be drawn from a failure to account for articles, marks etc and presence at the scene of a crime unless a special warning has been given.[25] The rules regarding the contents of a special warning are complex and are frequently inadequately dealt with by interviewing officers. The defence lawyer should listen to a taped interview to check that the form of any special warning complies with the requirements of the Codes of Practice. The lawyer should also consider the form of words used by the officer and whether it is likely that the child or young person would have understood the actual warning given.

15.44 Failures to account for information under Criminal Justice and Public Order Act 1994 ss36 and 37 may form part of the prosecution case and inferences may be drawn, whatever the nature of the case. The prosecutor may, therefore, open the facts by mentioning these failures.

15.45 Sections 36 and 37 do not include any reasonableness criterion which may justify the failure by the accused to account for presence, objects etc. However, this does not prevent the defence advocate from putting forward circumstances which the court might accept as nullifying any need to draw an inference.

Defences

15.46 Detailed examination of the prosecution and defence evidence may involve consideration of issues relating to defences to be raised at trial. The relevance of age to defences in criminal law is considered in chapter 6.

---

24 Criminal Justice and Public Order Act 1994 s34(1)(b).
25 Police and Criminal Evidence Act 1984, Codes of Practice Code C para 10.11.

Preparing the young defendant for trial

15.47   The majority of defendants will rarely have previously spoken in such stressful circumstances as a trial. Those who regularly attend court can forget how intimidating the formal atmosphere, even in the youth court, can be. It is important to remember that even the basic procedure of the trial may not be familiar to the child or young person. The defence lawyer must:

- explain the trial procedure to the client;
- ensure that the client is aware of all of the prosecution evidence;
- take full instructions using any available opportunity;
- send a copy of the instructions to the client to confirm as correct or alter as necessary (if appropriate, consider literacy issues);
- consider whether the particular circumstances of the defendant require further assessment by a psychologist or psychiatrist;
- consider whether there is information already in existence which would assist, eg assessment of special educational needs;
- consider a visit to the courtroom prior to trial;[26]
- consider whether trial modifications would assist the defendant.

15.48   When explaining the way that the trial will be conducted it may be helpful to use examples from television programmes, such as The Bill, which young people may have seen. It will be necessary to point out the inaccuracy of some of the things that a defendant may have seen or heard about the trial process. It is important to emphasise that the proceedings may seem slow. The young person should be encouraged to ask questions about matters which they do not understand. Where the defendant is to give evidence, the importance of making sure that a question being asked of her/him in evidence has been understood and asking for a break if needed should be emphasised.

Modifications to the trial procedure

15.49   Concerns as to how to ensure a fair trial for children and young defendants and the importance of their ability to effectively participate in their trials have been fully considered in chapter 10. Modifications to the trial procedure may be necessary in the youth court[27] and the in Crown Court.[28]

15.50   The *Consolidated Criminal Practice Direction* Part IV.39 applies to the trial hearing in the Crown Court and is reproduced in full at table 13 in chapter 10.

15.51   The role of expert evidence in advising on the appropriate modifications for an individual client is discussed in paras 10.30–10.38.

15.52   In summary, the overriding principle of the Practice Direction is to ensure that:

---

26   *Consolidated Criminal Practice Direction* IV.39.6.
27   *R (on the application of TP) v West London Youth Court* [2005] EWHC 2583 (Admin).
28   See chapter 10.

- the trial process itself should not expose the young defendant to avoidable intimidation, humiliation or distress;
- all possible steps should be taken to assist the young defendant to understand and participate in the proceedings;
- regard is had to the welfare of the defendant as required by Children and Young Persons Act 1933 s44.[29]

15.53 Any steps taken to comply with the Part IV.39 of the *Consolidated Criminal Practice Direction* should be judged to take account of the age, maturity and development (intellectual and emotional) of the young defendant on trial and all the other circumstances of the case.[30]

15.54 Part IV.39 of the *Consolidated Criminal Practice Direction* states that the issue of any modifications to the trial process should be considered at the plea and directions hearing. These hearings have been replaced by plea and case management hearings. Before the matter is listed for trial the judge should:

- consider the question of severing the young defendant from any adult with whom he or she is jointly charged;
- make appropriate directions for modifying the trial procedure; and
- impose reporting restrictions.[31]

15.55 The court should ordinarily order the separate trial of a child or young person unless it is of the opinion that a joint trial:

- would be in the interests of justice; and
- would not be unduly prejudicial to the welfare of the young defendant.[32]

15.56 This aspect of the *Consolidated Criminal Practice Direction* places the obligation on the court to decide why a joint trial should take place. It may be that the Crown Court does not always consider this issue in the way envisaged in Part IV.39 of the Practice Direction and the legal representative at the plea and case management hearing will wish to bring its full contents to the attention of the judge.

Modifications

15.57 Depending on the circumstances of the case, some or all of the following modifications may be appropriate to the trial procedures and should be considered:

- the defendant should be able to sit in a place which permits easy informal communication with his/her legal representative;
- the defendant should be allowed to sit with members or his/her family;
- the trial should take place in a courtroom where all the participants are on the same or almost the same level;

---

29 *Consolidated Criminal Practice Direction* IV.39.2.
30 Ibid, IV.39.3.
31 Ibid, IV.39.4–IV.39.8.
32 Ibid, IV.39.4.

- the court should have frequent and regular breaks if the defendant is unable to concentrate for long periods of time;
- wigs and gowns to be removed unless the defendant wishes them to be worn or the court orders them for good reason;
- the court should explain the course of proceedings in terms the young defendant can understand;
- the trial should, so far as practicable, be conducted in language which the defendant can understand;
- any persons responsible for the security of the defendant who is in custody should not be in uniform;
- there should be no recognisable police presence in the courtroom save for good reason;
- there should be restrictions on the numbers of members of the public and press allowed to attend the trial proceedings.[33]

15.58   This list of suggested modifications is not exclusive. The court will consider any other proposed changes to usual procedure in the light of the overriding principle set out in para 15.52 above.

15.59   The defence lawyer may need to consider instructing a psychologist with an expertise in children and adolescents to advise on the necessary modifications.[34]

The trial hearing

Role of the parent or guardian

15.60   Where the defendant is under 16 years of age, a parent must attend unless the court dispenses with this requirement.[35] This may cause particular problems when the parent is also a witness in the proceedings. This must be considered in advance and arrangements need to be made for the other parent or another adult relative or friend to attend in addition to the witness/parent.

15.61   When a parent is present during the trial, s/he will normally sit beside the young defendant. The parent should be advised that any comments the child or young person makes to the parent should be communicated to the advocate so that an assessment may be made of its relevance and further instructions taken. With a defence lawyer present, the parent will not be expected to play any part in the trial itself (other than as a witness) and this should be adequately explained before the trial commences. In contrast, where the child or young person is not legally represented, the court must allow the parent or guardian to conduct the case on behalf of the defendant.[36]

---

33   *Consolidated Criminal Practice Direction* IV.39.9–IV.39.16.
34   See chapter 10.
35   Children and Young Persons Act 1933 s34A.
36   Criminal Procedure Rules 2005 r38.2.

Taking instructions during the trial

15.62 It may be necessary to take instructions as the trial proceeds, either because the prosecution failed to disclose evidence in advance or because new matters arise. Depending on the age of the defendant it may be necessary to request that the trial is stood down so that instructions may be taken in private and away from the pressure of the courtroom, or even to apply for an adjournment to another date. The court may be more indulgent of such delay in the case of a child or young person as long as it is in the interests of justice, but this is not an invariable approach. Some courts may need to be presented with strong reasons for such an application and the defence lawyer should always remind the court of its duty to consider the welfare of the child or young person.[37]

Fast tracking

15.63 The trial court must not know that the defendant is regarded by the court administration as a persistent young offender.[38] This would have the same effect as a trial court knowing that the defendant has previous convictions. The only exception would be where the prosecution had made a successful application to admit bad character evidence in the form of previous convictions.

Defendant giving evidence

15.64 The defendant who chooses to give evidence is a witness, however the position of the defendant differs from that of other witnesses in a number of ways.

Right to have genuine choice whether to give evidence

15.65 In a fair trial process, the defendant must have a genuine choice whether or not to give evidence in his/her own defence.[39] A young defendant may be vulnerable as a witness by reason of age, cognitive and emotional immaturity, mental disorder, a history of abuse or poor educational attainment. The defence lawyer needs, therefore, to consider what extra help the young defendant will need to achieve best evidence.

Defendant excluded from statutory special measures

15.66 Part II of the Youth Justice and Criminal Evidence Act 1999 creates statutory provision for special measures for eligible witnesses.[40] The defendant

---

37 Children and Young Persons Act 1933 s44.
38 See paras 2.104–2.106.
39 Per Eady J in *R (on the application of S) v Waltham Forest Youth Court* [2004] EWHC 715 (Admin); [2004] 2 Cr App R 335.
40 See paras 16.12–16.27.

is the only witness excluded from the scope of these provisions.[41] In *R v Camberwell Green Youth Court ex p D (a minor)*[42] it was unsuccessfully argued that excluding the defendant from the statutory scheme was a breach of Article 6 of the European Convention on Human Rights as it forced the defendants to present their cases under a substantial disadvantage vis-à-vis prosecution witnesses, thereby offending the principle of equality of arms.[43] Commenting on this argument Lord Roger stated:

> As a general rule ... a provision that is designed to allow truthful witnesses for both sides to give their evidence to the best of their ability cannot make a trial unfair, simply because there is no corresponding provision designed to allow a truthful defendant to give his evidence to the best of his ability. The facts that the defendant does not need to give evidence, and that he has a legal representative to assist him if he chooses to do so, have hitherto been regarded as adequate arguments against the need to make such provision for child defendants in England and Wales.[44]

15.67 Whilst agreeing that the exclusion of the defendant from the statutory scheme of special measures did not itself breach Article 6, Baroness Hale did acknowledge serious problems were still to be addressed:

> Mr Carter Stephenson was concerned that we should understand the realities of life in the Youth Court. The child defendants appearing there are often amongst the most disadvantaged and the least able to give a good account of themselves. They lack the support and guidance of responsible parents. They lack the support of the local social services authority. They lack basic educational and literacy skills. They lack emotional and social maturity. They often have the experience of violence or other abuse within the home. Increasing numbers are being committed for trial in the Crown Court where these disadvantages will be even more disabling.

> These are very real problems. But the answer to them cannot be to deprive the court of the best evidence available from other child witnesses merely because the 1999 Act scheme does not apply to the accused. That would be to have the worst of all possible worlds. Rather, the question is what, if anything, the court needs to do to ensure that the defendant is not at a substantial disadvantage compared with the prosecution and any other defendants (see *Delcourt v Belgium* (1970) 1 EHRR 355, para 28). That can only be judged on a case by case basis at trial and on appeal.[45]

What help is available to the defendant?

15.68 The court has wide and flexible inherent powers to ensure that the accused receives a fair trial, and this includes a fair opportunity of giving the best evidence s/he can.[46] In relation to the defendant, these common law powers

41 See Youth Justice and Criminal Evidence Act 1999 ss16(1) and 17(1).
42 [2005] UKHL 4.
43 See *Dombo Beheer BV v Netherlands* (1993) 18 EHRR 213.
44 [2005] UKHL 4 at [16]. The last sentence refers to the original arguments for excluding the defendant from the statutory scheme of the 1999 Act – see Home Office, *Speaking Up for Justice: Report of the Inter-departmental Working Group on the Treatment of vulnerable or Intimidated Witnesses in the Criminal Justice System* (1998).
45 Ibid, [56]–[57].
46 *R v SH* [2003] EWCA Crim 1208 and see also opinion of Baroness Hale in *R v Camberwell Green Youth Court ex p D (a minor)* [2005] UKHL 4.

survive the introduction of the statutory special measures regime by virtue of Youth Justice and Criminal Evidence Act 1999 s19(6).[47]

15.69   When considering whether to use those inherent powers, the court should:

- take such steps as are necessary to promote the defendant's ability to understand and participate in the proceedings;[48] and
- have regard to the defendant's welfare.[49]

15.70   In recent judgments the appellate courts have considered the possible use of the following help for a defendant testifying:

- screens;
- pre-recorded video of defendant's evidence in chief;
- evidence via closed circuit television link;
- use of a facilitator;
- refreshing memory of defendant;
- excluding the public from the courtroom.

Screens

15.71   The court has a common law power to order that a witness be shielded by the use of a screen during the giving of his/her evidence.[50] Although this power is generally thought of as a protection from the defendant, it has been described as part of the court's armoury in choosing how to regulate a criminal trial.[51] It is submitted that a vulnerable defendant could be allowed to testify behind a screen if that would help him/her to give his/her best evidence.

15.72   The presence of a screen might help a young defendant to give his/her best evidence by:

- removing the distractions of a large courtroom, thereby helping him/her to concentrate and focus on the questions;
- stopping the young defendant from being overawed by a large or crowded courtroom; or
- preventing the young defendant from being intimidated by the presence of the public, and in particular, the complainant and his/her family or supporters.

Pre-recorded video of defendant's evidence in chief

15.73   The Court of Appeal has ruled that it would not be permissible for the defendant's evidence in chief to be given by way of a pre-recorded video.[52]

---

47   *R v Camberwell Green Youth Court ex p D (a minor)* [2005] UKHL 4, per Lord Roger (at para 17) and per Baroness Hale (at para 63).

48   *T v United Kingdon, V v United Kingdom* (2000) 30 EHRR 121, 179 at para 86.

49   Children and Young Persons Act 1933 s44.

50   *R v DJX and others* (1990) 2 Cr App R 36, CA.

51   *R (on the application of S) v Waltham Forest Youth Court* [2004] EWHC 715 (Admin); [2004] 2 Cr App R 335.

52   *R v SH* [2003] EWCA 1208.

Evidence via closed circuit television link

15.74   In *R (on the application of S) v Waltham Forest Youth Court*[53] Eady J held that
there was no common law power to order that the defendant give his/her
evidence from outside the courtroom via a closed circuit television link on
the basis that parliament had sought since 1988 to provide exclusively for
the circumstances in which a link might be used in a criminal trial. In *R
v Camberwell Green Youth Court ex p D (a minor)*[54] Baroness Hale questioned obiter whether this argument could be correct as the Youth Justice
and Criminal Evidence Act 1999 (as evidenced by section 19(6)) does not
purport to make exclusive provision for any of the special measures that
it prescribes. Without reaching a final conclusion on this point, Baroness
Hale did state that the situations of defendants and other witnesses are so
different that it would only very rarely be necessary for a defendant to give
evidence by live link.[55]

Use of facilitator

15.75   In *R v SH*[56] the adult defendant had a significant learning disability which
meant that he had limited communication skills. To deal with this problem
Kay LJ suggested the following:

> We can see no reason at all why such a person in the exercise of the court's
> inherent powers should not, if the judge finds it necessary and appropriate, be
> allowed to act in a role equivalent to an interpreter when the defendant is in the
> witness box. Thus if either counsel or the judge are having difficulty in putting
> questions to the defendant, because he is failing to understand their choice of
> language, a person with understanding of his problems may be in a position
> where they can act as interpreter to make clear by putting into language which
> he will understand the nature of the question that he is being asked.

15.76   There would seem to be no reason why such help could not also be made
available to a young defendant who had significant communication
problems.

Refreshing a defendant's memory

15.77   Where an adult defendant had a poor memory which hampered his ability
to give evidence, Kay LJ in *R v SH*[57]offered the following guidance:

> The judge thought that this could be achieved by a very detailed defence state-
> ment could be drawn [sic] and that since he had power to say what use could
> then be made of that defence statement, he could himself cause it to be read to
> the jury so that they would have that material before them and be able to hear
> the defendant's evidence in the light of that coherent account of what he wanted
> to say.
>
> We can see no difficulty with that course. But we suggest as another possible
> course open to the judge, which he may want to consider, the following. Any
> witness is entitled to refer to a document with the leave of the court if it assists

them properly to give their evidence. Clearly courts are reluctant with prosecution witnesses to over extend that facility because it may be unfair to a defendant. But where the only way in which a defendant can properly deal with a matter is by reference to some coherent account he has given in the past, then it seems to us that if the judge thinks it necessary he can permit that course to take place. Of course, this appellant has the difficulty that he cannot read, but we can see no problems at all, if it is necessary, with the judge concluding that he can be asked leading questions that come from a document which he has already identified.

15.78   Again, there would seem to be no reason why such help could not also be provided to a young defendant whose problems with recall are as a result of cognitive immaturity.

Excluding public from the courtroom

15.79   There is a common law power to exclude the public from the courtroom while an intimidated witness is giving evidence, if it is strictly necessary to do so.[58] The use of this power to help an intimidated defendant while s/he gives evidence in the Crown Court has been implicitly accepted by Eady J in *R (on the application of S) v Waltham Forest Youth Court*.[59]

15.80   It should also be noted that Children and Young Persons Act 1933 s37(1) permits a court to direct that all or any persons, not being members of or officers of the court or parties to the case, their counsel or solicitors, or persons otherwise directly concerned in the case, be excluded from the court during the taking of the evidence of a child or young person called as a witness in any proceedings in relation to an offence against, or any conduct contrary to, decency or morality. There would seem to be no reason why this power could not be exercised when the young defendant is called to give evidence.

What help is available to prevent intimidation by a co-defendant?

15.81   In *R (on the application of S) v Waltham Forest Youth Court*[60] the 13-year-old applicant with a learning disability had been arrested on suspicion of robbery. In her police interview she made certain allegations against her co-defendants who were aged 14 to 16 years. An application was made for her to be permitted to testify at her trial from outside the courtroom by way of a closed circuit television link. It was said that the applicant wanted to testify in her own defence but was too scared to do so in the physical presence of her co-defendants. A district judge refused to grant the application, ruling that he had no power to make such an order. The ruling was the subject of a judicial review. Although the Administrative Court agreed that there was no power to permit the defendant to testify from outside the courtroom via a closed circuit television link, it was accepted by Eady J that in a case where the defendant's right to choose to give evidence is effectively undermined

58   *R v Richards* (1999) 163 JP 246, CA.
59   See *R (on the application of S) v Waltham Forest Youth Court* [2004] 2 Cr App R 335, [2004] EWHC 715 (Admin), [35]–[37] and *R v Camberwell Green Youth court ex p D (a minor)* [2005] UKHL 4.
60   [2004] 2 Cr App R 335; [2004] EWHC 715 (Admin).

by fear or threats, the court may wish to consider redressing the balance by some proportionate procedural step. The nature of those steps would depend on the facts of the case and would have to take into account the co-defendant's right to confront his/her accuser and the practical problem of formulating a suitable warning to a jury in a Crown Court trial regarding the use of a screen.[61]

Separate trials?

15.82   In *R (on the application of S) v Waltham Forest Youth Court*[62] the court considered whether the difficulties of the defendant could be resolved by the ordering of separate trials. In *R v Grondkowski*[63] Lord Goddard stated:

> Prima facie it appears to the court that where the essence of the case is that the prisoners were engaged on a common enterprise, it is obviously right and proper that they should be jointly indicted and jointly tried, and in some cases it would be as much in the interest of the accused as of the prosecution that they should be.

15.83   The court approved this view, stating that once a joint trial had commenced, the circumstances in which a separation would take place during the trial process would be exceptional. The court left the possibility of the ordering of a separate trial from the outset as a possibility if it was found to be just to do so.[64]

Failure to testify

15.84   Criminal Justice and Public Order Act 1994 s35 allows a court to draw such inferences as appear proper from the defendant's failure to give evidence or refusal to answer questions once in the witness box unless it appears to the court that the physical or mental condition of the accused makes it undesirable for him/her to give evidence. 'Physical or mental condition' is not defined further in the statute.

15.85   The court will require evidence to be adduced before accepting that it would be undesirable for the defendant to give evidence. It could not be proper for a defence advocate to give the jury reasons for his/her client's silence at trial in the absence of evidence to support such reasons.[65]

15.86   No inference may be drawn unless the court is satisfied at the conclusion of the prosecution case that the accused is aware that s/he can give evidence and that an adverse inference may be drawn if s/he does not.[66] The younger the accused, the more important it is this is observed and that the position is explained to the accused in non-technical language.

---

61   [2004] 2 Cr App R 335; [2004] EWHC 715 (Admin), [77]–[78].

62   [2004] EWHC 715 (Admin); [2004] 2 Cr App R 335.

63   [1946] KB 369, para 371.

64   *R (on the application of S) v Waltham Forest Youth Court* [2004] EWHC 715 (Admin); [2004] 2 Cr App R 335, para 79. See also *Consolidated Criminal Practice Direction*, IV.39.4.

65   *R v Cowan* [1996] 1 Cr App R 1, CA.

66   Criminal Justice and Public Order Act 1994 s35(2) and *Consolidated Criminal Practice Direction*, IV.44

15.87   In *R v Friend*[67] the Court of Appeal looked at the application of section 35 to a young defendant. The defendant was a 15-year-old boy who stood trial for murder. Shortly after his remand in custody he was given psychometric testing which indicated that his full scale IQ was 56. Later testing nearer the trial date found his IQ to be 63. In evidence it was suggested by the clinical psychologist that this higher reading was explicable by reference to the defendant's improved concentration. He was not found to be suggestible. At trial the defendant was estimated to have a mental age of between 9 and 10 years. At the trial hearing it was not suggested that the defendant was unfit to plead. Instead it was argued that his low mental age meant that he had a mental condition making it undesirable for him to give evidence. This argument was rejected by the trial judge and the defendant was convicted. The defendant appealed his conviction, arguing that the trial judge was wrong to allow the jury to draw an adverse inference from his failure to testify.

15.88   Applying a test of *Wednesbury* reasonableness, the Court of Appeal refused to interfere with the judge's decision. In giving judgment Otton LJ held:

(i)   It will only be in very rare cases that a judge will have to consider whether it is undesirable for an accused to give evidence on account of his/her mental condition. In the majority of cases there will be evidence that s/he is unfit to plead.

(ii)   A 'mental condition' might include latent schizophrenia where the experience of giving evidence might trigger a florid state.

(iii) The trial judge properly took into account the following:
       (a) it is not unusual to see witnesses of 8 years and above give evidence in the Crown Court;
       (b) it was significant that the defendant was not considered suggestible; and
       (c) a judge's role includes ensuring that all witnesses (including a defendant) are not put under undue pressure whilst testifying.

15.89   In the light of this judgment it will be all the more important that the court gives as much help as possible to a defendant who may have any difficulties testifying in his/her own defence.[68]

Proceeding in the absence of the defendant

15.90   A youth court or adult magistrates' court may proceed with a trial in the absence of the defendant.[69] The court must exercise its discretion to proceed in the absence of the defendant with the utmost care and caution, the overriding concern being to ensure that any such trial is as fair as circumstances permit and leads to a just outcome.[70] The circumstances in which it is appropriate to proceed in the absence of the defendant are less likely to arise in the Crown Court.

67 [1997] 2 Cr App R 231, CA.
68 See paras 15.68–15.83.
69 Magistrates' Courts Act 1980 s11(1).
70 *Consolidated Criminal Practice Direction*, I.13.18.

15.91   Before the court decides to proceed in absence, it should consider all the circumstances of the case. The circumstances to be taken into account include:

- the conduct of the defendant;
- the disadvantage to the defendant;
- public interest;
- the effect of any delay;
- whether the attendance of the defendant could be secured on another date;
- seriousness of the offence;
- the likely outcome if the defendant is found guilty; and
- in summary matters, the possibility of appeal by way of rehearing and the power to reopen proceedings under Magistrates' Courts Act 1980 s142.[71]

15.92   Where the defendant has been remanded into local authority accommodation the position may be different.[72] The defendant is not on bail and would not face a charge under Bail Act 1976 s6 when s/he next appeared in court.[73] Where the defendant is a young person, there is a comparatively low threshold of prejudice and fairness that needs to be shown to establish that a finding of guilt is unsafe, where a court has decided to proceed in absence.[74]

The role of the defence lawyer

15.93   Where a court decides to proceed with a trial in the absence of the defendant, the defence lawyer is placed in a difficult situation and has to decide whether to remain to challenge the prosecution evidence or to withdraw from the case. The decision may be affected by the extent to which instructions have been taken on the prosecution case prior to the hearing.

15.94   In *R v Jones*[75] Lord Bingham expressed the view that:

> ... it is generally desirable that a defendant be represented even if he has voluntarily absconded. The task of representing at trial a defendant who is not present, and who may well be out of touch, is of course rendered much more difficult and unsatisfactory, and there is no possible ground for criticising the legal representatives who withdrew from representing the appellant at trial in this case. But the presence throughout the trial of legal representatives, in receipt of instructions from the client at some earlier stage, and with no object other than to protect the interests of that client, does provide a valuable safeguard against the possibility of error and oversight. For this reason trial judges routinely ask counsel to continue to represent a defendant who has absconded during the trial, and counsel in practice accede to such an invitation and defend their absent client as best they properly can in the circumstances.

---

71 *Consolidated Criminal Practice Direction* I.13.19, see also *R v Jones* [2003] AC 1; [2002] UKHL 5.

72 *R v Dewsbury Magistrates' Court ex p K (a minor)* (1994) *Times* 16 March.

73 See para 13.195.

74 *R (on the application of R (a juvenile)) v Thames Youth Court* (2002) 166 JP 613. In this case the defendant was detained in a police station and the court proceeded with knowledge of the circumstances of the defendant's absence.

75 [2003] AC 1; [2002] UKHL 5, para 15.

15.95   Whilst it may assist the court if the defendant's lawyer remains during a trial which proceeds in the absence of the defendant, in practice the lawyer frequently withdraws from the trial. The Law Society and the Bar Council do not give definitive guidance on this issue and it will be for the advocate to decide how best to deliver his/her duties to the client.

The child or young person as witness

Introduction

16.1   This chapter has been included because trials of children and young people involve a disproportionate number of young witnesses, both for the prosecution and the defence, compared to the trials of adult defendants. The witness could be of the same or similar age as the defendant. The law may treat the witness as needing additional assistance in giving evidence. Good practice may require additional considerations relating to their age and level of maturity.

The Witness Service

16.2   The charitable organisation Victim Support runs the Witness Service in all criminal courts. The Witness Service is available to give information and support to witnesses, victims, their families and friends when they go to court. This service is equally available to defence witnesses.

16.3   Volunteers are able to assist witnesses with what to expect when they go into court and will usually be able to make witnesses familiar with any special measures or procedures, such as a live link.[1] Facilities are available to enable witnesses to wait to give their evidence away from the court waiting area. Where there are prosecution and defence witnesses waiting, difficulties can arise if there is no separate additional waiting area.

16.4   The Witness Service encourages defence practitioners to make use of their facilities.

16.5   Further assistance for witnesses may be found in 'The Young Witness Pack' which is designed to prepare young witnesses for court.[2] The pack includes a video which shows court proceedings in real courtrooms.

Competence and compellability

Competence

16.6   All persons, whatever their age, are competent to give evidence unless it appears to the court that the person is:

- unable to understand the questions put to him/her; and
- unable to answer them in a way that can be understood.[3]

16.7   The question of whether a witness is competent to give evidence can be raised by a party to the proceedings or by the court of its own motion. It is for the party calling the witness to satisfy the court, on the balance of probabilities, that the witness is competent. In determining this question, the court shall treat the witness as having the benefit of any special measures directions which the court has, or may intend to give. Any such proceedings in the Crown Court shall take place in the absence of the jury, and any

---

1   See paras 16.43–16.46.
2   Available from the National Society for the Prevention of Cruelty to Children or Childline. See appendix 14 for contact details.
3   Youth Justice and Criminal Evidence Act 1999 s53.

questioning of the witness shall be conducted by the court in the presence of the parties.[4] Expert evidence may be received. The competence of a witness may need to be reviewed once s/he has given evidence.[5]

16.8   A witness shall not give sworn evidence unless:

- s/he has attained the age of 14 years; and
- s/he has a sufficient appreciation of the solemnity of the occasion and of the particular responsibility to tell the truth which is involved in taking the oath.[6]

16.9   It is for the party seeking to have the witness sworn to satisfy the court, on the balance of probabilities that these conditions are satisfied. Unsworn evidence may be received by the court and no conviction is to be regarded as unsafe solely for that reason.[7] The provisions in relation to sworn evidence also apply to the defendant.[8]

Compellability

16.10   A competent witness may be compelled to attend court to testify. In the youth court this will be done by the issue of a summons or arrest warrant under Magistrates' Courts Act 1980 s97.[9] A magistrates' court will issue a witness summons against a child or young person once it has determined that the witness could give material evidence and that it is in the interests of justice to issue the summons. The duty to consider the welfare of a child or young person cannot be relevant at this stage. The welfare principle is, however, relevant at the moment when it is desired to call the child or young person.[10]

16.11   If a witness under the age of 18 attending or brought before the court refuses to give evidence, the court's powers are extremely limited. In the case of an adult, the witness may be fined or committed to custody.[11] Children and young persons are excluded from this power by virtue of Criminal Justice Act 1982 s1(1). They are similarly excluded from the power to commit to custody for contempt of court.[12]

Special measures for vulnerable witnesses

16.12   Youth Justice and Criminal Evidence Act 1999 Part II modifies orthodox trial arrangements in an attempt to reduce stress and assist eligible, vulnerable and intimidated witnesses to give more effective and reliable evidence in criminal proceedings. The purpose of the provisions is to improve the quality of the evidence received by the court.

---

4   Youth Justice and Criminal Evidence Act 1999 s54.
5   *R v Powell* [2006] EWCA Crim 03.
6   Youth Justice and Criminal Evidence Act 1999 s55(2).
7   Ibid, s56.
8   Criminal Justice Act 1982 s72(1).
9   Amended by Serious Organised Crime and Police Act 2005 s169.
10   *R v Highbury Corner Magistrates' Court ex p Deering* (1997) 161 JP 138; [1997] Crim LR 59, QBD.
11   Magistrates' Courts Act 1980 s97(4).
12   See paras 22.80–22.89.

16.13   The legislation specifically excludes the defendant from use of these measures:

> ... a witness in criminal proceedings (other than the accused) is eligible for assistance ...[13]

16.14   This has been held not to be a breach of the defendant's right to a fair trial.[14] The provisions apply in the Crown Court, adult magistrates' court and youth court.

16.15   In order to qualify for special measures, the witness must fall within a category prescribed by the Act. Witnesses may be eligible for the measures on grounds of:

- youth;
- incapacity; or
- because of the fear or distress they are likely to suffer when giving evidence.[15]

16.16   There are additional provisions relating to young witnesses in certain categories of cases – see para 16.22 below.

Age or incapacity – vulnerable witnesses

16.17   A witness is eligible for assistance if:

- the witness is under the age of 17 at the time of the hearing; or
- the court considers that the quality of the evidence given by the witness is likely to be diminished by reason that the witness:
  - (i)   suffers from mental disorder within the meaning of the Mental Health Act 1983; or
  - (ii) has a significant impairment of intelligent and social functioning; or
  - (iii) has a physical disability or is suffering from a physical disorder.[16]

16.18   'The time of the hearing' in relation to a witness's age is the time when it falls to the court to make a special measures determination.[17]

Intimidated witnesses

16.19   A witness is eligible for assistance if the court is satisfied that the quality of evidence given by the witness is likely to be diminished by reason of fear or distress on the part of the witness in connection with testifying in the proceedings. In determining whether a witness falls within these provisions, the court must take into account, in particular:

- the nature and alleged circumstances of the offence to which the proceedings relate;

---

13   Youth Justice and Criminal Evidence Act 1999 ss16(1) and 17(1). See paras 15.64–15.83.

14   *R v Camberwell Green Youth Court ex p D (a minor)* [2005] UKHL 4.

15   Youth Justice and Criminal Evidence Act 1999 s17.

16   Ibid, s16(1) and (2).

17   Ibid, s16(3).

- the age of the witness;
- such of the following as appear to the court to be relevant:
  (i) the social and cultural background and ethnic origins of the witness;
  (ii) the domestic and employment circumstances of the witness;
  (iii) any religious beliefs or political opinions of the witness;
- any behaviour towards the witness on the part of:
  (i) the accused;
  (ii) members of the family or associates of the accused; or
  (iii) any other person who is likely to be an accused or a witness in the proceedings.[18]

16.20 The court must also consider any views expressed by the witness.[19] In sexual offences, a complainant who is witness in the proceedings is eligible for assistance by way of special measures, without the need for any of the other provisions to apply, unless the witness has informed the court that s/he does not wish to have the protection of special measures.[20]

Special provisions relating to young witnesses

16.21 A witness who is under 17 years of age will fall into one of three categories:
  (i) a witness giving evidence in cases of sexual offences;
  (ii) a witness giving evidence in cases involving offences of violence, cruelty, abduction or neglect; or
  (iii) a witness giving evidence in all other cases.

16.22 Young witnesses in cases involving sexual offences or offences of violence, cruelty, abduction or neglect are defined as being 'in need of special protection' and benefit from strong presumptions about how they will give evidence.[21]

16.23 A witness is 'in need of special protection' if the offence (or any of the offences) to which the proceedings in which they are to give evidence relate is:

- an offence under the Protection of Children Act 1978 or under Sexual Offences Act 2003 Part 1; or
- an offence involving kidnapping, false imprisonment or under Child Abduction Act 1984 s1 or s2;
- an offence under Children and Young Persons Act 1933 s1;
- any other offence which involves an assault on, or injury or threat of injury to, any person.[22]

16.24 This means that child witnesses in any allegation of violence, including robbery and common assault, will be 'in need of special protection' and presumed to be entitled to the protection of appropriate special measures.

18 Youth Justice and Criminal Evidence Act 1999 s17(2).
19 Ibid, s17(3).
20 Ibid, s17(4).
21 Ibid, s21.
22 Ibid, s35(3).

Young witnesses – the primary rule

16.25   The 'primary rule' in the case of any child witness is that the court must give a special measures direction in relation to the witness, which:

- provides for any relevant video recording of the witness's evidence in chief to be admitted; and
- must provide for any evidence given by the witness in the proceedings which is not given by means of a video recording to be given by means of a live link.[23]

16.26   If the witness is 'in need of special protection' the court will presume that the witness is entitled to the protection of these special measures and is not required to consider whether the measures will improve the quality of the witness's evidence.[24]

16.27   In other cases, the rule does not apply to the extent that the court is satisfied that compliance would not be likely to maximise the quality of the evidence given by the witness.[25] In determining whether any special measure or measures would or would not be likely to improve or to maximise the quality of evidence given by a witness the court must consider all the circumstances of the case including, in particular:

- any views expressed by the witness; and
- whether the measure or measures might tend to inhibit such evidence being effectively tested by a party to the proceedings.[26]

Special measures directions

Application

16.28   Special measures directions apply equally to eligible prosecution and defence witnesses, including the alleged victim. Applications must be made in the prescribed form and within specified time limits.[27] In the youth court, the application must be received within 28 days of the date on which the defendant first appears before the court in connection with the offence.[28] In the magistrates' court the application must be received within 14 days of the defendant indicating his intention to plead not guilty to any charge brought against him and in relation to which a special measures direction may be sought.[29]

16.29   In the Crown Court the application must be received within 28 days of:

- committal to the Crown Court; or
- consent being given to a voluntary bill of indictment; or
- service of notice of transfer; or
- sending for trial; or[30]

23   Youth Justice and Criminal Evidence Act 1999 s21(3).
24   Ibid, s21(5).
25   Ibid, s21(4)(c).
26   Ibid, s19(3).
27   *Consolidated Criminal Practice Direction*, Annexe D and Criminal Procedure Rules 2005 Part 29.
28   Criminal Procedures Rules 2005 r29.1(4).
29   Ibid, r29.1(4).
30   Crime and Disorder Act 1998 s51.

- service of a notice of appeal from a decision of a youth court or an adult magistrates' court.[31]

16.30 The timing of these applications and the form in which they must be made is set out in the *Consolidated Criminal Practice Direction* and Part 29 of the Criminal Procedure Rules 2005.[32] The application may be made by a party to the proceedings or permission may be granted by the court of its own motion.

16.31 Whilst the rules contain strict time limits, the court has discretion to waive those time limits, on specific application, and to raise the issue of special measures of its own motion. The time limits are directory, not mandatory.[33]

Opposing the application

16.32 Where a party wishes to oppose the application, notification to the applicant and the court must be given in writing within 14 days of the date on which the application was served. Reasons for opposing the application must be given.[34] Where an application for a special measures direction is made in relation to a child witness 'in need of special protection' in relation to that witness giving evidence by means of a live link, the application cannot be opposed on the basis that the direction is not likely to maximise the quality of the witness's evidence.[35]

Hearing the application

16.33 Where an application is not opposed, the court may determine the application in favour of the applicant without a hearing.[36] Where notification has been given that an application is opposed, there must be a hearing of the application.[37] Where an application has been refused by the court the application may be renewed if there is a material change of circumstances since the court refused the application.

Time limits and the court's powers

16.34 The court has a discretion to waive the time limits, although provisions do allow for leave to be sought for late applications. The court also has the power to raise the issue of special measures of its own motion.[38] Where no application for a special measures direction has been made in relation to a child witness 'in need of special protection' who is to be called as a witness for either the prosecution or the defence, the court should raise the issue of special measures of its own motion. The defence lawyer may have to consider raising the issue on the date of trial when witnesses attend without prior notice.

31 Criminal Procedure Rules 2005 r29.1(4).
32 SI No 384.
33 *R v Brown* [2004] EWCA Crim 1401.
34 Criminal Procedure Rules 2005 r29.1(6).
35 Ibid, r29.1(7).
36 Ibid, r29.1(9) and Youth Justice and Criminal Evidence Act 1999 s20(6).
37 Criminal Procedure Rules 2005 r29.1(10).
38 Youth Justice and Criminal Evidence Act 1999 s19(1)(b).

16.35   Justices who have ruled on an application for special measures are not disqualified from hearing a subsequent trial.[39]

What factors should the court consider?

16.36   Where an application relates to the admission of video evidence or the giving of evidence by way of live link and the witness is a child witness 'in need of special protection', the court will start from the statutory presumption that there is nothing intrinsically unfair in the witness giving evidence in this way. There is very limited discretion in relation to the way in which such witnesses give their evidence.[40] In other cases, the question of the likelihood of improvement to the quality of evidence given by the witness by the provision of special measures must be considered. In deciding whether or not a measure or measures will be likely to improve or maximise the quality of the evidence, the court must consider all the circumstances including, in particular:

- any views expressed by the witness; and
- whether the measure or measures might tend to inhibit such evidence being effectively tested by a party to the proceedings.[41]

Does the court have any remaining discretion?

16.37   The court may discharge or vary a special measures direction if it appears to the court to be in the interest of justice to do so, and may do so either:

- on an application made by a party to the proceeding if there has been a material change of circumstances; or
- of its own motion.[42]

16.38   In *R v Camberwell Green Youth Court ex p D (a minor)*[43] the circumstances in which this discretion might be applied were considered in relation to child witnesses 'in need of special protection'. In her judgment Baroness Hale stated:

> ... it is unlikely to arise much, if at all, in relation [video recorded evidence and live link evidence] because both may be disapplied by the trial judge or magistrates in the interest of justice.[44]

16.39   The court suggested that such discretion might be limited to particular circumstances, eg where the machinery is not working properly, where the child is sliding down so as not to be seen by the camera, or where the child was positively anxious to give evidence in the courtroom and the court considered that it would be contrary to the interest of justice to require the

---

39   *KL (a juvenile) v DPP, LAK (a juvenile) v DPP* [2001] EWHC Admin 1112; (2002) 166 JP 369, QBD.

40   *R v Camberwell Green Youth Court ex p D (a minor)* [2005] UKHL 4.

41   Youth Justice and Criminal Evidence Act 1999 s19(3).

42   Ibid, s20(2).

43   [2005] UKHL 4.

44   *R v Camberwell Green Youth Court ex p D (a minor)*, para 33.

use of the live link.[45] However, the court made it clear that such departures from the primary rule were intended to be exceptional:

> ... the court must always start from the statutory presumption that there is nothing intrinsically unfair in children giving evidence in this way.[46]

16.40 It is important that child witnesses know, from an early stage, that they will not have to go into the courtroom.

Special measures available

Screens

16.41 A special measures direction may provide for the witness, while giving testimony or being sworn in court, to be prevented by means of a screen or other arrangement from seeing the accused. The screen or other arrangement must not prevent the witness from being able to see, and to be seen by:

- the judge or justices (or both) and the jury (if there is one);
- legal representatives acting in the proceedings; and
- any interpreter or other person appointed (in pursuance of a direction or otherwise) to assist the witness.[47]

16.42 Where two or more legal representatives are acting for a party to the proceedings, the witness needs to be able, at all material times, to see and be seen by at least one of them.[48]

Evidence by live link

16.43 A 'live link' means a live television link or other arrangement by which a witness, while not in the courtroom or other place where the proceedings are being held, is able to see and hear persons in the courtroom.[49] The witness is to be seen and heard by:

- the judge, or justices (or both) and the jury (if there is one);
- legal representatives acting in the proceedings; and
- any interpreter or other person appointed (in pursuance of a direction or otherwise) to assist the witness.[50]

16.44 Where a direction provides for the witness to give evidence by means of a live link, the witness may not give evidence in any other way without the permission of the court.[51] A live link is a closed circuit television link.

16.45 Unfortunately the list of persons who should be able to hear and see the live link in the courtroom does not include the defendant. This was discussed by Baroness Hale in her judgment in *R v Camberwell Green Youth Court ex p D (a minor)*[52] where she observed that this omission arose

---

45 *R v Camberwell Green Youth Court ex p D (a minor)*, para 35.
46 Ibid, para 46.
47 Youth Justice and Criminal Evidence Act 1999 s23.
48 Ibid, s23(3).
49 Ibid, s24.
50 Ibid, ss24(8) and s23(2)(a)–(c).
51 Ibid, s24.
52 [2005] UKHL 4, para 27.

as the list of persons who should be able to see the live link was taken from the list referring to the use of screens, the whole purpose of which is to prevent the witness seeing and being seen by the accused. She states at para 27:

> ... this is not an exclusive definition. If the accused is in the courtroom, the court would and normally should, in the exercise of its power to ensure a fair trial, arrange matters so that [the accused] can see the witness.

16.46   Difficulties can arise where witnesses giving evidence through the live link are commenting on exhibits such as photographs or plans. The witness may also make reference to evidence in relation to their own height or size which would not be fully visible to the judge, justices or jury.

16.46A   Where a special measures direction is made enabling a vulnerable, intimidated or child witness to give evidence by means of a live television link, the court should make a direction as to the identity of the person who will be in the live link room with the witness. This person is known as the witness supporter. The witness supporter should be completely independent of the witness and his or her family and have no previous knowledge of or personal involvement in the case. The supporter should also be suitably trained so as to understand the obligations of, and comply with, the National Standards relating to witness supporters. Providing these criteria are met, the witness supporter need not be an usher or court official. Thus, for example, the functions of the witness supporter may be performed by a representative of the Witness Service.[53]

Evidence given in private

16.47   A special measures direction may provide for the exclusion from the court, during the giving of the witness's evidence, of persons of any description specified in the direction.[54] The persons who may be so excluded do not include:

- the accused;
- the legal representatives acting in the proceedings; or
- any interpreter or other person appointed to assist the witness.[55]

16.48   Where the press are to be excluded, if there has been one person nominated to represent all the press, that person shall be allowed to attend the proceedings.[56]

16.49   A direction for the exclusion of persons from the courtroom may only be made where:

- the proceedings relate to a sexual offence; or
- it appears to the court that there are reasonable grounds for believing that any person other than the accused has sought or will seek to intimidate the witness in connection with testifying in the proceedings.[57]

---

53 *Consolidated Criminal Practice Direction* III.29.2.
54 Youth Justice and Criminal Evidence Act 1999 s25(1).
55 Ibid, s25(2).
56 Ibid, s25(3).
57 Ibid, s25(4).

16.50   A sexual offence is defined as any offence under Sexual Offences Act 2003 Part 1.[58]

Removal of wigs and gowns

16.51   In the Crown Court, a special measures direction may provide for the wearing of wigs and gowns to be dispensed with during the giving of the witness's evidence.[59]

Video recorded evidence in chief

16.52   A special measures direction may provide for a video recording of an interview of the witness to be admitted as evidence in chief of the witness.[60] The video recording, or part of it, may not be admitted if the court is of the opinion, having regard to all the circumstances of the case, that it is in the interests of justice the recording, or part of it, should not be admitted.[61]

16.53   This direction is available for children and vulnerable adults in the Crown Court and for child witnesses 'in need of special protection' in the magistrates' court (including the youth court).[62] The admissibility of video recorded evidence in chief is considered in paras 16.62–16.65.

Video recorded cross-examination and re-examination

16.54   These provisions are set out in Youth Justice and Criminal Evidence Act 1999 s28 and are not yet in force.

Examination of a witness through an intermediary

16.55   A special measures direction may provide for any examination of the witness (however and wherever conducted) to be conducted through an interpreter or other person approved by the court (an intermediary).[63] The function of an intermediary is to communicate:

- to the witness, questions put to the witness; and
- to any persons asking such questions, the answers given by the witness in reply to them and to explain such questions or answers so far as necessary to enable them to be understood by the witness or person in question.[64]

16.56   Any such examination must take place in the sight and hearing of at least the judge or justices and the legal representatives acting in the proceedings. The examination may be video recorded. Except in the case of video recorded examination, the jury (if there is one) must be able to see and hear the examination of the witness. Communication with the intermediary must be possible for those watching.[65]

---

58 Youth Justice and Criminal Evidence Act 1999 s62(1).
59 Ibid, s26. Modification of the trial in the Crown Court is discussed in chapters 10 and 15.
60 Ibid, s27(1).
61 Ibid, s27(2).
62 Currently piloted for intimated witnesses and witnesses in fear or distress at Wood Green and Sheffield Crown Courts.
63 Youth Justice and Criminal Evidence Act 1999 s29(1).
64 Ibid, s29(2).
65 Ibid, s29(3).

16.57   This provision is being piloted for child witnesses and vulnerable adult witnesses.[66]

Aids to communication

16.58   A special measures direction may provide for the witness, while giving evidence (whether by testimony in court or otherwise), to be provided with such devices as the court considers appropriate with a view to enabling questions or answers to be communicated to or by the witness despite any disability or other impairment which the witness has or suffers from.[67] This is only available for child witnesses and witnesses who are vulnerable adults.

Availability

16.59   The special measures provisions are available subject to the receipt of notification from the Home Office of their availability. The majority of the measures came into force on 24 July 2002, but use of an approved intermediary was only brought into force on 23 February 2004. The provisions relating to the use of an approved intermediary and communication aids are not available for witnesses eligible only by reason of fear or intimidation.

Status of evidence

16.60   A statement made by a witness in criminal proceedings in accordance with a special measures direction, other than by direct oral testimony, forms part of the witnesses' evidence in the proceedings and is therefore admissible evidence of any fact of which direct oral testimony would be admissible.[68]

16.61   In assessing the weight to be attached to such evidence the court must have regard to all the circumstances from which an inference can reasonably be drawn as to the accuracy of the statement or otherwise. At a trial on indictment the judge must give the jury such warning (if any) as the judge considers necessary to ensure that the fact that the special measures direction was given in relation to the witness does not prejudice the accused.[69]

Admission of video recorded evidence

16.62   A video recording of a witness's evidence in chief, or part of that recording, may not be admitted if the court is of the opinion that, having regard to all the circumstances of the case, in the interest of justice, the recording (or part of it) should not be admitted.[70] Unless the parties have agreed otherwise, any witness whose evidence in chief is to be given by way of video recording must be available for cross-examination (whether by live link or

---

66 The pilot areas are Merseyside, Thames Valley, West Midlands, Norfolk, South Wales and Devon and Cornwall. National implementation is planned for 2006/7.

67 Youth Justice and Criminal Evidence Act 1999 s30.

68 Ibid, s31.

69 Ibid, s32.

70 Ibid, s27(2).

otherwise).[71] Where it is proposed that a child witness 'in need of special protection' is to give his/her evidence in chief by way of video recording, this cannot be challenged on the grounds that the interests of justice will be better served by 'live' evidence unless there is some specific reason relating to the recording or the circumstances of the case.[72] The court may exclude part of the video recording in the interests of justice, but it must consider whether any prejudice to the accused resulting from the admission of that part is outweighed by the desirability of showing the whole of the recorded interview.[73] Where the recording contains inadmissible material but the evidence could not be understood without the whole of it being played, there should be a direction to ignore inadmissible material.[74]

16.63   Detailed guidance on the interviewing of child witnesses is found in *Achieving Best Evidence in Criminal Proceedings: Guidance for Vulnerable or Intimidated Witnesses, including Children,* (2001) Home Office and others[75] and the court will have regard to these provisions in considering whether to exclude all or part of any video evidence of a witness. Non-compliance with the Guidance does not make the interview inadmissible, unless it is not in the interest of justice to admit it. Delay in interviewing young witnesses may affect their ability to give reliable evidence.[76] The large Guidance document is essential to any defence practitioner.

16.64   It is unlikely that the resources are available for defence witnesses to be interviewed in this way, but where witnesses have been tendered to the defence by the Crown, any video recorded evidence obtained in relation to that witness may be adduced by the defence in a similar way.

16.65   In the Crown Court there is specific provision for the duties of the party adducing video evidence in relation to any edits to be made.[77] Any other provisions relating to the exclusion of evidence will also apply to video recorded evidence.[78]

Defence witnesses

16.66   The special measures provisions will apply equally to prosecution and defence witnesses. The defence lawyer may not have sufficient notice to make prior application for a special measures direction as young witnesses may attend for the first time on the day of trial. The notice provisions are discretionary and application may have to be made to the trial court. Where no application is made, the court may raise the issue of its own motion.

16.67   Lawyers also have to consider that not all witnesses wish to have special measures applied. Such witnesses need to be told of the court's power to raise the issue of special measures of its own motion. The role of the defence lawyer in relation to defence witnesses is discussed more fully in paras 15.14–15.20.

71   Youth Justice and Criminal Evidence Act s27(4)(a).

72   *R v Camberwell Green Youth Court ex p D (a minor)* [2005] UKHL 4.

73   Youth Justice and Criminal Evidence Act 1999 s27(3).

74   *R [CPS Harrow] v Brentford Youth Court* [2003] EWHC 2409 (Admin).

75   Available at www.cps.gov.uk/publications/prosecution.

76   *R v Powell* [2006] EWCA Crim 03.

77   *Consolidated Criminal Practice Direction*, para.IV.40.

78   Police and Criminal Evidence Act 1984 s78.

Sentencing: general principles

Purposes of sentencing

17.1   When dealing with offenders under the age of 18, the principal aim of sentencing is to prevent further offending by children and young persons.[1]

Sentencing Guidelines Council

17.2   The Council was established by Criminal Justice Act 2003 s167. The council may issue sentencing or allocation guidelines.[2] Where a court is sentencing an offender it must have regard to any definitive guidelines issued by the Council which are relevant to the offender's case.[3]

Determining offence seriousness

17.3   In considering the seriousness of any offence, the court must consider:
- the offender's culpability in committing the offence; and
- any harm which the offence caused, was intended to cause or might foreseeably have caused.[4]

Culpability

17.4   The Sentencing Guidelines Council has identified four levels of criminal culpability. These are where the offender:

(i)   has the intention to cause harm, with the highest culpability when an offence is planned. The worse the harm intended, the greater the seriousness;

(ii)   is reckless as to whether harm is caused –that is, where the offender appreciates at least some harm would be caused but proceeds giving no thought to the consequences even though the extent of the risk would be obvious to most people;

(iii) has knowledge of the specific risks entailed by his/her actions even though s/he does not intend to cause the harm that results;

(iv)   is guilty of negligence.[5]

---

1   Crime and Disorder Act 1998 s37(1). Where the offender has attained 18 before conviction, the sentencing court would instead have to have regard to the following purposes of sentencing: the punishment of offenders; the reduction of crime (including its reduction by deterrence); the reform and rehabilitation of offenders; the protection of the public; and the making of reparation by offenders to persons affected by their offences: Criminal Justice Act 2003 s142(1).

2   Criminal Justice Act 2003 s170.

3   Ibid, s172.

4   Ibid, s143(1).

5   Sentencing Guidelines Council, *Overarching Principles: Seriousness* (2004), paras 1.6 and 1.7.

Harm

17.5 Harm may have been caused to individual victims or the community at large. Individual victims may suffer physical injury, sexual violation, financial loss, damage to health or psychological distress.[6] In some cases no actual harm may have resulted and the court will be concerned with considering the likelihood of harm occurring and the gravity of harm that could have resulted.[7] Harm to the community may include economic loss, harm to public health or interference with the administration of justice.[8]

Aggravating and mitigating factors

17.6 When considering the circumstances of an offence, the court will identify any aggravating or mitigating factors. These may affect the offender's culpability or the degree of harm caused.

Aggravating factors

17.7 The Sentencing Guidelines Council has identified a number of aggravating factors applicable to more than one offence. These are listed in table 19 below.

Mitigating factors

17.8 The Sentencing Guidelines Council has identified some factors which may indicate that an offender's culpability is unusually low. These are:

- a greater degree of provocation than normally expected;
- mental illness or disability;
- youth, where it affects the responsibility of the individual defendant; and
- the fact that the offender played only a minor role in the offence.[9]

Relevance of previous convictions

17.9 In considering the seriousness of the current offence committed by an offender who has one or more previous convictions, the court must treat each previous conviction as an aggravating factor if the court considers that it can reasonably be so treated having regard, in particular, to:

- the nature of the offence to which the conviction relates and its relevance to the current offence; and
- the time that has elapsed since the conviction.[10]

---

6   SGC, *Overarching Principles: Seriousness* (2004) para 1.9.
7   Ibid, para 1.11.
8   Ibid, para 1.12.
9   Ibid, paras 1.24 and 1.25.
10 Criminal Justice Act 2003 s143(2).

Table 19: Aggravating factors

Factors indicating higher culpability:

- Offence committed whilst on bail for other offences
- Failure to respond to previous sentences
- Offence was racially or religiously aggravated
- Offence motivated by, or demonstrating, hostility to the victim based on his or her sexual orientation (or presumed sexual orientation)
- Offence motivated by, or demonstrating, hostility based on the victim's disability (or presumed disability)
- Previous conviction(s), particularly where a pattern of repeat offending is disclosed
- Planning of an offence
- An intention to commit more serious harm than actually resulted from the offence
- Offenders operating in groups or gangs
- 'Professional' offending
- Commission of the offence for financial gain (where this is not inherent in the offence itself)
- High level of profit from the offence
- An attempt to conceal or dispose of evidence
- Failure to respond to warnings or concerns expressed by others about the offender's behaviour
- Offence committed whilst on licence/supervision element of detention and training order
- Offence motivated by hostility towards a minority group, or a member or members of it
- Deliberate targeting of vulnerable victim(s)
- Commission of an offence while under the influence of alcohol or drugs
- Use of a weapon to frighten or injure victim
- Deliberate and gratuitous violence or damage to property, over and above what is needed to carry out the offence
- Abuse of power
- Abuse of a position of trust

Factors indicating a more than usually serious degree of harm:

- Multiple victims
- An especially serious physical or psychological effect on the victim, even if unintended
- A sustained assault or repeated assaults on the same victim
- Victim is particularly vulnerable
- Location of the offence (for example, in an isolated place)
- Offence is committed against those working in the public sector or providing a service to the public
- Presence of others, eg relatives, especially children or partner of the victim
- Additional degradation of the victim (eg taking photographs of a victim as part of a sexual offence)
- In property offences, high value (including sentimental value) of property to the victim, or substantial consequential loss (eg where the theft of equipment causes serious disruption to a victim's life or business)

Offence committed on bail

17.10 In considering the seriousness of any offence committed while the offender was on bail, the court must treat the fact that it was committed in those circumstances as an aggravating factor.[11]

Increase in sentences for racial or religious aggravation

17.11 If the offence was racially or religiously aggravated, the court:
- must treat that fact as an aggravating factor; and
- must state in open court that the offence was so aggravated.[12]

17.12 An offence is racially or religiously aggravated if:
- at the time of committing the offence, or immediately before or after doing so, the offender demonstrates towards the victim of the offence hostility based on the victim's membership (or presumed membership) of a racial or religious group; or
- the offence is motivated (wholly or partly) by hostility towards members of a racial or religious group based on their membership of that group.[13]

17.13 It is immaterial whether or not the offender's hostility is also based, to any extent, on any other factor.[14]

Increase in sentences for aggravation related to disability or sexual orientation

17.14 When considering the seriousness of the offence, the court shall treat as an aggravating factor the fact:

(a) that, at the time of committing the offence, or immediately before or after doing so, the offender demonstrated towards the victim of the offence hostility based on:
  (i) the sexual orientation (or presumed sexual orientation) of the victim; or
  (ii) a disability (or presumed disability) of the victim; or
(b) that the offence is motivated (wholly or partly):
  (i) by hostility towards persons who are of a particular sexual orientation; or
  (ii) by hostility towards persons who have a disability or a particular disability.

17.15 'Disability' is defined to include any physical or mental impairment.[15] When considering the offender's motivation for the offence, it is immaterial whether or not the offender's hostility is also based, to any extent, on any other factor.[16]

---

11 Criminal Justice Act 2003 s143(3).
12 Ibid, s145(2).
13 Ibid, s145(3) and Crime and Disorder Act 1998 s28(1).
14 Crime and Disorder Act 1998 s28(3).
15 Criminal Justice Act 2003 s146(5).
16 Ibid, s146(4).

17.16   Where the court considers that such an aggravating factor exists, it must states so in open court.[17]

Plea of guilty

17.17   In determining what sentence to pass on an offender who has pleaded guilty to an offence, Criminal Justice Act 2003 s144(1) requires a court to take into account:

- the stage in the proceedings for the offence at which the offender indicated his/her intention to plead guilty; and
- the circumstances in which this indication was given.

17.18   The Sentencing Guidelines Council has issued guidelines in relation to the application of section 144.[18] Wherever practicable, the guidelines are to be applied in the youth court. These guidelines are summarised below.

General principles

17.19   A reduction in sentence is appropriate because a guilty plea avoids the need for a trial, shortens the gap between charge and sentence, saves considerable cost and, in the case of an early guilty plea, saves victims and witnesses from the concern about having to give evidence.

17.20   The court should address the issue of remorse, together with any other mitigating features present, such as admissions to the police in interview, separately, when deciding on the most appropriate length of sentence before calculating the reduction for the guilty plea. The effect of any offences to be taken into consideration should be reflected in the sentence before the reduction for a guilty plea. The guilty plea reduction has no impact on ancillary orders.

17.21   The guilty plea reduction may have the effect of reducing the appropriate sentence across sentencing thresholds (for example, by reducing the sentence from a custodial sentence to a community sentence).

Determining the level of reduction

17.22   The level of reduction should be a proportion of the total sentence, with the proportion based upon the stage in the proceedings at which the guilty plea was entered. The level of the reduction will be gauged on a sliding scale from a maximum of *one-third* (where a guilty plea was entered at the first reasonable opportunity), reducing to a maximum of *one-quarter* (where a trial date has been set) and to a maximum of *one-tenth* (for a guilty plea entered at the door of the court or after the trial has begun).

17.23   The first reasonable opportunity for the offender to indicate his/her willingness to admit guilt will vary from case to case. It could be the first time that a defendant appears before the court and has the opportunity to plead guilty but, in certain circumstances, it could even be during a police interview. In either case, the court would have to be satisfied that the defendant, and any defence lawyer, had sufficient information about the allegations.

17   Criminal Justice Act 2003 s146(3)(b).
18   Sentencing Guidelines Council, *Reduction in Sentence for a Guilty Plea*.

17.24   If after pleading guilty, there is a *Newton* hearing (see paras 19.40 onwards) and the offender's version of the circumstances of the offence is rejected, this should be taken into account in determining the level of reduction.

Withholding a reduction

17.25   The guilty plea reduction should not be withheld because:

- the offender was caught red-handed; or
- the maximum penalty for the offence is thought to be too low.

Personal mitigation

17.26   The sentencing court may reduce an offender's sentence by taking into account any such matters as, in the opinion of the court, are relevant in mitigation of sentence.[19] By taking into account mitigation, the court may pass a community sentence even though it is of the opinion that the offence, or the combination of the offence and one or more offences associated with it, was so serious that a community sentence could not normally be justified for the offence.[20]

17.27   Relevant factors could include:

- the welfare of the child or young person;
- co-operation with the police;
- youth;
- previous good character;
- signs of reform or settling down;
- completed previous supervision;
- additional hardship caused by conviction;
- has kept all bail conditions;
- remand in custody has had impact;
- custody would damage family relationships, accommodation, education, training or job;
- ill health;
- having voluntary help for alcohol, drugs or gambling problems;
- unrelated worthy conduct.

Welfare of the child or young person

17.28   The welfare principle enshrined in Children and Young Persons Act 1933 s44(1) conflicts with the due process framework of the Criminal Justice Act 1991. The starting point must always be the seriousness of the offence and a more restrictive sentence should never be imposed merely because the court has welfare concerns regarding the child or young person. Rather than resorting to the coercive means of a criminal sentence, such concerns should be addressed by the social services department by treating the child as a child in need or, in more extreme cases, by proceedings before the family proceedings court.

19 Criminal Justice Act 2003 s166(2).
20 Ibid, s166(2).

17.29   The principle may also be relevant to the question of the appropriate-ness of a community sentence. For example, a community sentence which involves group work with other offenders could be detrimental to a young, criminally inexperienced offender.

17.30   The welfare principle is both a factor relevant to personal mitigation and a reason for giving greater weight to other mitigation arising out of the young offender's background and personal circumstances. The court should take it into account when considering the custody threshold as well as the length of any custodial sentence. The principle cannot override the need for a deterrent sentence if the seriousness of the offence and other circumstances require it.[21]

Co-operation with the police

17.31   This is normally considered as part of the mitigation when the defendant has either admitted the offence in circumstances where it would have been difficult and time consuming for the police to gather evidence or where the defendant has admitted other offences for which the police did not suspect him/her. In extreme examples where the defendant surrendered and con-fessed to an offence for which s/he was not suspected, the discount upon any sentence could exceed 50 per cent.[22]

Youth

17.32   The age of the offender will usually be a significant consideration in miti-gation. Its relevance has been summarised as follows:

> Age does play a part in the sentencing process in appropriate circumstances. That is generally so when the court deals with criminal behaviour by young people. A difference of two and a half years or five years at that stage of develop-ment in the life of a person can be quite considerable in respect of responsibility for wrongdoing and its consequences and appreciation of its seriousness.[23]

17.33   The following factors may lead a court to reduce the proposed sentence because of the offender's youth:

- Young people are generally more easily influenced by their peers than adults, therefore it is more likely that they will be lead into criminal activity.
- They also have less experience of life, therefore they may not appreci-ate the consequences of their actions in the way that a mature adult would do.
- Offending for many young people is a passing phase. To allow the young person an opportunity to grow out of his/her offending without acquir-ing a serious criminal record, sentencing disposals should be kept to a minimum and involve the minimum intervention in an offender's life, commensurate with the duty to protect the public.
- As young offenders do not have significant emotional resources, a cus-todial sentence will have a greater impact upon a young offender than

21   *R v Ford* (1976) 62 Cr App R 303; [1976] Crim LR 391, CA.
22   *R v Claydon* (1994) 15 Cr App R (S) 526, CA.
23   *R v Pritchard* (1989) 11 Cr App R (S) 421, CA per Watkins LJ.

upon a mature adult. The impact of even the shortest custodial sentence will be significant.

Additional hardship caused by conviction

17.34 When dealing with adult offenders, sentencers have been willing to mitigate any sentence if the offence has resulted in a loss of employment. This would be equally applicable to young offenders and should include a loss of a training place too. It could have a wider application. As a result of an offence committed at school the young offender may have been permanently excluded from school. Increasingly it is proving difficult to place excluded pupils back into mainstream schools, and as a consequence a young person may be left with limited tuition leading to few or no qualifications.

Has kept all bail conditions

17.35 Successful compliance with onerous bail conditions may demonstrate an ability to comply with a high tariff community penalty. Furthermore, it may establish that the young offender is not a risk to the public if sufficient supervision in the community is provided.

Remand in custody has had impact

17.36 It may be possible to demonstrate to the court that a young offender has changed substantially as a result of a remand in custody or into secure accommodation. It would also be important to make the court aware of any particular problems, such as bullying, suffered by the young person while on remand.

Damaging effect of custody

17.37 Imposing a custodial sentence upon a young offender may have a devastating effect upon the relationship with the offender's family and any dependants. It may also result in the loss of the offender's accommodation, education, training or employment.

Relationship with family

17.38 The younger the offender the more important family contact will be. Removal from a close-knit family to a custodial institution can only have a damaging effect upon the development of a child or young person.

Dependants

17.39 Adverse effects upon dependants should be brought to the court's attention. This could be the effect upon an offender's own children or a disabled or sick parent for whom the offender is caring.

Accommodation

17.40   Young offenders living independently stand to lose their accommodation if imprisoned. Some local authorities will allocate housing to care leavers as young as 16 or 17 years old. Imposing even the shortest custodial sentence puts that accommodation at risk. Rent arrears may accrue and in many inner city areas there will be the constant threat of squatters moving in.

Education, training or employment

17.41   Courts are under a statutory duty to consider the welfare of the child or young person and in particular to ensure suitable education and training. Any custodial sentence will inevitably disrupt an education course and result in the loss of a job or training course. As young people are at the start of their employment careers, such disruption will have even greater consequences. It may be useful to obtain reports from teachers, trainers or employers to confirm good progress and identify future prospects which will be jeopardised by a custodial sentence.

Ill health

17.42   The fact that the offender suffers from a serious illness may be relevant mitigation. However, there has been a reluctance to accept that ill health is sufficient reason for not imposing a custodial sentence. Nevertheless, it is accepted that an illness which will make serving a custodial sentence a severe hardship may be a reason to reduce a sentence below the custody threshold,[24] as would the fact that the offender suffered from an illness requiring specialist treatment unavailable in custody without which s/he could die.[25]

Having voluntary help for alcohol, drugs or gambling problems

17.43   The fact that offences were committed to feed an addiction is not mitigation.[26] A court may be inclined to look more favourably on an offender who has already demonstrated (by taking practical steps to that end) a genuine, self-motivated determination to address his/her addiction.[27]

Unrelated worthy conduct

17.44   Decisions of the Court of Appeal have given a sentencing discount for meritorious conduct while awaiting trial (for example, saving children from a fire[28]). This principle has been extended to cover the conduct of a young offender's parents. In *R v Catterall*[29] the father of a 19-year-old informed the police that his son was dealing in ecstasy. The Court of Appeal reduced the sentence passed by the trial judge making specific reference to the father's actions serving the public interest.

24   *R v Leatherbarrow* (1992) 13 Cr App R (S) 632, CA.
25   *R v Green* (1992) 13 Cr App R (S) 613, CA.
26   *R v Lawrence* (1988) 10 Cr App R (S) 463, CA.
27   *R v Howells* [1999] 1 All ER 50, CA.
28   *R v Reid* (1982) 4 Cr App R (S) 280, CA.
29   (1993) 14 Cr App R (S) 724, (1993) *Times* 29 March, CA.

Length of sentence

Concurrent or consecutive?

17.45   When passing sentence upon an offender convicted of more than one offence, the court must impose a separate sentence for each offence. Sentences may be ordered to run concurrently or consecutively to each other. In addition, they may be ordered to run concurrently or consecutively to existing sentences. On passing sentence the court must indicate whether a sentence is to run concurrently or consecutively. If it is not specified at the time, the sentence is presumed to run concurrently.

17.46   In general, offences arising out of the same criminal transaction will be dealt with by concurrent sentences. A consecutive sentence may be appropriate in the following circumstances:

- where the second offence was committed whilst on bail for the first;
- for an offence of violence against a police officer or member of the public in an attempt to resist arrest for another offence;
- where the offender carries a firearm to carry out another offence.

Totality of sentence

17.47   When cases of multiplicity of offences come before the court, the court must not content itself by doing the arithmetic and passing the sentence which the arithmetic produces. It must look at the totality of the criminal behaviour and ask itself what is the appropriate sentence for all the offences.[30]

This principle applies as much to financial orders and community sentences as it does to custodial sentences. It is of particular relevance to young offenders who have not previously served a custodial sentence.[31]

---

30 Per Lawton LJ, quoted in Thomas, *Principles of sentencing* (Heineman, 1979).
31 *R v Koyce* (1979) 1 Cr App R (S) 21, CA.

CHAPTER 18

Preparing for the sentencing hearing

Introduction

18.1   Preparing for the sentencing hearing of a child or young person can in many cases be considerably more complicated than in the case of an adult defendant. The youth of the client may mean that it is more difficult to obtain relevant information from him/her. The welfare principle will mean that a number of agencies may provide information to the court and be in a position to offer support to the young person to prevent further offending. As a consequence, the defence lawyer must be prepared both to work closely with the youth offending team and to lobby for resources to ensure that the best sentencing package is offered to the court.

Relevance of age

18.2   The chronological age of the young offender is important both as an obvious indication of immaturity and as a determinant of the sentencing powers available to the court. The age at the date of the offence will be relevant to the sentencing powers of the court (see para 19.6) and the age at the date of conviction will be relevant to which sentences are available to the court (see para 19.5). Accordingly, it is good practice when preparing for a sentencing hearing to note all of the following:

- age at the date of the offence;
- age at the date of conviction; and
- age at the date of sentence.

18.3   By noting all three ages as a matter of routine, the defence lawyer is unlikely to miss any significant mitigation or procedural issue related to the age of the young offender.

Relevance of developmental maturity

18.4   The defence lawyer should always take into account the stage of development reached by the young offender when preparing mitigation (see chapter 4). Developmental maturity is relevant to:

- the young offender's culpability;
- the expression of remorse;
- the assessment of risk; and
- the appropriate disposal.

Culpability

18.5   Psychological features of adolescence which may reduce a young offender's culpability include:

- poor reasoning and problem-solving skills;
- the tendency for sensation-seeking;
- increased impulsivity; and
- susceptibility to peer pressure.

18.6　These factors may be even more prominent where the young offender also has a learning disability or mental disorder which adversely affects cognitive functioning (such as hyperactivity or autistic spectrum disorders).

Remorse

18.7　In the criminal justice system, the expression of remorse is treated as a mitigating factor. Conversely, the failure to express remorse will have a negative impact on the sentencer. Moreover, an ability to express remorse will be relevant to the pre-sentence report writer's assessment of victim empathy. An absence of victim empathy is normally seen as a risk factor for further offending, as well as relevant to whether the offender presents a risk of serious harm to others.

18.8　When dealing with young offenders, it is important to consider that their developmental maturity may explain the absence of remorse. The psychologist Thomas Grisso explains:

> [T]he mere fact that a youth appears to lack concern or remorse for a past harmful behaviour is not necessarily a sign of narcissism, psychopathy, or an enduring, trait-like deficiency of empathy. Developmental psychologists have long identified egocentrism as a typical feature of adolescent development, during which youths have not yet developed a capacity to fully see the world as others see it. The capacity for empathy requires the development of the ability to think abstractly and hypothetically. These abilities usually are developed by early adolescence, but, but for many youths it is delayed. For the latter, their apparent lack of empathy is not necessarily an enduring condition, and it should be given less weight for long-range estimates of future harmful aggression.[1]

18.9　It should also be noted that young people who have a learning disability or an autistic spectrum disorder will have a significantly limited capacity for empathy even in middle to late adolescence.

Risk assessment

18.10　Risk assessment has become a major feature of sentencing, particularly with the introduction of sentences for public protection under the Criminal Justice Act 2003 (see paras 24.117 onwards). Making an assessment of the future risk of serious harm posed by an adolescent can be considerably more problematic than a similar assessment for an adult. In *The forensic evaluation of juveniles*[2] the psychologist Thomas Grisso explains:

- there has been little research into he accuracy of clinical predictors of violence in adolescents;
- because so many adolescents engage in delinquent behaviour, there are few 'predictors' that do a good job of distinguishing which youth will engage in further delinquent acts and which will not; and
- delinquent and violent behaviour usually desists after adolescence.[3]

1　T Grisso *Forensic evaluation of juveniles*, Professional Resource Press, 1998 pp142–143.

2　Ibid.

3　Ibid, pp128–132.

18.11   In relation to the last point, Grisso states:

> The fact that most violent adolescents do not continue their violence in adult-hood also suggests how we should begin our reasoning process when weighing various risk factors for future violence. Despite a youth's violent behaviour in the past, and even if we believe that the youth presents a substantial immediate risk, we should begin with the hypothesis that the youth will not represent a substantial long-range risk of violence (i.e. upon reaching adulthood). Then we should reach the opposite conclusion only when factors in the case have carried the burden of proving it to us.[4]

Suitability of community order or additional requirement

18.12   The developmental status of a young client is relevant to both to the type of community sentence to be passed and the nature of any additional require-ments. Community punishment may be appropriate for a developmentally mature 16-year-old but not for a developmentally immature 17-year-old. Equally, community orders with onerous requirements may be beyond the capabilities of a developmentally immature offender.

Allocation in the juvenile secure estate

18.13   The fact that a young client is developmentally immature is a factor which should be brought to the attention of the Youth Justice Board Clearing House (see allocation procedure at para 26.12).

Preparing mitigation

Obtaining background information

18.14   The defence lawyer should aim to collect information regarding the following:

- family circumstances;
- care history (if any);
- care plan (if relevant);
- education;
- training;
- employment/career plans;
- leisure activities;
- financial resources.

Sources of information

18.15   The first source of information will obviously be the young client. How-ever, obtaining background information about a young client can be con-siderably more difficult than in the case of an adult client. Many young defendants have troubled home lives or care histories. As a result, they may be unable or reluctant to discuss what may be painful memories. The

---

4   T Grisso *Forensic evaluation of juveniles*, Professional Resource Press, 1998, p132.

defence lawyer may, therefore, need to ask the young client for permission to talk to:

- parent(s) or other carers;
- youth offending team workers;
- social workers;
- teachers; and
- health care professionals.

18.16　Any information obtained from other sources will obviously have to be checked with the young client.

18.17　　It is not good practice to rely upon the author of the pre-sentence report to provide all the relevant background information for the court. The report writer may not have the time to produce a comprehensive report and, in any event, his/her focus may be on analysis of the offence and assessment of risk rather than personal information which could provide compelling mitigation.

Supervising officer

18.18　Where a child or young person has had recent contact with the youth offending team it may be useful to contact the team member who had contact with him/her. The information provided may avoid the need for a pre-sentence report. A good response in the past could also be good mitigation.

Social worker

18.19　A child or young person may have contact with a social worker because of support offered to the family or because the child or young person has been looked after by the local authority. In some cases the social services files will cover most of the young client's life.

18.20　　Where it is known that the young client has contact with a social worker, the defence lawyer would be well-advised to contact him/her. It would be useful to establish:

- the history of contact between the young client and the local authority;
- the number and types of placement (if any); and
- the current care or pathway plan.

18.21　In cases where the client has had a very troubled history in care, the defence lawyer may wish to gain access to the social services files on behalf of the client. Access to personal files is governed by the Data Protection Act 1998 (for which see appendix 3). Where the files are too bulky to copy, the defence lawyer should consider arranging to visit the social services office to read them. The travel to and attendance at the social services offices will need to be specifically justified on the file for the purposes of taxation of the bill.

Teacher

18.22　After parents or other carers, teachers are the adults who spend the most time with the majority of children and young persons. They may, therefore, be a useful source of information about a young client. Teachers will often be willing to provide a more personal assessment of a pupil than that contained in a pre-sentence report. Research has demonstrated that youth court magistrates do place great store on the views of teachers.[5] Contacting a teacher may also reveal that the young client has a statement of special educational needs.

Health care professional

18.23   Consideration should be given to contacting:

- the family GP, who may be able to confirm relevant health problems of the young offender or (with that person's consent) any physical or psychiatric problems of a parent or carer which may have adversely affected the young offender's upbringing; and
- any psychiatrist, psychologist or therapist who may have worked with the young offender in the past.

Character witnesses

18.24   It may also be fruitful to identify potential character witnesses from whom statements may be taken or letters of support obtained. Such statements may still be of considerable use even if the writer gives some negative information about the offender. As much as anything, their importance is in identifying good qualities and a chance of rehabilitation. Possible referees could include:

- a family friend;
- a foster parent or care worker;
- another parent/relative for whom the young person has done babysitting;
- a school teacher;
- a youth training supervisor;
- an employer (including Saturday/holiday/after-school jobs);
- a youth worker;
- a religious leader;
- a community leader; and
- a sports coach (eg amateur youth league etc).

Obtaining details of previous convictions

18.25   Where the young offender has significant previous convictions, the defence lawyer may need to obtain the relevant case papers from the firm's file archive or from another firm which dealt with the case. This will be of particular importance when the young offender is to be sentenced for a specified offence and s/he has previously been convicted of specified offences. Even though the statutory presumption of dangerousness does not apply to children or young persons with previous convictions for specified offences, they will still be highly relevant to the determination of the sentencer. Perusal of the prosecution witness statements, trial notes and

---

5   C Ball and J Connolly 'Requiring school attendance: a little used sentencing power' [1999] Crim LR 183.

any basis of plea may reveal useful details that would not be available to the court from the information supplied by the prosecution.

Obtaining an expert assessment

18.26　In serious or complex cases, the defence lawyer should consider whether the young client needs be assessed by a psychologist or psychiatrist prior to sentence. A report may be valuable, not just for the sentencing hearing but also to identify exceptional vulnerability when the young offender's allocation is being considered during a custodial sentence.[6]

Issues to address

18.27　A chartered psychologist could use psychometric testing to identify:

- a learning disability;
- the existence of relevant mental disorders (such as autistic spectrum or hyperactivity disorders); and
- personality traits relevant to the assessment of risk.

18.28　A child and adolescent psychiatrist may be able to give a clinical opinion on:

- the young offender's developmental maturity;
- the risk of self-harm in custody;
- the existence of relevant mental disorders (such as autistic spectrum or hyperactivity disorders);
- whether the young offender presents a risk of serious harm to others.

Public funding

18.29　The cost of a report by a chartered psychologist or child and adolescent psychiatrist may be claimed as a disbursement under the representation order. Prior authority for the report should be sought from the Criminal Defence Service. Only if the court has ordered the report and the purpose is to enable disposal under the Mental Health Act or a community rehabilitation order requiring medical treatment, will a prior authority be refused as the cost of the report would be payable out of central funds.[7] The application for prior authority will need to explain why ordering a report is reasonable and justified.[8]

Frequent offenders

18.30　When a lawyer represents a child or young person who has been arrested and charged with many offences, the greatest challenge can simply be to keep track of all the offences. Cases may be in different courts, some awaiting sentence, some awaiting trial. In addition, there may be outstanding cases at police stations.

6　For the allocation criteria see paras 26.12 and 26.17 onwards.
7　Criminal Defence Service, *Criminal Bills Assessment Manual* (April 2006) para 4.3.12 and CRIMLA 3.
8　Ibid.

18.31   Traditionally lawyers organise their caseload by reference to individual court cases rather than individual clients, and it may therefore be difficult to maintain a clear picture of the young client's cases. Yet the defence lawyer is likely to be the only person who is in a position to be aware of the full picture. Preparing a schedule of outstanding offences may help to provide a clearer picture of the cases. With fast-tracking of defendants deemed to be persistent young offenders, it may also help the defence lawyer to prepare a strategy to deal with all the cases expeditiously and most advantageously for the young client.

18.32   The defence lawyer will wish to make full use of the power to remit for sentence so that offences can be collected together for sentence. S/he may also wish to make representations to the prosecution that it is not in the public interest to continue with the prosecution of some offences, in the light of the likely penalty. Similar arguments could be used to persuade a prosecutor to agree to offences being taken into consideration at another court.

18.33   If a child or young person is given a custodial sentence and other offences are still outstanding, the defence lawyer should again consider writing to the prosecution suggesting discontinuance. Alternatively, some police forces may wish to speak to the young offender with a view to 'clearing up' outstanding offences. It has also been held that if the prosecution decides to proceed with offences known to be outstanding, the police should not wait until after the offender serves his/her sentence before charging him/her with the other offences. Instead, prompt steps should be taken to initiate proceedings.[9]

Serious offenders

18.34   In the case of a child or young person, the defence lawyer should rarely assume that a lengthy custodial sentence is inevitable, when a defendant is convicted of a very serious offence. By adopting a proactive role and preparing a well thought out alternative to custody, it may well be possible to persuade a youth court or Crown Court judge not to impose a lengthy custodial sentence.

On committal/sending for trial

18.35   In the case of grave crimes, the defence lawyer should ensure that the relevant youth offending team has activated the early warning system so that in the event of the child or young person receiving a sentence of section 91 detention,[10] there is the greatest chance of allocation to a local authority secure children's home or secure training centre.[11]

---

9 *R v Fairfield* (1987) 9 Cr App R (S) 49, CA.
10 See para 24.59.
11 See para 26.23.

Exploring the alternatives

18.36   The defence lawyer will need to be familiar with the various local projects and establishments available in the area. Whether a particular option is realistic in a particular case will depend to a large extent on local resources, the willingness of the local authority or health trust to pay and the reputation that a particular criminal justice project or establishment has in the eyes of local Crown Court judges.

18.37   Funding sources for projects working with young people are diverse and there will be many local projects not known to sentencers. The defence lawyer should be alert to this and ensure that the project has information literature or a representative at court to answer any questions the sentencer may have.

18.38   Possible alternatives to a custodial sentence include:

- high tariff community penalties;
- community orders with treatment for drug, alcohol or mental condition;
- community orders with residence requirements; and
- secure accommodation orders.

High tariff community penalties

18.39   These would include:

- a supervision order with specified activities;
- a supervision order with an intensive supervision and surveillance programme;
- a community rehabilitation order with a requirement to attend a community rehabilitation centre; and
- a community punishment and rehabilitation order.

18.40   In many youth offending team areas the intensive supervision and surveillance programme is provided by voluntary organisations which may not operate from the youth offending team office. Where the young offender is eligible for an intensive supervision and surveillance programme, the defence lawyer should ensure that the pre-sentence report writer refers the young person for assessment. As such programmes are a scarce resource, the defence lawyer may also have to present arguments to the youth offending team justifying the allocation of the programme to the young client.

18.41   It should also be borne in mind that a curfew order may be imposed in addition to a supervision order.[12]

Community orders with residence requirements

18.42   These could include:

- a supervision order with a requirement to reside in local authority accommodation;
- a supervision order with an intensive fostering requirement (pilot areas only); and
- a community rehabilitation order with a condition of residence (at a place other than the home address).

12   Powers of Criminal Courts (Sentencing) Act 2000 s64A.

Table 20:　Personal mitigation – a checklist

- **Family**
  - Composition
  - Principal carer(s) – current and previous
  - Parental occupation(s)
  - Achievements/criminal history of siblings
  - Problems in home life (eg domestic violence, parental drug dependency or mental illness)
  - History of social services intervention (eg placement on 'at risk' register)
- **History in care (if relevant)**
  - History of periods when looked after child
  - Reason for being looked after
  - Type and number of placements
  - Care plan/pathway plan
  - Relationship with current social worker
- **Health and developmental problems**
  - Physical conditions or disabilities
  - Any history of psychiatric problems
- **Schooling**
  - History
  - Truancy
  - Exclusions
  - Achievements (academic, sporting or extra-curricular) and examination prospects/results
  - Statement of special educational need (if any)
- **Training/employment**
  - Periods in training – YTS or Modern Apprenticeship
  - Vocational qualifications (eg NVQ or City and Guilds)
  - History of paid employment (if any)
  - Career plans
- **Leisure**
  - Use of leisure time
  - Involvement in organised youth activities (eg amateur sport leagues or youth clubs)
- **Financial resources**
- **Offending history**
  - Types of offences
  - Dates of offences
  - Disposals
  - Case papers relating to past convictions (particularly if dangerousness may be an issue)
  - History of contact with youth offending team (if any)
- **Consider character references**

Secure accommodation

18.43 If a local authority is willing to allocate the resources to pay for secure accommodation, a court could be asked to consider a supervision order with a condition of residence in local authority accommodation, in the expectation that the local authority would then apply to the family proceedings court for authority to detain the offender.[13] Such an arrangement would ensure that the offender is kept in a child care establishment whilst ensuring that the public is protected. As the authority to detain in secure accommodation is permissive only, the local authority would have discretion to remove the offender from secure accommodation when it is considered that the public are no longer at risk.

13 See chapter 14 for the law and procedure relating to secure accommodation applications.

CHAPTER 19

Sentencing: powers and procedure

The age of the offender

Determining the offender's age

19.1 Powers of Criminal Courts (Sentencing) Act 2000 s164(1) provides:

> For the purposes of any provision of this Act which requires the determination of the age of a person by the court or the Secretary of State, his age shall be deemed to be that which it appears to the court or (as the case may be) the Secretary of State to be after considering any available evidence.

19.2 This provision applies to all sentences which may be imposed upon children and young persons with the exception of sentences for dangerous offenders under sections 226 and 228 of the Criminal Justice Act 2003.

19.3 For the purposes of any sentencing provision contained in the Criminal Justice Act 2003, there is a similar rule contained in section 305(2) of the Act.

19.4 The application of section 164(1) may be illustrated by reference to two decisions of the Court of Appeal which had to interpret an identically worded provision contained in the Criminal Justice Act 1982 (now repealed). In *R v Brown*[1] a 20-year-old was sentenced to a term of imprisonment because the judge mistakenly believed him to be 21 years old. On appeal it was argued that the sentence had to be quashed because Criminal Justice Act 1982 s1(1) prohibited the passing of a sentence of imprisonment upon an offender under the age of 21. The argument was rejected by reference to section 1(6) of the Act, which required the sentencing court to determine the offender's age 'as that which appears to the court after considering any available evidence'. The court held that all the evidence before the judge on the day of sentence indicated that the offender was 21 years old. The sentence of imprisonment was consequently not invalidated. This decision may be contrasted with the case of *R v Harris*[2] where a sentence of imprisonment was later quashed because, although the judge believed that the offender had attained the age of 21, the police antecedent form gave his correct age of 20 years. Distinguishing the case of *Brown*, the court ruled that, as the sentencing judge had before him evidence showing the true age, section 1(6) could not be invoked to save the sentence.

Relevant age

19.5 For the purposes of sentence, the relevant age is the age on the date of conviction (ie the date that the defendant pleads guilty or is found guilty).[3] This rule is of importance where a particular sentence is not available until the offender has attained a minimum age.

---

1   (1989) 11 Cr App R (S) 263, CA.
2   (1990) 12 Cr App R (S) 318, CA.
3   *R v Danga* (1992) 13 Cr App R (S) 408, CA, confirmed in relation to detention and training orders by *R v Cassidy* (2000) *Times* 13 October, CA.

Age at date of offence

19.6 In *R v Ghafoor* [4] the Court of Appeal outlined the approach to be adopted where a defendant crosses a significant age threshold between the date of the commission of an offence and the date of conviction:

1 The starting point is the sentence that the defendant would have been likely to receive if he had been sentenced at the date of the commission of the offence – not the maximum sentence that could lawfully have been imposed.

2 Justice requires there to be good reason to pass a sentence higher than would have been passed at the date of the commission of the offence.

3 The starting point may be tempered in certain cases, eg cases where there has been a long interval between the date of the commission of the offence and the date of conviction.

4 A somewhat higher sentence than the starting point may be appropriate if circumstances have changed significantly, eg the offender has subsequently been revealed as a dangerous criminal, a fact which was not apparent at the time of the offence, or if the tariff for the offence has increased.

5 Where the date of conviction is only a few months after the date of the offence, it would rarely be appropriate to pass a longer sentence that that which could have been passed at the date of the offence.

19.7 In *Ghafoor* a 17-year-old was charged with riot (section 91 detention not available, as the maximum penalty in the case of a person who has attained the age of 21 is ten years' imprisonment). He was committed for trial at the Crown Court as he was jointly charged with adults. At the Crown Court he pleaded guilty and was eventually sentenced to 54 months' detention in a young offender institution. On appeal it was held that the proper sentence was 18 months' detention in a young offender institution, as the maximum sentence he could have faced at the time of the commission of the offence was a two-year detention and training order. Bearing in mind the duty to give a discount for a guilty plea, the likely sentence that he would have received at the time of the commission of the offence was no more than 18 months, therefore that was the appropriate sentence.

Youth court

Available sentences

19.8 The youth court has an extensive range of sentencing options available to it. It can impose the following sentences:

- absolute and conditional discharges;
- fine;
- reparation order;
- referral order;
- attendance centre order;

---

4 [2002] EWCA Crim 57; [2003] 1 Cr App R (S) 84; [2002] Crim LR 739.

- curfew order;
- exclusion order (*pilot areas only*);
- action plan order;
- supervision order;
- community rehabilitation order;
- community punishment order;
- community punishment and rehabilitation order;
- drug treatment and testing order; and
- detention and training order.

Committal for sentence

19.9   The general power to commit indictable offences for sentence at the Crown Court was abolished by the Crime and Disorder Act 1998.

19.10   With implementation of the dangerous offender provisions of the Criminal Justice Act 2003, a new section 3C of the Powers of Criminal Courts (Sentencing) Act 2000 now allows committal for sentence in relation to specified offences committed on or after 4 April 2005 if the youth court considers that the criteria for the imposition of a sentence under sections 226(3) or 228(2) would be met (see also para 24.128).

19.11   When section 41 of and Schedule 3 to the Criminal Justice Act 2003 are implemented, there will also be a power, in relation to grave crimes only, to commit for sentence but only if the offender indicated a plea before venue.[5]

Remittal for sentence

19.12   Where any offender aged under 18 is convicted of an offence, the youth court may remit the case for sentence to the youth court acting for the place where the offender habitually resides.[6]

19.13   The remitting court may remand the offender on bail or in custody.[7] It must send to the local court a certificate setting out the nature of the offence and stating:

- that the offender has been convicted of the offence; and
- that the case has been remitted for the purpose of being sentenced.[8]

19.14   The local court dealing with the offender may deal with him/her in any way in which it might have dealt with him/her if the offender had been tried and convicted by that court.[9]

Discretion to remit

19.15   A youth court may have a good reason for not exercising its power under this section – for example, if the defendant can be sentenced immediately or it is considered desirable to sentence co-defendants from different areas

---

5   See appendix 13.
6   Powers of Criminal Courts (Sentencing) Act 2000 s8(1) and (2).
7   Ibid, s8(4)(a).
8   Ibid, s8(4)(b).
9   Ibid, s8(3).

Table 21: Sentencing options by age

Sentence	Age 10	11	12	13	14	15	16	17	18–20
	Child				*Young Person*				*Young Offender*
Discharges	✓	✓	✓	✓	✓	✓	✓	✓	✓
Fine	✓	✓	✓	✓	✓	✓	✓	✓	✓
Fine or one day									✓
Compensation	✓	✓	✓	✓	✓	✓	✓	✓	✓
Referral order	✓	✓	✓	✓	✓	✓	✓	✓	
Reparation order	✓	✓	✓	✓	✓	✓	✓	✓	
Exclusion order	✓	✓	✓	✓	✓	✓	✓	✓	✓
Curfew order	✓	✓	✓	✓	✓	✓	✓	✓	✓
Action plan order	✓	✓	✓	✓	✓	✓	✓	✓	
Supervision order	✓	✓	✓	✓	✓	✓	✓	✓	
Attendance centre order	✓	✓	✓	✓	✓	✓	✓	✓	✓
Community rehabilitation order							✓	✓	✓
Community punishment order							✓	✓	✓
Community punishment & rehabilitation order							✓	✓	✓
Drug treatment & testing order							✓	✓	✓
Detention and training order*			✓	✓	✓	✓	✓	✓	
S91 detention**	✓	✓	✓	✓	✓	✓	✓	✓	
Extended sentence**	✓	✓	✓	✓	✓	✓	✓	✓	✓
Detention for public protection**	✓	✓	✓	✓	✓	✓	✓	✓	✓
Detention for life	✓	✓	✓	✓	✓	✓	✓	✓	✓
S90 detention (HMP)***	✓	✓	✓	✓	✓	✓	✓	✓	✓
Custody for life									✓
Hospital order	✓	✓	✓	✓	✓	✓	✓	✓	✓
Guardianship order							✓	✓	✓
Restriction order****	✓	✓	✓	✓	✓	✓	✓	✓	✓

*   Only available for those aged 12, 13 or 14 where deemed to be a persistent offender.

**   Only available in Crown Court.

***   Only available in Crown Court. Offence must have been committed whilst under the age of 18.

**** Applies only in Crown Court. No power to commit until the age of 14.

together to avoid disparity of sentence. However, in the absence of such reasons it is desirable for the case to be remitted. The young defendant (and parent or guardian) will then not have to travel so far to court and s/he will appear before a youth court where workers from the local youth offending team are available to identify any outstanding welfare concerns.

Where the offender habitually resides

19.16   Courts will normally interpret this to be the local justice area where the young offender is currently living at the time of the conviction. However, it is fairly common that offenders accommodated by a local authority are actually residing outside the area of that authority. In such circumstances, it is suggested that the court consider remitting to the local justice area served by the local authority accommodating the young offender. The use of 'habitually' does seem to allow a more practical interpretation of this power.

Right of appeal

19.17   There is no right of appeal against the decision to remit, but the offender retains the right to appeal against the conviction.[10] In addition, s/he may appeal against any decision of the court to which the case is remitted as if s/he had been found guilty by that court.[11] In practice this will mean that any appeal against conviction will have to wait until the offender is sentenced by the second court. A notice of appeal would then be lodged with the clerk to the court receiving the remittal.

Remittal for sentence to the adult magistrates' court

19.18   Where a person who appears or is brought before a youth court charged with an offence subsequently attains the age of 18, the youth court may, at any time after conviction and before sentence, remit him/her for sentence in an adult magistrates' court acting for the same local justice area as the youth court.[12] Although not expressly excluded by statute, it makes no sense to remit indictable-only offences to the adult court as the magistrates' court has no power to sentence an offender for such an offence.[13] The remitting youth court may remand the offender on bail or in custody.[14]

19.19   There is no right of appeal against the decision to remit, but the offender may appeal against an order made in respect of the offence by the court to which s/he is remitted.[15]

19.20   The adult magistrates' court to which the offender is remitted may deal with the case in any way in which it would have power to deal with it if all proceedings relating to the offence which took place before the youth court took place before it.[16]

---

10   Powers of Criminal Courts (Sentencing) Act 2000 s8(5).
11   Ibid.
12   Ibid, s9(1).
13   *R (Denny) v Acton Youth Court* [2004] EWHC 948 (Admin) per Maurice Kay LJ at [9].
14   Powers of Criminal Courts (Sentencing) Act 2000 s9(2)(a).
15   Ibid, s9(3).
16   Ibid, s9(2)(b).

19.21   Remitting to the adult court will not result in any greater powers of sentence, and for that reason the power is rarely exercised. It may, however, be useful where the offender already has outstanding cases in the adult magistrates' court due for sentence.

Adult magistrates' court

Available sentences

19.22   In practice, when dealing with a child or young person an adult magistrates' court is limited to the following disposals:

- absolute discharge;
- conditional discharge;
- fine;
- parental bindover;
- referral order; and
- any other order the court has the power to make when absolutely or conditionally discharging an offender.

Remittal for sentence

19.23   Where a magistrates' court finds a child or young person guilty of an offence, it must remit the case to a youth court for sentence, unless it is of the opinion that the case is one which can properly be dealt with by one of the above orders.[17] If remittal for sentence is to take place, there seems to be no reason why the magistrates' court cannot order a pre-sentence report to be prepared for the next hearing in the youth court. This has the advantage of reducing the number of future hearings and consequently avoiding unnecessary delays.

To which youth court?

19.24   The adult magistrates' court may remit the young offender to a youth court acting for:

- the same local justice area as the adult court; or
- the local justice area where the offender habitually resides.[18]

Right of appeal

19.25   There is no right of appeal against the decision to remit, but the offender retains the right to appeal against the conviction.[19] In addition, s/he may appeal against any decision of the court to which the case is remitted as if s/he had been found guilty by that court.[20] In practice this will mean that any appeal against conviction will have to wait until the offender is sentenced by the second court. A notice of appeal would then be lodged with the clerk to the court receiving the remittal.

17 Powers of Criminal Courts (Sentencing) Act 2000 s8(2), (6)–(8).
18 Ibid, s8(2)(b).
19 Ibid, s8(5).
20 Ibid.

Crown Court

Available sentences

19.26   The Crown Court has all the powers available to the youth court (except the making of a referral order) and in addition it has available the following custodial sentences:

- detention under Powers of Criminal Courts (Sentencing) Act 2000 s91, 'section 91 detention';
- extended sentence of detention;
- detention for public protection;
- detention for life; and
- detention during Her Majesty' pleasure.

Remittal for sentence

19.27   Having convicted a child or young person, a Crown Court should remit him/her for sentence to a youth court, unless the judge is satisfied that it would be undesirable to do so.[21] Remittal may only be to the youth court acting for the local justice area where the offender was committed or sent for trial.[22]

19.28   Guidance on the exercise of this discretion was provided in *R v Lewis*[23] where Lord Lane CJ stated:

> Possible reasons that it would be undesirable to [remit to the youth court] are as follows – these of course are by no means comprehensive: that the judge who presided over the trial will be better informed as to the facts and circumstances; that there is, in the sad and frequent experience of this Court, a risk of unacceptable disparity if co-defendants are to be sentenced in different courts on different occasions; thirdly, that as a result of the remission there will be delay, duplication of proceedings and fruitless expense; and finally the provisions for appeal which are, as to conviction in the Crown Court an appeal to the Court of Appeal (Criminal Division) and as to orders made in the [youth court] an appeal to the Crown Court.

> However, it may become desirable to remit the case where a report has to be obtained and the Judge will be unable to sit when the report becomes available ...

19.29   Some commentators have taken the decision in *R v Lewis* as authority to say that a Crown Court should never remit a child or young person to a youth court for sentence. However, the last sentence of the quotation above demonstrates that Lord Lane did contemplate circumstances when it would be appropriate to remit the young offender for sentence. As the formality of the procedure and language usually makes the Crown Court unsuited to young offenders, it is submitted that the court should always consider carefully whether grounds such as those identified by Lord Lane exist in the case to make it unreasonable to remit.

---

21   Powers of Criminal Courts (Sentencing) Act 2000 s8(2).
22   Ibid, s8(2)(a).
23   (1984) 79 Cr App R 94; (1984) 6 Cr App R (S) 44; (1984) 148 JP 329, CA.

19.30   In the case of grave crimes where the use of section 91 detention remains a real possibility, remittal to the youth court will clearly not be an option. In other cases, however, there may well be persuasive reasons why a remittal should be considered. When all defendants plead guilty, relevant considerations may include the following:

- the judge will not have any special knowledge of the case;
- an adjournment for the preparation of pre-sentence reports may be necessary in any event;
- disparity of sentence is almost inevitable when sentencing a child or young person at the same time as an adult;
- in the case of an offender with no previous convictions, a referral order is only available in the youth court;
- the youth court will have special knowledge of the availability and nature of special programmes and activities designed for young offenders;
- the extra expense of a remittal may be balanced against the saving of a cheaper hearing in the youth court without the need for representation by both a barrister and solicitor; and
- with a plea of guilty, there is no duplication of appeal rights.

19.31   A further factor in favour of remittal is that the defendant may have other offences (possibly more serious ones) for sentence before a youth court. Remittal would allow all these offences to be dealt with together, since there is no power to commit these matters to the Crown Court for sentence.

Statutory time limits

19.32   Prosecution of Offenders Act 1985 s22A allows the Home Secretary to specify a time limit to run between conviction and sentence. This provision was piloted from November 1999 to April 2003. The provision is no longer in force in pilot areas and at the time of writing there is no plan to implement the provision nationally.

Sentencing procedure

Disparity of sentence

19.33   When a court has before it more than one defendant, it will normally be desirable to ensure that all co-defendants are sentenced together to avoid the risk of disparity of sentence and the consequent possibility of appeal.[24] For example, when one defendant pleads guilty while others plead not guilty, sentencing should normally be adjourned until after the conclusion of the trial. It is submitted, however, that this principle is less persuasive in the youth court where sentencing is much more defendant-oriented and welfare concerns may favour prompt disposal of the case for the defendant pleading guilty or remittal to a local youth court.

---

24 *R v Weekes* (1980) 2 Cr App R (S) 377, CA.

Adjourning cases for sentence

19.34   By Magistrates' Courts Act 1980 s10(3A) a youth court shall not be required to adjourn any proceedings for an offence by reason only of the fact:

- that the court commits the accused for trial for another offence; or
- that the accused is charged with another offence.

Accused committed for trial for another offence

19.35   Where a defendant comes before the youth court for a number of unrelated offences, it is possible for the court to commit the offender for trial in relation to the grave crime, thereby leaving other matters in the youth court. The youth court will then need to decide whether to proceed to sentence on the remaining matters. The court needs to balance the desirability of disposing with cases promptly against the risk of practical problems arising for the sentencing judge at the Crown Court. Problems are most likely to arise at the Crown Court where the youth court imposes a custodial sentence for offences which post-date the grave crime committed for trial.[25]

Sentencing offences together

19.36   Some young offenders may have a large number of outstanding cases before the courts at any one time. In *R v Bennett*[26] the Court of Appeal gave some guidance applicable to such situations. If a defence lawyer is aware that a client has other outstanding cases awaiting sentence, s/he should do everything possible to ensure that all outstanding offences are dealt with in the same court, by the same sentencer and on the same occasion. Such an approach both saves public money and avoids the unsatisfactory result that a community penalty is quickly followed by a custodial sentence for other outstanding offences. This guidance cannot, of course, override the defence lawyer's duty of confidentiality owed to the client and there will be occasions when it is not in the interests of the defendant to have all outstanding cases brought together for sentence.

19.37   In the youth court, the guidance in *R v Bennett* must now be read in the light of section 10(3A). It should be noted that a youth court is not prohibited from adjourning to link up cases. The effect of section 10(3A) is simply to emphasise that there is no presumption that an adjournment should take place to join up proceedings. It is submitted, however, that there will be many occasions when an adjournment would be the most sensible option to allow matters to be linked together. In many instances, such a course of action will not involve significant delay.

---

25   These practical problems may be seen in *R v Abdul Khan* (1994) 158 JP 760, CA, but note that the guidance to youth courts given by Smith J has now been reversed by section 10(3A).

26   *R v Bennett* (1980) 2 Cr App R (S) 96, CA.

Establishing the factual basis

After a trial

19.38 When a child or young person has been found guilty after a trial the case will often be adjourned for a remittal to another court or the preparation of a pre-sentence report. S/he will then come before a different bench to the one which heard the evidence at trial. The court will sentence on the basis of the facts as set out by the prosecution, unless the trial bench indicated that certain elements of the allegation were not proved.

On a guilty plea

19.39 Upon a guilty plea it is the duty of the prosecution to give the court a summary of the offence which reveals not only any aggravating features but also any mitigating ones. The prosecutor should warn the defence lawyer if details of any aggravating features are to be given to the bench when it is anticipated that those features will be disputed. If a plea is to be tendered on facts different from those of the prosecution, it is the duty of the defence lawyer to notify the prosecutor prior to the hearing. In practice, the defence version will often be accepted as the basis for sentence.

Resolving factual disputes

19.40 When the prosecution will not accept the factual basis of the plea, the court may resolve the issue based on the information before it. Lord Lane CJ considered the options in the case of *R v Newton*.[27] Faced with a factual dispute, the court had the following options:

(i)   to have a trial on the issue (for example, when the dispute is whether an assault was with the necessary intent for a charge under Offences Against the Person Act 1861 s18);
(ii) to hear submissions from both the prosecution and the defence;
(iii) for the sentencer to hear evidence and determine the factual dispute (a '*Newton* hearing').

Hearing submissions

19.41 If there is a substantial conflict between the two versions of events, the court should accept the defendant's version of events as much as possible, otherwise a *Newton* hearing should be held.

Newton hearing

19.42 Such a hearing will only be held if the difference on facts makes a material difference to the sentence.[28] Ultimately the decision whether to hold a *Newton* hearing rests with the court, not the prosecution or the defence.[29]

---

27   (1983) 77 Cr App R 13.
28   *R v Sweeting* (1987) 9 Cr App R (S) 372, CA.
29   *R v Costley* (1989) 11 Cr App R (S) 357, CA.

A defendant risks losing a substantial proportion of the credit for a guilty plea if his/her version of events is not accepted by the sentencer.[30]

19.43   At a *Newton* hearing the prosecution must prove any disputed facts beyond reasonable doubt. The usual rules of evidence apply, but as the hearing is not to determine guilt, adverse inferences under the Criminal Justice and Public Order Act 1994 may not be drawn from the exercise of the right to silence.

Pre-sentence drug testing (*not in force*)

The power

19.44   Where a person aged 14 or over is convicted of an offence and the court is considering passing a community sentence, it may order the offender to provide samples for the purposes of ascertaining whether s/he has heroin or cocaine in his/her body.[31]

19.45   It should be noted that unlike other drug testing provisions, there is no need for the conviction to relate to a trigger offence.

19.46   Where the offender has not attained the age of 17, the order must provide for the samples to be provided in the presence of an appropriate adult, defined as:

- the offender's parent or guardian, or if the offender is in the care of a local authority or voluntary organisation, a person representing that authority or organisation; or
- a social worker of a local authority social services department; or
- if no person falling into the above two categories is available, any responsible person aged 18 or over who is not a police officer or a person employed by the police.[32]

19.47   A court may not order an offender to provide a drugs sample unless it has been notified by the Home Secretary that the power to make such orders is exercisable by the court and the notice has not been withdrawn.[33]

Failure to comply with the order

19.48   If it is proved to the satisfaction of the court that the offender has, without reasonable excuse, failed to comply with an order to provide a drugs sample, it may fine him/her.[34]

19.49   Refusal to provide a drugs sample would allow the sentencing court to sentence an offender to a custodial sentence even though the seriousness threshold has not been satisfied.[35]

---

30 Sentencing Guidelines Council, *Reduction in a Sentence for a Guilty Plea* (December 2004). See also earlier case-law, eg *R v Costen* (1989) 11 Cr App R (S) 182, CA.
31 Criminal Justice Act 2003 s161(1).
32 Ibid, s161(3) and (8).
33 Ibid, s161(6).
34 Ibid, s161(4).
35 Ibid, s152(3)(b).

Offences to be taken into consideration

19.50   It is not uncommon with persistent young offenders that the police charge the offender with a small number of offences and suggest that other offences should be taken into consideration (often referred to as TICs). A court may take into consideration other offences admitted by the defendant when it is sentencing. Normally these offences to be taken into consideration will be of a similar nature to those for which the defendant is being sentenced. Such offences are associated offences for the purposes of determining the seriousness of the offences to which the defendant has pleaded guilty.[36]

19.51   A schedule of the offences to be taken into consideration will be prepared and shown to the defendant before the sentencing hearing. It is important that the defence lawyer checks that the child or young person agrees that s/he is responsible for each offence on the list. If the list is accepted, it should be signed by the defendant. In court the signed list should be handed to the court clerk who will confirm orally that the defendant admits all the offences contained in the list and that s/he wishes them to be taken into consideration by the magistrates when sentencing. When the bench announces sentence, it should make specific reference to the offences being taken into consideration and the court register should be noted accordingly.

Police antecedents

19.52   This would cover both previous convictions and a record of any reprimands or warnings.

Previous convictions

19.53   It is the duty of the prosecution to provide the court with a list of previous convictions. In some youth courts the youth offending team will also provide a list of convictions recorded against a child or young person; in many others details of previous convictions will be set out in any pre-sentence report.

19.54   Before a sentencing bench is given details of any recorded convictions, the list should be shown to the defence lawyer and the defendant. It should be determined that the defendant accepts the convictions listed. The defence lawyer should also check that every matter listed is in fact a conviction. It is not unknown for the police to provide courts with a computer print-out of all their contacts with a particular child or young person. Such a list will include arrests for which no further action was taken or charges which resulted in acquittals.

19.55   If the defendant disputes that s/he is the person named on the list of previous convictions, the prosecution will have to prove that the defendant is indeed the person against whom the convictions are recorded. This

---

36   Powers of Criminal Courts (Sentencing) Act 2000 s161(1)(b) and Criminal Justice Act 2003 s305(1).

is normally done by a fingerprint analysis.[37] If individual offences are disputed, then the court should ignore them for the purposes of sentencing, unless the prosecution indicates it wishes to prove the conviction by obtaining a memorandum of conviction from the relevant court. In such circumstances the sentencing hearing would have to be adjourned.

Reprimands and warnings

19.56 The prosecutor may cite in court a reprimand, warning or failure by the defendant to participate in a rehabilitation programme in the same circumstances as a conviction may be cited.[38] Where the offender was cautioned before the introduction of reprimands and warnings, the first caution is deemed to be a reprimand and any subsequent caution is deemed to be a warning.[39]

19.57 The defence lawyer should confirm with the defendant that the cited reprimand or warning is accepted. S/he should also attempt to establish whether a rehabilitation programme was offered following a warning. The fact that such a programme was not offered should be brought to the sentencing court's attention, as it demonstrates that no intervention by the youth offending team took place prior to an appearance at court.

19.58 If it is claimed that the defendant did not participate in a rehabilitation programme, the defence lawyer should attempt to confirm whether this is accepted by the child or young person and his/her parent or guardian. Any explanation for the non-participation needs to be identified. Where there is a good excuse (for example, the family moved to a new address outside the area of the youth offending team, or an adult carer was too ill to escort a child to the programme) this needs to be brought to the court's attention.

19.59 It should also be noted that where there has been non-participation in a rehabilitation programme, there is no defence of reasonable excuse. Moreover, the decision whether to record non-participation rests solely with the youth offending team organising the programme.

The sentencing hearing

19.60 In general, the procedure for sentencing a child or young person is the same as for an adult, however, the Criminal Procedure Rules 2005[40] impose specific requirements upon justices sitting both in the youth court and in the adult magistrates' court.

Presence in court

19.61 Normally an offender will be present in court throughout his/her sentencing hearing. The same would apply to any parent or guardian present. However, it is possible for the justices to require the young offender or the

---

37 Criminal Justice Act 1948 s39.
38 Crime and Disorder Act 1998 s66(5).
39 Crime and Disorder Act 1998 Sch 9 para 5.
40 SI No 384.

parent/guardian to withdraw from court if it is considered necessary in the interests of the child or young person.[41] Such a break with the principles of natural justice would only happen in the most unusual of circumstances.

19.62 The defence lawyer may wish to invite a youth court to use this power to hear submissions or some mitigation in the absence of the defendant. It may be considered important to provide the court with information about a parent's terminal illness or a traumatic incident experienced by the young defendant. It may be extremely distressing for a young defendant to hear such information related dispassionately in the courtroom. If it is not possible to provide the information in written form, the lawyer should seek the client's consent to providing the information in the defendant's absence. In the authors' opinion, the client should still be made aware of the general nature of the information that will be given in his/her absence.

Consideration of reports

19.63 Any reports may be received and considered without being read aloud.[42] In normal circumstances a copy of the report will have been made available to the young offender, his/her parent or guardian as well as the defence lawyer.[43]

Making a statement

19.64 The court must give the child or young person and his/her parent or guardian, if present, an opportunity of making a statement.[44] This right is rarely exercised when the young offender is legally represented.

Passing sentence

19.65 Having considered its sentence, the court must inform the defence lawyer and child or young person of the manner in which it proposes to dispose of the case. Representations by the defence lawyer, child or young person or parent/guardian must be allowed.[45] The final sentence must then be announced and its general effect and nature explained to the child or young person.[46]

Deferring sentence

19.66 The Criminal Justice Act 2003 substantially reworked the provisions for deferring sentence. In particular, it made provision for the court to outline requirements to be complied with during the period of deferment and introduced a power to appoint a supervisor to monitor compliance with

---

41 Criminal Procedure Rules 2005 r44.1(2)(e).
42 Ibid, r44.1(d).
43 Access to the reports is considered in more detail at para 20.62.
44 Criminal Procedure Rules 2005 r44.1(2)(a).
45 Ibid, r44.2(1).
46 Ibid, r44.2(2).

the requirements. There will therefore be much greater scrutiny of the young offender during the period of deferment. This may mean that the power is exercised more frequently. The Sentencing Guidelines Council has issued guidance on the use of the revised power to defer sentence in *New Sentences: Criminal Justice Act 2003*.

Power to defer

19.67 A court may defer passing sentence on an offender for the purposes of enabling the court, or any other court to which it falls to deal with him, to have regard in dealing with him to:

- his/her conduct after conviction (including, where appropriate, the making by him/her of reparation for his/her offence); or
- any change in his/her circumstances.[47]

19.68 A court may only defer sentence if:

- the offender consents;
- the offender undertakes to comply with any requirements as to his/her conduct during the period of the deferment that the court considers it appropriate to impose; and
- the court is satisfied, having regard to the nature of the offence and the character and circumstances of the offender, that it would be in the interests of justice to exercise the power.[48]

19.69 On deferring sentence, the court must specify the date on which the offender must return to court. This may not be more than six months after the date of deferment.[49] A sentence may only be deferred once.[50]

19.70 On deferring sentence, the court is deemed to be adjourning sentence.[51] It may not remand the offender on bail.[52]

Requirements

19.71 The court may include a requirement as to the residence of the offender during the whole or any part of the period of deferment.[53]

19.72 The Sentencing Guidelines Council guidance indicates that the requirements could be specific requirements as set out in the provisions for community sentences, or requirements that are drawn more widely. These should be specific, measurable conditions so that the offender knows exactly what is required and the court can assess compliance; the restriction on liberty should be limited to ensure that the offender has a reasonable expectation of being able to comply whilst maintaining his or her social responsibilities.[54]

---

47 Powers of Criminal Courts (Sentencing) Act 2000 s1(1) as substituted by Criminal Justice Act 2003 s278 and Sch 23.
48 Ibid, s1(3).
49 Ibid, s1(4).
50 Ibid.
51 Ibid, s1D(1).
52 Ibid, s1(6).
53 Ibid, s1A(1).
54 Sentencing Guidelines Council, *New Sentences: Criminal Justice Act 2003*, para 1.2.8.

Appointment of a supervisor

19.73 Where an offender has undertaken to comply with requirements, the court which is deferring sentence may appoint as the offender's supervisor:

- an officer of a local probation board; or
- any other person whom the court thinks appropriate.[55]

19.74 In the case of a young offender, the other appropriate person could be a member of a youth offending team.

19.75 A supervisor may not be appointed without his/her consent.[56]

19.76 The duties of the supervisor are:

- to monitor the offender's compliance with the requirements; and
- to provide the sentencing court with such information as the court may require relating to the offender's compliance with the requirements.[57]

Procedure when deferring sentence

19.77 Given the need for clarity in the mind of the offender and the possibility of sentence by another court, the court should give a clear indication (and make a written record) of the type of sentence it would be minded to impose if it had not decided to defer and ensure that the offender understands the consequences of failure to comply with the court's wishes during the deferral period.[58]

Final sentencing hearing

19.78 When passing sentence at the end of a period of deferment, the court may deal with the young offender in respect of the offence in any way in which the original court could have dealt with him/her if it had not deferred passing sentence.[59] The relevant age for the purposes of sentence is the age of the offender at the date of conviction, not the date of final sentence.[60]

19.79 In order to determine compliance with the requirements of the deferment, the court may request the attendance of the supervisor at the sentencing hearing. If the supervisor will not attend voluntarily, the court may summons him/her to attend as a witness.[61]

19.80 If the offender does not attend the deferred sentencing hearing, the court may issue a summons or a warrant for his/her arrest.[62]

---

55 Powers of Criminal Courts (Sentencing) Act 2000 s1A(2).
56 Ibid, s1A(3).
57 Ibid, s1A(4).
58 Sentencing Guidelines Council, *New Sentences: Criminal Justice Act 2003*, para 1.2.9.
59 Powers of Criminal Courts (Sentencing) Act 2000 s1D(2).
60 Cf *R v Danga* (1992) 13 Cr App R (S) 408, CA.
61 Powers of Criminal Courts (Sentencing) Act 2000 s1D(4) and (5).
62 Ibid, s1D(1).

Dealing with the offender before the deferred sentence date

19.81   The court may deal with the offender before the deferred sentence date if:

- the supervisor reports that the offender has not complied with the requirements of deferment;[63] or
- the offender has been convicted of an offence committed since sentencing was deferred.[64]

19.82   If the offender is not already before the court, it may issue a summons or warrant for his/her arrest.[65]

19.83   Where a different court is dealing with offences committed during the period of deferment, it may also deal with the offence(s) for which sentence was deferred, except that:

- a youth court may not deal with offences where sentence was deferred by the Crown Court; and
- the Crown Court, in dealing with an offence for which sentence was deferred by a youth court, is limited to the sentencing powers of the youth court.[66]

When is it appropriate to defer sentence?

19.84   In providing advice on the use of deferred sentences in relation to adult offenders, the Sentencing Guidelines Council suggests that the decision to defer sentence is likely to be used in very limited circumstances, given the range of sentences available including the power to suspend a sentence of imprisonment.[67] As suspended sentences are not available to young offenders, it is arguable that deferred sentences could be considered more widely than with adults.

19.85   The Sentencing Guidelines Council does provide useful guidance on the types of cases when deferral would be appropriate:

> A deferred sentence enables the court to review the conduct of the defendant before passing sentence, having first prescribed certain requirements. It also provides several opportunities for an offender to have some influence as to the sentence passed–
> a) it tests the commitment of the offender not to re-offend;
> b) it gives the offender an opportunity to do something where progress can be shown within a short period;
> c) it provides the offender with an opportunity to behave or refrain from behaving in a particular way that will be relevant to sentence.
>
> Given the new power to require undertakings and the ability to enforce those undertakings before the end of the period of deferral, the decision to defer sentence should be predominantly for a small group of cases at either the custody threshold or the community sentence threshold where the sentencer feels that there would be particular value in giving the offender the opportunities listed because, if the offender complies with the requirements, a different sentence

---

63   Powers of Criminal Courts (Sentencing) Act 2000 s1B(2).
64   Ibid, s1C(2).
65   Ibid, s1C(4).
66   Ibid, s1C(3).
67   Sentencing Guidelines Council, *New Sentences: Criminal Justice Act 2003*, para 1.2.6.

will be justified at the end of the deferment period. This could be a community sentence instead of a custodial sentence or a fine or discharge instead of a community sentence ...[68]

Lifting reporting restrictions on conviction

19.86   The protection from publicity normally given to children and young persons appearing in criminal proceedings may be lifted upon conviction. Increasingly the lifting of the reporting restrictions is being seen as part of the sentencing process, either as a means of encouraging young offenders to face up to the consequences of their offending or as part of a deterrent sentence.

International standards

19.87   Article 40(2)(b)(vii) of the United Nations Convention on the Rights of the Child establishes for defendants under the age of 18 the right to privacy at all stages of criminal proceedings. More specifically, rule 8 of the United Nations Standard Minimum Rules for the Administration of Juvenile Justice (the 'Beijing Rules') recommends that, in principle, information leading to the identification of a offender under the age of 18 should not be published. In *T v United Kingdom, V v United Kingdom*[69] the European Court of Human Rights noted these provisions and considered that they represented 'an international tendency in favour of the protection of the privacy of juvenile defendants'.

Youth court

19.88   The youth court has a power to dispense to any specified extent with the reporting restrictions where it is in the interests of justice to do so.[70] This power extends to proceedings relating to any of the following:

- the prosecution or conviction of the offender for the offence;
- the manner in which the offender, or his/her parent or guardian, should be dealt with in respect of the offence;
- the enforcement, amendment, variation or revocation or discharge of any order made in respect of the offence;
- where an attendance centre order is made in respect of the offence, the enforcement of the Attendance Centre Rules 1995;[71] or
- where a detention and training order is made, the enforcement of any requirement of the supervision part of that order.

19.89   Before exercising this power the court must give all parties an opportunity to make representations and must take such representations into account

---

68 SGC, *New Sentences: Criminal Justice Act 2003* paras 1.2.6 and 1.2.7.
69 [2000] 2 All ER 1024 (Note); (2000) 30 EHRR 121; 7 BHRC 659, ECtHR.
70 Children and Young Persons Act 1933 s49(4A).
71 SI No 3281.

when making its decision.[72] This may include considering representations from a representative of the press.[73]

Exercise of the power

19.90 Guidance on the use of this power was issued in 1998 by the Home Office and the Lord Chancellor's Department.[74] The circular reminds youth court magistrates of the duty to prevent offending and the duty to have regard to the welfare of the child or young person. It continues:

> Lifting reporting restrictions could be particularly appropriate in cases where:
> - the nature of the young person's offending is persistent or serious or has impacted on a number of people or his or her community in general;
> - alerting others to the young person's behaviour would prevent further offending by him or her.
>
> There will of course be circumstances in which the lifting of reporting restrictions will not be in the best interests of justice. Factors which courts will wish to consider are whether:
> - naming the young offender would reveal the identity of a vulnerable victim and lead to unwelcome publicity for that victim;
> - publicity may put the offender or his/her family at risk of harassment of harm;
> - the offender is particularly young or vulnerable;
> - the offender is contrite and has shown himself or herself ready to accept responsibility for his or her actions by, for example, an early guilty plea.[75]

19.91 The exercise of the power has been subsequently considered in the light of the European Court of Human Rights decision in *T v United Kingdom, V v United Kingdom.*[76] In *McKerry v Teesdale and Wear Valley Justices*[77] Lord Bingham CJ reviewed the relevant provisions of the United Nations Convention on the Rights of the Child and the Beijing Rules and then gave the following general guidance:

> It is a hallowed principle that justice is administered in public, open to full and fair reporting of the proceedings in court, so that the public may be informed about the justice administered in their name. That principle comes into collision with another important principle, also of great importance and reflected in the international instruments ... that the privacy of a child or young person involved in legal proceedings must be carefully protected, and very great weight must be given to the welfare of such child or young person. It is in my judgement plain that power to dispense with anonymity, as permitted in certain circumstances by section 49(4A), must be exercised with very great care, caution and circumspection. It would be wholly wrong for any court to dispense with a juvenile's prima facie right to anonymity as an additional punishment. It is also very difficult to see any place for 'naming and shaming'. The court must be satisfied that the statutory criterion that it is in the public interest to dispense

---

72 Children and Young Persons Act 1933 s49(4B).
73 *McKerry v Teesdale and Wear Valley Justices* (2000) 164 JP 355; [2000] Crim LR 594, QBD.
74 *Opening Up Youth Court Proceedings* (issued 11 June 1998).
75 Ibid, paras 16 and 17.
76 See n 69.
77 (2000) 164 JP 355; [2000] Crim LR 574, QBD.

with the reporting restriction is satisfied. This will be very rarely the case, and justices making an order under section 49(4A) must be clear in their minds why it is in the public interest to dispense with the restrictions.

Remedies if reporting restrictions lifted

19.92   The decision to lift reporting restrictions following conviction would seem to be an order made on conviction with the meaning of Magistrates' Courts Act 1980 s108. It should therefore be possible to appeal the decision to the Crown Court.

19.93   When the youth court has made an order to lift reporting restrictions, the defence lawyer must act quickly if the decision is to be challenged otherwise any damage will be done when the local press report the young offender's name. If there is a risk that the details will be published the same day, a notice of appeal should be lodged immediately. The lawyer should then ask the youth court to suspend its decision pending the appeal. The appeal proceedings before the Crown Court will be automatically covered by reporting restrictions.[78]

Crown Court

19.94   A Crown Court judge may consider whether to revoke the order imposing reporting restrictions after a child or young person has been convicted of a particularly serious offence. There may even be a request from a representative of the press for the order to be lifted.

19.95   The Divisional Court considered when it might be proper to lift the reporting restrictions in the case of *R v Leicester Crown Court ex p S (a minor)*[79] which involved a 12-year-old boy convicted of arson causing damage estimated at £2.5 million. Watkins LJ stated:

> In our judgment, the correct approach to the exercise of the power given by section 39 of the Children and Young Persons Act 1933 is that proceedings should not be restricted unless there are reasons to do so to outweigh the legitimate interest of the public in receiving fair and accurate reports of criminal proceedings and knowing the identity of those in the community who have been guilty of criminal conduct and who may, therefore, present a danger or threat to the community in which they live. The mere fact that the person before the court is a child or young person will normally be a good reason for restricting reports of the proceedings in the ways permitted by section 39 and it will, in our opinion, only be in rare and exceptional cases that directions under section 39 will not be given or having been given will be discharged.

19.96   This formulation of principle was subsequently considered by the Court of Appeal in *R v Lee*.[80] The defendant in this case was a 14-year-old boy convicted of robbery and possession of a firearm. These offences were committed whilst he was on bail for rape. Referring to the opinion of Watkins LJ that the restrictions should only be lifted in 'rare and exceptional cases', Lloyd LJ stated:

> For our part, we would not wish to see the court's discretion fettered so strictly. There is nothing in section 39 of the Children and Young Persons Act 1933

78 By virtue of Children and Young Persons Act 1933 s49(2)(b).
79 (1992) 94 Cr App R 153; [1993] 1 WLR 111.
80 (1993) 96 Cr App R 188; [1993] 1 WLR 103.

about rare or exceptional cases. There must of course be good reason for making an order under section 39, just as there must be a good reason for lifting the restriction on publicity of proceedings in the [youth] court under section 49 [of the 1933 Act], namely to avoid injustice to the child. The rule under section 49 ... is the reverse of the rule under section 39. The onus is, so to speak, the other way round. If the discretion under section 39 is too narrowly confined, we will be in danger of blurring the distinction between proceedings in the [youth] courts and proceedings in the Crown Court, a distinction which Parliament clearly intended to preserve.

19.97   This latter view has been preferred by the Divisional Court in both *R v Central Criminal Court ex p S and P (minors)* [81] and *R v Central Criminal Court ex p W.* [82] In the latter case Rose LJ also stated that the decision in *McKerry v Teesdale and Wear Valley Justices* [83] was limited to the decision in relation to section 49.

19.98   When considering whether to lift reporting restrictions, the judge must consider all relevant factors. The judge must have regard to the welfare of the child or young person. Considerable weight should be given to the age of the offender and to the potential damage to a young person of public identification as a criminal before s/he has the benefit or burden of adulthood. [84] The court should also consider the damage caused to any rehabilitation programme proposed in a custodial setting or in the community by adverse publicity. [85] It may also be relevant in the case of sex offenders to consider any increased risk of physical attack whilst in custody occasioned by publicity which names the offender. [86] In the case of very serious offences it is permissible to consider naming the offender so that it served as a deterrent to others, but it would be improper to allow his/her naming solely to ensure that the severity of any sentence was reported widely. [87] The judge should consider any grounds of appeal against conviction before deciding whether to lift the reporting restrictions as a successful appeal is likely to result in a re-trial. [88]

Remedies if a section 39 order is lifted

19.99   A member of the press who wishes to challenge the existence of reporting restrictions may appeal to the Court of Appeal by virtue of Criminal Justice Act 1988 s159. The defendant, however, cannot use this provision, and moreover it would seem that s/he cannot seek to have the restrictions re-imposed by the Court of Appeal as part of an appeal against sentence as the power under Children and Young Persons Act 1933 s39 only applies to proceedings before the court making the order. [89]

19.100   The only possible remedy may be to seek judicial review of the decision to remove the reporting restrictions. However, it has been questioned on

81   (1998) *Times* 26 October, CO/2702/98, (1998) 16 October, QBD.
82   CO/1927/2000, (2000) 24 July, QBD.
83   See n 77 above.
84   *R v Inner London Crown Court ex p Barnes (Anthony)* (1995) *Times* 7 August, QBD.
85   *R v Leicester Crown Court ex p S (a minor)*, n 79 above.
86   *R v Central Criminal Court ex p S and P (minors)*, n 81 above.
87   *R v Inner London Crown Court ex p Barnes (Anthony)*, n 84 above.
88   *R v Manchester Crown Court ex p H and D* [2000] 1 Cr App R 262, QBD.
89   *R v Lee*, n 80 above.

a number of occasions whether judicial review is an available remedy. It has been argued that the making of a section 39 order is a matter which relates to trial on indictment and therefore the High Court's jurisdiction is excluded by Supreme Court Act 1981 s29(3). In *R v Leicester Crown Court ex p S (a minor)*[90] this argument was rejected and in successive decisions the jurisdiction of the High Court does not seem to have been challenged. More recently the debate has been reopened. Judicial review was held *to be available* in *R v Cardiff Crown Court ex p M (a minor)*[91] A section 39 order was considered to be a separate child protection power and therefore not a matter relating to trial on indictment. This argument was rejected by a differently constituted court in the subsequent case of *R v Winchester Crown Court ex p B (a minor)*[92] which held that a section 39 order was in fact integral to the administration of justice so that Supreme Court Act 1981 s29(3) applied. Subsequently in *R v Manchester Crown Court ex p H and D*[93] the divisional court has once again held that judicial review is available at least after conviction and sentence. It is the opinion of the authors that this view is to be preferred. In the light of the decision in *R v Lee*[94] that there is no effective right of appeal to the Court of Appeal, the contrary view that the making of a section 39 order relates to a matter of trial on indictment deprives the young offender of any means of challenging the decision to lift the reporting restrictions.

19.101   In *R v Leicester Crown Court ex p S (a minor)*[95] Watkins LJ suggested that the Divisional Court would interfere with the decision of the Crown Court judge if s/he had failed to take into account relevant matters; failed to give reasons for the decision to lift the section 39 order or if the decision was *Wednesbury* unreasonable.[96] If there is any risk that the young offender's name will be published that same day or the following morning, the judge should be asked to suspend the lifting of the section 39 order until leave to move for judicial review can be applied for.

---

90 See n 79 above.
91 162 JP 527, QBD.
92 [1999] 1 WLR 788, QBD.
93 [2000] 1 Cr App R 262.
94 See para 19.99.
95 See n 79.
96 (1992) Cr App R 153, at p157.

CHAPTER 20

Reports

Introduction

20.1   Reports play a very important role in the sentencing of children and young persons. In many cases, background information is needed before the court is in a position to comply with its statutory duty to consider the welfare of the defendant under Children and Young Persons Act 1933 s44.

20.2   A youth court is required to consider available background information regarding an offender before disposing of a case. If sufficient information is not available, the court will usually adjourn to obtain a pre-sentence report, and more unusually an education or medical report.

20.3   The information contained in a report obviously depends on the co-operation of the offender. Nevertheless, the quality of reports concerning children and young persons varies alarmingly. The defence lawyer can play a role in identifying sources of information regarding the offender. S/he should also attempt to contact the report writer before the report is finalised to discuss the contents and the recommendation.

Obligation to consider background information

20.4   Children and Young Persons Act 1969 s9 places a duty upon local authority social services departments and local education authorities to make investigations and provide information relating to the home surroundings, school record, health and character of the child or young person appearing before a criminal court. Normally no such information would be made available unless there has been a finding of guilt.

20.5   A youth court is under an obligation to consider the background of the young offender. Criminal Procedure Rules 2005[1] r44.2 states:

(b) the court shall take into consideration all the available information as to the general conduct, school record and medical history of the relevant minor and, in particular, shall take into account such information as aforesaid which is provided in pursuance of section 9 of the Act of 1969,

(c) if such information as aforesaid is not fully available, the court shall consider the desirability of adjourning the proceedings for such inquiry as may be necessary.

20.6   This obligation must be seen in the context of the general duty to consider the welfare of the child or young person imposed on all courts.[2] A youth court will normally seek the background information required by adjourning the case and requesting written reports regarding the defendant.

Adjourning for reports

Power to adjourn

20.7   By Magistrates' Courts Act 1980 s10(3) a youth court may adjourn after conviction to obtain further information regarding the offender but the adjournment shall not be for more than four weeks at a time unless the

---

1   SI No 384.
2   Children and Young Persons Act 1933 s44(1).

defendant is remanded in custody (or in local authority accommodation), in which case the remand shall not be for more than three weeks.

20.8   This power must be considered in the light of Children and Young Persons Act 1933 s48(3) which provides:

> When a youth court has remanded a child or young person for information to be obtained with respect to him, any youth court acting in the same local justice area –
> (a) may in his absence extend the period for which he is remanded, so, however, that he appears before a court or a justice of the peace at least once in every twenty-one days;
> (b) when the required information has been obtained, may deal with him finally.

20.9   This provision seems to conflict with the power granted under Magistrates' Courts Act 1980 s10(3). However, the editors of *Justice of the Peace* argue persuasively that section 48(3) must take precedence as Magistrates' Courts Act 1980 s152 states that any procedural rule contained in the 1980 Act is subject to any rule specifically relating to a youth court.[3]

Is an adjournment necessary?

20.10   Because of the welfare ethos in the youth court, pre-sentence reports are ordered in some circumstances where no such report would be considered in an adult magistrates' court. A defence lawyer should always consider, therefore, whether it may be possible to persuade the court to dispose of the case without adjourning for reports. It may be possible, for example, to arrange for the supervisor of an existing community sentence to provide a letter for the court hearing describing the response to supervision or the other requirement of the sentence. Alternatively, if a supervisor is at court, s/he could be asked to provide a short oral report about the offender's progress.

Indications of seriousness

20.11   It is the practice in most courts for an indication of seriousness to be given before adjourning for reports. This practice is of great benefit to the writer of a pre-sentence report as it allows a more focused report to be prepared. Such an indication should always be noted by the defence lawyer for the benefit of the advocate at the sentencing hearing.

Implied promises

20.12   It has been held to be good practice when adjourning for reports before sentence for the court to warn the defendant that the request for reports in itself does not indicate that custody has been ruled out.[4] Nevertheless, if the court fails to give this warning, it will not by itself raise in the defendant's mind a legitimate expectation that s/he will not be given a custodial

---

3   (1995) 159 JPN 292.
4   *R v Norton and Claxton* (1989) 11 Cr App R (S) 143, CA.

sentence.[5] This is even more the case if the adjournment for a report was required by the statutory rules now contained in the Criminal Justice Act 2003.[6] However, if the court postpones sentence so that an alternative to custody can be examined and that alternative is found to be satisfactory, then the court ought to adopt the alternative.[7] The test is whether the court's actions have led the defendant to expect that a particular community penalty will be imposed if the assessment is favourable.[8]

Failure to co-operate with the preparation of reports

20.13   In normal circumstances reports will be prepared without any significant practical problems. However, in a number of cases young offenders may fail to co-operate with the report writer. If appointments are not kept, the report writer is likely to submit a letter to the court detailing the missed appointments. This is generally referred to as a non-report.

20.14   Faced with such non-cooperation, the court has two powers:

(i) to impose a condition of bail that the young offender should co-operate with the preparation of the report; or

(ii) to refuse bail.

Condition of bail

20.15   The court may impose a condition that the young offender must co-operate with the preparation of the report. If the report writer is able to suggest a particular appointment, it is open to the court to phrase the condition to require attendance at that appointment. Such a condition should not be imposed as a matter of routine.

20.16   Once such a condition has been imposed, failure to attend appointments as required is a breach of bail which makes the offender liable for arrest by the police to be returned to court. Furthermore, the member of the youth offending team preparing the report will be expected by the court to report any missed appointments to the police as a breach of bail.

20.17   When an up-to-date report is considered important, the defence lawyer may wish to draw the court's attention to this power and emphasise that the risk of arrest by the police should act as a powerful incentive to the young offender to attend the necessary appointments.

Refusal of bail

20.18   If a court refuses bail to a 17-year-old, s/he will be remanded into custody. If it refuses bail to a juvenile, s/he will be remanded to local authority accommodation under Children and Young Persons Act 1969 s23. If the sole reason for refusing bail is the failure to co-operate with the preparation of reports, it is unlikely that the criteria of section 23(5) will be satisfied justifying a secure remand.

5   *R v Moss* (1983) 5 Cr App R (S) 209, CA.
6   *R v Woodin* [1994] Crim LR 72, CA.
7   *R v Gillam* (1980) 2 Cr App R (S) 267, CA.
8   *R v Stokes* (1983) 5 Cr App R (S) 449, CA.

20.19   As part of a remand to local authority accommodation, the court may impose a condition upon the offender requiring co-operation with the preparation of the report.[9] This would have the same practical effect as a bail condition.

Pre-sentence reports

Definition

20.20   A pre-sentence report is defined as a report which:

- with a view to assisting the court in determining the most suitable method of dealing with an offender, is made or submitted by an appropriate officer; and
- contains information as to such matters, presented in such manner, as may be prescribed by rules made by the secretary of state.[10]

20.21   A pre-sentence report should be in writing.[11]

20.22   Where the offender is aged under 18, 'appropriate officer' means an officer of a local probation board, a social worker of a local authority social services department or a member of a youth offending team.[12]

Format

20.23   A pre-sentence report must be written using the following format:

- front sheet;
- sources of information, including whether an *Asset* has been completed;
- offence analysis, including impact of offence on victim(s);
- assessment of young person;
- assessment of risk to the community, including the risk of re-offending and dangerousness; and
- conclusion, including proposal for sentencing.[13]

20.24   A pre-sentence report must be based on:

- an *Asset* assessment (see para 2.23 onwards);
- a minimum of one interview with the young defendant;
- an interview with at least one parent and/or carer where possible;
- victim personal statements where available; and
- information from all relevant sources.[14]

---

9 Children and Young Persons Act 1969 s23(7).
10 Criminal Justice Act 2003 s158(1).
11 Youth Justice Board: *National Standards for Youth Justice Services* (2004) para 7.8. Note there is no longer a statutory requirement that pre-sentence reports be in writing.
12 Criminal Justice Act 2003 s158(2).
13 Youth Justice Board: *National Standards for Youth Justice Services* (2004) para 7.10.
14 Ibid, para 7.3.

When is a pre-sentence report required?

Custodial sentence

20.25   A court must obtain and consider a pre-sentence report before:

- forming an opinion that the offence, or the combination of the offence and one or more offences associated with it, was so serious that neither a fine alone nor a community sentence can be justified for the offence; or
- determining the appropriate length of a custodial sentence; or
- concluding that there is a significant risk to members of the public of serious harm occasioned by the commission by the offender of further specified offences.[15]

Community sentences

20.26   A court must obtain and consider a pre-sentence report before:

- forming an opinion that the offence, or the combination of the offence and one or more offences associated with it, was serious enough to warrant a community sentence; or
- determining what restrictions on liberty are commensurate with the seriousness of the offence, or the combination of the offence and one or more offences associated with it; or
- determining the suitability for the offender of the particular requirement or requirements to be imposed by the community order.[16]

Other penalties

20.27   No pre-sentence report is required before a court may sentence a defendant to the following sentences:

- absolute discharge;
- conditional discharge;
- fine; or
- referral order.

20.28   A written report (usually termed a 'specific sentence report') is required before a court may sentence an offender to a reparation order.[17]

Sentencing without an up-to-date pre-sentence report

20.29   A new pre-sentence report need not be ordered, if in the circumstances of the case, the sentencing court is of the opinion that it is unnecessary to do so.[18] Where the offender is aged under 18, the court must not form this opinion unless:

---

15   Criminal Justice Act 2003 s156(3)(a).
16   Ibid, s156(3)(b).
17   Powers of Criminal Courts (Sentencing) Act 2000 s73(5) – see 20.35 below.
18   Criminal Justice Act 2003 s156(4).

- there exists a previous pre-sentence report obtained in respect of the offender; and
- the court has had regard to the information contained in that report, or, if there is more than one report, the most recent report.[19]

20.30 Failure to obtain a pre-sentence report as required by the above rules does not invalidate the sentence passed, but on appeal the appellate court must obtain and consider a pre-sentence report if none was obtained by the court below.[20]

20.31 The appellate court need not obtain a pre-sentence report if it is of the opinion:

- that the court below was justified in forming an opinion that it was unnecessary to obtain a pre-sentence report; or
- that, although the court below was not justified in forming that opinion, in the circumstances of the case at the time it is before the appellate court, it is unnecessary to obtain a pre-sentence report.[21]

20.32 In the case where an offender is aged under 18, the appellate court must not form the opinion that a pre-sentence report is unnecessary unless:

- there exists a previous pre-sentence report obtained in respect of the offender; and
- the court has had regard to the information contained in that report, or, if there is more than one such report, the most recent report.[22]

20.33 In the quest for speedier proceedings, a inter-departmental government circular has been issued which does address the issue of using old reports in the youth court.[23] It reminds magistrates of the possibility of using an old report in certain circumstances. The guidance then goes further and suggests that magistrates should avoid acceding to routine requests for adjournments to provide up-to-date reports where an old report exists. When considering such a request the magistrates are recommended to take into account whether the request is likely to cause delays in sentencing and whether a verbal update might be more appropriate.[24]

20.34 The use of an old report may be unsatisfactory for a number of reasons. An old report will not deal with the defendant's attitude to the current offence(s) which could reveal unusual immaturity on the part of the defendant. As many defendants who come before the youth court regularly have troubled and unstable backgrounds, the information contained in a previous report may rapidly become out of date. With significant changes in an adolescent's life, or even simply increasing maturity, community penalties previously discounted may now be suitable for the defendant.

---

19 Criminal Justice Act 2003 s156(5).
20 Ibid, s156(6).
21 Ibid, s156(7).
22 Ibid, s156(8).
23 *Tackling Delays in the Youth Justice System* (issued 15 October 1997 jointly by the Lord Chancellor's Department, Home Office, Department of Health, Welsh Office, Attorney-General and the Department for Education and Employment).
24 Ibid, para 39.

Specific sentence reports

Reparation order

20.35   Before making a reparation order, a court shall obtain and consider a written report from an officer of a local probation board, a social worker of a local authority social services department or a member of a youth offending team indicating:

- the type of work that is suitable for the young offender; and
- the attitude of the victim or victims to the requirements proposed to be included in the order.[25]

Action plan order

20.36   Before making an action plan order, the court shall obtain and consider a written report from an officer of a local probation board, a social worker of a local authority social services department or a member of a youth offending team indicating:

- the requirements proposed by the youth offending team member to be included in the order;
- the benefits to the young offender that the proposed requirements are designed to achieve; and
- the attitude of a parent or guardian of the young offender to the proposed requirements.[26]

20.37   Where the offender is under the age of 16, the report should also include information about his/her family circumstances and the likely effect of the order on those circumstances.[27]

20.38   The requirement to obtain and consider a specific sentence report before imposing an action plan order, would seem to apply even if the court has an old pre-sentence report before it.

Format of a specific sentence report

20.39   A specific sentence report must:

- be based on *Asset* (see para 2.23 onwards);
- assess the young defendant's suitability for the specific order envisaged by the court;
- be a written report, which may be present verbally;
- other than in exceptional circumstances, be available on the day of request where a recent *Asset* is available; and
- exceptionally, be produced within five working days where there is no recent *Asset* available.[28]

20.40   Where it will facilitate the prompt conclusion of a case and where a recent *Asset* and other relevant information is available, the youth offending team

---

25 Crime and Disorder Act 1998 s73(5).
26 Ibid, s69(6)(a).
27 Ibid, s69(6)(b).
28 Youth Justice Board: *National Standards for Youth Justice* (2004), para 7.12.

may prepare a report on the same day as a court hearing on a stand down basis.[29]

Education reports

20.41   A court may order a written report from the offender's school or from the local education authority. Local practice in relation to such reports varies enormously. In some local authority areas an education report is not requested but the writer of the pre-sentence report will routinely contact an offender's school and incorporate relevant information into the report. However, even where such local arrangements exist a court may still seek a report regarding an offender's schooling if there is concern regarding the adequacy of educational provision. This applies in particular when an offender is currently excluded from school.

Guidance from the Department for Education and Skills

20.42   In the past there has been considerable concern regarding the content of educational reports as surveys have discovered an alarming proportion of reports containing irrelevant and often highly prejudicial information.[30]

20.43   As a result of this concern, the Department for Education and Skills has issued guidance to schools regarding the preparation of such reports. The most recent version of this guidance is contained in Annex E of DFES Circular 10/99 *Social Inclusion: Pupil Support*.[31]

General principles

20.44   Reports should:
- have a clear educational focus;
- be based on fact;
- be balanced, describing strengths as well as weaknesses;
- avoid race and gender stereotyping;
- reflect the fact that the school's knowledge of the pupil, although detailed about time spent in school, is not by its nature comprehensive.

Pupil achievements

20.45   The report should:
- present information in layperson's language;
- mention any statement of special educational needs (a court request is an exception to the rule that a statement may only be disclosed with the consent of the child's parents);
- relate the pupil's performance to their age and potential, and compared with peers;

---

29   Ibid, para 7.14.
30   NACRO, *School Reports to the Juvenile Court: Could Do Better* (1988).
31   Available on the website of the Department for Education and Skills – see appendix 14.

- identify successes as well as failures, and positive as well as negative attributes;
- mention application and motivation, for example if a pupil with low attainment tries hard or is helpful in class;
- cover the pupil's other skills and achievements including extra-curricular activities.

Attendance details

20.46   The report should:

- state the number of half days (sessions) attended out of the total possible number over two consecutive terms or a full academic year;
- compare the attendance record with normal pattern for the year group in the school;
- draw attention to any special factors (eg seasonal incidence of illness at the school);
- say if post-registration truancy is a particular problem;
- give the reasons for absence, and whether authorised or unauthorised;
- briefly describe the school's policy on truancy and any action the school or education welfare officer has taken on the pupil concerned.

Behaviour details

20.47   The report should:

- support judgments and opinions by reference to serious incidents, regular occurrences of misbehaviour, any periods of exclusion, or time spent in a pupil referral unit;
- note any change in the pupil's pattern of behaviour and the reason(s) with dates;
- set behaviour in the context of the standard of the pupil's class or year group;
- if behaviour has fallen short of the standard expected, indicate what steps the school has taken to improve this and the results;
- give information about the pupil's relationship with other pupils and staff;
- not mention hearsay comments about behaviour out of school hours.

Health details

20.48   Schools may report information about a pupil's health where it is relevant to the pupil's attendance, attainment and behaviour.

Information on home circumstances

20.49   The guidance states that the court's main source of information on the young offender's home circumstances will be the pre-sentence report. The school report should be confined to:

- any known special difficulties at home such as family illness, bereavement, parental separation or divorce;
- particular factors working against parental involvement.

Discussing report with the young person and the parent or guardian

20.50   If there is no locally established procedure, schools should ask their local court whether the school can show the parent the written school report before the hearing. It is always good practice to discuss the report's general content with the pupil and parents allowing them to correct any factual inaccuracies.

Failure to follow guidance

20.51   The defence lawyer may wish to object to an education report being used at a sentencing hearing if it does not follow this guidance, particularly if the contents are biased or contain unsubstantiated opinions.

Medical reports

Adjourning for a report

20.52   A youth court or adult magistrates' court may adjourn to allow a medical report to be prepared, if the court is of the opinion that an inquiry ought to be made into the accused's physical or mental condition, provided:

- the accused has been charged with an imprisonable offence; and
- the court is satisfied that the accused did the act or made the omission alleged; but
- it is of the opinion that an inquiry ought to be made into the accused's physical or mental condition before the method of dealing with him/her is determined.[32]

20.53   The period of adjournment may be for a maximum of four weeks if the defendant is on bail, or three weeks if in custody or remanded to local authority accommodation.[33]

20.54   If the court remands the defendant on bail, it shall impose conditions requiring him/her:

- to undergo a medical examination by a registered medical practitioner or, where the inquiry is into his/her mental condition and the court so directs, two such practitioners; and
- for that purpose, to attend such an institution or place, or on such practitioner, as the court directs, and where the inquiry is into his/her mental condition, to comply with any other directions which may be given to him/her for that purpose by any person (or class of persons) specified by the court.[34]

Remand to hospital

20.55   A youth court may remand a defendant to hospital for the preparation of a psychiatric report on his/her mental condition.

32   Powers of Criminal Courts (Sentencing) Act 2000 s11(1).

33   Ibid, s11(2).

34   Ibid, s11(3).

20.56   The power may only be exercised if:

- the accused has been found guilty of an imprisonable offence or the court is satisfied that s/he did the act or made the omission charged or the accused has consented;[35]
- the court is satisfied, on the written or oral evidence of a registered medical practitioner, that there is reason to suspect that the accused is suffering from mental illness, psychopathic disorder, severe mental impairment or mental impairment; and
- the court is of the opinion that it would be impracticable for a report on his/her mental condition to be made if s/he were remanded on bail.[36]

20.57   A remand to hospital may not be for more than 28 days at a time and for no more than 12 weeks in total. The court may terminate the remand at any time if it appears to the court that it is appropriate to do so.[37]

When is a medical report required?

20.58   The sentencing court must consider a medical report before imposing any of the following orders:

- custodial sentence (upon defendant who appears mentally disordered);
- hospital order (or interim hospital order);
- guardianship order;
- supervision or community rehabilitation order with requirement of treatment for mental condition.

Custodial sentence upon mentally disordered offender

20.59   Where the young offender is or appears to be mentally disordered, the court must obtain and consider a medical report before passing a custodial sentence, unless, in the circumstances of the case, the court is of the opinion that it is unnecessary to do so.[38]

20.60   A 'medical report' is a report as to the offender's mental condition made or submitted orally or in writing by a registered medical practitioner who is approved for the purposes of section 12 of the Mental Health Act 1983.[39]

20.61   Before passing a custodial sentence other than one fixed by law on an offender who is or appears to be mentally disordered, a court must consider:

- any information before it which relates to his/her mental condition (whether given in a medical report, pre-sentence report or otherwise); and
- the likely effect of such a sentence on that condition and on any treatment which may be available for it.[40]

---

35   Mental Health Act 1983 s35(2).
36   Ibid, s35(3).
37   Ibid, s35(7).
38   Criminal Justice Act 2003 s157(1) and (2).
39   Ibid, s157(6).
40   Ibid, s157(3).

Access to reports

Right to access

20.62 Where a court obtains a pre-sentence report, it must give a copy of the report:

- to the young offender or his/her lawyer;
- if the offender is aged under 18, to any parent or guardian who is present in court; and
- to the prosecutor.[41]

20.63 In relation to other types of court reports made by a member of a youth offending team or an officer of a local probation board, there is no corresponding requirement to provide a copy to the prosecutor.[42]

20.64 Where a prosecutor has received a copy of a pre-sentence report under these provisions, no information obtained may be used or disclosed otherwise than for the purpose of:

- determining whether representations as to matters contained in the report need to be made to the court; or
- making such representations to the court.[43]

Withholding disclosure at the order of the court

20.65 If the offender is aged under 18 and it appears to any court that the disclosure to the offender or to any parent or guardian of any information contained in the report would be likely to create a risk of significant harm to the offender, a complete copy of the report need not be given to the offender or, as the case may be, to that parent or guardian.[44]

20.66 A youth court may direct that a copy of any report should not be disclosed to the child or young person, if it considers that disclosure is:

- impracticable having regard to his/her age and understanding; or
- undesirable having regard to potential serious harm which might thereby be suffered by him/her.[45]

20.67 Such a direction would also bind the defence lawyer representing the child or young person.

20.68 If an unrepresented child or young person has been denied access to a copy of any written report, the court must still tell him/her the substance of any part of the information given to the court bearing on his/her character or conduct which the court considers to be material to the manner in which the case should be dealt with, unless it appears to be impracticable to do so having regard to his/her age and understanding.[46]

---

41 Criminal Justice Act 2003 s159(1) and (2).
42 Ibid, s160(1) and (2).
43 Ibid, s159(5).
44 Ibid, s159(3).
45 Criminal Procedure Rules 2005 r44.1(3)(c).
46 Ibid, r44.1(4)(a).

Use of reports beyond the sentencing hearing

20.69   The Court of Appeal has suggested that interviews conducted in the course of preparing a pre-sentence report are in a confidential relationship and made in the interests of the child. Accordingly, it would be contrary to the public interest for information contained in a pre-sentence report to be used for any purpose other than the sentencing of the child or young person.[47]

20.70   Copies of any reports before the court at the sentencing hearing should be forwarded by the youth offending team to the secure establishment where a young offender is being held within 24 hours of the court hearing.[48] The reports should then inform the establishment's sentence planning as well as help to fulfil its duty to safeguard the young offender's welfare.

Challenging the contents of a report

20.71   The defence lawyer should always go through the contents of a report with his/her client. S/he will also wish to discuss its contents with any parent or guardian present. If the client disagrees with the factual content of the report, the errors may be dealt with when addressing the court in mitigation. If it is necessary to challenge the opinions expressed in the report, the author of the report may have to be called to be cross-examined. Ultimately it is up to the sentencing bench or judge to decide whether the report is adequate for the purposes of sentencing.[49]

20.72   If a report is considered to have been inadequate, the child or young person (or a parent or guardian on his/her behalf) may make a complaint to the relevant youth offending team.

---

47   *Lenihan v West Yorkshire Metropolitan Police* (1981) 3 Cr App R (S) 42.
48   Youth Justice Board: *National Standards for Youth Justice Services* (2004), para 11.4.
49   *R v Okinikan* (1993) 96 Cr App R 431, CA.

Referral orders

Introduction

21.1   Introduced by the Youth Justice and Criminal Evidence Act 1999, and later re-enacted in Part III of the Powers of Criminal Courts (Sentencing) Act 2000, the referral order is the mandatory sentence for most first-time defendants who plead guilty. It is a unique disposal. When the defendant pleads guilty s/he is referred to a youth offending panel established by the youth offending team. The court specifies the length of the referral but it is for the panel to draw up a contract with the offender specifying the reparation and activities that the young offender will carry out. Compliance is monitored by the youth offending team. If the contract is successfully completed, the offender's conviction is immediately spent under the Rehabilitation of Offenders Act 1974. If the offender fails to comply with a contract drawn up, s/he will be returned to the youth court to be re-sentenced.

Power to make order

21.2   Referral orders may only be made by a youth court or an adult magistrates' court.[1] If a Crown Court judge considers that a referral order should be made, the offender will have to be remitted for sentence to a youth court under Powers of Criminal Courts (Sentencing) Act 2000 s8 (see paras 19.12 onwards).

21.3   A referral order cannot be made if:

- the penalty for the offence is fixed by law; or
- the offender has previously been convicted of a criminal offence in any court in the United Kingdom or been bound over in criminal proceedings in England and Wales or in Northern Ireland to keep the peace or to be of good behaviour.[2]

21.4   For the purposes of this provision, a conditional discharge is counted as a conviction, but an absolute discharge is not.[3]

Compulsory referral conditions

21.5   Referral to a youth offender panel must take place where the offender pleads guilty to an imprisonable offence and to any associated offence(s).[4]

Discretionary referral conditions

21.6   A court may also refer an offender to a panel where:

- s/he has pleaded guilty to all offences and all the offences are non-imprisonable;[5] or

---

1   The restrictions on the adult court's powers to sentence a child or young person do not prevent the making of a referral order: Powers of Criminal Courts (Sentencing) Act 2000 s8(7).
2   Powers of Criminal Courts (Sentencing) Act 2000 ss16(1)(a), 17(1)(b) and (c).
3   Ibid, s17(5).
4   Ibid, ss16(2) and 17(1).
5   Ibid, s17(1A).

- s/he is being dealt with for the offence and one or more connected offences (whether or not any of them is imprisonable) and, although s/he has pleaded guilty to at least one offence, s/he has also pleaded not guilty to at least one of them.[6]

21.7 For the purposes of this provision an offence is connected with another if the offender falls to be dealt with for it at the same time as s/he is dealt with for the other offence (whether or not s/he is convicted of the offences at the same time or by or before the same court).[7]

Alternative disposals

21.8 If the conditions for the making of a referral order are satisfied, the court may still impose one of the following disposals:

- absolute discharge;
- hospital order;
- custodial sentence.[8]

Prohibited disposals

21.9 When the court makes a referral order, it may not also impose any of the following:

- community sentence;
- fine;
- reparation order;
- conditional discharge;
- bindover to keep the peace or be of good behaviour; or
- parental bindover.[9]

21.10 The previous prohibition on making a parenting order has been removed.[10]

21.11 Where the compulsory referral conditions apply, the court may not defer sentence.[11]

Power to adjourn or remit

21.12 Where the compulsory referral conditions are satisfied, the court may not be sure whether one of the other permitted disposals would be more appropriate. In such circumstances, before making a final decision as to the appropriate disposal, the court may do any of the following:

- adjourn for pre-sentence reports;
- remit to the youth court for sentence;
- remand to hospital for reports;
- make an interim hospital order.[12]

---

6 Powers of Criminal Courts (Sentencing) Act 2000 s17(2).
7 Ibid, s16(4).
8 Ibid, s16(1)(b) and (c).
9 Ibid, s19(4)and (5).
10 Criminal Justice Act 2003 s324 and Sch 34 para 3.
11 Powers of Criminal Courts (Sentencing) Act 2000 s19(7).
12 Ibid.

Procedural requirements

21.13   When making a referral order the court must:

- specify the youth offending team responsible for implementing the order;
- require the offender to attend each of the meetings of the panel;
- require the attendance of an appropriate person;
- specify the length of time within which the contact between offender and panel shall have effect;[13] and
- explain to the offender in ordinary language the effect of the order and the consequences of failure to agree a contract or breach of any contract made.[14]

Determining the length of the order

21.14   When considering the length of the referral order, relevant considerations include:

- the seriousness of the offence;
- whether the offender pleaded guilty to all offences;
- when the offender pleaded guilty;
- the age of the offender;
- any mitigation in relation to the offence; and
- any personal mitigation.

Attendance of an appropriate person

21.15   On making a referral order the court may require the appropriate person, or if there are two or more appropriate persons, any one of more of them to attend the meetings of the panel.[15]

21.16   Where the offender is aged under 16 when a court makes a referral order it must require the attendance of at least one appropriate person, unless it is satisfied that it would be unreasonable to do so.[16]

21.17   'Appropriate person' is defined as each person who is a parent or guardian of the offender. Guardian has the same meaning as contained in the Children and Young Persons Act 1933 (for which see para 31.14).[17]

21.18   In the case of a looked after child, an appropriate person is defined as:

- a representative of the local authority; and
- each person who is a parent or guardian of the offender with whom the offender is allowed to live.[18]

21.19   If the appropriate person required to attend the panel meetings is not present when the court makes the referral order, s/he shall be sent a copy of the order forthwith.[19]

---

13   Powers of Criminal Courts (Sentencing) Act 2000 s18(1).
14   Ibid, s18(3).
15   Ibid, s20(1).
16   Ibid, s20(2) and (3).
17   Ibid, s164(1).
18   Ibid, s20(5) and (6).
19   Ibid, s20(7).

Practical considerations for the defence lawyer

Previous convictions

21.20   As a referral order may only be made if the offender has no previous convictions, the court may wish to confirm that the information on the police national computer is up to date. Frequently courts will ask the youth offending team to check the team's records to establish that no convictions are known. Where this is the local practice, the defence lawyer would be well advised to ensure that the youth offending team checks its records before the hearing to avoid the case being put back in the list.

Confirming the basis of plea

21.21   As the young offender is unlikely to be legally represented in the meetings of the youth offending panel, it is important that the basis of plea is clear at the time that it is entered. To avoid problems later on, it is suggested that the court could be asked to make a written record of the agreed facts of the offence which could then be forwarded to the youth offending team convening the panel. The defence lawyer could also write directly to the youth offending team to confirm the basis of plea.

21.22   In most cases where the referral conditions are satisfied, the defence lawyer will have to be prepared to mitigate immediately after plea, as it is very unlikely that the court will consider adjourning for reports unless the offence may warrant a custodial sentence.

Serious offences

21.23   Usually where there is a substantial risk of a custodial sentence, the pre-sentence report will give details of a high tariff community sentence which is proposed as an alternative to a detention and training order. As part of the mitigation, the defence lawyer will be able to draw the sentencing court's attention to the exacting nature of the requirements of the alternative community sentence. In contrast, where a referral order is the only realistic alternative, the report is unlikely to provide any information about the possible requirements of the sentence as the terms of the contract will only be drawn up by the panel after sentence. To reduce this problem, the defence lawyer could encourage the writer of the pre-sentence report to include information in the report about the type of conditions which might be imposed upon the particular defendant in a youth offending contract.

21.24   In cases where there is a high risk of a custodial sentence, one youth offending team known to the authors is willing to convene a panel before the sentencing hearing so that a draft contract can be drawn up. This draft contract is then attached to the pre-sentence report. This allows the sentencing court to have a much better idea of the likely requirements of a contract if a referral order were to be made.

Youth offender panel

21.25 Where a referral order has been made, it is the duty of the specified youth offending team to establish a panel for the offender and to arrange meetings of that panel.[20]

21.26 At each of its meetings a panel shall consist of at least:

- one member appointed by the youth offending team from among its members; and
- two members so appointed who are not members of the team.[21]

21.27 The Secretary of State may issue regulations setting out the qualification criteria for the panel members drawn from the local community.[22]

Before the first panel meeting

21.28 A representative of the youth offending team should contact the young offender within five working days of the referral order being made. An assessment of the offender's circumstances should be carried out (or updated). This will involve completion of the *Asset* profile. The youth offending team representative should also collate information regarding the offender's family circumstances as well his/her education and health needs. It is intended that all this background information will be available to the panel members.[23]

21.29 The defence lawyer may wish to submit further written information to the youth offending team with the consent of the young offender. This could include a written basis of plea which highlights any mitigating factors relevant to the offence, as well as copies of relevant documents obtained or commissioned during the proceedings. These could include:

- character references;
- education reports; or
- psychological or psychiatric reports.

21.30 In addition to the assessment of the young offender, a youth offending team representative should contact the victim of the offence to explain the panel procedure and to establish whether s/he wishes to participate in the panel meeting or in any reparation.[24]

Attendance at panel meetings

21.31 The specified youth offending team must notify the offender and any appropriate person of the time and place at which they are required to attend the meeting.[25]

21.32 The panel may also allow the following to attend:

20 Powers of Criminal Courts (Sentencing) Act 2000 s21(1).
21 Ibid, s21(3).
22 Ibid, s21(4).
23 Home Office/LCD/Youth Justice Board, *Referral Orders and Youth Offender Panels* (February 2002) Section 7.
24 Ibid, para 6.4.
25 Powers of Criminal Courts (Sentencing) Act 2000 s22(1).

- a person over 18 chosen by the offender;
- a person who is capable of having a good influence on the offender; and
- a victim of the offence.

Adult chosen by the offender

21.33   The offender has the right to nominate, with the agreement of the panel, a person over the age of 18 to accompany him/her to the panel meetings.[26] The same person need not attend each meeting of the panel. This adult could be a sibling, family friend or possibly even a children's rights advocate.

21.34   As the defence lawyer is unlikely to attend the panel meetings, it is important to advise the young offender of the right to nominate an adult to attend with him/her. The lawyer may need to help the client to identify a suitable adult. If a person is identified, it would be advisable to inform the representative of the youth offending team so that notification of the date and time of the first panel meeting can be sent directly to the adult.

Person capable of having a good influence upon the offender

21.35   The panel may also invite any other adult who appears to be capable of having a good influence on the offender.[27] Such an invitation would not appear to require the consent of either the young offender or his/her parent or guardian.

Victim of offence

21.36   The panel may invite any person who appears to the panel to be a victim of, or otherwise affected by, the offence, or any of the offences, in respect of which the offender was referred to the panel.[28] Where a victim wishes to attend the meeting, the panel may allow him/her to be accompanied by one person. The choice of person to accompany the victim is subject to the agreement of the panel.[29]

Presence of a defence lawyer

21.37   The legislation does not expressly prohibit legal representation of the young offender at the panel hearings, but any representation order issued for the proceedings will not cover attendance at the panel hearings.[30] Consequently the vast majority of young offenders will have no choice but to attend the panels without legal representation.

21.38   Defence lawyers who are instructed privately or agree to act pro bono should be aware that youth offender panels are strongly advised to exclude legal representation:

> Young people will not be legally represented at panel meetings and supporters should not act as legal representatives. This could hinder the process of

26   Powers of Criminal Courts (Sentencing) Act 2000 s22(3).
27   Ibid, s22(4)(b).
28   Ibid, s22(4)(a).
29   Ibid, s22(5).
30   *Criminal Bills Assessment Manual*, para 3.10.1.

directly involving the young people, enabling them to take responsibility for their offending and future behaviour. Lawyers may be present as parents, carers or supporters, but wherever possible offenders should speak for themselves throughout the youth offender panel process.[31]

Failure of offender to attend meetings

21.39   If the offender fails to attend any part of a meeting the panel may:

- adjourn the meeting to such place and time as it may specify; or
- end the meeting and refer the offender back to the appropriate court.[32]

21.40   The Home Office guidance states:

> Where the young person fails to attend the initial panel meeting the youth offending team member should attempt to establish the reason. Where there appear to be reasonable grounds for the absence (for example, ill health) and a reasonable prospect of attendance in the future, the meeting should be rearranged.[33]

Failure of appropriate person to attend meetings

21.41   If a parent or guardian named as an appropriate person in the referral order fails to attend the panel meeting without good reason, s/he can be referred by the panel to a youth court acting for the local justice area in which it appears to the panel that the offender resides or will reside. Such a referral may only take place if the offender is still under the age of 18 on the date when the parent or guardian fails to attend the meeting.[34] The purpose of the referral is for the court to consider whether a parenting order should now be made (see paras 31.101–31.104).

The first panel meeting

21.42   The panel members will consider the report prepared by the youth offending team worker. This should have been received prior to the hearing.

21.43   The panel will want to discuss with the offender the offence for which the order was made. The Home Office guidance suggests:

> The panel meeting must not be used as an opportunity for a 'retrial'. The facts of the offence, as found by the court, should be accepted. The panel should concentrate on the consequences of the offence for the victim and the wider community, how the offence came to be committed, how the harm is to be repaired and the risk of re-offending minimised.[35]

21.44   The panel will then normally consider the terms of the youth offender contract.

31 Home Office/LCD/Youth Justice Board, *Referral Orders and Youth Offender Panels* (February 2002) para 8.9.
32 Powers of Criminal Courts (Sentencing) Act 2000 s22(2).
33 Home Office/LCD/Youth Justice Board, *Referral Orders and Youth Offender Panels* (February 2002), para 8.13.
34 Powers of Criminal Courts (Sentencing) Act 2000 s22(2A) inserted by Criminal Justice Act 2003 Sch 34.
35 Home Office/LCD/Youth Justice Board, Referral Orders and Youth Offender Panels (February 2002) para 8.5.

Youth offender contract

21.45   At the first meeting of the panel, the members of the panel shall seek to reach agreement with the offender on a programme of behaviour. The aim of this programme is the prevention of re-offending by the offender.[36]

Terms of the programme

21.46   The programme may include provision for any of the following:

- financial or other reparation to any person who appears to the panel to be a victim of, or otherwise affected by, the offence or any of the offences, for which the offender was referred to the panel;
- the offender to attend mediation sessions with any such victim or other person;
- the offender to carry out unpaid work or service in or for the community;
- the offender to be at home at times specified in the programme;
- attendance by the offender at a school or other educational establishment or at a place of work;
- the offender to participate in specified activities;
- the offender to present him/herself to specified persons at times and places specified in or determined under the programme;
- the offender to stay away from specified places or persons (or both);
- enabling the offender's compliance with the programme to be supervised and recorded.[37]

21.47   The programme may not, however, provide:

- for the monitoring of the offender's whereabouts (electronically or otherwise); or
- for the offender to have imposed on him/her any physical restriction on his/her movements.[38]

21.48   No condition requiring anything to be done to or with any victim or other person affected by the offence(s) may be included in the programme with the consent of the victim or other person.[39]

21.49   When considering the terms of the contract, the Home Office guidance suggests:

- the two main aspects of every referral order should be reparation to the victim and/or the wider community and a programme of interventions delivered or organised by the youth offending team which addresses the factors likely to be associated with any re-offending;
- contracts must take into account the offender's school or work attendance, and, in the case of a young person claiming Job Seeker's Allowance, the terms of any Job Seekers Agreement;

36   Powers of Criminal Courts (Sentencing) Act 2000 s23(1).
37   Ibid, s23(2).
38   Ibid, s23(3).
39   Ibid, s23(4).

- community reparation should as far as possible be determined by the impact of the offence on the community and may include physical work (such as clearing up litter, graffiti or vandalism) and/or social work (such as working with elderly or disabled people, or helping to get messages across to other young people at risk of offending);
- the amount of community reparation should be proportionate to the seriousness of the offence;
- a panel should normally expect to specify three to nine hours of reparation in a three- or four-month order; 10 to 19 hours in a five- to seven-month order; 20–29 hours in an eight- or nine-month order; and more than 30 hours in an order of ten months or longer;
- there should be a face-to-face meeting between the offender and a member of the youth offending team at least once every two weeks for the first half of the order, and at least once every month for the second half of the order.[40]

Record of the programme

21.50 Where a programme has been agreed between the offender and the panel, the panel shall cause a written record of the programme to be prepared forthwith. This record should be in language capable of being readily understood by, or explained to, the offender.[41] The offender will then be expected to sign the agreed contract. It is not clear whether it would be open to the young offender to seek an adjournment of the panel meeting at that point to obtain legal advice on the contents of the draft programme.

Youth offender contract

21.51 Once the record has been signed by both the offender and a member of the panel on behalf of the panel, the terms of the programme take effect as the terms of a 'youth offender contract'.[42] A copy of the record must be given or sent to the offender.[43] Although there is no statutory requirement to give a copy of the contract to the parent or guardian, the government guidance recommends that a copy of the contract should be given to the parent or guardian as well as anyone who will be assisting the offender in complying with the terms of the contract.[44]

21.52 The contract will be in effect from the day when it is signed for the length of the referral order made by the court.[45] It is the duty of the specified youth offending team to make arrangements for supervising the offender's compliance with the terms of the contract and to ensure that records are kept of that compliance.[46]

---

40 Home Office/LCD/Youth Justice Board, *Referral Orders and Youth Offender Panels* (February 2002) paras 8.20–8.37.
41 Powers of Criminal Courts (Sentencing) Act 2000 s23(5).
42 Ibid, s23(6).
43 Ibid.
44 Home Office/LCD/Youth Justice Board, *Referral Orders and Youth Offender Panels* (February 2002) para 8.44.
45 Powers of Criminal Courts (Sentencing) Act 2000 s24(2).
46 Ibid, s29(2).

Failure to agree contract

21.53 It is clearly intended that a youth offender contract will be agreed at the first meeting of the panel. However, where it is considered appropriate to do so, the panel may end the first meeting without reaching agreement and resume consideration of the offender's case at a further meeting of the panel.[47]

21.54 Where it appears to the panel at the first or any such further meeting that there is no prospect of agreement being reached with the offender within a reasonable period after the making of the referral order, the panel may chose to refer the offender back to the appropriate court to be re-sentenced.[48] Before exercising this power it is suggested that the panel could end the meeting and advise the young offender to seek legal advice before the panel meets again to consider his/her case.

21.55 If at a meeting of the panel, agreement is reached with the offender but s/he does not sign the record and his/her failure to do so appears to the panel to be unreasonable, the panel shall end the meeting and refer the offender back to the appropriate court.[49]

Progress meetings

21.56 At any time after a youth offender contract has taken effect and before the expiry of the period for which the contract has effect, the panel may request the specified youth offending team to arrange a further meeting of the panel. Such meetings are referred to as progress meetings.[50]

Request initiated by the panel

21.57 A progress meeting may be requested if it appears to the panel to be expedient to review:

- the offender's progress in implementing the programme of behaviour contained in the contract; or
- any other matter arising in connection with the contract.[51]

21.58 A progress meeting must be requested if it appears to the panel that the offender is in breach of any terms of the contract.[52]

21.59 The government guidance states that a progress meeting must be ordered at least once every three months.[53]

Request initiated by the young offender

21.60 The panel must request a progress meeting if the offender has notified the panel that:

- s/he wishes to seek the panel's agreement to a variation in the terms of the contract; or

47 Powers of Criminal Courts (Sentencing) Act 2000 s25(1).
48 Ibid, s25(2).
49 Ibid, s25(3).
50 Ibid, s26(1).
51 Ibid, s26(2).
52 Ibid, s26(3)(b).
53 Home Office/LCD/Youth Justice Board, *Referral Orders and Youth Offender Panels* (February 2002) para 9.2.

- s/he wishes the panel to refer him/her back to the appropriate court with a view to the referral order (or orders) being revoked on account of a significant change in his/her circumstances making compliance with any youth offender contract impractical.[54]

21.61 The example of a significant change of circumstances given in the legislation is the offender being taken to live abroad. The Home Office guidance contemplates a wider use of the power:

> A variation of the contract may be requested for one or more of the following reasons:
> (i) a difficulty with a specific element of the contract (for example, coping with victim/offender mediation)
> (ii) a change in circumstances which makes some aspect of [the] contract difficult to comply with (for example, starting a new course of study or employment which could clash with programmed meetings or activities) and
> (iii) a belief that the contract, if fully complied with, would be unacceptably onerous.[55]

Final meeting

21.62 When the compliance period of a youth offender contract is due to expire, the youth offending team must arrange a final meeting of the panel. This meeting must take place before the expiry of the contract.[56] It can take place in the absence of the offender.[57]

21.63 At the final meeting the panel shall:

- review the extent of the offender's compliance with the terms of the contract; and
- decide, in the light of that review, whether the offender's compliance with those terms justify the conclusion that, by the time the contract expires, s/he will have satisfactorily completed the contract.[58]

21.64 The final meeting may not be adjourned to a time after the end of the period of the youth offender contract.[59]

21.65 If the panel determines that the offender's compliance has been satisfactory, it shall give him/her written confirmation of its decision.[60] This will also mean that the referral order will be discharged as from the end of the period of the contract.[61] If the panel concludes that the offender's compliance has not been satisfactory, it shall refer him/her back to the appropriate court.[62]

---

54 Powers of Criminal Courts (Sentencing) Act 2000 s26(3)(a).
55 Home Office/LCD/Youth Justice Board, *Referral Orders and Youth Offender Panels* (February 2002) para 9.14.
56 Powers of Criminal Courts (Sentencing) Act 2000 s27(1).
57 Ibid, s27(5).
58 Ibid, s27(2).
59 Ibid, s27(6).
60 Ibid, s27(2).
61 Ibid, s27(3).
62 Ibid, s27(4).

Challenging decisions of the panel

21.66 There is no right of appeal against any of the decisions of the panel; however, it is arguable that decisions of the panel are subject to judicial review, if the panel has exceeded its statutory powers or acted contrary to the rules of natural justice.

Referral back to appropriate court

21.67 A youth offending panel may refer an offender back to court if:

- the offender fails to attend any panel meeting;
- it appears that there is no prospect of agreement being reached with the offender within a reasonable time after the making of the referral order;
- the offender unreasonably refuses to sign a contract which has been agreed at a meeting;
- the offender unreasonably refuses to sign an amended contract;
- the panel considers that the offender is in breach of the contract;
- the offender requests such a referral with a view to the referral order being revoked on account of a significant change in circumstances making compliance with any contract impractical.

21.68 The procedure at court for dealing with a referral is dealt with at paras 27.27–27.35.

The effect of further convictions

21.69 When a defendant subject to a referral order appears before a court for other offences, the court has two options:

- to extend the compliance period of the existing referral order; or
- to revoke the order.

Extending the compliance period of the referral order

21.70 The power of the court to do this depends on whether the offence was committed before or after the making of the referral order. The period of compliance may not be extended beyond 12 months.[63] The court may not therefore exercise this power where the original referral order was for the maximum 12 months.

Offences committed before the making of the referral order

21.71 Where the defendant is under the age of 18, the court may sentence him/her by making an order extending the compliance period of the existing referral order. This power may only be exercised if this is the only other

---

63 Powers of Criminal Courts (Sentencing) Act 2000 Sch 1 para 13(1).

time that the defendant has been sentenced in a court in any part of the United Kingdom.[64] The extension will be for a period commensurate with the seriousness of the current offence and in the opinion of the authors it does not need to be for a minimum period.

Offences committed after the making of the referral order

21.72   Where the defendant is under the age of 18, the court may sentence him/her by making an order extending the compliance period of the existing referral order, but only if it is satisfied, on the basis of a report made by the relevant body, that there are exceptional circumstances which indicate that, even though the offender has re-offended, extending his/her compliance period is likely to prevent further re-offending.[65] If the court is satisfied that this exception exists, it must state in open court that it is so satisfied and why it is.[66]

21.73   The 'relevant body' is defined as:

- the panel to which the offender was referred; or
- if no contract has yet taken effect, the youth offending team specified in the order.[67]

Revocation of the referral order

21.74   When a defendant is sentenced for another offence other than by way of an absolute discharge or an extension of the referral order, any existing referral order is automatically revoked.[68]

21.75   If it appears to be in the interests of justice, the court may deal with the offender for the offence in respect of which the referral order was made in any manner in which s/he could have been dealt with for that offence by the court which made the order.[69] The relevant age is therefore the offender's age at the time when s/he entered a guilty plea to the original offence. When re-sentencing, the court shall have regard to the extent of the offender's compliance with the youth offending contract.[70]

64   Powers of Criminal Courts (Sentencing) Act 2000 Sch 1 para 11.
65   Ibid, Sch 1 para 12(1) and (2)(a).
66   Ibid, Sch 1 para 12(2)(b).
67   Ibid, Sch 1 para 12(3).
68   Ibid, Sch 1 para 14(1).
69   Ibid, Sch 1 para 14(3).
70   Ibid, Sch 1 para 14(4).

Discharges, financial orders and other powers

Absolute and conditional discharges

22.1   Where a court by or before which a person is convicted of an offence (not being an offence the sentence for which is fixed by law or subject to a mandatory minimum sentence) is of the opinion, having regard to the circumstances including the nature of the offence and the character of the offender, that it is inexpedient to inflict punishment, the court may make an order either:

- discharging the person absolutely;
- if the court thinks fit, discharging the person subject to the condition that s/he commits no offence during such period, not exceeding three years from the date of the order, as may be specified in the order.[1]

Absolute discharge

22.2   This disposal is very rare. It is imposed where the offender is considered to be blameless or guilty only because of a technicality. With the policy of diversion from the criminal justice system it is unlikely that a court will have before it a young offender whose offence could be considered to warrant an absolute discharge.

22.3   It is the practice of some courts to use an absolute discharge as the nominal sentence for an offence dealt with at the same time that a custodial sentence is imposed upon the offender. Other courts achieve the same result by announcing that no separate penalty has been imposed.

Conditional discharge

22.4   When a court imposes a conditional discharge upon an offender it should announce the length of the discharge and explain to the offender in ordinary language that if s/he commits another offence during the period of conditional discharge s/he will be liable to be sentenced for the original offence.[2]

Restrictions on the use of a conditional discharge

22.5   Where a child or young person has received a warning (see chapter 9) within two years of the date of the commission of current offence, the court shall not conditionally discharge him/her unless it is satisfied that there are exceptional circumstances relating to the offence or the offender which justify its doing so.[3] Where a court does discharge the young offender in such circumstances, it must state in open court the reasons for considering that there are exceptional circumstances.[4]

---

1   Powers of Criminal Courts (Sentencing) Act 2000 s12(1).
2   Ibid, s12(4).
3   Crime and Disorder Act 1998 s56(4)(a).
4   Ibid, s56(4)(b).

Effect of a discharge

22.6 A discharge is not generally deemed to be a conviction except for the purposes of the proceedings in which the order was made and any subsequent proceedings for breach of the discharge.[5] This applies even if the child or young person is re-sentenced for the offence.

22.7 There are a number of exceptions to this general rule. A conditional discharge does count as a previous conviction which would prohibit the making of a referral order.[6] It is also a conviction for the purposes of triggering the requirement to register as a sex offender.[7]

22.8 A discharge is not counted as a conviction for the purposes of reprimands and warnings. It may be possible, therefore, to receive a reprimand or warning after receiving an absolute or conditional discharge at court.

Security for good behaviour

22.9 When making an order for a condition discharge the court may allow any person who consents to do so to give security for the good behaviour of the offender, if it thinks it is expedient for the purpose of the reformation of the offender.[8]

22.10 This power is extremely rarely used and would seem to be largely redundant in the case of children and young persons as the court already has a general power to bind over a parent or guardian.[9]

Breach of a conditional discharge

22.11 An offender will be in breach of a conditional discharge if s/he is convicted of a further offence which occurred during the period of conditional discharge. When this has happened, the offender is liable to be sentenced for the original offence and the sentencing court will have available to it all sentencing powers that would be available if the offender had just been convicted of the offence.[10] Where a custodial sentence would not have been available at the time of the commission of the offence due to the offender's age, it is submitted that following the principles set out in *R v Ghafoor*[11] (see para 19.6) the court would not be able to impose a detention and training order on re-sentence.

22.12 The procedure for dealing with the breach depends upon whether the discharge was imposed by a magistrates' court or Crown Court.

---

5 Powers of Criminal Courts (Sentencing) Act 2000 s14(1).
6 Ibid, s17(5).
7 Sexual Offences Act 2003 s134(1). For convictions prior to 1 May 2005, a conditional discharge does not count as a conviction: *R v Longworth* [2006] UKHL 1.
8 Powers of Criminal Courts (Sentencing) Act 2000 s12(6).
9 Ibid, s150 – see para 31.52.
10 Ibid, s13(6) and (8).
11 [2002] EWCA 1857; [2003] 1 Cr App R (S) 84; [2002] Crim LR 739.

Discharge imposed by youth court or magistrates' court

22.13 The breach of the discharge will usually be discovered by the court which is dealing with the new offence, conviction for which puts the offender in breach. In practice it is therefore more convenient for this court to deal with the breach. This is possible provided the court obtains the consent of the original court to deal with the breach.[12] A Crown Court does not need to obtain the consent of a magistrates' court or youth court before dealing with a breach.[13]

22.14 If such consent is obtained, the offender will be asked to confirm that s/he admits both the fact that the conditional discharge was imposed and that the new conviction means that the discharge has been breached. If the breach is admitted, the court may proceed to sentence. If the breach is not admitted, the original conviction would have to be proved by the production of a memorandum of conviction.

22.15 It is also possible for the original court to deal with the breach. This is the case even if the original court was a youth court and the offender has now attained the age of 18.[14]

22.16 Upon receipt of an information, a justice of the peace for the original court may issue a summons requiring the offender to appear before the court at a time specified if it appears that the offender has been convicted of an offence committed during the period of discharge and s/he has been dealt with for this new offence. A warrant for the offender's arrest may be issued if the information is in writing and on oath.[15]

22.17 If a youth or adult magistrates' court conditionally discharge a young person for an indictable-only offence and the offender has attained the age of 18 before s/he is dealt with for any breach, the court's powers are:

- to fine the offender (maximum level £5,000); or
- to deal with the offence for that offence in any way in which a magistrates' court could deal with him/her if it had just convicted him/her of an offence punishable with imprisonment for a term not exceeding six months.[16]

Discharge imposed by the Crown Court

22.18 When an offender is convicted of an offence before a magistrates' or youth court which places him/her in breach of a conditional discharge imposed by a Crown Court, the justices may commit the offender on bail or in custody, to appear at the Crown Court.[17] If an offender is committed, the court shall send a memorandum of the conviction signed by the justices' chief executive to the Crown Court.[18]

---

12 Powers of Criminal Courts (Sentencing) Act 2000 s13(8).
13 Ibid, s13(7).
14 Children and Young Persons Act 1933 s48(2).
15 Powers of Criminal Courts (Sentencing) Act 2000 s13(1) and (3).
16 Ibid, s13(9).
17 Ibid, s13(5).
18 Ibid.

Fine

Power to fine

22.19　In the youth court or magistrates' court an offender convicted of an offence may be fined. If the offence is summary only, the court's powers will be limited depending on the level of the offence and the standard scale.

Level on the scale	Amount of fine £
1	200
2	500
3	1,000
4	2,500
5	5,000

22.20　For offences triable on indictment there is a statutory maximum of £5,000.

22.21　Powers of Criminal Courts (Sentencing) Act 2000 s135 imposes lower maxima when fining children and young persons. An offender under the age of 14 is subject to a maximum of £250 and an offender aged 14 to 17 is subject to a maximum of £1,000. In the Crown Court the judge is not subject to a statutory maximum. The Crown Court judge is required to fix a period of imprisonment to be served in default of payment of the fine.[19] In relation to a child or young person, this requirement would seem to be redundant as a child or young person may not be detained for default.[20]

A fine or one day

22.22　It is common for magistrates to impose a fine but declare that an alternative period of imprisonment may be served. This disposal is most commonly used where the offender has already spent a period of time in custody.

22.23　This disposal is not available in relation to a child or young person as there is no power to commit a child or young person to prison for default[21] and the power to commit to detention for default only exists if the offender is not less than 18 years of age.[22] The disposal would of course be available to a court dealing with a young offender who has attained the age of 18 during the proceedings.

19　Powers of Criminal Courts (Sentencing) Act 2000 s139(2).
20　Ibid, s108 – see also *R v Basid* [1996] Crim LR 67, CA which considered the position of a young person in relation to the previous identical statutory enactment of this provision.
21　Ibid, s89.
22　Ibid, s108.

Ordering the parent or guardian to pay

22.24   In the case of a child or young person the court is required to order a parent or guardian to pay any fine imposed against an offender aged under 16 and gives the court a discretion to order such payment in the case of an offender aged 16 or 17.[23] If a local authority has parental responsibility it may be ordered to pay the fine instead of the young offender. This power and the criteria for considering its use are considered in detail in chapter 31.

Determining the level of the fine

22.25   Before fixing the amount of any fine, a court shall inquire into the financial circumstances of the offender.[24] The amount of any fine fixed by a court shall be such as, in the opinion of the court, reflects the seriousness of the offence.[25] In fixing the amount of any fine, a court shall take into account the circumstances of the case including, among other things, the financial circumstances of the offender so far as they are known, or appear, to the court.[26]

Financial circumstances order

22.26   Before imposing a fine or other financial penalty, the court may make a financial circumstances order in relation to the young offender.[27] This is an order requiring him/her to give the court, within such period as may be specified in the order, such a statement of his/her financial circumstances as the court may require.[28] A person who without reasonable excuse fails to comply with a financial circumstances order shall be liable on summary conviction to a fine.[29]

Seriousness of the offence

22.27   The court is required to consider any aggravating or mitigating features of the offence as well as any personal mitigation before fixing the level of the fine. Account should also be taken of any guilty plea.

Means

22.28   Determining a young offender's financial circumstances will often be extremely straightforward simply because s/he has limited income and no financial commitments.

22.29   In the case of young offenders living with parents or guardians or in children's homes, the defence lawyer should check whether any weekly allowance includes travel to school or college and any lunch money while at school. In the case of young offenders who live independently, the defence

---

23 Powers of Criminal Courts (Sentencing) Act 2000 s137.
24 Ibid, s128(1).
25 Ibid, s128(2).
26 Ibid, s128(3).
27 Ibid, s126(1).
28 Ibid, s126(3).
29 Ibid, s126(4).

lawyer will need to ensure that a full list of outgoings is also recorded (eg water rates, estimated weekly expenditure on gas or electricity key meters etc.).

Time to pay

22.30 If the person ordered to pay does not have the means to pay the fine ordered immediately, the court may order that the full amount be paid within a specified period or it may order the payment of the fine in instalments. In normal circumstances it should be possible to pay the fine in 12 months, however, there is nothing wrong in principle with a period of payment longer than a year, provided that it was not an undue burden and too severe a punishment, having regard to the nature of the offence and the offender.[30]

22.31 When ordering payment by instalments, the court may fix a return date when the offender must attend court for payments of the fine to be reviewed. The court may also place the offender under the supervision of a person appointed by the court to ensure payment is made. If the young offender is under 18 at the date of sentence, the court should not make a collection order under Courts Act 2003 Sch 5 para 12 as this provision only applies to a person aged 18 or over.[31]

Rehabilitation of Offenders Act 1974

22.32 It should be noted that an offence for which a child or young person is found guilty and fined is only spent after the expiry of two-and-a-half years from the date of the conviction. This contrasts with a conditional discharge where the offence is spent at the end of the period of discharge. Defence lawyers should ensure that courts bear this difference in mind when selecting the appropriate penalty. It could have a significant effect on a young person's ability to obtain employment.

Compensation order

Power to order compensation

22.33 A court by or before which a person is convicted of an offence, instead of or in addition to dealing with him/her in any other way, may, on application or otherwise, make a compensation order requiring the offender:

- to pay compensation for any personal injury, loss or damage resulting from that offence or any other offence which is taken into consideration by the court in determining sentence; or
- to make payments for funeral expenses or bereavement in respect of a death resulting from any such offence, other than a death due to an accident arising out of the presence of a motor vehicle on a road.[32]

---

30 *R v Olliver and Olliver* (1989) 11 Cr App R (S); [1989] Crim LR 387, CA.
31 Courts Act 2003 Sch 5 para 1(1).
32 Powers of Criminal Courts (Sentencing) Act 2000 s130(1).

22.34   If there is more than one claimant for compensation, individual orders should be made[33] and the available money apportioned between the various complainants on a pro rata basis.[34] It is, however, possible in rare cases to select certain complainants to receive the money available for compensation.[35]

Ordering the parent or guardian to pay

22.35   In the case of a child or young person, the court is required to order a parent or guardian to pay any compensation order imposed against an offender aged under 16 and gives the court a discretion to order such payment in the case of an offender aged 16 or 17.[36] If a local authority has parental responsibility it may be ordered to pay the fine instead of the young offender. This power and the criteria for considering its use are considered in detail in chapter 31.

What loss may be compensated?

Personal injury

22.36   Guidance for common injuries may be found in the appendix to the Home Office Circular 53/1993 *Compensation in the Criminal Courts*. An award may be made if the injury may fairly be said to have resulted from the offence. For example, it was held lawful to order an offender convicted of affray to pay compensation to a person injured during the disturbance even though it could not be shown that the offender directly caused the injury.[37] A victim may also be compensated for any distress and anxiety caused by the offence.[38] Home Office Circular 53/1993 offers the following guidance:

> The assessment of compensation in such cases is not always easy, but some factors which can be taken into account are any medical or other help required, the length of any absence from work and a comparison with the suggested levels of compensation for physical injury.

Items of sentimental value

22.37   Home Office Circular 53/1993 gives the following guidance:

> [I]n the case of stolen or damaged items of sentimental value or where the value can no longer be ascertained, it may be possible to draw common sense comparisons with other property losses and the likely effect on the victim. The fact that an exact value cannot be established should not necessarily deter courts from attempting to assess compensation and from making an order; victims will otherwise take away the impression that their losses have been ignored.

33   *R v Grundy* [1974] 1 WLR 139.
34   *R v Miller* [1976] Crim LR 694.
35   *R v Amey* [1983] 1 WLR 345; [1983] 1 All ER 865; (1983) 76 Cr App R 206.
36   Powers of Criminal Courts (Sentencing) Act 2000 s137.
37   *R v Taylor* (1993) 14 Cr App R (S) 276.
38   *Bond v Chief Constable of Kent* [1983] 1 All ER 456.

Motor vehicles

22.38 Compensation arising out of the presence of a motor vehicle on a road may only be ordered if:

- it is in respect of damage to property resulting from an offence under the Theft Act 1968; or
- it is in respect of injury, loss or damage with respect to which the offender is uninsured in relation to the use of the vehicle, and compensation is not payable under any arrangements to which the secretary of state is a party (ie agreements with the Motor Insurers' Bureau).[39]

22.39 Compensation may be ordered for the loss of an owner's no claims bonus.[40]

Determining the amount of the order

Determining the loss

22.40 Compensation shall be of such amount as the court considers appropriate, having regard to any evidence and to any representations that are made by or on behalf of the accused or the prosecutor.[41] If the loss claimed by the complainant is not accepted by the offender, the court should not make a compensation order without receiving any evidence.[42] The claim will normally be supported by documentary evidence, for example a repair bill for materials and labour. The court should enquire whether the offender (or his/her parent or guardian) accepts the stated amount of loss. If s/he does not, the court should attempt to resolve the dispute on the evidence available, however, a complicated investigation where the court is asked to resolve questions of fact and law should not be undertaken.[43] In such circumstances the complainant should be left to pursue his/her civil remedies.

Means

22.41 A court must have regard to the offender's means so far as they appear or are known to the court before determining the amount of any compensation order.[44] When the parent or guardian is ordered to pay it is their means which should be assessed.

22.42 If the means of the person ordered to pay are insufficient to pay the compensation ordered immediately the court may allow time to pay or may order payment by instalments. According to Home Office Circular 53/1993 wherever possible the period of payment should not be more than 12 months. However, there is nothing wrong in principle with a period of payment longer than a year, provided that it was not an undue burden and too severe a punishment, having regard to the nature of the offence and the offender.[45]

---

39 Powers of Criminal Courts (Sentencing) Act 2000 s130(6).
40 Ibid, s130(7).
41 Ibid, s130(4).
42 *R v Horsham Justices ex p Richards* (1985) 7 Cr App R (S) 158, QBD.
43 *Hyde v Emery* (1984) 6 Cr App R (S) 206, QBD.
44 Powers of Criminal Courts (Sentencing) Act 2000 s130(11).
45 *R v Olliver and Olliver* (1989) 11 Cr App R (S) 10; [1989] Crim LR 387, CA.

22.43   Where the offender lacks the money to pay both a fine and a compensation order, a court should give priority to a compensation order.[46] All defendants found guilty of an offence are jointly and severally responsible for any loss, therefore, if more than one defendant is being sentenced for an offence, it is quite proper for the court to order one to pay all the compensation if s/he is the only one who has any means.[47]

Costs

Prosecution costs

22.44   A court may order an accused convicted of an offence to pay such prosecution costs as the court considers just and reasonable.[48] In the case of an offender under the age of 18, the amount of any costs ordered to be paid shall not exceed the amount of any fine imposed.[49]

22.45   In the case of a child or young person, the court is required to order a parent or guardian to pay any compensation order imposed against an offender aged under 16 and gives the court a discretion to order such payment in the case of an offender aged 16 or 17.[50] If a local authority has parental responsibility it may be ordered to pay the fine instead of the young offender. This power and the criteria for considering its use are considered in detail in chapter 31.

Defence costs

22.46   A court may make an order in favour of an accused for a payment to be made out of central funds in respect of his/her costs where:

- any information charging a person with an offence is not proceeded with;
- a defendant is discharged at committal proceedings;
- any information is dismissed at summary trial.[51]

22.47   Such an order is referred to as a defendant's cost order.

22.48   The Crown Court may also make a defendant's costs order where the accused is not tried for the offence or s/he has been tried and acquitted.[52]

22.49   For the purposes of this provision, 'accused' includes the parent or guardian of a child or young person, so that a defendant's costs order may be made in favour of a local authority.[53] In normal circumstances a defendant may expect to receive his/her costs to be paid out of central funds in any of the circumstances listed above.[54]

46 Powers of Criminal Courts (Sentencing) Act 2000 s130(12).
47 *R v Beddow* (1987) 9 Cr App R (S) 235, CA.
48 Prosecution of Offences Act 1985 s18(1).
49 Ibid, s18(5).
50 Ibid, s137.
51 Ibid, s16(1).
52 Ibid, s16(2).
53 *R v Preston Crown Court ex p Lancashire County Council* [1999] 1 WLR 142; [1998] 3 All ER 765, DC.
54 *R v Birmingham Juvenile Courts ex p H* (1992) *Times* 4 February.

22.50   Defence costs may also be claimed if the prosecution serve a written notice of discontinuance under the Prosecution of Offences Act 1985 s23. It is not necessary for the accused to return to court to claim his/her costs; instead a written request may be made to the clerk of the court.[55]

22.51   As the legal representation for young defendants will almost always be funded by the Criminal Defence Service, the main expense to be covered by a defendant's costs order is likely to be travel expenses for attending court. The cost of a child minder to look after other children while a parent is at court with the defendant may also be claimed for.

Enforcement of financial orders

Enforcement against the offender

22.51A If the young offender was ordered to pay the fine, compensation order or costs personally, any enforcement proceedings will be against the child or young person. Enforcement proceedings against a child or young person should be undertaken by the youth court unless the offender has attained the age of 18, in which case the appropriate court is the adult magistrates' court.

Enforcement against the parent or guardian

22.51B If the parent or guardian has been ordered to pay the financial order under Powers of Criminal Courts (Sentencing) Act 2000 s137, the magistrates' court has the power to enforce the order. Enforcement proceedings in these circumstances may only be against the parent or guardian not against the child or young person.

Means enquiry

22.51C If the young offender is in default the court may issue a summons requiring the child or young person to attend at a specified time and date or the court may issue a warrant for his/her arrest.[56] In normal circumstances the court will first issue a summons against the child or young person and only if s/he fails to attend will a warrant be issued. If on sentence a return date was set and the child or young person does not attend as required, the court is much more likely to issue a warrant straightaway.

22.51D When the defaulter is before the court, s/he will be asked to go into the witness box and take the oath. The court will then ask why the money has not been paid. It will also carry out a means enquiry. If the young person is living independently or for any other reason has significant financial commitments, it is advisable for any defence lawyer or social worker attending with him/her to prepare a list of income and outgoings before going into court.

---

55 *DPP v Denning* [1991] Crim LR 699; [1991] 3 All ER 439.
56 Magistrates' Courts Act 1980 s83(1).

Powers of the court

22.51E The court has the following powers in relation to a child or young person in default:

- remission of whole or part of a fine (Magistrates' Courts Act 1980 s85);
- giving more time to pay (Magistrates' Courts Act 1980 s75);
- making a money payment supervision order (Magistrates' Courts Act 1980 s88);
- imposing an attachment of earnings order (Attachment of Earnings Act 1971);
- issuing a distress warrant (Magistrates' Courts Act 1980 s76(1));
- imposing an attendance centre order (Powers of Criminal Courts (Sentencing) Act 2000 s60);
- imposing a curfew order or, if aged 16 or over, a community punishment order (Crime (Sentences) Act 1997 s35);
- ordering the offender's parent/guardian to enter into a recognizance to ensure payment by the young offender (Magistrates' Courts Act 1980 s81(1)(a)); and
- ordering the parent/guardian to pay instead of the young offender (Magistrates' Courts Act 1980 s81(1)(b)).

22.51F For offenders who have attained the age of 18, the court's powers are determined by Courts Act 2003 Sch 5 and the Collection of Fines (Final Scheme) Order 2006 SI No 1737. There will also be a power to commit the offender to detention in a young offender institution for default where the court finds wilful refusal or culpable neglect.[57]

Reparation order

22.52 A reparation order requires the offender to make reparation specified in the order to either a person or persons specified in the order (the victim(s) of the offence) or the community at large.[58]

Pre-conditions

22.53 A reparation order may be passed upon a child or young person convicted of any offence for which the sentence is not fixed by law.[59] A reparation order is not a community sentence, therefore the court does not need to consider whether the offence is serious enough to merit such an order.

22.54 A reparation order may not be made at the same time as:

- a custodial sentence;
- a generic community sentence;
- a supervision order with includes any additional requirements;

---

57 Magistrates' Courts Act 1980 ss76 and 82. 'Wilful refusal or culpable neglect' means something more than negligence, it must be sufficiently blameworthy to justify immediate imprisonment in the absence of mitigating factors: *R v Poole Justices ex p Benham* (1991) *Times* 10 October, QBD.
58 Powers of Criminal Courts (Sentencing) Act 2000 s73(1).
59 Ibid, s73(1).

- an action plan order; or
- a referral order.[60]

Age

22.55 A reparation order may be imposed upon any offender aged 10 to 17.[61]

Length of order

22.56 The order shall not require the offender to work for more than 24 hours in aggregate.[62] It must be completed within three months of the date of sentence.[63]

Procedural requirements

22.57 Before making a reparation order the court shall obtain and consider a written report by an officer of a local probation board, a social worker of a local authority social services department or a member of a youth offending team indicating:

- the type of work that is suitable for the offender; and
- the attitude of the victim or victims to the requirements proposed to be included in the order.[64]

22.58 Before making the order the court shall explain to the offender in ordinary language:

- the effect of the order and of the requirements proposed to be included in it;
- the consequences of a breach of the order; and
- that the court has power to review the order on the application either of the offender or of the responsible officer.[65]

22.59 The court shall give reasons if it does not make a reparation order in a case where it has power to do so.[66]

22.60 The order must name the local justice area in which it appears that the offender resides or will reside.[67]

Responsible officer

22.61 'Responsible officer' means one of the following specified in the order:

- an officer of a local probation board;
- a social worker of a local authority social services department; or
- a member of a youth offending team.[68]

60 Powers of Criminal Courts (Sentencing) Act 2000 s73(4).
61 Ibid, s73(1).
62 Ibid, s74(1).
63 Ibid, s74(8)(b).
64 Ibid, s73(5).
65 Ibid, s73(7).
66 Ibid, s73(8).
67 Ibid, s74(4).
68 Ibid, s74(5).

Requirements of the order

22.62   The requirements specified in the order shall be such as in the opinion of the court are commensurate with the seriousness of the offence, or the combination of the offence and one or more offences associated with it.[69]

22.63   Guidance issued by the Home Office[70] suggests that reparation may vary from a letter of apology to several hours a week of practical activity which benefits an individual victim or the community at large. Where possible, the nature of the reparation should be linked as closely as possible to the type of offence itself. The guidance gives the following examples:

- A 15-year-old boy is found guilty of daubing graffiti on the walls of a newsagent's shop. He is sentenced to a reparation order which, with the agreement of the newsagent, requires the offender to clean the graffiti from the walls, and to spend one hour under supervision every Saturday morning for two months helping the newsagent to sort out his stock.

- A 12-year-old girl is found guilty of vandalising an elderly lady's garden and shouting abusive language at her. She is sentenced to a reparation order which requires her, with the victim's agreement, to meet with the victim in order to hear her describe the effect that this behaviour has had on her and to allow the offender to explain why he has behaved in this way, and to apologise. This meeting might be arranged and supervised by a local voluntary organisation working with victims and offenders, in support of the youth offending team.

- A 16-year-old boy has caused damage to a local children's playground. The court sentences him to a reparation order. As there is no obvious, specific victim in this case, the reparation is designed to benefit the community at large, many of whom use the playground; the offender is required to spend one hour every weekend under supervision helping to repair the damage he has caused.

22.64   As far as is practicable the requirements of the order shall be such as to avoid:

- any conflict with the offender's religious beliefs;
- any interference with the times, if any, at which the offender normally works or attends school or any other educational establishment; or
- any conflict with the requirements of any community order to which s/he may be subject.[71]

Binding over

22.65   Binding over is a procedure whereby the court seeks to avoid anticipated breaches of the peace by asking a person to enter into an agreement to be of good conduct for a specified period of time not exceeding three years. As part of this agreement the person being bound over will enter into a recognizance for a specified sum of money. If the court subsequently finds

---

69 Powers of Criminal Courts (Sentencing) Act 2000 s74(2).
70 The Crime and Disorder Act – Guidance Document: Reparation Order.
71 Powers of Criminal Courts (Sentencing) Act 2000 s74(3).

that the person has broken the agreement s/he is liable to forfeit some or all of the recognizance in a procedure called estreatment.

22.66 In relation to children and young persons, the courts have powers to bind over both the young defendant and the parent or guardian. The circumstances when parents or guardians may be bound over are considered in chapter 31.

22.67 Any court with a criminal jurisdiction may bind over a person before it. Two distinct powers exist:

- on complaint under Magistrates' Courts Act 1980 s115;
- under common law powers.

Magistrates' Courts Act 1980 s115

22.68 A person normally appears before the court under this section after the police have exercised their common law powers of arrest when a breach of the peace has taken place. If the police consider there is a continuing risk of a breach of the peace, the person will be held in custody until s/he may be brought before a court.

Which court?

22.69 The hearing of complaints under this section is not a matter which has been specifically assigned to the youth court under Children and Young Persons Act 1933 s46 and therefore it could be argued that a child or young person should be taken before the adult magistrates' court. As discussed elsewhere, the authors consider that section 46 does not exclusively define the competence of the youth court and it would clearly be preferable for a youth court to deal with any alleged breach.

Procedure

22.70 In court, the defendant will be asked whether s/he admits the breach of the peace. If it is admitted, the court will proceed to consider whether to bind over the defendant. If the breach is not admitted it must be proved beyond reasonable doubt that there had been a use of violence or the threat of violence.[72]

Appeal

22.71 There is a right of appeal against a bind over to the Crown Court.[73] The appeal is by way of a complete rehearing.

Common law powers

22.72 These powers of the court are a form of preventative justice when the court has material before it leading it to the conclusion that there is a risk of a breach of the peace in the future. The power may be exercised after the prosecution discontinue proceedings, when a defendant is convicted or even when there is an acquittal.

---

72 *Percy v DPP* (1994) *Times* 13 December, QBD.
73 Magistrates' Courts (Appeals from Binding Over Orders) Act 1956.

22.73   If the court is considering binding over a defendant, it is good practice to warn him/her and give an opportunity for representations to be made either by the defendant or his/her lawyer. Unless the court intends to fix the recognizance at a trivial sum, the court should allow the defendant to give information about his/her means.

Can a child or young person be compelled to consent to be bound over?

22.74   In the case of adults, the court may imprison anyone who refuses to be bound over. In the case of children and young persons, this power does not exist. In *Veater v Glennon*[74] it was held that no other sanction existed and accordingly a bind over could not be imposed. Notwithstanding this decision, a bind over may be imposed if the child or young person agrees to be bound over.[75]

22.75   *Veater v Glennon* predates the Powers of Criminal Courts (Sentencing) Act 2000 and it may be questioned whether it is still accurately describes the law. Section 89(1) of the Act forbids the use of imprisonment for anyone under the age of 21. Section 60(1)(b) of the Act allows a court to impose an attendance centre order upon a person under the age of 21 where:

> ... a court would have power, but for section 89 ... to commit a person aged under 21 to prison in default of any sum of money or for failing to do or abstain from doing anything required to be done or left undone ...

22.76   It could be argued that this section gives a court the power to impose an attendance centre order upon a child or young person who refuses to be bound over.

Application to children and young persons

22.77   When a child or young person is charged with a minor assault or public order offence in circumstances where a caution is unrealistic, the defence lawyer may wish to canvas the possibility of the prosecution being discontinued if the young defendant consents to being bound over. It is not necessary for the defendant to admit a past use of violence to justify a court binding him/her over.[76]

Estreatment

22.78   Estreatment is the legal process by which some or all of the recognizance may be forfeited to the court. Proceedings start by way of complaint and the person who entered into the recognizance will be summonsed to attend court.

22.79   Estreatment proceedings against a child or young person is not a matter which is expressly assigned to the youth court under Children and Young

---

74 [1981] 1 WLR 567; [1981] 2 All ER 306; 145 JP 158, QBD.
75 *Conlan v Oxford* (1983) 5 Cr App R (S) 237; (1984) 148 JP 97.
76 *Hourihane v Metropolitan Police Commissioner* (1995) *Independent*, 18 January.

Persons Act 1933 s46(1). Nevertheless, it is the opinion of the authors that the appropriate court to hear the proceedings would be the youth court.[77]

Contempt of court

What constitutes contempt?

22.80 Contempt of Court Act 1981 s12 provides that it is a contempt of court where a person:

- wilfully insults the justice or justices, any witnesses or officer of the court or any solicitor or counsel having business in the court, during his/her or their sitting or attendance at court or in going to or returning from the court; or
- wilfully interrupts the proceedings of the court or otherwise misbehaves in court.

22.81 'Otherwise misbehaves' could include assaulting anyone concerned in the proceedings and disrespectful behaviour which impairs the authority of the court.

22.82 It is also a contempt of court for a witness to refuse to give evidence without just cause. It would be a defence to show that the witness was refusing to testify because of duress[78] or because of a well-founded fear of attack.[79]

Procedure

22.83 Faced with gross contempt of the court which is disrupting proceedings, a court may take immediate action by detaining the contemnor to stop the disruption. This power would also seem to apply to children and young persons. However, it must be stressed that it would only extend to detention in the court cells until at the latest the end of the court sitting.

22.84 Before any final decision as to how the contempt will be dealt with, the contemnor has the right to legal representation. The court should not act in the heat of the moment, but instead should leave itself some time for reflection. Before reaching a final decision as to whether to impose any sanction, the court should allow the contemnor the opportunity to apologise for his/her behaviour.[80]

22.85 If the court is dealing with a witness who refuses to give evidence, it should allow a period for reflection, perhaps even overnight, and the witness should be allowed the opportunity to have legal advice.

What sanctions are available against a child or young person?

22.86 It is not completely clear what sanctions are available, but in any event it would seem that the court's powers are extremely limited.

---

77 See paras 11.22 onwards.
78 *R v K* (1984) 148 JP 410.
79 *R v Lewis (James John)* (1993) 96 Cr App R 412.
80 *R v Moran* (1985) 81 Cr App R 51.

Detention and training order

22.87 No one under the age of 18 may be imprisoned for contempt of court.[81] Powers of Criminal Courts (Sentencing) Act 2000 s100 allows a court to sentence a person aged 12 to 17 convicted of an imprisonable offence to a detention and training order. A person found to be in contempt of court is not a person convicted of an offence[82] and therefore there is no power to impose a detention and training order for contempt. If a person has attained the age of 18 s/he may be committed to detention for contempt pursuant to section 108 of the 2000 Act.

Community penalty

22.88 As a finding of contempt is not 'a conviction for an offence' it has been held that it was not possible to impose a probation order (later renamed a community rehabilitation order) upon the contemnor as being convicted of an offence is a pre-condition for the sentence.[83] The same principle would seem to apply to other community orders.

Financial order

22.89 It would seem that a fine is the only penalty available for a child or young person. It would also seem to be possible to bind over the person if a further breach of the peace is feared.

Forfeiture order

General power

22.90 A court may make a forfeiture order where a person is convicted of an offence and the court is satisfied that any property lawfully seized from him/her or which was in his/her possession or under his/her control at the time when s/he was apprehended for the offence:

- has been used for the purpose of committing, or facilitating the commission, of any offence; or
- was intended by the offender for that purpose.[84]

22.91 A court may order the forfeiture of, for example, a screwdriver used to break into cars or cans of spray paint used to put graffiti on trains.

Specific powers

22.92 There also exist a number of specific powers of forfeiture available to the courts. The ones most applicable to young offenders allow for the forfeiture of:

---

81   Powers of Criminal Courts (Sentencing) Act 2000 s108.
82   *R v Byas* [1995] Crim LR 439, CA.
83   *R v Palmer* (1992) 13 Cr App R (S) 595, [1992] 1 WLR 568.
84   Powers of Criminal Courts (Sentencing) Act 2000 s143(1).

- drugs;[85]
- offensive weapons;[86]
- firearms and prohibited weapons.[87]

Recommendation for deportation

22.93 A youth court or Crown Court may recommend that an offender should be deported, but only if:

- the offender is not a British citizen;[88]
- s/he has attained the age of 17 by the date of conviction;[89]
- the offence is imprisonable in the case of an adult.

Procedure

22.94 A person liable to deportation must be given at least seven days' written notice. This is usually given by the police at the time of charge. If this has not been done, the case must be adjourned for seven days.

22.95 The offender should be given warning that the court is considering exercising the power to recommend deportation. The defence lawyer will need to address the issue specifically. The court must give reasons for its decision to recommend deportation.[90] Once a court has recommended deportation, the offender is automatically detained under the Immigration Act 1971 unless the court grants bail.

Grounds for recommendation

22.96 The court must be of the opinion that the offender's continuing presence in the United Kingdom would be detrimental to the community, and relevant considerations include the seriousness of the offence, the offender's record and the likely detrimental effect upon third parties.[91]

22.97 A recommendation may be inappropriate if the young offender has spent all his formative years in the United Kingdom.[92] In the case of a young person, regard must be had to the right to family life contained in Article 8 of the European Convention on Human Rights. It is arguable that a young person should not be deported to a country where s/he has never lived and where his/her family live in the United Kingdom.[93]

---

85 Misuse of Drugs Act 1971 s27.
86 Prevention of Crime Act 1953 s1(2).
87 Firearms Act 1968 s52.
88 Defined in the British Nationality Act 1981, Part I: EU nationals may only be deported in limited circumstances specified in EU Directive 64/221 articles 3 and 9 (see also *R v Bouchereau* [1978] QB 732).
89 A person is deemed to have attained the age of 17 if, on consideration of any available evidence, s/he appears to the court to have done so: Immigration Act 1971 s6(3)(a).
90 *R v Rodney* (1996) 2 Cr App R (S) 230, CA and *R v Bozat* [1997] 1 Cr App R (S) 270, CA.
91 *R v Nazari* [1980] 1 WLR 1366, CA.
92 *R v Dudeye* [1998] 2 Cr App R (S) 430, CA.
93 See, eg, *Lamguindaz v UK* (1994) 17 EHRR 213.

Appeal

22.98   A recommendation for deportation may be appealed in the same way as any other part of the sentence. Representations may also be made to the Immigration and Nationality Department to persuade the Home Secretary not to act upon the recommendation.

Binding over to come up for judgment

22.99   This common law power is only available to the Crown Court. On conviction, the offender may be bound over on specified conditions. A recognizance will also be taken. If the offender breaks any of the conditions during a specified period, s/he may be brought back before the court for sentence.

22.100   The power has been used to require an offender to leave the country. In *R v Williams*[94] an 18-year-old had been convicted of theft and he had a number of previous convictions. He was British-born of Jamaican parents. The Crown Court judge bound him over to come up for judgment on condition that he accompanied his mother to Jamaica and did not return to the United Kingdom for five years. It was held that such a condition could not be imposed upon the defendant as he was a British citizen and it should generally be used sparingly, for example to require an offender to return to a country of which he was a citizen and where s/he normally resided.

Disqualification and endorsement of driving licences

22.101   When a person is found guilty of a road traffic offence and certain other offences related to motor vehicles, the court has extra powers on sentencing which relate to the offender's driving licence. These powers are:

- to impose penalty points;
- to endorse the offender's licence;
- to disqualify the offender from driving.

Penalty points

22.102   For most road traffic offences the court is required to impose penalty points in addition to any other sentence. The number of penalty points to be imposed vary depending on the offence (see table 22).

22.103   If an offender does not have a driving licence or is too young to apply for one, the court should still impose penalty points for the offence. The Driving Vehicle Licence Agency will then be informed and any licence issued subsequently will be endorsed with any outstanding points.

22.104   New drivers are subject to a two-year probationary period beginning with the day that the driving test is passed. A probationary driver will have his/her full licence revoked if s/he receives six or more penalty points in

94 [1982] 1 WLR 1398, CA.

respect of offences committed within three years of the latest offence(s).[95] Revocation is not the same as disqualification. The young offender will still be able to drive but his/her licence will revert to a provisional one. The offender will need to take the ordinary driving test again.

Endorsement

22.105 An endorsement is a record on the offender's licence that s/he has been found guilty of an offence. The endorsement will also record how many penalty points have been imposed for the offence. For many road traffic offences the court is required to order the endorsement. No endorsement is made if the offender is disqualified at the same time; instead the fact that s/he is now disqualified is recorded.

Disqualification

22.106 An offender may be disqualified by a court as part of the sentence or s/he may be disqualified as a result of an accumulation of penalty points by what is usually termed the 'totting up' system. For any endorsable offence the court will have a discretionary power to order disqualification. In addition, some offences require the court to disqualify.

Discretionary disqualification

22.107 All offences which carry penalty points give the court a discretion to disqualify. The power should only be exercised in cases involving bad driving, persistent motoring offences or the use of the vehicle for the purposes of crime.[96] With young defendants, the court should also consider the serious consequences that disqualification may have on his/her future employment prospects.

Mandatory disqualification

22.108 Certain offences carry a mandatory disqualification. In such cases the minimum disqualification is for 12 months unless the court for special reasons thinks fit to order the offender to be disqualified for a shorter period or not to order him/her to be disqualified.[97] In the case of aggravated vehicle-taking, the fact that the offender did not actually drive the car shall not be regarded as special reason for departing from the minimum period of disqualification.[98]

22.109 Special rules apply to an offender convicted of any of the following offences under the Road Traffic Act 1988:

- driving or attempting to drive while unfit (section 4(1));
- causing death by careless driving while under the influence of drink or drugs (section 3A);
- driving or attempting to drive with excess alcohol (section 5(1)(a));

---

95 Road Traffic (New Drivers) Act 1995 s2.
96 *R v Callister* [1993] RTR 70 per Morland J.
97 Road Traffic Offenders Act 1988 s34(1).
98 Ibid, s34(2).

- failing to provide a specimen for analysis or laboratory test, where the specimen was required to ascertain ability to drive or proportion of alcohol at time offender was driving or attempting to drive (section 7(6)).

22.110 If the offender has been convicted of one of the offences listed above and, at any time in the previous ten years s/he was convicted of any of the offences on the list, the minimum period of disqualification following the second conviction is three years.[99]

Interim disqualification

22.111 It is possible to make an interim disqualification where the court:
- commits the offender for sentence to the Crown Court; or
- defers sentence; or
- adjourns for the preparation of a pre-sentence report.[100]

22.112 Although not specifically mentioned, it is arguable that the power applies when a court remits for sentence under Powers of Criminal Courts (Sentencing) Act 2000 s8.

Totting up

22.113 If an offender receives 12 or more penalty points in respect of offences committed within three years of the latest offence(s), the court must disqualify him/her for a minimum period of six months.[101] If the offender has a previous disqualification imposed within three years of the commission of the current offence(s), the minimum period of disqualification is 12 months. If there are two such disqualifications, the minimum is two years' disqualification.

Length of period of disqualification

22.114 Subject to the minimum periods of disqualification applicable in certain circumstances, the following principles apply:
- where there is a real chance that the ability to drive will improve a young offender's employment prospects, the court should keep any disqualification to a minimum;[102]
- a lengthy period of disqualification should be avoided, particularly when imposed at the same time as a custodial sentence as it may have an adverse effect upon the defendant's chances of rehabilitation;[103]
- with defendants who seem incapable of leaving motor cars alone, a lengthy period of disqualification will only invite the offender to commit further offences in relation to motor cars which would be counterproductive and so contrary to the public interest;[104]

---

99 Road Traffic Offenders Act 1988 s34(3).
100 Ibid, s26(1) and (2).
101 Ibid, s35.
102 *R v Aspden* [1975] RTR 456, CA.
103 *R v Russell* [1993] RTR 249, CA.
104 *R v Thomas* [1983] 1 WLR 1490 (two years under totting up procedure reduced to 12 months).

Table 22: Disqualification and endorsement

Offence	Disqualification	Penalty Points
Road Traffic Act 1988		
Dangerous driving: section 2	Mandatory*	3–11
Careless driving: section 3	Discretionary	3–9
Driving while unfit: section 4(1)	Mandatory	3–11
Drunk in charge: section 4(2)	Discretionary	10
Driving with excess alcohol: section 5(1)	Mandatory	3–11
Failing to give specimen for breath test: section 6	Discretionary	4
Failing to give specimen for laboratory test: section 7	Mandatory	3–11
No headgear: section 16	–	–
Failing to comply with traffic directions: section 35	Discretionary**	3
Using vehicle in dangerous condition: section 40A	Discretionary	3
No test certificate: section 47	–	–
Driving otherwise than in accordance with licence: section 87(1)	Discretionary	3–6
Causing or permitting above: section 87(2)	–	–
Driving whilst disqualified: section 103(1)(b)	Discretionary	6
Driving without insurance: section 143	Discretionary	6–8
Failing to stop after accident: section 170(4)	Discretionary	5–10
Theft Act 1968		
Aggravated vehicle taking: section 12A	Mandatory	3–11
Theft/attempted theft of motor vehicle	Discretionary	–
Taking without consent: section 12	Discretionary	–
Going equipped to steal (in relation to the theft of motor vehicles): section 25	Discretionary	–

* Offender must be required to take special driving test before s/he may receive full licence: Road Traffic Offenders Act 1988 s36(1) and (2).

** If directions given by a police officer or traffic warden.

- where a defendant's record demonstrates that his/her driving constitutes a risk to the public, a lengthy period of disqualification is proper to enable the young offender to mature.[105]

Disqualification as a sentence for any offence

22.115 The court by or before which a person is convicted of an offence may, in addition to or instead of dealing with him/her in any other way, order him/her to be disqualified, for such period as it thinks fit, for holding or obtaining a driving licence.[106] A court which makes such an order shall require the offender to produce any driving licence held by him/her.[107]

22.116 Although not specifically dealt with in the statute, this power is presumably only exercisable where the offender is of sufficient age to be able to hold a driving licence.

---

105 *R v Gibbons* (1987) 9 Cr App R (S) 21, CA. See also *R v Sharkey and Daniels* (1995) 16 Cr App R (S) 257, CA, where five years' disqualification upheld after convictions for aggravated vehicle-taking.

106 Powers of Criminal Courts (Sentencing) Act 2000 s146(1).

107 Ibid, s146(4).

Community orders

Introduction

23.1   A community order is defined as any of the following orders:

(i)   a curfew order;
(ii)   an exclusion order;
(iii)   an attendance order;
(iv)   an action plan order;
(v)   a supervision order;
(vi)   a community rehabilitation order;
(vii)   a community punishment order;
(viii) a community punishment and rehabilitation order; or
(ix)   a drug treatment and testing order.[1]

23.2   The first five orders may also be referred to as youth community orders.[2]

Curfew order

23.3   By Powers of Criminal Courts (Sentencing) Act 2000 s37, where a offender has been convicted of any offence, the court may make a curfew order, that is an order requiring him/her to remain, for periods specified in the order, at a specified place. As well as the power to order an offender to stay indoors at a particular time, the court may order the monitoring of the offender's compliance by means of electronic tagging of the offender.

Pre-conditions

23.4   A curfew order may only be imposed if the court considers:

- the offence, or the combination of the offence and associated offences; to be serious enough; and
- the order to be the most suitable for the offender.[3]

23.5   The order may be imposed for any offence whether or not it is imprisonable.

Age

23.6   A curfew order may be imposed on any offender who has attained the age of 10.

Length of the order

23.7   The order may not last beyond six months from the day on which it was made.[4]

---

1   Criminal Justice Act 2003 s147(1) and Criminal Justice Act 2003 (Commencement Order No 8 and Transitional and Saving Provisions) Order 2005 SI No 950, Sch 2 para 10.
2   Criminal Justice Act 2003 s147(2).
3   Ibid, s148(1).
4   Powers of Criminal Courts (Sentencing) Act 2000 s37(3)(a).

23.8   In the case of an offender aged under 16 on conviction, the maximum length of the order is three months.[5] This restriction will be removed upon implementation of Anti-social Behaviour Act 2003 Sch 2 para 2(2).[6]

Requirements of the order

23.9   The order will specify the period of each day when the offender must not leave a specified place (usually, but not necessarily, the offender's home address). More than one specified place may be specified and the court may specify different times for different days of the week. The order may not specify a period of less than two hours or more than 12 hours in any one day.[7]

23.10   As part of the curfew order, the court may include a requirement for securing the electronic monitoring of the offender's whereabouts during the curfew periods specified in the order.[8] Electronic monitoring will be by way of a tag fitted to the young offender's ankle (or occasionally his/ her wrist) and the installation of monitoring equipment in the curfew address(es).

23.11   The court may not include a electronic monitoring requirement unless:

- it has been notified by the secretary of state that electronic monitoring arrangements are available in the area in which the place proposed to be specified in the order is situated; and
- it is satisfied that the necessary provision can be made under those arrangements.[9]

23.12   The requirements of a curfew order shall, as far as is practicable, be such as to avoid:

- any conflict with the offender's religious beliefs; or
- any conflict with the requirements of any other community order to which s/he may be subject; and
- any interference with the times, if any, at which s/he normally works or attends school or any other educational establishment.[10]

Procedural requirements

23.13   The court is not required to obtain a pre-sentence report before imposing a curfew order. However, the court is required to obtain and consider information about the place proposed to be specified in the order (including information as to the attitude of the persons likely to be affected by the enforced presence there of the offender).[11] It is submitted that this is particularly important in the case of young offenders where the court is likely

---

5 Powers of Criminal Courts (Sentencing) Act 2000 s37(4).
6 By the Anti-social Behaviour Act 2003 (Commencement No 4) Order 2004 SI No 2168 the restriction has been repealed in the pilot areas listed in appendix 12.
7 Powers of Criminal Courts (Sentencing) Act 2000 s37(3)(b).
8 Ibid, s36B(1).
9 Ibid s36B(2).
10 Ibid, s37(5).
11 Ibid, s37(8).

to be requiring them to remain in the parental home. Requiring a child or young person to remain at a particular address may, for example, have child protection implications or interfere with the child care arrangements made by parents who have separated.

23.14 Before making the order, the court shall explain to the offender in ordinary language:

- the effect of the order (including the effect of any electronic tagging);
- the fact that on breach the court may impose a fine, community service order or re-sentence; and
- that the court has the power to review the order at the application of either the supervisor or the offender.[12]

23.15 An offender need not consent before a curfew order is imposed.

Combining a curfew order with other community orders

23.16 A curfew order may be made at the same time as a supervision order.[13] This is most commonly done in conjunction with an Intensive Supervision and Surveillance Programme.

Responsible officer

23.17 The responsible officer will be:

- where the offender is also subject to a supervision order, the person who is the supervising officer in relation to the supervision order; and
- in any other case, the person who is responsible for monitoring the offender's whereabouts during the curfew periods specified in the order.[14]

23.18 In the latter case, this will be an employee of the private company contracted to provide electronic monitoring in the court's area.[15]

Amendment of the order

Legal representation

23.19 If a representation order was granted to the offender in the original proceedings, this order will cover representation at the hearing to determine an application for variation. Attendance at any hearings and other work done in relation to an application to vary must be justified as reasonable.[16] If a claim has already been submitted to the Criminal Defence Service, then a supplementary claim can be made after the conclusion of the application to vary.[17]

---

12 Powers of Criminal Courts (Sentencing) Act 2000 s37(10).
13 Ibid, s64A.
14 Ibid, s37(12) as amended by Anti-social Behaviour Act 2003 Sch 2 para 2(3).
15 Curfew (Responsible Officer) Order 2001 SI No 2234 amended by SI 2001 No 3344.
16 Criminal Defence Service, *Criminal Costs Manual*, para 3.10.
17 Ibid, para 3.10.4.

Amendment by reason of change of residence

23.20 While a curfew order is in force, a youth court may, and on the application of the responsible officer shall, amend the order by substituting a new place in the new local justice area for the place specified in the order.[18]

23.21 A court shall not amend under this provision a curfew order which contains requirements which, in the opinion of the court, cannot be complied with unless the offender continues to reside in the local justice area specified in the original order, unless it:

- cancels those requirements; or
- substitutes for those requirements other requirements which can be complied with if the offender ceases to reside in that area.[19]

Amendment of requirements of order

23.22 A youth court for the local justice area in which the place for the time specified in the order is situated may, on application by the offender or the responsible officer, amend a curfew order:

- by cancelling any of the requirements of the order; or
- by inserting in the order (either in addition to, or in substitution for, any of its requirements) any requirement which the court could include if it were then making the order.[20]

23.23 A youth court shall not amend a curfew order by extending the curfew periods beyond the end of six months from the date of the original order.[21]

Revocation of order

Powers of youth court

23.24 Application may be made either by the offender or the responsible officer to a youth court acting for the local justice area specified for the time being in the order.

23.25 If, after having regard to the circumstances which have arisen since the imposition of the order, the court is satisfied that it would be in the interests of justice that the order be revoked or that the offender be dealt with in another manner, it may:

- revoke the order; or
- revoke the order and deal with the offender, for the offence in respect of which the order was made, in any manner in which it could deal with him/her if s/he had just been convicted by the court of the offence.[22]

23.26 In re-sentencing an offender, the court shall take into account the extent to which the offender has complied with the requirements of the original order.

---

18 Powers of Criminal Courts (Sentencing) Act 2000 Sch 3 para 15(1) and (2).
19 Ibid, Sch 3 para 15(3).
20 Ibid, Sch 3 para 16(1).
21 Ibid, Sch 3 para 16(2).
22 Ibid, Sch 3 para 10(1) and (3).

23.27   No application for revocation may be made by the offender while an appeal against sentence is pending.[23]

Powers of Crown Court

23.28   Where a curfew order made by the Crown Court is still in force, the Crown Court may revoke the order:

- on the application of the offender or the responsible officer; or
- where the offender has been convicted of an offence before the Crown Court.

23.29   If it appears to the Crown Court to be in the interests of justice to do so, having regard to the circumstances which have arisen since the order was made, the Crown Court may:

- revoke the order; or
- revoke the order and deal with the offender for the offence in respect of which the order was made, in any manner in which it could deal with him/her if s/he had just been convicted by the court of the offence.[24]

23.30   In re-sentencing an offender the Crown Court shall take into account the extent to which the offender has complied with the requirements of the curfew order.[25]

Revocation following custodial sentence by youth court unconnected with order

23.31   A curfew order may also be revoked by a youth court at the time of sentence for another offence. This power may only be exercised where:

- an offender in relation to whom a curfew order is in force is convicted of an offence by a youth court not acting for the local justice area specified in the order;
- the court has imposed a custodial sentence on the offender; and
- it appears to the court, on the application of the offender or the responsible officer, that it would be in the interests of justice to exercise its powers having regard to circumstances which have arisen since the order was made.[26]

23.32   The youth court may:

- if the order was made by a youth court, revoke it; or
- if the order was made by the Crown Court, commit the offender in custody or on bail until s/he can be brought or appear before the Crown Court.[27]

23.33   Where an offender is brought or appears before the Crown Court and it appears to the Crown Court to be in the interests of justice to do so, having

---

23 Powers of Criminal Courts (Sentencing) Act 2000 Sch 3 para 10(7).
24 Ibid, Sch 3 para 11(2).
25 Ibid, Sch 3 para 11(3).
26 Ibid, Sch 3 para 12(1).
27 Ibid, Sch 3 para 12(3).

regard to circumstances which have arisen since the original order was made, the Crown Court may revoke the order.[28]

Exclusion order (*pilot areas only*)

23.34 Where a person is convicted of an offence, the sentencing court may make an exclusion order prohibiting the offender from entering a specified place for a specified period.

23.35 The Home Office has given the following guidance on the making of orders in the original pilot areas:

> A court may wish to consider an exclusion order where it believes the offender should be kept away from a particular address or addresses (such as the home of a victim), or from particular types of establishment in a limited area (such as specified public houses or a shopping mall at particular times) or from an area (such as a town centre at night). As in all cases, care should be taken that the prohibition is not disproportionate. For example, it may not be necessary to exclude an offender from a town centre at all times if his offending typically takes place at night and where a day-time exclusion would interfere with his need to shop, or take part in any intervention set out as part of an ISSP programme, i.e. meetings with his ISSP supervising officer.
>
> Exclusion order proposals will be made via a full PSR during the assessment stage. They will usually be made in cases where custody is the only other likely option. Exclusion orders can be used as the sole order of a community sentence but are most likely to be considered as one element of a programme of intensive interventions where, for example, it can be used alongside ...a supervision order or community rehabilitation order to deliver an ISSP.[29]

Age

23.36 The order may be imposed on any offender over the age of 10.

Length of order

23.37 In the case of an offender who has attained the age of 16, the order may be for any period up to a maximum of 24 months.[30]

23.38 In the case of an offender under 16 on conviction, the maximum period is three months.[31]

Requirements of the order

23.39 In making the order the court may specify one or more areas which the offender must not enter. The court may specify that the offender not enter the exclusion zone at any hour during the duration of the order or at specified times of day during the order.

---

28 Powers of Criminal Courts (Sentencing) Act 2000 Sch 3 para 13.
29 Home Office Circular 61/2004, paras 6.2 and 6.7.
30 Powers of Criminal Courts (Sentencing) Act 2000 s40A(1).
31 Ibid, s40A(4).

23.40   It is obviously important that the extent of any exclusion zone is clear. The Home Office advises that the writer of the pre-sentence report should be very specific about the details of the proposed zone(s) and should represent them on a map showing the zone(s).[32]

23.41   The requirements shall, as far as practicable, be such as to avoid:

- any conflict with the offender's religious beliefs or with the requirements of any other community order to which s/he may be subject; and
- any interference with the times, if any, at which s/he normally works or attends school or any other educational establishment.[33]

23.42   A court may include in the exclusion order requirements for securing the electronic monitoring of the offender's compliance with any other requirements of the order.[34]

23.43   A court shall not make an exclusion order unless the court has been notified by the secretary of state that arrangements for monitoring the offender's whereabouts are available in the area where the proposed exclusion zone is situated and the notice has not been withdrawn.[35]

Procedural requirements

23.44   Before making an exclusion order in respect of an offender who on conviction is under 16, the court shall obtain and consider information about his/her family circumstances and the likely effect of such an order on those circumstances.[36]

23.45   If an electronic monitoring requirement is not practicable without the co-operation of a person other than the offender, it may not be included in the exclusion order without the consent of that person.[37]

23.46   Before making an exclusion order, the court shall explain to the offender in ordinary language:

- the effect of the order, including any additional requirements for electronic monitoring;
- the consequences which may follow if the offender breaches the order; and
- that the court has power to review the order on the application of the offender, the responsible officer or any affected person.[38]

23.47   After the order is made, the court must give a copy of the order to the offender and the responsible officer.[39] The court must also give any affected

---

32 Home Office Circular 61/2004 para 6.9.
33 Powers of Criminal Courts (Sentencing) Act 2000 s40A(5).
34 Ibid, s36B(1).
35 At the time of writing arrangements are only available in the pilot areas specified in appendix 12. For more information regarding the form of the monitoring, see Home Office Circular 61/2004.
36 Powers of Criminal Courts (Sentencing) Act 2000 s40A(9).
37 Ibid, s36B(3).
38 Ibid, s40A(10).
39 Ibid, s40A(11)(a).

person any information relating to the order which the court considers it appropriate for him/her to have.[40] A person is an affected person if:

- electronic monitoring is included in the order by virtue of his/her consent; or
- a prohibition is included in the order for the purpose of protecting him/her from being approached by the offender.[41]

Responsible officer

23.48 When making an exclusion order the court must include provision for making a person responsible for monitoring the offender's whereabouts during the periods when the prohibition operates.[42] This responsible officer shall be an employee of the regional contractor delivering the monitoring service.[43]

Amendment of the order

Legal representation

23.49 If a representation order was granted to the offender in the original proceedings this order will cover representation at the hearing to determine an application for variation. Attendance at any hearings and other work done in relation to an application to vary must be justified as reasonable.[44] If a claim has already been submitted to the Criminal Defence Service, then a supplementary claim can be made after the conclusion of the application to vary.[45]

Amendment by reason of change of residence

23.50 While an exclusion order is in force, a youth court may, and on the application of the responsible officer shall, amend the order by substituting the other local justice area for the area specified in the order.[46]

Amendment of requirements of order

23.51 A youth court for the local justice area in which the place for the time specified in the order is situated may, on application by the offender or the responsible officer, amend an exclusion order:

- by cancelling any of the requirements of the order; or
- by inserting in the order (either in addition to, or in substitution for, any of its requirements) any requirement which the court could include if it were then making the order.[47]

---

40 Ibid, s40A(11(b).
41 Ibid, s40A(13).
42 Powers of Criminal Courts (Sentencing) Act 2000 s40A(6).
43 The current contractors are Premier Monitoring Services and Securicor Justice Services: Exclusion Order (Monitoring of Offenders) Order 2005 SI No 979.
44 Criminal Defence Service, *Criminal Costs Manual* (2005), para 3.10.
45 Ibid, para 3.10.4.
46 Powers of Criminal Courts (Sentencing) Act 2000 Sch 3 para 15(1) and (2).
47 Ibid, Sch 3 para 16(1).

23.52   A youth court shall not amend an exclusion order by extending the period for which the offender is prohibited from entering the place in question beyond the end of three months from the date of the original order.[48]

Revocation of the order

Powers of youth court

23.53   Application may be made either by the offender or the responsible officer to a youth court acting for the local justice area specified for the time being in the order.

23.54   If, after having regard to the circumstances which have arisen since the imposition of the order, the court is satisfied that it would be in the interests of justice that the order be revoked or that the offender be dealt with in another manner, it may:

- revoke the order; or
- revoke the order and deal with the offender, for the offence in respect of which the order was made, in any manner in which it could deal with him/her if s/he had just been convicted by the court of the offence.[49]

23.55   In re-sentencing an offender, the court shall take into account the extent to which the offender has complied with the requirements of the original order.

23.56   No application for revocation may be made by the offender while an appeal against sentence is pending.[50]

Powers of Crown Court

23.57   Where an exclusion order made by the Crown Court is still in force, the Crown Court may revoke the order:

- on the application of the offender or the responsible officer; or
- where the offender has been convicted of an offence before the Crown Court.

23.58   If it appears to the Crown Court to be in the interests of justice to do so, having regard to the circumstances which have arisen since the order was made, the Crown Court may:

- revoke the order; or
- revoke the order and deal with the offender for the offence in respect of which the order was made, in any manner in which it could deal with him/her if s/he had just been convicted by the court of the offence.[51]

23.59   In re-sentencing an offender, the Crown Court shall take into account the extent to which the offender has complied with the requirements of the exclusion order.[52]

---

48   Powers of Criminal Courts (Sentencing) Act 2000 Sch 3 para 16(3).
49   Ibid, Sch 3 para 10(1) and (3).
50   Ibid, Sch 3 para 10(7).
51   Ibid, Sch 3 para 11(2).
52   Ibid, Sch 3 para 11(3).

Revocation following custodial sentence by youth court unconnected with order

23.60   An exclusion order may also be revoked by a youth court at the time of sentence for another offence. This power may only be exercised where:

- an offender in relation to whom an exclusion order is in force is convicted of an offence by a youth court not acting for the local justice area specified in the order;
- the court has imposed a custodial sentence on the offender; and
- it appears to the court, on the application of the offender or the responsible officer, that it would be in the interests of justice to exercise its powers having regard to circumstances which have arisen since the order was made.[53]

23.61   The youth court may:

- if the order was made by a youth court, revoke it; or
- if the order was made by the Crown Court, commit the offender in custody or on bail until s/he can be brought or appear before the Crown Court.[54]

23.62   Where an offender is brought or appears before the Crown Court and it appears to the Crown Court to be in the interests of justice to do so, having regard to circumstances which have arisen since the original order was made, the Crown Court may revoke the order.[55]

Attendance centre order

23.63   Attendance centres used to be managed by the Home Office and were largely staffed by police officers. In April 2000 responsibility for the management of the centres was passed to the Youth Justice Board. The local youth offending manager will act as the Board's local agent and is responsible for appointing the officer in charge of the attendance centre. In some areas, youth offending team staff are involved in the programme of activities at individual attendance centres, which are still usually held in school premises on alternate Saturdays. The occupation and instruction given at a centre should include a programme of group activities designed to assist offenders to acquire or develop personal responsibility, self-discipline skills and interests.[56]

Power

23.64   Powers of Criminal Courts (Sentencing) Act 2000 s60 provides that an attendance centre order may be imposed:

- on conviction for any imprisonable offence;
- in default of payment of any fine or order for compensation or costs.

---

53   Powers of Criminal Courts (Sentencing) Act 2000 Sch 3 para 12(1).
54   Ibid, Sch 3 para 12(3).
55   Ibid, Sch 3 para 13.
56   Attendance Centre Rules 1995 SI No 3281 r4(1).

23.65   It may also be imposed as a sanction for failure to comply with the requirements of:

- a reparation order;[57]
- an action plan order;[58] or
- a supervision order.[59]

Pre-conditions

23.66   An attendance centre order may be imposed upon a child or young person by a youth court or by a Crown Court. It may only be imposed if:

- the offence is imprisonable;
- the offence, or the combination of the offence and associated offences, is serious enough;
- the order is the most suitable for the offender;
- the court has been notified by the secretary of state that an attendance centre is available for the reception of persons of the offender's description;[60]
- the court is satisfied that the centre is reasonably accessible to the offender, having regard to the offender's age, the means of access available to him/her and any other circumstances.[61]

23.67   A pre-sentence report will normally be required before an attendance centre order is imposed (see para 20.26).

Available for the reception of persons of the offender's description

23.68   This means that the court must be satisfied that a centre exists which caters both for the age of the offender and his/her gender. Attendance centres may be classed as either junior or senior centres. Junior centres cater for all offenders aged 10 to 15. In addition, subject to local arrangements, they may also cater for offenders aged 16 and 17. Senior centres cater for offenders aged 18 to 20, and may also accept offenders aged 16 and 17. Junior centres normally run for two hours each session, whereas senior centres may run for three-hour sessions. Most centres cater for male offenders only, but in larger conurbations some mixed centres exist.

23.69   If there is a choice of a junior and senior centre available for an offender aged 16 or 17, Home Office Circular 72/1992 suggests that the offender should always be sent to the senior centre if the order is for more than 24 hours and in the case of a shorter order the court should select the centre according to suitability. When considering suitability, the Circular suggests the court take into account the maturity of the offender.

Reasonably accessible

23.70   The court is clearly expected to make enquiries of the offender and his/her parent or guardian to ascertain how the offender would travel to the centre if the order were imposed.

---

57 Powers of Criminal Courts (Sentencing) Act 2000 Sch 8 para 2(2)(a)(iii) and 4.
58 Ibid.
59 Ibid, Sch 7 paras 2(2)(a)(iii) and 4.
60 Ibid, s60(1).
61 Ibid, s60(6).

23.71 The Home Office has provided guidance to courts regarding reasonable distances for travelling to attendance centres. Offenders should not normally be expected to travel for more than 90 minutes each way, although courts may consider that less demanding travelling requirements are appropriate to younger attenders.[62]

23.72 In normal circumstances the cost of travelling to the centre must be borne by the offender or his/her parents, but in cases of hardship officers in charge of the centre may pay all or part of the expenses incurred.[63]

Age

23.73 An attendance centre order may be imposed upon any offender aged from 10 to 20 inclusive.[64]

23.74 The age of a person shall be deemed that which it appears to the court to be after considering any available evidence.[65]

Length of the order

23.75 The length of the order shall be such as is, in the opinion of the court, commensurate with the seriousness of the offence, or the combination of the offence and other offences associated with it.[66]

Minimum

23.76 The minimum number of hours shall be 12 unless the offender is aged under 14 and, having regard to the offender's age or any other circumstances, the court is of the opinion that 12 hours would be excessive.[67]

Maximum

23.77 The aggregate number of hours shall not exceed 12 except where the court is of the opinion, having regard to all the circumstances, that 12 hours would be inadequate. In such circumstances the court may order attendance to a maximum of 24 hours for an offender under 16 years of age and up to 36 hours for an offender aged 16 or over.[68]

Multiple orders

23.78 It is possible for a court to impose an attendance centre order upon an offender who is still completing an existing attendance centre order. If a court does this, it may determine the number of hours for the new order without regard to the number specified in the previous order or to the fact that the previous order is still in effect.[69]

---

62 *National Standard for Attendance Centres* (1995) para 11.
63 Ibid, para 12.
64 Powers of Criminal Courts (Sentencing) Act 2000 s60(1)(a).
65 Ibid, s164(1).
66 Criminal Justice Act 2003 s148(2)(b).
67 Powers of Criminal Court (Sentencing) Act s60(3).
68 Ibid, ss60(4).
69 Ibid, s60(5).

Procedural requirements

23.79   On making the order, the court must specify the centre and the day and time of the offender's first attendance which should be recorded in the order.[70]

23.80   The offender is not required to consent to the order.

Requirements of the order

23.81   The first time at which an offender is required to attend at the attendance centre shall be the time at which the centre is available for his/her attendance in accordance with the notification of the Secretary of State.[71] The subsequent times shall be fixed by the officer in charge of the centre, having regard to the young offender's circumstances.[72]

23.82   An offender may not be required to attend an attendance centre on more than one occasion on each day or for more than three hours on one occasion.[73] The times of attendances should, as far as practicable, be such as to avoid:

- any conflict with the offender's religious beliefs or with the requirement of any other community order to which s/he may be subject; and
- any interference with the times, if any, at which the offender normally works or attends school or any other educational establishment.[74]

Amendment of the order

23.83   Either the offender or the officer in charge of the centre may apply to an appropriate court for a variation of the order.[75]

23.84   The appropriate court is:

- a magistrates' court acting for the local justice area in which the attendance centre specified in the order is situated; or
- (except in the case of an order made by the Crown Court) the magistrates' court which made the order.[76]

23.85   The court may vary the starting date of the order or the time when the offender is required to attend. It may also change the centre specified in the order, provided it is satisfied that the new centre is reasonably accessible to the offender, having regard to his/her age, the means of access available to him/her and any other circumstances.[77]

23.86   A copy of any amended order should be supplied to the offender and the officer in charge of the centre.[78]

---

70 Powers of Criminal Courts (Sentencing) Act 2000 s60(8).
71 Ibid, s60(8).
72 Ibid, s60(9).
73 Ibid, s60(10).
74 Ibid, s60(7).
75 Ibid, Sch 5 para 5(1).
76 Ibid, Sch 5 para 5(2).
77 Ibid, Sch 5 para 5(1).
78 Ibid, Sch 5 para 5(3).

23.87   If a representation order was granted to the offender in the original proceedings, this order will cover representation at the hearing to determine an application for variation. Attendance at any hearings and other work done in relation to an application to vary must be justified as reasonable.[79] If a claim has already been submitted to the Criminal Defence Service, then a supplementary claim can be made after the conclusion of the application to vary.[80]

Revocation of the order

23.88   Either the offender or the officer in charge of the centre may apply to an appropriate court for the order to be revoked.[81]

23.89   An appropriate court is the Crown Court which made the order but only if the original order contains a direction that the power to revoke the order is reserved to that court.[82] In any other case the appropriate court is;

- the youth court for the local justice area in which the attendance order specified in the order is situated; or
- the youth court which made the order.[83]

23.90   On discharge the court has the power to deal with the offender in any manner in which s/he could have been dealt with for the offence by the court which made the order if the order had not been made.[84] There is surprisingly no statutory requirement to take account of the extent to which the order has been completed prior to discharge but it is submitted that the court should take this into account as it would if the discharge had followed breach proceedings.[85]

23.91   When an order is revoked, the court must send a copy of the revoking order to the offender and the officer in charge.[86]

23.92   An offender re-sentenced by the youth court following revocation of the original order may appeal to the Crown Court against the substituted sentence.[87]

Action plan order

23.93   Action plan orders were introduced by the Crime and Disorder Act 1998. Initially piloted in a number of court areas, the orders have been implemented throughout England and Wales since 1 June 2000.

23.94   Action plan orders are intended to be 'a short but intensive and individually tailored response to offending behaviour and associated risks'.[88] The

---

79 Criminal Defence Service, *Criminal Costs Manual*, para 3.10.
80 Ibid, para 3.10.4.
81 Powers of Criminal Courts (Sentencing) Act 2000 Sch 5 para 4(1).
82 Ibid, Sch 5 para 4(2)(a).
83 Ibid, Sch 5 para 4(2)(b).
84 Ibid, Sch 5 para 4(3).
85 Cf s19(5A) – see para 27.41.
86 Powers of Criminal Courts (Sentencing) Act 2000 Sch 5 para 4(5).
87 Ibid, Sch 5 para 4(4).
88 Youth Justice Board, *National Standards for Youth Justice Services* (2004), para 8.37.

Home Office has issued guidance to courts and youth offending teams regarding the use of action plan orders. This guidance states

> The action plan order is ... intended to be imposed for relatively serious offending, but it is also intended to offer an early opportunity for targeted intervention to help prevent further offending. courts may wish to consider the action plan order when a young person has first been convicted of an offence serious enough for a community sentence.[89]

Pre-conditions

23.95   An action plan order may be imposed by a youth court or a Crown Court. It may be imposed for any offence, the penalty for which is not fixed by law, but only if:

- the offence, or the combination of the offence and associated offences, is serious enough;
- the order is the most suitable for the offender; and
- the court is of the opinion that it is desirable to pass such an order in the interests of securing the offender's rehabilitation or of preventing the commission by him/her of further offences.[90]

Age

23.96   An action plan order may be passed upon any offender under the age of 18.[91] The age of a person shall be deemed that which it appears to the court to be after considering any available evidence.[92]

Length of order

23.97   The order shall last for a period of three months beginning with the date of the order.[93]

Requirements of order

23.98   A young offender subject to an action plan order may be required to do any of the following:

- to participate in activities specified in the requirements or directions at a time or times so specified;
- to present him/herself to a person or persons specified in the requirements or directions at a place or places and at a time or times so specified;

---

89 Home Office, *The Crime and Disorder – Guidance Document: Action Plan Order*, para 2.2.
90 Powers of Criminal Courts (Sentencing) Act 2000 s69(3).
91 Ibid, s69(1).
92 Ibid, s164(1).
93 Ibid, s69(1)(a).

- to attend at an attendance centre specified in the requirements or directions for a specified number of hours (only in case of imprisonable offence);
- to stay away from a place or places specified in the requirements or directions;
- to comply with any arrangements for his/her education specified in the requirements or directions;
- to make reparation specified in the requirements or directions;
- to undergo drug treatment and testing (*pilot areas only*); and
- to attend any review hearing as fixed by the court.[94]

23.99 As far as is practicable, the requirements of the order shall be such as to avoid:

- any conflict with the offender's religious beliefs;
- any interference with the times, if any, at which the offender normally works or attends school or any other educational establishment; or
- any conflict with the requirements of any community order to which s/he may be subject.[95]

Ordering attendance at an attendance centre

23.100 Although there is no statutory limit on the number of hours at an attendance centre which can be specified in the order, Home Office guidance suggests:

- that it would not be appropriate for the number of hours to exceed those which may be included in a free-standing attendance order (see paras 23.75–23.78); and
- when specifying the number of hours, regard should be had to the frequency and number of hours the relevant attendance centre is open, to ensure that the specified hours are appropriate to enable some worthwhile work to be undertaken with the offender within the three-month period of the action plan order.[96]

Ordering the making of reparation

23.101 Making reparation is reparation by the offender other than the payment of compensation.[97]

23.102 The court or responsible officer may specify a person to whom reparation is to be made but only if:

- that person is identified by the court or responsible officer as a victim of the offence or otherwise affected by it; and
- s/he consents to the reparation being made.[98]

---

94 Powers of Criminal Courts (Sentencing) Act 2000 s70(1).
95 Ibid, s70(5).
96 Home Office, *The Crime and Disorder – Guidance Document: Action Plan Order*, para 4.5.
97 Powers of Criminal Courts (Sentencing) Act 2000, s70(3).
98 Ibid, s70(4).

Ordering drug treatment and testing (pilot areas only)

23.103 The sentencing court may include a requirement for the offender to undergo drug treatment and testing where it is satisfied:

- that the offender is dependent on, or has a propensity to misuse, drugs; and
- that his/her dependency or propensity is such as requires and may be susceptible to treatment.[99]

23.104 The requirement must specify:

- the period for which the offender must submit to treatment ('the treatment period') and
- the person with the necessary qualifications and experience who will provide directions to the offender for his/her treatment ('the treatment provider').[100]

23.105 The drug treatment shall be:

- treatment as a resident in such institution or place as may be specified in the order; or
- treatment as a non-resident at such institution or place, and at such intervals as may be so specified.[101]

23.106 A drug treatment requirement may not be included in an action plan order:

(a) in any case, unless:
- the court is satisfied that arrangements have been or can be made for the treatment intended to be specified in the order (including arrangements for the reception of the offender where s/he is to be required to submit to treatment as a resident); and
- the requirement has been recommended to the court as suitable for the offender by an officer of a local probation board or a member of a youth offending team; and

(b) in the case of an order made in respect of an offender aged 14 or over, unless s/he consents to its inclusion.[102]

23.107 A testing requirement is a requirement that, for the purpose of ascertaining whether the offender has any drug in his/her body during the treatment period, the offender shall during that period, at such times or in such circumstances as may be determined by the responsible officer or the treatment provider, provide sample of such description as may be so determined.[103]

23.108 A drug testing requirement may not be included in an action plan order unless:

- the offender is aged 14 or over and s/he consents to its inclusion; and

---

99 Powers of Criminal Courts (Sentencing) Act 2000 s70(4A) as inserted by Criminal Justice Act 2003 Sch 24 para 1(2).

100 Ibid, s70(4B).

101 Ibid, s70(4C).

102 Ibid, s70(4D).

103 Ibid, s70(4E).

- the court has been notified by the secretary of state that arrangements for implementing such requirements are in force in the area proposed to be specified in the order.[104]

23.109 A testing requirement shall specify for each month the minimum number of occasions on which samples are to be provided.[105]

23.110   An action plan order including a testing requirement shall provide for the results of tests carried out on samples provided by the offender in pursuance of a requirement to a person other than the responsible officer to be communicated to the responsible officer.[106]

Procedural requirements

23.111 Before making an action plan order, a court shall obtain and consider a written report by an officer of a local probation board, social worker of a local authority social services department or a member of a youth offending team, indicating:

- the requirements proposed to be included in the order;
- the benefits to the offender that the proposed requirements are designed to achieve; and
- the attitude of a parent or guardian of the offender to the proposed requirements.[107]

23.112 In the case of offenders under the age of 16, the report should also contain information regarding the offender's family circumstances and the likely effect of the order on those circumstances.[108]

23.113   Before making an action plan order, a court shall explain to the offender in ordinary language:

- the effect of the order and of the requirements proposed to be included in it;
- the consequences which may follow if the order is breached;
- that the court has power to review the order on the application of either the offender or the responsible officer.[109]

23.114 An action plan order may not be imposed upon a young offender already the subject of an action plan order.[110] It also cannot be combined with any of the following orders:

- a custodial sentence;
- a community rehabilitation order;
- a community punishment order;
- a community punishment and rehabilitation order;
- an attendance centre order;

---

104 Powers of Criminal Courts (Sentencing) Act 2000 s70(4F). At the time of writing only the courts for the areas listed in appendix 12 have received notification letters.
105 Ibid, s70(4G).
106 Ibid, s70(4H).
107 Ibid, s69(6)(a).
108 Ibid, s69(6)(b).
109 Ibid, s70(2).
110 Ibid, s69(5)(a).

- a supervision order; or
- a referral order.[111]

Responsible officer

23.115   A responsible officer in relation to an offender subject to an action plan order shall be one of the following who is specified in the order, namely:

- an officer of a local probation board;
- a social worker of a local authority social services department;
- a member of a youth offending team.[112]

Review hearing

23.116   Immediately after making an action plan order, a court may fix a further hearing for a date not more than 21 days after the making of the order. The court may also direct the responsible officer to make at that hearing a report (oral or written) as to the effectiveness of the order and the extent to which it has been implemented.[113]

23.117   The Home Office has given the following advice to courts regarding the need for review hearings:

> This further hearing is discretionary; it is not expected that courts will feel generally it to be necessary. Its purpose is to allow the court to review the initial stages of the action plan order, and to make any alterations – variations or cancellations of certain requirements, and/or their replacement with alternative ones – in the action plan which are necessary or appropriate. It may be particularly where the court was unclear at the time of sentencing that a particular requirement in the order was practicable or could be delivered.[114]

23.118   The young offender will normally be required to attend any review hearing as a requirement of the action plan order. S/he cannot be bailed to the review hearing as sentencing has taken place and the criminal proceedings have concluded. However, if the offender fails to attend the hearing when required to do so as part of the order, the non-attendance will be a breach of the order. This on its own could lead to breach proceedings, but in practice is only likely to do so if the offender has also failed to comply with other requirements of the action plan order since it was imposed.

23.119   At the review hearing the court shall consider the responsible officer's report and may, on the application of the responsible officer or the offender, vary the order by cancelling any provision contained in it or by inserting in it (either in addition to or in substitution for any of its provisions) any provision that the court could originally have included in it.[115]

23.120   Attendance at a review hearing may be covered by the original representation order but it will rarely, if ever, be justified.[116] Attendance may be justified if the defence lawyer has been notified that there will be an

---

111   Powers of Criminal Courts (Sentencing) Act 2000 s69(5)(b).

112   Ibid, s69(4).

113   Ibid, s71(1).

114   Home Office, *The Crime and Disorder – Guidance Document: Action Plan Order*, para 9.2.

115   Powers of Criminal Courts (Sentencing) Act 2000 s71(2).

116   Criminal Defence Service, *Criminal Costs Manual*, para 3.10.

application to amend the terms of the order in a significant way. If a claim has already been submitted to the Criminal Defence Service, then a supplementary claim can be made for reasonable work done in relation to the review hearing.[117]

Variation and discharge of the order

23.121 While the action plan order is in force, an application for variation or discharge of the order may be made by either the offender or the responsible officer.[118] Application should be made to the youth court acting for the local justice area named in the order.[119]

Powers of the court

23.122 The order may be varied either by inserting in it (in addition to or substitution for) any provision which could have been included in the order if the court had then had the power to make it and were exercising the power.[120]

23.123 Where an application for discharge of an action plan order has been dismissed, no further discharge application may be made without the consent of the youth court acting for the local justice area named in the order.[121]

Guidance

23.124 The Home Office has offered the following advice on the need for varying an order:

> There may be a range of reasons why the need might arise to vary an action plan order. For example, the offender in question may move and it may be necessary for a youth offending team in another area to take over responsibility for the order; the offender's family circumstances may alter making one or more requirements of the order impossible to comply with; or a particular requirement of the order may be proving completely unsuccessful in helping the offender to address his or her offending behaviour and the responsible officer may believe that it could usefully be replaced with an alternative requirement.[122]

Legal representation

23.125 If a representation order was granted to the offender in the original proceedings, this order will cover representation at the hearing to determine an application for variation. Attendance at any hearings and other work done in relation to an application to vary must be justified as reasonable.[123] If a claim has already been submitted to the Criminal Defence Service, then a supplementary claim can be made after the conclusion of the application to vary.[124]

---

117 *Criminal Costs Manual*, para 3.10.4.
118 Powers of Criminal Courts (Sentencing) Act 2000 Sch 8 para 5(1).
119 Ibid, Sch 8 para 1.
120 Ibid, Sch 8 para 5(1).
121 Ibid, Sch 8 para 5(3) – to be repealed on implementation of the Criminal Justice and Courts Services Act 2000 Sch 7.
122 Home Office, *The Crime and Disorder – Guidance Document: Action Plan Order*, para 10.2.
123 Criminal Defence Service, *Criminal Costs Manual*, para 3.10.
124 Ibid, para 3.10.4.

Right of appeal

23.126   An offender may appeal to the Crown Court against any decision to vary the requirements of the order or to dismiss an application to discharge the order. The right of appeal does not extend to appealing a decision:

- discharging the order;
- cancelling a requirement of the order;
- altering the relevant local justice area named in the order; or
- changing the responsible officer.[125]

Supervision order

23.127   The supervision order is the most flexible youth court sentence. With its wide range of additional requirements it can be the suitable disposal for a relatively minor offence, as well as the disposal for some of the most serious offences. In contrast to the action plan order, the supervision order is appropriate when a more extended period of supervision is required because of the frequency or seriousness of the offending.[126]

Pre-conditions

23.128   A supervision order may be imposed in relation to any offence, provided the court considers that:

- the offence, or the combination of the offence and associated offences is serious enough; and
- the order is the most suitable for the offender.

23.129   The consent of the young offender is not required except if the court is considering imposing upon an offender who has attained the age of 14 any of the following additional requirements:

- requirement to submit to drug treatment and testing; or
- requirement as to treatment for mental condition.

Age

23.130   A supervision order may be imposed upon any offender under 18 years of age.[127] The relevant age will be that at the date of conviction, however, by virtue of Children and Young Persons Act 1963 s29(1), a young offender who attains 18 during the proceedings may still be dealt with as though s/he had not attained that age and therefore a supervision order may be available.

23.131   The age of a person shall be deemed that which it appears to the court to be after considering any available evidence.[128]

---

125 Powers of Criminal Courts (Sentencing) Act 2000 Sch 8 paras 6(9) and 7.
126 Youth Justice Board, *National Standards for Youth Justice Services* (2004), para 8.38.
127 Children and Young Persons Act 1969 s7(7).
128 Powers of Criminal Courts (Sentencing) Act 2000 s164(1).

Length of the order

23.132 There is no minimum period for an order, however, in practical terms it is unlikely that a court would impose a supervision order for less than six months, particularly as the option of a three-month action plan order now exists.

23.133 The maximum period is three years from the date the order was made by the court.[129]

23.134 The length of the order shall be such as is, in the opinion of the court, commensurate with the seriousness of the offence, or the combination of the offence and other offences associated with it.[130] A court should not therefore impose a supervision order because of welfare concerns unless the seriousness of the offence warrants it, and equally, the period of supervision should not be extended beyond that which is commensurate with the seriousness of the offence by reference to the offender's welfare.

Procedural requirements

23.135 The court shall in the order name the area of the local authority and the local justice area in which it appears the supervised person resides or will reside.[131] A court may make an order placing the offender under the supervision of a local authority designated in the order, an officer of a local probation board or a member of a youth offending team.[132]

23.136 A court shall not designate a local authority as the supervisor unless the authority agrees or it appears to the court that the supervised person resides or will reside in the area of the authority.[133] Where the supervisor is to be a probation officer, s/he shall be an officer appointed for or assigned to the local justice area named in the order.[134] Where a supervision order places a person under the supervision of a member of a youth offending team, the supervisor shall be a member of the team established by the local authority within whose area it appears to the court that the supervised person resides or will reside.[135]

23.137 Wherever there is a possibility of dispute between local authorities regarding the proper authority to designate in the order, the court should make arrangements for the relevant authorities to be represented, if they consider it appropriate, in order to make submissions at the sentencing hearing.[136] The decision of the sentencing court as to which authority to designate is part and parcel of the sentencing process and therefore in the Crown Court the decision is not amenable to judicial review by reason of Supreme Court Act 1981 s29(3).[137]

---

129 Powers of Criminal Courts (Sentencing) Act 2000 s63(7).
130 Criminal Justice Act 2003 s164(1).
131 Powers of Criminal Courts (Sentencing) Act 2000 s63(6)(a).
132 Ibid, s11.
133 Ibid, s64(1).
134 Ibid, s64(2).
135 Ibid, s64(3).
136 *R (Kirklees Metropolitan Council) v Preston Crown Court* [2001] EWHC 510 (Admin).
137 Ibid.

23.138   A copy of the order shall be sent forthwith:

- to the supervised person, and if the supervised person is a child, to his/her parent or guardian;
- to the supervisor;
- where the supervised person is required to reside with an individual or to undergo treatment by or under the direction of an individual or at any place, to the individual or the person in charge of that place; and
- if the local justice area named in the order is not that for which the court acts, to the designated officer for the local justice area so named (and the court shall also be sent such documents and information relating to the case as the court considers likely to be of assistance to them).[138]

Role of supervisor

23.139   While a supervision order is in force, the supervisor shall advise, assist and befriend the offender.[139]

Requirements of the order

23.140   A making of a supervision order does not automatically impose any requirements on the offender. It may, however, contain such prescribed provisions as the court making the order considers appropriate for facilitating the performance by the supervisor of his/her duty to advise, assist and befriend the supervised person, including any prescribed provisions for requiring visits to be made by the offender to the supervisor.[140]

23.141   In the youth court the prescribed provisions are contained in the Magistrates' Courts (Children and Young Persons) Rules 1992.[141] Rule 29(2) states that the following requirements may be included in an order:

(a) That [the offender] shall inform the supervisor at once of any change in his/her address or employment;

(b) That [the offender] shall keep in touch with the supervisor in accordance with such instructions as may from time to time be given by the supervisor, and in particular, that he/she shall, if the supervisor so requires, receive visits from the supervisor at his/her home.

23.142   Failure to include such requirements in the supervision order is likely to cause difficulties if the supervised person fails to co-operate with the order.

23.143   The minimum contact with the offender must be twice a week for the first 12 weeks, weekly for the next three months and fortnightly thereafter, unless the offender is assessed as presenting a high level of risk, in which case contact should revert to at least twice weekly contact.[142]

---

138   Powers of Criminal Courts (Sentencing) Act 2000 s63(8).

139   Ibid, s64(4).

140   Ibid, s63(6)(b).

141   SI No 2071.

142   Youth Justice Board: *National Standards for Youth Justice Services* (2004), para 8.40.

Additional requirements

23.144 The possible additional requirements of a supervision order are listed in Schedule 6 to the Powers of Criminal Courts (Sentencing) Act 2000. These additional requirements are:

- to attend a specified place at specified times (non-specified activities);
- to take part in specified activities (including Intensive Supervision and Surveillance Programme (ISSP));
- to make reparation to specified persons or the community at large;
- to refrain from taking part in specified activities;
- to live at a particular place (residence as specified);
- to live in local authority accommodation;
- to live with a local authority foster parent (*pilot areas only*);
- to attend school or comply with other arrangements for his/her education;
- to submit to drug treatment and testing (*pilot areas only*); and
- to receive treatment for a mental condition.

23.145 It is no longer possible to impose a night restriction as an additional requirement.[143] This little used provision was repealed as the Home Office considered that a curfew order was a more practical option for a sentencing court.

Activities at the direction of the supervisor

23.146 The offender must comply with any directions given from time to time by the supervisor and requiring him/her to:

- present himself/herself to a person or persons specified in the directions at a place or places and on a day or days so specified; and/or
- to participate in activities specified in the directions on a day or days so specified.[144]

23.147 It shall be for the supervisor to decide:

- whether and to what extent s/he exercises any power to give directions conferred on him/her under this provision; and
- the form of any directions.[145]

23.148 The court must specify the number of days on which the offender may be required to comply with directions from the supervisor. The total number of days may not exceed 90 days.[146]

23.149 Although the court would be required to consider a pre-sentence report before imposing a requirement to comply with directions of the supervisor, it is not required to have consulted the supervisor about the feasibility of

---

143 Powers of Criminal Courts (Sentencing) Act 2000 Sch 6 paras 3(2)(e) and 4 repealed by Anti-social Behaviour Act 2003 Sch 2 para 4(3) and (4) with effect from 30 September 2004: Anti-social Behaviour Act 2003 (Commencement No 4) Order 2004 SI No 2168.

144 Powers of Criminal Courts (Sentencing) Act 2000 Sch 6 para 2(1)(a) and (b).

145 Ibid, Sch 6 para 2(4).

146 Ibid, Sch 6 para 2(5). In pilot areas this limit has been increased to 180 days: Anti-social Behaviour Act 2003 Sch 2 para 4(3). For pilot areas see appendix 12.

imposing the requirement. It is, however, submitted that it would be best practice to consult in any event.

Specified activities

23.150   The offender must:

- present him/herself to a person or persons in the order for a period or periods so specified;
- participate in activities specified in the order on a day or days so specified.[147]

23.151   The court may not impose a specified activities requirement unless:

(a) it has first consulted the supervisor as to:
  (i) the offender's circumstances; and
  (ii) the feasibility of securing compliance with the requirements;
  and is satisfied, having regard to the supervisor's report, that it is feasible to secure compliance with them;

(b) having regard to the circumstances of the case, it considers the requirements necessary for securing the good conduct of the supervised person or for preventing a repetition by him/her of the same offence or the commission of other offences; and

(c) if the offender is aged under 16, it has obtained and considered information about his/her family circumstances and the likely effect of the requirements on those circumstances.[148]

23.152   Prior to sentencing, the court will have considered a specified activities programme which will set out the type of activity proposed for each session during the programme. By imposing such a requirement the court removes the discretion from the supervising officer and should the programme need to be varied for any reason the supervising officer will have to apply to the court for a variation of the order.

23.153   The court must specify the number of days on which the offender must participate in the specified activities. The total number of days may not exceed 90 days.[149]

Intensive Supervision and Surveillance Programme (ISSP)

23.154   This is a form of specified activities (see para 23.1502ff above). A young offender may only be placed on an Intensive Supervision and Surveillance Programme if s/he meets the criteria laid down by the Youth Justice Board (see para 2.33). As part of the sentence it is usual for the young offender also to be made subject to a curfew order.

23.155   In pilot areas where the maximum number of days for a specified activities additional requirement has been increased to 180 days,[150] a longer than normal Intensive Supervision and Surveillance Programme may be

---

147 Powers of Criminal Courts (Sentencing) Act 2000 Sch 6 para 3(2)(b) and (c).

148 Ibid, Sch 6 para 3(4).

149 Ibid, Sch 6 para 3(3). In pilot areas this limit has been increased to 180 days: Anti-social Behaviour Act 2003 Sch 2 para 4(3). For pilot areas see appendix 12.

150 Anti-social Behaviour Act 2003 Sch 2, para 4(3)(b) – for pilot areas see appendix 12.

imposed. In relation to such longer programmes the Youth Justice Board has given the following guidance:

> [A]dditional days might be sought (with a recommended limit of 150) if the scheme:
> * believes the risk posed by the young person is such that longer supervision is needed;
> * believes the young person has acute needs that would require it to be able to direct the young person's attendance at a specific programme for longer;
> * is struggling to deliver a credible programme in the low intensity phase as young people have refused to attend more than the five hours a week minimum.[151]

Reparation requirement

23.156 The offender is required to make reparation specified in the order to a person or persons or to the community at large.[152]

23.157 The court may not impose a reparation requirement unless:

(a) it has first consulted the supervisor as to:
(i) the offender's circumstances; and
(ii) the feasibility of securing compliance with the requirements,
and is satisfied, having regard to the supervisor's report, that it is feasible to secure compliance with them;

(b) having regard to the circumstances of the case, it considers the requirements necessary for securing the good conduct of the supervised person or for preventing a repetition by him/her of the same offence or the commission of other offences; and

(c) if the offender is aged under 16, it has obtained and considered information about his/her family circumstances and the likely effect of the requirements on those circumstances.[153]

23.158 The court must specify the number of days on which the offender must participate in the specified activities. The total number of days may not exceed 90 days.[154]

Refraining from specified activities

23.159 The offender must refrain from participating in activities specified in the order:

* on a specified day or days during the period for which the supervision order is in force; or
* during the whole of that period or a specified portion of it.[155]

23.160 This is an additional requirement which is very rarely imposed. It may conceivably be considered where there has been shown to be a pattern of offending linked to a particular leisure activity – for example, football matches.

---

151 Youth Justice Board, *ISSP Management Guidance* (2005), p46.
152 Powers of Criminal Courts (Sentencing) Act 2000 Sch 6 para 3(2)(d).
153 Ibid, Sch 6 para 3(4).
154 Ibid, Sch 6 para 3(3).
155 Ibid, Sch 6 para 3(2)(f).

23.161   The court may not impose a requirement to refrain from specified activities unless:

(a) it has first consulted the supervisor as to:
   (i) the offender's circumstances; and
   (ii) the feasibility of securing compliance with the requirements,
   and is satisfied, having regard to the supervisor's report, that it is feasible to secure compliance with them;

(b) having regard to the circumstances of the case, it considers the requirements necessary for securing the good conduct of the supervised person or for preventing a repetition by him/her of the same offence or the commission of other offences; and

(c) if the offender is aged under 16, it has obtained and considered information about his/her family circumstances and the likely effect of the requirements on those circumstances.[156]

Residence at direction of supervisor

23.162 The offender must live at a place or places specified in the directions for a period or periods so specified.[157]

23.163   It shall be for the supervisor to decide:

- whether and to what extent s/he exercises any power to give directions conferred on him/her under this provision; and
- the form of any directions.[158]

23.164 The court must specify the number of days for which the offender may be required to reside at the direction of the supervisor. The total number of days may not exceed 90 days.[159]

Residence at a place specified by the court

23.165 The offender must live at a place or places specified in the order for a period or periods so specified.[160]

23.166   The court may not impose a requirement to reside at a specified place unless:

(a) it has first consulted the supervisor as to:
   (i) the offender's circumstances; and
   (ii) the feasibility of securing compliance with the requirements,
   and is satisfied, having regard to the supervisor's report, that it is feasible to secure compliance with them;

(b) having regard to the circumstances of the case, it considers the requirements necessary for securing the good conduct of the supervised person or for preventing a repetition by him/her of the same offence or the commission of other offences; and

---

156 Powers of Criminal Courts (Sentencing) Act 2000 Sch 6 para 3(4).
157 Ibid, Sch 6 para 2(1)(a) and (b).
158 Ibid, Sch 6 para 2(4).
159 Ibid, Sch 6 para 2(5).
160 Ibid, Sch 6 para 3(2)(a).

(c) if the offender is aged under 16, it has obtained and considered information about his/her family circumstances and the likely effect of the requirements on those circumstances.[161]

Local authority residence requirement

23.167 The offender must live for a specified period (not exceeding six months) in local authority accommodation.[162] The requirement may stipulate that the supervised person is not to live with a named person.[163]

23.168 A local authority residence requirement must designate the local authority who are to receive the offender, and that authority shall be the authority in whose area the offender resides.[164]

23.169 Such a requirement may only be made if the following pre-conditions are satisfied:

- the court has first consulted with the designated authority;[165] and

- a supervision order has previously been made in respect of the child or young person; and

- the supervision order in existence includes an additional requirement under paragraphs 1, 2, 3, or 7 of Powers of Criminal Courts (Sentencing) Act 2000 Sch 6 (any requirement other than a requirement for treatment for mental condition); and

- the supervised person has either failed to comply with the additional requirement or been found guilty of an offence committed while that order was in force; and

- the court is satisfied that:
  (i) the failure to comply with the requirements, or the behaviour which constituted the offence, was due to a significant extent to the circumstances in which the supervised person was living; and
  (ii) the imposition of the residence requirement will assist in his/her rehabilitation.[166]

23.170 A court may not impose a local authority residence requirement on an offender who is not legally represented at the relevant time unless:

- s/he was granted a representation order but this was later withdrawn because of his/her behaviour; or
- s/he was informed of his/her right to apply for a representation order but nevertheless refused or failed to do so.[167]

23.171 The relevant time means the time when the court is considering whether or not to impose the requirement.[168]

---

161 Powers of Criminal Courts (Sentencing) Act 2000 Sch 6 para 3(4).
162 Ibid, Sch 6 para 5(1).
163 Ibid, Sch 6 para 5(5).
164 Ibid, Sch 6 para 5(3).
165 Ibid, Sch 6 para 5(4).
166 Ibid, Sch 6 para 5(2).
167 Ibid, Sch 6 para 5(7).
168 Ibid, Sch 6 para 5(8)(a).

23.172 A supervision order imposing a local authority residence requirement may also impose any of the other possible additional requirements.[169]

Local authority accommodation

23.173 This is defined as 'accommodation provided by or on behalf of a local authority (within the meaning of the Children Act 1989)'.[170] This could include a placement with family, relatives or any suitable person (for example, a foster parent) as well as accommodation in a children's home.[171]

23.174 The court has no power to specify a particular placement for the offender. The order, therefore, leaves the social services department with considerable discretion subject to the court naming a particular person with whom the offender is not to reside.

Application

23.175 This requirement clearly involves a substantial restriction of liberty and this fact is reflected in the legislation by the fact that the offender must be legally represented before it may be imposed. The court should clearly only impose such a requirement where there has been a full assessment of the young offender's home circumstances. The Department of Health has given the following guidance on the use of this requirement:

> The purpose of the residence requirement is not punitive; it is designed to help a young person to work through his problems. A young person's circumstances may contribute to his offending: for example, he may be living rough and stealing to survive; he may have experienced a lack of parental control; or his life at home may be unsatisfactory in other respects. The residence requirement is designed to remove such a young person from the surroundings that are contributing to his offending behaviour, and to place him in local authority accommodation while the local authority enables him to work through the problems associated with his home surroundings. The aim must be to assist the young person to deal with his problems, and to stop him re-offending, even when he does return to his home surroundings. It therefore follows that the role of the social workers responsible for him must be to care for and assist him, and not simply to act as warders.[172]

Foster parent residence requirement (pilot areas only)

23.176 This provision was introduced by Anti-social Behaviour Act 2003 Sch 2 para 4(5). It was implemented on 30 September 2004[173] but is being piloted from October 2004 for an unspecified period.[174] For details of the pilot areas see appendix 12.

23.177 A court in a pilot area may impose a requirement that an offender live for a specified period with a local authority foster parent if:

---

169 Powers of Criminal Courts (Sentencing) Act 2000 Sch 6 para 5(9).
170 Ibid, s70(1).
171 Children Act 1989 s23(2).
172 *The Children Act 1989 Guidance and Regulations* (HMSO, 1991), Vol 1, Court Orders, para 6.26.
173 Anti-social Behaviour Act (Commencement No 4) Order 2004 SI No 2168.
174 Home Office Circular 66/2004 para 6.

(a) the offence is punishable with imprisonment in the case of an offender aged 18 or over;

(b) the offence, or the combination of the offence and one or more offences associated with it, was so serious that a custodial sentence would normally be appropriate (or, if the offender is aged 10 or 11, would normally be appropriate if the offender were aged 12 or over); and

(c) the court is satisfied that:

   (i) the behaviour which constituted the offence was due to a significant extent to the circumstances in which the offender was living; and

   (ii) the imposition of a foster parent residence requirement will assist in his/her rehabilitation.[175]

23.178   On sentence, a foster parent residence requirement may not be specified to last longer than 12 months.[176] It is, however, possible to apply subsequently for the order to be varied up to a maximum period of 18 months.[177]

23.179   A foster parent residence requirement may be imposed at the same time as any of the following additional requirements:

- participation in non-specified activities;
- participation in specified activities or an ISSP;
- a reparation requirement;
- refraining from specified activities;
- requirement as to education; and
- requirement as to psychiatric treatment.[178]

23.180   On making a foster parent residence requirement, the court shall designate the local authority in whose area the offender lives as the authority who are to place the offender with a foster parent under Children Act 1989 s22(2)(a).[179]

23.181   A court shall not impose a foster parent residence requirement unless:

- the court has been notified by the secretary of state that arrangements for implementing such a requirement are available in the area of the designated authority;
- the notice has not been withdrawn; and
- the court has consulted the designated authority.[180]

23.182   A court may not impose a foster parent residence requirement on an offender who is not legally represented at the relevant time unless:

- s/he was granted a representation order but this was later withdrawn because of his/her behaviour; or
- s/he was informed of his/her right to apply for a representation order but nevertheless refused or failed to do so.[181]

---

175 Powers of Criminal Courts (Sentencing) Act 2000 Sch 6 para 5A(1) and (2).
176 Ibid, Sch 6 para 5A(5).
177 Ibid, Sch 7 para 5(2A).
178 Ibid, Sch 6 para 5A(8).
179 Ibid, Sch 6 para 5A(3).
180 Ibid, Sch 6 para 5A(4). At the time of writing, notification has only been received by courts in the pilot areas listed in appendix 12.
181 Ibid, Sch 6 para 5A(6).

23.183   The relevant time is the time when the court is considering whether or not to impose the requirement.[182]

23.184   Whilst a supervision order imposing a foster parent residence requirement is in force, there may be occasions when no suitable foster parent is available. This is most likely to occur when the offender's behaviour has meant that s/he has had to be removed from a placement and no other foster parent is able or willing to look after the offender. If no foster parent is available for whatever reason, the order shall be deemed to include a requirement to reside in local authority accommodation instead, provided the supervisor has informed the offender that no suitable foster parent is available and that an application to vary or revoke the order has been or will be made.[183]

Requirement as to education

23.185   The offender, if s/he is of compulsory school age, must comply, for as long as s/he is of that age and the order remains in force, with such arrangements for his/her education as may from time to time be made by his/her parent, being arrangements for the time being approved by the local education authority.[184]

23.186   The court shall not include such a requirement unless:

- it has consulted the local education authority with regard to its proposal to include the requirement; and
- it is satisfied that in the view of the local education authority arrangements exist for the offender to receive efficient full-time education suitable to his/her age, ability and aptitude and to any special educational need s/he may have.[185]

23.187   The court may not include a requirement as to education unless it has first consulted the supervisor as to the offender's circumstances and, having regard to the circumstances of the case, it considers the requirement necessary for securing the good conduct of the offender or for preventing a repetition by him/her of the same offence or the commission of other offences.[186]

23.188   This additional requirement appears to be very rarely used by magistrates.[187]

Drug treatment and testing (pilot areas only)

23.189   A court may include a requirement for the supervised person to undergo drug treatment and testing where it is satisfied:

- that the offender is dependent on, or has a propensity to misuse, drugs; and

---

182   Powers of Criminal Courts (Sentencing) Act 2000 Sch 6 para 5A(7)(a).
183   Ibid, Sch 6 para 5A(9).
184   Ibid, Sch 6 para 7(2).
185   Ibid, Sch 6 para 7(3).
186   Ibid, Sch 6 para 7(5).
187   In 1995 only 22 such orders were made: see Ball and Connolly, *Requiring school attendance: a little used sentencing power* [1999] Crim LR 183.

- that his/her dependency or propensity is such as requires and may be susceptible to treatment.[188]

23.190 The requirement must specify:

- the period for which the offender must submit to treatment ('the treatment period'); and
- the person with the necessary qualifications and experience who will provide directions to the offender for his/her treatment ('the treatment provider').[189]

23.191 The drug treatment shall be:

- treatment as a resident in such institution or place as may be specified in the order; or
- treatment as a non-resident at such institution or place, and at such intervals as may be so specified.[190]

23.192 A drug treatment requirement may not be included in a supervision order:

(a) in any case, unless:

- the court is satisfied that arrangements have been or can be made for the treatment intended to be specified in the order (including arrangements for the reception of the offender where s/he is to be required to submit to treatment as a resident); and
- the requirement has been recommended to the court as suitable for the offender by an officer of a local probation board or a member of a youth offending team; and

(b) in the case of an order made in respect of an offender aged 14 or over, unless s/he consents to its inclusion.[191]

23.193 A testing requirement is a requirement that, for the purpose of ascertaining whether s/he has any drug in his/her body during the treatment period, the offender shall during that period, at such times or in such circumstances as may be determined by the supervising officer or the treatment provider, provide samples of such description as may be so determined.[192]

23.194   A drug testing requirement may not be included in a supervision order unless:

- the offender is aged 14 or over and s/he consents to its inclusion; and
- the court has been notified by the secretary of state that arrangements for implementing such requirements are in force in the area proposed to be specified in the order.[193]

23.195 A testing requirement shall specify for each month the minimum number of occasions on which samples are to be provided.[194]

---

188 Powers of Criminal Courts (Sentencing) Act 2000 Sch 6 para 6A(1) as inserted by Criminal Justice Act 2003 Sch 24 para 2(3).
189 Ibid, Sch 6 para 6A(2).
190 Ibid, Sch 6 para 6A(3).
191 Ibid, Sch 6 para 6A(4).
192 Ibid, Sch 6 para 6A(5).
193 Ibid, Sch 6 para 6.A(6).
194 Ibid, Sch 6 para 6A(7).

23.196   A supervision order including a testing requirement shall provide for the results of tests carried out on samples provided by the offender in pursuance of a requirement to a person other than the supervising officer to be communicated to the responsible officer.[195]

Requirement as to treatment for mental condition

23.197   The offender is required to submit, for a period specified in the order, to treatment of one of the following descriptions:

- treatment as a resident patient in an independent hospital or care home within the meaning of the Care Standards Act 2000 or a hospital within the meaning of the Mental Health Act 1983 but not a hospital which high security psychiatric services within the meaning of that Act are provided;
- treatment as a non-resident patient at an institution or place specified in the order;
- treatment by or under the direction of a registered medical practitioner specified in the order; and
- treatment by or under the direction of a chartered psychologist specified in the order.[196]

23.198   The court must be satisfied, on the evidence of a registered medical practitioner approved for the purposes of section 12 of the Mental Health Act 1983, that the mental condition of the offender:

- is such as requires and may be susceptible to treatment; but
- is not such as to warrant the making of a hospital or guardianship order.[197]

23.199   The requirement may not be included in a supervision order:

- in any case, unless the court is satisfied that arrangements have or can be made for the treatment in question and, in the case of treatment as a resident patient, for the reception of the patient; and
- in the case of an order made or to be made in respect of a person aged 14 or over, unless s/he consents to its inclusion.[198]

23.200   The requirement may last as long as the supervision order itself, except that it may not continue in force after the supervised person has attained the age of 18.[199]

Amendment of the order

23.201   While a supervision order is in force, a relevant court may, on the application of the supervisor or the offender, make an order amending the supervision order:

---

195 Powers of Criminal Courts (Sentencing) Act 2000 Sch 6 para 6A(8).
196 Ibid, Sch 6 para 6(2).
197 Ibid, Sch 6 para 6(1).
198 Ibid, Sch 6 para 6(3).
199 Ibid, Sch 6 para 6(3).

- by cancelling any additional requirement or any requirement imposed by the court under Powers of Criminal Courts (Sentencing) Act 2000 s63(6)(b); or
- by inserting in it (either in addition or in substitution for any of its provisions) any provision which could have been included in the order if the court had then had power to make it and were exercising the power.[200]

23.202 The relevant court is the youth court acting for the local justice are for the time being named in the order.[201] If an application is made to a youth court and while it is pending the offender to whom it relates attains the age of 18, the youth court shall deal with the application as if s/he had not attained that age.[202]

23.203 A court may not amend an order by inserting a requirement as to treatment for a mental condition after the end of three months beginning with the date when the order was originally made, unless it is in substitution for such a requirement already included in the order.[203]

Amendment of order on report of practitioner

23.204 An application may be made to the relevant court to vary or cancel a requirement for treatment for a mental condition following a report from the medical practitioner by whom or under whose direction the offender is being treated for his/her mental condition.[204]

23.205 The practitioner must make a report in writing to the supervisor if:

(a) s/he is of the opinion:
- that the treatment of the offender should be continued beyond the period specified in the original order;
- that the offender needs different treatment;
- that the offender is not susceptible to treatment; or
- that the offender does not require further treatment; or

(b) s/he is for any reason unwilling to continue to treat or direct the treatment of the offender.[205]

23.206 Where the supervisor receives such a report, s/he must refer it to the court acting for the local justice area for the time being named in the order.[206]

Restriction on power to amend order

23.207 A youth court shall not amend a supervision order except in a case where the court is satisfied that the offender either is unlikely to receive the care and or control s/he needs unless the court makes the order or is likely to receive it notwithstanding the order.[207]

---

200 Powers of Criminal Courts (Sentencing) Act 2000 Sch 7 para 5(1).
201 Ibid, Sch 7 para 1(1).
202 Ibid, Sch 7 para 1(2).
203 Ibid, Sch 7 para 5(3).
204 Ibid, Sch 7 para6(3).
205 Ibid, Sch 7 para 6(2).
206 Ibid, Sch 7 para 6(3).
207 Ibid, Sch 7 para 8(1)

23.208   Where the offender has attained the age of 14, the court may not amend the order without the consent of the offender, unless it is to remove an additional requirement or to reduce the length of that requirement.[208]

Application to amend by parent or guardian

23.209   An application to amend a supervision order may be made by the offender's parent or guardian on his/her behalf.[209] This power extends to a person who was a guardian of the offender at the time when the supervision order was originally made.[210]

Legal representation

23.210   If a representation order was granted to the offender in the original proceedings, this order will cover representation at the hearing to determine an application for variation. Attendance at any hearings and other work done in relation to an application to vary must be justified as reasonable.[211] If a claim has already been submitted to the Criminal Defence Service, then a supplementary claim can be made after the conclusion of the application to vary.[212]

Revocation of the order

23.211   While a supervision order is in force a relevant court may, on the application of the supervisor or the offender, make an order revoking the supervision order.[213]

23.212   The relevant court is the youth court acting for the local justice area for the time being named in the order.[214] If an application is made to a youth court and while it is pending the offender to whom it relates attains the age of 18, the youth court shall deal with the application as if s/he had not attained that age.[215]

23.213   Where an application to revoke is dismissed, no further application for its revocation shall be made by any person during the period of three months beginning with the date of the dismissal except with the consent of the court having jurisdiction to entertain such an application.[216]

Restriction on power to revoke order

23.214   A youth court shall not make an order to revoke a supervision order except in a case where the court is satisfied that the offender either is unlikely to receive the care and or control s/he needs unless the court makes the order or is likely to receive it notwithstanding the order.[217]

---

208   Powers of Criminal Courts (Sentencing) Act 2000 Sch 7 para 9.
209   Ibid, Sch 7 para 12(1).
210   Ibid, Sch 7 para 12(2).
211   Criminal Defence Service, *Criminal Costs Manual*, para 3.10.
212   Ibid, para 3.10.4.
213   Powers of Criminal Courts (Sentencing) Act 2000 Sch 7 para 5(1).
214   Ibid, Sch 7 para 1(1).
215   Ibid, Sch 7 para 1(2).
216   Ibid, Sch 7 para 5(1)(a).
217   Ibid, Sch 7 para 8(1)

23.215 Where the offender has attained the age of 14, the court may not amend the order without the consent of the offender, unless it is to remove an additional requirement or to reduce the length of that requirement.[218]

Application to revoke by parent or guardian

23.216 An application to revoke a supervision order may be made by the offender's parent or guardian on the offender's behalf.[219] This power extends to a person who was a guardian of the offender at the time when the supervision order was originally made.[220]

Community rehabilitation order

Pre-conditions

23.217 A probation order may be imposed for any offence whether imprisonable or non-imprisonable. However, it may not be imposed unless the court considers:

- the offence, or the combination of the offence and associated offences to be serious enough;[221]
- the requirements of the order to be the most suitable for the offender;[222]
- the offender's supervision is desirable in the interests of securing his rehabilitation or protecting the public from harm from him/her or preventing the commission by him/her of further offences.[223]

Age

23.218 A probation order may only be imposed upon an offender who has attained the age of 16.[224] The relevant age is the age at the date of conviction for the offence.

Length of the order

23.219 A probation order may be imposed for any period between six months and three years.[225]

Requirements of the order

23.220 The offender shall be under the supervision of a 'responsible officer', defined as:

- an officer of a local probation board appointed for or assigned to the local justice area specified in the order; or

218 Powers of Criminal Courts (Sentencing) Act 2000, Sch 7 para 9.
219 Ibid, Sch 7 para 12(1).
220 Ibid, Sch 7 para 12(2).
221 Criminal Justice Act 2003 s148(1).
222 Ibid s148(2)(a).
223 Powers of Criminal Courts (Sentencing) Act 2000 s41(1).
224 Ibid.
225 Ibid.

- a member of a youth offending team established by a local authority specified in the order.[226]

23.221 An offender in respect of whom a community rehabilitation order is made shall keep in touch with the reasonable officer in accordance with such instructions as s/he may be given from time to time by that officer, and shall notify the officer of any change of address.[227]

Additional requirements

23.222 In addition to the general requirements of the order, the court may impose additional requirements upon the offender. The possible requirements are as follows:

- requirements as to residence;
- requirements to participate in activities (including Intensive Supervision and Surveillance Programme);
- requirements as to attendance at community rehabilitation centres;
- requirements for sex offenders;
- requirements as to treatment for mental condition;
- requirements as to drugs or alcohol dependency; and
- curfew requirements.

Requirements as to residence

23.223 A court may attach to the community rehabilitation order a requirement to live at a place specified by the court.[228] The type of accommodation where the offender may be required to reside is not specified by the legislation. As well as being a probation hostel or other institution dealing with offenders, it could presumably also cover a requirement for a young offender to reside with a named member of the family. If the required residence is a probation hostel or other institution, the order must specify the period for which the offender is required to reside there.[229] Before making a community rehabilitation order with a residence requirement, the court shall consider the home surroundings of the offender.[230]

Requirements as to activities

23.224 An offender may be required to:

(a) present him/herself to a person or persons specified in the order at a place or places so specified;

(b) to participate in activities specified in the order on a day or days so specified or during the probation period or a portion of it as specified.[231]

---

226 Powers of Criminal Courts (Sentencing) Act 2000 s41(5) and (6).
227 Ibid, s41(11).
228 Ibid Sch 2 para 1(1).
229 Ibid, Sch 2 para1(3).
230 Ibid, Sch 2 para 1(2).
231 Ibid, Sch 2 para 2(1).

23.225 The offender is required to attend or participate in activities as directed by the responsible officer for not more than 60 days in the aggregate.[232] While attending as required, s/he must comply with the instructions of the person in charge.[233]

23.226   The court may only impose such a requirement if:

- it has consulted an officer of a local probation board or a member of a youth offending team; and
- it is satisfied that it is feasible to secure compliance with the requirement.[234]

23.227 Instructions given by the offender's responsible officer shall, as far as practicable, be such as to avoid:

- any conflict with the offender's religious beliefs or with the requirements of any other community order to which s/he may be subject; and
- any interference with the times, if any, at which s/he normally works or attends school or any other educational establishment.[235]

Intensive Supervision and Surveillance Programme (ISSP)

23.227A An Intensive Supervision and Surveillance Programme is a variant of the requirement as to activities (see para 23.224 above). The Youth Justice Board has given guidance which discourages the use of such a requirement with a community rehabilitation order:

> The [community rehabilitation order] is reserved for 16 and 17-year-olds, although they can also receive a Supervision Order (sic) and the Board would prefer this sentence wherever possible because the [community rehabilitation order] only allows for a truncated version of ISSP to be offered (only 60 days of specified activity is available). The recommended length for a [community rehabiliation order] with ISSP is one year.[236]

Requirements as to attendance at community rehabilitation centres

23.228 A court may require an offender during the community rehabilitation period to attend at a community rehabilitation centre on not more than 60 days.[237] A community rehabilitation centre is defined as 'premises at which non-residential facilities are provided for use in connection with the rehabilitation of offenders ...'.[238] Attendance at such a centre may include attendances elsewhere than at the centre for the purpose of participating in activities in accordance with instructions given by, or under the authority of, the person in charge of the centre.[239]

---

232 Powers of Criminal Courts (Sentencing) Act 2000 Sch 2 para 2(4)(a) and (6)(a).

233 Ibid, Sch 2 para 2(4)(b) and (6)(b).

234 Ibid, Sch 2 para 2(2).

235 Ibid, Sch 2 para 2(7).

236 Youth Justice Board, *ISSP Management Guidance* (2005), p46.

237 Ibid, Sch 2 para 3(1) and (4).

238 Ibid, Sch 2 para 3(8)(a).

239 Ibid, Sch 2 para 3(6).

23.229   A court shall not include such a requirement in a community rehabilitation order unless:

- it has consulted either an officer of a local probation board or a member of a youth offending team;[240] and
- it is satisfied that arrangements can be made for the offender's attendance at a centre and the person in charge of the centre consents to the inclusion of the requirement.[241]

23.230   An offender subject to such a requirement shall be required:

- to attend the centre in accordance with instructions given by the responsible officer; and
- while attending there to comply with instructions given by, or under the authority of, the person in charge of the centre.[242]

23.231   Instructions given by the offender's responsible officer shall, as far as practicable, be such as to avoid:

- any conflict with the offender's religious beliefs or with the requirements of any other community order to which s/he may be subject; and
- any interference with the times, if any, at which s/he normally works or attends school or any other educational establishment.[243]

Extension of requirements for sex offenders

23.232   A court has the power in the case of an offender convicted of a sexual offence to impose a requirement to participate in activities or attend a community rehabilitation centre for any period beyond the normal maximum period of 60 days.[244]

Requirement as to treatment for mental condition

23.233   Where it appears that a young offender is mentally ill, the court may impose a requirement to submit to treatment with a view to the improvement of the offender's mental condition.[245]

Medical evidence

23.234   The court must be satisfied, on the evidence of a medical practitioner approved under Mental Health Act 1983 s12, that the mental condition of the offender is such as requires and may be susceptible to treatment but is not such as to warrant the making of a hospital order or guardianship order.[246]

Type of treatment

23.235   The treatment required in the order must be of the description of one of the following:

---

240 Powers of Criminal Courts (Sentencing) Act 2000 Sch 2 para 3(2).
241 Ibid, Sch 2 para 3(3).
242 Ibid, Sch 2 para 3(4).
243 Ibid, Sch 2 para 3(5).
244 Ibid, Sch 2 para 4.
245 Ibid, Sch 2 para 5(2).
246 Ibid, Sch 2 para 5(1).

- treatment as a resident patient in an independent hospital or care home within the meaning of the Care Standards Act 2000 or a hospital with the meaning of the Mental Health Act 1983, but not hospital premises at which high security psychiatric services within the meaning of that Act are provided;
- treatment as a non-resident patient at such institution or place as may be specified in the order; and
- treatment by or under the direction of such registered medical practitioner or chartered psychologist (or both) as may be so specified.[247]

23.236 The actual nature of the treatment may not be specified by the court beyond the categories listed above.

Length of the requirement

23.237 The court may require the offender to submit to the treatment during the whole of the community rehabilitation period or such part of that period as is specified in the order.[248]

Procedural requirements

23.238 A court may not impose a requirement as to mental treatment for mental condition unless:

- it is satisfied that arrangements have been or can be made for the treatment specified in the order; and
- the offender has expressed his/her willingness to comply with such a requirement.[249]

During course of treatment

23.239 While the offender is under treatment as a resident patient in pursuance of this requirement, the responsible officer shall carry out the supervision of the offender to such extent only as may be necessary for the purpose of revocation or amendment of the order.[250]

23.240 Where the medical practitioner or chartered psychologist by whom or under whose direction an offender is being treated for his/her medical condition is of the opinion that part of the treatment can be better or more conveniently given in or at an institution or place not specified in the order s/he may, with the consent of the offender, make arrangements for the offender to be treated accordingly.[251]

Requirements as to treatment for drug or alcohol dependency

23.241 A court may include a requirement that an offender shall submit, during the whole period of the community rehabilitation order or during such part of the period as may be specified in the order, to treatment with a view

---

247 Powers of Criminal Courts (Sentencing) Act 2000 Sch 2 para 5(3).
248 Ibid, Sch 2 para 5(2).
249 Ibid, Sch 2 para 5(4).
250 Ibid, Sch 2 para 5(5).
251 Ibid, Sch 2 para 5(6).

to the reduction or elimination of the offender's dependency on drugs or alcohol.[252] The court may only impose such a requirement if it is satisfied:

- that the offender is dependent on drugs or alcohol;
- that the dependency caused or contributed to the offence in respect of which the order is proposed to be made; and
- that the dependency is such as requires and may be susceptible to treatment.[253]

Dependent on drugs or alcohol

23.242 Dependent includes 'having a propensity towards the misuse of drugs or alcohol'.[254]

Treatment

23.243 The order must specify the type of treatment to be followed. It may comprise any of the following:

- treatment as a resident in such institution or place as may be specified in the order;
- treatment as a non-resident in or at such institution or place as may be so specified; or
- treatment by or under the direction of such person having the necessary qualifications or experience as may be so specified.[255]

23.244 A court shall not impose such a requirement as to treatment for drug or alcohol dependency unless:

- it is satisfied that arrangements have been or can be made for the treatment intended to be specified in the order (including arrangements for the reception of the offender as a resident); and
- the offender has expressed his/her willingness to comply with such a requirement.[256]

Curfew requirement

23.245 The court may require the offender to remain, for periods specified in the order, at a place so specified.[257] There appears to be no provision for the curfew to be electronically monitored.

23.246   The court may specify different places or periods for different days, but shall not specify:

- periods which fall outside the period of six months beginning with the day on which the order is made; or
- periods which amount to less than two hours or more than 12 hours in any one day.[258]

---

252 Powers of Criminal Courts (Sentencing) Act 2000, Sch 2 para 6(2).
253 Ibid, Sch 2 para 6(1).
254 Ibid, Sch 1A para 6(9).
255 Ibid, Sch 2 para 6(4).
256 Ibid, Sch 2 para 6(5).
257 Ibid, Sch 2 para 7(1).
258 Ibid, Sch 2 para 7(2).

23.247 Before making a curfew requirement, the court shall obtain and consider information about the place proposed to be specified in the requirement (including information as to the attitude of persons likely to be affected by the enforced presence there of the offender).[259]

23.248   A curfew requirement shall, as far as practicable, be such as to avoid:

- any conflict with the offender's religious beliefs or with the requirements of any other community order to which s/he may be subject; and
- any interference with the times, if any, at which s/he normally works or attends school or any other educational establishment.[260]

Amendment

23.249 Application may be made by either the offender or his/her responsible officer to a youth court (or to a magistrates' court if the offender has attained 18) for the amendment of the requirements of a community rehabilitation order. The court may:

- substitute another local justice area for the one named in the order;
- cancel any requirement;
- insert in the order (either in addition or in substitution for any existing requirements) any requirements which the court could include if it were then making the order.[261]

23.250 A court may not amend the order:

- by reducing the community rehabilitation period, or by extending that period beyond the end of three years from the date of the original order; or
- by inserting in it a requirement that the offender shall submit to treatment for his/her mental condition, or his/her dependency on drugs or alcohol, unless the offender agrees to the amendment and the amending order is made within three months after the date of the original order.[262]

Revocation

23.251 Application may be made either by the offender or the supervisor to a youth court (or to a magistrates' court if the offender has attained 18) for the community rehabilitation order to be revoked. If after having regard to the circumstances which have arisen since the imposition of the order, the court is satisfied that it would be in the interests of justice that the order be revoked or that the offender be dealt with in another manner, it may:

- revoke the order; or
- revoke the order and deal with the offender, for the offence in respect of which the order was made, in any manner in which it could deal with him/her if s/he had just been convicted by the court of the offence.[263]

259 Powers of Criminal Courts (Sentencing) Act 2000 Sch 2 para 7(8).
260 Ibid, Sch 2 para 7(3).
261 Ibid, Sch 3 paras 12 and 13.
262 Ibid, Sch 3 para 13(2).
263 Ibid, Sch 3 para 10(1) and (3).

23.252   If the order was made by the Crown Court, the court may not revoke the order itself but it may commit the offender to the Crown Court for that purpose.[264]

23.253   In either case, if a court does re-sentence the offender, the extent to which s/he complied with the probation order must be taken into account.[265]

23.254   The circumstances in which a community rehabilitation order may be revoked shall include the offender's making good progress or his responding satisfactorily to supervision.[266]

Community punishment order

23.255   A community punishment order is an order that the offender perform unpaid work.[267]

Pre-conditions

23.256   An order may not be imposed unless:
- the offence is imprisonable;[268]
- the court considers the offence, or the combination of the offence and associated offences to be serious enough;[269]
- the court considers the requirements of the order to be the most suitable for the offender.[270]

Age

23.257   A community service order may not be imposed upon an offender who has not attained the age of 16 years.[271] The relevant age is the age at the date of conviction.

Length of the order

23.258   The number of hours shall be in the aggregate not less than 40 and not more than 240.[272] The court may impose more than one community punishment order at the same time. If it does so, it may specify that the orders are to run concurrently or consecutively.[273]

23.259   A court may also impose a community punishment order upon an offender already subject to such an order. The court may then specify that the new order is to run concurrently with the existing order or to run

---

264 Powers of Criminal Courts (Sentencing) Act 2000 Sch 3 para 11.
265 Ibid, Sch 3 paras 10(3) and 11(2).
266 Ibid, Sch 3 para 10(4).
267 Ibid, s46(1) and (2).
268 Ibid, s46(1).
269 Criminal Justice Act 2003 s148(1).
270 Ibid, s148(2)(a).
271 Powers of Criminal Courts (Sentencing) Act 2000 s46(1).
272 Ibid, s46(3).
273 Ibid, s46(8).

consecutively. If the order is made consecutively, it is undesirable for the offender to be subject to orders totalling more than 240 hours.[274] This principle refers to the hours of the various orders rather than the actual number of hours which remain to be completed.[275]

Procedural requirements

23.260 A court may not make a community punishment order unless, after hearing (if the court thinks it necessary) an officer of a local probation board or a member of a youth offending team, the court is satisfied that the offender is a suitable person to perform work under the order.[276]

23.261 On making the order, the court shall forthwith give copies of the order to an officer of a local probation board assigned to the court or to a member of a youth offender team so assigned.[277]

Responsible officer

23.262 The functions of a responsible officer shall be discharged by:

- an officer of a local probation board; or
- a member of a youth offending team established by a local authority specified in the order.[278]

Requirements of the order

23.263 An offender subject to a community punishment order shall:

- keep in touch with the responsible officer in accordance with such instructions as s/he may from time to time be given by that officer and notify the officer of any change of address; and
- perform for the number of hours specified in the order such work at such times s s/he may be instructed by the responsible officer.[279]

23.264 Instructions given by the offender's responsible officer shall, as far as practicable, be such as to avoid:

- any conflict with the offender's religious beliefs or with the requirements of any other community order to which s/he may be subject; and
- any interference with the times, if any, at which s/he normally works or attends school or any other educational establishment.[280]

23.265 The order should be completed within one year of the date of sentence.[281] If the order is to run beyond this, the supervisor should apply to the court for an extension. This may be granted if it appears to the court that it would

---

274 *R v Evans* [1977] 1 All ER 228, [1977] 1 WLR 27, 141 JP 141.
275 *R v Anderson* (1989) 11 Cr App R (S) 417; [1990] Crim LR 130, CA.
276 Powers of Criminal Courts (Sentencing) Act 2000 s46(4) and (5).
277 Ibid, s46(11).
278 Ibid, s47(5).
279 Ibid, s47(1).
280 Ibid, s47(2).
281 Ibid, s47(3).

be in the interests of justice to do so having regard to circumstances which have arisen since the order was made.[282].

Amendment

23.266   Application may be made by either the offender or his/her supervisor to a youth court (or to a magistrates' court if the offender has attained 18) for the substitution of a different local justice area to the one specified in the order. The court may only substitute the new local justice area if it is satisfied that provision exists for the offender to perform such work in that area.[283]

Revocation

23.267   Application may be made either by the offender or the supervisor to a youth court (or to a magistrates' court if the offender has attained 18) for the community punishment order to be revoked. If, after having regard to the circumstances which have arisen since the imposition of the order, the court is satisfied that it would be in the interests of justice that the order be revoked or that the offender be dealt with in another manner, it may:

- revoke the order; or
- revoke the order and deal with the offender, for the offence in respect of which the order was made, in any manner in which it could deal with the offender if s/he had just been convicted by the court of the offence.[284]

23.268   If the order was made by the Crown Court, the court may not revoke the order itself but it may commit the offender to the Crown Court for that purpose.[285]

23.269   In either case, if a court does re-sentence the offender, the extent to which s/he complied with the probation order must be taken into account.[286]

23.270   The circumstances in which a community punishment order may be revoked shall include the offender's making good progress.[287]

Community punishment and rehabilitation order

Pre-conditions

23.271   A community punishment and rehabilitation order may only be imposed if:

- the offence is imprisonable;[288]
- the court considers the offence, or the combination of the offence and associated offences to be serious enough;[289]

---

282   Powers of Criminal Courts (Sentencing) Act 2000, Sch 3 para 22.
283   Ibid, Sch 3 para 18.
284   Ibid, Sch 3 para 10(1) and (3).
285   Ibid, Sch 3 para 11.
286   Ibid, Sch 3 paras 10(3) and 11(2).
287   Ibid, Sch 3 para 10(4).
288   Ibid, s51(1).
289   Criminal Justice Act 2003 s148(1).

- the court considers the order to be the most suitable for the offender;[290] and
- the court is of the opinion that the making of the order is desirable in the interests of:
  (a) securing the rehabilitation of the offender; or
  (b) protecting the public from further harm from him/her or preventing the commission by him/her of further offences.[291]

Age

23.272 The offender must have attained the age of 16.[292] The relevant age is that at the date of conviction.

Length of the order

23.273 The community rehabilitation element of the order may be for a minimum of 12 months and a maximum of three years.[293] The community punishment element may be for a minimum in the aggregate of 40 hours and a maximum in the aggregate of 100 hours.[294]

Requirements of the order

23.274 The offender will be required to comply with the requirements imposed by both the community rehabilitation element and the community punishment element.

23.275 The community rehabilitation part of the order may include any of the additional requirements specified in Schedule 2 to the Powers of Criminal Courts (Sentencing) Act 2000.[295]

Amendment

23.276 Application may be made by either the offender or his/her responsible officer to a youth court (or to a magistrates' court if the offender has attained 18) for the amendment of the requirements of a community rehabilitation order. The court may:

- substitute another local justice area for the one named in the order;
- cancel any requirement;
- insert in the order (either in addition to, or in substitution for, any existing requirements) any requirements which the court could include if it were then making the order.[296]

---

290 Criminal Justice Act 2003 s148(2)(a).
291 Powers of Criminal Courts (Sentencing) Act 2000 s51(3).
292 Ibid, s51(1).
293 Ibid, s51(1)(a).
294 Ibid, s51(1)(b).
295 See para 23.222.
296 Powers of Criminal Courts (Sentencing) Act 2000 Sch 3 paras 12 and 13.

23.277 A court may not amend the order:

- by reducing the community rehabilitation period, or by extending that period beyond the end of three years from the date of the original order; or
- by inserting in it a requirement that the offender shall submit to treatment for his/her mental condition, or his/her dependency on drugs or alcohol, unless the offender agrees to the amendment and the amending order is made within three months after the date of the original order.[297]

Revocation

23.278 Application may be made either by the offender or the supervisor to a youth court (or to a magistrates' court if the offender has attained 18) for the community rehabilitation order to be revoked. If after having regard to the circumstances which have arisen since the imposition of the order, the court is satisfied that it would be in the interests of justice that the order be revoked or that the offender be dealt with in another manner, it may:

- revoke the order; or
- revoke the order and deal with the offender, for the offence in respect of which the order was made, in any manner in which it could deal with the offender if s/he had just been convicted by the court of the offence.[298]

23.279 If the order was made by the Crown Court, the court may not revoke the order itself but it may commit the offender to the Crown Court for that purpose.[299]

23.280 In either case, if a court does re-sentence the offender, the extent to which s/he complied with the probation order must be taken into account.[300]

23.281 The circumstances in which a community punishment and rehabilitation order may be revoked shall include the offender's making good progress or his/her responding satisfactorily to supervision.[301]

Drug treatment and testing order

23.282 A drug treatment and testing order is designed for repeat offenders whose offending is driven by drug dependence. Such offenders would often be those who would otherwise be sent to prison for a significant period of time.[302]

23.283 No court shall make a drug treatment and testing order unless it has been notified by the secretary of state that arrangements for implementing such orders are available in the local justice area proposed to be named in the order and the notice has not been withdrawn.[303]

---

297 Powers of Criminal Courts (Sentencing) Act 2000 Sch 3 para 13(2).
298 Ibid, Sch 3 para 10(1) and (3).
299 Ibid, Sch 3 para 11.
300 Ibid, Sch 3 paras 10(3) and 11(2).
301 Ibid, Sch 3 para 10(4).
302 *R v Woods and Collins* [2005] EWCA 2065, [2005] Crim LR 982.
303 Powers of Criminal Courts (Sentencing) Act 2000 s52(5).

Pre-conditions

23.284 A drug treatment and testing order may be imposed unless the court is satisfied that:

- the offender is dependent on or has a propensity to misuse drugs; and
- his/her dependency or propensity is such as requires and may be susceptible to treatment.[304]

Age

23.285 A drug treatment and testing order may only be imposed upon an offender who has attained the age of 16.[305] The relevant age is that on the date of conviction.

Length of the order

23.286 The order shall be for a minimum of six months and a maximum of three years.[306]

Pre-sentence drug testing

23.287 To determine whether the offender is dependent on or has a propensity to misuse drugs, the court may order the offender to provide samples of such description as the court may specify in order to ascertain whether the offender has any drug in his body. The court shall not make such an order unless the offender expresses his/her willingness to comply with its requirements.[307]

Procedural requirements

23.288 A court shall not make a drug treatment and testing order unless it is satisfied that arrangements have been or can be made for the treatment intended to be specified in the order (including arrangements for the reception of the offender where s/he is to be required to submit to treatment as a resident).[308]

23.289   A court may not make a drug treatment and testing order unless the offender expresses his/her willingness to comply with its requirements.[309]

Responsible officer

23.290 The responsible officer shall be an officer of a local probation board responsible for the offender's supervision.[310]

---

304 Powers of Criminal Courts (Sentencing) Act 2000 s52(3).
305 Ibid, s52(1).
306 Ibid, s52(1)(a).
307 Ibid, s52(4).
308 Ibid, s53(3).
309 Ibid, s52(7).
310 Ibid, s54(3).

Requirements of the order

23.291 The offender is required to keep in touch with the responsible officer in accordance with such instructions as s/he may from time to time be given by that officer, and to notify him/her of any change of address.[311]

23.292   The offender is required to submit during the whole period of the order to treatment by or under the direction of a specified person. The treatment should have the aim of reducing or eliminating the offender's dependency on or propensity to misuse drugs.[312] It may be residential treatment at an institution specified in the order or treatment as an out-patient at such institution or place, and at such intervals, as specified in the order.[313]

23.293   The offender is required during the period of the order to provide samples of such description as may be so determined for the purposes of ascertaining whether s/he has any drug in his/her body.[314] These samples must be given at such times or in such circumstances as determined by the treatment provider. The court will specify the minimum number of samples to be provided in any one month.[315]

Periodic reviews

23.294 The court must order review hearings which must take place at least once a month. The offender must attend the hearings and the responsible officer must provide a written report to the court describing the offender's progress on the order.[316]

23.295   At a review hearing the court may amend any requirement or provision of the order.[317] The offender must consent to any amendment of the order.[318] If such consent is not forthcoming, the court may revoke the order and deal with the offender for the offence in respect of which the order was made in any manner in which it could deal with him/her if the offender had just been convicted by the court of the offence.[319] If re-sentencing the offender, the court must take into account the extent to which the offender has complied with the requirements of the order.[320] A custodial sentence may be imposed, notwithstanding the restrictions imposed by Criminal Justice Act 2003 s152.[321] In the case of an indictable-only offence, the maximum penalty on re-sentence is six months' detention.[322]

23.296   Attendance at a review hearing may be covered by the original representation order but it will rarely, if ever, be justified.[323] Attendance may

311 Powers of Criminal Courts (Sentencing) Act 2000 s54(4)(a).
312 Ibid, s53(1).
313 Ibid, s53(2).
314 Ibid, s53(4).
315 Ibid, s53(5).
316 Ibid, s54(6).
317 Ibid, s55(1).
318 Ibid, s55(2).
319 Ibid, s55(3).
320 Ibid, s55(4)(a).
321 Ibid, s55(4)(b).
322 Ibid, s55(5).
323 Criminal Defence Service, *Criminal Costs Manual*, para 3.10.

be justified if the defence lawyer has been notified that there will be an application to amend the terms of the order in a significant way. If a claim has already been submitted to the Criminal Defence Service, then a supplementary claim can be made for reasonable work done in relation to the review hearing.[324]

324 Ibid, para 3.10.4.

CHAPTER 24

Custodial sentences

General

Definition of custodial sentence

24.1   In relation to offenders under the age of 18 there are the following possible custodial sentences:

- detention and training order;
- detention under Powers of Criminal Courts (Sentencing) Act 2000 s91 ('section 91 detention');
- detention for public protection;
- detention for life; and
- detention during Her Majesty's pleasure.

24.2   Secure training orders for the 12- to 14-year-old age group were abolished on 1 April 2000.

24.3   Detention in a young offender institution was abolished for offenders under the age of 18 on 1 April 2000. The sentence will also be abolished for 18- to 20-year-olds upon implementation of section 61 of the Criminal Justice and Court Services Act 2000.

Offender to be legally represented

24.4   A court may not impose a custodial sentence upon a child or young person unless s/he is legally represented.[1] This restriction applies whether or not the offender has previously received a custodial sentence.

24.5   An offender is treated as legally represented if, but only if, s/he has the assistance of a solicitor or barrister to represent him/her in the proceedings in that court at some time after s/he was found guilty and before s/he is sentenced.[2] This requirement is subject to the following exceptions:

- the offender was granted a representation order but that order was withdrawn because of his/her conduct; or
- having been informed of his/her right to apply for a representation order and having had the opportunity to do so, the offender refused or failed to apply.[3]

24.5A   From 2 October 2006 Criminal Defence Service Act 2006 s4 will create a further exception, namely where legal representation has been refused because the offender's means are such that s/he is not eligible for legal representation.

Statutory restrictions

24.6   Save in the case of offences for which the penalty is fixed by law or subject to a minimum term, a court must not impose a custodial sentence unless it is of the opinion that the offence, or the combination of the offence and one or more offences associated with it, was so serious that neither a fine alone nor a community sentence can be justified for the offence.[4]

---

1   Powers of Criminal Courts (Sentencing) Act 2000 s83(2).
2   Ibid, s83(4).
3   Ibid, s83(3).
4   Criminal Justice Act 2003 s152(1) and (2).

24.7   This general principle is subject to two exceptions, where:

- the young offender fails to express his/her willingness to comply with a requirement which is proposed by the court to be included in a community order and which requires an expression of such willingness; or
- in the case of offenders who have attained the age of 14, the offender fails to comply with an order for pre-sentence drug testing.[5]

Offence seriousness

24.8   This is the most common reason for imposing a custodial sentence. A court must firstly consider the seriousness of the offence and any offences associated with it. In making this assessment the court must consider the aggravating and mitigating features known to the court. Relevant features are considered in chapter 17.

24.9   The Sentencing Guidelines Council has issued a definitive guideline *Overarching Principles: Seriousness* (2004). Although this is intended to provide guidance on sentencing adult offenders, much of it is also applicable to children and young persons. The Council advises that in applying the custody threshold test, sentencers should note that:

- the clear intention of the threshold test is to reserve detention as a punishment for the most serious offences;
- it is impossible to determine definitively which features of a particular offence make it serious enough to merit a custodial sentence;
- passing the custody threshold does not mean that a custodial sentence should be deemed inevitable, and custody can still be avoided in the light of personal mitigation or where there is a suitable intervention in the community which provides sufficient restriction (by way of punishment) while addressing the rehabilitation of the offender to prevent further crime.[6]

Refusal to express willingness to comply with additional requirements

24.10   The offender is required to express willingness to comply with the following:

(a) an action plan order with a requirement of drug treatment and testing (offenders aged 14 and over);

(b) supervision order with additional requirements relating to:
  (i) drug treatment and testing (offenders aged 14 and over);
  (ii) mental treatment.

(c) community rehabilitation order with additional requirements relating to:
  (i) treatment for mental condition
  (ii) treatment for drug or alcohol dependency.

(d) drug treatment and testing order.

Pre-sentence drug testing

24.11   See paras 19.44–19.49.

---

5   Criminal Justice Act 2003 s152(3).
6   Sentencing Guidelines Council, *Overarching Principles: Seriousness* (2004), para 1.31.

Determining the length of the sentence

24.12   Having determined that only a custodial sentence is justified, the court must then consider the length of that sentence. Except in the case of offences subject to a minimum sentence, this must be the shortest term (not exceeding the permitted maximum) that in the opinion of the court is commensurate with the seriousness of the offence, or the combination of the offence and one or more offences associated with it.[7]

24.13   The court is still required to take into account any personal mitigation when determining the length of sentence. In particular with young offenders the courts have always been anxious to ensure that any custodial sentence is for the shortest possible period.

Giving of reasons

24.14   When any court passes a custodial sentence it must state in open court that it is of the opinion that the offence, or the combination of that offence and one or more offences associated with it, is so serious that neither a fine alone nor a community sentence can be justified for the offence.[8] There is no such requirement if the custodial sentence is being passed because the young offender has refused to consent to a requirement of a community sentence or to pre-sentence drug testing.[9] The court must also explain to the young offender in open court and in ordinary language why it is imposing a custodial sentence upon him/her.[10] A youth court must record the stated reasons for passing a custodial sentence in the court register.[11]

Mandatory minimum sentences

24.15   There has been a mandatory sentence for murder since the 1960s, but the Crime (Sentences) Act 1997 introduced the concept of mandatory minimum sentences. Their application to children and young persons will be considered below.

Firearms possession

24.16   For offences of firearms possession under Firearms Act 1968 s5(1)(a), (ab), (aba), (ac), (ad), (af) or (c) (prohibited weapons) or under subsection (1A)(a) of that Act, there is now (save in exceptional circumstances) a mandatory minimum sentence of three years' detention if:

- the offence was committed on or after 22 January 2004; and
- the offender had attained the age of 16 by the date of the offence.[12]

24.17   For offenders aged less that 16 on the date of the offence, the court would be limited to a detention and training order and no minimum sentence would apply.

7 Criminal Justice Act 2003 s153(2).
8 Ibid, s174(2)(b).
9 Ibid.
10 Ibid, s174(1)(a) and (2)(b).
11 Ibid, s174(5).
12 Firearms Act 1968 s51A as inserted by Criminal Justice Act 2003 s287.

Third domestic burglary

24.18 Where an offender is to be sentenced for a domestic burglary, Powers of Criminal Courts Sentencing Act 2000 s111 requires a court to impose a custodial sentence of at least three years where the offender has been convicted in England and Wales of two previous domestic burglaries and one of those other burglaries was committed after s/he had been convicted of the other and both of them were committed after 30 November 1999.

24.19 This requirement only applies if the offender was 18 or over on the date of the commission of the third burglary. Nevertheless, the existence of the minimum sentence will mean that a young offender who would be caught by the provision but for his/her age can expect a sentence of at least two years' detention.[13] The young offender should also be warned that offences committed when aged under 18 will count as qualifying convictions for section 111 once s/he attains 18.

Third class A drug trafficking offence

24.20 When an offender is to be sentenced for a class A drug trafficking offence, Powers of Criminal Courts (Sentencing) Act 2000 s110 requires the court to impose a custodial sentence of at least seven years where the offender has been convicted prior to the commission of the third offence in any part of the United Kingdom of two other class A drug trafficking offences and one of those offences was committed after the offender has been convicted of the other.

24.21 This requirement does not apply unless the offender had attained the age of 18 before the commission of the third offence. The young offender should also be warned that offences committed when aged under 18 will count as qualifying convictions for s110 once s/he attains 18.

Detention and training order

24.22 Detention and training orders were implemented throughout England and Wales on 1 April 2000. Half of the order is served in custody and for the remainder of the order the young offender is subject to supervision by his/her local youth offending team.

24.23 Guidance on the operation of the order was issued jointly be the Home Office, Lord Chancellor's Department (now Department for Constitutional Affairs) and the Youth Justice Board on 9 February 2000 and 30 March 2000.[14]

Age

24.24 The order is currently available to young offenders aged from 12 to 17 inclusive.[15] There is provision for the age limit to be reduced by the Home

---

13 *R v McInerney, R v Keating* [2002] EWCA Crim 3003; [2002] 1 All ER 1089.
14 The guidance is available on the Youth Justice Board website.
15 Powers of Criminal Courts (Sentencing) Act 2000 s100(1) and (2).

Secretary by way of statutory instrument to include 10- and 11-year-olds.[16] At the time of writing this provision had not been implemented.

24.25   The relevant age would normally be the age of the offender on the date of conviction, that is the date on which the offender pleaded guilty or was found guilty after trial.[17] Children and Young Persons Act 1963 s29(1) may allow a court to impose a detention and training order upon an offender who attained 18 before conviction. Section 29(1) applies to proceedings in respect of a young person who attains the age of 18 before the conclusion of the proceedings. In such cases, the court may continue to deal with the case and make any order which it could have made if s/he had not attained 18. In *DPP v Aldis*[18] an 18-month detention and training order for an offence of wounding with intent contrary to Offences Against the Person Act 1861 s 18 was upheld against an offender who had attained 18 before conviction. The Administrative Court considered that it had been an important consideration at the mode of trial hearing that the youth court could sentence the offender (then 17) to a detention and training order for up to 24 months. Section 29(1) should therefore allow such a sentence to be passed now that the offender was 18.

24.26   If there is any doubt about the offender's age, his/her age shall be deemed to be that which it appears to the court to be after considering any available evidence.[19]

Pre-conditions

24.27   A court may not impose a detention and training order unless:

- the accused is legally represented;[20]
- the offence before the court is imprisonable;[21]
- the court is of the opinion that the offence, or the combination of the offence and one or more offences associated with it, was so serious that neither a fine alone nor a community sentence can be justified;[22] and
- the court is of the opinion that the offence was sufficiently serious to warrant the minimum period of the order, namely four months.[23]

Defendants aged 12–14

24.28   In addition to the pre-conditions set out in para 24.27 above, where the offender is below the age of 15, a court may not impose a detention and training order, unless it is of the opinion that the child or young person is a persistent offender.[24]

16 Powers of Criminal Courts (Sentencing) Act 2000 s100(2)(b)(ii).
17 *R v Cassidy* (2000) *Times* 13 October, CA.
18 [2002] EWHC 403 (Admin), [2002] Crim LR 435.
19 Powers of Criminal Courts (Sentencing) Act 2000 s164(1).
20 Ibid, s83(2) – see para 24.4 above.
21 Ibid, s100(1)(a).
22 Criminal Justice Act 2003 s152(2).
23 Ibid, s153(2).
24 Powers of Criminal Courts (Sentencing) Act 2000 s100(2)(a).

24.29   There is no statutory definition of the term 'persistent offender' and no general definition has been suggested by the appellate courts. A small number of appeal decisions have addressed the question of determining when a child or young person. The decisions provide the following (rather limited) guidance:

- the Home Office definition for fast tracking persistent young offenders (see para 2.105) is not applicable;[25]
- a court may take into account offences for which the young offender received a caution (and by extension a reprimand or warning);[26]
- an offender sentenced for two serious robberies committed over a 24-hour period may be treated as a persistent offender even though he had not previously been convicted of any offence;[27]
- it would be wrong to treat a defendant as a persistent offender if the offence before the court for sentence is of a different character to a previous conviction or caution.[28]

24.30   There are unfortunately contradictory decisions of the Court of Appeal regarding the question of when the child or young person has to satisfy the criterion of persistent offender. Should it be at the date of the offence or should it be at the date of sentence? In *R v DR*[29] the court considered it should be the former; in *R v LM*[30] the Court considered it should be the latter. In the opinion of the authors, the latter view is to be preferred as it conforms with the principles established in *R v Ghafoor*[31] regarding the relevance of crossing a significant age threshold (see para 19.6).

Defendants aged 10 or 11

24.31   If the use of detention and training orders is extended to 10 and 11-year-olds, they may only be imposed if the pre-conditions outlined in para 24.27 are satisfied and the court is of the opinion that:

- the child is a persistent offender;[32] and
- only a custodial sentence would be adequate to protect the public from further offending by him/her.[33]

Length of order

24.32   Detention and training orders are subject to both a minimum and maximum term.

25 *R v Charlton* (2000) 164 JP 685, CA.
26 *R v AD (a juvenile)* (2001) 1 Cr App R (S) 59; [2000] Crim LR 867, CA.
27 *R v Smith* (2000) 164 JP 681, [2000] Crim LR 613, CA.
28 *R v JD* (2001) 165 JP 1, CA.
29 [2002] EWCA Crim 178.
30 [2002] EWCA Crim 3047, [2003] Crim LR 205, sub nom *R v M* [2002] All ER (D) 35 (Dec).
31 [2002] EWCA Crim 1857, [2003] 1 Cr App R (S) 84, [2002] Crim LR 739.
32 See para 24.29.
33 Powers of Criminal Courts (Sentencing) Act 2000 s100(2)(b)(i).

Minimum term

24.33   The minimum term is four months.[34] The minimum order applies to each offence not the aggregate sentence.[35]

24.34   At the time of writing, the fact that the minimum term is four months means that there are offences whose maximum penalty is too low to permit the imposition of a detention and training order. Such offences include:

- being found on enclosed premises (Vagrancy Act 1824 s4);
- criminal damage under £5,000 (Criminal Damage Act 1971 s1 and Magistrates' Courts Act 1980 s33);
- failure to surrender (Bail Act 1976 s6);
- motor vehicle interference (Criminal Attempts Act 1981 s9);
- obstructing a police officer in the execution of his duty (Police Act 1996 s89(2));
- refusing to give drugs sample on charge (Police and Criminal Evidence Act 1984 s63C); and
- trespassing with a weapon of offence (Criminal Law Act 1977 s8).

24.35   When the increase in magistrates' courts' sentencing powers is introduced by the Criminal Justice Act 2003 s154 there will be a consequent increase in the maximum penalties for the above offences under Schedule 26 to the Act, which will mean that a four- or six-month order could be imposed for these offences.[36]

24.36   Even if the maximum penalty allows a detention and training order to be imposed, the defence lawyer still needs to consider whether the seriousness of the offence warrants a four-month order, especially when the court should be giving credit for a guilty plea or taking into account a period in secure accommodation on remand.

Maximum term

24.37   The maximum term for a summary-only offence is six months.[37] The maximum term for an indictable offence is 24 months.[38]

Determining the length of the order

24.38   When determining the length of a detention and training order, the court is restricted to imposing orders of 4, 6, 8, 10, 12, 18 or 24 months.[39]

---

34   Powers of Criminal Courts (Sentencing) Act 2000 s101(1).
35   *R v Ganley*, unreported, 200000359/Z1 following decision of *R v Kent Youth Court ex p K (a minor)* [1997] 1 WLR 27, in relation to minimum term of detention in a young offender institution.
36   This change is not anticipated before November 2006.
37   At the time of writing, this maximum is by virtue of the maximum penalty available for the offence. When magistrates' courts sentencing powers are increased by the Criminal Justice Act 2003, the six-month maximum will remain by virtue of a new subsection (2A) inserted into s101 of the 2000 Act by Criminal Justice Act 2003 s298(3).
38   Powers of Criminal Courts (Sentencing) Act 2000 s101(2).
39   Ibid, s101(1).

Aggregate term

24.39 A court has the same power to pass consecutive detention and training orders as if they were sentences of imprisonment. This applies where the offender:

- is being sentenced for more than one offence at the same time; or
- is already subject to a detention and training order.

24.40 A court may not make, in respect of an offender, a detention and training order the effect of which would be that s/he would be subject to orders for an aggregate term which exceeds 24 months.[40] Where the aggregate term of the orders to which an offender would otherwise be subject exceeds 24 months, the excess shall be treated as remitted.[41] Where a 'new' detention and training order is made in relation to an offender who is already subject to a detention and training order under which the period of supervision has already begun, the old order shall be disregarded for the purposes of determining whether the aggregate exceeds 24 months.[42]

24.41 When dealing with one or more summary-only offences, the youth court is not subject to the usual restrictions in relation to custodial sentences imposed by Magistrates' Courts Act 1980 s133. Accordingly it may impose consecutive detention and training orders to an aggregate of more than six months, provided that the term of each order does not exceed six months.[43]

Time spent on remand

24.42 When determining the term of the order, the court must take into account any period for which the offender has been remanded in custody in connection with the offence, or any other offence the charge for which was founded on the same facts or evidence.[44] Where a court proposes to make detention and training orders for two or more offences, it shall take account of the total period for which the offender was remanded in custody in connection with any of the offences, or any other offence the charge for which was founded on the same facts or evidence.[45] Once a period of remand in custody has been taken account of in relation to a detention and training order in respect of an offender for any offence or offences, it shall not subsequently be taken into account in relation to another order made in respect of other offences.[46]

24.43 A reference to being remanded in custody shall include any period where the young offender was:

- held in police detention;
- remanded to or committed to custody by an order of a court;

---

40 Powers of Criminal Courts (Sentencing) Act 2000 s101(4).
41 Ibid, s101(5).
42 Ibid, s101(7).
43 *C (a child) v DPP* [2001 EWHC Admin 453, [2002] 1 Cr App R (S) 45, [2001] Crim LR 671.
44 Powers of Criminal Courts (Sentencing) Act 2000 s101(8).
45 Ibid, s101(9).
46 Ibid, s101(10).

- remanded or committed to local authority accommodation under Children and Young Persons Act 1969 s23 and placed and kept in secure accommodation or detained in a secure training centre; or
- remanded, admitted or removed to hospital under Mental Health Act 1983 s35, s36, s28 or s48.[47]

24.44   In the light of the obligation to take account of remand time, it is the unavoidable duty of the sentencing court to acquaint itself in every case where it is proposed to make a detention and training order with the precise amount of time spent in custody on remand.[48] Prior to a sentencing hearing the defence lawyer will need to calculate the period of time which could count as remand time. S/he may be the only professional in the courtroom who has access to the necessary information.

24.45   Although there is a duty to take remand time into account, the appellate courts have consistently held that there is no duty to make a precise reflection of the remand time when determining the length of the detention and training order, particularly if the remand time is only a matter of a day or two.[49] In the case of *R v Fieldhouse and Watts*[50] Rose LJ gave the following practical advice to sentencing courts:

> [T]he proper approach can perhaps best be illustrated by taking by way of example a defendant who has spent four weeks in custody on remand – that is the equivalent of a two month term. The court is likely to take such a period into account in different ways according to the length of the detention and training order which initially seems appropriate for the particular offence and offender. If that period is four months, the court may conclude that a non-custodial sentence is appropriate. If that period is six, eight, 10 or 12 months, the court is likely to impose a period of four, six, eight or 10 months respectively. If that period is 18 or 24 months, the court may well conclude that no reduction can properly be made from 18 or 24 months, although the court will of course bear in mind in such a case, as in all others involving juveniles, the continuing importance of limiting the period in custody to the minimum necessary.

Taking account of a guilty plea

24.46   On sentence the court is required to take account of the fact that the offender pleaded guilty.[51] Where a court is imposing a detention and training order, it should give credit for a guilty plea even if the court thinks that the two-year maximum order is too short to be commensurate with the seriousness of the offence(s).[52] The fact that the prosecution chose not to proceed with a grave crime is not justification for refusing to give credit for a guilty plea.[53]

---

47   Powers of Criminal Courts (Sentencing) Act 2000 s101(11).
48   *R v Haringey Youth Court ex p A (a minor)* (2000) *Times* 30 May, QBD.
49   See, for example, *R v Inner London Crown Court ex p I (a minor)* (2000) *Times* 12 May, QBD; *R v B* [2001] 1 Cr App R (S) 89, CA; *R v Inner London Crown Court ex p N and S (minors)* [2000] Crim LR 871, QBD.
50   [2000] Crim LR 1020, CA.
51   Criminal Justice Act 2003 s144 – see 17.17.
52   *R v Sharkey and Daniels* (1995) 16 Cr App R (S) 257; [1994] Crim LR 866, CA; *R v Kelly* [2001] EWCA Crim 1030; *R v Marley* [2002] 2 Cr App R (S) 73, CA.
53   *R v March* [2002] EWCA Crim 551, [2002] Crim LR 509.

24.47   A 24-month order may, however, be imposed in the Crown Court on a guilty plea to a grave crime, if the discount for the guilty plea is actually the court's decision not to use its power to impose section 91 detention.[54]

24.48   Under the current law, this exception to the general rule could never apply in the youth court as section 91 detention is not an option at the sentencing hearing. When plea before venue in introduced for grave crimes (see appendix 6), this principle will apply if the youth court makes it clear that the credit for the guilty plea is reflected in a decision not to commit for sentence at the Crown Court.

Offender already subject to a sentence of section 91 detention

24.49   A court may not order a detention and training order to run consecutively to a sentence of section 91 detention.[55]

Procedural requirements

24.50   The court must consider a pre-sentence report before imposing a detention and training order. This may be a report prepared specifically for the current proceedings or an old report if the court considers that a new report is unnecessary in the circumstances of the case (for more see para 20.25).

24.51   A youth court should record the stated reasons for passing the detention and training order in the court register.[56]

Place of detention

24.52   An offender shall serve the period of detention and training under a detention and training order in such secure accommodation as may be determined by the Home Secretary or by such other person as may be authorised by him for that purpose.[57] Currently the choice of institution is made by the Youth Justice Board. The young offender may be placed in a young offender institution, secure training centre or a local authority secure children's home. The allocation decision is considered at para 26.27.

The period of detention and training

24.53   The period of detention and training under a detention and training order shall be one-half of the term of the order.[58] The young offender may in certain circumstances be released earlier than the half-way point (see paras 26.43 and 26.47). S/he may also be kept in custody longer than the half-way point on the authority of a youth court (see para 26.55).

24.54   An offender detained in pursuance of a detention and training order shall be deemed to be in legal custody.[59]

---

54 *R v Fieldhouse and Watts* [2000] Crim LR 1020, CA.
55 *R v Hayward and Hayward* [2001] 2 Cr App R (S) 149, CA.
56 Criminal Justice Act 1991 s1(5).
57 Powers of Criminal Courts (Sentencing) Act 2000 s102(1).
58 Ibid, s102(2).
59 Ibid, s102(6).

The period of supervision

24.55   Upon release from custody, the young offender is subject to supervision by a youth offending team until the term of the order ends (for more see para 26.59).

Offences during currency of order

24.56   Where an offender is subject to a detention and training order, a court may order him/her to be returned to custody if s/he is convicted of a new imprisonable offence committed after his/her release and before the date on which the term of the order ends.[60] The power to recall to custody exists whether or not the young offender is convicted of the new offence before the expiry of the existing order.[61]

24.57   The court by or before which the offender is convicted of the new offence may, whether or not it passes any other sentence on the offender, order him/her to be detained for the whole or any part of the period which:

- begins with the date of the court's order; and
- is equal in length to the period between the date on which the new offence was committed and the date on which the term of the existing order ends.[62]

24.58   The court may order that the recall to custody be served before any sentence imposed for the new offence or concurrently with that sentence.[63] In either case, the period of recall to custody shall be disregarded in determining the appropriate length of the sentence for the new offence.[64] Where the new offence is found to have been committed over a period of two or more days or at some time during a period of two or more days, it shall be taken for the purposes of calculating the recall period to have been committed on the last of those days.[65]

Section 91 detention

Grave crimes

24.59   Section 91 detention is only available if the offence can be defined as a 'grave crime'. An offence may be defined as a grave crime if it is punishable in the case of an adult with imprisonment for 14 years or more.[66] A list of offences which could be defined as grave crimes is contained in appendix 6.

---

60   Powers of Criminal Courts (Sentencing) Act 2000 s105((1) and (2).
61   Ibid, s105(1)(b).
62   Ibid, s105(2).
63   Ibid, s105((3)(a).
64   Ibid, s105(3)(b).
65   Ibid, s105(4).
66   Ibid, s91(1)(a).

Sexual offences

24.60 The following sexual offences may be treated as grave crimes notwithstanding the fact that the maximum sentence is less than 14 years:

- sexual assault contrary to Sexual Offences Act 2003 s3;
- child sex offences committed by children and young persons contrary to Sexual Offences Act 2003 s13;
- sexual activity with a child family member contrary to Sexual Offences Act 2003 s25; and
- inciting a child family member to engage in sexual activity contrary to Sexual Offences Act 2003 s26.[67]

Firearms possession

24.61 Even thought the maximum penalty is only 10 years, offences under Firearms Act 1968 s5(1)(a), (ab), (aba), (ac), (ad), (af) or (c) (prohibited weapons) or under subsection (1A)(a) of that section may also be grave crimes, provided:

- the offence was committed after 22 January 2004; and
- at the time of the offence the offender had attained 16; and
- the court is of the opinion that there are no exceptional circumstances justifying its not imposing at least the mandatory minimum sentence of three years' detention.[68]

Fatal driving offences

24.62 Prior to 27 February 2004 the offences of causing death by dangerous driving and causing death by careless driving whilst under the influence of drink or drugs were only punishable in the case of an adult with ten years' imprisonment. Express statutory provision allowed these offences to be treated as grave crimes but only in the case of an offender who had attained the age of 14.

24.63 With the implementation on 27 February 2004 of Criminal Justice Act 2003 s285, the maximum penalty was increased to 14 years for the following offences:

- causing death by dangerous driving contrary to Road Traffic Act 1988 s1;
- causing death by careless driving whilst under influence of drink or drugs contrary to Road Traffic Act 1988 s3A;
- aggravated vehicle-taking resulting in death contrary to Theft Act 1968 s12A(4).

24.64 Criminal Justice Act 2003 s 285 does not have retrospective effect, therefore it is only for offences committed on or after 27 February 2004 that these three offences may now be treated as grave crimes for any child or young person.[69]

67 Powers of Criminal Courts (Sentencing) Act 2000 s91(1)(b)–(e).
68 Ibid, s91(1A).
69 Criminal Justice Act 2003 s285(8).

Age

24.65 Section 91 detention is available for all young offenders aged 10–17, except in the following cases:

- offences of firearms possession subject to the statutory minimum (see para 24.61 above); and
- offences of causing death by dangerous driving and causing death by careless driving whilst under influence of drink or drugs committed before 27 February 2004 (see paras 24.62–24.64 above).

24.66 The relevant age for the purposes of section 91 detention is the age on the date of conviction.[70] This means that the sentence must still be imposed upon an offender who attains the age of 18 between the date of conviction and the date of sentence. By Children and Young Persons Act 1963 s29(1) the court is also given the discretion to use the sentence in the case of a young person who attains the age of 18 after proceedings have commenced but prior to conviction. If there is any doubt about the offender's age, his/her age shall be deemed to be that which it appears to the court to be after considering any available evidence.[71]

Convicted on indictment

24.67 At the time of writing, section 91 detention is only available when the young offender has been committed to stand trial on indictment at the Crown Court. This will be when:

- the offence was one of homicide or firearms possession; or
- the offence was a grave crime and a youth court considered that the powers of section 91 should be available; or
- the offence was a specified offence within the meaning of Schedule 15 to the Criminal Justice Act 2003 and the offender was sent for trial as a dangerous offender; or
- the young offender was jointly charged with an adult and the magistrates' court considered it to be in the interests of justice that the child or young person stand trial together with the adult.

24.68 When section 41 of and Schedule 3 to the Criminal Justice Act 2003 are in force, it will be possible for the youth court to commit a child or young person for sentence, if the offence is a grave crime and a guilty plea was indicated at the plea before venue stage. Committal in such circumstances will then allow the Crown Court to impose a sentence of section 91 detention.[72]

No other method suitable

24.69 The Crown Court judge is required to consider whether any other disposal would be suitable to deal with the offender.[73]

---

70 *R v Robinson* (1993) 14 Cr App R (S) 448, CA.
71 Powers of Criminal Courts (Sentencing) Act 2000 s164(1).
72 Implementation of s41 and Sch 3 is expected in November 2006. See appendix 13.
73 Powers of Criminal Courts (Sentencing) Act 2000 s91(3).

Place of detention

24.70   An offender sentenced to section 91 detention may be detained in such place and under such conditions as the Home Secretary may direct or as the Home Secretary may arrange with any person.[74] The offender could be detained in a local authority secure children's home, a secure training centre or a young offender institution. The type of establishment will be determined in the early part of the sentence as part of the allocation procedure.[75]

Guidelines

24.71   The principles for the use of detention under Children and Young Persons Act 1933 s53, the predecessor of section 91 detention, were set out in the judgments of the Court of Appeal in *R v Fairhurst*[76] and *R v AM*.[77] In general, these judgments are still taken as outlining relevant principles for the use of section 91 detention. Quotations from these two judgments have been amended to reflect legislative changes which do not affect the principles involved.

General principles

24.72   On the one hand there exists the desirability of keeping youths under the age of [18] out of long terms of custody ... On the other hand it is necessary that serious offences committed by youths of this age should be met with sentences sufficiently substantial to provide both the appropriate punishment and also the necessary deterrent effect, and in certain cases to provide a measure of protection to the public.

A balance has to be struck between these objectives. In our view it is not necessary, in order to invoke the provisions of [section 91], that the crime committed should be one of exceptional gravity, such as attempted murder, manslaughter, wounding with intent, armed robbery or the like. [78]

Offenders aged 15–17

24.73   [Section 91] may be properly invoked where the crime committed is one within the scope of the section, and is one that not only calls for a sentence of detention but detention for a longer period than 24 months.

The court should not exceed the 24 month limit for [a detention and training order] without much careful thought; but if it concludes that a longer sentence, even if not a much longer sentence, is called for, then the court should impose whatever it considers the appropriate period of detention under section [91].[79]

Offenders aged under 15

24.74   Section 91 detention will be the only custodial option for the Crown Court in relation to offenders under 15, unless the offender is aged 12–14 and is

---

74   Powers of Criminal Courts (Sentencing) Act 2000 s92(1).
75   See para 26.27.
76   (1986) 8 Cr App R (S) 346; [1986] 1 WLR 1374; [1997] 1 All ER 46; [1987] Crim LR 60.
77   [1998] 1 All ER 874; [1998] 2 Cr App R (S) 57.
78   *R v Fairhurst* (1986) 8 Cr App R (S) 346, per Lane LCJ at p349.
79   *R v AM* [1998] 2 Cr App R 57, per Bingham LCJ at p65.

deemed to be a persistent offender, in which case a detention and training order will also be available.

24.75   Where the seriousness of the offence warrants a sentence of more than two years, there is no doubt that a sentence of section 91 detention may be imposed. There are, however, conflicting lines of authority regarding the Crown Court's powers in relation to an offender aged under 15 years who cannot be deemed to be a persistent offender.

24.76   In *R v Gaskin*[80] it was held that where no other custodial sentence was available because of the offender's age, a sentence of section 53 detention (the predecessor of section 91 detention) could be imposed for a period shorter than two years. This approach was later endorsed by Lord Bingham CJ in *R v AM* and, after implementation of detention and training orders, followed in *R v J-R (a juvenile)*.[81]

24.77   This line of authorities was not followed in the cases of *R (on the application of D) v Manchester City Youth Court*[82] and *R (on the application of W) v Thetford Youth Court*.[83] Judgments in both cases were delivered by Gage J. In the *Thetford Youth Court* case, having reviewed the above line of authorities, Gage J said:

> There is no statutory restriction on a court, using its powers under section 91, passing a sentence of less than two years. But it seems to me that it will only be in very exceptional and restricted circumstances that it will be appropriate to do so, rather than making a detention and training order. The fact that an offender ... does not qualify for a detention and training order because he is not a persistent offender does not seem to me such an exceptional circumstance as to justify the passing of a period of detention of less that two years under section 91 of the Act of 2000.

> My conclusion is that the authorities do not alter my conclusions already expressed on the relationship between [the statutory provisions relating to section 91 detention and detention and training orders] ... I remain of the opinion that that where an offence or offences are likely to attract a sentence of less than two years' custody the appropriate sentence will be a detention and training order. In the case of an offender under 15, who is not a persistent offender or a child under 12, the most likely sentence will be a non-custodial sentence ...

> However, I accept that there may be cases, where despite the fact that the offender is under 15, and no detention and training order can be made, the only appropriate sentence is a custodial sentence pursuant to section 91 and possibly for a period of less than two years. In expressing my views, as I did, in *D v Manchester City Youth Court*, my use of the expression 'very exceptional' may be more restrictive than was strictly necessary or justified ... Perhaps it would be better to say that cases involving offenders under 15 for whom a detention and training order is not available will only rarely attract a period of detention under section 91; the more rarely if the offender is under 12.[84]

24.78   This judgment of Gage J was expressly endorsed by Lord Woolf CJ and Sedley LJ in *R (on the application of W) v Southampton Youth Court*.[85]

80   (1985) 7 Cr App R (S) 28, CA.
81   [2001] 1 Cr App R (S) 109; [2000] Crim LR 1022, CA.
82   [2001] EWHC 860 (Admin); (2001) 166 JP 15; [2002] 1 Cr App (S) R 573.
83   [2002] EWHC 1252 (Admin); [2002] Crim LR 681.
84   [2002] EWHC 1252 (Admin) at [28]–[30].
85   [2002] EWHC 1640 (Admin); 166 JP 569; [2002] Crim LR 750.

24.79 The practical effect of the judgments of Gage J would seem to be that, in the case of an offender aged under 15 who is not a persistent offender, the Crown Court would be faced with the choice of a sentence of section 91 detention for more than two years or a non-custodial sentence. This logic was rejected by the Court of Appeal in *R v Thomas*[86] where Hooper LJ held that the Administrative Court decisions following on from the *Manchester City Youth Court* case were not binding on the Court of Appeal and only in fact applied to the youth court decision regarding jurisdiction. In *Thomas* the sentencing judge had imposed two years' section 91 detention for a very serious robbery committed by a 14-year-old without previous convictions who had attained 15 by the time of his conviction. One of the co-defendants received a two-year detention and training order; the other received a supervision order. On appeal it was held that a custodial sentence was fully justified but that the length of the sentence was excessive. Hooper LJ considered that a shorter sentence of section 91 detention was possible, but instead ruled that a 12-month detention and training order could be imposed in the circumstances.

24.80 Although a decision of the Court of Appeal, the judgment of Hooper LJ in *Thomas* does appear to contradict an interpretation expressly endorsed by the then Lord Chief Justice, albeit whilst sitting in the Administrative Court. The decision in *Thomas* is also unsatisfactory as it results in a sentence of a detention and training order even though when the offence was committed such a sentence could not have been imposed as the appellant was not a persistent offender. This part of the judgment seems difficult to reconcile with the principles set out in the Court of Appeal in *R v Ghafoor* and *R v LM* (see paras 19.6 and 24.30 respectively).

24.81 In all the circumstances it is likely that the Court of Appeal will have to revisit the question of which line of authorities to follow in the future.

Sentencing for more than one grave crime together

24.82 [W]here more than one offence is involved for which section [91] is available, but the offences vary in seriousness, provided that at least one offence is sufficiently serious to merit section [91] detention, detention sentences of under two years' duration, whether concurrent or consecutive, may properly be imposed in respect of the other offences (see *Gaskin* (1985) 7 Cr.App.R.(S.) 28).[87]

Sentencing grave crimes together with non-grave crime

24.83 Where there are two offences committed by a 15 or 16 [or 17] year old and one of them (A) carries a maximum sentence of 14 years and the other (B) carries a lower maximum, then generally speaking it is not proper to pass a sentence of section [91] detention in respect of offence A which would not otherwise merit it in order to compensate for the fact that [a 24-month detention and training order] is grossly inadequate for offence B. Where, however, it can be truly said that the defendant's behaviour giving rise to offence B is part and parcel of the events giving rise to offence A such a sentence may properly be passed.[88]

---

86 [2004] EWCA Crim 2199.
87 *R v Fairhurst* (1986) 8 Cr App R (S) 346, per Lane LCJ at p349.
88 Ibid.

24.84 Since the introduction of the concept of associated offences for the purposes of determining seriousness, the seriousness of the grave crime could be treated as increased by the existence of the non-grave crime where it is an associated offence.[89] This is the approach followed in *R v McKay*.[90]

Offenders already serving a detention and training order

24.85 A court may not order a sentence of section 91 detention to run consecutively to a detention and training order.[91]

Determining the length of detention

24.86 The sentence of section 91 detention shall be for such term as in the opinion of the court is commensurate with the seriousness of the offence, or the offence and one or more offences associated with it.[92]

Light at the end of the tunnel

24.87 Although the court will often be dealing with extremely serious offences, consideration should still be given to the youth of the offender. In *R v Storey*[93] Mustill J stated the principle which has been followed on many occasions.

> There is another principle to which effect must, in our opinion, be given. These are young men not of outstanding intellectual attainments, and perhaps not very gifted in imagination. It is important , when using the powers under the Act, that the court should not impose a sentence, which, the far end of it, would to young men like this seem completely out of sight. True it always lies in the administrative powers of the appropriate authorities to release the offender substantially before the end of the period fixed by the court. Nevertheless it is not always easy for a 16 year old to appreciate this. The court must take care to select a duration for the order upon which the offender can fix his eye, so that he could buckle down to taking advantage of the structured environment in a place like Aycliffe School, with a view to emerging from it in the foreseeable future improved by his study there.

Deterrence

24.88 Using section 91 detention to impose a deterrent sentence has been held to be compatible with the court's statutory duty to consider the welfare of the child or young person.[94] It has been established that the possibility of a deterrent sentence survived the Criminal Justice Act 1991[95] and the Court of Appeal has further confirmed that a deterrent sentence may be proper in the context of detention under Children and Young Persons Act 1933 s53(2)

---

89 *R v AM* [1998] 2 Cr App R 57, per Bingham LCJ at p67.
90 [2000] 1 Cr App R (S) 17, CA.
91 *R v Lang* [2001] 2 Cr App R (S) 175, CA.
92 Criminal Justice Act 2003 s153(2).
93 (1984) 6 Cr App R (S) 104, CA.
94 *R v Ford* (1976) 82 Cr App R 303, CA, per Scarman LJ.
95 *R v Cunningham* [1993] 1 WLR 183; (1993) 14 Cr App R (S) 444, CA.

and (3) (now section 91 detention).[96] Nevertheless, the court should take account of the offender's youth:

> It is not inappropriate to impose a deterrent sentence; there may be a very real need to deter others and indeed young others from offending in a like manner. But when one is passing ... a deterrent sentence, it is necessary to keep a balance between that aspect of the matter, the youth of the offender and the effect of a long sentence upon the perception of the offender, it being trite to observe that young offenders see time stretching ahead of them in a different way to that in which adults see it.[97]

Remand time (offences committed before 4 April 2005)

24.89 The actual time to be served by the offender in custody will be treated as reduced by the relevant period. This is defined as the following:

- any period during which the offender was in police custody in connection with the offence for which the sentence was passed;
- any period for which s/he was remanded in custody for the offence; or
- any period when the offender was remanded or committed to local authority accommodation and placed in accommodation provided for the purpose of restricting liberty.[98]

24.90 The calculation will be made by the Section 53/92 Casework Unit now located at the Youth Justice Board.

Time in police custody

24.91 This includes time spent in the police station as a suspect prior to charge, time spent after charge if bail was refused and any time spent in a police station following a court remand to police custody.

24.92 In the case of young offenders who have been sentenced to a custodial sentence for a series of offences committed over a period of time, there may be a significant number of days to be deducted from the sentence. The defence lawyer may be the only person who would be able to calculate the time spent in police custody and s/he should be prepared to confirm the figure in writing to the Section 53/92 Casework Unit.

Time spent remanded in custody

24.93 This will not count if the offender is serving a custodial sentence at the same time.

Remanded in local authority accommodation provided for the purpose of restricting liberty

24.94 Such a period will only be counted by the secure institution if the offender was detained in a local authority secure children's home or secure training centre.[99]

---

96 *R v Marriott and Shepherd* (1995) 16 Cr App R (S) 428; *R v Arrowsmith* [1996] 16 Cr App R (S) 6.

97 *R v Marriott and Shepherd*, above, n92 per Ebsworth LJ.

98 Criminal Justice Act 1967 s67(1).

99 *R v Secretary of State for the Home Office ex p A (a juvenile)* [2000] 2 AC 276; [2000] 2 Cr App R (S) 263, HL.

Calculating the relevant time on re-sentence

24.95 If an offender is being re-sentenced following revocation of a community rehabilitation order or a community punishment order or breach of a conditional discharge, any period on remand before the passing of the order should not be deducted from the custodial sentence passed.[100] Instead, the court imposing the custodial order on re-sentence should take into account any time spent on remand prior to the original order and reduce the order accordingly.[101]

24.96   It should be noted that supervision, attendance centre, reparation and action plan orders are not covered by this exception and it is submitted that any remand time before the imposition of the original sentence should be credited by the Section 53/92 Casework Unit and deducted from the actual period served in custody.

Remand time (offences committed on or after 4 April 2005)

24.97 Where a court sentences an offender to section 91 detention, it must normally direct that the number of days for which the offender was remanded in custody in connection with the offence or a related offence is to count as time served by him/her as part of the sentence.[102]

24.98   The court has a discretion to ignore time spent on remand or to direct that only some of the time should count as time served, if it considers it just in all the circumstances to do so.[103]

24.99   The court may exercise the same power in the case of:

- a remand in custody which is wholly or partly concurrent with a sentence of detention; or
- sentences of detention for consecutive terms or for terms which are wholly or partly concurrent.[104]

24.100 Such a decision must be in accordance with rules issued by the Home Secretary.[105]

24.101   Where the court makes a direction, it shall state in open court:

- the number of days for which the offender was remanded in custody; and
- the number of days which will count as time served.[106]

24.102 If the court does not direct that all days spent on remand are to be credited towards the actual sentence served, it shall state in open court:

- that its decision is in accordance with rules issued by the Home Secretary in relation to concurrent detention; or
- that it is of the opinion that it is just in all the circumstances not to count some or all of the period spent on remand.[107]

---

100 Criminal Justice Act 1967 s67(1).
101 *R v McDonald* (1988) 10 Cr App R (S) 458, CA.
102 Criminal Justice Act 2003 s240(1) and (3).
103 Ibid, s240(4)(b).
104 Ibid, s240(4(a).
105 Ibid. See Home Office Circular 37/2005.
106 Ibid, s240(5).
107 Ibid, s240(6).

24.103 For the purposes of this provision, remand in custody means:

- remanded or committed to custody by order of a court;
- remanded or committed to local authority accommodation pursuant to Children and Young Persons Act 1969 s23 and kept in secure accommodation or a secure training centre; or
- remanded, admitted or removed to hospital under Mental Health Act 1983 s35, s36, s38 or s48.[108]

24.104 Note that the sentencing court is no longer required to take into account time spent in police custody.

Procedural requirements

24.105 The court must consider a pre-sentence report before imposing section 91 detention. This may be a report prepared specifically for the current proceedings or an old report if the court considers that a new report is unnecessary in the circumstances of the case (for more see para 20.25).

24.106   It is essential that the Crown Court judge makes it clear that s/he is using the extended powers of section 91. There have been a surprising number of cases where the judge passed lengthy sentences of custody without specifying that s/he was using section 91. In such cases, the Court of Appeal has ruled that the part of the sentence in excess of 24 months is automatically remitted.[109] It has been held, however, that the mistake may be rectified if the case is brought back before the sentencing judge within the 28 days required by Supreme Court Act 1981 s47(2).[110]

Longer than normal sentences (offences before 4 April 2005)

24.107 In relation to an offender convicted of a violent or sexual offence committed before 4 April 2005, the court has the following options:

- a longer than normal sentence under Powers of Criminal Courts (Sentencing) Act 2000 s80(2)(b);
- an extended period of licence under Powers of Criminal Court (Sentencing) Act 2000 s85; or
- detention for life under Powers of Criminal Courts (Sentencing) Act 2000 s91(3).

Longer than normal sentence

24.108 The court may impose a sentence of section 91 detention for such longer term (not exceeding the maximum) as in the opinion of the court is necessary to protect the public from serious harm from the offender.[111]

24.109   When a court passes a longer than normal sentence, it shall:

- state in open court that such a sentence is necessary to protect the public from serious harm; and

---

108 Criminal Justice Act 2003 s242(2)
109 *R v Edgell* (1993) 15 Cr App R (S) 509 and *R v Venison* (1993) 15 Cr App R (S) 624.
110 *R v Anderson* (1992) 13 Cr App R (S) 325.
111 Powers of Criminal Courts (Sentencing) Act 2000 s80(2)(b).

- explain to the offender in open court and in ordinary language why the sentence is for such a term.[112]

Extended period of licence

24.110 A court may order that an offender be subject to a longer period of supervision on release if the court:

- proposes to impose a custodial sentence for a sexual or violent offence committed on or after 30 September 1998; and
- considers that the period for which the offender would otherwise be subject to licence would not be adequate for the purpose of preventing the commission by him/her of further offences and securing his/her rehabilitation.[113]

24.111 The court would impose an extended sentence, defined as a custodial sentence the term of which is equal to the aggregate of:

- the term of the custodial sentence that the court would have imposed if it had passed a custodial sentence otherwise than under this provision ('the custodial term'); and
- a further period ('the extension period') for which the offender is to be subject to a licence and which is of such length as the court considers necessary for the purpose of preventing further offences and securing the offender's rehabilitation.[114]

24.112 In the case of a violent offence, the court may not impose an extended sentence the custodial term of which is less than four years.[115]

24.113   The extension period shall not exceed:

- ten years in the case of a sexual offence; and
- five years in the case of a violent offence.[116]

24.114 The term of an extended sentence passed in respect of an offence shall not exceed the maximum term permitted for that offence.[117]

Discretionary life sentence

24.115 It is possible to order that a young offender be detained for life under section 91 provided the maximum penalty for the offence so provides.[118] In the case of a violent or sexual offence, a life sentence may be imposed in preference to a lengthy determinate sentence where the offender is a person of mental instability who is likely to re-offend and present a grave danger to the public and in view of the offender's mental condition s/he will remain an potential danger for a long or uncertain period. A life sentence should only be imposed upon a young offender in exceptional cases where there is a marked degree of mental instability.[119] Where the available evidence

---

112 Powers of Criminal Courts (Sentencing) Act 2000 s80(3).
113 Ibid, s85(1).
114 Ibid, s85(2).
115 Ibid, s85(3).
116 Ibid, s85(4).
117 Ibid, s85(5).
118 *R v Abbott* (1963) 47 Cr App R 110, CA.
119 *R v Turton* (1986) 8 Cr App R (S) 174, CA.

before the court cannot given any assurances to the court as to when the young offender will cease to present a serious danger to the public, detention for life has been upheld on appeal.[120] A psychiatric report should be obtained and considered before imposing detention for life.[121]

24.116 When detention for life is imposed, the sentencing judge must determine the minimum term to be served before release on licence may be considered by the Parole Board.[122] In determining the minimum term the judge must take into account:

- the seriousness of the offence, or of the combination of the offence and one or more offences associated with it;
- any period spent on remand in secure accommodation.[123]

Dangerous offenders

24.117 The Criminal Justice Act 2003 introduced new provisions to provide public protection against dangerous offenders. With modifications, these provisions also apply to offenders under the age of 18. It was the government's expectation that the provisions would be rarely used in the case of offenders under the age of 18.[124]

24.118 The provisions only apply to certain offences committed on or after 4 April 2005.

Definitions

Specified offence

24.119 A violent or sexual offence listed in Schedule 15 to the Criminal Justice Act 2003 (see appendix 7).

Serious offence

24.120 A specified offence punishable in the case of a person aged 18 or over by:

- life imprisonment; or
- imprisonment for a determinate period of ten years or more.[125]

Serious harm

24.121 'Serious harm' means death or serious person injury, whether physical or psychological.[126] This definition is familiar from Criminal Justice Act 1991 s2(2)(b), and case-law regarding that earlier provision is still relevant.[127]

---

120 Eg *R v Bell* (1989) 11 Cr App R (S) 472, [1990] Crim LR 206, CA; *R v Stanley* [1999] 2 Cr App R (S) 31, CA; *R v JM* [2002] EWCA Crim 1636, [2003] 1 Cr App R (S) 51.
121 *R v Pither* (1979) 1 Cr App R (S) 209, CA.
122 Powers of Criminal Courts (Sentencing) Act 2000 s82A(1) and (2).
123 Ibid, s82A(3).
124 Hilary Benn, Hansard, HC Debates col 705W, 18 March 2003.
125 Criminal Justice Act 2003 s224(2).
126 Ibid.
127 *R v Lang and others* [2005] EWCA Crim 2864, [11].

24.122   Examples of such authorities cited:

- sexual assaults which are relatively minor physically may lead to serious psychological injury: *R v Bowler* (1994) 15 Cr App R (S) 78, CA
- downloading indecent images of children may cause serious psychological injury child arising not only from what that child has been forced to do but also from the knowledge that others will see what they were doing: *R v Collard* [2004] Crim LR 757, CA.

Members of the public

24.123   The following definition has been given by Rose LJ:

> This seems to be an all-embracing term. It is wider than 'others', which would exclude the offender himself. We see no reason to construe it so as to exclude any particular group, for example prison officers or staff at mental hospitals, all of whom, like the offender, are members of the public. In some cases, particular members of the public may be more at risk than members of the public generally, for example when an offender has a history of violence to cohabitees or of sexually abusing children of cohabitees, or ... where the offender has a particular problem in relation to a particular woman.[128]

The assessment of dangerousness

24.124   The sentencing court must consider whether the young offender poses a significant risk of serious harm from the commission of further specified offences. In making this assessment, the court starts from a 'neutral' position, as the existence of previous convictions for specified offences does not create a presumption of dangerousness as it does in the case of persons aged 18 or over at the time of the offence.

24.125   In making the assessment, the court:

- must take into account all such information as is available to it about the nature and circumstances of the offence;
- may take into account any information which is before it about any pattern of behaviour of which the offence forms part; and
- may take into account any information about the offender which is before it.[129]

24.126   In *R v Lang and others*[130] Rose LJ sought to give general guidance on the way to approach the assessment of dangerousness. The parts of that guidance relevant to young offenders is set out below:

> **Meaning of 'significant risk'**
> The risk identified must be significant. This is a higher threshold than mere possibility of occurrence and in our view can be taken to mean (as in the Oxford Dictionary) 'noteworthy, of considerable amount or importance [para 17(i)].
>
> Significant risk must be shown in relation to two matters: first, the commission of further specified, but not necessarily serious, offences; and secondly, the causing thereby of serious harm to members of the public [para 7].

---

128   *R v Lang and others* [2005] EWCA Crim 2864, [19].
129   Criminal Justice Act 2003 s229(2).
130   [2005] EWCA Crim 2864.

Risk of further offences
In assessing the risk of further offences being committed, the sentencer should take into account the nature and circumstances of the current offence; the offender's history of offending including not just the kind of offence but its circumstances and the sentence passed, details of which the prosecution must have available, and, whether the offending demonstrates any pattern; social and economic factors in relation to the offender including accommodation, employability, education, associates, relationships and drug or alcohol abuse; and the offender's thinking, attitude towards offending and supervision and emotional state. Information in relation to these matters will most readily, though not exclusively, come from antecedents and pre-sentence probation and medical reports ... [para 17(ii)].

Risk of serious harm
If the foreseen specified offence is serious, there will clearly be some cases, though not by any means all, in which there may be a significant risk of serious harm. For example, robbery is a serious offence. But it can be committed in a wide variety of ways many of which do not give rise to a significant risk of serious harm. Sentencers must therefore guard against assuming there is a significant risk of serious harm merely because the foreseen specified offence is serious. If the foreseen specified offence is not serious, there will be comparatively few cases in which a risk of serious harm will properly be regarded as significant. The huge variety of offences in Schedule 15, includes many which, in themselves, are not suggestive of serious harm. Repetitive violent or sexual offending at a relatively low level without serious harm does not of itself give rise to a significant risk of serious harm in the future. There may, in such cases, be some risk of future victims being more adversely affected than past victims but this, of itself, does not give rise to significant risk of serious harm [para 17(iv)].

Importance of reports regarding the young offender
A pre-sentence report should usually be obtained before any sentence is passed which is based on significant risk of serious harm. In a small number of cases, where the circumstances of the current offence or the history of the offender suggest mental abnormality on his part, a medical report may be necessary before risk can properly be assessed [para 17(iii)].

The sentencer will be guided, but not bound by, the assessment of risk in such reports. A sentencer who contemplates differing from the assessment in such a report should give both counsel the opportunity of addressing the point [para 17(ii)].

A developmental perspective
When sentencing young offenders, to bear in mind that, within a shorter time than adults, they may change and develop. This and their level of maturity may be highly pertinent when assessing what their future conduct may be and whether it may give rise to significant risk of serious harm [para 17(vi)].

In relation to a particularly young offender, an indeterminate sentence may be inappropriate even where a serious offence has been committed and there is a significant risk of serious harm from further offences ... [para 17(vii)].

Giving reasons
Sentencers should usually, and in accordance with section 174(1)(a) of the Criminal Justice Act 2003 give reasons for all their conclusions: in particular, that there is or is not a significant risk of further offences or serious harm ... and for not imposing an extended sentence under section ... 228. Sentencers should, in giving reasons, briefly identify the information which they have taken into account [para 17(ix)].

Challenging the assessment of risk of serious harm

24.127   The risk assessment carried out by the writer of the pre-sentence report is likely to be very important in determining whether the young offender is deemed to present a risk of serious harm. The defence lawyer may therefore wish to challenge the basis of any assessment. In *R v S and others*[131] Rose LJ gave the following guidance:

> Whether or not the author of a pre-sentence report ought to be cross-examined is essentially and pre-eminently a matter for the sentencing judge, whatever the terms of that report may be. The assessment of risk contained in such a report is, of course, an important factor when the judge is assessing risk but it is not determinative. The judge has to look at all the circumstances of the case and make his assessment in the light of the material before him. It is only likely to be in very rare cases that it will be incumbent on a judge to permit the author of a pre-sentence report to be cross-examined in relation to assessment of seriousness. It is, of course, open to counsel to make submissions about the contents of a report in relation to a defendants' history of criminal offending and all other material matters.

Committal for sentence

24.128   If a youth court concludes that an offender convicted of a specified offence presents a significant risk of serious harm, it must commit him/her to the Crown Court for sentence.[132] It is important to remember that when this happens it is still for the Crown Court judge to reach his/her own decision regarding the offender's dangerousness. The pre-sentence report prepared for the Crown Court sentencing hearing should, therefore, still provide a reasoned assessment of the risk of serious harm posed by the offender.

Sentences for dangerous offenders

24.129   Where the young offender has been held to pose a significant risk of serous harm, the fundamental question to be addressed by the court is whether an extended sentence is adequate to protect the public.[133] If the requirements of sections 37 and 41 of the Mental Health Act 1983 are satisfied, the court may still make a restriction order.[134]

Extended sentence

24.130   A Crown Court must pass an extended sentence unless:

- the specified offence is a serious offence; and
- the case requires the imposition of detention for public protection or detention for life.[135]

---

131 [2005] EWCA 3616.
132 Powers of Criminal Courts (Sentencing) Act 2000 s3C(2).
133 *R v Lang and others* [2005] EWCA Crim 2864, [14].
134 Ibid, [22]. For the criteria for the imposition of a restriction order see paras 30.25–30.27.
135 Criminal Justice Act 2003 s228(1).

24.131 The extended sentence comprises:

- the appropriate custodial term; and
- an extension period when the offender will be subject to a licence.[136]

24.132 The appropriate custodial term must be at least 12 months and not exceed the maximum term of imprisonment permitted for the offence in the case of an adult.[137]

24.133 The extension period may be of such length as the court considers necessary for the purpose of protecting members of the public from serious harm occasioned by the commission of the offender of further specified offences up to a maximum of:

- five years in the case of a specified violent offence; and
- eight years in the case of a specified sexual offence.[138]

24.134 The aggregate of the custodial term and extension period may not exceed the maximum term of imprisonment permitted in the case of an adult.[139]

24.135 The extension period starts upon the expiry of the custodial term, even if the offender has been released before the end of the custodial term.[140]

Detention for life

24.136 The Crown Court must impose detention for life where:

- a person aged under 18 is convicted of a serious offence punishable with life imprisonment in the case of an adult; and
- the court is of the opinion that there is a significant risk to members of the public of serious harm occasioned by the commission by him/her of further specified offence; and
- the court considers that the seriousness of the offence, or the offence and one or more offences associated with it, is such as to justify the imposition of a sentence of detention for life.[141]

24.137 When considering whether the seriousness of the offence justifies detention for life, the court must consider the culpability of the offender as well as the seriousness of the offence.[142]

Detention for public protection

24.138 A court must pass a sentence of detention for public protection where:

- a person aged under 18 is convicted of a serious offence committed on or after 4 April 2005; and
- the court is of the opinion that there is a significant risk to members of the public of serious harm occasioned by the commission by him/her of further specified offences; and

136 Criminal Justice Act 2003 s228(2).
137 Ibid, s228(3).
138 Ibid, s228(4).
139 Ibid, s228(5).
140 *R v S and others* [2005] EWCA Crim 3616.
141 Ibid, s226(1) and (2).
142 *R v Lang and others* [2005] EWCA Crim 2864, [8]; cf criteria for a discretionary life sentence: *R v Chapman* [2000] 1 Cr App R (S) 77, CA.

- (in the case of an offence punishable in the case of an adult with life imprisonment) the seriousness of the offence is not such as to justify the imposition of a sentence of detention for life (see above); and
- the court considers that an extended sentence would not be adequate for the purpose of protecting the public from serious harm occasioned by the commission by the offender of further specified offences.[143]

24.139   A sentence of detention for public protection is a sentence of an indeterminate period subject to the early release provisions of Chapter 2 of Part 2 of the Crime (Sentences) Act 1997.[144]

Minimum term

24.140   When passing a sentence of detention for life or detention for public protection, the court must announce the minimum term to be served before the offender can be released on licence.[145] This may not be a 'whole life' tariff.[146]

24.141   Taking into account the seriousness of the offence or the combination of the offence and one or more offences associated with it, the court must identify the notional determinate sentence which would have been imposed if life detention or detention for public protection had not been required. This should not exceed the maximum permitted for the offence. Care should be taken not to incorporate in the notional determinate sentence an element for risk which is already covered by the indeterminate sentence. Half of that notional term should normally be taken as the minimum term.[147]

24.142   In calculating the minimum term, an appropriate deduction should be allowed for a plea of guilty.[148] Time spent on remand should be deducted from the minimum term.[149]

Detention during Her Majesty's pleasure

24.143   Detention during Her Majesty's pleasure is the mandatory sentence for murder where the offender was under the age of 18 at the time of the offence.[150] The sentence is indeterminate.

Minimum term

24.144   The sentencing judge must determine the minimum period the offender will spend in custody before release on licence can be considered.[151]

---

143   Criminal Justice Act 2003 s226(1) and (3).
144   Ibid, s226(4).
145   Powers of Criminal Courts (Sentencing) Act 2000 s82A(2).
146   Ibid, s82A(4A).
147   *R v Lang and others* [2005] EWCA Crim 2864, [10].
148   Sentencing Guidelines Council *Guideline for a Guilty Plea*, para 5.1.
149   Powers of Criminal Courts (Sentencing) Act 2000 s82A(3)(b).
150   Ibid, s90.
151   Criminal Justice Act 2003 s269(2).

This period will be such as the court considers appropriate, taking into account:

- the seriousness of the offence, or of the combination of the offence and anyone or more offences associated with it; and
- any period of remand in custody.[152]

24.145 For an offender under the age of 18 at the time of the offence, the sentencing judge must take as his/her starting point a figure of 12 years.[153] To determine the minimum term, the judge should then increase or decrease the starting point, bearing in mind the aggravating and mitigating factors listed in Schedule 21 to the Criminal Justice Act 2003 (see table 23).

24.146 On passing sentence, the judge must state in open court and in ordinary language his/her reasons for deciding on the length of the minimum term.[154]

24.147 The offender may appeal the length of the minimum period.[155] The Attorney-General may appeal against an unduly lenient minimum term.[156]

Place of detention

24.148 An offender ordered to be detained during Her Majesty's pleasure may be detained in such place and under such conditions as the Home Secretary may direct or as the Home Secretary may arrange with any person.[157] The offender could be detained in a local authority secure children's home, a secure training centre or a young offender institution. The type of establishment will be determined in the early part of the sentence as part of the allocation procedure.[158]

Offenders who have attained 18 before conviction

Which custodial sentence?

24.149 Except in the case of murder, the relevant age for the purposes of selecting the type of custodial sentence is the age on the date of conviction, that is, the date on which the offender pleads guilty or is found guilty after a trial.[159] It therefore follows that an offender who is 18 on conviction will receive an adult custodial sentence, whereas an offender who attains 18 between conviction and sentence will receive a detention and training order or a sentence of section 91 detention.

152 Criminal Justice Act 2003 s269(3).
153 Ibid, s269(5) and Sch 21 para 7.
154 Ibid, s270.
155 Criminal Appeal Act 1968 s1(1A) as inserted by Criminal Justice Act 2003 s271(1).
156 Criminal Justice Act 1988 s36.
157 Criminal Justice Act 2003 s92(1).
158 See paras 26.13 onwards.
159 *R v Danga* [1992] QB 476, [1992] 2 WLR 277, (1992) 13 Cr App R (S) 408, CA.

> ## Table 23: Statutory aggravating and mitigating factors for determining minimum term for sentence of detention during Her Majesty's pleasure
>
> **Aggravating factors:**
>
> - A significant degree of planning or premeditation
> - The fact that the victim was particularly vulnerable because of age or disability
> - The abuse of a position of trust
> - The use of duress or threats against another person to facilitate the commission of the offence
> - The fact that the victim was providing a public service or performing a public duty
> - Concealment, destruction or dismemberment of the body
> - Abduction of the victim
> - Sexual or sadistic motive
> - Use of firearm or explosive
> - Murder for gain
> - Murder involving killing of two or more persons
> - Racially or religiously motivated or aggravated by sexual orientation
> - Intended to obstruct or interfere with the course of justice
>
> **Mitigating factors:**
>
> - An intention to cause serious bodily harm rather than to kill
> - Lack of premeditation
> - The fact that the offender suffered form any mental disorder or mental disability which lowered his/her degree of culpability
> - The fact the offender was provoked (for example, by prolonged stress) in a way not amounting to a defence of provocation
> - The fact that the offender acted to any extent in self-defence
> - A belief by the offender that the murder was an act of mercy
> - The age of the offender

Limit on the length of the custodial sentence

24.150 Where an offender attains the age of 18 between the commission of the offence and conviction, the stating point for sentence is the sentence that s/he would have been likely to receive if dealt with at the time the offence was committed.[160]

---

160 *R v Ghafoor* [2002] EWCA Crim 1857, [2003] 1 Cr App R (S) 84, [2002] Crim LR 739 – for more information see para 19.6.

Imposing a sentence of detention in a young offender institution

24.151 Detention in a young offender institution under Powers of Criminal Courts (Sentencing) Act 2000 s96 is the current custodial sentence for offenders aged 18–20 years on the date of conviction. This sentence will be abolished upon implementation of Criminal Justice and Court Service Act 2000 s61.

24.152 Detailed consideration of the rules relating to the sentence of detention in a young offender institution is beyond the scope of this book, but the following are worthy of note:

1 The minimum term is 21 days.[161] This minimum term is not applicable where an offender is being sentenced for a breach of a licence requirement under Criminal Justice Act 1991 s65(6).

2 The minimum term applies to the sentence for each offence rather than to the aggregate term.[162]

3 When imposing a sentence of detention in a young offender institution upon an offender who attained 18 before conviction, the sentencing court should take into account the sentencing restrictions applicable to a detention and training order and only impose a sentence of 4, 6, 8, 10, 12, 18, or 24 months.[163]

---

161 Powers of Criminal Courts (Sentencing) Act 2000 s97(2).
162 *R v Kent Youth Court ex p K (a minor)* [1999] 1 WLR 27, [1999] Crim LR 168, QBD.
163 *R v Jones* [2003] EWCA Crim 1609, [2003] Crim LR 639.

Appeals

Introduction

25.1   A child or young person has the same rights of appeal as an adult. Save in the case of appeal by way of case stated, the young offender may exercise his/her right of appeal in his/her own name. No parental consent is required.

25.2   A child or young person found guilty in the youth court or magistrates' court may appeal his/her conviction and/or sentence to the Crown Court. On a point of law, either a conviction or sentence may be challenged in the Administrative Court by way of case stated or judicial review. A person tried in the Crown Court may appeal conviction or sentence to the Court of Appeal (Criminal Division).

25.3   Following conviction and sentence, the defence lawyer is under a duty to advise his/her client of any grounds of appeal. This advice is covered by the existing representation order.

Appeal to the Crown Court

25.4   Following sentence in the youth court or adult magistrates' court, a child or young person may appeal his/her conviction and/or sentence to the Crown Court.[1]

Legal representation

25.5   A representation order for an appeal may be granted by the magistrates' court from which the appeal originates or by the Crown Court which will hear the appeal.[2] An application for a representation order should be lodged with the youth court at the same time as the notice of appeal. An order is almost invariably granted to a child or young person for an appeal to the Crown Court.

Notice of appeal

25.6   A written notice of appeal should be given to a court officer for the magistrates' court and to the prosecutor.[3] The notice should state, in the case of an appeal arising out of conviction of a youth court, whether the appeal is against conviction or sentence or both.

Time limit

25.7   Notice of intention to appeal must be lodged within 21 days of the date of the court's order, that is the sentence of the court.[4] This time limit applies even if the appeal is against conviction only, except in the case of a deferred

---

1   Magistrates' Courts Act 1980 s108.
2   Criminal Defence Service (General) (No 2) Regulations 2001 SI No 1437 reg 9(1)(a) and (f).
3   Criminal Procedure Rules 2005 SI No 384 r63.2(2).
4   Ibid, r63.2(3).

sentence where the time limit for an appeal against conviction runs from the date when the sentence is deferred and not from the day when final sentence is passed.[5]

Calculating the time limit

25.8   The 21-day time limit is calculated by excluding the day of the court's order but including the 21st day thereafter. This means that if a court sentences a young offender on the 1st of the month, the notice of appeal must be received by the court clerk before midnight on the 22nd.[6]

Appealing out of time

25.9   If the notice of appeal is not lodged within this period, an application must be made to the Crown Court for leave to appeal out of time. This application must be in writing and it must explain the reasons why the appeal was not lodged in time.[7] If leave is then granted, the Crown Court will notify the clerk to the justices. It is for the defence lawyer to notify the Crown Prosecution Service that an extension to the time limit has been granted.[8]

Bail pending appeal

25.10   Where magistrates have imposed a custodial sentence upon a child or young person, they may grant him/her bail pending the determination of the appeal provided a written notice of appeal has been received.[9] If the magistrates refuse bail, a further application may be made to the Crown Court.[10] Bail will only be granted in exceptional circumstances.[11]

Withdrawing an appeal

25.11   An appeal may be withdrawn at any time with the leave of the Crown Court. It may also be abandoned without the leave of the Crown Court if written notice is given not less than the third day before the day fixed for hearing the appeal.[12] Written notice of the abandonment must be served on the justices' chief executive and upon the Crown Court.[13]

The appeal hearing

25.12   Appeals are heard by a Crown Court judge sitting with two lay magistrates. When hearing an appeal from the youth court, the Crown Court judge shall sit with two justices, each of whom is a member of the youth court panel and who are chosen so that the court shall include a man and

---

5   Criminal Procedure Rules 2005.
6   Ibid.
7   Ibid, r63.2(6).
8   Ibid, r63.2(7).
9   Magistrates' Courts Act 1980 s113.
10   Supreme Court Act 1981 s81(1)(b).
11   *R v Watton* (1979) 68 Cr App R 293; [1979] Crim LR 249, CA.
12   Criminal Procedure Rules 2005 r63.5.
13   Ibid.

a woman.[14] Appeals against conviction are complete re-hearings of the evidence and the burden of proof is on the prosecution.

Powers of the court

25.13 On hearing an appeal against sentence, the Crown Court may confirm, reverse or vary any part of the decision appealed against.[15] The sentence may be increased, however it may not exceed the maximum sentence which the magistrates' court could have imposed.[16]

25.14   If only part of a sentence is appealed, the whole sentence is still at large and the Crown Court may increase the penalty in relation to any part of the sentence.[17]

Appealing by way of case stated

25.15 A child or young person may apply to the Administrative Court to argue that a conviction or sentence of a youth court or adult magistrates' court was wrong in law or in excess of jurisdiction.[18] Once an application for case stated has been made, the applicant loses the right to appeal to the Crown Court.[19]

Legal representation

25.16 The representation order which covers the proceedings in the youth court or the adult magistrates' court also covers steps relating to the stating of a case. For the actual hearing, a fresh application for a representation order must be made to the Administrtive Court.[20]

Litigation friend

25.17 Litigants under the age of 18 in civil proceedings are treated as litigants under a disability. A litigation friend is therefore required for a child or young person to appeal by way of case stated.[21]

25.18   The litigation friend will usually be a parent or guardian. If the applicant is looked after by a local authority, it may be appropriate to ask a social worker who knows the young person to act as the litigation friend. If neither a parent or social worker is willing to act, any other responsible adult may be approached. If no other adult known to the young client is suitable, it may be possible to persuade the Official Solicitor of the Supreme Court to act as the litigation friend.

---

14 Criminal Procedure Rules 2005 r63.7.
15 Supreme Court Act 1981 s48(2).
16 Ibid, s48(4).
17 *Dutta v Westcott* [1987] QB 291.
18 Magistrates' Courts Act 1980 s111(1).
19 Ibid, s111(4).
20 General Criminal Contract, para 4A-004.
21 Civil Procedure Rules 1998 SI No 3132 r21.2(2).

The application

25.19 The application must be in writing and must be sent to a court officer for the magistrates' court whose decision is questioned. It must identify the question or questions of law or jurisdiction on which the opinion of the High Court is sought. If it is thought that the court could not have reached its decision on the evidence, the application should identify the particular finding(s) of fact which it is claimed cannot be supported by the evidence.[22]

25.20 The application must be signed by or on behalf of the applicant.[23] There is no required form for the application and it can be simply contained in the form of a letter to the court.

Time limits

25.21 The application should be received by the court within 21 days of the date of the decision which is being challenged.[24]

Bail pending appeal

25.22 Where magistrates have imposed a custodial sentence upon a child or young person, they may grant him/her bail pending the determination of the appeal provided a written request to state a case has been received.[25] If the magistrates refuse bail, a fresh application may be made to a High Court judge in chambers.

Procedure for stating a case

25.23 The procedure is governed by Criminal Procedure Rules 2005[26] Part 64 and Civil Procedure Rules 1998[27] Part 52. In summary the procedure is as follows:

- upon receipt of the application the court should produce a draft case which should be served upon the applicant's lawyer and the Crown Prosecution Service as respondent within 21 days;
- the parties have 21 days in which to submit representations and amendments;
- within a further 21 days the court serves the final version of the case upon the applicant's solicitor;
- the applicant's solicitor should then lodge it at the Administrative Court within ten days;
- within seven days thereafter the applicant's solicitor must notify the respondent that the appeal has been lodged and forward a copy of the case.

22 Civil Procedure Rules 1998 r64.1.
23 Ibid.
24 Magistrates' Courts Act 1980 s111(2).
25 Ibid, s113.
26 SI No 384.
27 SI No 3132.

25.24 There is provision for the granting of extensions to the time limits applicable to the preparation of the case.[28]

The content of a case

25.25 The case must include the facts as found by the justices and the question or questions of law or jurisdiction on which the opinion of the High Court is sought. A statement of evidence should not normally be included.[29] If, however, it is contended that a particular finding of fact cannot be supported by the evidence before the court, the disputed finding of fact should be specified and a statement of evidence included.[30]

Powers of the High Court

25.26 Upon the hearing and determination of the case, the High Court may:

- reverse, affirm or amend the determination of the youth or adult magistrates' court; or
- remit the matter to the justice(s) with the opinion of the court.[31]

Appeal to the Court of Appeal

Representation

25.27 The representation order which covers representation in the Crown Court automatically covers an advice on appeal against conviction and/or sentence. This advice should normally be in writing and should be drafted by counsel instructed in the case. If counsel advises that there are grounds for an appeal, the representation order also covers the drafting the grounds of appeal.

25.28 Representation orders to cover advocacy at the appeal hearing are granted by the Registrar of Criminal Appeals. An order is normally only granted once leave has been given. In the case of an appeal against sentence, the order will only be granted for representation by counsel.

Notice of appeal

25.29 Notice of appeal should be sent to the Crown Court. The following documents should be included:

- notice of appeal;
- grounds of appeal signed by counsel.

25.30 The notice of appeal is normally completed by the solicitor. It may be signed personally be the appellant or his/her solicitor.[32] The grounds of appeal

---

28 Criminal Procedure Rules 2005 r64.4.

29 Ibid, r64.6(1).

30 Ibid, r64.6(2) and (3).

31 Supreme Court Act 1981 s28A(3).

32 If signed by the solicitor, s/he must certify that the appellant has been advised that the Court of Appeal may order that the time spent awaiting the appeal hearing should not count towards the sentence.

will normally be drafted by counsel and may be supported by a written advice on appeal.

Time limits

25.31 Notice of appeal should be received by the court within 28 days of the decision which is being appealed. In the case of an appeal against conviction, this time limit starts to run from the day when the jury returns its verdict even if sentence is then adjourned for the preparation of pre-sentence reports.

25.32 If the notice is not lodged within that time, an application for leave to appeal out of time must be made. An explanation for the delay must be included in the grounds of appeal.

Leave to appeal

25.33 In normal circumstances, the application will be considered by a single judge reading the written application. The decision of the judge will be sent directly to counsel who drafted the grounds of appeal and to the appellant.

25.34 If the application is refused, the appellant has the right to renew the application before a full court. Oral arguments may be made at this hearing but legal aid will not be available and therefore a young appellant is only likely to be legally represented if the barrister involved is willing to appear without payment.

25.35 Both a single judge or the full court on refusing leave to appeal may make directions that the time spent in custody pending the determination of an appeal should not count towards the custodial sentence.[33] This power may not be exercised where leave to appeal or a certificate for appeal has been granted.[34] A direction concerning loss of time would not normally be made where leave is refused after an application where the grounds are settled by counsel and supported by a written advice.

Powers of the court

25.36 In an appeal against conviction, the Court of Appeal may quash the conviction[35] and, if it appears to be in the interests of justice, order a retrial.[36]

25.37 In an appeal against sentence, the court may, if it thinks that the appellant should be sentenced differently for the offence(s), quash any sentence or order and in its place pass such sentence as is appropriate, provided that a Crown Court had power to impose the sentence. The court may not deal with the appellant more severely than the original sentence.[37]

---

33 Criminal Appeal Act 1968 s29(1).
34 Ibid, s29(2).
35 Criminal Appeal Act 1968 s2(2).
36 Ibid, s7(1).
37 Ibid, s11(3).

Appeals against sentence by the prosecution

25.38   The Attorney-General may ask the Court of Appeal to review a sentence passed because it is considered to be unduly lenient.[38] This power only exists if the sentencing of the offender took place in the Crown Court. The power to refer the case to the Court of Appeal only exists if the offence is indictable-only or an either-way offence specified in the Criminal Justice Act 1988 (Reviews of Sentencing) Order 2006 SI No 1116.

25.39   The power to appeal an unduly lenient sentence applies to children and young persons sentenced in the Crown Court even though by virtue of Magistrates' Courts Act 1980 s24 indictable-only offences may be tried summarily.[39]

Procedure

25.40   The Attorney-General must give notice of an application for leave to refer a case to the Court of Appeal within 28 days of sentence being passed. The offender has no right to be present at any leave hearing. If leave is granted, legal aid will be granted to the offender to oppose the reference.

Grounds for increasing a sentence

25.41   In considering references of sentences as unduly lenient, the Court of Appeal has adopted the test of whether the sentence is outside the range of sentences which a judge, applying his/her mind to all relevant factors, could reasonably consider appropriate.[40] Even if the court reaches the conclusion that the sentence was unduly lenient, it is not obliged to increase the sentence.

Other remedies

Rectification of mistakes

25.42   A youth or adult magistrates' court may vary or rescind a sentence or other order imposed or made by it, if it appears to be in the interests of justice to do so.[41] This power may be exercised by any subsequent bench at any time. As the power is in relation to an offender, it would appear that the power may only be exercised after conviction.

25.43   A power to rectify mistakes also exists in the Crown Court where it is commonly referred to as the 'slip rule'.[42] Unlike the power in a magistrates' court, it may only be exercised by the same judge within 28 days of the original decision.

---

38   Criminal Justice Act 1988 s35.
39   Attorney-General's Reference No 3 of 1993 [1993] Crim LR 472, CA.
40   Attorney-General's Reference No 4 of 1989 (1989) 11 Cr App R (S) 517.
41   Magistrates' Courts Act 1980 s142 as amended by Criminal Appeal Act 1995 s25.
42   Supreme Court Act 1981 s47(2).

Judicial review

25.44　Magistrates' courts and youth courts are creations of statute and are therefore subject to the supervisory jurisdiction of the Administrative Court. The court may exercise this jurisdiction when the youth or magistrates' court:

- has acted outside its statutory powers (ultra vires);
- has breached the rules of natural justice;
- has wrongly exercised its discretion by taking into account irrelevant factors or ignoring relevant factors; or
- has acted irrationally or wholly unreasonably.

25.45　Judicial review is a discretionary remedy governed by the Civil Procedure Rules 1998 Part 54. The procedure for such an application is beyond the scope of this book.[43]

43　See Manning, J. *Judicial Review Proceedings: a practitioner's guide*, Legal Action Group, 2nd edition (2004).

CHAPTER 26

Serving a custodial sentence

Introduction

26.1   From April 2000 the Youth Justice Board took over responsibility for the juvenile secure estate. The Board does not directly manage any secure institution. Instead it contracts with the Prison Service, local authorities and private security companies to provide a number of beds for juvenile prisoners on remand or serving custodial sentences. Through its Clearing House, the Board also decides on the particular institution that a young offender will be sent to.

Types of secure institution

26.2   There are three types of institution where a young offender may serve his/her sentence:

- young offender institution;
- secure training centre; and
- local authority secure children's home.

Young offender institution

26.3   The Youth Justice Board has contracted with the Prison Service to provide beds in young offender institutions across England and Wales.

26.4   For male trainees the institutions are:

- Ashfield (South Gloucestershire);
- Castington (Northumbria);
- Feltham (Hounslow, west London);
- Hindley (near Wigan);
- Huntercombe (Oxfordshire);
- Lancaster Farms (Lancashire);
- Thorn Cross (Cheshire);
- Warren Hill (Suffolk); and
- Werrington (Staffordshire).

26.5   For 17-year-old female trainees the institutions are:

- Cookham Wood (Kent);
- Downview (Surrey);
- Eastwood Park (Gloucestershire); and
- New Hall (Yorkshire).

26.6   The regime in a young offender institution is governed by the Young Offender Institution Rules 2000[1] (as amended) made under the Prisons Act 1952 s47 and Prison Service Order (PSO) 4960. Young offender institutions are subject to inspection by HM Inspectorate of Prisons.

---

1   SI No 3371.

Secure training centre

26.7 At the time of writing four secure training centres have been established:

- Medway in Kent;
- Rainsbrook in Rugby
- Hassockfield in County Durham; and
- Oakhill in Milton Keynes.

26.8 Each centre is managed under contract from the Home Office by a private security company. The centres are much smaller than young offender institutions, none holding more than 100 trainees aged from 12 to 17. There is also a much higher staff to trainee ratio (a minimum of three staff members to eight trainees).

26.9 The regime at a secure training centre is governed by the Secure Training Centre Rules 1998[2] made under the Prisons Act 1952 s47. The Home Office has also confirmed that secure training centres will be run in conformity with the underlying principles of the Children Act 1989. Secure training centres are subject to inspection by the Commission for Social Care Inspection.[3]

Secure children's home

26.10 With the exception of Orchard Lodge in south-east London, secure children's homes are all run by local authorities.[4] They tend to be small institutions – the largest holding less than 40 young people. In total there are 460 beds in England and Wales. About a third of these beds are used for young people detained under Children Act 1989 s25 on welfare grounds.

26.11 Secure children's homes are run in accordance with the principles of the Children Act 1989. They are subject to inspection by the Commission for Social Care Inspection.

Allocation to secure institutions

Offenders sentenced to detention and training orders

26.12 The Youth Justice Board's Secure Accommodation Clearing House allocates offenders sentenced to a detention and training order. The Clearing House operates in accordance with a Placement Protocol (last issued in November 2004). This protocol states:

1. The Youth Offending Team must complete a **Youth Justice Board Placement Alert Form** in full and send it by fax or secure email to the YJB Placement Team in advance of the court hearing. Ideally this should be no later than the day before the court appearance. This new form replaces the current Secure Facilities Placement Booking Form ....

2 SI No 472.
3 Reports of inspectors may be found on the website of the Commission for Social Care, see appendix 14.
4 Criminal Justice and Public Order Act 1994 s19 introduced the possibility of voluntary or private organisations running secure units. Orchard Lodge was purchased by Glen Care on 31 March 2006.

2. If the Yot has assessed the young person as vulnerable supporting documents must be sent with the completed form to the placement team.

3. The placement alert form together with any accompanying documents will provide to the YJB Placement Team information as to the particular characteristics of the young person such as:
   - Has the Yot assessed her/him as vulnerable?
   - Has she/he attempted self-harm or suicide?
   - Was she/he in local authority accommodation at the time of the placement request?
   - Is she/he on a full care order?
   - Is she/he currently or in the past been on the child protection register? And if so under which category?
   - Is she/he receiving treatment for a diagnosed mental health problem?
   - Nature of the offence
   - Background information on the young person's individual circumstances

4. On the day of the court appearance a senior member of the YJB Placement Team will read all the information that has been provided on each young person who fit the following criteria:
   - All young people assessed as vulnerable by the Youth Offending Team (Yot),
   - All males aged 14 and under,
   - All girls aged 16 and under,
   - Those young people not assessed as vulnerable by the Yot but with the following, as the YJB Placement Team are required to monitor these categories:
     – Sex offence
     – Murder/manslaughter offence
     – Other grave offence where a S91 or life sentence is possible
     – With media interest
     – Pregnant girls or mothers
     – Self-harm or suicide or mental health needs

   The member of the team undertaking this exercise will complete an internal form, which will record the risk factors identified by the Yot. These factors are listed under the following headings and will assist the YJB in determining the most appropriate placement for the young person.
   - risk of harm to self;
   - welfare indicators;
   - risk to others;
   - other significant factors.

5. In order for the YJB to make a final judgement as to which particular placement or type of establishment is the most suitable for each young person the following factors are considered:
   - Yot assessment of vulnerability, and in particular risk of self harm or suicide;
   - Age and gender of the young person which informs which type of accommodation is legal and suitable;
   - Type of offence;
   - Information from the Yot and other sources;
   - Previous offending history and whether they have previously been in a secure facility;
   - What particular services they may need due to their individual circumstances (healthcare, substance misuse, anti-natal care);
   - Where places are available in relation to their home.

6. Where there are competing cases for the available beds in LASCH and STC accommodation those beds are normally prioritised as follows, although individual circumstances are considered on a case by case basis:

- 12–14 males or 12–16 females subject to DTO/S90/1 sentences;
- 12–14 males or 12–16 females made subject to a court ordered secure remand;
- 15–16 males assessed by a Yot as at risk of, or having previously made, a serious attempt of self harm or suicide either on remand or sentenced;
- 15–16 males assessed as vulnerable by a Yot where a high number of risk factors are present where self harm or suicide is not evident;
- 17 year old sentenced males or females assessed by a Yot as at risk of, or having previously made, a serious attempt of self harm or suicide.

7. In order to ascertain the available beds staff from the placement team contact each secure facility daily and produce vacancy information which is then circulated to all stakeholders.

8. The final decision on placement will be made taking into account the available vacancies, current circumstances of the young person and the total number of young people requiring non prison beds.

9. If the Yot's assessment is that the young person is not vulnerable boys aged 15 and over and 17 year old girls will be placed in their catchment YOI.

Offenders sentenced to section 91 detention

26.13 Young offenders sentenced to section 91 detention shall be liable to be detained in such place and under such conditions:

- as the Home Secretary may direct; or
- as the Home Secretary may arrange with any person.[5]

26.14 A person detained pursuant to the directions or arrangements made by the Home Secretary shall be deemed to be legal custody.[6]

26.15 At present this will be in one of the following:

- a young offender institution;
- a local authority secure children's home; or
- a secure training centre.

26.16 The allocation of young offenders sentenced to section 91 detention is normally delegated to a designated civil servant from the Section 53/92 Casework Unit which is now located at the Youth Justice Board headquarters (previously based at Prison Service Headquarters).[7] The policy on allocating offenders sentenced to section 91 detention is set out in Prison Service Order (PSO) 4960.[8]

General considerations

26.17 PSO 4960 para 5.4.2 states:

The designated officer's decision on the placement of Section 90/91 offenders under 18 must be made on the merits of each individual case and by reference

---

5 Powers of Criminal Courts (Sentencing) Act 2000 s92(1).
6 Ibid, s92(2).
7 For contact details see appendix 14.
8 Available on the Prison Service website – see appendix 14.

to a number of factors, including the age of the young person, the nature of their offence, the length of their sentence, their relative vulnerability or maturity, their ability to cope in a structured environment, their previous behaviour in detention, any history of self-harm or evidence of a propensity for it, their educational needs, their health needs (both physiological and psychological), the proximity of their family or other support and ease of access for visiting. In addition to these factors the designated officer must also take into account the Youth Justice Board's views on the best use of the accommodation available when competing

Female offenders

26.18   PSO 4960 para 5.4.3 states that female offenders under 18 will, in the normal course of events, and subject to individual assessment, be placed in secure children's homes. In practice this only applies to female offenders under the age of 17. Seventeen-year-old offenders will be placed in one of the four special juvenile units at the young offender institutions listed in para 26.5 above.

Male offenders aged under 15 years

26.19   As a matter of policy, section 90/91 offenders under the age of 15 are not held in a young offender institution and will therefore be placed initially in a secure children's home or a secure training centre.[9]

Male offenders aged 15–17

26.20   Boys aged 15 or over will normally be placed in a young offender institution, unless having regard to the factors in para 26.17 above and any other relevant factors presented by the individual case, it is deemed that their needs can only be adequately be met with the local authority secure estate. In such circumstances, the young person will normally be placed in a local authority secure unit, provided that a place is available and he can be safely contained.

26.21   Fifteen-year-olds and vulnerable 16- or 17-year-olds may be allocated to an enhanced unit when higher staffing levels permit closer attention to individual needs.[10] At the time of writing, enhanced units exist at HMYOI Warren Hill (Oswald Unit) and HMYOI Castington (Carford Unit).

26.22   Boys aged 15–17 will, save in exceptional circumstances, be placed in a young offender institution designated for juvenile prisoners. Where the offender is deemed to present significant security or control problems or he requires specific programmes or medical or other special needs not available elsewhere, he may be placed in a young offender institution with prisoners aged 18 to 20.[11]

Early warning system

26.23   The Section 53/92 Casework Unit operates an early warning system for young persons expected to receive a sentence of section 91 detention. This

---

9   PSO 4960 para 5.5.1.
10   PSO 4960, para 5.5.3.
11   PSO 4960, para 5.5.2.

allows the Unit to make a provisional booking of a secure bed for a young person prior to the sentencing hearing.

26.24 The youth offending team should alert the Section 53/92 Casework Unit to the possibility of a sentence of section 91 detention and forward the following:

- a completed Secure Facilities Placement Booking Form;
- the *Asset* Core Profile and any *Asset* Risk of Serious Harm;
- a pre-sentence report; and
- any other relevant information (eg psychiatric reports).[12]

26.25 The fact that the youth offending team has used the early warning system is not a matter that would be brought to the attention of the sentencing judge.

26.26 The defence lawyer should ensure that the youth offending team has activated the early warning system, as it gives the best chance of an appropriate placement being found for the young client facing section 91 detention. Consideration should also be given to supplying any documents or reports which might influence the decision regarding placement.

Allocation Boards

26.27 Where an offender starts a section 91 sentence by being sent from the Crown Court to the nearest young offender institution, the governor of that institution, in partnership with the supervising officer, must arrange for an Allocation Board to be held within 20 working days of reception.[13] In preparation for the meeting, the governor must order reports from the offender's personal officer, the wing officer and, where appropriate the seconded probation officer as well as from the medical officer and education staff.[14] The supervising officer must attend the Allocation Board.[15]

26.28 The Allocation Board must consider all reports and other relevant information about the young offender and make an allocation recommendation which should be forwarded immediately by the Governor to the Section 53/92 Casework Unit.

26.29 The Allocation Board may recommend that the young offender:

- remains in the establishment where he is currently detained; or
- is transferred to another Prison Service under-18 establishment (or, exceptionally, to a young offender institution for young adults); or
- is transferred to an enhanced unit; or
- is transferred to a secure children's home.[16]

26.30 Having received the recommendation of the Allocation Board, the designated officer in the Section 53/92 Casework Unit must then decide on the appropriate placement. The officer is not bound to follow the recommendation of the Allocations Board, particularly where there is substantial further background information from the supervising officer, or where there are conflicting opinions.[17]

---

12 PSO 4960, para 3.1.2.
13 PSO 4960, para 5.6.1.
14 Ibid.
15 Youth Justice Board, *National Standards for Youth Justice Services* (2004), para 12.9.
16 PSO 4960, para 5.6.2.
17 PSO 4960, para 5.6.3.

Transfer of juvenile prisoners

26.31   A young offender placed initially in a local authority secure unit may not serve his/her whole sentence in a secure unit. The Section 53/92 Casework Unit will keep every case under continuous review and transfer to a young offender institution will be made if it is considered that the offender's needs can be met outside the local authority secure estate.[18] Because of the need to use local authority secure children's homes for offenders aged under 15, many offenders will be transferred to a young offender institution after their 15th birthday.

Transfer of prisoners attaining 18

26.32   Prisoners who have reached their 18th birthday will normally be moved out of the juvenile secure estate within one month, unless good reasons exist not to. Good reasons could include being in the middle of a course of study or similar activity or being near the end of the sentence.[19] In any event, offenders may not be held in a local authority secure unit after their 19th birthday.[20]

Offender serving a detention and training order

Sentence planning meeting

26.33   A full assessment must be made of each young person admitted to custody within ten working days of admission. The assessment should cover the health, social, education, vocational and any other needs of the young person.[21]

26.34   A sentencing planning meeting must be convened within ten working days of admission. The offender's parent(s) or carer(s) should be encouraged to attend the meeting, including the local authority social worker if the young person is a looked after child. Independent visitors appointed under the Children Act 1989 are to be invited as appropriate.[22] The planning meeting needs to ensure that the views of the home education and health authorities are represented, as are those of the young person him/herself. Relevant education staff from the secure establishment should contribute to the sentence plan.[23]

26.35   Although it is not anticipated that trainees will be legally represented at sentence planning and review meetings, a trainee may involve a defence lawyer or other personal advocate if s/he so wishes.[24] It is unlikely that attendance by a defence lawyer could be publicly funded.

---

18   PSO 4960, para 5.7.1.

19   PSO 4960, para 5.7.4.

20   Children and Young Persons Act 1969 s30.

21   Youth Justice Board, *National Standards for Youth Justice Services* (2004), para 10.10.

22   Ibid, para 11.5.

23   Ibid, para 11.6.

24   Home Office/LCD/YJB Guidance *The Detention and Training Order* (9 February 2000), para 2.87.

Sentence plan

26.36 The sentencing plan must address objectives to be achieved during the custodial phase and how they will be measured, and objectives to be achieved post-transfer. It must include objectives addressing the factors that contributed to the offending. The training plan must describe the contribution each agency involved with the offender will make in meeting the objectives, and the timescales in which services will be delivered.[25] Education, health and accommodation needs on transfer to the community must be addressed from the beginning of the sentence and firm arrangements agreed for accommodation and education, training or employment arrangements to form a seamless post-release transition.[26]

26.37 The supervising officer must ensure that the plan is distributed, that the offender and the parent(s) or carer(s) understand it, and that the offender has indicated the extent of his/her agreement with the plan by signing it.[27]

Review meetings

26.38 Within one month of the initial planning meeting, the supervising officer must hold a case discussion with the trainee's key worker or personal officer and the trainee. The purpose of this discussion is to ensure that the training plan, including the individual education plan, is being implemented as agreed.[28]

26.39 A review meeting involving, where possible, those who attended the initial planning meeting, must be held at least every three months (after two months if the order is of eight months or less). The review meetings should also consider the trainee's suitability for early release.[29]

26.40 One month before the discharge date, a resettlement meeting should be held to confirm arrangements for discharge including arrangements for education, training, employment, offending behaviour work, accommodation, health provision and other relevant issues.[30]

26.41 The final review meeting must detail the specific release arrangements, including reporting details and where the young person will be living in the community.[31]

Release from custody

26.42 The offender will normally serve the first half of the sentence in custody and the second half under supervision in the community.[32]

---

25 Youth Justice Board, *National Standards for Youth Justice Services* (2004), para 11.8.
26 Ibid, para 11.9.
27 Ibid, para 11.9.
28 Ibid, para 11.12.
29 Ibid, para 11.12.
30 Ibid, para 11.13.
31 Ibid, para 11.14.
32 Powers of Criminal Courts (Sentencing) Act 2000 s102(2).

Compassionate early release

26.43   The Home Secretary may, at any time, release the offender if he is satisfied that exceptional circumstances exist which justify the offender's release on compassionate grounds.[33]

26.44   An application for compassionate early release should be submitted to the Young Offender Group at Prison Service Headquarters.

26.45   The Joint Home Office/Lord Chancellor's Department/Youth Justice Board Circular gives the following guidance on the grant of compassionate early release:

> This is a wholly exceptional provision, intended for use where the trainee's circumstances rather than behaviour warrant some special action. It is not possible to set out the range of circumstances in which the provision might be needed. Examples might be where the trainee has a serious illness from which he or she is not expected to recover during the custodial part of the order, or where very difficult family circumstances following a bereavement reasonably require the trainee's presence for a prolonged period. In such cases it must be clear that the exceptional step of release from the custodial part of the order is the only course, and that there is no risk of danger to the public and minimal risk of further offending during the remainder of the order.[34]

26.46   Any offender released on compassionate grounds will be subject to supervision in the community for the remainder of the order. Supervision will normally be by the local youth offending team.[35]

Early release

26.47   The Home Secretary may release the offender:

- in the case of an order for a term of eight months or more but less than 18 months, one month before the half-way point of the term of the order; and
- in the case of an order for a term of 18 months or more, one month or two months before that point.[36]

26.48   There is no provision for the period of early release to be extended or shortened, even by a few days. Trainees who qualify must be released exactly one or two months before the halfway point of the term of the order.[37] The only two exceptions to release exactly one or two months before the halfway point are:

- where the trainees' early release falls on a weekend or public holiday – in that case, the trainee should be released on the day immediately before the weekend/public holiday(s); or
- where the paperwork has been completed and the trainee has been notified of his/her early release date, but the release date has passed without

---

33   Powers of Criminal Courts (Sentencing) Act 2000 s102(3).

34   Home Office/Youth Justice Board, *The Detention and Training Order* (9 February 2000), para 2.97.

35   Ibid, para 2.99.

36   Powers of Criminal Courts (Sentencing) Act 2000 s102(4).

37   Home Office/Youth Justice Board, *The Detention and Training Order: Preparing for Electronically-Monitored Early Release* (6 May 2003), para 4.

the release being effected – in such circumstances, the trainee must be released as soon as the error comes to light.[38]

26.49 There is a presumption that early release will be granted unless the offender demonstrates his/her unsuitability through negative actions or behaviour or s/he falls into one of the specific exceptions.[39]

Grounds for denial of early release

26.50 Early release may be denied if:

- the trainee has exhibited violent or dangerous behaviour to other trainees or staff within the secure facility;
- the trainee has exhibited destructive behaviour that has led to serious damage to the fabric of the secure facility, or the property of others;
- the trainee has made exceptionally bad progress against the training plan as a result of consistent failure to co-operate or failure to take responsibility for his/her behaviour.[40]

Exceptions

26.51 The presumption in favour of early release does not apply to offenders serving sentences for:

- sexual offences as defined by Powers of Criminal Courts (Sentencing) Act 2000 s161(2);
- homicide;
- arson with intent to endanger life (Criminal Damage Act 1971 s1(2), (3));
- wounding or causing grievous bodily harm with intent (Offence Against the Person Act 1861 s18)
- possession a firearm while committing an offence specified in Schedule 1 to the Firearms Act 1968 (Firearms Act 1968 s17(2));
- kidnapping and/or false imprisonment (common law offences).[41]

26.52 In such cases, early release may only be granted where the offender has made exceptional progress against his/her training plan.[42]

Right of appeal

26.53 The young person may appeal a decision not to grant early release. In a Prison Service establishment this is initially made through the requests and complaints procedure.

Legal representation

26.54 Defence solicitors may advise on an application for early release (and any appeal) as Advice and Assistance under the Prison Law Class of work,

---

38 *The Detention and Training Order: Preparing for Electronically-Monitored Early Release*, para 5.

39 Home Office/Youth Justice Board, *The Detention and Training Order: Revised Guidance on Electronically-Monitored Early Release* (23 May 2002), para 8.

40 Ibid, para 12.

41 Ibid, para 15.

42 Ibid, para 16.

provided that the young person is financially eligible and the sufficient benefit test is met.[43]

Late release

26.55   The Home Secretary may apply to a youth court for the period of detention to be extended. If the youth court grants such authority, the offender must be released:

- in the case of an order for a term of eight months or more but less than 18 months, one month after the half-way point of the term of the order; and
- in the case of an order for a term of 18 months or more, one month or two months after that point.[44]

26.56   An application for late release should result from particularly poor progress against the training plan and not be used as a means of supplementing disciplinary sanctions.[45] Circumstances outside the offender's control (such as lack of suitable accommodation or family problems) should not be used as a reason to apply for late release.[46]

26.57   An application for late release should normally be made to the youth court for the offender's home area.[47] The application should:

- explain how the offender has made particularly poor progress against the objectives and targets which were reasonably set for him/her in the training plan;
- record the reviews undertaken, the decisions reached and the reasons for these; and
- set out how the additional period in custody would be used and what it would contribute to preventing further offending by the offender on release (eg tackling offending behaviour and providing basic skills teaching).[48]

26.58   Such an application falls within the definition of 'criminal proceedings' in Access to Justice Act 1999 s12(2) and therefore the young person may make an application for a representation order to the youth court considering the application.[49] If the court considering the application is the same one which made the original order, then the original representation order covers the proceedings and a supplementary bill should be submitted.[50]

Supervision following release

26.59   The period of supervision begins with the offender's release and ends when the term of the order ends. During the period of supervision, the

---

43   Criminal Defence Service *Criminal Bills Assessment Manual*, section 3.11, para 12.
44   Powers of Criminal Courts (Sentencing) Act 2000 s102(5).
45   Joint Home Office/LCD/Youth Justice Board Circular, *The Detention and Training Order* (9 February 2000), para 2.77.
46   Ibid, para 2.79.
47   Ibid, para 2.95.
48   Ibid, para 2.94.
49   Criminal Defence Service, *Criminal Bills Assessment Manual*, part 3.11 para 15.
50   Ibid.

young offender will be under the supervision of a probation officer, a social worker of a local authority social services department or a member of a youth offending team.[51] Any probation officer appointed shall be from the local justice area within which the offender resides for the time being.[52] Any social worker or member of a youth offending team appointed shall be from the local authority area within whose area the offender resides for the time being.[53]

26.60   Before being released on supervision, the young offender must be given a notice specifying:

- the category of person responsible for his/her supervision;
- any requirements with which s/he must comply with whilst on supervision.[54]

Electronic monitoring following release

26.61   The conditions attached to the supervision element of the order may include:

- conditions for securing the electronic monitoring of his compliance with any other conditions of the offender's release; or
- conditions for securing the electronic monitoring of the offender's whereabouts (otherwise than for the purpose of securing his/her compliance with other conditions of his/her release).[55]

26.62   Electronic monitoring may be imposed whether or not the offender is released early. Where early release is granted to the offender, s/he must (save in exceptional circumstances) be released subject to an electronically-monitored curfew until the half-way point of the sentence.[56] The standard curfew hours are 7.00 pm to 7.00 am, although these may be adapted to suit the individual circumstances of the case.[57]

Intensive Supervision and Surveillance Programme

26.63   As a condition of the supervision, an offender may be required to comply with an Intensive Supervision and Surveillance Programme. This may be a requirement from the date of early release.[58] The Youth Justice Board has given the following guidance:

> The Board expects the post-custody option to be considered for any young person who is eligible [for which see para 2.33]. It should particularly be used where:
> - there are concerns about managing the young person's risk in the community

---

51 Ibid, s76(3).
52 Ibid, s76(4).
53 Ibid, s76(5).
54 Ibid, s76(6).
55 Criminal Justice and Court Services Act 2000 s62(1), (2) and (5)(a).
56 Home Office/Youth Justice Board, *The Detention and Training Order: Revised Guidance on Electronically-Monitored Early Release* (23 May 2002), para 24.
57 Ibid, para 28.
58 Ibid, para 25.

- the structure of ISSP will help the transition from custody to the community.

The expectation is that those leaving custody will undertake the full pro-gramme of core elements:

- if the licence is six months or more, the high intensity period should be at least three months, and at least three months should be spent under the low intensity requirements – the exact time spent on ISSP should be based on the risk assessment
- if the licence is less than six months, at least half the time should be spent on high intensity and at least one third on the low intensity (to help the young person readjust to independence).[59]

Drug testing following release (*not yet implemented*)

26.64   The Home Secretary may impose a drug testing requirement as part of the supervision where:

(a) the offender has attained the age of 14; and
(b) a responsible officer is of the opinion:
   (i) that the offender has a propensity to misuse heroin or cocaine; and
   (ii) that the misuse by the offender of heroin or cocaine caused or con-tributed to any offence of which s/he has been convicted, or is likely to cause or contribute to the commission of further offences.[60]

26.65   A 'responsible officer' is defined as:

- an officer of a local probation board; or
- a member of a youth offending team.[61]

26.66   The requirement is for the offender to provide, when instructed to do so, any sample mentioned in the instruction for the purpose of ascertaining whether s/he has heroin or cocaine in his/her body.[62]

26.67   An offender under the age of 17 years may not be required to provide a drug sample unless in the presence of an appropriate adult, namely:

- his/her parent or guardian, or if s/he is in the care of a local author-ity or voluntary organisation, a person representing that authority or organisation;
- a social worker of a local authority social services department; or
- if no person falling into the above two categories is available, any responsible person aged 18 or over who is not a police officer or a person employed by the police.[63]

Breach of requirements of supervision

26.68   When an offender fails to comply with the requirements of the supervision element, the youth offending team will initiate breach proceedings in the youth court (see chapter 27).

59 Youth Justice Board, *ISSP Management Guidance* (2005), pp46–47.
60 Criminal Justice and Court Services Act 2000 s64(1) and (5)(a) as amended by Criminal Justice Act 2003 s266.
61 Ibid, s64(6) as amended inserted by Criminal Justice Act 2003 s266.
62 Ibid, s64(3).
63 Ibid, s64(4A) and (6) as inserted by Criminal Justice Act 2003 s266.

Offender sentenced to section 91 detention

Duty to release prisoners

26.69 The provisions for release from a determinate sentence of section 91 detention depend on the date of the offence(s) for which the offender has received the sentence. The position may be summarised as follows:

(i) For offences committed before 4 April 2005 the offender will generally be released automatically after serving one half of his/her sentence.[64] The only exception to this rule is where the offender was sentenced to a term of detention of four years or more. In such a case s/he will only be released after serving half the sentence if the Parole Board so recommends. If the Parole Board refuses to authorise release on licence, the offender may re-apply every 12 months but will be released automatically after serving two thirds of the sentence.[65]

(ii) For offences committed on or after 4 April 2005, an offender serving a determinate sentence of section 91 detention of any length must be released on licence after serving one half of his/her sentence.[66]

Early release (home detention curfew)

26.70 A young offender sentenced to section 91 detention may be released on licence up to 135 days before the halfway point in the sentence.[67] S/he may not be granted early release unless:

- s/he has served at least four weeks of the sentence; and
- at least a quarter of the total sentence.[68]

Curfew condition

26.71 Release on licence before the half-way point must be subject to an electronically-monitored curfew condition.[69] The condition may specify different places or different periods for different days but may not specify periods which amount to less than nine hours in any one day. The standard curfew condition is from 7.00 pm to 7.00 am. The curfew condition is to remain in force until the halfway point of the sentence.[70]

---

64 Criminal Justice Act 1991 s33(1)(a) as retained by Criminal Justice Act 2003 (Commencement Order No 8 and Transitional and Saving Provisions) Order 2005 SI No 950 Sch 2 para 19.

65 Criminal Justice Act 1991 ss33(2) and 35(1) as retained by Criminal Justice Act 2003 (Commencement Order No 8 and Transitional and Saving Provisions) Order 2005 SI No 950 Sch 2 paras 16 and 19.

66 Criminal Justice Act 2003 s244(1) and (3) and Criminal Justice Act 2003 (Commencement Order No 8 and Transitional and Saving Provisions) Order 2005 SI No 950 Sch 1 para 19.

67 Criminal Justice Act 2003 s246(1)(a).

68 Ibid, s246(2).

69 Ibid, s253(1).

70 Ibid, s253(2).

Statutory restrictions to power to release early

26.72   It is not possible to release an offender early where:

- s/he is subject to an extended sentence under Criminal Justice Act 2003 s228;
- the sentence is for an offence under Prisoners (Return to Custody) Act 1995 s1;
- the prisoner is subject to a hospital order, hospital direction or transfer direction under Mental Health Act 1983 s37, s45A or s47;
- s/he is subject to the notification requirements of Part 2 of the Sexual Offences Act 2003;
- s/he is liable to removal from the United Kingdom;
- s/he has been previously released on licence during the currency of the sentence, and has been recalled to custody; or
- in the case of a prisoner to whom a direction regarding remand time relates, the interval between the date on which the sentence was passed and the halfway point of the sentence is less than 14 days.[71]

Presumption in favour of granting a home detention curfew

26.73   Unless they have requested not to be considered, prisoners must normally be released on home detention curfew unless there is considered to be:

- an unacceptable risk to the victim or to members of the public;
- a pattern of offending which indicates a likelihood of re-offending during the home detention curfew period;
- a likelihood of failure to comply with the conditions of the curfew;
- a lack of suitable accommodation for home detention curfew; or
- too short a period of time for an effective curfew requirement.[72]

Right of appeal

26.74   In the first instance, the young offender may seek a review of the refusal of home detention curfew by using the internal requests and complaints procedure. If still refused, the young offender may appeal to the relevant Area Manager at Prison Service Headquarters.

Recall of offenders on home detention curfew

26.75   An offender subject to a home detention curfew may be recalled to custody under section 255 of the Criminal Justice Act 2003, if it appears to the Home Secretary that:

- s/he has failed to comply with any condition included in the his/her licence; or
- his/her whereabouts can no longer be electronically monitored at the place for the time being specified in the curfew condition included in the licence.

---

71   Criminal Justice Act 2003 s246(4).
72   Prison Service Order PSO6700, *Home Detention Curfew*, para 5.13.3.

26.76 When an offender is recalled to custody under section 255:

- s/he may make representations in writing with respect to the revocation; and
- on his/her return to custody, must be informed of the reasons for the revocation and of his/her right to make representations.

26.77 After considering any representations or any other matters, the Home Secretary may cancel a revocation of an offender's licence, in which case the offender is treated as if s/he had not be recalled to custody under section 255.[73] In any event, the young offender recalled under section 255 should be re-released on licence at the halfway point of the sentence.[74]

Release on licence

26.78 When released from a sentence of section 91 detention, the young offender will be on licence.

Duration of licence

26.79 For offences committed before 4 April 2005, the licence period will run from the date of release to the three-quarter point of the sentence.[75]

26.80 For offences committed on or after 4 April 2005, the licence will remain in force for the remainder of the sentence.[76]

Conditions

26.81 Any licence in respect of a prisoner serving a sentence of section 91 detention:

- must include the standard conditions prescribed by the Home Secretary; and
- may include conditions relating to electronic monitoring or drug testing (see below).[77]

26.82 The standard conditions will include requirements:

- to keep in touch with the supervising officer in accordance with any instructions that may be given;
- if required, to receive visits from the supervising officer at the offender's place of residence;
- to reside at an address approved by the supervising officer and notify him/her in advance of any proposed change of address or any proposed stay away from that approved address;

---

73 Criminal Justice Act 2003 s255(4).

74 See para 26.78 onwards.

75 Criminal Justice Act 1991 s37(1) as preserved by Criminal Justice Act 2003 (Commencement Order No 8 and Transitional and Saving Provisions) Order 2005 SI No 950 Sch 2 para 19.

76 Criminal Justice Act 2003 s249(1) and Criminal Justice Act 2003 (Commencement Order No 8 and Transitional and Savings Provisions) Order 2005 SI No 950 Sch 1 para 19.

77 Criminal Justice Act 2003 s250(4).

- to undertake only such work (including voluntary work) approved by the supervising officer and notify him/her in advance of any proposed change;
- not to travel outside the United Kingdom without obtaining the prior permission of the supervising officer (which will be given in exceptional circumstances only); and
- to be well behaved, not commit any offence and not do anything which could undermine the purposes of the supervision, which are to protect the public, prevent further offending and help re-settlement into the community.[78]

26.83   A prisoner subject to licence must comply with such condition as may for the time being be specified in the licence.[79]

Electronic monitoring following release

26.84   The conditions attached to the supervision element of the order may include:

- conditions for securing the electronic monitoring of his compliance with any other conditions of his release; or
- conditions for securing the electronic monitoring of the offender's whereabouts (otherwise than for the purpose of securing his/her compliance with other conditions of his/her release).[80]

Intensive Supervision and Surveillance Programme

26.84A As a condition of the licence, an offender may be required to comply with a Intensive Supervision and Surveillance Programme (see para 26.63 above).

Drug testing following release (*not yet implemented*)

26.85   The Home Secretary may impose a drug testing requirement as part of the supervision where:

(a) the offender has attained the age of 14; and

(b) a responsible officer is of the opinion:

   (i) that the offender has a propensity to misuse specified class A drugs; and

   (ii) that the misuse by the offender of any specified class A drug caused or contributed to any offence of which s/he has been convicted, or is likely to cause or contribute to the commission of further offences.[81]

26.86   A responsible officer is defined as:

- an officer of a local probation board; or
- a member of a youth offending team.[82]

---

78   PSO 6000 Chapter 10.
79   Criminal Justice Act 2003 s252.
80   Criminal Justice and Court Services Act 2000 s62(1), (2) and (5)(d).
81   Ibid, s64(1) and (5)(a) as amended by Criminal Justice Act 2003 s266.
82   Ibid, s64(6) as amended inserted by Criminal Justice Act 2003 s266.

26.87 The requirement is for the offender to provide, when instructed to do so, any sample mentioned in the instruction for the purpose of ascertaining whether s/he has any specified class A drug in his/her body.[83]

26.88 An offender under the age of 17 years may not be required to provide a drug sample unless in the presence of an appropriate adult, namely:

- his/her parent or guardian, or if s/he is in the care of a local authority or voluntary organisation, a person representing that authority or organisation;
- a social worker of a local authority social services department; or
- if no person falling into the above two categories is available, any responsible person aged 18 or over who is not a police officer or a person employed by the police.[84]

Recall whilst on licence

26.89 The secretary of state may, in the case of any prisoner released on licence, revoke his/her licence and recall him/her to custody.[85] This decision will be made by the Early Release and Recall Section of the National Offender Management Service. Recall will ordered where the offender is not complying with the conditions of his/her licence or that the prisoner poses a risk of harm or of re-offending.

26.90 Once an offender's licence has been revoked, s/he shall be liable to be detained in pursuance of his/her sentence. If the offender remains at liberty, s/he shall be treated as being unlawfully at large.[86]

26.91 On his/her return to custody, an offender must be informed of:

- the reasons for his/her recall; and
- his/her right to make representations.[87]

Review of the recall decision

26.92 The decision to recall an offender must be referred to the Parole Board, whether or not the offender makes representations. As part of this review process, a recall review dossier will be prepared by the Early Release and Recall Section of the Prison Service. This dossier will contain the original pre-sentence report, information provided by secure institution and information provided by the youth offending team regarding the offender's compliance with his/her licence conditions. The expectation is that the contents of the dossier will be shared with the offender, but there are arrangements for the non-disclosure of information.

26.93 As part of the review process the offender may submit representations. These may be prepared by the defence lawyer by way of Advice and Assistance under the Prison Law Class of Work.[88]

---

83 Criminal Justice and Court Services Act 2000 s64(3).
84 Ibid, s64(4A) and (6) as inserted by Criminal Justice Act 2003 s266.
85 Ibid, s254(1).
86 Ibid, s254(6).
87 Ibid, s254(2).
88 General Criminal Contract, Contract Specification Part A rule 5.2.

Parole Board decision

26.94 The Parole Board must review the recall decision and decide whether the original recall decision was justified or not.[89] Prison Service Order 6000 – *Parole, Release and Recall* gives the following advice regarding the decision to be made:

> The Parole Board assesses the risk that the prisoner presents, in terms of harm to the public, and re-offending. The presumption will be that the prisoner will be re-released, unless the risk is unmanageable in the community and/or the likelihood of future compliance with licence conditions is small. The Parole Board may make a decision that the recall decision, based on the information received at the time, was not justified, but this will not automatically lead to the immediate release of the prisoner. The Parole Board, in assessing the information given by the [youth offending team], may still consider the risk of harm, or re-offending, to be sufficiently high, so as to be unmanageable in the community. If this is the case, the Parole Board may decide that although the recall decision was not justified, the offender should remain in custody for the time being.

26.95 An offender may request that the Parole Board convenes an oral hearing to consider his/her representations against recall. The hearing is held in the custodial establishment with the prisoner present. S/he may be legally represented.[90]

26.96   Having considered the original recall, the Parole Board must order:

- immediate release;
- release at a future date;
- further review; or
- release at the sentence expiry date (if less than 12 months away).[91]

Offender sentenced to extended detention

Release from custodial part of sentence

26.97 A prisoner sentenced to extended detention under Criminal Justice Act 2003 s228 does not have an automatic date of release from custody. Instead s/he is eligible to be released on licence when s/he has served one-half of the appropriate custodial term (determined by the sentencing court – see para 24.132).[92]

Early release (home detention curfew)

26.98 An offender sentenced to extended detention may not be released prior to the half-way point on home detention curfew.[93]

---

89 PSO 6000 para 7.10.1
90 PSO 6000, para 7.10.5. For more information on the procedure of an oral hearing see H Arnott and S Creighton, *Parole Board Hearings: Law and Practice*, Legal Action Group (2006).
91 PSO 6000, para 7.10.3.
92 Criminal Justice Act 2003 s247(1) and (2).
93 Ibid, s246(4)(a).

Applying for release on licence

26.99 Application for release after serving half the appropriate custodial term must be made to the Parole Board, which may not direct the prisoner's release unless the Board is satisfied that it is no longer necessary for the protection of the public that the prisoner should be confined.[94]

26.100 A parole dossier will be prepared by the parole clerk, if the offender is in a Prison Service establishment, or by the Section 53/92 Casework Unit currently based at the Youth Justice Board, if the offender is in a secure children's home or a secure training centre.

26.101 The dossier will contain details of the offence, the pre-sentence report, reports from the secure establishment staff as well as reports from the youth offending team supervising the sentence. The dossier will be forwarded to the Parole Board Secretariat.

26.102 The offender has a right to see the contents of the dossier and make representations to the Parole Board. Those representations may be prepared by the defence lawyer by way of Advice and Assistance under the Prison Law Class of Work.[95]

26.103 An offender serving an extended sentence has a right to an oral hearing before the Parole Board.[96] S/he may be legally represented at this hearing. The defence lawyer may provide representation as Advocacy Assistance under the Prison Law Class of Work.[97]

26.104 If the Parole Board direct release on licence, the offender must be so released. If release on licence is refused, it must be reviewed every 12 months during the custodial part of the sentence. A prisoner who has served the whole appropriate custodial term must be released on licence unless s/he has previously been recalled.[98]

Release on licence

26.105 If released on licence, the offender is subject to licence for the balance of the appropriate custodial term and then the extension period for which the offender has been ordered to be subject to licence.

26.106 Any licence in respect of a prisoner serving an extended sentence:

- must include the standard conditions prescribed by the Home Secretary; and
- may include conditions relating to electronic monitoring or drug testing (see below).[99]

26.107 A prisoner subject to licence must comply with such condition as may for the time being be specified in the licence.[100]

---

94 Criminal Justice Act 2003 s247(3).
95 General Criminal Contract, Contract Specification, Part A rule 5.2
96 Parole Board Rules 2004 rule 12.
97 General Criminal Contract, Contract Specification, Part A rule 5.2.
98 Criminal Justice Act 2003 s247(4).
99 Ibid, s250(4) – for more details see paras 26.84–26.88 above.
100 Ibid, s252.

Recall on licence

26.108   The secretary of state may, in the case of any prisoner released on licence, revoke his/her licence and recall him/her to custody.[101] This decision will be made by the Early Release and Recall Section of the National Offender Management Service. Recall will ordered where the offender is not complying with the conditions of his/her licence or that the prisoner poses a risk of harm or of re-offending.

Review of recall

26.109   The review procedure is the same as for offenders serving section 91 detention (for which see paras 26.92–26.96 above) except that the offender serving an extended sentence has a right to an oral hearing before the Parole Board.

Offender sentenced to detention for public protection or detention for life

26.110   Where the offender has served the minimum term, s/he may require the Home Secretary to refer his/her case to the Parole Board.[102] The Parole Board may direct his/her released if satisfied that his continued detention is no longer necessary for the protection of the public. The offender will then remain on licence indefinitely.

26.111   In the case of an offender serving a sentence of detention for public protection, s/he may apply to the Parole Board for the licence to be revoked, provided:

- s/he has been released on licence for at least ten years; and
- if s/he has made a previous application for revocation, a period of at least 12 months has expired since the disposal of that application.[103]

Regime in a secure establishment – general principles

26.112   In accordance with Article 3.1 of the United Nations Convention on the Rights of the Child, every public authority concerned with issues relating to the care and management of children and young persons in custody must take their interests as a primary consideration.[104]

26.113   Children and young persons in custody must also be afforded the following rights and entitlements, so far as they are consistent with their custodial status:

(i)   the entitlement of such protection and care as is necessary for their well-being;

(ii)   the right to maintain personal relationships and direct contact with both their parents on a regular basis;

101 Criminal Justice Act 2003 s254(1).
102 Crime (Sentences) Act 1997 s28(7).
103 Ibid, s31A(3).
104 *R (SR) v Nottingham Magistrates' Court* [2001] EWHC Admin 802, [66]; 166 JP 132.

(iii)   the right to a standard of living adequate for their physical, mental, spiritual, moral and social development;

(iv)   the right to insist that any period of imprisonment must be in conformity with the law and used as a measure of last resort and for the shortest appropriate period of time;

(v)   the entitlement, when deprived of liberty, to be treated with humanity and respect for the inherent dignity of the human person and in a manner which takes into account the needs of persons of their age;

(vi)   the entitlement, when deprived of liberty, to be separated from adults unless it is considered in their best interests not to be so separated;

(vii) the entitlement, when deprived of liberty, to maintain contact with their family through correspondence and visits, save in exceptional circumstances; and

(viii) when it is alleged or recognised that they have infringed the penal law, the right to be treated in a manner consistent with the promotion of their dignity and worth.[105]

26.114   The Youth Justice Board has issued a Code of Practice for managing behaviour applicable to all juvenile secure estate institutions.[106]

Regime in a secure unit or secure training centre

26.115   *The National Standards for Youth Justice Services* (2004) set out the minimum standards for the regime that must be provided to a detainee serving a sentence in a secure unit or secure training centre. The most important requirements are outlined below.

Learning and skills

26.116   There must be an educational assessment on arrival. Educational needs must be continually addressed in the individual training plan with appropriate goals.[107] All young people held in secure establishments must participate in education and training. Those serving six months or more must have their educational attainment continually assessed including on departure.[108]

Constructive activity

26.117   Detainees must have access to a range of stimulating activities at weekends and evenings as well as time for reflection and homework.[109] Each detainee must be given the opportunity of fresh air for at least one hour per day.[110]

26.118   Detainees must not be locked in their rooms more than 14 hours a day. In exceptional circumstances the director of the institution may authorise

---

105 Ibid – summarising UNCRC Articles 3.2, 9.3, 27.1, 37(b) and (c), and 40.1.

106 Youth Justice Board, *Managing Children and Young People's Behaviour in the Secure Estate; Code of Practice* (2006).

107 Youth Justice Board, *National Standard for Youth Justice Services* (2004), para 10.38.

108 Ibid, para 10.42.

109 Ibid, para 10.33.

110 Ibid, para 10.35.

longer periods as a result of bad behaviour or the detainee presenting a risk to others.[111]

External contact

26.119 On reception all detainees must be given the opportunity to telephone someone who may be concerned about their welfare.[112] Frequent telephone contact, visits and letters between young people and their parent(s)/carers should be encouraged.[113]

26.120 Parents or carers must be notified of significant events that affect the young person whilst in custody.[114]

Physical restraint

26.121 Physical restraint must be used only as a last resort and then following approved, accredited methods. The minimum necessary force must be applied and incidents documented, recorded and audited.[115]

Complaints

26.122 There must be a complaints procedure that is clear, published and free of discrimination. Young people must be free to raise complaints without fear of sanction. Staff dealing with complaints must provide at least an interim response within seven days and a full response within 21 days.[116]

Regime in a young offender institution

26.123 Serving prisoners under the age of 18 are referred to as juvenile prisoners. The rules and guidance regarding their conditions of detention are to be found in:
- Young Offender Institution Rules 2000 SI No 3371 (as amended by SI 2002 No 2117 and SI 2005 No 897);[117]
- Prison Service Order 4950 – Regime for Juveniles;
- National Standards for Youth Justice Services (2004) Standards 10–12.

Human Rights Act 1998 and the Prison Service

26.124 In *R (Howard League for Penal Reform) v Secretary of State for the Home Department*[118] Munby J concluded that:

1 Articles 3 and 8 of the European Convention on Human Rights afforded protection to juvenile prisoners from actions by members of the Prison

---

111 *National Standard for Youth Justice Services* para 10.32.
112 Ibid, para 10.28.
113 Ibid, para 10.30.
114 Ibid, para 10.29.
115 Ibid, para 10.20.
116 Ibid, paras 10.25 and 10.26.
117 A consolidated version of the Rules may be found on the Prison Service website – see appendix 14.
118 [2002] EWHC 2497 (Admin).

Service which constitute inhuman and degrading treatment or punishment or which impact adversely and disproportionately on the inmate's physical or psychological integrity.

2   Articles 3 and 8 of the European Convention on Human Rights, read in the light of Articles 3 and 37 of the UN Convention on the Rights of the Child and Article 24 of the European Charter, impose positive obligations to take reasonable and appropriate measures designed to ensure that:

   (i)   children in young offender institutions are treated, both by members of the Prison Service and by fellow inmates, with humanity, with respect for their inherent dignity and personal integrity as human beings, and not in such a way as to humiliate or debase them;

   (ii) children in young offender institutions are not subjected to torture or to inhuman or degrading treatment or punishment by fellow inmates or to other behaviour by fellow inmates which impacts adversely and disproportionately on their physical or psychological integrity.

3   Such measure must strike a fair balance between the competing interests of the particular child and the general interests of the community as a whole (including the other inmates), but always having regard to:

   (i)   first, the principle that the best interests of the child are at all times a primary consideration;

   (ii) second, the inherent vulnerability of children in a young offender institution; and

   (iii) third, the need for the Prison Service to take deterrent steps to prevent, to take effective deterrent steps to prevent, and to provide children in young offender institutions with effective protection from, ill-treatment (whether at the hands of Prison Service staff or of other inmates) of which the Prison Service has or ought to have knowledge.

4   Where the Prison Service fails to meet its human rights obligations, the child may apply to the High Court for relief under Human Rights Act 1998 ss7 and 8. In the case of a child, such an applicant should be made to the Family Division.

Safeguarding children in prison

26.125   In *R (Howard League for Penal Reform) v Secretary of State for the Home Department*[119] Munby J was asked to consider the application of the Children Act 1989 to juvenile prisoners in young offender institutions. He concluded that:

- the Act does not confer or impose any functions, powers, duties, responsibilities or obligations on either the Prison Service (or any of its staff) or the Home Secretary; but

- the duties a local authority would otherwise owe to a child under section 17 (child in need) or section 47 (child protection investigation) of the Act do not cease to be owed merely because the child is currently detained in a young offender institution; however

119 [2002] EWHC 2497 (Admin).

- a local authority's functions, powers duties and responsibilities under the Act, and specifically under sections 17 and 47, take effect and operate subject to the necessary requirements of imprisonment.

26.126 As a result of this judgment, the Prison Service have issued revised guidance requiring governors to maintain a child protection policy and to have arrangements for referring child protection concerns to local authorities. The duties under Children Act 1989 ss17 and 47 fall on the local authority where the child is currently detained (see para 3.117).

Female inmates with babies

26.127 The Home Secretary may, subject to any conditions he thinks fit, permit a female inmate to have her baby with her in a young offender institution, and everything necessary for the baby's maintenance and care may be provided there.[120] Current policy in relation to mother and baby units is set out in Prison Service Order (PSO) 4801 *Management of Mother and Baby Units* (3rd edn).

Education and training

26.128 Provision must be made for the education of inmates by means of programmes of class teaching or private study with the working week and, so far as practicable, programmes of evening and weekend educational class or private study.[121] Provision should also be made for the training of inmates by means of training courses, which should, as far as practicable, be such as to enable inmates to acquire suitable qualifications.[122]

Trainees of compulsory school age

26.129 In the case of an inmate of compulsory school age, arrangements shall be made for his/her participation in education or training courses for at least 15 hours a week within the normal working week.[123]

Trainees with special educational needs

26.130 In the case of an inmate aged 17 or over who has special educational needs, arrangements shall be made for education appropriate to his/her needs, if necessary within the normal working week.[124]

Physical activity

26.131 Provision shall be made for the physical education of inmates within the normal working week, as well as evening and weekend physical recreation.[125]

120 The Young Offender Institution Rules 2000, rule 25.
121 Ibid, rule 38(1).
122 Ibid, rule 39.
123 Ibid, rule 38(2).
124 Ibid, rule 38(3).
125 Ibid, rule 41(1).

Mandatory drug testing

26.132 An inmate may be required to provide a urine or other sample for the purposes of testing for the presence of controlled drugs in his/her body.[126]

Removal from association

26.133 Where it appears desirable for the maintenance of good order and discipline, or in his/her own interests, that an inmate should not associate with other inmates, either generally or for particular purposes, the governor may arrange for the inmate's removal for association accordingly. An inmate may not be removed from association for the maintenance of good order and discipline or in his/her own interests for a period of more than three days without the authority of a member of the board of visitors or of the Home Secretary. Any authority given may not be for a period not exceeding 14 days, but may be renewed from time to time for a like period.

26.134   Before a juvenile prisoner is removed from association, fairness requires that s/he be given the opportunity to make representations unless reasons of good order, discipline or urgency required that the order should be made without any opportunity for representations.[127]

Restraint

26.135 The governor may order an inmate to be put under restraint where this is necessary to prevent to prevent the inmate from injuring him/herself or others, damaging others, damaging property or creating a disturbance.[128] The governor may not order an inmate under 17 to be put under restraint, except that s/he may order such an inmate be placed in handcuffs where it is necessary to prevent the inmate injury him/herself or others, damaging property or creating a disturbance.[129] An inmate shall not be kept under restraint longer than necessary, nor shall s/he be so kept for longer than 24 hours without a direction in writing by a member of the board of visitors or by an officer of the Home Office. No inmate shall be put under restraint as a punishment.[130]

Disciplinary charges

Offences against discipline

26.136 These are set out in rule 55 of the Young Offender Rules 2000.[131] Some, such as assault, may also be a criminal offence.

---

126 The Young Offender Institution Rules 2000, rule 53.
127 *Secretary of State for the Home Department v SP* [2004] EWCA Civ 1750.
128 The Young Offender Institution Rules 2000, rule 52(1).
129 Ibid, rule 52(5).
130 Ibid, rule 52(7).
131 SI No 3371.

Laying a charge against prison discipline

26.137 A charge against prison discipline must be laid as soon as possible and, save in exceptional circumstances, within 48 hours of the discovery of the offence the charge must be in sufficient detail for the prisoner to know exactly what is alleged against him/her.

26.138 An inmate who is to be charged with an offence against discipline may be kept apart from other inmates pending the governor's first inquiry or determination.[132] After first inquiry, segregation is only possible for the maintenance of good order and discipline.

Adjudications by governors

26.139 Every charge must be first inquired into by the governor the next day (excluding Sundays or public holidays).[133] If the governor considers that the offence is so serious that additional days should be awarded for the offence if the inmate is found guilty, s/he should refer the charge to an independent adjudicator.[134]

Referral to independent adjudicator

26.140 Independent adjudicators are District Judges (Magistrates' Court) who travel to the institution for the hearing. Where a charge has been referred to an independent adjudicator, s/he must conduct a first hearing within 28 days of the referral.[135]

26.141 At a hearing before an independent adjudicator, the inmate has a right to be legally represented.[136] Advocacy Assistance may be provided by solicitors who hold a Legal Services Commission contract in crime or prison law.

Conduct of adjudication hearing

26.142 At an adjudication hearing, the inmate shall be given an opportunity of hearing what is alleged against him/her and of presenting his/her own case.[137] The adjudicator must ascertain the facts and must be prepared to question in a spirit of impartial inquiry the accused, the reporting officer and any witnesses.[138]

Governor's punishments

26.143 If found guilty of an offence against discipline, the governor may impose one or more of the following punishments:

- caution;
- forfeiture of privileges (maximum period 21 days);

132 The Young Offender Institution Rules 2000, rule 58(4).
133 Ibid, rule 58(2)(a).
134 Ibid, rule 58A(1) and (2).
135 Ibid, rule 58(3)(b).
136 Ibid, rule 59(3).
137 Ibid, rule 59(2).
138 Prison Discipline Manual, para 1.2.

- loss of association (maximum 21 days);
- stoppage of or deduction from earnings (maximum 42 days);
- removal from wing or living unit (maximum 21 days).[139]

26.144 These punishments are available to all inmates under the age of 18. Placement in segregation as a punishment is not available to inmates under the age of 18 at the date of the commission of the offence.[140]

Adjudicator's punishments

26.145 An adjudicator may impose any of the punishments available to a governor, and in addition s/he may make an award of additional days not exceeding 42 days.[141] If the inmate is found guilty of more than one offence against discipline, the adjudicator may order additional days to run consecutively but in any case the total period shall not exceed 42 days.[142] Additional days can only be awarded to an inmate serving section 91 detention, extended detention, detention for public protection or detention for life.

Referral to police

26.146 If the offence against discipline is also a criminal offence, it may be referred to the police for investigation. A disciplinary charge should still be laid against the inmate, but the governor should adjourn the adjudication pending the outcome of the police investigation. If no criminal proceedings commence, the governor may re-convene the adjudication hearing.

Complaints

26.147 A complaint may be made either orally or in writing to the governor or the Board of Visitors.[143] If the complaint is not resolved to the young offender's satisfaction, it may be renewed to the Prison Service Area Manager.

26.148 Complaints not resolved by the Area Manager may be made to the Prison Service Ombudsman.[144]

---

139 Young Offender Institution Rules 2000, rule 60(1).
140 Ibid, rule 60(1)(f).
141 Ibid, rule 60A(1).
142 Ibid, rule 60A(3).
143 Ibid, rule 8.
144 For contact details see appendix 14.

CHAPTER 27

Breach proceedings

Enforcement of community and other court orders

Management of community and other court orders

27.1   The Youth Justice Board gives the following guidance to youth offending teams managing community orders:

> Court orders confer rights and responsibilities on the young offenders. On the making of an order a written, signed agreement should be made with the young offender setting these out. The agreement should include:
> * acceptable and unacceptable absence criteria;
> * the right to be treated fairly and with respect;
> * the requirement to behave acceptably (in a non-abusive or discriminatory way); and
> * time keeping.
>
> Contact with the offender is expected to take place twice a week for the first 12 weeks of all orders and thereafter once a week unless the assessed level of risk requires contact to be maintained at a higher level of intensity. A contact is a planned meeting with the young person by the Supervising Officer, another member of the YOT, a member of another agency, or a volunteer authorised to see the young person, in respect of the supervision of his or her court order
>
> Failure to attend (FTA) must be recorded as acceptable or unacceptable. Unexplained FTAs must always be followed up within one working day by telephone, home visit or letter to seek an explanation. General principles must be agreed in the YOT about what constitutes an acceptable and unacceptable reason for non-attendance. These must be defensible to the general public. Sickness or work commitments should be evidenced where possible. If an absence is deemed unacceptable a warning must be issued to the young offender in writing.
>
> Unacceptable failures to comply with the requirements of the order must result in the issuing of a formal written warning. During the order if the offender receives two formal warnings and then fails to comply a further time breach action must be initiated within five days of the most recent failure to comply. Breach action can only be stayed in exceptional circumstances with the authorisation of the YOT manager. The reason must be noted on the file. When breach action has been initiated the young offender should be allowed to continue the order until the date of the court hearing unless it would be disruptive for the individual or other offenders on orders for him/her to do so.[1]

27.2   Enforcement of the detention and training order supervision element should be in line with the same guidelines.[2]

Who prosecutes breach proceedings?

27.3   In relation to most community orders and reparation orders, the general rule is that breach proceedings will be initiated by the responsible officer (normally a member of the youth offending team).

Referral orders

27.4   The youth offending team will initiate breach proceedings on behalf of the youth offender panel.

---

1   Youth Justice Board *National Standards for Youth Justice Services* (2004), paras 8.4, 8.6, 8.7 and 8.8.
2   Ibid, para 11.20.

Curfew and exclusion orders

27.5 In relation to a curfew order, breach proceedings will be initiated by the monitoring company.

Attendance centre orders

27.6 Breach proceedings will be initiated by the youth offending team on behalf of the officer in charge of the centre.[3]

Community rehabilitation and community punishment orders

27.7 Where a young offender is in breach of one of these orders, the breach may be prosecuted by the relevant probation service or, in some areas, by the youth offending team on its behalf.

Legal representation

27.8 Proceedings for breach of a community or other court order are not covered by the representation order for the original proceedings. There will, therefore, need to be a fresh application for a representation order.

27.9 If the breach proceedings are dealt with at the same time as new offences, then a separate standard fee is not payable, irrespective of whether there is any nexus between the breach proceedings and any other proceedings being heard at the same time. If breach proceedings are heard alone, then they will attract a separate standard fee.[4]

Initiating breach proceedings

27.10 The responsible officer must prepare an information which will be lodged with the relevant court. Where the breach is on the basis of missed appointments, it is appropriate to draw up one information which specifies all the dates. Where, however, the breach proceedings are on the basis of breach of more than one requirement of the order, then separate informations should be drawn up for each requirement breached.[5]

Before the hearing

27.11 The defence lawyer may be fortunate enough to receive advance warning of a breach hearing. If that happens, s/he should:

(a) make contact with the youth offending team or other organisation prosecuting the breach to establish:
   (i) how much of the order has been complied with;
   (ii) details of the alleged breach; and

---

3 *National Standards for Youth Justice Services*, para 8.56.
4 Criminal Defence Service, General Criminal Contract, Part B, Rule 5.8 para 8 and *Criminal Bills Assessment Manual*, para 3.8.2.
5 *S v Doncaster Youth Offending Team* [2003] EWHC 1128 (Admin) [12]–[14].

   (iii) whether the offender is able to continue with the order while the breach is being prosecuted;

(b) obtain a copy of the information(s) laid for the purposes of the breach proceedings;

(c) obtain a copy of the original order;

(d) obtain details of the offence(s) for which the order was originally made (eg charge sheet, witness statements and any pre-sentence report).

Information from the prosecuting organisation

27.12 The prosecuting organisation will prepare a breach report to present to the court. In these reports it is common for the breach officer to identify missed appointments or other instances of non-compliance without providing details of when the offender did comply with the requirements of the order. The defence lawyer should attempt to establish a complete history of contact between the responsible officer and the young offender. Where the responsible officer is a member of a youth offending team, the history of contact will usually be available as a contact log on the standard database, Youth Offender Information System (YOIS), used by most youth offending teams.

27.13   If the young offender is not continuing with the order after being breached, the defence lawyer should establish if the offender would be accepted back. It would clearly be in the young offender's interests to show the court that s/he has been able to comply with the requirements of the order during the period that it took the case to come to court. If the responsible officer is not willing to allow the young offender to continue with the order, the reasons should be established.

Copy of the court order

27.14 It is important for the defence lawyer to obtain a copy of the original court order to establish that the order is valid and, in the case of additional requirements, that those requirements were actually imposed. If the responsible officer cannot provide a copy of the order, the defence lawyer should contact the court which passed sentence.

Details of the original offences

27.15 In breach proceedings for a community order, the court always has the power to re-sentence for the original offence. The defence lawyer therefore needs to be aware of the details of the original offence to identify mitigating factors of the offence, including whether the offender pleaded guilty in the original proceedings. The pre-sentence report may reveal important information about the offence, how co-defendants were dealt with and personal information regarding the offender which was relevant to the commission of the offence.

Taking instructions

27.16 Having spoken to the supervisor, instructions should be taken from the young person to establish which, if any, of the alleged breaches are accepted.

It should also be considered whether there is a reasonable excuse for any of the breaches. Documentary evidence of this must be obtained before the court hearing. It should also be discussed with the young person whether it would be advisable to continue with the order while awaiting the court hearing. The young person should be advised that the court is obliged to take such attendances into account even if it decides to re-sentence and it will be much harder for the court to decide that the offender has wilfully and persistently failed to comply with the requirements of the order.

The first hearing

27.17   At the first hearing the young offender will be asked if s/he admits the information(s). If the information(s) are denied, the court will adjourn to allow the responsible officer to call evidence to prove the alleged breach(es).

27.18   If the offender admits the information(s), the court must then decide how to proceed. If the offender indicates that s/he will comply with the order in the future, it will often be possible to persuade a youth court to adjourn the proceedings for a period of time to monitor attendance. If attendance is then regular and satisfactory, the defence lawyer should seek to persuade the bench that it would not be in the interests of the child or young person to impose any extra penalty for the breach.

The contested breach hearing

27.19   The contested breach hearing will be subject to the normal criminal rules of evidence. The burden of proof is upon the responsible officer who will have to call evidence of the breach. The factual basis of the breach must be proved beyond reasonable doubt.[6] Where a failure is alleged of an requirement to comply with a specific order (such as to live as a specified address or attend on a specific occasion), the person who gave that order should, if it is disputed, be at court to give evidence about it.[7]

Re-sentencing for the original offence: general considerations

Is a pre-sentence report required?

27.20   When re-sentencing the offender, Criminal Justice Act 2003 s156 would apply and the court may be required to consider a pre-sentence report. If the original sentencing hearing was some time ago, the defence lawyer will wish to argue that a new report should be ordered to give up-to-date information concerning the young offender.

---

6   *West Yorkshire Probation Board v Boulter* [2005] EWHC 2342 (Admin), [2006] 1 WLR 232.
7   *S v Doncaster Youth Offending Team* [2003] EWHC 1128 (Admin) [18].

Extent to which the offender has complied

27.21   In taking into account the extent of the offender's compliance, the court must consider not only the number of hours for which the offender has attended at a youth offending team, but also how far s/he has accepted the supervision of the youth offending team.[8] No guidance has yet been given as to how the compliance will actually affect the length of any custodial sentence subsequently imposed.

Sentencing to custody

27.22   The fact that the original sentencing court did not impose a custodial sentence does not mean that the offence itself is not so serious that only a custodial sentence could be justified.[9] It may be, therefore, that after reviewing the seriousness of the offence and the weight to be attached to the personal mitigation, the court now determines that a custodial sentence is indeed the only sentence justified.

Wilfully and persistently failed to comply

27.23   Wilful and persistent failure to comply with the requirements of a community order may be grounds for imposing a custodial sentence even though the original offence did not cross the custody threshold. It should be noted that this provision is only applicable to relevant orders to which Schedule 3 to the Powers of Criminal Courts (Sentencing) Act 2000 applies (see paras 27.65 and 27.78 below). It is not applicable to supervision orders, attendance centre orders, action plan orders or reparation orders.

Time spent on remand prior to original sentence

27.24   When a court is determining the length of a detention and training order, Powers of Criminal Courts (Sentencing) Act 2000 s101(8) requires it to take into account any period for which the offender has been remanded in custody in connection with the offence. The requirement of section 101(8) would seem to extend to the imposition of a detention and training order on re-sentence. It would therefore follow that there is a duty to take into account any time spent on remand prior to the imposition of the original sentence.

Provisions specific to particular orders

27.25   There are specific rules relating to breach proceedings for the following orders:
- referral order;
- attendance centre order;
- reparation and action plan orders;
- supervision order;

8   *R v Neville* [1993] Crim LR 463, CA.
9   *R v Cox* (1993) 19 Cr App R (S) 479, CA; *R v Oliver and Little* [1993] Crim LR 147, CA.

- other community orders (curfew, exclusion, community rehabilitation, community punishment and drug treatment and testing orders); and
- detention and training order supervision.

27.26 The specific rules relating to these orders will be considered below.

Referral order

27.27 Breach proceedings are regulated by Schedule 1 to the Powers of Criminal Courts (Sentencing) Act 2000.

Which court?

27.28 Any referral is to the youth court acting for the local justice area in which it appears to the youth offender panel that the offender resides or will reside.[10]

27.29 Where a youth offender contract has been signed, the court may deal with any breach even after the expiry of the period of the contract.[11]

Determination to be made by the court

27.30 The court must decide whether:

- the panel was entitled to make any finding of fact; and
- any exercise of discretion was reasonably exercised.[12]

27.31 In performing this role, it is not clear whether the court is acting as a tribunal of fact requiring the alleged breach to be proved or as a supervisory body only rejecting wholly unreasonable decisions. As the young offender would have no access to legal representation at the panel meeting, it is submitted that the former role should be adopted by the court.

Powers of the court

27.32 If the court upholds the panel's decision to refer the offender back to court, it may either order the referral order to continue or revoke it.[13] If further referral orders were made at a subsequent sentencing hearing, these orders would also be automatically revoked.[14]

27.33 When a court revokes a referral order, it may deal with the offender in any manner in which s/he could have been dealt with for that offence by the court which made the referral order.[15] This means that the relevant age is the age on the date of conviction for the offence.

27.34 When re-sentencing, the court must have regard to:

- the circumstances of the offender's referral back to the court; and
- the extent to which the offender complied with any contract that had been agreed.[16]

10 Powers of Criminal Courts (Sentencing) Act 2000 Sch 1 para 1(1)(a).
11 Ibid, Sch 1 para 5(6).
12 Ibid, Sch 1 para 5(1).
13 Ibid, Sch 1 para 5(2).
14 Ibid, Sch 1 para 5(3).
15 Ibid, Sch 1 para 5(5)(a).
16 Ibid, Sch 1 para 5(5)(b).

27.35   A court may not revoke a referral order and re-sentence the offender unless s/he is present before it.[17]

Attendance centre order

27.36   Breach proceedings are regulated by Schedule 5 to the Powers of Criminal Courts (Sentencing) Act 2000.

Which court?

27.37   Breach proceedings may be dealt with by the youth court:
- for the area where the attendance centre is situated; or
- which originally imposed the order.[18]

Breach of the order

27.38   It must be proved to the satisfaction of the court that the offender has:
- failed to attend without reasonable excuse; or
- while attending, committed a breach of the Attendance Centre Rules 1995[19] which cannot be adequately dealt with under those rules.[20]

Power of the youth court

27.39   If the court is satisfied that the offender is in breach, it may allow the order to continue and for the breach it may:
- take no action at all; or
- fine the offender up to £1,000 (£250 in the case of an offender under the age of 14).[21]

27.40   Alternatively, in the case of a youth court order, the court may deal with the offender, for the offence for which the order was made, in any way in which s/he could have been dealt with for that offence by the court which made the order if the order had not been made.[22]

27.41   When re-sentencing, the court:
- shall take into account the extent to which the offender has complied with the requirements of the attendance centre order; and
- in the case of an offender who has wilfully and persistently failed to comply with those requirements, may impose a custodial sentence, notwithstanding the fact that the original offence does not cross the custody threshold.[23]

Crown Court orders

27.42   If the original order was made by a Crown Court, the youth court may commit the offender to that court either on bail or in custody.[24]

---

17 Powers of Criminal Courts (Sentencing) Act 2000 Sch 1 para 5(6).
18 Ibid, Sch 5 para 1(2).
19 SI No 3281.
20 Powers of Criminal Courts (Sentencing) Act 2000 Sch 5 para 1(1).
21 Ibid, Sch 5 para 2(1)(a).
22 Ibid, Sch 5 para 2(1)(b).
23 Ibid, Sch 5 para 2(5).
24 Ibid, Sc 5 para 2(1)(c).

Supervision order

27.43 Breach proceedings are regulated by Schedule 7 to the Powers of Criminal Courts (Sentencing) Act 2000.

Which court?

27.44 The application should be made to the relevant court for the local justice area for the time being named in the supervision order.[25] Relevant court is defined as follows:

- in the case of an offender who has not attained 18, a youth court;
- in the case of an offender who has attained 18, a magistrates' court.[26]

27.45 A youth court may still deal with breach proceedings in relation to a young offender who attains the age of 18 while the supervisor's application is pending.[27] In such circumstances the court shall deal with the application as if the offender had not attained the age of 18.

Breach of the order

27.46 It must be proved to the satisfaction of the court that the young offender has failed to comply with:

- any requirement included in the supervision order in pursuance of Powers of Criminal Courts Act 2000 s63(6)(b) (see para 23.140 onwards); or
- any additional requirements included in the supervision order.[28]

27.47 It should be noted that there is no statutory defence of reasonable excuse.

Powers of the youth court

27.48 If the breach is admitted or proved, the court may vary the requirements or it may discharge the order. Whether or not the court exercises these powers, in relation to the breach, it may:

- take no action; or
- impose a fine not exceeding £1,000 (maximum of £250 if aged under 14 years); or
- impose an attendance centre order; or
- impose a curfew order.[29]

27.49 If the court decides to discharge a youth court supervision order, it may deal with the offender for the original offence in any manner in which s/he could have been dealt with by the court which made the order if the order had not been made.[30]

27.50 The offender must, therefore, be re-sentenced on the basis of his/her age at the time of the original sentencing hearing and it is important that

---

25 Powers of Criminal Courts (Sentencing) Act 2000 Sch 7 para 2(1).
26 Ibid, Sch 7 para 1(1).
27 Ibid, Sch 7 para 1(2): the term 'pending' is not defined, but it is arguable that an application is pending as soon as it is received by the relevant court.
28 Ibid, Sch 7 para 2(1).
29 Ibid, Sch 7 para 2(2)(a).
30 Ibid, Sch 7 para 2(2)(b).

the defence lawyer establishes when the original finding of guilt was made and, based on that, determine which sentences would have been available to the court at that time.

27.51   If the supervision order was made by a Crown Court, the youth court or magistrates' court may commit the offender in custody or release him/her on bail until s/he can be brought or appear before the Crown Court.[31] Where a youth or adult magistrates' court commits the offender to the Crown Court, it shall send a certificate signed by a justice of the peace giving particulars of the supervised person's failure to comply with the requirements of the order. Such a certificate shall be admissible as evidence of the failure before the Crown Court. If it is proved to the satisfaction of the Crown Court that the supervised person has failed to comply with the requirements of the order, the Crown Court may deal with him/her for the offence in respect of which the order was made, in any manner in which it could have dealt with him/her for that offence if it had not made the order.[32] Again, the relevant age is the age at the date of the original conviction.

27.52   When either the youth court or the Crown Court re-sentence for the original offence, account must be taken of the extent to which the offender has complied with the requirements of the supervision order.[33]

Reparation and action plan orders

27.53   Breach proceedings for reparation and action plan orders are regulated by Schedule 8 to the Powers of Criminal Courts (Sentencing) Act 2000.

Which court?

27.54   To commence breach proceedings, an application should be made by the responsible officer to the appropriate court. The appropriate court is the youth court acting for the local justice area for the time being named in the order.[34]

Requiring attendance at court

27.55   On the application of the responsible officer, an appropriate court may issue:

- a summons requiring the young offender (and parent or guardian, if still under the age of 18) to attend at a specified time and place;
- a warrant under Powers of Criminal Courts (Sentencing) Act 2000 Sch 8 para 6(2); or
- a warrant under Magistrates' Courts Act 1980 s1.

27.56   Where a young offender is arrested in pursuance of a warrant issued under Powers of Criminal Courts (Sentencing) Act 2000 Sch 8 para 6(2) and cannot be brought immediately before the appropriate court, the person in whose custody s/he is:

---

31 Powers of Criminal Courts (Sentencing) Act 2000 Sch 7 para 2(2)(c).
32 Ibid, Sch 7 para 2(4).
33 Ibid, Sch 7 para 2(7).
34 Ibid, Sch 8 para 1.

- may make arrangements for his/her detention in a place of safety for a period of not more than 72 hours from the time of arrest; and
- shall within that period bring him/her before a youth court.[35]

27.57 Where a young offender is brought before a youth court other than the appropriate court, that court may release the offender forthwith or remand him/her to local authority accommodation.[36] Where the offender is aged 18 or over at the time when s/he is brought before the court, the offender shall not be remanded to local authority accommodation but may instead be remanded into custody.[37]

Powers of the court

27.58 If, while a reparation order or action plan order is in force, it is proved to the satisfaction of the court that the offender is in breach of the order, the court may allow the order to continue and for the breach it may:

- take no action at all;
- fine the young offender up to £1,000 (£250 in the case of an offender under the age of 14);
- impose an attendance centre order; or
- impose a curfew order.[38]

27.59 Alternatively, the court may decide that the offender should be re-sentenced for the offence. If the order was made by a youth court, the court may discharge the order and re-sentence the offender for the original offence.[39] If the order was made by a Crown Court, the court may commit the offender to that court on bail or in custody.[40]

Discharge and re-sentencing

27.60 When the court discharges a reparation order or action plan order, it may deal with the offender in any manner in which s/he could have been dealt with by the court which made the order if the order had not been made.[41]

27.61 The offender must, therefore, be re-sentenced on the basis of his/her age at the time of the original sentencing hearing and it is important that the defence lawyer establishes when the original finding of guilt was made and, based on that, determine which sentences would have been available to the court at that time.

27.62 When sentencing the offender, the court is required to take into account the extent to which s/he has complied with the requirements of the order.[42] The court should, therefore, reduce any new sentence in proportion to the extent that the reparation order or action plan order has been completed.

35 Powers of Criminal Courts (Sentencing) Act 2000 Sch 8 para 6(4).
36 Ibid, Sch 8 para 6(5).
37 Ibid, Sch 8 para 6(7).
38 Ibid, Sch 8 para 2(2)(a).
39 Ibid, Sch 8 para 2(2)(b).
40 Ibid, Sch 8 para 2(2)(c).
41 Ibid, Sch 8 para 2(2)(b).
42 Ibid, Sch 8 para 2(7).

Breach of an order imposed by the Crown Court

27.63   Breach proceedings are started in the usual way by the issue of a summons or warrant by the youth court. If the breach is proved to the satisfaction of the court, in addition to the power to impose a sanction for the breach, it may commit the offender to the Crown Court either on bail or in custody.[43] If an offender is committed in these circumstances, the youth court should send the Crown Court a certificate signed by a justice of the peace giving particulars of the offender's failure to comply with the requirement in question and such other particulars of the case as may be desirable.[44] A certificate purporting to be so signed shall be admissible as evidence of the failure of the breach before the Crown Court.[45]

27.64   Breach proceedings are heard by a Crown Court judge sitting alone. If it is proved to the satisfaction of the court that the offender has failed to comply with the requirements of the order, it may deal with him/her in any manner in which it could have dealt with him/her for the original offence if it had not made the order.[46] Where the Crown court re-sentences an offender, it shall revoke the original order, if it is still in force.[47]

Other community orders

Relevant orders

27.65   A 'relevant order' means any of the following orders:

- curfew order;
- exclusion order;
- community rehabilitation order;
- community punishment order;
- community punishment and rehabilitation order; and
- drug treatment and testing order.[48]

27.66   Breach proceedings for relevant orders are regulated by Schedule 3 to the Powers of Criminal Courts (Sentencing) Act 2000.[49]

Instituting proceedings

27.67   If at any time while a relevant order is in force in respect of an offender, it appears on information to a justice of the peace acting for the local justice area concerned that the offender has failed to comply with any of the requirements of the order, the justice may:

- issue a summons requiring the offender to appear at the place and time specified in it; or

---

43   Powers of Criminal Courts (Sentencing) Act 2000 Sch 8 para 2(2)(c).
44   Ibid, Sch 8 para 2(3).
45   Ibid, Sch 8 para 2(3).
46   Ibid, Sch 8 para 2(4).
47   Ibid, Sch 8 para 2(5).
48   Ibid, Sch 3 para 1(1).
49   Schedule 3 is the original version, not that substituted by the Criminal Justice Act 2003 Sch 32 para 125 – see Criminal Justice Act 2003 (Commencement Order No 8 and Transitional and Saving Provisions) Order 2005 SI No 950 article 4.

- if the information is in writing and on oath, issue a warrant for his/her arrest.[50]

27.68 Any summons or warrant shall direct the offender to appear or be brought:

- in the case of a drug treatment and testing order, before the court responsible for the order;
- in the case of any other relevant order which was made by the Crown Court and included a direction that any failure to comply with any of the requires of the order be dealt with by the Crown court, before the Crown Court; and
- in the case of a relevant order which is neither of the above, before a youth court acting for the local justice area for the time being specified in the order.[51]

27.69 If the offender has attained the age of 18, breach proceedings will start in the adult magistrates' court rather than the youth court.

Powers of youth court

27.70 If the youth court is satisfied that the offender has failed to comply with any requirement without reasonable excuse, it may allow the order to continue and for the breach:

- take no action;
- impose a fine not exceeding £1,000;
- impose a community service order of 40–60 hours (if the existing order is a community punishment order, the total of both orders must not exceed 240 hours);
- if the relevant order is a community rehabilitation order or a community punishment and rehabilitation order, impose an attendance centre order in addition.[52]

27.71 If the order was made by a youth court, the court may revoke the order and deal with the offender for the original offence in any way in which in which it could deal with him/her if s/he had just been convicted by the court of the offence.[53] When re-sentencing, the youth court must take into account the extent to which the offender has complied with the requirements of the relevant order.[54] In the case of an offender who has wilfully and persistently failed to comply with the requirements of the order, the court may impose a custodial sentence notwithstanding the fact that the original sentence does not cross the custody threshold.[55]

27.72 Where the offender has attained 18 and the proceedings relate to an indictable-only offence, the adult magistrates' court may only re-sentence to a maximum of six months' detention in a young offender institution.[56]

50 Powers of Criminal Courts (Sentencing) Act 2000 Sch 2 para 2(1).
51 Ibid, Sch 3 para 1(2)(b).
52 Ibid, Sch 3 para 4(1)(a)–(c).
53 Ibid, Sch 3 para 4(1)(d).
54 Ibid, Sch 3 para 4(2)(a).
55 Ibid, Sch 3 para 4(2)(b).
56 Ibid, Sch 3 para 9(3).

27.73   If the order was made by a Crown Court, the court may commit the offender either on bail or in custody to be dealt with by the Crown Court.[57]

Powers of the Crown Court

27.74   If the Crown Court is satisfied that the offender has failed without reasonable excuse to comply with any of the requirements of an order, it may deal with the offender in any of the following ways:

- take no action;
- impose a fine not exceeding £1,000;
- impose a community service order of 40–60 hours (if the existing order is a community punishment order, the total of both orders must not exceed 240 hours);
- if the relevant order is a community rehabilitation order or a community punishment and rehabilitation order, impose an attendance centre order in addition.[58]

27.75   In the alternative, the Crown Court may deal with the offender for the original offence in any way in which it could deal with the offender if s/he had just been convicted before the Crown Court of the offence.[59] When re-sentencing, the Crown Court must take into account the extent to which the offender has complied with the requirements of the relevant order.[60] In the case of an offender who has wilfully and persistently failed to comply with the requirements of the order, the Crown Court may impose a custodial sentence notwithstanding the fact that the original sentence does not cross the custody threshold.[61]

What constitutes a breach of the requirements?

27.76   An offender required by a community rehabilitation order to submit to treatment for a mental condition or a dependency on drugs or alcohol, shall not be treated as having failed to comply with that requirement on the ground only that s/he has refused to undergo any surgical, electrical or other treatment if, in the opinion of the court, his/her refusal was reasonable having regard to all the circumstances.[62]

27.77   An offender who is convicted of a further offence while a relevant order is in force shall not, on that account, be liable to be dealt with for breach of the requirements of the order.[63]

'Wilfully and persistently'

27.78   In the absence of any case-law on the interpretation of the phrase 'wilfully and persistently', it may be helpful to consider the dictionary definitions.

---

57   Powers of Criminal Courts (Sentencing) Act 2000 Sch 3 para 4(4).
58   Ibid, Sch 3 para 5(1).
59   Ibid, Sch 3 para 5(1)(d).
60   Ibid, Sch 3 para 5(2)(a).
61   Ibid, Sch 3 para 5(2)(b).
62   Ibid, Sch 3 para 6(2).
63   Ibid, Sch 3 para 6(1).

The Concise Oxford English Dictionary gives the following definitions:

> **wilful**, *adjective*, (Of action or state) for which compulsion or ignorance or accident cannot be pleaded as excuse, intentional, deliberate, due to perversity or self-will.

> **persistent**, *adjective*, enduring, constantly repeated.

27.79 It should be noted that the court must find that both are satisfied before assuming that the offender has refused to consent to a community penalty requiring his/her consent.

27.80 Any explanation as to why the young offender has not complied with the order should be put to the court, even if it could not constitute a reasonable excuse. Such explanations may show that the offender's non-compliance was not wilful. It is also submitted that erratic compliance may not be persistent.

Detention and training order supervision

27.81 Where a detention and training order is in force in respect of an offender and it appears on information to a justice of the peace that the offender has failed to comply with requirements of supervision, the justice may:

- issue a summons requiring the offender to appear before a youth court; or
- if the information is in writing and on oath, issue a warrant for the offender's arrest.[64]

Which court?

27.82 The supervisor may seek a summons from a youth court for a relevant local justice area. The court is in a relevant local justice area if:

- the order was made by the youth court acting for it; or
- the offender resides in it for the time being.[65]

Breach of supervision requirements

27.83 The supervision requirements will be set out in a written notice which should have been given to the young offender by the secure establishment prior to his/her release. Some of the requirements will be standard requirements; others will be specific to the young offender (see para 26.59 onwards). The defence lawyer should always confirm the requirements imposed by requesting a copy of the notice.

27.84 Direct evidence of proof of service of the notice upon the offender is not required, provided that there is some evidence from which the court can infer that service has taken place – for example, when the offender attends an appointment at the youth offending team offices on the day of the offender's release as specified in the notice.[66]

27.85 It should be noted that the legislation provides for no defence of reasonable excuse.

---

64 Powers of Criminal Courts (Sentencing) Act 2000 s104(1).
65 Ibid s104(2).
66 *S v Doncaster Youth Offending Team* [2005] EWHC 1128 (Admin).

Court powers

27.86   If it is proved to the satisfaction of the youth court before which an offender appears, that s/he has failed to comply with requirements of the supervision, that court may:

- do nothing about the breach; or
- fine the offender up to £1,000 (£250 if the offender is still under the age of 14); or
- order the offender to be detained in such secure accommodation as determined by the secretary of state for up to three months or for the remainder of the order, whichever is the shorter.[67]

27.87   In the first two possibilities the supervision presumably continues, although the legislation does not deal specifically with the point.

27.88   There is no power to commit the offender to the Crown Court, even if the original order was made at that court.

---

67 Powers of Criminal Courts (Sentencing) Act 2000 s104(3).

Criminal records and public protection

Introduction

28.1   Having a criminal record potentially affects employment prospects and access to some other services such as insurance and credit from financial institutions. As many young clients are approaching the age when they will be seeking employment, a criminal record will be a matter of concern for them and their parents. The defence lawyer should be prepared to advise on the consequences of a criminal conviction.

28.2   Unlike some jurisdictions, there is no rule that removes a young person's criminal record when s/he attains the age of 18. Instead, the general policy has been to allow most offenders to be formally rehabilitated by the passage of time. This policy has been given effect by the Rehabilitation of Offenders Act 1974. The effects of having a criminal record will be felt even more acutely with the establishment of the Criminal Records Agency. For the first time, any employer will be able to obtain independent confirmation of a job applicant's criminal record.

28.3   Parallel to this general policy are a number of provisions aimed to protect the public from certain offenders. Local authorities and probation services have long kept registers of offenders who have committed violent or sexual offences against children ('Schedule 1 offences'). More recently, offenders convicted of a wide range of sex offences have been required to register with the police. Both of these schemes apply to offenders aged under 18. The restrictions they impose on the offender can have long-term consequences for the child or young person.

Rehabilitation of Offenders Act 1974

28.4   The intention of the Rehabilitation of Offenders Act 1974 is to provide a mechanism whereby a person convicted of a criminal offence may be rehabilitated for most official purposes. This is effected by deeming offences to have been 'spent' after a fixed period of time.

Spent convictions

28.5   The Act provides that a criminal conviction becomes spent after a certain period of time. The rehabilitation period depends upon the sentence imposed by the court and is set out in section 5 of the Act. The period starts to run in most cases from the date of conviction. As a further concession to youth, the rehabilitation period is halved where the sentence was imposed on a person who was under 18 years of age at the date of conviction.[1] The various rehabilitation periods are set out in table 24 below.

28.6   Once a conviction is spent, the Act deems that the person concerned shall be treated as though s/he were never convicted of the offence. In practical terms, a spent conviction need not be declared when applying for a job or for services (eg mortgages, credit, insurance etc).[2] Convictions are never spent for the purposes of criminal proceedings.[3]

---

1   Rehabilitation of Offenders Act 1974 s5(2(a).
2   Ibid, s4.
3   Ibid, s7(2)(a).

Excluded sentences

28.7   Certain sentences may never be rehabilitated. These include:

- detention under Powers of Criminal Courts (Sentencing) Act 2000 s91 for terms exceeding 30 months;
- extended detention under Criminal Justice Act 2003 s228;
- detention for life or detention for public protection under Criminal Justice Act 2003 s226; and
- detention during Her Majesty's pleasure.[4]

Excluded occupations

28.8   The provisions of the Act do not apply in relation to the following professions and occupations:

- all health professionals;
- veterinary surgeons;
- pharmacists;
- solicitors and barristers;
- accountants;
- probation officers;
- prison staff;
- police officers;
- traffic wardens;
- teachers;
- employees of social services departments (or voluntary organisations) who in the course of ordinary duties would have access to various vulnerable groups (eg elderly, mentally ill, disabled etc);
- any employment concerned with the provision of services to persons under the age of 18.[5]

Criminal record checks

28.9   The Police Act 1997 introduced a new system of certificates which detail information held on police computer records. The issuing of certificates is done by the Criminal Records Bureau.

28.10   The 1997 Act creates three types of certificate:

(i)   **Criminal conviction certificate** – details convictions which are not spent under the Rehabilitation of Offenders Act 1974 or confirms that no conviction is recorded.

(ii)   **Criminal record certificate (or standard record certificate)** – details both convictions and cautions and will include offences which are spent.

(iii) **Enhanced criminal record certificate** – details not only convictions and cautions recorded against the offender but also police intelligence which could include unsubstantiated allegations.

---

4   Rehabilitation of Offenders Act 1974 s5(1).
5   Rehabilitation of Offenders Act 1974 (Exceptions) Order 1975 SI No 1023 Sch 1.

Table 24: Rehabilitation of Offenders Act 1974: rehabilitation periods

Sentence	Period
Absolute discharge	6 months
Conditional discharge	1 year or until the order expires, whichever is the longer
Fine or compensation order	2 and a half years
Reparation order	2 and a half years
Referral order	When youth offender contract completed
Attendance centre order	1 year after the order ceases
Curfew order	2 and a half years
Action plan order	2 and a half years
Supervision order	1 year or until the order ceases, whichever is the longer
Community rehabilitation order	2 and a half years
Community punishment order	2 and a half years
Community punishment and rehabilitation order	2 and a half years
Detention and training order:	
if aged 15 or over:	
less than 6 months	3 and a half years
6 to 24 months	5 years
if aged less than 15	1 year after the date on which the order ceases to have effect
Section 91 detention:	
less than 6 months	3 years
6 to 30 months	5 years

Unless otherwise specified, the rehabilitation period runs from the date of conviction.

28.11   At the time of writing, the Criminal Records Bureau only offers standard or enhanced certificates. Checks will be carried out where the employment involves working with children or vulnerable adults, in establishments that are wholly or mainly for children or in healthcare. Checks will also be carried out if a person applies to be a foster carer, adoptive parent or a childminder.

Schedule 1 offenders

28.12   Special provisions relate to persons convicted of offences against children and young persons which are specified in Children and Young Persons Act 1933 Schedule 1. These offences include:

- murder or manslaughter of a child or young person;
- infanticide;
- causing or allowing the death of a child (Domestic Violence, Crime and Victims Act 2004 s5);
- any offence involving bodily injury to a child or young person;
- common assault or battery;
- any offence against a child or young person under any of Sexual Offences Act 2003 ss1–41, 47–53, 57–61, 66 and 67, or any attempt to commit such an offence;
- any offence under Sexual Offences Act 2003 s62 or 63 where the intended offence was an offence against a child or young person, or any attempt to commit such an offence.

28.13   The list of offences indicates that the aim of the provisions is to ensure that local authorities can carry out their child protection duties more effectively. Children and young persons who offend against their age peers will fall within the definition of Schedule 1 offender, without in most cases posing a continuing risk to minors.

Registers of Schedule 1 offenders

28.14   Most local authority social services departments maintain registers of Schedule 1 offenders known to be living in their areas. The fact that a Schedule 1 offender is known to live in the same household as children may prompt a child protection investigation. The fact that a person is on the Schedule 1 offenders list may also rule out certain types of employment involving contact with children, as well as the possibility of fostering or adopting children. Classification would stay with the offender for life.

Release from custody

28.15   Guidance to the Prison Service[6] requires prison officers to identify any prisoner of whatever age who has Schedule 1 convictions. This includes not just the current offence(s), but also previous convictions. The local social services department and probation service should be notified. Classification as a Schedule 1 offender will restrict the opportunities for temporary

6   Release of Prisoners Convicted of Offences Against Children or Young Persons under the Age of 18 (IG 54/1994).

release and parole. It could also result in licence conditions prohibiting the offender from living in a household containing children.

28.16   This whole procedure can be dispensed with, but only if the Director of Social Services (now the Director of Children's Services) for the area where the offender lives certifies in writing to the Prison Service that no child protection issues are involved. The guidance suggests that an example would be cases of minor physical violence between young persons of similar age or development. Because of the serious consequences of being classified as a Schedule 1 offender, the defence lawyer should make representations to the relevant social services department asking that confirmation be sent to the young offender institution where the young offender is being held

Review of Schedule 1 and child protection

28.17   In 2004 the Home Office established a multi-agency working group to review existing agency procedures for identifying those person who present a risk of harm to children. As a consequence of this ongoing review, the Home Office has issued Home Office Circular 16/2005.[7] This suggests that the use of the term 'Schedule 1 offender' may be unhelpful, as it focuses on offending history rather than ongoing risk to children. Accordingly, the Circular recommends that agencies involved in child protection should instead use the term 'person identified presenting a risk, or potential risk, to children'. The Circular contains a consolidated list of the major offences against children. The Circular makes it clear that the professionals involved in child protection must still exercise their judgment when considering whether a particular offender poses a risk of harm to children. This guidance may be of particular benefit to young people convicted of Schedule 1 offences.

Registration as a sex offender

Applicable offences

28.18   A child or young person is subject to sex offender notification requirements if convicted of an offence listed in appendix 9.

Notification requirement

28.19   The notification requirement applies to a person, if s/he is:

- convicted of a sexual offence listed in appendix 9; or
- cautioned in respect of such an offence; or
- found not guilty of such an offence by reason of insanity, or to be under a disability and to have done the act charged against him in respect of such an offence.[8]

---

7   The Department for Education and Skills has issued similar guidance to local authorities – see LASSL (2005) *Identification of individuals who present a risk to children*.

8   Sexual Offences Act 2003 s80(1).

Table 25: Sexual Offences Act 2003: Applicable period for offenders aged under 18

Disposal	Applicable period
Sentence of s91 detention for a term of 30 months or more	Indefinite
Restriction order	Indefinite
Custodial sentence for a term of more than 6 months but less than 30 months*	5 years
Custodial sentence for a term of 6 months or less*	3 and a half years
Non-custodial sentence	2 and a half years
Conditional discharge	The period of conditional discharge
Reprimand/warning	1 year

* In the case of a detention and training order the length refers to the custodial part of the order only: *R v Slocombe* [2005] EWCA Crim 2297; [2006] 1 WLR 328.

A conditional discharge is a conviction for these purposes notwithstanding section 14(1) of the Powers of Criminal Courts (Sentencing) Act 2000.[9] An absolute discharge does not count as a conviction by virtue of section 14(1) of the 2000 Act.

28.20   It also applies to an offender who on 1 May 2004 is serving a custodial or community sentence for an applicable offence or is subject to supervision after being released from a custodial sentence for such an offence.[10]

Length of requirement of notification

28.21   The period for which an offender is subject to a requirement of notification depends on the sentence received for the offence. It is referred to as the applicable period.

28.22   The applicable period for offenders aged under 18 on the date of conviction are shown in table 25.[11]

9 Sexual Offences Act 2003 s134.
10 Ibid, s81(1) and (3).
11 Ibid, s82 (1) and (2).

Certificates

28.23   The court before which the offender is convicted will certify that the offence is one for which the registration requirement applies.[12] In the case of a reprimand or warning, the police officer administering the reprimand or warning will issue a certificate confirming that the offence is one to which the registration requirement applies.[13]

Initial notification to police

28.24   Within three days of the conviction (that is, conviction at trial or plea of guilt rather than date of sentence)[14] or the administering of the reprimand or warning, a relevant offender must provide to the police the following information:

- his/her name;
- any other names used;
- date of birth;
- national insurance number (where the offender has attained 16);
- home address;
- any other premises in the United Kingdom at which s/he regularly resides or stays.[15]

28.25   If a young person lives part of the week with one parent and the rest of the week with the other parent, both addresses will need to be registered. The same considerations will apply where a young person is at a residential boarding school during the week but returns home at the weekends and school holidays.

Notification to police

Change in circumstances

28.26   A relevant offender must also notify the police within three days of:

- his/her using a name not previously notified to police;
- any change of his/her home address;
- his/her having resided or stayed for a qualifying period at any premises in the United Kingdom the address of which has not been notified to the police; or
- his release from custody (whether on remand, on release from a sentence or a hospital order).[16]

28.27   'Qualifying period' is defined as a period of seven days or two or more periods, in any 12-month period which taken together amount to seven days.[17]

---

12   Sexual Offences Act 2003 s92(2).
13   Ibid, s92(4).
14   *R v Longworth* [2006] UKHL 1; [2006] 1 WLR 313.
15   Sexual Offences Act 2003 s83(1) and (5).
16   Ibid, s84(1).
17   Ibid, s84(6).

Periodic notification

28.28 Having given initial notification, a relevant offender must re-notify the details required of him/her on initial notification within 12 months of the last time s/he was required to notify. The 12-month time limit runs from whichever of the following occurred most recently:

- initial notification;
- notification of a change of circumstances; or
- the most recent annual re-notification.[18]

Travel outside the United Kingdom

28.29 A relevant offender who intends to leave the United Kingdom for three days or longer must provide the police with certain information regarding the trip abroad.[19] Notification must be made by attending at a prescribed police station in the young person's area. The information should normally be provided not less than seven days prior to departure. If the trip is arranged at shorter notice, or the necessary information is not known at the time, the information should be provided at least 24 hours before travelling.

28.30 The following information (if known) must be provided:

- the date of departure from the United Kingdom;
- the destination country (or, there is more than one, the first);
- the point of arrival in that country;
- his/her point(s) of arrival in any countries s/he will be visiting in addition to the initial destination;
- the carrier(s) s/he intends to use to leave and return to the United Kingdom or any other point(s) of arrival while s/h is outside the United Kingdom;
- details of his/her accommodation arrangements for his/her first night outside the United Kingdom;
- his/her date of re-entry to the United Kingdom;
- his/her point of arrival on his/her return to the United Kingdom.[20]

28.31 Where the young person has provided the required information and at any time prior to his/her departure the information provided becomes inaccurate or incomplete, s/he must provide the up-to-date information at least 24 hours before travelling.[21]

28.32 Within three days of his/her return to the United Kingdom, the young person must attend a specified police station in his/her local police area to notify the police of the date of his/her return and his/her point of arrival in the United Kingdom. This need not be done if the expected date of return and point of re-entry was provided before travelling and the young person returned as stated.[22]

---

18 Sexual Offences Act 2003 s85(1) and (2).
19 Sexual Offences Act 2003 (Travel Notification Requirements) Regulations 2004 SI No 1220 reg 5.
20 Ibid, reg 6.
21 Ibid, reg 7.
22 Ibid, reg 8.

Parental directions

28.33   The court dealing with the young offender may make a parental direction in relation to any person with parental responsibility. Such a direction means that:

- the obligations in relation to police notification that would be imposed on the young offender are to be treated instead as obligations on the parent; and
- the parent must ensure that the young offender attends at the police station with him/her, when a notification is being given.[23]

28.34   A parental direction applies until the offender attains the age of 18, or for such shorter period as the court may, at the time the direction is given, direct.[24]

28.35   Even where the sentencing court does not make a parental direction, a chief officer of police, by complaint to any magistrates' court whose commission area includes any part of his police area, may apply for a parental direction in respect of a relevant offender:

- who resides in his police are, or who the chief officer believes is in or is intending to come to his police area; and
- who the chief officer believes to be under 18.[25]

28.36   It is possible to apply for an order varying, renewing or discharging a parental direction.[26] Application is made to the court which made the order (or the Crown Court in the case of a direction made by the Court of Appeal).[27] Application may be made by any of the following:

- the young offender;
- the parent;
- the chief officer of police for the area in which the young offender resides;
- a chief officer of police who believes that the young offender is in, or is intending to come to, his/her police area;
- a chief officer of police who has previously applied to a court for the making of a parental direction.[28]

Criminal offences relating to notification

28.37   It is a criminal offence:

- to fail without reasonable excuse to comply with a notification requirement; or
- to provide false information as part of a notification; or
- for a parent subject to a parental direction, to fail without reasonable excuse to ensure that the young offender attends at the police station with him/her when a notification is being given.[29]

23 Sexual Offences Act 2003 s89(2).
24 Ibid, s89(3).
25 Ibid, s89(4).
26 Ibid, s90(1).
27 Ibid, s90(5).
28 Ibid, s90(2).
29 Ibid, s91(1).

28.38   The above offences are punishable with a term of imprisonment for a term not exceeding five years.[30]

Disqualification from working with children

Offence against a child

28.39   An individual commits an 'offence against a child' if:

- s/he commits any offence in Criminal Justice and Court Services Act 2000 Sch 4 para 1;
- s/he commits against a child any offence mentioned in paragraph 2 of that Schedule, or
- s/he falls within paragraph 3 of that Schedule.

28.40   Schedule 4 to the Criminal Justices and Court Services Act 2000 is reproduced at appendix 10.

Compulsory disqualification

28.41   A Crown Court judge must make an order disqualifying the offender from working with children if:

- s/he is convicted of an offence against a child committed at a time when s/he was under the age of 18;
- the sentence passed was one of the following:
  (a) a detention and training order for a term of 12 months or more;
  (b) section 91 detention for a period of 12 months or more;
  (c) detention in a young offender institution for a period of 12 months or more;
  (d) extended detention under Criminal Justice Act 2003 s228;
  (e) detention for public protection under Criminal Justice Act 2003 s226;
  (f) detention for life under Criminal Justice Act 2003 s226; and
  (g) detention during Her Majesty's pleasure; and
- the court is satisfied, having regard to all the circumstances, that it is likely that the individual will commit a further offence against a child.[31]

28.42   If the requirement to make a compulsory disqualification order is overlooked at the time of sentence, the prosecutor may apply at any time to the sentencing court for an order to be made.[32] The court must then make the order if it is satisfied, having regard to all the circumstances, that it is likely that the individual will commit a further offence against a child.[33]

---

30   Sexual Offences Act 2003 s91(2).
31   Criminal Justice and Court Services Act 2000 s29(2), (3) and (4).
32   Ibid, s29B(1)(b).
33   Ibid, s29B(2)(b).

Discretionary disqualification

28.43   A Crown Court may order an offender to be disqualified from working with children if:

- s/he is convicted of an offence against a child; and
- the court is satisfied, having regard to all the circumstances, that it is likely that the individual will commit a further offence against a child.[34]

28.44   A discretionary disqualification may be imposed whatever the sentence passed.

Scope of disqualification

28.45   'Work' includes work of any kind, whether paid or unpaid and whether under a contract of service or apprenticeship, under a contract for services, or otherwise under a contract.[35] This would extend as far as prohibiting babysitting and acting as a volunteer at a youth club or with a youth sports team.

Breach of the disqualification order

28.46   A person subject to a disqualification order commits an offence if s/he knowingly applies for, offers to do, accepts or does any work in a regulated position.[36] 'Regulated position' is defined by Criminal Justice and Court Services Act 2000 s36; it covers all positions where there is substantial access to children.

Sexual offences prevention order

28.47   A sexual offences prevention order prohibits a defendant from doing anything described in the order.[37] The only prohibitions which may be included in the order are those necessary for the purpose of protecting the public or any particular members of the public from serious sexual harm from the defendant.[38]

28.48   The court making the order must specify whether the order is to be for a determinate period (minimum period of five years) or indefinite.[39]

28.49   The Home Office has issued guidance on the sexual offences prevention order which indicates that an application for an order against a person under the age of 18 should only be considered exceptionally.[40]

---

34 Criminal Justice and Court Services Act 2000 s29A(1) and (2).
35 Ibid, s42(1).
36 Ibid, s35(1).
37 Sexual Offences Act 2003 s107(1)(a).
38 Ibid, s107(2).
39 Ibid, s107(1)(b).
40 Home Office, *Guidance on Part 2 of the Sexual Offences Act 2003*, p36, para 4.

Order made on conviction

28.50 A court may make a sexual offences prevention order where:

- the offender has been convicted of an offence specified in Sexual Offences Act 2003 Sch 3 or Sch 5; and
- it is satisfied that it is necessary to make such an order for the purpose of protecting the public or any particular members of the public from serious sexual harm from the defendant.[41]

28.51 There is also power to make the order if the defendant has been found not guilty of the offence by reason of insanity, or to be under a disability and to have done the act charged against him/her.[42]

28.52 The defendant may appeal the making of a sexual offences prevention order made on conviction as if the order were a sentence passed on him/her for the offence.[43]

Civil order

28.53 A chief officer of police may by complaint to a magistrates' court apply for an order in respect of a person who resides in his police area or who the chief officer believes is in, or intending to come to, his police area if it appears t the chief officer that:

- the person is a qualifying offender; and
- the person has, since the date when s/he was convicted of a relevant offence, acted in such a way as to give reasonable cause to believe that it is necessary for such an order to be made.[44]

28.54 A 'qualifying offender' means a person:

- convicted of an offence listed in Sexual Offences Act 2003 Sch 3 (other than at paragraph 60) or in Sexual Offences Act 2003 Sch 5;
- found not guilty of such an offence by reason of insanity;
- found to be under a disability and to have done the act charged against him/her in respect of the offence;
- cautioned for such an offence;
- convicted in a country outside the United Kingdom of an offence which would have constituted such an offence if committed in the United Kingdom.[45]

28.55 Before applying for an order in relation to a person aged under 18, the police should consult the social services department and youth offending team for the area, who may have assessed or supervised the child or young person following their earlier offending, or have other relevant contact with the child or young person or their families.[46]

---

41 Sexual Offences Act 2003 s104(1) and (2).
42 Ibid, s104(1) and (3).
43 Ibid, s110(1)(a).
44 Ibid, s104(1)(4).
45 Ibid, s106(5)–(7) and (9).
46 Home Office, *Guidance on Part 2 of the Sexual Offences Act 2003*, page 40, para 22.

Criteria for making order

28.56   The court may make a sexual prevention order if it is satisfied that the defendant's behaviour since the date when s/he was first convicted of a relevant offence makes it necessary to make such an order for the purpose of protecting the public or any particular members of the public from serious sexual harm from the defendant.

Interim order

28.57   On making the main application, the police may also request that an interim order be made whilst the main application is being considered.[47] The court may, if it thinks it just to do so, make an interim order prohibiting the defendant from doing anything described in the order.[48] The interim order must be for a specified period.[49]

Appeal against making of order

28.58   The young person may appeal the making of both an interim or full order.[50]

Breach of a sexual offences prevention order

28.59   It is a criminal offence to breach the terms of an interim or a full sexual offences prevention order.[51]

Multi-agency public protection arrangements (MAPPA)

28.60   Multi-agency protection panel arrangements were introduced by the Criminal Justice and Court Services Act 2000 to provide protection from offenders who are considered to present a risk of serious harm to members of the public. The provisions were substantially altered by the Criminal Justice Act 2003.

28.61   The responsible authority, that is the chief officer of police, the local probation board and the Prison Service acting jointly must establish arrangements for the purpose of assessing and managing the risks posed in each area by relevant offenders.[52]

28.62   A duty to cooperate with the responsible authority is placed on, amongst others:

- youth offending teams;
- local education authorities;
- local housing authorities;
- registered social landlords;

---

47   Sexual Offences Act 2003 s109(2).
48   Ibid, s109(3).
49   Ibid, s109(4).
50   Ibid, s110(1) and (2).
51   Ibid, s113(1).
52   Criminal Justice Act 2003 s325(1).

- social services authorities;
- Primary Care Trusts;
- NHS trusts; and
- designated providers of electronic monitoring services.

28.63 The core functions of MAPPA are to:

- identify relevant offender;
- share relevant information with those agencies involved in risk assessment;
- assess the risk of serious harm; and
- manage that risk.

Relevant offender

28.64 A young offender will be made the subject of a MAPPA referral if s/he is:

- subject to the notification requirements of Sexual Offences Act 2003 Part 2 (see para 28.19); or
- convicted by a court in England and Wales of murder or an offence specified in Criminal Justice Act 2003 Sch 15 (see appendix 7); or
- is found not guilty by a court in England and Wales of murder or a specified offence by reason of insanity or to be under a disability and to have done the act charged against him/her in respect of such an offence but only if the court makes a hospital order or guardianship order; or
- convicted of an offence against a child (see appendix 10) where a qualifying sentence (see para 28.41) was imposed; or
- charged with an offence against a child (see appendix 10) and made the subject of a hospital order or guardianship order following a finding that s/he did the act or omission charged.[53]

Levels of risk management

28.65 When considering whether to refer to MAPPA, the relevant agency must assess the level of risk that the young offender poses to the public. In the case of youth offending teams this will involve completion of *Asset* Core Profile and *Asset* Risk of Serious Harm. Referrals will be made at three levels (see table 26).

Violent and Sexual Offenders Register

28.66 Referral to MAPPA will also trigger entry onto the new Violent and Sexual Offenders Register (ViSOR). Established in 2005, ViSOR is a national police database of offenders' details. The information is held by the local police public protection unit. It is planned that the National Probation Service and Prison Service will also have access to the information.

---

53 Criminal Justice Act 2003 s327.

Table 26: MAPPA: levels of risk management

Level 1 *Ordinary management*
Risk is managed by the youth offending team through supervision in accordance with National Standards.

Level 2 *Local inter-agency risk management*
This is where a young person poses a high risk of harm, with associated needs. The case must be referred to a local risk-management meeting, where agencies must be involved in a co-ordinated approach to planning and management.

Level 3 *Referral to multi-agency public protection panel (MAPPA)*
This is intended for the few young people who meet one or more of the following criteria:
- They are assessed as posing a high or very high risk of causing serious harm.
- The risks have to be managed by a plan that necessitates close co-operation at a senior level, due to the complexity of the case, or a need for the commitment of additional resources.
- Although not assessed as being high or very high risk, the case may attract media scrutiny or community interest, and there is a need to ensure public confidence in the public protection work of agencies and the criminal justice system is maintained.

28.67   The information recorded on the database is intended to help with the investigation of crime. It may include information regarding:
- personal details;
- offending history;
- supervision;
- details of risk assessment and management;
- relationships;
- employment/education; and
- victims.

Preventing youth crime and disorder

Introduction

29.1   The Crime and Disorder Act 1998 introduced a range of measures intended to reduce the incidence of crime and disorder. The original Act has been substantially expanded by subsequent legislation. For young people under the age of 18 the following have implications:

- acceptable behaviour contracts;
- anti-social behaviour orders;
- powers to remove truants to designated premises;
- child curfew schemes;
- child safety orders; and
- dispersal orders.

29.2   Some of the provisions, particularly breaches of anti-social behaviour orders, create criminal offences whilst others involve youth offending teams in preventing offending. The defence lawyer will need to be aware of the law relating to these measures and the consequences for a young client made subject to them.

Acceptable behaviour contract

29.3   Some local authorities have used acceptable behaviour contracts in an attempt to deal with anti-social behaviour, without recourse to legal proceedings. The acceptable behaviour contract is a written agreement between the person who has been involved in anti-social behaviour and one or more local agencies whose role it is to prevent such behaviour. In practice, the contracts are most commonly used for young people, and are offered prior to, or during, the consideration of an application for an anti-social behaviour order.

29.4   The contract will specify a list of anti-social acts, which it is said have been committed by the person who is signing the contract. They will then agree not to continue those acts. The guidance on the making of acceptable behaviour contracts can be found in the joint Home Office, Association of Chief Police Officers and Youth Justice Board publication *A guide to anti-social behaviour and acceptable behaviour contracts.*[1]

29.5   The guide suggests that the terms of the contract should be agreed at a meeting with the person to be made the subject of the contract and the local agencies involved in the prevention of anti-social behaviour. A parent or guardian should be encouraged to attend. Where possible, the young person should be involved in drawing up the contract. The contract would usually be for a period of six months, but it could be for longer. Support to address the underlying causes of the behaviour should be offered in parallel to the contract.

29.6   Any failures to adhere to the terms of the contract can be dealt with by verbal or written warnings and by threats of prosecution by way of an application for an anti-social behaviour order or possession proceedings, where relevant. The contract has no legal force, but failures to agree a contract or

---

1   March 2003. This guide can be downloaded from www.crimereduction.gov.uk.

to adhere to its terms are likely to be used as evidence of the necessity for an anti-social behaviour order in any subsequent application.

Anti-social behaviour order

29.7   Crime and Disorder Act 1998 s1 introduced the anti-social behaviour order. It originally arose only as a stand-alone order. Breach of an anti-social behaviour order is a criminal offence. The Crime and Disorder Act 1998 has subsequently been amended and added to substantially by:

- Police Reform Act 2002;
- Anti-social Behaviour Act 2003;
- Serious Organised Crime and Police Act 2005.

29.8   An anti-social behaviour order can now arise in the following ways:

- an application to the adult magistrates' court sitting in its civil jurisdiction;[2]
- on application to a county court where there are existing proceedings against defendants;[3]
- an order after conviction for an offence in the youth court, adult magistrates' court or Crown Court;[4]
- the Crown Court may make an order on appeal from an anti-social behaviour order made in the magistrates' court.[5]

29.9   County court orders are beyond the scope of this book and are not mentioned further in this section.

29.   The order is similar to an injunction as its terms are prohibitive, and it is designed to prevent serious anti-social behaviour of a criminal or near criminal kind. Interim orders may also be made pending the determination of an application for a full order. Interim orders can be made in relation to an application for a stand-alone order or an order following conviction.[6]

Applicable age

29.10   An anti-social behaviour order may be made against any person aged 10 years or over.[7]

Legal representation

29.11   Public funding is available for any proceedings under Crime and Disorder fflAct 1998 ss1 and 4 relating to anti-social behaviour orders, including

---

2   Crime and Disorder Act 1998 s1.
3   Ibid, s1B.
4   Ibid, s1C.
5   Ibid, s4. For the purposes of applications to vary or discharge, the order it will be treated as if it were an order of the magistrates' court from which the appeal was brought.
6   Ibid, s1D and s1D(1) and (2), as inserted by Serious Organised Crime and Police Act 2005 s139, in force 1 July 2005 (SI 2005 No 1521).
7   Ibid, s1(1).

interim orders. The Criminal Defence Service, *General Criminal Contract* allows for the self-grant of Advocacy Assistance to an extendable upper financial limit of £1,500.[8] There are no financial criteria for the grant of Advocacy Assistance save that it must not be provided where it appears unreasonable in the particular circumstances of the case, or whether the interests of justice test are not met.[9] As there is a real risk of imprisonment if an anti-social behaviour order is made and subsequently breached, this may be a powerful factor in applying the interests of justice test. The defence lawyer needs to complete Form CDS3. Representation orders are not available in these proceedings. Advocacy Assistance is also available for proceedings in the Crown Court in relation to an appeal. The merits test in these cases is based only on a general test of reasonableness.

29.12   Where an anti-social behaviour order is considered post-conviction, the proceedings are covered by the representation order for the original proceedings. This order will also cover an application to vary or discharge the anti-social behaviour order. Such applications will be part of the same case as the original proceedings.[10]

29.13   A breach of an anti-social behaviour order is a criminal offence. Legal representation is by way of a representation order granted by the magistrates' court.

Anti-social behaviour order or order on conviction to prevent further anti-social acts?

29.14   The legislation, as now substantially amended, refers to stand-alone orders arising under Crime and Disorder Act 1998 s1 as 'anti-social behaviour orders' and orders arising under section 1C as 'orders on conviction to prevent further anti-social acts'. In hearing appeals relating to orders arising in either circumstance, the Court of Appeal and the Divisional Court have referred to both types of orders as anti-social behaviour orders. It seems that this distinction has not been one that has arisen in argument before them. In the view of the authors, it is a largely academic distinction with little relevance in practice. It is only in relation to the ancillary orders dealt with at paras 29.61 to 29.68 below that the difference may be of relevance.

29.15   In accordance with the practice of the appellate courts, this chapter refers to both types of order as anti-social behaviour orders.

Stand-alone order – adult magistrates' court

29.16   An application is made to the adult magistrates' court, and before making an order the court must be satisfied that the following criteria are fulfilled:

- that the person against whom the order is sought has acted in a manner that caused or was likely to cause harassment, alarm or distress to one or more persons not at the same household as him/herself; and

---

8   General Criminal Contract, Part B 4 and 6.3.
9   Access to Justice Act 1999 Sch 3.
10   Criminal Defence Service: *Criminal Bills Assessment Manual* para 10.4.

- that such an order is necessary to protect relevant persons, or persons elsewhere in England and Wales, from further anti-social acts by him/her.[11]

Who can apply

29.17 The application can only be made by a 'relevant authority', which includes any of the following:

- the council for a local government area;
- in England, a county council;
- the chief constable of police of any police force maintained for a police area;
- the chief constable of the British Transport Police;
- any person registered under Housing Act 1996 s1 as a social landlord;
- a housing action trust established by order in pursuance of Housing Act 1988 s62;
- an organisation with whom a relevant local authority makes arrangements under an order of the secretary of state.[12]

The statutory duty to consult

29.18 Before making an application for an order:

- the council for a local government area shall consult the chief of police of the police force for the police area within which that local government area lies;
- a chief officer of police shall consult the council for the local government area in which the person in relation to whom the application is to be made resides or appears to reside;
- any other relevant authority shall consult both the council for the local government area in which the person in relation to whom the application is to be made resides or appears to reside, and the chief officer of police of the police force for the police area within which that local government area lies.[13]

29.19 There is no requirement for agreement to be reached between the parties being consulted. There is no decided case-law on whether a failure to consult will render the application void. Evidence of consultation will be produced at the hearing of the application. Where an application is made by the police, the power of the Chief Constable and the duty to consult prior to any application can be delegated to any officer or officers judged suitable.[14]

---

11 Crime and Disorder Act 1998 s1(1).
12 Ibid, s1(1A) and s1F, as inserted by Serious Organised Crime and Police Act 2005 s142.
13 Ibid, s1(2) and s1E.
14 *R (Chief Constable of the West Midlands) v Birmingham Justices* [2002] EWHC 1087 (Admin).

Young people – Assessment of Needs

29.20   Children and young people are often the subject of applications for anti-social behaviour orders. It is likely that these young people will have needs which mean that they are, or should be, receiving support from the local authority in whose area they reside. Guidance on applications for anti-social behaviour orders has been issued jointly by the Home Office, Youth Justice Board and the Association of Chief Police Officers.[15] The guide contains useful information on the assessment of the needs of young people and how the application process relates to the statutory duties of the local authority:

> When applying for an Anti-Social Behaviour Order against a person aged 10 to 17 an assessment should be made of their circumstances and needs to ensure that appropriate services are provided for the young person concerned and for the courts to have the necessary information about him/her.

> It is vital that any assessment made does not cause any delay to the application for an order. The lead agency should therefore liaise closely with the local social services department or youth offending team from the start of the process so that where a new assessment is required it can begin quickly.

> Councils with social services responsibilities have a duty, arising from the Children Act 1989 s17, to safeguard and promote the welfare of children within their areas who may be in need. The assessment is expected to be carried out in accordance with the Framework for the Assessment of Children in Need and their Family. This guidance sets out the content and timescales for the initial assessment and the core assessment. A core assessment is required when an initial assessment has determined that the child is in need. The assessment will cover the child's needs, the capacity of his/her parents and wider family, and environmental factors. This enables councils to determine whether the child is a 'child in need' and what services may be necessary in order to address the assessed need. The assessment of the child's needs should run in parallel with evidence gathering and the application process.

> Statutory agencies, such as social services, the local education authority or the health authority have a statutory obligation to provide services to the under 18s. They should do so irrespective of whether an ASBO application is to be made and the timing of the application. The ASBO application does not prevent such support and can proceed in parallel, or indeed prior to that support.[16]

29.21   Further information on the *Framework for the assessment of children in need and their families*[17] and the statutory duties of local authorities is contained in chapter 3.

29.22   Where a local authority fails to invite a proposed defendant to give his/her views at an anti-social behaviour case conference convened prior to the decision to apply, this did not amount to an infringement of any European Convention on Human Rights provisions. The defendant was said to have a full opportunity to put his case in court.[18]

---

15   *A guide to anti-social behaviour orders and acceptable behaviour contracts* (March 2003). This guide can be downloaded from www.crimereduction.gov.uk.

16   Ibid, pp40–41.

17   Department of Health, 2000.

18   *Wareham v Purbeck District Council* [2005] EWHC 358 (Admin).

Local authorities applying for an order against a child in its care

29.23 Where a local authority applies for an anti-social behaviour order against a child over whom it holds a full care order and therefore has parental responsibility, there is an obvious risk of a conflict of interest between its duties to the public and its duties to the child under the Children Act 1989.

29.24 The need to protect the interests of the child by separating the functions of the local authority has been recognised by the courts. In the case of *R (on the application of M) v Sheffield Magistrates' Court*[19] the Administrative Court gave the following legal and practical guidance:

- A decision to apply for an anti-social behaviour order is a decision within the meaning of Children Act 1989 s22(4), which requires the authority to ascertain the 'wishes and feelings of the child and any person who is not a parent but has a parental responsibility for him/her and any other person whose wishes and feelings the authority considers to be relevant'. This duty can be discharged by officers who are discharging care duties for the child in question, taking the necessary steps and reporting in full to the authority.

- The material should be prepared and presented not as though it is for report for the anti-social behaviour order panel, but as a report for the authority on behalf of the child. The anti-social behaviour order panel should consider the material before it proceeds to make an application to the court. This is because considerations to which section 22(4) will give rise are likely to be relevant to the question whether it is necessary to apply for an anti-social behaviour order.

- If, having seen the full report, the 'lead' section of the authority decides to apply for an order, that decision must be communicated to all concerned. The social worker responsible for the child should not participate in the decision to apply for an order.

- The social services workers for the authority should be available to assist and be witnesses at court, if requested, as witnesses for the child. No court should (save where exceptional circumstances prevail) make an order against a child in care without someone from the social services who can speak to the issue.

- Where social services wish to support an application for an anti-social behaviour order, after detailed consideration with the child and relevant persons, different considerations may apply.

- The solicitor having responsibility for the authority's anti-social behaviour order application should not attend meetings with the child's solicitor and social services representatives. The need for an attendance of a solicitor for the officer should be rare.

- Once a decision has been taken to apply for an anti-social behaviour order, there should be no contact on the issue between the anti-social behaviour team and the social services section without the solicitor for the child being informed and consenting.

19 [2004] EWHC 1830 (Admin), at [49]–[53].

Applying for an order

29.25   The application for an anti-social behaviour order is made to the adult magistrates' court. An application for a stand-alone order cannot be made to a youth court. A separate application must be made against each named individual. The application must be in writing and in the prescribed form.[20] The application will be in the form of summons, and must be served on the person against whom the application is made. It should be served in person or sent by first class post to his/her last known address. A person with parental responsibility should also receive a copy of the summons. A parent or guardian may be required to attend the hearing and will be required to do so if the application is made in relation to a child or young person under the age of 16 years.[21]

29.26   The complaint leading to issue of the summons must be made within six months from the time when the final act of anti-social behaviour is said to have taken place.[22]

29.27   If the defendant does not attend court, a warrant for his/her arrest may be issued provided the complaint has been substantiated on oath.[23] The court may proceed in the defendant's absence,[24] although in practice this is uncommon. In either case the court must be satisfied that the summons was served upon the defendant within a reasonable time of the hearing.

The tests

29.28   In considering an application for an order, the court will be considering the following questions:

- Has the defendant acted in an anti-social manner to one or more persons not at the same household as him/herself?
- If so, is an order necessary to protect persons (whether relevant persons or persons elsewhere in England and Wales) from further anti-social acts by him/her?

What is anti-social behaviour?

29.29   'Anti-social behaviour' is defined in Crime and Disorder Act 1998 s1(1)(a) as:

> acting ... in a manner that caused or is likely to cause harassment, alarm or distress to one or more persons not at the same household as himself.

29.30   It is likely that these words will be given their ordinary natural meaning by the courts. Whether the conduct of an individual, on one or more than one occasion, amounts to anti-social behaviour will be a question of fact to be decided by the court.[25] This may be measured by the effect that the

---

20   Magistrates' Court (Anti-social Behaviour Orders) Rules 2002, SI No 2784.
21   Children and Young Persons Act 1933 s34A.
22   Magistrates' Courts Act 1980 s127.
23   Ibid, s55.
24   Ibid, s55(1).
25   *R v Manchester Crown Court ex p McCann, Clingham v Kensington and Chelsea Royal Borough Council* [2002] UKHL 39; [2002] 3 WLR 1313; [2002] 4 All ER 593, HL.

behaviour has, or is likely to have, on members of the community where the behaviour takes place. The behaviour alleged may or may not also constitute criminal activity.[26]

29.31 The scope of behaviour which is likely to be considered to be anti-social has been considered by the courts in a number of appeals in relation to the terms of orders made by lower courts (see paras 29.95 to 29.104).

Burden and standard of proof

29.32 The proceedings are civil but the applicant must prove, evidentially and legally, beyond reasonable doubt that the defendant has acted in an anti-social manner – namely in a manner that caused or was likely to cause harassment, alarm or distress. The standard of proof is to the criminal standard.[27] The statute does not require the applicant to show that the defendant intended their behaviour to be anti-social. The necessity test is not subject to the same considerations and is dealt with below.

Defence of reasonableness

29.33 When considering whether the grounds for an anti-social behaviour order are made out, the court shall disregard any act of the defendant which s/he shows was reasonable in the circumstances.[28]

Nature of evidence

29.34 The evidence relied on may vary considerably depending on the nature of the behaviour alleged and the circumstances in which it is said to have taken place. It may come from lay and professional witnesses. The joint Home Office, Association of Chief Police Officers and Youth Justice Board guide gives the following examples of evidence which may be relied on:

- breach of an acceptable behaviour contract;
- witness statements of officers who attended incidents;
- witness statements of people affected by the behaviour;
- evidence of complaints recorded by police, housing providers or other agencies;
- statements from professional witnesses, for example council officials, health visitors or truancy officers;
- video or CCTV evidence;
- supporting statements or reports from other agencies;
- previous successful civil proceedings which are relevant;
- previous relevant convictions; and
- information from witness diaries.[29]

---

26 *R v Manchester Crown Court ex p McCann*, n25, para 22.

27 Ibid.

28 Crime and Disorder Act 1998 s1(5).

29 Home Office, Association of Chief Police Officers and the Youth Justice Board, *A guide to anti-social behaviour orders and acceptable behaviour contracts*, March 2003 pp27 and 28.

29.35 The guide emphasises the importance of avoiding elaborate court files and focusing on what is most relevant and necessary to provide sufficient evidence for the court to arrive at a clear understanding of the issues. As the evidence being presented to the court will include the information being submitted in support of both the evidential and necessity tests, the distinction as to which evidence is to support which test is frequently not clearly made.

29.36 This is illustrated by the fact that incidents pre-dating the six-month time limit on applications by way of complaint in the magistrates' court under their civil jurisdiction may show a course of conduct and might be admitted in evidence to show the necessity of making an order.[30] Special measures are now available for witnesses.[31]

Hearsay evidence and weight

29.37 The purpose of the proceedings is preventative and as the proceedings are civil, hearsay evidence is admissible.[32] It is intended that hearsay and professional witness evidence will allow for the identities of those too fearful to give evidence to be protected.[33]

29.38 The types of hearsay evidence on which it is envisaged an applicant is likely to rely are:

- a signed and dated statement from a witness giving a direct account of events. This may also be accompanied by a statement from the witness stating that s/he is too frightened to attend court;
- an anonymous statement from a witness, giving a direct account of events and stating the reasons for not attending court or wishing to be identified;
- direct evidence from a professional witness telling the court what an identified (or anonymous) witness has told him/her and why that witness will not attend court.

29.39 In some cases the applicant may seek to rely on multiple hearsay by seeking to adduce the evidence of professional witnesses who give details of anonymous witnesses without calling the professional witness to give evidence. The Home Office guide emphasises that hearsay evidence should be relevant and should include specific details of dates, places, times and actions.

29.40 Hearsay notices put the other side on notice of the intention to adduce hearsay evidence and are used to try to give greater weight to hearsay evidence. The Magistrates' Courts (Hearsay Evidence in Civil Proceedings) Rules 1999[34] set out the requirements of hearsay notices and the power of the court to allow another party to call and cross-examine a witness in

---

30 *Stevens v South East Surrey Magistrates' Court* [2004] EWHC 1456 (Admin).
31 Crime and Disorder Act 1998 s1I as inserted by Serious Organised Crime and Police Act 2005 s143.
32 *R v Manchester Crown Court ex p McCann, Clingham v Kensington and Chelsea Royal Borough Council* [2002] UK HL 39; [2002] 3 WLR 1313; [2002] 4 All ER 593, HL.
33 Home Office, Association of Chief Police Officers and the Youth Justice Board, *A guide to anti-social behaviour orders and acceptable behaviour contracts*, March 2003 p28.
34 SI No 681.

relation to whom a hearsay notice is served. The Criminal Procedure Rules 2005 do not apply to applications for anti-social behaviour orders.[35]

29.41 The weight to be given to hearsay evidence is dealt with in Civil Evidence Act 1995 s4 which provides:

> In estimating the weight (if any) to be given to hearsay evidence in civil proceedings the court shall have regard to any circumstances from which any inference can reasonably be drawn as to the reliability or otherwise of the evidence.

> Regard may be had, in particular, to the following:
> (a) whether it would have been reasonable and practicable for the party by whom the evidence was adduced to have produced the maker of the original statement as a witness;
> (b) whether the original statement was made contemporaneously with the occurrence or existence of the matters stated;
> (c) whether the evidence involves multiple hearsay;
> (d) whether any person involved had any motive to conceal or misrepresent matters;
> (e) whether the original statement was an edited account, or was made in collaboration with another or for a particular purpose;
> (f) whether the circumstances in which the evidence is adduced as hearsay are such as to suggest an attempt to prevent proper evaluation of its weight.

29.42 The fact that there is no possibility of cross-examination in some circumstances does not automatically mean that the trial is unfair and contrary to Article 6 (right to a fair trial) of the European Convention on Human Rights. The court will have to consider the appropriate weight to give to the evidence in the light of the criticisms that can be made of hearsay evidence.[36]

Finding of facts

29.43 The forms to be used in the application for and making of anti-social behaviour orders are set out in the Schedules to the Magistrates' Courts (Anti-social Behaviour Orders) Rules 2002.[37]

29.44 They include provision for the setting out of the acts alleged by the applicant and the facts found by the court. This part of the procedure is important and the lack of similar provision in the Crown Court has caused the Court of Appeal concern.[38]

Necessity of an order

29.45 Once an applicant has shown beyond reasonable doubt that the person has acted in an anti-social manner, the court must determine whether the order is necessary to protect 'relevant persons' from further anti-social acts. 'Relevant persons' are defined as persons in the local government area, the police area or elsewhere in England and Wales.[39]

---

35 *R v W and F* [2006] EWCA Crim 686.

36 *R v Crown Court at Manchester ex p McCann, Clingham v Kensington and Chelsea Royal Borough Council* [2002] UKHL 39; [2002] 3 WLR 131; [2002] 4 All ER 593, HL.

37 SI No 2784.

38 *R v W and F* [2006] EWCA Crim 686.

39 Crime and Disorder Act 1998 s1(1B) and (6).

29.46   The test is an 'exercise of judgement or evaluation' rather than a test to which the civil or criminal standard is applied.[40] There is an element of looking into the future and considering whether past behaviour is likely to be repeated and would lead to further anti-social conduct. The considerations for the court in considering the necessity of an order are wide, and in relation to a child or young person the authors suggest that the court could be asked to consider the following:

- Has an acceptable behaviour contract been tried?
- Had the child or young person been assessed as a 'child in need'?
- Have appropriate services/support been offered to the child or young person and his/her family?
- Have substantial changes taken place in the circumstances of the child since the application was made?

29.47   The best interests of the young defendant are a primary consideration when determining whether to make an anti-social behaviour order.[41] Where the conduct complained of has ceased prior to the making of an order, an order can still be made.[42]

29.48   The 'necessity' test in relation to a post-conviction anti-social behaviour order is considered at paras 29.83–29.85. Many of the appeals relating to anti-social behaviour orders have examined the details of the terms imposed and whether they were necessary. These are discussed further at paras 29.88 to 29.104.

Length of the order

29.49   An anti-social behaviour order shall have a minimum length of two years and there is no maximum period.[43] The considerations of the court when deciding on the length of the order are dealt with below at paras 29.86 and 29.87.

Terms of the order

29.50   The terms of the order are decided by the court. There have been a number of decisions of the Divisional Court and the Court of Appeal in relation to the nature of the terms to be included in an order. These decisions are dealt with in paras 29.95–29.104 below.

Interim orders

29.51   Pending the determination of the main application for an anti-social behaviour order, the court may make an interim order if it considers that it is just to do so.[44] An interim order is for a fixed period and may be varied, renewed or discharged. It shall cease to have effect on the determination

---

40   *R v Crown Court Act Manchester ex p McCann, Clingham v Kensington and Chelsea Royal Borough Council* [2002] UKHL 39; [2002] 3 WLR 1313; [2002] 4 All ER 593, HL.
41   *R (Kenny and M) v Leeds Magistrates' Court* [2003] EWHC 2963.
42   *S v Poole Borough Council* [2002] EWHC 244 (Admin).
43   Crime and Disorder Act 1998 s1(7).
44   Ibid, s1D.

of the main application. An application for an interim order may be made without notice, with the leave of the justices' clerk.[45] Leave shall only be granted if the justices' clerk is satisfied that it is necessary for the application to be made without notice being given to the defendant.[46] The justices' clerk is likely to have regard to the nature of the behaviour alleged and the urgency of the situation in deciding whether to allow the interim application to be made without notice.[47]

29.52   There is nothing inherently unlawful in interim orders made without notice and the fact that criminal sanctions are attached to breach of an anti-social behaviour order does not render the procedure for interim orders without notice unlawful.[48] An interim order made without notice only takes effect when served upon the defendant and must be served personally on him/her. It shall cease to have effect, if not served, within seven days.[49]

29.53   The test to be applied in determining an application for an interim order is whether 'it is just to make an order under this section pending the determination of [the main] application'.[50] The court will consider the material relied upon by the parties seeking the interim order and any evidence or submissions made on behalf of the defendant, if the application is on notice. The burden is on the party seeking the order to demonstrate that it is just for there to be an interim order until the hearing of the main application.[51]

29.54   Consideration of whether it is just to make an order without notice is a balancing exercise. The court must balance the need to protect the public against the impact that the order sought will have on the defendant. It will need to consider the seriousness of the behaviour alleged, the urgency with which it is necessary to take steps to control such behaviour, and whether it is necessary for orders to be made without notice in order for them to be effective. The court will balance these considerations with the degree to which the order will impede the defendant's rights as a free citizen to go where s/he pleases and to associate with whosoever s/he pleases.[52]

29.55   The court does not have to apply the criminal standard of proof to the evidence being adduced, which may include hearsay evidence. The joint Home Office, Association of Chief Police Officers and Youth Justice Board guide suggests that the court determining the application for the interim order will consider whether the application for the full order is properly made and whether there is sufficient evidence of an urgent need to protect the community.[53] The court will need to consider carefully the evidence brought before it. In the case of *R (Kenny and M) v Leeds Magistrates' Court*[54] the Administrative Court decided that the District Judge who had dealt

---

45 Magistrates' Courts (Anti-social Behaviour Order) Rules 2002 r5(1).

46 Ibid, r5(2).

47 *R (Kenny) v Leeds Magistrates' Court* [2003] EWHC 2963 at [36].

48 Ibid, at [24].

49 Magistrates' Courts (Anti-social Behaviour Order) Rules 2002 r5(4) and (5).

50 Crime and Disorder Act 1998 s1D(2).

51 *R (Kenny) v Leeds Magistrates' Court* [2003] EWHC 2963.

52 Ibid, para 38.

53 Home Office, Association of Chief Police Officers and the Youth Justice Board, *A guide to anti-social behaviour orders and acceptable behaviour contracts* (March 2003) p19. This cn be downloaded from www.crimereduction.gov.uk.

54 [2003] EWHC 2963.

with the original applications for interim orders without notice had applied the appropriate test and, in carrying out the balancing exercise inherent in that test, had taken account of the relevant considerations. However, a close examination of the evidence in that case did not allow the conclusion that it was just to make an interim order.

29.56   Where a defendant is under the age of 18 years, the court must have regard to the principle that his/her best interests are a primary consideration when addressing the question of whether it is just to make an order.[55]

29.57   Where an interim order is granted without notice, the court will usually arrange an early return date. Where the court refuses to make an interim order without notice, it may direct that the application be made on notice.[56]

Discharge or variation of an interim order

29.58   An application can be made to vary or discharge an interim order and the appropriate forms are contained in the Magistrates' Courts (Anti-social Behaviour Orders) Rules 2002. If an interim order is made without notice and the defendant subsequently applies to the court for the order to be varied or discharged, the application to do so shall not be dismissed without the opportunity for him/her to make oral representations to the court.[57]

Making the full order

29.59   A copy of the order may be served on the defendant by post.[58] As the order needs to be understood by the defendant, it is good practice to announce the reasons for it being made and the terms of the order in open court. The courts have emphasised the importance of clarity of terms. Where the defendant's first language is not English, consideration should be given to translating the order where necessary.[59]

Applications to vary or discharge a full order

29.60   Except with the consent of both parties, no order can be discharged before the end of the period of two years beginning with the date of service of the order.[60] The application to vary or discharge is made on complaint and the application must specify the reasons that the order should be varied or discharged. The application is made on a form contained in the Magistrates' Courts (Anti-social Behaviour Orders) Rules 2002. Where the court considers that there are no grounds upon which it might conclude that the order should be varied or discharged, it may determine the application without hearing representations.[61]

---

55   [2003] EWHC 2963 para 42.
56   Magistrates' Courts (Anti-social Behaviour Orders) Rules 2002 r5(7).
57   Ibid, r5(8).
58   Ibid, r7(1).
59   See para 29.92 below.
60   Crime and Disorder Act 1998 ss1(9).
61   Magistrates' Courts (Anti-social Behaviour Orders) Rules 2002 r6.

Parenting orders

29.61 When an anti-social behaviour order is made in relation to a young person aged 16 years or under, the court must make a parenting order in respect of his/her parents if it considers that such an order will be desirable in the interests of preventing repetition of the behaviour which led to the making of the anti-social behaviour order. If the court does not make a parenting order in these circumstances, then it must give its reasons in open court.[62] Parenting orders are dealt with in chapter 31.

Individual support orders

29.62 Anti-social behaviour orders are preventative and therefore can only contain prohibitions.[63] In some cases the court may wish to place some positive requirements upon the young person. Where a court makes an anti-social behaviour order on a person aged 16 years or under it must also consider whether an individual support order should be made.[64] Before making an individual support order the court shall obtain from a social worker of the local authority social services department or a member of the youth offending team any information which it considers necessary to determine whether the individual support conditions are fulfilled or what requirements should be imposed by any individual support order.[65] As part of this assessment, it is submitted that the local authority should consider whether the young person is a child in need and, if so, what services should be provided to the young person and his/her family (see paras 3.20–3.34).

Pre-conditions

29.63 The conditions for the making of an individual support order are that:
- an individual support order would be desirable in the interests of preventing any repetition of the kind of behaviour which led to the making of the anti-social behaviour order;
- the defendant is not already subject to an individual support order; and
- the court has been notified by the secretary of state that arrangements for implementing individual support orders are available in the area in which the young person resides or will reside.[66]

Requirements

29.64 An individual support order will require the child or young person, for a period not exceeding six months, to comply with the requirements specified in the order and any directions given by a 'responsible officer'. The requirements may include:
- participation in specified activities;

---

62 Crime and Disorder Act 1998 s8(1b) as inserted by Anti-social Behaviour Act 2003 s85(8).
63 Ibid, s1(4).
64 Ibid, ss1AA and 1AB, inserted by Criminal Justice Act 2003 ss322 and 323.
65 Ibid, s1AA(9).
66 Ibid, s1AA(3).

- presenting him/herself to a specified person at places and times specified;
- complying with any arrangement for his/her education.[67]

29.65   The requirements or directions will not require the child or young person to attend on more than two days in any week.[68]

'Responsible officer'

29.66   A 'responsible officer' is defined by statute and means:

- a social worker of a local authority social services department; or
- a person nominated by the chief education officer under Education Act 1996 s532; or
- a member of the youth offending team.[69]

Procedural requirements

29.67   If the court is not satisfied that the conditions for the making of an individual support order are fulfilled, it should state this in open court and give reasons.[70]

Breach of order

29.68   Breach of an individual support order is a criminal offence punishable:

- if aged 14 years or over, on the date of conviction a fine not exceeding £1,000.
- if aged under 14 on the date of conviction a fine not exceeding £250.[71]

Termination of order

29.68A   Any individual support order will cease to have effect if the anti-social behaviour order to which it was linked ceases to have effect.[72]

Reporting restrictions

29.69   There is no restriction on the reporting of proceedings in the adult magistrates' court unless an order is made under Children and Young Persons Act 1933 s39. This section gives the court a discretionary power to impose reporting restrictions to prevent publication of anything that might lead to the identification of the young person involved in the proceedings. The provisions of Children and Young Persons Act 1933 s49, which impose automatic restrictions in the youth court, do not apply. Each case has to be considered in its own particular facts. The court must conduct a balancing exercise weighing up the considerations relating to the desirability of disclosure in the public interests against the welfare of the young person.[73]

---

67   Crime and Disorder Act 1998 s11AA(6).
68   Ibid, s11AA(7).
69   Ibid, s1AA(10).
70   Ibid, s4.
71   Ibid, s1AB(3).
72   Ibid, s1AB(5).
73   *Keating v Knowsley Metropolitan Borough Council* [2004] EWHC 1933 (Admin).

29.70   Where a court is asked to impose reporting restrictions, or to lift exist-ing reporting restrictions, the relevant considerations are:

- the welfare of the child or young person under Children and Young Persons Act 1933 s44;
- considerable weight should be given to the age of the young person and the potential damage caused by public identification;
- whether there are good reasons for naming the young person;
- the deterrent effect of being identified;
- the desire for open justice;
- the stage in the proceedings, as during interim proceedings no find-ings of fact may have been made;
- where an appeal has been made it may be relevant.[74]

29.71   Publicising the existence of an anti-social behaviour order engages Article 8 (right to respect for private and family life) of the European Convention on Human Rights, particularly where photographs taken by police, using their powers under the Police and Criminal Evidence Act 1984, are used. Publicity following the making of an anti-social behaviour order should be confined to what is reasonable and proportionate in the circumstances. In the case of serious anti-social behaviour by a group of teenagers over a considerable period of time, it was reasonable to publicise the making of orders by means of publication of their photographs along with their names and partial addresses.[75]

29.72   The defence lawyer needs to be prepared to argue for the imposition of restrictions, certainly until the final hearing of an application for an anti-social behaviour order, and in many circumstances following the making of a final order, using the welfare principle and the particular circumstanc-es of the young person.

Anti-social behaviour order on conviction

When an order can be made

29.73   An anti-social behaviour order can be made following conviction in the magistrates' court, youth court and Crown Court. In some cases, the local authority or Crown prosecutor will ask the court to consider the making of such an order following conviction. The court, however, can raise the issue of its own motion.[76] The order is in addition to a sentence imposed for the offence and this includes a conditional discharge.[77]

Adjourning the proceedings

29.74   The court may adjourn any proceedings in relation to the making of an anti-social behaviour order on conviction in criminal proceedings, even after sentencing. If the defendant does not appear for any adjourned

---

74 *R (T) v St Albans Crown Court* [2002] EWHC 1129 (Admin).
75 *R (Stanley) Metropolitan Police Commissioner and London Borough of Brent* [2004] EWHC 2229 (Admin).
76 Crime and Disorder Act 1998 s1C.
77 Ibid, s1C(4).

proceedings, the court may further adjourn the proceedings or issue a warrant for his/her arrest. The court may not issue a warrant unless it is satisfied that there has been adequate notice to the defendant of the time and place of the adjourned proceedings.[78]

Interim orders

29.75   If the court decides to adjourn the proceedings it may impose an interim order if it considers it just to do so.[79] In the view of the authors, the considerations for the court will be as set out in paras 29.51–29.57 above. The court may have decided some issues of fact as the consideration of an order arises following a conviction.

Procedure

29.76   Unlike the stand-alone order discussed above, there is no specific procedure for the making of an order following conviction. The court will have heard evidence in a trial, or in relation to a plea of guilty, and it can also consider evidence led by any applicant or the defendants themselves. It is immaterial whether that evidence would have been admissible in the proceedings in which the child or young person was convicted.[80]

The tests

29.77   Before making a post-conviction anti-social behaviour order, the court must be satisfied that:

- the offender has acted in a manner that caused or was likely to cause harassment, alarm or distress to one or more persons not at the same household as him/herself; and
- an order is necessary to protect persons in any place in England and Wales from further anti-social act by him/her.[81]

29.78   This is substantially the same test as for stand-alone applications.

Hearsay evidence

29.79   The consideration of an anti-social behaviour order following conviction is not part of the sentencing process. The proceedings are civil and not criminal, therefore hearsay evidence is admissible.[82] In the magistrates' court the same considerations apply in relation to the service of notices under the Magistrates' Courts (Hearsay Evidence in Civil Proceedings) Rules 1999 as apply in stand-alone applications.[83]

---

78   Crime and Disorder Act 1998 s1C(4A), (4B), (4C) as inserted by Serious Organised Crime and Police Act 2005 s139.

79   Ibid, s1D(1) and (2) as inserted by Serious Organised Crime and Police Act 2005 s139.

80   Ibid, s1C.

81   Ibid, s1C(2).

82   *R v W and F* [2006] EWCA Crim 686, following *R v Crown Court at Manchester ex p McCann, Clingham v Kensington and Chelsea Royal Borough Council* [2002] UKHL 39; [2002] 3 WLR 1313; [2002] 4 All ER 593, HL, and *W (a juvenile) v Acton Youth Court* [2005] EWHC 954 (Admin).

83   See para 29.40.

29.80   In the Crown Court the procedure for serving and adducing evidence in support of the application is not expressly governed by any one set of court rules. The Civil Evidence Act 1995 applies.[84] The use of hearsay evidence is dealt with more fully in paras 29.37 to 29.42 above.

Standard of proof

29.81   The standard of proof is to the criminal standard and is the same as in stand-alone applications (see para 29.32 above).

Findings of fact

29.82   The findings of fact which give rise to the making of the order must be recorded by the court. In the magistrates' court this is done on the form in the Magistrates' Court (Anti-social Behaviour Orders) Rules 2002. In the Crown Court the form on which this must be done is in the Consolidated Criminal Practice Direction.[85] In *R v W and F*[86] the Court of Appeal emphasised the importance of this part of the process. The findings of fact are likely to form the basis of the terms of the order.

Necessity of an order

29.83   In an application for an anti-social behaviour order following conviction the sentence of the court will be a relevant consideration in deciding whether an order is necessary. The court should not make an anti-social behaviour order where the underlying objective was to give the court higher sentencing powers in the event of future similar offending.[87] The making of an anti-social behaviour order should not be a normal part of the sentencing process where the case itself did not involve intimidation, harassment, alarm and distress.[88] The purpose of an anti-social behaviour order is not to punish an offender.[89] The court may have regard to the totality of the defendant's behaviour. It is not necessary to make an order not to commit a specified criminal offence if the sentence which could be passed on conviction for the offence should be sufficient deterrent.[90] Anti-social behaviour orders have serious consequences and all applications must be dealt with in a fair and thorough manner.[91]

29.84   Each case turns on its own facts, but it may be arguable that an anti-social behaviour order was not necessary, having regard to the fact that the custodial sentence would be effective.[92] It may be appropriate to make an order notwithstanding the imposition of a substantial custodial sentence.[93]

---

84 *R v W and F* [2006] EWCA Crim 686, at [34[–][36].

85 Annexe D.

86 [2006] EWCA Crim 686, at [41].

87 *C v Sunderland Youth Court* [2003]EWHC 2385 (Admin), *R v Kirby* [2005] EWCA Crim 1228, approved in *R v Boness and others* [2005] EWCA Crim 2395.

88 *R v Kirby* [2005] EWCA Crim 1228 at [11].

89 *R v Boness and others* [2005] EWCA Crim 2395 at [30].

90 Ibid, para [31].

91 *C v Sunderland Youth Court* [2003] EWHC 2385 (Admin).

92 Ibid.

93 *R v Vittles* [2005] 1 Cr App R (S) 31 (8) CA.

29.85   The decisions of the courts, dealt with at paras 29.94 to 29.104 below, illustrate that there can be considerable overlap between the necessity of an order and the appropriateness of its terms.

Length of the order

29.86 An anti-social behaviour order has a minimum length of two years and there is no maximum period.[94] An order comes into effect on the day it is made. The court may suspend any requirements of the order during periods of custody, until release.[95] Where a custodial sentence of more than a few months is passed and the offender was liable to release on licence, a geographical restraint contained in an order could properly supplement the licence in some circumstances.[96]

29.87   The courts have taken the view on a number of occasions that the age of the young person made subject to an order is a consideration in deciding the appropriate length, eg *R v H, Stevens and Lovegrove*.[97]

Terms of the order

29.88 The prohibitions that may be imposed are those necessary for the purpose of protecting persons in England and Wales from further anti-social acts by the defendant. The terms of the order must be proportionate, in that they must be commensurate with the risk to be guarded against. This is particularly important where an order may interfere with Articles 8 (right to respect for private and family life), 10 (freedom of expression) or 11 (freedom of assembly and association) of the European Convention on Human Rights.[98]

29.89   Each case must be analysed on its own facts and the prohibitions directed to the behaviour causing harassment, alarm or distress in that particular case. The terms of the order must be:

- clear and easily understood;
- enforceable;
- commensurate with the seriousness of the offence;
- commensurate with the risk of future conduct.[99]

29.90 While an order may last a minimum of two years, not all the terms in the order need to do so.[100]

29.91   The joint Home Office, Association of Chief Police Officers and Youth Justice Board guide suggests to applicants for orders that the terms proposed to the court should:

- cover the range of anti-social acts committed;
- be reasonable and proportionate;
- be realistic and practical;

94 Crime and Disorder Act 1998 s1(7) and s1C(a).
95 Ibid, s1C(5).
96 *R v P (Shane Tony)* [2004] EWCA Crim 284 at [35]; [2004] 2 Cr App R (S) 63 (343).
97 [2006] EWCA Crim 255.
98 *R v Boness and others* [2005] EWCA Crim 2395 at [38].
99 Ibid, approving *R v McGrath* [2005] EWCA Crim 353.
100 *R (Longergan) v Lewes Crown Court* [2005] 2 All ER 362.

- be clear, concise and easy to understand;
- be specific when referring to curfews or area restrictions, using a map where it assists;
- be in terms which make it easy to determine and prosecute a breach.[101]

29.92 A working group chaired by Thomas LJ for the Judicial Studies Board has issued *Anti-social behaviour order guidance for the judiciary*[102] in which elements of good practice adopted by the courts when dealing with the terms of an anti-social behaviour order are identified. This good practice has been approved in the leading case of *R v Boness and others*[103]and may be expressed as follows:

- the prohibition should be capable of being easily understood by the defendant;
- the condition should be enforceable in the sense that it should allow a breach to be readily identified and capable of being proved;
- exclusion zones should be clearly delineated with the use of clearly marked maps;
- individuals whom the defendant is prohibited from contacting or associating with should be clearly identified;
- in the case of a foreign national, consideration should be given to the need for the order to be translated.

29.93 Where an order is to be made, the defence lawyer should take full and detailed instructions on the likely impact on the defendant of proposed terms. This information will be needed by the court in finalising the terms of the order.

29.94 There have been a number of appeals relating to the making of and terms contained in anti-social behaviour orders, and the decisions in some of those cases are reviewed below. Recurring in the decided cases is the importance of the following:

- the terms imposed must be necessary;
- the terms must relate to the behaviour found by the court to have taken place;
- the terms must be clear and proportionate;
- the prohibitions must be tailor-made to the facts of the case and the circumstances of the offender;
- the court should not rubber-stamp the conditions proposed by an applicant local authority or police force, but give careful consideration to the terms of any order itself.

R v McGrath[104]

29.95 A defendant with an appalling record for car theft was made the subject of an anti-social behaviour order containing prohibitions preventing him

---

101 *A Guide to anti-social behaviour orders and acceptable behaviour contracts* (March 2003). See www.crimereduction.gov.uk.

102 June 2005. The document can be obtained from the websites of the Judicial Studies Board or the Youth Justice Board. See appendix 14 for contact details.

103 [2005] EWCA Crim 2395 at [23].

104 [2005] EWCA Crim 353.

from entering any car park in three named counties, preventing him from trespassing and preventing him from having in his possession tools or implements which could be used for breaking into motor vehicles. The Court of Appeal held that these terms were too wide and not justified.

R (on the application of W) v DPP[105]

29.96   A term in an anti-social behaviour order made in respect of a young offender prohibiting the offender from committing any criminal offence was held by the Divisional Court to be too wide and unenforceable. A general restriction was not necessary where specific behaviour restrictions were in place.

R v P (Shane Tony)[106]

29.97   A 15-year-old convicted of offences including robbery, assault and false imprisonment was made the subject of an order which included his exclusion from two parks and an airport. In the original judgment of Henriques J, the Court of Appeal appeared to doubt the relevance of an anti-social behaviour order to such offending. However, in the subsequent case of *R v Boness and others*[107] Hooper LJ commented on this case, stating that terms such as these in an order would give those responsible for the safety of the prescribed areas an opportunity to act before a robbery is committed by the offender.

R v Werner[108]

29.98   A defendant convicted of theft of credit cards and other items from hotel rooms and using the cards to obtain services and goods, was made the subject of an anti-social behaviour order prohibiting her from entering any hotel, guesthouse or similar premises anywhere within the Greater London area. The Court of Appeal commented that the forms of conduct which were envisaged in the Home Office guide as the kinds of behaviour that orders were intended to prevent were different in character from offences of dishonesty committed in private against individual victims. In *R v Boness and others*[109] it was observed that the main difficulty with the imposition of the prohibition in this case was its width, which would lead to difficulties in enforcement. As to whether an order was appropriate for this type of offending, the court seems to have taken the view that the facts of the offending might determine whether an order was necessary. If the offending had been in a limited number of establishments, it would be practical to supervise an order excluding her from them.

R v Boness and others[110]

29.99   This important case dealt with 11 co-joined appeals and reviewed and commented on a number of decided cases. It has been referred to and approved

105 [2005] EWCA Civ 1333.
106 [2004] EWCA Crim 284.
107 [2005] EWCA Crim 2395.
108 [2004] EWCA Crim 2931.
109 [2005] EWCA Crim 2395.
110 [2005] EWCA Crim 2395.

in subsequent appeals in the Court of Appeal. The principles confirmed and clarified are dealt with throughout the text of this chapter. The full judgment is essential reading to all practitioners in this area.

R v H, Stevens and Lovegrove[111]

29.100 A defendant who committed two offences of theft by shoplifting whilst on licence for supplying a class A drug should not have been made subject to an anti-social behaviour order prohibiting him from committing any act of theft and from entering a prescribed area. The offences of theft did not demonstrate that members of the public were likely to be harassed, distressed or alarmed by the behaviour and it was not necessary for the order to have been made. The terms of the order were not justified by the defendant's history or behaviour.

29.101   In a separate appeal heard at the same time, a 15-year-old with no previous convictions was sentenced to a period of detention for an offence of causing grievous bodily harm to a man who he believed to have committed sexual offences against children. The anti-social behaviour order imposed following conviction prevented contact with the victim and prohibited the defendant from entering an area, which included his family home, for a period of ten years. The Court of Appeal reduced the length of the order to five years 'to reflect a sufficient time for this young man to have reached the necessary level of maturity' and amended the area of exclusion. The court was concerned that the prospects of the defendant's successful rehabilitation would be reduced if he were unable to return home.

R (Mills) v Birmingham Magistrates' Court[112]

29.102 A defendant convicted of theft by shoplifting, with 86 previous convictions for similar offences, should not have been made subject to an anti-social behaviour order as the circumstances of the offending in this case was not likely to cause harassment, alarm or distress.

T v Crown Prosecution Service[113]

29.103 A 13-year-old had been made the subject of an anti-social behaviour order which included the term 'not to act in an anti-social manner in the City of Manchester'. The term was too vague and lacked clarity. It did not even include the explanatory words contained in the statutory definition. It lacked the essential element of clarity as to what the respondent was and was not permitted to do. The defendant was aged 13 to 15 years during the currency of the order and could not be taken to know the ambit of the words 'act in an anti-social manner'. He would probably not know the geographical ambit of the 'City of Manchester'.

29.104 In the view of the authors, this is an area of practice where the consideration of case-law is of great importance and the court may need to be referred to the text of individual judgments.

---

111 [2006] EWCA Crim 255.
112 [2005] EWHC 2732 (Admin).
113 [2006] EWHC 728 (Admin).

Making an order

29.105 The facts found by the court, the reasons for the order and its terms should be clearly stated by the court. The procedure adopted in some cases by magistrates' courts and Crown Courts has been criticised in a number of subsequent appeals.[114]

29.106 In *R v Parkin*[115] the Court of Appeal set out what should happen on the making of an order:

- the terms of the order must be precise and capable of being understood by the offender;
- findings of fact giving rise to the making of the order must be recorded;
- the order must be explained to the offender;
- the exact terms of the order must be pronounced in open court;
- the written order must accurately reflect the order pronounced.

29.107 The court should consider whether it should provide a copy of the order translated into the first language of the person to whom it relates.[116]

Parenting orders

29.108 There is an arguable position that the provisions of Crime and Disorder Act 1998 s8 do not apply where an order is made under section 1C.[117] In an application for an order following conviction, the court will have considered the necessity or otherwise of a parenting order as part of the sentencing process. This will mean that the question whether the provisions apply is an largely academic one.

Individual support orders

29.109 Similar arguments arise in relation to these orders.[118] Any sentence of the court on conviction is likely to involve some element of intervention from the youth offending team. It is therefore unlikely that an individual support order would be necessary in a post-conviction case.

29.110 It should be noted that the Youth Justice Board advice to practitioners states that the individual support order provisions do not apply to orders made post-conviction.[119] It is suggested that the provisions of Crime and Disorder Act 1998 s1AA only apply to orders made under section 1 and not under section 1C as this latter section refers to 'orders made following conviction to prevent anti-social behaviour'. However, for the reasons set out in the paragraph above, it is a largely academic argument for the purposes of the youth and Crown Courts.

---

114 For example, *C v Sunderland Youth Court* [2003] EWHC 2385 (Admin), *R v W and F* [2006] EWCA Crim 686.

115 [2004] EWCA Crim 287.

116 *R v Boness and others* [2005] EWCA Crim 2395. In Wales there is a duty under the Welsh Language Act 1993 to provide the document in Welsh. See chapter 2.

117 See para 29.14 above.

118 See para 29.14 above.

119 www.youth-justice-board.gov.uk/practitionersportal/preventionandinterventions/antisocialbehaviour/indidvidualsupportorders.

Reporting restrictions

29.111 The provisions of Children and Young Persons Act 1933 s49 which impose automatic reporting restrictions in the youth court, do not apply to the making of an anti-social behaviour order following conviction.[120] The court retains a discretionary power to restrict reporting under Children and Young Persons Act 1933 s39. See paras 29.69–29.72 above. It is submitted that the court will take account of similar matters as are considered in relation to civil applications.

Right of appeal

29.112 A defendant has a right of appeal against the making of an anti-social behaviour order. An appeal is made to the Crown Court.[121] Judicial review should not normally be used to challenge the grant of an order, including an interim order. Applications should first be made to the magistrates' court to vary or discharge an order, or appeal can be made to the Crown court.[122] On appeal to the Crown Court, the court has power to make any order which could be made by the magistrates' court. The right to appeal is not limited to the making of an order, but extends to the terms of the order. The Crown court can order reporting restrictions.[123]

Discharge or variation

29.113 The defendant or the applicant may apply by complaint to the court which made the anti-social behaviour order for it to be varied or discharged by a further order.[124] Except with the consent of both parties, no order shall be discharged before the end of the period of two years beginning with the date of service of the order.[125] Variation does not require the agreement of both parties. The procedure for discharge and variation of orders is covered by the Magistrates' Court (Anti-social Behaviour Order) Rules 2002.

Breach of an anti-social behaviour order

29.114 The breach of a condition of an anti-social behaviour order without reasonable excuse is a criminal offence. Where the defendant is under the age of 18 years s/he will be prosecuted in the youth court, regardless of which court originally made the order.

29.115 The penalties for breach of an order are:

- on a summary conviction, an adult can face imprisonment for up to six months and/or a fine not exceeding £5,000;

---

120 Crime and Disorder Act 1998 ss1C(9C)(b) and (10), inserted by Anti-social Behaviour Act 2003 s86(3) and (4).
121 Crime and Disorder Act 1998 s4.
122 *R (A) v Leeds Magistrates' Court* [2004] EWHC 554 (Admin).
123 Children and Young Persons Act 1933 s39.
124 Crime and Disorder Act 1998 s1(8).
125 Ibid, s1(9).

- on indictment, an adult can be sentenced to imprisonment for up to five years and/or a fine.[126]

29.116   The court may not conditionally discharge the defendant.[127] The effect of the specific provisions relating to children and young people is that the maximum sentence for breach of an anti-social behaviour order is a 24-month detention and a training order, where the defendant is aged 15 years or over or is aged 12–14 years and is a persistent offender.

29.117   A prosecution for an alleged breach of the requirements of an order is a matter for the police. The case will be referred to the Crown Prosecution Service and prosecuted in the same way as any other criminal allegation. Local authorities may prosecute breaches where the original proceedings were brought by them, although this is less common.

Legal representation

29.118   As proceedings in relation to breach of an anti-social behaviour order are criminal proceedings, a representation order may be granted by the court.

Evidence

29.119   A certified copy of the original order is admissible as evidence of the order having been made.[128] As proceedings are criminal, all the procedural and evidential provisions relating to criminal prosecutions apply.

Reasonable excuse

29.120   Acting under a reasonable misapprehension as to the scope and meaning of an order is capable of being a reasonable excuse for acting in a manner which is prohibited by the order. The issue is a question of fact.[129]

Sentencing for breach

29.121   A number of appeals against sentences imposed for breach of anti-social behaviour orders have reached the Court of Appeal and decisions which initially appeared to conflict have now been resolved. It is observed that the majority of these cases involve older offenders who have persistently breached anti-social behaviour orders.

29.122   A distinction can be drawn between cases where the breach involved further anti-social behaviour and cases where the breach involved the breaking of a prohibition, without further anti-social behaviour.[130] Where a breach does not involve further behaviour causing harassment, alarm or

---

126 Crime and Disorder Act 1998 s1(10).

127 Ibid, s1(11).

128 Ibid, s1(10C), inserted by Serious Organised Crime and Police Act 2005 s139.

129 *R v Evans (Dorothy)* [2005] 1 Cr App R 549 cited in *R v Nicholson* [2006], CA, 15 May.

130 *R v Lamb* [2005] EWCA Crim 3000, disapproving *R v Morrison* [2005] EWCA Crim 2237.

distress, a community order should be considered to assist the defendant to learn to live within the terms of the anti-social behaviour order.[131]

29.123   Persistent breaches without harassment, alarm or distress being caused may mean that it becomes necessary to impose a custodial sentence to 'preserve the authority of the court'. In these circumstances, custodial sentences should be kept as short as possible.[132] Where the breach amounts to further anti-social behaviour, the court will consider longer custodial sentences.[133] Any sentence given should be proportionate and reflect the impact of the anti-social behaviour. The court may wish to consider up-to-date pre-sentence reports. The court will also need to bear in mind the original reasons for the making of the order.

R v Braxton[134]

29.124   The defendant, who had numerous previous convictions, was subject to an order prohibiting him from entering Birmingham City for five years and from 'using or engaging in any threatening, abusive, offensive, intimidating, insulting language or behaviour or threatening or engaging in violence or damage against any person or property within the city centre'.

29.125   The first breach consisted of presence in the city and abusive and offensive language, but no actual violence. A four-year prison sentence was reduced to two years by the Court of Appeal. Three months after release, there were two further breaches which involved begging aggressively in the city centre. A three-and-a-half year sentence was upheld on appeal. The persistence of the conduct in breach of an order of the court and the protection of the public justified the sentence.

R v Tripp[135]

29.126   A sentence of eight months' imprisonment was substituted for the original sentence of 12 months' imprisonment by the Court of Appeal. The breach involved the defendant, when drunk, using abusive language to staff at a night shelter where he was known. He was subject to a community rehabilitation order and a conditional discharge at the time of sentence.

R v Lamb[136]

29.127   An 18-year-old defendant sentenced for three breaches of an anti-social behaviour order, none of which involved further anti-social behaviour, had a 22-month sentence reduced to two months' imprisonment to run consecutively on each breach. Leveson J disapproved the view expressed by Hughes J in *R v Morrison*[137] that if a breach is no more than a criminal offence for which the maximum penalty is prescribed by statute, it is

---

131   *R v Lamb* at [19].
132   Ibid.
133   Ibid, applying *R v Braxton* [2005] 1 Cr App R (S) 36, *R v Tripp* [2005] EWCA Crim 2253 and *R v Dickenson* [2005] 2 Cr App (S) 488.
134   [2005] 1 Cr App R (S) 167.
135   [2005] EWCA Crim 2253.
136   [2005] EWCA Crim 3000.
137   [2005] EWCA Crim 2237.

normally wrong in principle to pass a sentence for breach which exceeds the maximum sentence available for the substantive offence itself.

R v H, Stevens and Lovegrove[138]

29.128   The penalty for breach of an anti-social behaviour order is distinct from the sentence for any underlying offence and can, in an appropriate case, exceed the maximum sentence for that underlying offence.

Unenforceable conditions

29.129   In *R (on the application of W) v DPP*[139] Brooke LJ held that an a term in an anti-social behaviour order not to commit any criminal offence was plainly invalid and that on a prosecution for breach of that term a district judge was entitled to find that it was not a valid order.

29.130   In *T v Crown Prosecution Service*[140] this approach was criticised by Richards LJ, also in the Divisional Court. It was held that there was no power in a prosecution for breach to find a term of the original order invalid. The court could give effect to any concerns about the width and uncertainty of the order by considering whether the relevant provision lacked sufficient clarity to warrant a finding that the defendant's conduct amounted to a breach of the order; whether the lack of clarity provided a reasonable excuse for non-compliance with the order; and whether, if a breach was established, it was appropriate in the circumstances to impose any penalty for the breach.[141] There may be circumstances where it would be wrong in principle to impose any penalty additional to that imposed in respect of the underlying offence which led to a breach of an anti-social behaviour order.

29.131   This is an area where, in the view of the authors, the practitioner will be assisted by reading the relevant judgments.

Powers to remove truants to designated premises

29.132   The need to deal with the phenomenon of truancy has been explained by the government as follows:

> Failing to attend school regularly can have a major impact on children's education, their future and their life chances. Examination of data from 2004 shows a strong correlation between average absence levels in schools and their pupils' attainment. For example:
> - 88% of pupils gain 5 or more good GCSE grades at schools with average absence of 8 days or fewer per pupil. But only 26% at schools with average absence of more than 20 days per pupil, and
> - 86% of pupils reach Key Stage 2 Level 4 Maths in schools where pupils average fewer than 8 days absence a year but this drops to 57% in schools where average absence is more than 15 days.

138   [2006] EWCA Crim 255.
139   [2005] EWCA Civ 133.
140   [2006] EWHC 728 (Admin).
141   Ibid at [37].

The 2004 Youth Crime Survey showed that 45% of young people in mainstream education who have committed an offence say they have played truant from school, compared with just 18% who have not committed an offence. It also showed that 62% of 10-16 year olds who have committed criminal or anti-social behaviour have also truanted.[142]

29.133 Truancy patrols with education welfare officers and police officers working jointly have been a feature in some areas for a number of years. However, truancy is not an offence, and in reality police have had limited powers. Crime and Disorder Act 1998 s16 gives police officers the power to return truants to their schools or to other premises designated by the local authority.

Authorising the use of the power

29.134 The power to remove truants is not a power that may be exercised at any time. It may only be exercised when:
- the local authority have designated premises to which children and young persons may be taken;
- a police officer of at least the rank of superintendent has authorised the use of the power.[143]

29.135 In practice the power is only likely to be used for short periods of time when a campaign against truancy is to be mounted.

Exercising the power

29.136 A constable may remove a child or young person to designated premises or to the school from which the child or young person is absent if the constable has reasonable cause to believe that a child or young person found by him/her in a public place in a specified area during a specified period:
- is of compulsory school age; and
- is absent from a school without lawful authority.[144]

29.137 Although not specified in the Act, Department for Education and Skills guidance states that the power should be exercised by police officers in uniform, who, where practicable, should be accompanied by an education representative such as an education welfare officer.[145]

Compulsory school age

29.138 A person ceases to be of compulsory school age at the end of the school year in which s/he attains the age of 16. [146]

---

142 Department for Education and Skills, *Truancy Sweep Effective Practice and Advice* (July 2005). This can be downloaded from the dfes website.
143 Crime and Disorder Act 1998 s16(1), (2).
144 Ibid, s16(3).
145 Department for Education and Skills, *Truancy Sweep Effective Practice and Advice* (July 2005) paragraphs 13, 14 and 24.
146 Education Act 1996 s8.

Absent from school without lawful authority

29.139 A pupil's absence from a school shall be taken to be without lawful authority unless it falls within one of the reasons set out in Education Act 1996 s444, namely:

- leave;
- sickness;
- unavoidable cause; or
- day set apart for religious observance.[147]

29.140 Pupils on leave could include pupils on work experience placements arranged through the school and traveller children with leave of absence granted for purposes of travelling. Pupils excluded from school would be absent from school with authority and, therefore, not subject to the power to remove.

Designated premises

29.141 Designated premises could include the following:

- the school from which the child or young person is absent;
- the education welfare service office;
- offices within a shopping precinct maintained by the local education authority for the duration of the truancy operation.[148]

29.142 The designated premises will not include police stations.[149]

Public place

29.143 'Public place' has the same meaning as in Part II of the Public Order Act 1986.[150] This includes:

- any highway; and
- any place to which at the material time the public or a section of the public has access, on payment or otherwise, as of right or by virtue of express or implied permission.

29.144 This definition would include shopping centres, parks, amusements arcades and cinemas.

Reasonable force

29.145 Crime and Disorder Act 1998 s16 does not make truancy a criminal offence, nor does it create a power of arrest and detention. The government has, however, given some guidance on the use of force when exercising this power.

> [T]here may be occasional cases in which suspected truants refuse to comply. In such cases, if the police officer has reasonable grounds for believing that the child or young person is absent from school without authority, the power under

---

147 Crime and Disorder Act 1998 s16(4).
148 Department for Education and Skills, *Truancy Sweep Effective Practice and Advice* (July 2005) paragraph 37.
149 Ibid, paragraph 38.
150 Crime and Disorder Act 1998 s16(5).

section 16 will enable the officer to use such force as is necessary in the circumstances. What reasonable force might be will depend on the circumstances. It must be proportionate to the nature of the power and the behaviour of the child or young person concerned. If the child or young person resists with violence, that in itself might be an offence of assault and other powers would come into play.[151]

Child curfew schemes

29.146 The Home Office has explained the rationale for child curfew schemes as follows:

> The Government believes that early intervention before habits become ingrained and before a child has started to identify himself or herself as an offender will often be more effective than waiting until that child is old enough to end up in the criminal justice system.
>
> The Government believes that for a number of reasons children under the age of 10 should not be out late at night unsupervised. It may place them at risk and can create problems for the local community because such children, particularly when gathered in large groups, may become involved in anti-social or potentially criminal behaviour. Such behaviour should not be tolerated because people should have the right to live in a society which is safe and trouble free.[152]

29.147 Crime and Disorder Act 1998 s14 allows the police and local authorities to develop local child curfew schemes.

29.148 In consultation with the police and local community, a local authority or chief officer of police can produce a local child curfew scheme. Before a scheme may be implemented, it must be submitted to the Home Secretary for his/her approval. If the scheme is approved, the chief officer of police or local authority may impose a curfew notice.

Curfew notice

29.149 A curfew notice bans children of a specified age from being in a public place during specified hours unless they are under the effective control of a parent or a responsible person aged 18 or over.[153]

29.150 Any curfew notice shall be given by posting the notice in some conspicuous place or places within the specified area. The local authority may also use other means it considers desirable for giving publicity to the notice (eg leafleting local homes or advertising in the local news media).

Length of notice

29.151 A curfew notice may apply for a maximum of 90 days.[154]

---

151 Department for Education and Skills, *Truancy Sweep Effective Practice and Advice* (July 2005) paragraph 55.

152 Home Office, *Local Child Curfews Guidance Document* (July 2001) paragraphs 2.1 and 2.3. This guide can be downloaded from the Home Office website www.crimereduction.gov.uk.

153 Crime and Disorder Act 1998 s14(2).

154 Ibid, s14(1).

Applicable age

29.152 Child curfews are applicable to children up to the age of 16.

Specified hours

29.153 A child curfew notice may apply to any time period between the hours of 9.00 pm and 6.00 am.[155] The notice may specify different hours in relation to children of different ages.[156]

Public place

29.154 'Public place' has the same meaning as in Part II of the Public Order Act 1986.[157] This includes:

- any highway; and
- any place to which at the material time the public or a section of the public has access, on payment or otherwise, as of right or by virtue of express or implied permission.

Enforcement of the curfew

29.155 The Home Office suggests that the primary responsibility for enforcing a local child curfew will rest with the police, but that special operations in conjunction with the local authority and social services department might be mounted.

Removal of the child to his/her place of residence

29.156 Where a constable has reasonable cause to believe that a child is in contravention of a ban imposed by a curfew notice, s/he may remove the child to the child's place of residence unless s/he has reasonable cause to believe that the child would, if removed to that place, be likely to suffer significant harm.[158] Where the constable considers that significant harm is likely, s/he may take the child into police protection.[159]

Duty of local authority to investigate

29.157 Where a constable has reasonable cause to believe that a child is in contravention of a ban imposed by a curfew notice, s/he shall, as soon as practicable, inform the local authority for the area that the child has contravened the ban.[160] Upon receiving such notification, the social services department is under a duty to make such enquiries as they consider necessary to enable them to decide whether they should take action to promote the child's welfare.[161] Such enquiries must be commenced within 48 hours of the author-

---

155 Crime and Disorder Act 1998 s14(2).
156 Ibid, s14(6).
157 Ibid, s14(8).
158 Ibid, s15(1) and (3).
159 Children Act 1989 s46.
160 Crime and Disorder Act 1998 s15(1) and (2).
161 Children Act 1989 s47(1)(a)(iii) as inserted by Crime and Disorder Act 1998 s15(4).

ity receiving the notification from the police.[162] As a result of these enquiries, the social services department could offer support, or could apply to the family proceedings court for a child safety order (see below), or, if the threshold criteria are satisfied, a supervision or care order.

The child safety order

29.158　A child safety order places a child under the age of 10 under the supervision of a responsible officer and requires the child to comply with specified requirements. It is designed to protect children under 10 who are at risk of becoming involved in crime or who have already started to behave in an anti-social or criminal manner.[163] The provisions discussed in chapter 3 are likely to be of relevance to practitioners dealing with these orders.

29.159　　A court shall not make a child safety order unless it has been notified by the secretary of state that arrangements for implementing such orders are available in the area in which it appears to the court that the child resides or will reside, and the notice has not been withdrawn.

Applying for the order

29.160　To obtain a child safety order the local authority with social services responsibility must apply to a magistrates' court sitting as a family proceedings court.[164] The procedure is contained in the Family Proceedings Courts (Children Act 1989) Rules 1991.[165] The applications for child safety orders are not specified proceedings for the purposes of Children Act 1989 s41, consequently, the child is not a party to the proceedings and no children's guardian will be appointed. Notice of the application should be served on any person who is believed to have parental responsibility.

Grounds for an order

29.161　To make a child safety order, the court must be satisfied that one or more of the following conditions are fulfilled:

- the child has committed an act which, if s/he had been aged 10 or over, would have constituted an offence;
- a child safety order is necessary for the purpose of preventing the commission by the child of an offence;
- the child has contravened a ban imposed by a curfew notice; and
- the child has acted in a manner that caused or was likely to cause harassment, alarm or distress to one or more persons not of the same household as him/herself.[166]

162　Children Act 1989 s47(1)(a)(iii).
163　Home Office, *Child safety orders – guidance* (November 2005).
164　Crime and Disorder Act 1998 s11(6).
165　SI No 1395.
166　Crime and Disorder Act 1998 s11(3).

The hearing

29.162 Where the grounds for the application are contested by any of the parties present, the local authority must establish the grounds for the order to the civil burden of proof, namely on a balance of probabilities.[167]

29.163   Before making a child safety order, a court shall obtain and consider information about the child's family circumstances and the likely effect of the order on those circumstances.[168]

Length of the order

29.164 The maximum period permitted for a child safety order is normally three months.[169] Where the court is satisfied that the circumstances of the case are exceptional, the order may be for a maximum of 12 months.[170]

29.165   The Home Office provides the following advice:

> The local authority will need to provide compelling evidence to justify the making of a longer order given that three months' effective supervision in the life of a child under 10 is a substantial period which, if properly structured, should prove to be effective. By their nature, Acceptable circumstances cannot be precisely defined although these might arise in a situation where the child's actions would, if they had been committed by a child aged 10 or over, be criminally very serious.[171]

Responsible officer

29.166 A responsible officer may be one of the following:

- a social worker of a local authority social services department; or
- a member of a youth offending team.[172]

Requirements of the order

29.167 The requirements that may be specified are those which the court considers desirable in the interests of:

- ensuring that the child receives appropriate care, protection and support and is subject to proper control; or
- preventing any repetition of the kind of behaviour which led to the child safety order being made.[173]

29.168 The Home Office suggests that the order could include requirements that the child:

- attend school or extra-curricular activities;
- avoid contact with disruptive and possibly older children;
- does not attend certain places (such as shopping centres) unsupervised;

167 Crime and Disorder Act 1998 s11(6).
168 Ibid, s12(1).
169 Ibid, s11(4).
170 Ibid.
171 *Child safety orders – guidance*, para 6.2.
172 Crime and Disorder Act 1998 s11(8).
173 Ibid, s11(5).

- be at home during certain times, probably the evenings; or
- attend particular courses to address specific problems.[174]

29.169 The requirements specified in the order shall, as far as practicable, be such as to avoid:
- any conflict with the parent's religious beliefs; and
- any interference with the times at which the child normally attends school.[175]

29.170 There is no requirement to avoid a conflict with the child's religious beliefs where these are different from those of the parent with whom the child lives.

Procedural requirements

29.171 Before making the order, a court shall explain to the parent or guardian of the child in ordinary language:
- the effect of the order and the requirements proposed to be included in it;
- the consequences that may follow if the child fails to comply with the requirements of the order; and
- that the court may review the order on the application of the parent, guardian or responsible officer.[176]

29.172 The Home Office suggests that, where appropriate, the order should also be explained to the child.[177] Unless family proceedings courts change their practice regarding the attendance at court of children under the age of 10, it is unlikely that this possibility will arise.

Parenting order

29.173 When making a child safety order, the court may also make parenting order.[178]

Discharge or variation

29.174 The court which made the order may discharge or vary the order on the application of either the parent or guardian of the child or the responsible officer.[179] When varying the order, the court may delete a requirement or insert a new condition (either in addition to or in substitution of an existing provision) that could have been included when the court made the order.[180] The procedure for an application to vary or discharge the order is

---

174 *Child safety orders – guidance*, para 4.26.
175 Crime and Disorder Act 1998 s12(3).
176 Ibid, s12(2).
177 *Child safety orders – guidance*, para 4.23.
178 Crime and Disorder Act 1998 s8(1)(a) and (2). See chapter 31.
179 Ibid, s12(4).
180 Ibid.

covered by the Magistrates' Courts (Miscellaneous Amendments) Rules 1998.[181]

29.175   Home Office guidance suggests that orders may be varied where:

- the child moves;
- the requirements are not effective in meeting the objectives of the order;
- the child has made good progress.[182]

29.176   Where a court dismisses an application for discharge, no further application to discharge the order may be made except with the consent of the court which made the order.[183]

Breach of the requirements of the order

29.177   Where a child safety order is in force and it is proved to the satisfaction of the court which made the order, or another magistrates' court acting for the same petty sessions area, on the application of the responsible officer, that the child has failed to comply with any requirement included in the order, the court may:

- vary the order (by cancelling any provision or by inserting any provision that could have been included in the order if the court had then had power to make it and were exercising the power); or
- discharge the order and make a care order.[184]

29.178   The power to make a care order applies whether or not the court is satisfied that the usual threshold criteria contained in Children Act 1989 s31(2) are satisfied.[185]

Right of appeal

29.179   An appeal against the making of a child safety order is made to the High Court.[186]

Dispersal orders

29.180   Anti-social Behaviour Act 2003 ss30–36 gives the police the power to designate areas where they can disperse groups in areas where groups have been causing or are likely to cause intimidation, harassment, alarm or distress to the public. The powers conferred on the police are seen as a useful tool in ensuring that public areas such as shopping centres, bus stops, street corners and other open areas are kept free of groups who are perceived as

---

181   SI No 2167. Criminal Procedure Rules 2005 Part 50 deals with applications to vary other orders formerly dealt with under SI No 2167, but not child safety orders.

182   *Child safety orders – guidance,* para 8.3.

183   Crime and Disorder Act 1998 s12(5).

184   Ibid, 12(6).

185   Ibid, s12(7).

186   Ibid, s13(1).

causing a nuisance to the public and in protecting younger children from the risks of being unaccompanied on the streets late at night, particularly of older peers encouraging them into criminal activities.[187] These orders are likely to have an impact on young people who frequently spend their free time in public places, often having nowhere else to meet their friends. The provisions create a criminal offence for breach and include a separate power to remove persons under 16 years of age to their home.

Authorisation

29.181 Authorisation for the exercise of the powers contained in Anti-social Behaviour Act 2003 s30 can only to be given by a police officer of the rank of superintendent or above who has reasonable grounds for believing:

- that any members of the public have been intimidated, harassed, alarmed or distressed as a result of the presence or behaviour of groups of two or more persons in public places in any locality in his police area (the 'relevant locality'); and
- that anti-social behaviour is a significant and persistent problem in the relevant locality.[188]

29.182 An authorisation may not be given without the consent of the local authority or authorities whose areas include the whole or part of the relevant locality.[189] Any authorisation lasts for a maximum of six months.[190] This does not appear to prevent an appropriate officer granting subsequent authorities.[191]

29.183 The authorisation must:

- be in writing;
- be signed by the relevant officer;
- specify the relevant locality;
- specify the grounds on which the authorisation is given;
- specify the period during which the powers can be exercised.[192]

29.184 The *Practice advice on Part 4 of the Anti-social Behaviour Act 2003* produced on behalf of the Association of Chief Police Officers by the National Centre for Policing Excellence suggests that officers should consult widely and consider the negative impact of an authorisation on disadvantaged groups.[193]

---

187 Home Office Circular 04/2004 and Association of Chief Police Officers 2005: *Practice advice on Part 4 of the Anti-social Behaviour Act 2003*. A copy of these documents can be obtained from the Home Office and Association of Chief Police Officers websites. See appendix 14 for contact details .

188 Anti-social Behaviour Act 2003 ss30(1) and 36.

189 Ibid, s31(2).

190 Ibid, s30(2).

191 Association of Chief Police Officers, *Practice advice on Part 4 of the Anti-social Behaviour Act 2003* (2005), para 2.3.

192 Anti-social Behaviour Act 2003 s31(1).

193 Para 2.

Publicity of the authorisation

29.185 Publicity must be given to the authorisation by either or both of the following methods:

- publishing a notice in a local newspaper circulating in the relevant locality;
- posting a notice in some conspicuous place or places in the relevant locality.[194]

29.186 The publicity must take place before the beginning of the period of the order.[195] Consideration should be given to diversity issues and notices may need to be translated into other languages.[196] The *Practice advice* emphasises the importance of monitoring any notices to ensure that where they have been removed they are immediately replaced.

Police powers

29.187 A constable in uniform who has reasonable grounds for believing that the presence or behaviour of a group of two or more persons in any public place in the relevant locality has resulted or is likely to result in any members of the public being intimidated, harassed alarmed or distressed, may give one or more of the following directions, namely:

- a direction requiring the persons in the group to disperse (either immediately or by such time as s/he may specify and in such way as s/he may specify);
- a direction requiring any of those persons whose place of residence is not within the relevant locality to leave the relevant locality or any part of the relevant locality either immediately or by such time as s/he may specify and in such way as s/he may specify; and
- a direction prohibiting any of those persons whose place of residence is not within the relevant locality from returning to the relevant locality or any part of the relevant locality for such period (not exceeding 24 hours) from the giving of the direction as s/he may specify.[197]

29.188 A direction:

- may be given orally;
- may be given to any person individually or to two or more persons together; and
- may be withdrawn or varied by the person who gave it.[198]

29.189 A direction may not be given to those engaged in lawful industrial action or public processions.[199] Directions may also be given by designated community support officers.[200]

---

194 Anti-social Behaviour Act 2003 s31(3).
195 Ibid, s31(5).
196 Association of Chief Police Officers, *Practice advice on Part 4 of the Anti-social Behaviour Act 2003* (2005), para 2.8.
197 Anti-social Behaviour Act 2003 s30(3) and (4).
198 Ibid, s32(1).
199 Ibid, s30(5).
200 Ibid, s33.

29.190   The *Practice advice* notes that it is important that this power is used proportionately, reasonably and with discretion to comply with Article 11 (freedom of assembly and association) of the European Convention on Human Rights. There must be evidence of anti-social behaviour taking place for the power to be used.[201] It is also suggested that the provisions do not relate to persons of the same household.[202] The officer making a direction may also exercise the power to require a person to give his/her name and address.[203]

Contravention of a direction

29.191 A person who knowingly contravenes a direction given to him/her commits an offence punishable on summary conviction by a fine or imprisonment for term not exceeding three months.[204] A constable in uniform may arrest without warrant any person s/he reasonably suspects has knowingly contravened a direction.[205]

Power to remove persons under 16 to their place of residence

29.192 If an authorisation is in force, a further power to return juveniles to their places of residence is exercisable by constables (and designated community support officers).

29.193   If, between the hours of 9.00 pm and 6.00 am, a constable in uniform finds a person in any public place in the relevant locality who s/he has reasonable grounds for believing:

- is under the age of 16, and
- is not under the effective control of a parent or responsible person aged 18 or over,

s/he may remove that person to the person's place of residence unless s/he has reasonable grounds for believing that the person would, if removed to that place, be likely to suffer significant harm.[206]

29.194   Where this power is exercised, any local authority whose area includes the whole or part of the relevant locality must be informed.[207]

29.195   'Public place' is defined as:

- any highway, and
- any place to which at the material time the public or any section of the public has access, on payment or otherwise, as of right or by virtue of express or implied permission.[208]

---

201 Association of Chief Police Officers, *Practice advice on Part 4 of the Anti-social Behaviour Act 2003* (2005), para 3.1.

202 Ibid, paras 1.1 and 3.2, based on the definition of 'anti-social behaviour' in Anti-social Behaviour Act 2003 s36.

203 Police Reform Act 2002 s50.

204 Anti-social Behaviour Act 2003 s32(2). This means that at the time of publication custody is not available for a young person prosecuted under these provisions.

205 Ibid, s32(3). A designated police community support officer has no power of arrest but may detain to obtain details for the service of a summons or to await the arrival of a police officer to exercise the power of arrest.

206 Ibid, s30(6).

207 Ibid, s32(4).

208 Ibid, s36.

29.196 This would seem to include cinemas, restaurants, coffee bars and public houses.[209]

29.197   The *Practice advice* points out that there is no provision to deal with the situation where a child is removed and there is no responsible person at their normal place of residence. The police now have duties under the Children Act 2004 to safeguard and promote the welfare of children.[210]

Use of reasonable force

29.198 The meaning of the word 'remove' in Anti-social Behaviour Act 2003 s30(6) was considered in *R (on the application of W and PW) v Commissioner of Police for the Metropolis, London Borough of Richmond-on-Thames and Secretary of State for the Home Department* where it was held to mean 'take away using reasonable force if necessary'.[211]

Extent of the power

29.199 In *R (on the application of W and PW) v Commissioner of Police for the Metropolis, London Borough of Richmond-on-Thames and Secretary of State for the Home Department* the court decided that the power does not have a curfew effect:

> ... a constable exercising the power given by section 30(6) of the 2003 Act is not free to act arbitrarily. He is not free to act for a purpose other than that for which the power was conferred ... The power is not a power of arrest ... The purpose for which the power was conferred is, in our view, clear and largely uncontentious. It is to protect children under the age of 16 within a designated dispersal area at night from the physical and social risks of anti-social behaviour by others. Another purpose is to prevent children from themselves participating in anti-social behaviour within a designated dispersal area at night. The sub-section does not confer an arbitrary power to remove children who are not involved in, nor at risk from exposure to, actual or imminently anticipated anti-social behaviour. It does not confer a power to remove children simply because they are in a designated dispersal area at night. Children are, so far as this legislation goes, free to go there without fear of being removed, provided that they do not themselves participate in anti-social behaviour and provided that they avoid others who are behaving anti-socially. Furthermore, the Secretary of State accepts that the discretionary power can only be used if, in the light of its purpose, it is reasonable to do so; and the Commissioner accepts that, to act reasonably, constables must have regard to circumstances such as how young the child is; how late at night it is; whether the child is vulnerable or in distress; the child's explanation for his or her conduct and presence in the area; and the nature of the actual or imminently anticipated anti-social behaviour.[212]

---

209 *R (on the application of W and PW) v Commissioner of Police for the Metropolis, London Borough of Richmond-on-Thames and the Secretary of State for the Home Department* [2006] EWCA Civ 458, at [4].

210 Association of Chief Police Officers 2005: *Practice advice on Part 4 of the Anti-social Behaviour Act 2003*, para 3.5. For police duties to safeguard and promote children's welfare, see HM Government, *Statutory guidance on making arrangements to safeguard and promote the welfare of children under section 11 of the Children Act 2004* (2005), chapters 6 and 7 (available to download from Department for Education and Skills website – see appendix 14).

211 [2006] EWCA Civ 458, at [28].

212 Ibid, at [35].

Mentally disordered young offenders

Introduction

30.1 In chapter 1 it was noted that research indicates that there is a high rate of mental disorder among children and young persons involved in the youth justice system. Fortunately not all of the young people suffering from a mental disorder will need specialised mental health services or hospital treatment. However, where such a need arises the defence lawyer is likely to find the case particularly challenging because of the vulnerability of the young client and the paucity of forensic adolescent psychiatric services.

30.2 This chapter provides an overview of the mental health provision in youth offending teams and the National Health Service. It also outlines the disposals available to the criminal courts when dealing with a mentally disordered young person.

Risk factors for developing mental health problems

30.3 Risk factors are set out in table 27 below.

30.4 To the risk factors in table 27 should probably be added the simple fact that the child or young person is involved in the youth justice system. A 2002 survey[1] of previous research noted that there was evidence that young people involved in the criminal courts, and in particular the custodial system, cope poorly with the stress of the situation they find themselves in. Such difficulties with coping would increase the likelihood of the young person developing mental health problems.

Mental health screening in the youth justice system

30.5 Youth offending teams working with children and young persons are required to carry out an *Asset* needs assessment.[2] Part 8 of the *Asset* Core Profile deals with the young person's emotional and mental health. A high risk indicator in this section should prompt the use of more detailed screening tools as follows:

- **SQIfA** (Screening Questionnaire Interview for Adolescents) – a two-page questionnaire completed by a youth offending team worker who may have no specialist mental health training; and
- **SIfA** (Screening Interview for Adolescents) – an assessment tool which is designed to screen for eight mental disorders, completed by a mental health worker, if the young person rates a score of 3 or 4 (out of 4) on the SQIfA.

30.6 Where mental health problems are identified as part of this screening process, there will usually be a referral to more specialised mental health services.

---

1 Hagell, *The mental health of young offenders*, The Mental Health Foundation, 2002.
2 Youth Justice Board, *National Standards for Youth Justice Services*, 2004 para 4.1. For *Asset* see para 2.23 onwards.

Table 27: Factors that increase the risk of mental health problems in young people

1. Child risk factors

- Genetic influences
- Low IQ and learning disability
- Specific developmental delay
- Communication difficulty
- Difficult temperament
- Physical illness, especially if chronic and/or neurological
- Academic failure
- Low self-esteem

2. Family risk factors

- Overt parental conflict
- Family breakdown
- Inconsistent or unclear discipline
- Hostile and rejecting relationships
- Failure to adapt to the child's changing developmental needs
- Abuse – physical, sexual and/or emotional
- Parental psychiatric illness
- Parental criminality, alcoholism and personality disorder
- Death and loss – including loss of friendships

3. Environmental risk factors

- Socio-economic disadvantage
- Homelessness
- Disaster
- Discrimination
- Other significant life events

Source: Audit Commission, *Children in mind: child and adolescent mental health services* (1999)

Provision of mental health services

30.7   Mental health services for children and young persons will be provided by a wide range of professionals under the broad heading of the Child and Adolescent Mental Health Service. This is frequently referred to by the acronym CAMHS. Services are provided at four levels of specialism as shown in table 28 below.

Table 28: Child and Adolescent Mental Health Service provision

Tier 1

A primary level, which includes interventions by:
– GPs;
– health visitors;
– residential social workers;
– youth offending team workers;
– school nurses;
– teachers;
– social workers.

These non-specialist staff:
– identify mental health problems early in their development;
– offer general advice and, in certain cases, treatment for less severe mental health problems;
– pursue opportunities for promoting mental health and preventing mental health problems.

Tier 2

A level of serviced provided by professionals working on their own who relate to others through a network rather than with a team:
– clinical child psychologists;
– educational psychologists;
– paediatricians – especially community;
– community child psychiatric nurse/ nurse specialists;
– child and adolescent psychiatrists;
– mental health workers in youth offending teams.

CAMHS professionals offer:
– training and consultation to other professionals (who might be at Tier 1);
– consultation for professionals and families;
– outreach to identify severe or complex needs where children and families are unwilling to use specialist services;
– assessment which may trigger treatment at this level or in a different tier.

Tier 3

A specialist service for the more severe, complex and persistent disorders:
– child and adolescent psychiatrists;
– child and adolescent psychiatrists;
– clinical psychologists;
– community psychiatric nurses;
– occupational therapists;
– social workers;
– child psychotherapists.

This is usually a multi-disciplinary team or service working in a community child mental health clinic or child psychiatry outpatient service offering:
– assessment and treatment of child mental health disorders;
– assessment for referrals to Tier 4;
– contributions to the services. consultation and training at Tiers 1 and 2;
– participation in research and development projects.

Tier 4

Access to infrequently used but essential services such as day units, highly specialised out-patient teams and in-patient units for older adolescents who are severely mentally ill or at suicidal risk. These services may need to be provided on a supra-district level, as not all districts can expect to offer this level of expertise.

More specialist CAMHSs may provide for more than one district or region and might include:
– adolescent in-patient units and secure forensic adolescent units;
– specialist services for young people with learning difficulties;
– specialist forensic out-patient teams for risk assessment and offence specific treatments;
– specialist teams for neuro-psychiatric problems.

Source: Dimond et al, *Key elements of effective practice – mental health: source document*, Youth Justice Board, 2004.

Mental disorder – statutory definition

30.8   Mental Health Act 1983 s1(2) defines 'mental disorder' as mental illness, arrested or incomplete development of mind, psychopathic disorder and any other disorder or disability of mind.

30.9   Further definitions are provided as follows:

- 'severe mental impairment' – a state of arrested or incomplete development of mind which includes severe impairment of intelligence and social functioning and is associated with abnormally aggressive or seriously irresponsible conduct on the part of the person concerned;

- 'mental impairment' – a state of arrested or incomplete development of mind (not amounting to severe mental impairment) which includes severe impairment of intelligence and social functioning and is associated with abnormally aggressive or seriously irresponsible conduct on the part of the person concerned;

- 'psychopathic disorder' – a persistent disorder or disability of mind (whether or not including significant impairment of intelligence) which results in abnormally aggressive or seriously irresponsible conduct on the part of the person concerned.

In the police station

Appropriate adult

30.10   If a police officer has any suspicion, or is told in good faith, that a suspect of any age may be mentally disordered or otherwise mentally vulnerable, in the absence of clear evidence to dispel that suspicion, the person shall be treated as such for the purposes of the Police and Criminal Evidence Act Codes of Practice.[3]

30.11   Where a suspect is believed to be mentally disordered, the police must arrange for the attendance of an appropriate adult at the police station.[4] In relation to a mentally disordered suspect, the appropriate adult may be:

- a relative, guardian or other person responsible for the suspect's care or custody;

- someone experienced in dealing with mentally disordered or mentally vulnerable people but who is not a police officer or employed by the police;

- failing these, some other responsible adult aged 18 or over who is not a police officer or employed by the police.[5]

---

3   PACE Code C, para 1.4.
4   PACE Code C, para 3.15.
5   PACE Code C, para 1.7(b).

Place of safety

30.12   The Mental Health Act 1983 s135 gives a police constable a power to remove a mentally disordered person to a place of safety. The power is exercisable if:

- the person is found in a place to which the public have access; and
- s/he appears to be suffering from mental disorder within the meaning of the Act (see para 30.8 above) and in immediate need of care or control.

The constable must think it necessary to exercise the power in the interests of that person or for the protection of others. Wherever possible, the place of safety should be a hospital and not a police station.

Diversion

30.13   Home Office Circular 66/1990 *Provision for Mentally Disordered Offenders* identifies the desirability of ensuring effective cooperation between agencies to ensure that the best use is made of resources that mentally disordered persons are not prosecuted where this is not required by the public interest.

30.14   The circular suggests:

- alternatives to prosecution such as cautioning (now reprimands and warnings), civil admission to hospital under the Mental Health Act 1983 and informal support in the community by social services departments should be considered;
- after a mentally disordered person has been charged, wherever possible arrangements should be made with the health, probation and social services for his/her assessment with a view to ensuring that s/he receives any treatment that may be necessary;
- where a prosecutor is satisfied that the probable effect upon a person's mental health outweighs the interest of justice in the particular case, s/he will consider discontinuing the proceedings;
- where the form of mental disorder is present without there being any indication that proceedings will have an adverse effect, the prosecutor will take account of the public interest in attempting to ensure that the offence will not be repeated as well as having regard to the welfare of the person in question.

30.15   Home Office Circular 66/1990 does not deal specifically with children and young persons. Additional guidance specific to children and young persons may be found in the Legal Guidance issued by the Crown Prosecution Service:

> A youth offender who is mentally disordered is doubly vulnerable ... The term 'mental disorder' is used in the Mental Health Act 1983. This identifies four categories of mental disorder and defines three of them. These categories are the criteria for compulsory admission to hospital under Section 36 of the Act and are inevitably expressed by way of clinical classification ... These classifications can be unhelpful in relation to youth offenders; they fail to allow for behaviour, which falls short of a disposable condition, but which is neverthe-

less 'disturbed' in the ordinary sense of the word e.g. personality disorders. It follows that when considering a prosecution, reference to 'mental disorder' should not be restricted to the Mental Health Act definition as this could restrict decision-making.

Mentally disordered offenders will often commit offences that are more of a public nuisance than a danger to the public. However, in serious cases where the offender is a danger to the public, the public interest is likely to require a prosecution. In determining where the public interest lies the prosecutor should look particularly to:

- the seriousness of the offence;
- the circumstances of any previous offending;
- the nature of the youth offender's mental condition;
- the likelihood of repetition; and
- the availability of suitable alternatives to prosecution.

Reprimand and final warnings can be problematic. Both require sufficient evidence and full recognition of guilt by the offender.

Particular difficulties can arise when mens rea is a component of the offence. The prosecutor must be satisfied that any admissions are genuine. Particular care must be taken when considering whether to administer a reprimand or final warning in a case relying on admissions.

It may be that in a proportion of cases, which might otherwise have attracted such a disposal, that this is not an advisable option, either because of doubts about the truth of any admissions made (in cases where there is little or no supporting evidence), or because of the defendants level of understanding. In such cases taking no further action will usually be the only appropriate way of dealing with the matter short of prosecution. Prosecutors should try and ensure the police are alert to these difficulties and guard against the inappropriate use of the reprimand and final warning system.

The file should include the opinions of the relevant welfare agencies, particularly about the offender's stage of development or understanding of the offence and the perceived likelihood of repetition, the likely effect of proceedings on his or her mental state and the available welfare options.

Secure accommodation as an alternative disposal

30.16 In addition to voluntary hospital admission or compulsory admission under Mental Health Act 1983 ss2 and 3, placement in a secure children's home under a secure accommodation order may be an option.[6] Whether this is appropriate will depend on the available facilities and the young person's ability and willingness to consent to treatment.[7] Unless the young person is already a looked after child, the local authority will have to commence care proceedings to acquire the power to make the application.

---

6 For the criteria for a secure accommodation order see chapter 14.
7 For a consideration of the legal issues regarding the use of secure accommodation, see Harbour 'Children, psychiatric treatment and compulsion' in Bailey and Dolan (eds) *Adolescent forensic psychiatry*, Arnold, 2004. For guidance on young people consenting to treatment see Department of Health, *Seeking consent: working with children*, 2001.

Criminal sentencing disposals

30.17   Where there is concern about the mental health of a young offender, the court may consider the following disposals:

- supervision order with a requirement as to treatment for a mental condition – see para 23.197 onwards; and
- community rehabilitation order with a requirement as to treatment for mental condition (16 years and over) – see para 23.233 onwards.

30.18   Both of these disposals requires the sentencing court to consider the evidence of a registered medical practitioner approved for the purposes of section 12 of the Mental Health Act 1983 before making the order.

Disposals under the Mental Health Act 1983

30.19   Where a young defendant has more severe mental health problems, the appropriate disposal is likely to be under the Mental Health Act 1983. The available disposals are:

- a hospital order (with or without a restriction order); and
- a guardianship order.

Hospital order

30.20   This order may be made either by a youth court[8] or the Crown Court. The order transfers the offender to a psychiatric hospital where s/he is treated as being detained under the Mental Health Act in the same way as civil patients.

30.21   The court may make a hospital order if:

- the court is satisfied, on the written or oral evidence of two registered medical practitioners, that the offender is suffering from mental illness, psychopathic disorder, severe mental impairment or mental impairment; and
- the mental disorder from which the offender is suffering is of a nature or degree which makes it appropriate for him/her to be detained in a hospital for medical treatment and, in the case of psychopathic disorder or mental impairment, that such treatment is likely to alleviate or prevent a deterioration of his/her condition; and
- the court is of the opinion, having regard to all the circumstances including the nature of the offence and the character and antecedents of the offender, and to the other available methods of dealing with him/her, that the most suitable method of disposing of the case is by means of a hospital order.[9]

---

8   See *R (on the application of P) v Barking Youth Court* [2002] EWHC 734 (Admin); [2002] 2 Cr App R 19.
9   Mental Health Act 1983 s37(2).

30.22 When a court is considering making a hospital order, the defendant should, except in the rarest circumstances, be legally represented.[10]

Guardianship order

30.23 A guardianship order may be made by either a youth court or a Crown Court. The offender must have attained the age of 16.[11] The court may only make the order if it is satisfied that the relevant social services department or other person is willing to receive the offender into guardianship.[12]

30.24   The pre-conditions for the making of a guardianship order are as for a hospital order, except that there is no requirement that the mental disorder must be treatable. A guardianship order gives the local authority social services department or other person nominated in the order the power to determine the young person's place of residence, education or training. The young person may also be required to attend for treatment.

Restriction order

30.25 A restriction order is a hospital order where the court orders that the offender's release shall be subject to special restrictions. A restriction order may only be made by a Crown Court judge. The order may only be made when making a hospital order if it appears to the court, having regard to the nature of the offence, the antecedents of the offender and the risk of his/her committing further offences if set at large, that it is necessary for the protection of the public from serious harm from him/her.[13] Before the order can be made, at least one of the medical practitioners must give evidence orally before the court.[14]

30.26   A youth court or adult magistrates' court which has convicted a defendant, may commit him/her to the Crown Court with a view to a restriction order being made, but only if:

- s/he has attained the age of 14 by the date of conviction;
- the offence is imprisonable in the case of an adult;
- the conditions for a hospital order are satisfied (see above); and
- it appears to the court, having regard to the nature of the offence, the antecedents of the offender and the risk of his/her committing further offences if set at large, that if a hospital order is made a restriction order should also be made.[15]

30.27 If committal is made under this power, the offender shall be committed in custody to the Crown Court.[16] If the offender has not attained the age of 17, it is submitted that committal to custody should be construed subject to the provisions of Children and Young Persons Act 1969 s23.

---

10 *R v Blackwood* (1974) 59 Cr App R 170, CA.
11 Mental Health Act 1983 s37(2)(a)(ii).
12 Ibid, s37(6).
13 Ibid, s41(1).
14 Ibid, s41(2).
15 Ibid, s43(1).
16 Ibid.

Disposals in cases of insanity and unfitness to plead

30.28 Criminal Procedure (Insanity) Act 1964 s5 applies to an accused person who is found:

- not guilty by reason of insanity; or
- to be unfit to plead and to have done the act or made the omission charged against him/her.

30.29 In such cases the court's powers are limited to one of the following disposals:

- a hospital order (with or without a restriction order);
- a supervision order; or
- an absolute discharge.

Hospital order

30.30 Such an order may only be made if the conditions set out in Mental Health Act 1983 s37 are satisfied (see para 30.21 above).

Supervision order

30.31 This is a different order from the community order under the Powers of Criminal Courts (Sentencing) Act 2000. A supervision order under Schedule 1A to the Criminal Procedure (Insanity) Act 1964 is an order which requires the supervised person to be under the supervision of a social worker or an officer of a local probation board for a period specified in the order of not more than two years.[17] There appears to be no provision for the order to be supervised by a member of a youth offending team who is not a social worker or probation officer.

30.32 The order may require the supervised person, during the whole of that period or such part of it as may be specified in the order, to treatment by or under the direction of a registered medical practitioner.[18]

30.33 The court shall not make a supervision order unless it is satisfied that, having regard to all the circumstances of the case, the making of such an order is the most suitable means of dealing with the accused.[19]

30.34 The court shall not make a supervision order unless it is also satisfied:

- that the supervising officer intended to be specified in the order is willing to undertake the supervision; and
- that arrangements have been made for the treatment intended to be specified in the order.[20]

---

17 Criminal Procedure (Insanity) Act 1964 Sch 1A para 1(1).
18 Ibid, Sch 1A para 1(2); detailed provision for the treatment is contained in Sch 1A para 5.
19 Ibid, Sch 1A para 2(1).
20 Ibid, Sch 1A para 2(2).

Transfer from juvenile secure estate to hospital

30.35 The Youth Justice Board considers that there are up to 300 young people in secure establishments requiring transfer to specialist mental health facilities at any one time.[21] Transfer from the juvenile secure estate to a psychiatric hospital is possible on the direction of the Home Secretary. It should however be noted that there is a severe shortage of secure beds in hospitals which are available for adolescent patients.[22] It may therefore be extremely difficult in practice to arrange such a transfer.

Transfer notice – serving prisoners

30.36 The Home Secretary may by warrant direct that a person serving a custodial sentence be removed to and detained in such hospital as may be specified in the direction, provided:

(i) the Home Secretary is satisfied by reports from at least two registered medical practitioners:
   (a) that the prisoner is suffering from mental illness, psychopathic disorder, severe mental impairment or mental impairment; and
   (b) that the mental disorder from which the person is suffering is of a nature or degree which makes it appropriate for him/her to be detained in a hospital for medical treatment and, in the case of a psychopathic disorder or mental impairment, that such treatment is likely to alleviate or prevent a deterioration of his/her condition; and

(ii) having regard to the public interest and all the circumstances, the Home Secretary is of the opinion that it would be expedient to do so.[23]

30.37 A transfer direction shall cease to have effect at the expiration of the period of 14 days beginning with the date on which it is given unless within that period unless the person specified in the direction has been received into the hospital specified in the direction.[24] A transfer direction with respect to any person shall have the same effect as a hospital order made in his/her case.[25]

Transfer notice – remand prisoners

30.38 The Home Secretary may make a transfer direction in relation to a remand prisoner provided:

(i) the Home Secretary is satisfied by reports from at least two registered medical practitioners:
   (a) that the remand prisoner is suffering from mental illness or severe mental impairment of a nature or degree which makes it appropriate for him/her to be detained in a hospital for medical treatment; and
   (b) that s/he is in urgent need of such treatment; and

---

21 Audit Commission, *Youth Justice 2004: Bringing young people to justice* (2004).
22 Ibid.
23 Mental Health Act 1983 s47(1).
24 Ibid, s47(2).
25 Ibid, s47(3).

(ii) having regard to the public interest and all the circumstances, the Home Secretary is of the opinion that it would be expedient to do so.[26]

Arranging the transfer

30.39 Transfer of prisoners is authorised by the Mental Health Unit based at the Home Office. For prisoners in a young offender institution, the senior medical officer has responsibility for initiating the application for transfer. It is not clear who has responsibility for initiating the transfer application if the child or young person is detained in a secure children's home or secure training centre. It is suggested that the Youth Justice Board should be alerted to the problem.

26 Mental Health Act 1983 s48(1).

Parental involvement

Introduction

31.1   Under the Criminal Justice Act 1991 the concept of parental involvement was justified in terms of parents taking responsibility for criminal offences committed by their children. The scheme of the Act was explained in Home Office Circular 30/1992 *Criminal Justice Act 1991: young people and the youth court*, para 32:

> The Government believes that parents must be involved when the children under 16 come to court in criminal proceedings. It will often be right for the parents of 16 and 17 year olds to be involved. Most parents take their responsibilities seriously, but the purpose of the 1991 Act is to ensure that all parents do so.

> Under the Act ... courts have a duty, subject to exceptions, to involve the parents of children and young people under 16. The Act gives courts a power to involve the parents of 16 and 17 year olds when it is appropriate to do so. This reflects the general principle that the way in which courts deal with young people aged 16 and 17 should take account of the stage of their development, and, in particular, their dependence on or independence from their parents.

31.2   Parental involvement under the 1991 Act encompassed attendance at court, liability to pay financial penalties on behalf of the young offender and being bound over to exercise control over the young offender. Since the Crime and Disorder Act 1998, the focus has moved to poor parenting as a contributing factor in youth offending. The reason for this change is explained in the latest joint Home Office, Department for Constitutional Affairs and Youth Justice Board circular, *Parenting Contracts and Orders Guidance:*[1]

> Inadequate parental supervision is strongly associated with offending. For example, a Home Office study[2] showed that 42% of juveniles who had low or medium levels of parental supervision had offended, whereas for those juveniles who had experienced high levels of parental supervision the figure was only 20%. The same research showed that the quality of relationship between the parent and child is crucial. Research[3] also shows that the children of parents whose behaviour towards their children is harsh and erratic are twice as likely to offend.

> In the United States, a study as long ago as 1973 showed that by training parents in negotiation skill, in sticking to clear rules and rewarding good behaviour, offending rates were halved.[4] Parenting can also be an important protective factor that moderates a child's exposure to risk.[5]

---

1   February 2004, paras 2.1–2.3. This can be downloaded from www.youth-justice-board.gov.uk.

2   Graham and Bowling, *Young people and crime*, 1995, Home Office Research Study No 145.

3   Farrington, 'Family backgrounds in aggressive youths' in Hersov et al (eds), *Aggressive and anti-social behaviour in childhood and adolescence*, Pergamon Press, 1978.

4   Alexander and Parsons, 'Short-term behavioural intervention with delinquent families: impact on family process and recidivism' in *Journal of Abnormal Psychology*, 81(3) 1973.

5   See various pieces of Youth Justice Board research including 'Risk and protective factors associated with youth crime and effective interventions to Prevent it' (2001) and 'The evaluation of the validity and reliability of the Youth Justice Board's assessment for young offenders'. See also chapter 1.

Parenting programme are designed to develop parents' skills to reduce parenting as a risk factor and enhance parenting as a protective factor.

The Government believes that for many parents whose children get into trouble, help from trained professionals and contact with other parents in the same situation may prove invaluable.

31.3   The 1998 Act gave courts the power to impose a parenting order upon parents of a child or young person convicted of a criminal offence or where an anti-social behaviour order is made. The orders can include compulsory parenting programmes as well as other requirements imposed upon the parent with a view to preventing their children from offending.

31.4   The Anti-social Behaviour Act 2003 introduced the possibility of a 'middle-way' for youth offending teams working with parents. As well as voluntary work and the court-imposed parenting order, a formal contract could be drawn up in which both the youth offending team and the parent(s) agree to do certain things. This is known as a parenting contract. The contract is not enforceable through the courts, but failure to adhere to the terms of a contract may be cited in court as an illustration of the need for a parenting order.

31.5   The concept of parental involvement applies equally to the youth court, adult magistrates' court and the Crown Court. The application of the concept varies widely between different courts and different geographical regions and practitioners will be well advised to develop local knowledge about the prevailing attitude of magistrates and judges in the courts where they appear to represent children and young persons.

Involvement in pre-court disposals

31.6   When a child or young person is given a final warning by the police, there will be a referral to the youth offending team to determine whether the young offender should participate in a rehabilitation programme.[6] This programme could involve asking the parent to attend parenting classes on a voluntary basis. It could also involve arranging for the local authority social services department to provide help and support to the parent under Children Act 1989 s17.[7] The defence lawyer needs to be aware of any voluntary pre-court intervention, as it may affect the court's decisions in relation to financial orders, bindovers and parenting orders.

Obligation to attend court

31.7   Children and Young Persons Act 1933 s34A imposes a duty upon the court to involve in the court proceedings the adult responsible for the care of a child or young person.

6   Crime and Disorder Act 1998 s66. See chapter 7.
7   See chapter 3.

31.8   The purpose of this requirement is explained in Home Office Circular No 30/1992 as follows:

> There are a number of reasons why parents should be expected to attend court with their children. Their attendance:
> - provides support to their children in what may well be a confusing and intimidating experience;
> - ensures that parents understand the serious nature of the proceedings;
> - enables parents to participate in the proceedings as appropriate, and assist the court as necessary;
> - helps the court have confidence that any arrangements it makes will be properly understood and acted upon.

31.9   The obligation varies depending on the age of the defendant.

Defendants under 16

31.10   The court must require the attendance of the parent or guardian during all stages of the proceedings, unless and to the extent that it would be unreasonable, having regard to the circumstances of the case.[8]

Defendants aged 16 or 17

31.11   The court has a wider discretion in relation to 16- and 17-year-olds. With such defendants the court may require a parent or guardian to attend at court during all stages of the proceedings unless and to the extent that it would be unreasonable in all the circumstances of the case.[9]

Discharging the responsibility to attend court

31.12   The duty to attend court may be discharged by the following:
- parents;
- guardian;
- a local authority.

Parents

31.13   'Parent' is not defined for the purposes of Children and Young Persons Act 1933 s34A. It is likely that the word would be construed as referring to a person with parental responsibility under the Children Act 1989.[10]

Guardians

31.14   'Guardian' is defined by Children and Young Persons Act 1933 s107(1) as:

> any person, who in the opinion of the court having cognisance of any case in relation to the child or young person or in which the child or young person is concerned, has for the time being the care of the child or young person.

8   Children and Young Persons Act 1933 s34A(1)(b).
9   Ibid, s34A(1)(a).
10 Magistrates' Courts (Children and Young Persons) Rules 1992 SI No 2071 r2(2)(b) defined 'parent' in this way. These rules have been substantially replaced by the Criminal Procedure Rules 2005. The definition has not been expressly incorporated into the new rules, nor does it appear to have been repealed.

31.15 This definition would include step-parents, grandparents or other relatives who have day-to-day care of a child or young person.

Local authorities

31.16 A local authority may have an obligation to attend court with a defendant, but only when:

- the authority has parental responsibility; and
- the defendant is in their care or accommodated by the authority under the Children Act 1989.[11]

31.17 'Parental responsibility' has the same meaning as in the Children Act 1989.[12] A local authority will only have parental responsibility in the following circumstances:

- where a full care order under Children Act 1989 s31 is in force; or
- where an emergency protection order is in force.

31.18 When a local authority has an obligation to attend court, it should be discharged by the local authority social worker or other representative of the social services department with responsibility for the child or young person.[13] If the defendant is subject to a full care order but the local authority has placed him/her back at home, the obligation to attend court is shared by the parents and the authority.[14] In such circumstances it may be appropriate for both the parent(s) and a representative of the local authority to attend court.[15]

31.19 Where a child or young person has been remanded to local authority accommodation under Children and Young Persons Act 1969 s23, the authority does not acquire parental responsibility and therefore cannot be required to attend court. However, the authority will wish to consider whether it can fulfil its obligations to the court without arranging for the attendance of a representative.

Attending at all stages of the proceedings

31.20 The obligation is to attend at all stages of the proceedings, and some courts may seek to enforce the responsibility to attend at every hearing. In practice, however, many courts will be concerned to see that the responsibility to attend is discharged at any hearing where the liberty of the child or young person is at stake, either in the course of making a decision with regard to bail or sentence, or where substantive issues in the case are to be determined. This may include any first appearance at court, when the question of whether bail should be granted will always arise and important preliminary issues will be dealt with, such as confirmation of the defendant's name, address and date of birth. The court may be particularly concerned to ensure the attendance of a parent at a trial or other hearing where

11 Children and Young Persons Act 1933 s34A(2) and chapter 3.
12 See para 3.14.
13 Home Office Circular No 30/1992.
14 Children and Young Persons Act 1933 s34A(2).
15 Home Office Circular No 30/1992 para 35.

the child or young person may have to make decisions as to the conduct of the case or give evidence in the proceedings.

Unreasonable to require attendance?

31.21   What is unreasonable is a question of fact for the court to decide in the circumstances of each individual hearing. Where a parent fails to attend at a particular hearing, the court may accept that attendance would be unreasonable due, for example, to ill health or other unforeseen circumstances. Courts are generally more reluctant to accept that requiring attendance would be unreasonable when there is a general reason which will apply to all hearings. Relevant considerations could include:

- parental employment;
- other childcare responsibilities;
- where the defendant is estranged from his/her parent.

Enforcing the requirement to attend

31.22   Children and Young Persons Act 1933 s34A(1) states that the court may require the parent or guardian to attend court. The term 'require' is not further defined in the Act.

31.23   Criminal Procedure Rules 2005 r7.8 provides:

> Where a child or young person is charged with an offence, or is for any other reason brought before a court, a summons or warrant may be issued by a court to enforce the attendance of a parent or guardian under section 34A of the Act of 1933, in the same manner as if an information were laid upon which a summons or warrant could be issued against a defendant under the Magistrates' Courts Act 1980 and a summons to the child or young person may include a summons to the parent or guardian to enforce his attendance for the said purpose.

31.24   For the purposes of this rule a 'parent' is defined as:

- a local authority with parental responsibility; and
- in any other case, a parent with parental responsibility.[16]

31.25   'Guardian' has the same meaning as in Children and Young Persons Act 1933 s107(1).[17]

Liability for financial penalties

31.26   The power to order parents or guardians to pay financial orders on behalf of their children is set out in the Powers of Criminal Courts (Sentencing) Act 2000, s137. The precise powers of the court depend once again on the age of the defendant.

---

16   Magistrates' Courts (Children and Young Persons) Rules 1992 SI No 2071 r2(2). This rule was not repealed on the introduction of the Criminal Procedure Rules 2005.

17   Ibid, see para 31.14.

Definition of parent and guardian

31.27   'Parent' is not defined, but it is likely to be construed as the person or persons with parental responsibility.[18]

31.28   'Guardian' has the same meaning as in the Children and Young Persons Act 1933 s107(1).[19] It does not include a local authority[20] or a limited company which is contracted by a local authority to look after a young offender.[21]

Offenders aged under 16

31.29   The court *must* order the parent or guardian to pay the financial order unless:

- s/he cannot be found; or
- it would be unreasonable to make an order for payment, having regard to the circumstances of the case.[22]

Offenders aged 16 or 17

31.30   The court *may* order the parent or guardian to pay the financial order unless:

- s/he cannot be found; or
- it would be unreasonable in all the circumstances of the case.[23]

31.31   As the court is not required to order the parent or guardian to pay the financial order, it may take into account not only the above factors, but also the maturity of the offender.

Unreasonable to make a financial order

31.32   The circumstances when ordering the parent or guardian to pay would be unreasonable are not defined in the 2000 Act, however, as a matter of practice guidance may be sought from Home Office Circular No 3/1983, which suggests the following criteria:

- whether the parents had neglected to exercise due care and control of the juvenile;
- whether any such neglect had caused or contributed directly or indirectly to the commission of the offence;
- whether it is desirable that the child or young person should bear the responsibility him/herself;
- the relationship between the parent and juvenile and the likely effect on that relationship of ordering the parent or guardian to pay the sum adjudged; and
- the respective means of the parent or guardian and the juvenile.

---

18 See para 31.14.
19 Powers of Criminal Courts (Sentencing) Act 2000 s163.
20 *Leeds City Council v West Yorkshire Metropolitan Police* [1983] 1 AC 29, HL.
21 *Marlowe Child and Family Services Ltd v DPP* [1998] 2 Cr App R (S) 438, QBD.
22 Powers of Criminal Courts (Sentencing) Act 2000 s137(1).
23 Ibid, s137(3).

31.33   The higher courts have identified circumstances where it was unreasonable to order a parent to pay the financial order. In *R v Sheffield Crown Court ex p Clarkson*[24] the Court of Appeal quashed a compensation order made against a mother who it was accepted 'had done what she could to keep her son from criminal ways'. Her limited means would also have meant that she would have taken more than two years to pay off the order. In *TA v DPP*[25] it was held that it would be unreasonable to order a parent to pay a financial penalty for a child, who at the time of the offence was accommodated by the local authority under Children Act 1989 s20. Although the parent still had parental responsibility, the local authority had de facto charge of the child's day-to-day management.

31.34   More recently there have been contradictory decisions regarding the broader question of whether the sentencing court has to find fault with the way the parent has looked after his/her child before making a financial order under section 137. In *R (on the application of M) v Inner London Crown Court*[26] Henriques J stated that the policy underlying the legislation is to achieve the recovery of fines, costs and compensation imposed on children and young people in order to protect the public purse and/or the person in favour of whom the compensation order has been made. He further declared that it was in the public interest that the financial order should be recovered from the parent unless there were special circumstances which make that result inappropriate. He distinguished the above decisions as cases where special circumstances had been found to exist. A subsequent decision of the Court of Appeal appears to contradict this interpretation of the legislation. In *R v J-B*[27] the Crown Court judge had commented favourably on how well the parents had brought up the defendant. Nevertheless, he proceeded to make a compensation order for £1,000 against the father. This order was quashed by the Court of Appeal partly because the sentencing judge had failed to identify how the father had fallen down on his parental obligations. In giving judgment, Curtis J seems to assume that, in the absence of fault being attributable to the parent, it would be unreasonable to impose a financial order on the parent.

Procedure

Determining responsibility

31.35   Where both parents live together, the court may choose which of the parents should be ordered to pay the penalty. In practice it is likely to be a parent who is working. Where the parents are separated, the court is only likely to consider whether to order the parent who has a residence order in relation to the child or who has day-to-day care for him/her to pay.

24   [1986] Cr App R (S) 454.
25   [1997] 1 Cr App R (S) 1; [1996] Crim LR 606, QBD.
26   [2003] EWHC 301 Admin; [2003] 1 FLR 944.
27   [2004] EWCA Crim 14; [2004] Crim LR 390.

Giving the parent or guardian a right to be heard

31.36   The court cannot make a financial order against a parent or guardian without giving him/her an opportunity to be heard.[28] Where the court is considering making a financial order against a parent or guardian present during the sentencing hearing, s/he should be expressly asked whether s/he has anything to say about the making of such an order. The court should also establish not only the parent's income but also his/her expenses or other commitments.[29]

31.37   It is the practice in some courts to invite the defence lawyer to suggest why a financial order should not be made against the parents. The lawyer should consider carefully whether there is any potential conflict between his/her young client and the parent before accepting this invitation.

31.38   A parent or guardian would not be eligible for a representation order as they are not 'an individual involved in criminal investigations or criminal proceedings'.[30] In hearings before the youth court or adult magistrates' court the parent or guardian will be able to receive Advocacy Assistance from a solicitor other than the solicitor acting for the child or Advice and Assistance and Advocacy Assistance from the duty solicitor (if s/he is not also acting for the child), if a parenting order is being considered.[31] If a parental bindover is being considered, the duty solicitor may act for the parent.[32]

Making an order in the absence of the parent or guardian

31.39   A court may make an order against the parent or guardian in his/her absence where the court has required his/her attendance but the parent or guardian nonetheless fail to attend.[33]

Assessment of means

31.40   Where the court orders the parent or guardian to pay the financial order, the amount should be fixed in accordance with his/her means.[34] The maximum fine would be that applicable to the young defendant.[35]

31.41   Before making a financial order against the parent or guardian, the court may make a financial circumstances order with respect to the parent or guardian.[36]

31.42   Where the parent or guardian has failed to comply with a financial circumstances order or has otherwise failed to co-operate with the court in its inquiry into his/her financial circumstances, and the court considers that it has insufficient information to make a proper determination of the

---

28   Powers of Criminal Courts (Sentencing) Act 2000 s137(4).

29   *R v J-B* [2004] EWCA Crim 14; [2004] Crim LR 390.

30   Access to Justice Act 1999 s12.

31   Criminal Defence Service: *General Criminal Contract*, October 2005, Part A para 3.2.1(b), Part B paras 8.3.2(e) and (f).

32   Ibid, Part A para 3.2.1(b),

33   Powers of Criminal Courts (Sentencing) Act 2000 s137(5).

34   Ibid, s138(1).

35   See chapter 22.

36   Powers of Criminal Courts (Sentencing) Act 2000 s136(1).

parent's or guardian's financial circumstances, it may make such determination as it thinks fit.[37]

Right of appeal

31.43   The parent or guardian has a right of appeal against the making of an order. The right of appeal lies to the Crown Court in the case of a decision made by a youth or adult magistrates' court,[38] and to the Court of Appeal in the case of a decision made by a Crown Court judge.[39] Legal representation by way of Advocacy Assistance will only be available if the appeal is linked to an appeal against the making of a parenting order.[40]

Liability of local authorities

31.44   A local authority may be ordered to pay a financial order instead of a child or young person, but only if:

- the authority has parental responsibility for the defendant; and
- the defendant is in the authority's care or is accommodated by the authority under the Children Act 1989.[41]

31.45   Such occasions will be rare, as parental responsibility is only acquired with a full care order.[42]

Reasonable for the local authority to pay?

31.46   The court has the power to order the local authority to pay unless it would be unreasonable to do so. The authority has the same right as a parent or guardian to assert unreasonableness. However, it must be prepared to provide evidence to support its assertion.

31.47   The principles upon which to decide whether it would be reasonable to order an authority to pay are set out in two decisions of the Divisional Court. In *D and R v DPP*[43] Leggatt LJ accepted that local authorities could not be liable in the same way as natural parents. Biological parents have had the responsibility for their child's upbringing since birth. In contrast:

> A local authority may often be entrusted with the care of, or be obliged to provide accommodation for, a young person who is already an offender, or who is of criminal or anti-social propensity. The steps that the local authority should or lawfully can take to restrain such a young person may well be limited.

> Where therefore ... the local authority is found to have done everything that it reasonably and properly could to protect the public from the young offender, it would be wholly unreasonable and unjust that it should bear a financial penalty.

37 Powers of Criminal Courts (Sentencing) Act 2000 s138(3).
38 Ibid, s137(6).
39 Ibid, s137(7).
40 Criminal Defence Service: General Criminal Contract, October 2005, Part A para 3.2.1(d).
41 Powers of Criminal Courts (Sentencing) Act 2000 s137(8). 'Local authority' and 'parental responsibility' have the same meaning as in the Children Act 1989.
42 *North Yorkshire County Council v Selby Youth Court* [1994] 1 All ER 991, QBD.
43 (1995) 16 Cr App R (S) 1040; [1995] Crim LR 748.

31.48   In the subsequent case of *Bedfordshire County Council v DPP*[44] the court went even further and stated that a causative link between the authority's lack of care and the young person's offences would have to be established before a court should order the authority to pay the financial penalty.

Procedure

Right to be heard

31.49   The local authority has a right to be heard before any order is made against it. In the case of *Bedfordshire County Council v DPP*[45] the Divisional Court gave guidance on the procedure to follow when a court is minded to make a financial order against a local authority.

- The court should notify the local authority in writing of its right to make representations and also supply the authority with any documents provided in support of a claim for compensation.
- The local authority should notify the court whether there is any dispute regarding the amount of compensation or whether an order should be made.
- If there is any dispute, a hearing should be arranged on reasonable notice to the local authority.
- The local authority should supply the court and the prosecution with relevant documents which it intends to rely upon to assert unreasonableness.
- The hearing should be as simple as possible.

Assessment of means

31.50   There is no duty to enquire into the financial circumstances of the local authority.[46]

Right of appeal

31.51   The local authority has a right of appeal in the same way as a parent or guardian.[47]

Binding over parents

31.52   The power to bind over parents was originally introduced by the Criminal Justice Act 1991 and is now consolidated in the Powers of Criminal Courts (Sentencing) Act 2000. During the 1990s the power was invoked inconsistently with some youth courts showing a reluctance to impose bindovers while other courts imposed them in most cases. Since parenting orders have been introduced nationally, the use of parental bindovers appears to have declined.

---

44 [1996] 1 Cr App R (S) 322; [1995] Crim LR 962.
45 Ibid.
46 Powers of the Criminal Courts (Sentencing) Act 2000 s138(2).
47 See para 31.43.

Definition of 'parent' and 'guardian'

31.53   'Parent' is not defined, but it is likely to be construed as the person or persons with parental responsibility.[48]

31.54   'Guardian' has the same meaning as in Children and Young Persons Act 1933 s107(1).[49]

Power

31.55   Following conviction for any offence the court has a power to bindover the parent or guardian of a child or young person:

- to take proper care of, and exercise control over, the offender; and
- where a community sentence has been passed, to ensure that the offender complies with the requirements of that sentence.[50]

31.56   The court may require a recognizance of up to £1,000. In fixing the size of the recognizance the court must take into account, among other things, the means of the parent or guardian.[51]

31.57   The period of the bindover is in the discretion of the court, however no bindover may last for more than three years or beyond the offender's eighteenth birthday.[52]

31.58   A court may not bindover a parent or guardian without his/her consent. However, if consent is refused, and the court considers the refusal unreasonable, it may order the parent or guardian to pay a fine not exceeding £1,000.[53]

Exercise of the power

Offenders aged under 16

31.59   The court has a duty to bindover the parent or guardian if, having regard to the circumstances in the case, the court considers it desirable in the interests of preventing the commission by the young offender of further offences.[54]

31.60   If the court does not exercise its power in relation to the parents or guardian of an offender aged under 16 it must state in open court:

- that it is not satisfied that a bindover would help prevent the commission of further offences; and
- the reasons for that decision.[55]

31.61   It does not automatically follow that the conviction of a child or young person will result in the court exercising its power to bindover the parent

---

48 See para 31.13.
49 Powers of Criminal Courts (Sentencing) Act 2000 s163. See para 31.14.
50 Ibid, s150(1).
51 Ibid, s150(7)
52 Ibid, s150(4).
53 Ibid, s150(2)(b).
54 Ibid, s150(1)(a).
55 Ibid, s150(1)(b).

or guardian. The court must act judicially and consider the particular circumstances of the case. Relevant criteria were suggested by Home Office Circular No 30/1992:

> It is for the court to decide whether or not binding over the parents would help prevent the juvenile offending again, but the following factors may be relevant:
> - whether the juvenile is likely to be amenable to supervision and intervention by the parents;
> - whether the parents' authority over the juvenile would be strengthened;
> - whether the parents are physically in a position to exercise the necessary degree of care and control (e.g. the juvenile may be living away from the parents' home); and
> - the circumstances of the present offence (e.g. the juvenile, of previous good character, may have been drawn into an uncharacteristic slip in circumstances which are not likely to recur).

Offenders aged 16 or 17

31.62　The court has a discretion to bindover the parent or guardian if, having regard to the circumstances in the case, it considers it desirable in the interests of preventing the commission by the young offender of further offences. In the case of a 16- or 17-year-old the court is not required to give reasons for its failure to bindover a parent or guardian.

Bindover to ensure compliance with a community sentence

31.63　Powers of Criminal Courts (Sentencing) Act 2000 s150(2) provides:

> ... where the court has passed a community sentence on the offender, it may include in the recognizance a provision that the offender's parent or guardian ensure that the offender complies with the requirements of that sentence.

31.64　The wording of the provision makes it clear that:
- the power may only be exercised if the court has already decided to impose a parental bindover to prevent further offending; and
- there is no presumption that the requirement will be imposed on the parent or guardian of an offender under the age of 16.

31.65　Although it is not stated in the legislation, the part of the bindover relating to compliance with the order presumably expires with the end of the community order.

No bindover where a referral order is made

31.66　Where the sentence of the court is a referral order[56] the court cannot impose a parental bindover.[57]

56　See chapter 21.
57　Powers of Criminal Courts (Sentencing) Act 2000 s19(5).

Legal representation

31.67   When a court is considering a bindover, the parent or guardian may receive Advice and Assistance (including Advocacy Assistance) from the court duty solicitor.[58]

Variation or revocation of the order

31.68   Bindovers may be varied or revoked on the application of the parent or guardian, if the court considers that would be in the interests of justice to do so, having regard to any change of circumstances since the order was made.[59]

31.69   An obvious relevant change of circumstances would be that the child or young person no longer lives with the person bound over.

Right of appeal

31.70   The parent or guardian has a right of appeal against the making of a bindover. The appeal lies to the Crown Court from a decision of a youth court or adult magistrates' court, and to the Court of Appeal from the decision of a Crown Court judge after a trial on indictment.[60]

Estreatment of the recognizance

31.71   Estreatment is the process whereby a recognizance is forfeited. In the case of a parental bindover, estreatment is initiated by way of complaint under Magistrates' Courts Act 1980 s120.[61] The parent or guardian who entered into the recognizance will be summonsed to attend court. In practice it is likely to be the court itself which initiates the process.

Which court?

31.72   There has been some confusion as to the proper court to hear such a complaint under section 120. It has been argued that it should be the adult magistrates' court because the youth court is a court of summary jurisdiction only able to deal with cases against children and young people.[62] This is not the view taken by the Home Office, Lord Chancellor's Department and Crown Prosecution Service as expressed in a Home Office letter dated 9 May 1994 to the clerk to the justices in Leeds.[63] The letter said that the decision whether complaints would be heard in the youth court or adult magistrates' court should be made locally but a preference was indicated for such proceedings being in the youth court where magistrates '... are probably better able to judge whether the parent has tried to control the child or whether the child is out of parental control'. The authors prefer the

58   Criminal Defence Service: *General Criminal Contract*, Part B para 8.3.2(e).
59   Powers of Criminal Courts (Sentencing) Act 2000 s150(10).
60   Ibid, s150(8) and (9).
61   Ibid, s150(5).
62   See, for example, (1995) 159 JPN 611.
63   Reported in Gibson et al *The Youth Court one year onwards*, Waterside Press, 1994.

latter view and would see no jurisdictional problem with the youth court dealing with the complaint.[64]

Legal representation

31.73   A parent or guardian facing estreatment proceedings may be represented by the duty solicitor.[65]

The hearing

31.74   Forfeiture is not automatic upon the young offender being found guilty of a further offence. The justices must enquire as to the extent to which the parent or guardian is culpable.[66] The burden rests upon the parent or guardian that s/he exercised all reasonable control.

31.75   The court may order that the whole or part of the sum is to be forfeited. It may also order that the recognizance be remitted.[67] This would be appropriate when the court learns that the child or young person is no longer living with the parent who has been bound over.

Enforcement

31.76   Payment of any sum adjudged to be paid upon forfeiture will be enforced as if it were a fine.[68]

Appeal

31.77   The adjudication of forfeiture is not a conviction so there is no right of appeal to the Crown Court.[69]

Parenting contracts

31.78   Parenting contracts were introduced by Anti-social Behaviour Act 2003 ss19 and 25.

31.79   A local education authority or the governing body of a relevant school may enter into a parenting contract with a parent of the pupil or child where a child or young person has:

- been excluded on disciplinary grounds from a relevant school[70] for a fixed period or permanently;[71]
- failed to attend regularly at a relevant school where s/he is registered as a pupil.[72]

---

64   See discussion of the assignment of matters to the youth court in chapter 11.
65   Criminal Defence Service: *General Criminal Contract*, October 2005, Part B para 8.3.2 (b).
66   *R v Southampton Justices ex p Green* [1976] 1 QB 11; [1975] 2 All ER 1073.
67   Magistrates' Courts Act 1980 s120(3).
68   Ibid, s120(4).
69   *R v Durham Justices ex p Laurent* [1945] KB 33; [1944] 2 All ER 530.
70   Anti-social Behaviour Act 2003 s24, a qualifying school as defined in Education Act 2002 s1(3) or a pupil referral unit as defined in Education Act 1996 s19(2).
71   Anti-social Behaviour Act 2003 s19(1).
72   Ibid, s19(2).

31.80   Where a child or young person has been referred to a youth offending team, that team may enter into a parenting contract with a parent or guardian of that child or young person, if a member of that team has reason to believe that the child or young person has engaged, or is likely to engage, in criminal conduct or anti-social behaviour.[73]

31.81   Guidance issued jointly by the Home Office, Department for Constitutional Affairs and the Youth Justice Board contemplates the use of parenting contracts by youth offending teams:

- when a child or young person has been reprimanded or warned for an offence;
- when a child or young person has been convicted of an offence;
- where a child under 10 years is believed by the youth offending team to have committed an act which would have constituted a crime if the child had been older; and
- where a child is identified (by local initiatives such as youth inclusion projects or anti-social behaviour teams) as being at risk of offending.[74]

31.82   A parenting contract is a document which contains:

- a statement by the parent or guardian that s/he agrees to comply for a specified period with requirements specified in the contract; and
- a statement by the local education authority, school or youth offending team agreeing to provide support to the parent or guardian for the purposes of complying with the contract.[75]

31.83   The contract requirements imposed on a parent or guardian should have the purpose of preventing the child or young person from engaging in criminal conduct or anti-social behaviour if the contract is with the youth offending team under section 25. If the contract is with the local education authority or the school, the purpose of the contract requirements should be to improve the behaviour of the pupil or to ensure regular school attendance.[76] The contract may include a requirement for a parent or guardian to attend a counselling or guidance programme.[77]

31.84   A parenting contract must be signed by the parent and signed on behalf of the education authority, school or youth offending team.[78]

31.85   Education authorities, schools and youth offending teams must, in carrying out their functions in relation to parenting contracts, have regard to any guidance which is issued by the secretary of state from time to time for that purpose.[79]

31.86   Parenting contracts are a means of formalising voluntary contact with parents of children and young people who are having difficulties with their

---

73 Anti-social Behaviour Act 2003 s25(1) and(2).
74 *Parenting Contracts and Orders Guidance,* February 2004.
75 Anti-social Behaviour Act 2003 s19(4) and s25(3).
76 Ibid, s19(6) and s25(5).
77 Ibid, s19(5) and s25(4).
78 Ibid, s19(7) and s25(6).
79 Ibid, s19(9) and s25(8). There is current guidance from the Department for Education and Skills in relation to education related parenting contracts and guidance issued jointly by the Home Office, Department for Constitutional Affairs and Youth Justice Board: *Parenting Contracts and Orders Guidance.*

education or offending or who are seen as at risk of offending. The terms of the contract will be negotiated with the parent or parents. The contract does not create any enforceable obligations.[80] However, failure to agree on the terms to be included in a contract or to comply with the terms of the contract may be cited as a reason to impose a parenting order if the youth offending team decide to apply to the court for a 'free-standing' parenting order.[81]

Definition of parent

31.87 In relation to education cases under section 19, a 'parent' is defined as including a person with parental responsibility or who has care of the child or pupil in question.[82] This does not include a person who is not an individual, ie a local authority.

31.88 In relation to cases under section 25 where the youth offending team is involved, a 'parent' is defined only to include a guardian.[83] This is likely to mean the person who has for the time being care of the child or young person.

Parenting orders

31.89 Parenting orders were introduced by the Crime and Disorder Act 1998. The circumstances in which a parenting order can be made have subsequently been extended by the Anti-social Behaviour Act 2003 and the Criminal Justice Act 2003. The Home Office, Department for Constitutional Affairs and Youth Justice Board have jointly issued guidance on parenting orders.[84] In contrast with parenting contracts, parenting orders have criminal sanctions for breach.[85]

31.90 Parenting orders have been held to be compatible with Article 8 (right to respect for private and family life) of the European Convention on Human Rights.[86]

Definition of parent or guardian

31.91 'Parent' is not defined save to include guardian, but it is likely to be construed as the person or persons with parental responsibility or who for the time being has care of the child or young person.[87]

---

80 Anti-social Behaviour Act 2003 s19(8) and s25(7).
81 Ibid, s27(1)(a).
82 Ibid, s24, in accordance with Education Act 1996 s576, as amended by the School Standards Framework Act 1998 Sch 30 para 180.
83 Ibid, s29. 'Guardian' is defined as in Children and Young Persons Act 1933 s107.
84 Joint Home Office, Department of Constitutional Affairs, Youth Justice Board Circular *Parenting Contracts and Orders Guidance,* February 2004.
85 Crime and Disorder Act 1998 s9(7), see paras 31.145 and 31.146.
86 *R (On the application of M) v Inner London Crown Court* [2003] EWHC 30; [2003] 1 FLR 944.
87 See para 31.2.

31.92   'Guardian' has the same definition as in Children and Young Persons Act 1933 s107.[88]

Responsible officer

31.93   A responsible officer may be one of the following:

- a probation officer;
- a social worker of a local authority social services department;
- a person nominated by the local education department; or
- a member of a youth offending team.[89]

Power to make an order

31.94   A parenting order may be made in any of the following circumstances:

- on the conviction of the child or young person;
- on referral by a youth offender panel;
- on application by a youth offending team – 'free-standing' order;
- on the making of a anti-social behaviour order or sex offender order[90] in respect of the child or young person;
- on the conviction of the parent or guardian for failing to comply with a school attendance order or failure to secure regular attendance at school of a registered pupil (offences contrary to Education Act 1996 ss443 and 444); or
- on the making of a child safety order in respect of a child.

Order on conviction of the child or young person

31.95   A court may impose a parenting order upon the parent or guardian of a child or young person when the child or young person is convicted of an offence and the court considers that such an order would be desirable in the interests of preventing the commission of any further offence by the child or young person.[91]

31.96   Where the offender is aged under 16, the court must make a parenting order, if it is satisfied that the order would be desirable in the interests of preventing further offending. If the court is not satisfied that a parenting order would be desirable, it must state this in open court and give reasons.[92] Where the offender is aged 16 or 17 years, the court has the discretionary power to make a parenting order.

---

88 Crime and Disorder Act 1998 s117 and see para 31.14.

89 Ibid, s8(8).

90 The provisions of the Crime and Disorder Act 1998 relating to the making of sex offender orders were repealed by the Sexual Offences Act 2003, which introduced the sex offences prevention order and the risk of sexual harm order. However, Crime and Disorder Act 1998 s8 which deals with the making of a parenting order on the making of a sex offender order has not been amended. The Sexual Offences Act 2003 makes no mention of parenting orders. The view of the authors is that there is no power to make a parenting order on the making of a sex offences prevention order or a risk of sexual harm order.

91 Crime and Disorder Act 1998 s8(1)(c) and (6)(b).

92 Ibid, s9(1).

31.97   Before making a parenting order in the case of an offender under the age of 16, the court shall obtain and consider information about the family circumstances and the likely effect of the order on those circumstances.[93] This information will usually be in the form of a report, but there is no statutory requirement that it be in that form.

Where the sentence is a referral order

31.98   The court has power to make a parenting order where the sentence of the court in relation to a child or young person is a referral order.[94] Where the young person is under 16 years of age, the duty to make a parenting order does not apply where the court is considering whether to make a parenting order at the same time as sentencing by way of a referral order.[95]

31.99   In a case where the court is considering making a parenting order at the same time as a referral order, before making the parenting order the court shall obtain and consider a report by an appropriate officer:

- indicating the requirements proposed by that officer to be included in the parenting order;
- indicating the reasons why the officer considers the requirements would be desirable in the interests of preventing the commission of any further offences by the child or young person; and
- if the child or young person is under 16, containing information about the family circumstances and the likely effect of the order on those circumstances.[96]

31.100   In practice, the Home Office, Department of Constitutional Affairs and Youth Justice Board circular suggests that:

> Parenting orders would normally only be made at the same time as referral orders if there is enough already known about the parents and family circumstances to enable a satisfactory report to be written in the time before the hearing. This would usually be where the YOT has already attempted to engage with the parents, for instance where a young person has received a Final Warning with an intervention. In this case the YOT may be able to provide the court with a report describing the attempts to engage the parents, with an update of the original parenting assessment in the time between notification and court appearance.

> Where the parents are not already known to the YOT in this way, the court will want to provide the opportunity for the Youth Offender Panel to engage parents and young people in agreeing a contract which could include provision of parenting support on a voluntary basis or through a parenting order.[97]

---

93 Ibid, s9(2).
94 Powers of the Criminal Courts (Sentencing) Act 2000 Sch 1 Part 1A, inserted by Criminal Justice Act 2003 s324 and Sch 34.
95 Crime and Disorder Act 1998 s9(1A), inserted by Criminal Justice Act 2003 Sch 34 para 2.
96 Ibid, s9(2A) and (2B), inserted by Criminal Justice Act 2003 Sch 34 para 2.
97 Joint Home Office, Department of Constitutional Affairs, Youth Justice Board Circular *Parenting Contracts and Orders Guidance* (February 2004) paras 6.12 and 6.13.

Order on referral by a youth offender panel

31.101   If the parent or guardian named in a referral order fails to attend the subsequent panel meetings, s/he can be referred by the panel to a youth court
acting for the local justice area in which it appears to the panel that the
offender resides or will reside. Such a referral may only take place if the
offender is still under the age of 18 on the date when the parent or guardian
fails to attend the meeting.[98]

31.102   The youth offender panel shall make the referral by sending a report to
the youth court explaining why the parent or guardian is being referred.[99]
Where a youth court receives such a report it may secure the attendance of
the parent or guardian by issuing a summons or, if the report is substantiated on oath, by issuing a warrant.[100]

31.103   Where the parent or guardian is brought before the youth court, it may
make a parenting order in respect of the parent or guardian if:

- it is proved to the satisfaction of the court that the parent or guardian
  has failed without reasonable excuse to comply with an order to attend
  the panel meetings; and
- the court is satisfied that the parenting order would be desirable in the
  interests of preventing the commission of any further offence by the
  offender.[101]

31.104   Before making a parenting order under this provision in the case of an
offender under the age of 16, the court shall obtain and consider information about the offender's family circumstances and the likely effect of the
order on those circumstances.[102]

Order on application by a youth offending team – 'free-standing' order

31.105   A youth offending team may apply to a magistrates' court for a parenting
order in respect of the parent or guardian of a child or young person who
has been referred to the team.[103]

31.106   What constitutes 'referral' to the youth offending team is not defined in
statute. The referral could be as a result of:

- the administering of a reprimand;
- the administering of a warning;
- the making of a mandatory or discretionary referral order; or
- referral through a local agency.

The tests

31.107   When an application is made, the court may make a parenting order if it is
satisfied that:

---

98 Powers of Criminal Courts (Sentencing) Act 2000 s22(2A).
99 Ibid, Sch 1 Part 1A para 9B.
100 Ibid, Sch 1 Part 1A para 9C.
101 Ibid, Sch 1 Part 1A para 9D(1).
102 Ibid, Sch 1 Part 1A para 9D(6).
103 Anti-social Behaviour Act 2003 s26(1) and (2).

- the child or young person has engaged in criminal conduct or anti-social behaviour; and
- making the order would be desirable in the interests of preventing the child or young person from engaging in further criminal conduct or further anti-social behaviour.[104]

Standard of proof

31.108 The court must make a finding in relation to the alleged criminal conduct or anti-social behaviour. There is no standard of proof set out in the Act, although the joint Home Office, Department of Constitutional Affairs and Youth Justice Board circular suggests that the criminal standard will apply as in the case of anti-social behaviour orders.[105] The question of the desirability of making an order is likely to be a question of judgment or evaluation rather than to a standard of proof.[106]

Factors to be considered

31.109 Before making a parenting order under this provision in the case of an child or young person under the age of 16, the court shall obtain and consider information about the child or young person's family circumstances and the likely effect of the order on those circumstances.[107]

31.110 In deciding whether to make a parenting order, a court must take into account (amongst other things):

- any refusal by the parent to enter into a parenting contract in respect of the child or young person; and
- if the parent or guardian has entered into such a parenting contract, any failure by the parent or guardian to comply with the requirements specified in the contract.[108]

Procedure

31.111 Applications for free-standing parenting orders should be made by complaint and in the form set out in Annexe D of the Practice Direction.[109] The joint Home Office, Department of Constitutional Affairs and Youth Justice Board guidance suggests the application should be made to the adult magistrates' court.[110] The guidance also suggests that, to comply with the time limit imposed by Magistrates' Courts Act 1980 s127, any complaint must be made within six months of the criminal or anti-social behaviour concerned.[111]

---

104 Anti-social Behaviour Act 2003 s26(3).
105 See chapter 29 and *R (McCann) v Manchester Crown Court* [2002] UKHL 39; [2003] 1 AC 787, *Parenting orders and contracts for criminal conduct and anti-social behaviour*, February 2004, para 5.6.
106 Ibid.
107 Anti-social Behaviour Act 2003 s27(2).
108 Ibid, s27(1).
109 Available through the Department of Constitutional Affairs website. See appendix 14 for full contact details.
110 *Parenting Contracts and Orders Guidance* (February 2004), para 5.11.
111 Ibid, para 5.12.

31.112   Difficulties may arise where applications are made in the adult court to justices who are not members of the youth panel and therefore are not familiar with the practice and procedure of the youth court. The court will also need to consider the imposition of reporting restrictions to prevent the identification of the child or young person.[112]

Order on the making of an anti-social behaviour order or sex offender order[113]

31.113   A court may impose a parenting order upon the parent or guardian of a child or young person made the subject of an anti-social behaviour order, if the court considers that the making of a parenting order would be desirable in the interests of preventing any repetition of the kind of behaviour which led to the anti-social behaviour order.[114]

31.114   When a court makes an anti-social behaviour order against a person under the age of 16, it must make a parenting order if it considers that the order would be desirable in the interests of preventing a repetition of the anti-social behaviour. If the court does not make a parenting order in such circumstances, it must state this in open court and explain why no order has been made.[115]

31.115   Before making a parenting order under this provision in the case of a child or young person under the age of 16, the court shall obtain and consider information about the child or young person's family circumstances and the likely effect of the parenting order on those circumstances.[116]

Order on the conviction of the parent or guardian of an offence under Education Act 1996 ss443 and 444

31.116   When a parent or guardian is convicted of an offence under Education Act 1996 ss443 or 444 (failing to comply with a school attendance order or failure to secure regular attendance at school of a registered pupil), the court may make a parenting order if the making of the order would be desirable in the interests of preventing any further offences under sections 443 and 444.[117]

31.117   Before making a parenting order under this provision in the case of a child or young person under the age of 16, the court shall obtain and consider information about the child or young person's family circumstances and the likely effect of the parenting order on those circumstances.[118]

112 See para 11.104.
113 See fn 90 above. As, in the view of the authors, there is no power to make a parenting order under the Sexual Offences Act 2003 and sex offender orders under the Crime and Disorder Act 1998 have been repealed, the remainder of this chapter will not refer to provisions of the Crime and Disorder Act 1998 which relate to the making of a parenting order on the making of a sex offender order, even though these provisions have not been specifically amended or repealed.
114 Crime and Disorder Act 1998 s8(1)(b) and (6)(a), and see chapter 29.
115 Ibid, s9(1)(b).
116 Ibid, s9(2).
117 Ibid, s8(1)(d) and (6)(c).
118 Ibid, Sch 1 para 9D(6).

31.118   The Department for Education and Skills has issued guidance on the making and implementation of parenting orders under this provision.[119] The reader is referred to this guidance for further information.

Order on the making of a child safety order

31.119 Where a child safety order is made in relation to a child, a court may make a parenting order against the parent or guardian of the child, if it considers that such an order would be desirable in the interests of preventing any repetition of the behaviour which led to the child safety order.[120] These applications will be made in the family proceedings court.

31.120   Before making a parenting order under this provision, the court shall obtain and consider information about the offender's family circumstances and the likely effect of the order on those circumstances.[121]

Assessment by a youth offending team

31.121 In most cases, the youth offending team will complete an *Asset* assessment of the child or young person.[122] Information may also be available from other agencies.

31.122   The Home Office, Department of Constitutional Affairs and Youth Justice Board circular suggests that a detailed assessment of a parent or parents should identify:

- parenting risk and protective factors;
- the individual needs and circumstances of the parents;
- whether a programme could support the parents so they can positively influence their child and if so, what form it should take and whether it should involve a parenting contract or an order;
- any cultural, racial, linguistic, literacy, religious or gender-specific issues that may affect the kind of programme that will be effective for a particular parent;
- the facts relating to a particular parent or child without invalid assumptions relating to culture, race or gender;
- whether the parent has any disability, special educational need or mental health problem that would affect the parent's ability to participate in a programme and if so, how it can be accommodated;
- any other issue that could affect a parent's ability to participate (such as transport or childcare).[123]

31.123 The parenting assessment and the *Asset* assessment may be presented in court if a youth offending team applies for or recommends a parenting

---

119 Department for Education and Skills, *Guidance on education-related parenting contracts, parenting orders and penalty notices* (2004). The guidance is available on the department website and full contact details are contained in appendix 14.

120 Crime and Disorder Act 1998, s8(1) and (6)(a), see chapter 29.

121 Ibid, s9(2).

122 See chapter 2.

123 *Parenting Contracts and Orders Guidance* (February 2004) , para 2.18.

order. Any intervention should be in accordance with any existing child protection plan or care plan.[124]

Is a parenting order desirable?

31.124 The test to be applied is not defined and the question of desirability will be for the judgment of the court having considered all the information available to it. The joint Home Office, Department of Constitutional Affairs and Youth Justice Board circular states that:

> The court has discretion to consider all the circumstances of the case in deciding whether it is desirable to make a parenting order. The court may wish to consider, for example, how much help, support and encouragement the parent or guardian has offered the child, and whether they are willing to receive assistance and support from the [youth offending team] or other provider on a voluntary basis. Where the parent is fully co-operating or willing to co-operate voluntarily a parenting order will not usually be desirable. If a parent has attended a programme without changing his or her behaviour, then an order might be called for.[125]

31.125 In *R (on the application of M) v Inner London Crown Court*[126] the Divisional Court reviewed a parenting order made following conviction in the Crown Court as to whether it was irrational and perverse. The court indicated that it had paid particular attention to the views of the writer of the pre-sentence report, a member of the youth offending team who had interviewed both mother and daughter in that case and had observed the family circumstances:

> Her views are not of course decisive, but occasions are likely to be limited when a court decides that it is desirable to make a parenting order contrary to the views of those whose task it will be to administer the regime as the responsible officer.[127]

Legal representation

31.126 When a court is considering whether to make a parenting order, the parent or guardian may receive Advice and Assistance (including Advocacy Assistance) from the court duty solicitor.[128] This would not be appropriate where the court duty solicitor was acting for the child. The parent or guardian can also receive Advocacy Assistance from a solicitor acting under a Legal Services Commission Criminal Contract.[129]

---

124 *Parenting Contracts and Orders Guidance* (February 2004) , para 2.20, and see chapter 3.
125 Ibid, para 6.6.
126 [2003] EWHC 31; [2003] 1 FLR 944.
127 Ibid at 71].
128 Criminal Defence Service: *General Criminal Contract*, October 2005, Part B para 8.3.2(f).
129 Ibid, Part A para 3.2.1(b).

Making an order against more than one person

31.127 Orders may be made against more than one person depending on the circumstances of the family. The guidance suggests that this should include any parent or guardian who could be supported to positively influence their child. This may include stepparents, a parent's partner, grandparents or any other adult who is significantly involved in the child's upbringing.

> The evaluation of the [Youth Justice Board's] parenting programmes has shown that few fathers have been involved in parenting programmes. However, when both parents are participating in the upbringing of a child, even when they live separately, a parenting intervention is likely to be more effective if both the mother and the father are involved, unless a parent is estranged, for instance because of domestic violence or abuse ... By contrast, working with only one of the parents means that positive results achieved through one of them can be undermined by the influence of the other. Encouraging one parent to set consistent and fair boundaries will have less effect if the other parent continues to be inconsistent and unfair. Whether or not both should go on the same programme will depend on the particular needs of the parents and whether the presence of one parent is likely to reduce the impact of the programme on the other. In some cases the [youth offending team] will be able to work with one parent voluntarily but may have to explore the use of a parenting order to engage the other.[130]

Procedure on making the order

31.128 Before making the order, the court shall explain to the parent in ordinary language:
- the effect of the order and the requirements proposed to be included in it;
- the possibility of being fined if found in breach of any of the requirements of the order; and
- the court may review the order on the application of the parent or responsible officer.[131]

31.129 If the parent is present at the court hearing, this information will be given orally.

Requirements of the order

31.130 A parenting order may include:
- a requirement to participate in counselling and guidance;
- a requirement to go on a residential parenting course; and
- specific requirements relating to the supervision of the child or young person.[132]

31.131 The order will be made in a specified form.[133]

---

130 *Parenting Contracts and Orders Guidance* (February 2004) , para 2.17.
131 Crime and Disorder Act 1998 s9(3).
132 Ibid, s8(4).
133 Criminal Procedure Rules 2005 r50.2.

Counselling and guidance programme

31.132 A counselling and guidance programme may not last longer than three months. Such programmes are usually referred to as 'parenting programmes'. The Home Office, Department of Constitutional Affairs and Youth Justice Board circular states that all parenting orders should include a parenting programme unless the parent or guardian has already received a parenting order.[134]

Residential courses

31.133 A counselling or guidance programme which a parent or guardian is required to attend may consist wholly or in part of a residential course, but only if the court is satisfied that:

- the attendance of the parent at a residential course is likely to be more effective than his/her attendance at a non-residential course in preventing the commission of any further offence; and
- any interference with family life which is likely to result from the attendance of the parent or guardian at a residential course is proportionate in all the circumstances.[135]

31.134 The Home Office, Department of Constitutional Affairs and Youth Justice Board circular suggests that a residential component might be justified where the parent's home life is so chaotic that s/he needs a structured setting where sustained counselling and guidance can be undertaken.[136] The circular also indicates that the residential component need not be continuous and could comprise a number of residential weekends structured within a wider non-residential programme.[137]

Specific requirements

31.135 On the making of a parenting order, the court has a discretion to impose on the parent or guardian specific requirements for not more than 12 months.[138] The court may impose such conditions as it considers desirable to prevent any further offence by the child or young person or any repetition of the behaviour which led to the anti-social behaviour, sex offender order or child safety order.[139]

31.136   As examples of possible requirements, the circular suggests that the parent or guardian could be required to ensure that the child or young person:

- attends school or other relevant educational activities, such as mentoring in literacy or numeracy or a homework club;
- attends a programme or course to address relevant problems such as anger management or drug or alcohol misuse;
- avoids contact with disruptive and, possibly, older children;

---

134 *Parenting Contracts and Orders Guidance* (February 2004), para 8.2
135 Crime and Disorder Act 1998 s8(7A).
136 *Parenting Contracts and Orders Guidance* (February 2004), para 8.9.
137 Ibid, para 8.10.
138 Crime and Disorder Act 1998 s8(4)(a).
139 Ibid, s8(7).

- avoids unsupervised visits to certain areas, such as shopping centres;
- is at home during certain hours at night and is effectively supervised.[140]

Duty to avoid conflict with religious beliefs and work/educational commitments

31.137 The requirements specified in the order shall, as far as practicable, be such as to avoid:

- any conflict with the parent's religious beliefs; and
- any interference with the times, if any, at which the parent normally works or attends an educational establishment.[141]

Discharge or variation

31.138 A court may discharge or vary the order on the application of either a parent or the responsible officer. When varying the order it may delete a requirement or insert a new condition (either in addition to or in substitution of an existing provision) that could have been included if the court had then had power to make the order.[142]

31.139 An application shall be made to the magistrates' court which made the order, and shall specify the reason why the applicant for variation or discharge believes the court should vary or discharge the order.[143]

31.140 Where a court dismisses an application for discharge, no further application to discharge the order may be made except with the consent of the court which made the order.[144]

Right of appeal

31.141 In the case of a parenting order imposed following the conviction of a child or young person and in the case of an order imposed in relation to failure to attend school, the parent has the same right of appeal against the making of the order as if it were a sentence imposed on him/her.[145] It would therefore be possible to appeal to the Crown Court or to appeal by way of case stated. If the parenting order were made in the Crown Court, appeal would be to the Court of Appeal.

31.142 In the case of a parenting order imposed following the making of an anti-social behaviour order, appeal is to the Crown Court.[146] In the case of a parenting order imposed following the making of a child safety order, appeal is to the High Court by way of case stated.[147]

---

140 *Parenting Contracts and Orders Guidance* (February 2004), para 8.13.
141 Crime and Disorder Act 1998 s9(4).
142 Ibid, s9(5).
143 Criminal Procedure Rules 2005 r50.3(2).
144 Crime and Disorder Act 1998 s9(6).
145 Ibid, s10(4) and (5).
146 Ibid, s10(1)(b).
147 Ibid, s10(1)(a).

31.143   Parenting orders introduced by the Anti-social Behaviour Act 2003 have a right of appeal to the Crown Court.[148]

31.144   On appeal, the Crown Court has power to vary the terms of the order by cancelling or inserting any provisions which the court imposing the original order has or could have made. The Crown Court can also discharge the order.[149]

Enforcement

31.145   If a parent fails to comply with a requirement of a parenting order without a reasonable excuse for so doing, s/he shall be liable on summary conviction to a fine not exceeding level 3 on the standard scale.[150] The court could also make the parent the subject of a conditional discharge, community order or a curfew order.

31.146   The circular issued jointly by the Home Office, the Department of Constitutional Affairs and the Youth Justice Board anticipates that the responsible officer will report the alleged breach to the police, who will carry out a criminal investigation. The matter will then be referred to the Crown Prosecution Service to determine whether a prosecution should be brought.[151] The prosecution will take place in the adult magistrates' court. There is a six-month time limit for bringing proceedings in relation to breach of an order.[152]

---

148 Anti-social Behaviour Act 2003 s22 and s28.
149 Crime and Disorder Act 1998 s9(5) and (6).
150 Ibid, s9(7).
151 *Parenting Contracts and Orders Guidance* (February 2004) , para 9.20–9.21.
152 Magistrates' Courts Act 1980 s127.

APPENDICES

Children's services: a glossary of terms

This glossary is intended to provide an introduction to key terms and acronyms that are used by children's services. A fuller list of terms may be found in *Multi-agency Working: Glossary* published by the Department for Education and Skills.

Accommodated child	Child provided with accommodation by a local authority on a voluntary basis. The parents retain parental responsibility.
Allocated worker	A member of staff, usually a social worker, with case responsibility.
Approved social worker	A social worker with powers under the Mental Health Act including compulsory detention in a hospital.
Asset	Assessment tool used by youth offending teams See 2.23.
At risk	Used by social workers to describe a child at risk of significant harm. Can have other meanings, ie at risk of offending.
Attention deficit hyperactivity disorder (ADHD)	A psychiatric or paediatric diagnosis reflecting serious and persistent inattentiveness or hyperactivity. For more see appendix 2.
Autistic spectrum disorder	Autistic spectrum disorder sufferers find it difficult to understand and use both verbal and non-verbal communication, to understand social behaviour (this affects their ability to interact with children and adults). For more see appendix 2.
Behaviour support plan	Plan to support children with behavioural difficulties within school.
Behavioural, emotional and social difficulty (BESD)	Used to define a type of special educational need. Until recently, the term 'emotional and behavioural difficulty' was used.
CAMHS	See Child and Adolescent Mental Health Service
Care order	An order made under Children Act 1989 s31. Places a child compulsorily in the care of a designated local authority and enables the local authority to exercise parental responsibility for the child. See 3.11.
Care plan	A plan that details the needs and plans for a child who is accommodated or on a care order.
Child and Adolescent Mental Health Service	Used broadly the term covers all types of provision and intervention, from mental health promotion and prevention, specialist community-based services, through to in-patient care for children and young people with mental illness. See 30.7.
Child protection	General term used to describe work by social services with children who have been identified as requiring protection from harm.

Child protection plan	Inter-agency plan to protect a child on the child protection register who is vulnerable due to emotional, physical or sexual abuse.
Child protection register	Statutory register held by a local authority of children who are at risk of significant harm.
Child safety order	A family court order made on a child under 10 who has committed an offence, breached a child curfew, or who has caused harassment, distress or alarm to others. Under a child safety order, a social worker or officer from the youth offending team supervises the child. See 29.158.
Children in need	A child is in need if: • s/he is unlikely to achieve or maintain, or have the opportunity of achieving or maintaining, a reasonable standard of health or development without the provision of services by a local authority; • his or her health or development is likely to be significantly impaired, or further impaired, without the provision of such services; or • s/he is disabled. See 3.20.
Children's Commissioner for England	Established by Children Act 2004 s1, the Children's Commissioner for England has a number of functions including advising the government of children's views and interests as well as encouraging organisations whose activities affect children to take account of children's views. The Commissioner is able to hold inquiries into cases of individual children that have wider policy relevance.
Children's Commissioner for Wales	Established by the Children's Commissioner for Wales Act 2001, the Commisioner reviews legislation and policy in Wales which affects children in the Principality.
Children's guardian	Formerly known as a guardian ad litem, the children's guardian is appointed by a family proceedings court in specified proceedings (includes applications for a care order or a civil secure accommodation order).
Children's services department	Created under the Children Act 2004, local government department with responsibility for education and social services.
Children's trust	Created under the Children Act 2004, arrangements that are put in place between children's services departments, health services and other partners to provide integrated services to children and families.
Common Assessment Framework (CAF)	An assessment tool that can be used by a range of professionals to assess a child's needs.
Compulsory school age	Defined as beginning from the start of the term commencing on or after the child's fifth birthday. A child continues to be of compulsory school age until the last Friday of June in the school year that s/he reaches 16.
Conduct disorder	A psychiatric diagnosis for a pattern of persistent and serious misbehaviour in children and young people. The misbehaviour must be much worse than would normally be expected from other children of a similar age. For more see Appendix 2.
Connexions Service	Responsible for the provision of advice and guidance to young people aged 13 to 19 including regarding education, training and employment.

Developmental delay	The failure of a child to achieve specific milestones at an age when it would be expected that most children would have achieved those milestones.
Director of Children's Services	Statutory local government post with responsibility for children's education, social services and leaving care. Key responsibilities include the safeguarding of children.
Disabled child	By Children Act 1989 s17, a child is disabled if she is blind, deaf or dumb or suffers from mental disorder of any kind, or is substantially and permanently handicapped by illness, injury or congenital or other such disability as may be prescribed. A disabled child is also a child in need.
Dyslexia	Children with dyslexia have a marked and persistent difficulty in learning to read, write and spell, despite progress in other areas. They may have poor reading comprehension, handwriting and punctuation.
Education maintenance allowance (EMA)	Means tested allowance to young people aged 16 – 18 years who are in full-time education. Depending on household income the allowance is paid weekly by the Department for Education and Skills directly to the young person at the rate of £10, £20 or £30. It is intended to cover the cost of travel to the place of education and the purchase of books and other study materials.
Education supervision order	This order is made under Children Act 1989 s36 in a family proceedings court on the application of a local education authority. It may only be made if the court is satisfied that a child of compulsory school age is not being properly educated. The order cannot be made in relation to a child in care. The supervisor will be an education social worker or welfare officer whose duty is to advise, assist and befriend, and give directions to the child and parents to secure proper education of the child. Failure to comply with such directions is an offence.
Education welfare officer (EWO)	Education welfare officers (also known as education social workers or attendance advisers) are employed by local education authorities to resolve problems of children and young people regularly missing school. Education welfare officers fulfil local authorities' responsibilities in relation to prosecuting for non-attendance, penalty notices, parenting contracts and parenting orders for attendance, education supervision orders, and truancy sweeps.
Emergency protection order	A court order made by a family proceedings court under Children Act 1989 s44. An order is initially limited to eight days and is made to ensure the safety of a child where there is reasonable cause to believe the child would otherwise suffer significant harm if not moved to (or kept in) accommodation provided for by the applicant (usually a local authority). While an emergency protection order is in force it gives the applicant parental responsibility.
Emotional and behavioural difficulties (EBD)	See Behavioural, emotional and social difficulty.
Excluded from school	Disciplinary sanction used by head teachers for bad behaviour or refusal to comply with school rules. Exclusion may be fixed-term or permanent. Pupils have a right of appeal against a decision to exclude them permanently.

Family therapy	A way of working with families when one or more family members are experiencing problems. It is based on the idea that the behaviour of people is influenced and maintained by the way in which they interact with others, particularly within strong social systems such as a family.
Fraser competent	See Gillick competent.
Gillick competent	Arises from case of *Gillick v West Norfolk and Wisbech AHA* [1986] 1 AC 112 where a mother challenged the legality of providing contraceptive advice to a child under 16. The House of Lords ruled that young people who are under 16 are competent to give valid consent to a particular intervention if they have sufficient understanding and intelligence to enable them to understand fully what is proposed and are capable of expressing their own wishes. Lord Fraser delivered the leading opinion, hence also Fraser competent.
Home school agreement	All state schools have written home-school agreements. Non-binding statements explaining the school's aims and values, the responsibilities of both the school and parents, and what the school expects of its pupils.
Independent reviewing officer	Registered social worker who must chair statutory review meetings for looked after children.
Independent visitor	A local authority must appoint an independent visitor for a child they are looking after if it appears that: • communication between the child and his/her parent or any other person with parental responsibility has been infrequent: or • s/he has not visited or been visited by (or lived with) any such person during the preceding twelve months; and in either case • it would be in the child's best interests to appoint such a visitor. An independent visitor has the duty of visiting, advising and befriending the child.
Individual education plan	An individual learning programme devised by a school for a child who has been identified as having special educational needs
Lead professional	Social worker, teacher, youth worker or other professional providing the lead in service provision to a child and their family.
Learning support unit	School based centres providing short-term teaching and support programmes for pupils who are disaffected, at risk of exclusion, or vulnerable because of social or family issues.
Local safeguarding children board	Established under Children Act 2004 s13 the function of a board is to co-ordinate what is done by each person or body represented on the Board for the purposes of safeguarding and promoting the welfare of children in the area of the authority by which it is established and to ensure the effectiveness of what is done by each such person or body for those purposes.
Looked after child	Any child who is in the care of the local authority or who is provided with accommodation by the local authority department for a continuous period of more than 24 hours.

Mentor	An adult who works usually in a one-to0ne relationship with a young person at risk. The mentoring may involve coaching and encouraging, constructively criticising, listening and guiding a young person to achieve his or her goals. Mentors can provide young people with extra support and a positive role model and therefore a protective factor to divert the young person from offending. Group mentoring schemes exist where one mentor works with a group of young people.
Moderate learning difficulties	Term used by education professionals. Children with moderate learning difficulties will have attainments significantly below expected levels in most areas of the curriculum, despite appropriate interventions.
Onset	An assessment tool developed on behalf of the Youth Justice Board for use in early intervention crime prevention programmes to help target resources for young people who may become involved in offending behaviour.
Parental responsibility	All the rights, duties, powers, responsibilities and authority which, by law, a parent of a child has in relation to the child and his property: Children Act 1989 s3.
Pathway plan	Plan drawn up by a local authority for a care leaver. See para 3.84.
Personal adviser	Connexions personal advisers provide information, advice and guidance, support for young people aged 13 to 19, including vulnerable young people requiring more substantial one-to-one support. Their key objective is to support young people to remain in learning and to fulfil their potential (see also Connexions Service). Care leavers should also have a personal adviser appointed by the local authority. See 3.89.
Police protection	Under Children Act 1989 s46 any police constable who has reasonable cause to believe that a child is at risk of significant harm can remove the child to a place of safety, or prevent the child being removed from somewhere where the child is safe (eg a hospital). This is known as police protection; it is the most immediate form of protection available for any child or young person who has experienced, or is likely to experience, abuse or exploitation, in that it can be put into effect straightaway without reference to a court. Police protection can remain in force for up to 72 hours. Any police officer can make the order (sometimes referred to as a police protection order), but it must be confirmed by an officer of at least the rank of inspector as soon as possible and it must be reported to the local authority, which will take action to ensure the child's safety, often by applying for an emergency protection order in the first instance.
Positive Activities for Young People (PAYP)	Programme launched by the Youth Justice Board in 2003 to provide a broad range of constructive activities for 8- to 19-year-olds at risk of social exclusion. It is targeted specifically at young people who are not fully engaged in education, as well as those with a low level of academic achievement. The programme aims to reduce crime, truancy and anti-social behaviour, both in the short term and the long term, and to ensure that young people return to education, have opportunities to engage in new activities, and can mix with others from different backgrounds.

Pupil referral unit (PRU)	A school that is established and maintained by a local authority providing education for children who are excluded, sick or otherwise unable to attend mainstream school.
Resettlement and aftercare provision (RAP)	Established in 2004 in 50 youth offending team areas, this resource is targeted as young people with substance misuse problems. It provides a high level of support during the community part of a detention and training order and for up to six months afterwards.
Residence order	An order made under Children Act 1989 s8 by a family proceedings court which stipulates who a child is to live with. An order normally lasts until the child reaches age 16.
School attendance order	Issued under Education Act 1996 s437 on the application of a local education authority where a child of compulsory school age is not receiving a suitable education, either by regular attendance at school or otherwise.
Secure children's home (secure unit)	Provide accommodation for young people placed under a secure accommodation order for the protection of themselves or others (ie on welfare grounds), and those vulnerable young people placed under criminal justice legislation by the Youth Justice Board.
Significant harm	The threshold that justifies compulsory intervention in family life in the best interests of a child. Children Act 1989 s47.
Special educational needs	The Education Act 1996 defines a pupil as having a special educational need if he or she has 'a learning difficulty which calls for special educational provision to be made for him'. For the purposes of the Act, children are defined as having a learning difficulty if they: • have a significantly greater difficulty in learning than most children of the same age; • have a disability that prevents or hinders them from making use of educational facilities generally provided for children of the same age; or • are under compulsory school age and would be likely to fall within one of the above definitions if special provision was not made for them. The Act imposes duties on schools and local education authorities to identify, assess and meet children's special educational needs. The presumption is that, wherever possible, those needs will be met within a mainstream school.
Statement of special educational needs (SEN)	A statement of special educational needs sets out in detail a pupil's special educational needs, the provision required to meet those needs, and the type and name of school that the pupil should attend.
Statutory review	Refers to the process for reviewing (and changing as necessary) care plans for looked after children.
Supervision Order (made in family proceedings)	Made on the same basis as a care order, in that the court believes that the child is suffering, or is likely to suffer, significant harm that is directly attributable to the care being provided by the child's parents (or carers), or because the child is beyond the parents' control. Children Act 1989 s31.

Unaccompanied asylum-seeking child.	A child (under 18) who is applying for asylum in his or her own right, and who is separated from both parents and is not being cared for by an adult who, by law or custom, has responsibility to do so.
Voluntary care	Non-statutory term used to identify those children in care who are not on a care order.
Well-being	Local authorities and other agencies are required to make arrangements to improve the well-being of children relating to the five 'outcomes' first set out in the Green Paper, *Every Child Matters*. As defined by Children Act 2004 s10, these five outcomes are:

- Physical and mental health and emotional well-being;
- Protection from harm and neglect;
- Education, training and recreation;
- The contribution made by children to society; and
- Social and economic well-being.

Youth inclusion project (YIP)	Established in 2000, the programmes target 13- to 16-year olds who are engaged in crime or are identified as being most at risk of offending, truancy or social exclusion. The projects operate in 72 of the most deprived/high crime estates in England and Wales. The projects offer activities, help with education and careers guidance.
Youth worker	Youth workers (also known as youth and community workers) promote young people's personal and social development through a range of non-formal educational activities that combine enjoyment and challenges. They work with young people between the ages of 11 and 25, but for the most part, with 13- to 19-year-olds. Youth workers are usually employed by a local authority's education department, but may sometimes be employed by the leisure, recreation or social services department. They may also be employed by voluntary organisations. They may be based in youth clubs or other community centres. Some youth workers are 'detached', which means that rather than work in a traditional youth centre, they meet young people in informal settings such as amusement arcades, shopping centres, on the streets, or wherever young people gather.

Mental disorders

This appendix provides a basic explanation of some of the most common mental disorders found in adolescents. It is intended to help the defence lawyer to be aware of the significance of a disorder both to a client's culpability and the way that the defence case is prepared.

Attention deficit hyperactivity disorder (ADHD)

The principal features of the disorder are impaired attention and over-activity. Both are necessary for the diagnosis and should be evident in more than one situation (eg home or school). The characteristic behaviour problems should be of early onset (before the age of six) and of long duration.[1]

A young person with ADHD may display the following:

- short attention span;
- distractibility;
- inability to foresee consequences of behaviour;
- low self-esteem;
- lack of impulse control;
- excitability;
- low frustration tolerance;
- high rate of activity;
- poor coordination.

Young people with ADHD frequently suffer from other disorders as well, the most common being conduct disorder, tic disorder, learning disabilities and epilepsy.

ADHD is diagnosed in boys more frequently than girls (ratio of 4:1). To meet the diagnostic criteria the symptoms must be evident from an early age and in at least two settings, e.g. home and school. Treatment can include medication (stimulants such as methylphidate (Ritalin) and dexamphetamine (Dexedrine)) or behavioural therapy.

Autistic spectrum disorders

A pervasive developmental disorder defined by the presence of abnormal and/or impaired development that is manifest before the age of three years and by the characteristic type of abnormal functioning in the areas of social interaction, communication and restricted repetitive behaviour.[2] The group of disorders will include autism and Asperger's syndrome.

A young person with an autistic spectrum disorder may display:

- an inability to empathise with others;
- a lack of understanding of rules governing social interaction;
- a lack of reciprocity in social interactions;
- impaired ability to form loving relationships;
- a lack of social conversation;

---

1 World Health Organisation, *International Classification of Diseases* (1992, 1996) referred to as ICD-10.
2 Ibid.

- inappropriate emotional expression;
- self-harming behaviour (eg head-banging or biting);
- stereotyped behaviour patterns, routines and rituals; and
- a resistance to change (and occasionally intense negative emotional response to change).

Autistic spectrum disorders are diagnosed in boys more often than girls (ratio 3 or 4: 1).

For more information about autism refer to the National Autism Society website www.nas.org.uk.

Conduct disorder

Conduct disorders are characterised by a repetitive and persistent pattern of dissocial, aggressive, or defiant conduct. Such behaviour, when at its most extreme for the individual, should amount to major violations of age-appropriate social expectations, and is therefore more severe than ordinary childish mischief or adolescent rebelliousness. Isolated criminal acts are not in themselves grounds for a diagnosis of conduct disorder which requires a enduring pattern of behaviour.[3]

Examples of behaviours on which the diagnosis is based include the following:
- excessive levels of fighting or bullying;
- cruelty to animals or other people;
- severe destructiveness to property;
- fire setting;
- stealing;
- repeated lying;
- truancy from school and running away from home;
- unusually frequent and severe temper tantrums;
- defiant, provocative behaviour; and
- persistent and severe disobedience.

Depression

In a typical depressive episode the individual suffers from depressed mood, loss of interest and enjoyment and reduced energy. A depressive episode may involve the young person displaying some of the following features:
- perceptual bias towards negative events;
- negative view of self, world and future;
- excessive guilt;
- ideas or acts of self-harm or suicide;
- inability to concentrate;
- inability to experience pleasure;
- irritable mood;
- anxiety and apprehension;
- disturbance of sleep;
- loss of appetite or overeating;
- change of mood during day (worse in the morning);
- deterioration in family relationships;
- withdrawal from peer relationships.

Learning disability

A learning disability is a reduced level of intellectual functioning resulting in diminished ability to adapt to the daily demands of the normal social environ-

---

3 World Health Organisation, *International Classification of Diseases* (1992, 1996) referred to as ICD-10.

ment.[4] A learning disability will have a significant impact on the way that a young person develops intellectually, emotionally and socially.

The assessment of intellectual level may involve psychometric tests to establish an intelligence quotient (IQ). For adolescents the psychometric test is likely to be the Wechsler Intelligence Scale for Children, Fourth Edition (WISC-IV) which provides a full-scale IQ as well as verbal and performance IQs. The average IQ is 100 and those with an IQ below 70 are considered to be learning disabled. The World Health Organisation further classifies IQ scores as follows:

IQ between 50 and 69	Mild mental retardation
IQ between 35 and 49	Moderate mental retardation
IQ between 20 and 34	Severe mental retardation
IQ below 20	Profound mental retardation

The learning disability is usually present from birth but may be acquired later in life (usually as a result of a head injury).

Among the general population approximately two per cent have an IQ below 70. Studies suggest that a much higher proportion of young offenders have an IQ which falls below that figure.

Adolescents with a low IQ may display the following features:
- limited internal control;
- impulsivity;
- poor ability to 'read' people or situations;
- poor planning ability;
- inattention and distractibility;
- poor language processing skills;
- tendency to speak aloud to organise themselves;
- reduced empathy and role-taking skills;
- high suggestibility; and
- limited ability to extricate themselves from difficult social situations leading to verbal or physical aggression.

Post-traumatic stress disorder (PTSD)

The disorder is defined as a delayed and/or protracted response to a stressful event or situation of an exceptionally threatening or catastrophic nature, likely to cause pervasive stress in almost anyone. The disorder may be caused by the child being involved in a serious accident, witnessing the violent death of another person, being the victim of a violent crime or sexual abuse. In the case of refugee children it could be caused by experiences during war or natural disaster.[5]

Typical symptoms include
- episodes of reliving the trauma in intrusive memories (flashbacks) or dreams;
- sense of numbness or emotional blunting;
- detachment from people;
- avoidance of activities and situations reminiscent of the trauma;
- disturbed sleep; and
- reduced appetite.

Specific learning disability

A young person who significantly underachieves in a specific scholastic skill or skills (for example, reading or arithmetic) relative to his/her age and general level of intelligence (IQ) is said to have a specific learning disability. In common usage, dyslexia is used to refer to a person who has a specific impairment in literacy skills.

---

4   World Health Organisation, *International Classification of Diseases* (1992, 1996) referred to as ICD-10.
5   Ibid.

Access to education, social services and health records

The right of access to personal files is governed by the Data Protection Act 1998. Legal guidance on the working of the Act has been provided by the Information Commissioner.[1]

The Act places duties upon 'data controllers', that is a person who (either alone or jointly or in common with other persons) determines the purposes for which and the manner in which any personal data are, or are to be, processed.[2] This definition will cover those individuals or organisations who hold a young client's education, social services and health records. Any request for access to those records by the defence lawyer on behalf of the client will be made under these provisions.

Right to information

Any individual is entitled:
- to be given a description of the personal data held by a data controller; and
- to have communicated to him or her in an intelligible form the information constituting the personal data.[3]

The right extends to personal data held in both manual and computerised records.

Access to specific types of information

Social services records

A person under 18 may request information from social services records. Where such a request is made, the local authority will need to decide whether or not s/he has sufficient understanding of the nature of the request. If the authority determines that s/he does, it should comply with the request.[4] If the person is deemed not to have sufficient understanding to make his/her own request, a person with parental responsibility can make the application on his/her behalf, provided the authority is satisfied that the request made is in the child's interest.[5]

A young client who has capacity to ask for information in his or her own name may appoint the defence lawyer as their agent to access the information on his or her behalf. The defence lawyer should provide written authority from the client. If an agent has been appointed, the local authority must treat any request from the defence lawyer as if it had been made by the child.[6]

Access need not be granted where the disclosure to the applicant would be likely to prejudice the carrying out of social work, by causing serious harm to the physical or mental health, or condition, of the applicant or another person.[7]

1 Information Commissioner, *Data Protection Act 1998 - Legal Guidance*. An electronic version of this guidance may be downloaded from the Commissioner's website. See appendix 14.
2 Data Protection Act 1998 s1.
3 Ibid, s7(1).
4 Department of Health, LASSL(2000)2 issuing *Data Protection Act 1998: Guidance to Social Services*, para 5.8.
5 Ibid, para 5.9
6 Ibid, para 5.13.
7 The Data Protection (Subject Access Modification) (Social Work) Order 2000 SI No 415.   737

Education record

'Education record' includes any information record which:
- is processed by or on behalf of the governing body or a teacher;
- relates to any person who is or has been a pupil at a school;
- originated from or was supplied by or on behalf of an employee of a local education authority or a teacher or educational psychologist employed by a voluntary aided, or foundation school.[8]

Pupils of any age may request access to their education records unless it is obvious that they do not understand what they are asking for.[9] Parents have a right of access to their children's education records until their child attains 18.[10]

Access need not be granted where disclosure of information contained in the education record would be likely to cause serious harm to the physical or mental health or condition of the applicant or to some other person or, in some circumstances, where disclosure would reveal that the applicant is, or may be, at risk of child abuse.[11]

A statement of special educational need should not generally be disclosed without the parent's consent. Relevant exceptions to this rule are:
- disclosure is to persons to whom, in the opinion of the authority concerned, the statement should be disclosed in the interests of the child; and
- on the order of any court or for the purposes of any criminal proceedings.[12]

Health records

Health records do not need to be disclosed where the data relates to the physical or mental health or condition of the child or young person to the extent which disclosure would cause serious harm to the physical or mental health or condition of the child or young person or any other person.[13] Where social services hold health records, they are required to consult a health professional responsible for the clinical care of the child or young person, before deciding whether this exemption applies.[14]

Form of application

The application to supply information must be in writing.[15] A fee may be charged subject to a statutory maximum of £10.00. There is however an exception for a request to access medical records. A maximum fee of £50.00 may be charged for granting access to manual records, or to a mixture of manual and automated records, where the request for access will be granted by supplying a copy of the records.

Disclosure of information

A data controller must comply with a request for information promptly and in any event before the end of 40 days.[16] This time limit runs from the date on which any fee required has been paid. It is therefore suggested that the statutory maximum fee of £10.00 is sent with the original request for information.

---

8 Data Protection Act 1998 s68 and Sch 11.
9 DfES Circular 15/2000 *Pupil Records and Reports*, p4.
10 Education (Pupil Information) England) Regulations 2000 SI No 1437 reg 5.
11 Education (The Data Protection (Subject Access Modifications) (Education)) Order 2000 SI No 414.
12 Education (Special Educational Needs) Regulations 1994 SI No 1047 reg 19, expressly preserved by The Data Protection (Miscellaneous Subject Access Exemptions) Order 2000 SI No 419.
13 Health Protection (Subject Access Modification) (Health) Order 2000 SI No 413 reg 5(1).
14 Ibid, reg 5(2).
15 Data Protection Act 1998 s7(2)(a).
16 Ibid, s7(8) and (10).

Third party information

Where the data controller cannot comply with the request without disclosing information relating to another individual who can be identified from that information, it is not obliged to comply with the request unless:

- the other individual has consented to the disclosure of the information to the person making the request, or
- it is reasonable in all the circumstances to comply with the request without the consent of the other individual.[17]

In determining whether it is reasonable in all the circumstances to comply with the request without the consent of the third party, the data controller shall have regard in particular to:

- any duty of confidentiality owed to the other individual;
- any steps taken by the data controller with a view to seeking the consent of the other individual;
- whether the other individual is capable of giving consent; and
- any express refusal of consent by the other individual.[18]

Statutory crime exemption

Data Protection Act 1998 s29 provides that a data controller need not disclose personal data where the controller considers that disclosure would be likely to prejudice criminal investigations or crime prevention. This exception should only be invoked where there is a 'substantial chance' of such prejudice.[19]

Appeals procedure

If disclosure is refused the applicant may:

- lodge a complaint with the Information Commissioner;[20] or
- seek compensation from the civil courts.[21]

---

17 Data Protection Act 1998 s7(4).
18 Ibid, s7(6).
19 Information Commissioner, *Data Protection Act 1998 – Legal Guidance*, para 3.37.
20 Data Protection Act 1998 s30(1) and Data Protection (Subject Access Modification) (Health) Order 2000 SI No 413.
21 Data Protection Act 1998 s7(9).

Extracts from legislation

(i) Mode of trial (law on publication)[1]

Magistrates' Courts Act 1980

Summary trial of information against child or young person for indictable offence

24A (1)Where a person under the age of 18 appears or is brought before a magistrates' court on an information charging him with an indictable offence other than one falling within subsection (1B) below, he shall be tried summarily unless –

(a) the offence is such as is mentioned in subsection (1) or (2) of section 91 of the Powers of Criminal Courts (Sentencing) Act 2000 (under which young people convicted on indictment of certain grave crimes may be sentenced to be detained for long periods) and the court considers that if he is found guilty of the offence it ought to be possible to sentence him in pursuance of subsection (3) of that section; or

(b) he is charged jointly with a person who has attained the age of 18 and the court considers it necessary in the interests of justice to commit them both for trial;

and accordingly in a case falling within paragraph (a) or (b) of this subsection the court shall commit the accused for trial if either it is of the opinion that there is sufficient evidence to put him on trial or it has power under section 6(2) above so to commit him without consideration of the evidence.

(1A) Where a magistrates' court –

(a) commits a person under the age of 18 for trial for an offence falling within subsection (1B) below; or

(b) in a case falling within subsection (1)(a) above, commits such a person for trial for an offence,

the court may also commit him for trial for any other indictable offencw with which he is charged at the same time if the charges for both offences could be joined in the same indictment.

(1B) An offence falls within this subsection if –

(a) it is an offence of homicide; or

(b) each of the requirements of section 51A(1) of the Firearms Act 1968 would be satisfied in respect to –

(i) the offence; and

(ii) the person charged with it,

if he were convicted of the offence.

(2) Where, in a case falling within subsection (1)(b) above, a magistrates' court commits a person under the age of 18 for trial for an offence with which he is charged jointly with a person who has attained that age, the court may also commit him for trial for any indictable offence with which he is charged at the same time (whether jointly with that person who has attained that age or not) if the charges for both offences could be joined in the same indictment.

(3) If on trying a person summarily in pursuance of subsection (1) above the court finds him guilty, it may impose a fine of an amount not exceeding £1,000 or may exercise the same powers as it could have exercised if he had been found guilty

---

1 See appendix 13 for the forthcoming law.

of an offence for which, but for section 89(1) of the said Act of 2000, it could have sentence him to imprisonment for a term not exceeding –

(a) the maximum term of imprisonment for the offence on conviction on indict-ment; or

(b) six months,

whichever is the less.

(4) In relation to a person under the age of 14 subsection (3) above shall have effect as if for the words '£1,000' there were substituted the words '£250'.

Crime and Disorder Act 1998

No committal proceedings for indictable-only offences

51 (1) Where an adult appears or is brought before a magistrates' court ('the court') charged with an offence triable only on indictment ('the indictable-only offence'), the court shall send him forthwith to the Crown Court for trial-

(a) for that offence, and

(b) for any either-way or summary offence with which he is charged which fulfils the requisite conditions (as set out in subsection (11) below).

(2) Where an adult who has been sent for trial under subsection (1) above subsequent-ly appears or is brought before a magistrates' court charged with an either-way or summary offence which fulfils the requisite conditions, the court may send him forthwith to the Crown Court for trial for the either-way or summary offence.

(3) Where –

(a) the court sends an adult for trial under subsection (1) above;

(b) another adult appears or is brought before the court on the same or a subse-quent occasion charged jointly with him with an either-way offence; and

(c) that offence appears to the court to be related to the indictable-only offence,

the court shall where it is the same occasion, and may where it is a subsequent occa-sion, send the other adult forthwith to the Crown Court for trial for the either-way offence.

(4) Where a court sends an adult for trial under subsection (3) above, it shall at the same time send him to the Crown Court for trial for any either-way or summary offence with which he is charged which fulfils the requisite conditions.

(5) Where –

(a) the court sends an adult for trial under subsection (1) or (3) above; and

(b) a child or young person appears or is brought before the court on the same or a subsequent occasion charged jointly with the adult with an indictable offence for which the adult is sent for trial,

the court shall, if it considers it necessary in the interests of justice to do so, send the child or young person forthwith to the Crown Court for trial for the indictable offence.

(6) Where a court sends a child or young person for trial under subsection (5) above, it may at the same time send him to the Crown Court for trial for any either-way or summary offence with which he is charged which fulfils the requisite conditions.

(7) The court shall specify in a notice the offence or offences for which a person is sent for trial under this section and the place at which he is to be tried; and a copy of the notice shall be served on the accused and given to the Crown Court sitting at that place.

(8) In a case where there is more than one indictable-only offence and the court includes an either-way or a summary offence in the notice under subsection (7) above, the court shall specify in that notice the indictable-only offence to which the either-way offence or, as the case may be, the summary offence appears to the court to be related.

(9) The trial of the information charging any summary offence for which a person is sent for trial under this section shall be treated as if the court had adjourned

it under section 10 of the 1980 Act and had not fixed the time and place for its resumption.

(10) In selecting the place of trial for the purpose of subsection (7) above, the court shall have regard to –

(a) the convenience of the defence, the prosecution and the witnesses;

(b) the desirability of expediting the trial; and

(c) any direction given by or on behalf of the Lord Chief Justice with the concurrence of the Lord Chancellor under section 75(1) of the Supreme Court Act 1981.

(11) An offence fulfils the requisite conditions if –

(a) it appears to the court to be related to the indictable-only offence; and

(b) in the case of a summary offence, it is punishable with imprisonment or involves obligatory or discretionary disqualification from driving.

(12) For the purposes of this section –

(a) 'adult' means a person aged 18 or over, and references to an adult include references to a corporation;

(b) 'either-way offence' means an offence which, if committed by an adult, is triable either on indictment or summarily;

(c) an either-way offence is related to an indictable-only offence if the charge for the either-way offence could be joined in the same indictment as the charge for the indictable-only offence;

(d) a summary offence is related to an indictable-only offence if it arises out of circumstances which are the same as or connected with those giving rise to the indictable-only offence.

Sending cases to the Crown Court: children and young persons

51A(1) This section is subject to sections 24A and 24B of the Magistrates' Courts Act 1980 (which provide for certain offences involving children or young persons to be tried summarily).

(2) Where a child or young person appears or is brought before a magistrates' court ('the court') charged with an offence and any of the conditions mentioned in subsection (3) below is satisfied, the court shall send him forthwith to the Crown Court for trial for the offence.

(3) Those conditions are –

(a) [*Not in force.*];

(b) [*Not in force.*];

(c) [*Not in force.*];

(d) that the offence is a specified offence (within the meaning of section 224 of the Criminal Justice Act 2003) and it appears to the court that if he is found guilty of the offence the criteria for the imposition of a sentence under section 226(3) or 228(2) of that Act would be met.

(4) Where the court sends a child or young person for trial under subsection (2) above, it may at the same time send him to the Crown Court for trial for any indictable or summary offence with which he is charged and which-

(a) (if it is an indictable offence) appears to the court to be related to the offence mentioned in subsection (2) above; or

(b) (if it is a summary offence) appears to the court to be related to the offence mentioned in subsection (2) above or to the indictable offence, and which fulfils the requisite condition (as defined in subsection (9) below).

(5) Where a child or young person who has been sent for trial under subsection (2) above subsequently appears or is brought before a magistrates' court charged with an indictable or summary offence which-

(a) appears to the court to be related to the offence mentioned in subsection (2) above; and

(b) (in the case of a summary offence) fulfils the requisite condition,

the court may send him forthwith to the Crown Court for trial for the indictable or summary offence.

(6) Where –

(a) the court sends a child or young person ('C') for trial under subsection (2) or (4) above; and

(b) an adult appears or is brought before the court on the same or a subsequent occasion charged jointly with C with an either-way offence for which C is sent for trial under subsection (2) or (4) above, or an either-way offence which appears to the court to be related to that offence,

the court shall where it is the same occasion, and may where it is a subsequent occasion, send the adult forthwith to the Crown Court for trial for the either-way offence.

(7) Where the court sends an adult for trial under subsection (6) above, it shall at the same time send him to the Crown Court for trial for any either-way or summary offence with which he is charged and which –

(a) (if it is an either-way offence) appears to the court to be related to the offence for which he was sent for trial; and

(b) (if it is a summary offence) appears to the court to be related to the offence for which he was sent for trial or to the either-way offence, and which fulfils the requisite condition.

(8) The trial of the information charging any summary offence for which a person is sent for trial under this section shall be treated as if the court had adjourned it under section 10 of the 1980 Act and had not fixed the time and place for its resumption.

(9) A summary offence fulfils the requisite condition if it is punishable with imprisonment or involves obligatory or discretionary disqualification from driving.

(10) In the case of a child or young person charged with an offence –

(a) if the offence satisfies any of the conditions in subsection (3) above, the offence shall be dealt with under subsection (2) above and not under any other provision of this section or section 51 above;

(b) subject to paragraph (a) above, if the offence is one in respect of which the requirements of subsection (7) of section 51 above for sending the child or young person to the Crown Court are satisfied, the offence shall be dealt with under that subsection and not under any other provision of this section or section 51 above.

(11) The functions of a magistrates' court under this section, and its related functions under section 51D below, may be discharged by a single justice.

(12) [*Not reproduced.*]

Provisions supplementing section 51

52 (1) Subject to section 4 of the Bail Act 1976, section 41 of the 1980 Act, regulations under section 22 of the 1985 Act and section 25 of the 1994 Act, the court may send a person for trial under section 51 above –

(a) in custody, that is to say, by committing him to custody there to be safely kept until delivered in due course of law; or

(b) on bail in accordance with the Bail Act 1976, that is to say, by directing him to appear before the Crown Court for trial.

(2) Where –

(a) the person's release on bail under subsection (1)(b) above is conditional on his providing one or more sureties; and

(b) in accordance with subsection (3) of section 8 of the Bail Act 1976, the court fixes the amount in which a surety is to be bound with a view to his entering into his recognisance subsequently in accordance with subsections (4) and (5) or (6) of that section,

the court shall in the meantime make an order such as is mentioned in subsection (1)(a) above.

(3) The court shall treat as an indictable offence for the purposes of section 51 above an offence which is mentioned in the first column of Schedule 2 to the 1980 Act (offences for which the value involved is relevant to the mode of trial) unless it is clear to the court, having regard to any representations made by the prosecutor or the accused, that the value involved does not exceed the relevant sum.

(4) In subsection (3) above 'the value involved' and 'the relevant sum' have the same meanings as in section 22 of the 1980 Act (certain offences triable either way to be tried summarily if value involved is small).

(5) A magistrates' court may adjourn any proceedings under section 51 above, and if it does so shall remand the accused.

(6) Schedule 3 to this Act (which makes further provision in relation to persons sent to the Crown Court for trial under section 51 above) shall have effect.

Powers of Criminal Courts (Sentencing) Act 2000

Committal for sentence of dangerous young offenders

3C(1) This section applies where on the summary trial of a specified offence a person aged under 18 is convicted of the offence.

(2) If, in relation to the offence, it appears to the court that the criteria for the imposition of a sentence under section 226(3) or 228(2) of the Criminal Justice Act 2003 would be met, the court must commit the offender in custody or on bail to the Crown Court for sentence in accordance with section 5A(1) below.

(3) Where the court commits a person under subsection (2) above, section 6 below (which enables a magistrates' court, where it commits a person under this section in respect of an offence, also to commit him to the Crown Court to be dealt with in respect of certain other offences) shall apply accordingly.

(4) Nothing in this section shall prevent the court from committing a specified offence to the Crown Court for sentence under section 3B above if the provisions of that section are satisfied.

(5) In this section, references to a specified offence are to a specified offence within the meaning of section 224 of the Criminal Justice Act 2003.

Offenders under 18 convicted of certain serious offences: power to detain for specified period

91 (1) Subsection (3) below applies where a person aged under 18 is convicted on indictment of –

(a) an offence punishable in the case of a person aged 21 or over with imprisonment for 14 years or more, not being an offence the sentence for which is fixed by law; or

(b) an offence under section 3 of the Sexual Offences Act 2003 (in this section, 'the 2003 Act') (sexual assault); or

(c) an offence under section 13 of the 2003 Act (child sex offences committed by children or young persons); or

(d) an offence under section 25 of the 2003 Act (sexual activity with a child family member); or

(e) an offence under section 26 of the 2003 Act (inciting a child family member to engage in sexual activity).

(1A) Subsection (3) also applies where-

(a) a person aged under 18 is convicted on indictment of an offence –

(i) under subsection (1)(a), (ab), (aba), (ac), (ad), (ae), (af) or (c) of section 5 of the Firearms Act 1968 (prohibited weapons), or

(ii) under subsection (1A)(a) of that section,

(b) the offence was committed after the commencement of section 51A of that Act and at at iem when he was aged 16 or over, and

(c) the court is of the opinion mentioned in section 51A(2) of that Act (exceptional circumstances which justify its not imposing required custodial sentence).

(2) [*Repealed.*]

(3) If the court is of the opinion that neither a community sentence nor a detention and training order is suitable, the court may sentence the offender to be detained for such period, not exceeding the maximum term of imprisonment with which the offence is punishable in the case of a person aged 21 or over, as may be specified in the sentence.

(4) Subsection (3) above is subject to (in particular) section 152 and 153 of the Criminal Justice Act 2003.

(5) Where subsection (2) of section 51A of the Firearms Act 1968 requires the imposition of a sentence of detention under this section for a term of at least the required minimum term (within the meaning of that section), the court shall sentence the offender to be detained for such period, of at least that term but not exceeding the maximum term of imprisonment with which the offence is punishable in the case of a person aged 18 or over, as may be specified in the sentence.

(ii) Custodial remands

Children and Young Persons Act 1969

Version applicable to boys aged 12 to 14 and girls aged 12 to 16.

Remand to local authority accommodation, committal of young persons of unruly character, etc

23 (1) Where –

    (a) a court remands a child or young person charged with or convicted of one or more offences or commits him for trial or sentence; and

    (b) he is not released on bail,

the remand or committal shall be to local authority accommodation; and in the following provisions of this section (except subsection (1A)), any reference (however expressed) to a remand shall be construed as including a reference to a committal.

(1A) Where a court remands a child or young person in connection with extradition proceedings and he is not released on bail the remand shall be to local authority accommodation.

(2) A court remanding a person to local authority accommodation shall designate the local authority who are to receive him; and that authority shall be –

    (a) in the case of a person who is being looked after by a local authority, that authority; and

    (b) in any other case, the local authority in whose area it appears to the court that he resides or the offence or one of the offences was committed.

(3) Where a person is remanded to local authority accommodation, it shall be lawful for any person acting on behalf of the designated authority to detain him.

(4) Subject to subsections (5), (5ZA) and (5A) below, a court remanding a person to local authority accommodation may, after consultation with the designated authority, require that authority to comply with a security requirement, that is to say, a requirement that the person in question be placed and kept in secure accommodation.

(5) A court shall not impose a security requirement in relation to a person remanded in accordance with subsection (1) above except in respect of a child who has attained the age of twelve, or a young person, who (in either case) is of a prescribed description, and then only if –

    (a) he is charged with or has been convicted of a violent or sexual offence, or an offence punishable in the case of an adult with imprisonment for a term of fourteen years or more; or

    (b) he is charged with or has been convicted of one or more imprisonable offences which, together with any other imprisonable offences of which he has been convicted in any proceedings –

  (i) amount, or

  (ii) would, if he were convicted of the offences with which he is charged, amount, to a recent history of repeatedly committing imprisonable offences while remanded on bail or to local authority accommodation,

and (in either case) the condition set out in subsection (5AA) below is satisfied.

(5ZA) A court shall not impose a security requirement in relation to a person remanded in accordance with subsection (1A) above unless –

  (a) he has attained the age of twelve and is of a prescribed description;

  (b) one or both of the conditions set out in subsection (5ZB) below is satisfied; and

  (c) the condition set out in subsection (5AA) below is satisfied.

(5ZB) The conditions mentioned in subsection (5ZA)(b) above are –

  (a) that the conduct constituting the offence to which the extradition proceedings relate would if committed in the United Kingdom constitute an offence punishable in the case of an adult with imprisonment for a term of fourteen years or more;

  (b) that the person has previously absconded from the extradition proceedings or from proceedings in the United Kingdom or the requesting territory which relate to the conduct constituting the offence to which the extradition proceedings relate.

(5ZC) For the purposes of subsection (5ZB) above a person has absconded from proceedings if in relation to those proceedings –

  (a) he has been released subject to a requirement to surrender to custody at a particular time and he has failed to surrender to custody at that time, or

  (b) he has surrendered into the custody of a court and he has at any time absented himself from the court without its leave.

(5AA) The condition mentioned in subsections (5) and (5ZA) above is that the court is of the opinion, after considering all the options for the remand of the person, that only remanding him to local authority accommodation with a security requirement would be adequate –

  (a) to protect the public from serious harm from him; or

  (b) to prevent the commission by him of imprisonable offences.

(5A) A court shall not impose a security requirement in respect of a child or young person who is not legally represented in the court unless –

  (a) he was granted a right to representation funded by the Legal Services Commission as part of the Criminal Defence Service but the right was withdrawn because of his conduct *or because it appeared that his financial resources were such that he was not eligible to be granted such a right*; [or]

  (aa) *he applied for such representation and the application was refused because it appeared that his financial resources were such that he was not eligible to be granted a right to it; or*

  (b) having been informed of his right to apply for such representation and had the opportunity to do so, he refused or failed to apply.[2]

(6) Where a court imposes a security requirement in respect of a person, it shall be its duty –

  (a) to state in open court that it is of such opinion as is mentioned in subsection (5AA) above; and

  (b) to explain to him in open court and in ordinary language why it is of that opinion;

and a magistrates' court shall cause a reason stated by it under paragraph (b) above to be specified in the warrant of commitment and to be entered in the register.

---

2 Words in italics in subsection (5A) inserted by the Criminal Defence Service Act 2006 s4(2)(a), (3)(a) and (b) as of 2 October 2006.

(7) Subject to section 23AA below, a court remanding a person to local authority accommodation without imposing a security requirement may, after consultation with the designated authority, require that person to comply with

(a) any such conditions as could be imposed under section 3(6) of the Bail Act 1976 if he were then being granted bail; and

(b) any conditions imposed for the purpose of securing the electronic monitoring of his compliance with any other condition imposed under this subsection.

(7A) Where a person is remanded to local authority accommodation and a security requirement is imposed in respect of him –

(a) the designated local authority may, with the consent of the Secretary of State, arrange for the person to be detained, for the whole or any part of the period of the remand or committal, in a secure training centre; and

(b) his detention there pursuant to the arrangements shall be lawful.

(7B) Arrangements under subsection (7A) above may include provision for payments to be made by the authority to the Secretary of State.

(8) Where a court imposes on a person any such conditions as are mentioned in sub-section (7) above, it shall be its duty to explain to him in open court and in ordinary language why it is imposing those conditions; and a magistrates' court shall cause a reason stated by it under this subsection to be specified in the warrant of commit-ment and to be entered in the register.

(9) A court remanding a person to local authority accommodation without imposing a security requirement may, after consultation with the designated authority, impose on that authority requirements –

(a) for securing compliance with any conditions imposed on that person under subsection (7) above; or

(b) stipulating that he shall not be placed with a named person.

(10) Where a person is remanded to local authority accommodation, a relevant court –

(a) may, on the application of the designated authority, impose on that person any such conditions as could be imposed under subsection (7) above if the court were then remanding him to such accommodation; and

(b) where it does so, may impose on that authority any requirements for securing compliance with the conditions so imposed.

(11) Where a person is remanded to local authority accommodation, a relevant court may, on the application of the designated authority or that person, vary or revoke any conditions or requirements imposed under subsection (7), (9) or (10) above.

(12) In this section –

'court' and 'magistrates' court' include a justice;

'children's home' has the same meaning as in the Care Standards Act 2000;

'extradition proceedings' means proceedings under the Extradition Act 2003;

'imprisonable offence' means an offence punishable in the case of an adult with imprisonment;

'prescribed description' means a description prescribed by reference to age or sex or both by an order of the Secretary of State;

'relevant court' –

(a) in relation to a person remanded to local authority accommodation under sub-section (1) above, means the court by which he was so remanded, or any mag-istrates' court having jurisdiction in the place where he is for the time being;

(b) in relation to a person remanded to local authority accommodation under sub-section (1A) above, means the court by which he was so remanded;

'requesting territory' means the territory to which a person's extradition is sought in extradition proceedings;

'secure accommodation' means accommodation which is provided in a children's home in respect of which a person is registered under Part II of the Care Standards Act 2000 for the purpose of restricting liberty, and is approved for that purpose by the Secretary of State or the National Assembly for Wales;

'sexual offence' means an offence specified in Part 2 of Sch 15 to the Criminal Justice Act 2003;

'violent offence' means murder or an offence specified in Part 1 of Sch 15 to the Criminal Justice Act 2003;

'young person' means a person who has attained the age of fourteen years and is under the age of seventeen years;

but, for the purposes of the definition of 'secure accommodation', 'local authority accommodation' includes any accommodation falling within s61(2) of the Criminal Justice Act 1991.

(13) In this section –

(a) any reference to a person who is being looked after by a local authority shall be construed in accordance with section 22 of the Children Act 1989;

(b) any reference to consultation shall be construed as a reference to such consultation (if any) as is reasonably practicable in all the circumstances of the case; and

(c) any reference, in relation to a person charged with or convicted of a violent or sexual offence, to protecting the public from serious harm from him shall be construed as a reference to protecting members of the public from death or serious personal injury, whether physical or psychological, occasioned by further such offences committed by him.

(14) This section has effect subject to –

(a) ...

(b) section 128(7) of that Act (remands to the custody of a constable for periods of not more than three days),

but section 128(7) shall have effect in relation to a child or young person as if for the reference to three clear days there were substituted a reference to twenty-four hours.

Children and Young Persons Act 1969

Section 23 as modified in respect of 15 and 16-year old males by the Crime and Disorder Act 1998 s98:

Remand to local authority accommodation, committal of young persons of unruly character, etc

23 (1) Where –

(a) a court remands a child or young person charged with or convicted of one or more offences or commits him for trial or sentence; and

(b) he is not released on bail, and

(c) is not remanded in connection with proceedings under the Extradition Act 2003.

the remand or committal shall be to local authority accommodation; and in the following provisions of this section (except subsection (1A)), any reference (however expressed) to a remand shall be construed as including a reference to a committal.

(1A) Where a court remands a child or young person in connection with extradition proceedings and he is not released on bail the remand shall be to local authority accommodation.

(2) A court remanding a person to local authority accommodation shall designate the local authority who are to receive him; and that authority shall be –

(a) in the case of a person who is being looked after by a local authority, that authority; and

(b) in any other case, the local authority in whose area it appears to the court that he resides or the offence or one of the offences was committed.

(3) Where a person is remanded to local authority accommodation, it shall be lawful for any person acting on behalf of the designated authority to detain him.

(4) Where a court after consultation with an officer of an local probation board, a social worker of a local authority social services department or a member of youth offending team, declares a person to be one to whom subsection (5) below applies-

    (a) it shall remand him to local authority accommodation and require him to be placed and kept in secure accommodation, if –

        (i) it also, after such consultation, declares him to be a person to whom subsection (5A) below applies; and

        (ii) it has been notified that secure accommodation is available for him; or

    (b) (repealed);

    (c) if paragraph (a) above does not apply , it shall remand him to a prison.

(4A) A court shall not declare a person who is not legally represented in the court to be a person to whom subsection (5) below applies unless-

    (a) he was granted a right to representation funded by the Legal Services Commission as part of the Criminal Defence Service but the right was withdrawn because of his conduct *or because it appeared that his financial resources were such that he was not eligible to be granted such a right; [or]*

    (aa) he applied for such representation and the application was refused because it appeared that his financial resources were such that he was not eligible to be granted a right to it; or

    (b) having been informed of his right to apply for such representation and had the opportunity to do so, he refused or failed to apply.[3]

(5) This subsection applies to a person who –

    (a) is charged with or has been convicted of a violent or sexual offence, or an offence punishable in the case of an adult with imprisonment for a term of fourteen years or more; or

    (b) he is charged with or has been convicted of one or more imprisonable offences which, together with any other imprisonable offences of which he has been convicted in any proceedings –

        (i) amount, or

        (ii) would, if he were convicted of the offences with which he is charged, amount, to a recent history of repeatedly committing imprisonable offences while remanded on bail or to local authority accommodation,

and (in either case) the condition set out in subsection (5AA) below is satisfied.

(5ZA)A court shall not impose a security requirement in relation to a person remanded in accordance with subsection (1A) above unless –

    (a) he has attained the age of twelve and is of a prescribed description;

    (b) one or both of the conditions set out in subsection (5ZB) below is satisfied; and

    (c) the condition set out in subsection (5AA) below is satisfied.

(5ZB)The conditions mentioned in subsection (5ZA)(b) above are –

    (a) that the conduct constituting the offence to which the extradition proceedings relate would if committed in the United Kingdom constitute an offence punishable in the case of an adult with imprisonment for a term of fourteen years or more;

    (b) that the person has previously absconded from the extradition proceedings or from proceedings in the United Kingdom or the requesting territory which relate to the conduct constituting the offence to which the extradition proceedings relate.

(5ZC)For the purposes of subsection (5ZB) above a person has absconded from proceedings if in relation to those proceedings –

---

3 Words in italics in subsection (4A) inserted by the Criminal Defence Service Act 2006 s4(2)(a), (3)(a) and (b) as of 2 October 2006.

(a) he has been released subject to a requirement to surrender to custody at a particular time and he has failed to surrender to custody at that time, or

(b) he has surrendered into the custody of a court and he has at any time absented himself from the court without its leave.

(5AA)The condition mentioned in subsections (5) and (5ZA) above is that the court is of the opinion, after considering all the options for the remand of the person, that only remanding him to a remand centre or prison, or to local authority accommodation with a requirement that he be placed and kept in secure accommodation would be adequate –

(a) to protect the public from serious harm from him; or

(b) to prevent the commission by him of imprisonable offences.

(5A) This subsection applies to a person if the court is of the opinion that , by reason of his physical or emotional immaturity or a propensity of his to harm himself, it would be undesirable from him to be remanded to a remand centre or a prison.

(6) Where a court declares a person to be one to whom subsection (5) above, it shall be its duty –

(a) to state in open court that it is of such opinion as is mentioned in subsection (5AA) above; and

(b) to explain to him in open court and in ordinary language why it is of that opinion;

and a magistrates' court shall cause a reason stated by it under paragraph (b) above to be specified in the warrant of commitment and to be entered in the register.

(7) Subject to section 23AA below, a court remanding a person to local authority accommodation without imposing a security requirement (that is to say, a requirement imposed under subsection (4)(a) above that the person be placed and kept in secure accommodation may, after consultation with the designated authority, require that person to comply with

(a) any such conditions as could be imposed under section 3(6) of the Bail Act 1976 if he were then being granted bail; and

(b) any conditions imposed for the purpose of securing the electronic monitoring of his compliance with any other condition imposed under this subsection.

(7A) Where a person is remanded to local authority accommodation and a security requirement is imposed in respect of him –

(a) the designated local authority may, with the consent of the Secretary of State, arrange for the person to be detained, for the whole or any part of the period of the remand or committal, in a secure training centre; and

(b) his detention there pursuant to the arrangements shall be lawful.

(7B) Arrangements under subsection (7A) above may include provision for payments to be made by the authority to the Secretary of State.

(8) Where a court imposes on a person any such conditions as are mentioned in subsection (7) above, it shall be its duty to explain to him in open court and in ordinary language why it is imposing those conditions; and a magistrates' court shall cause a reason stated by it under this subsection to be specified in the warrant of commitment and to be entered in the register.

(9) A court remanding a person to local authority accommodation without imposing a security requirement may, after consultation with the designated authority, impose on that authority requirements –

(a) for securing compliance with any conditions imposed on that person under subsection (7) above; or

(b) stipulating that he shall not be placed with a named person.

(9A) Where a person is remanded to local authority accommodation without the imposition of a security requirement, a relevant court may, on the application of the designated authority, declare him to be a person to whom subsection (5) above applies, and on its doing so, subsection (4) above shall apply.

(10) Where a person is remanded to local authority accommodation, a relevant court –

(a) may, on the application of the designated authority, impose on that person any such conditions as could be imposed under subsection (7) above if the court were then remanding him to such accommodation; and

(b) where it does so, may impose on that authority any requirements for securing compliance with the conditions so imposed.

(11) Where a person is remanded to local authority accommodation, a relevant court may, on the application of the designated authority or that person, vary or revoke any conditions or requirements imposed under subsection (7), (9) or (10) above.

(12) In this section –

'court' and 'magistrates' court' include a justice;

'children's home' has the same meaning as in the Care Standards Act 2000;

'extradition proceedings' means proceedings under the Extradition Act 2003;

'imprisonable offence' means an offence punishable in the case of an adult with imprisonment;

'prescribed description' means a description prescribed by reference to age or sex or both by an order of the Secretary of State;

'relevant court' –

(a) in relation to a person remanded to local authority accommodation under subsection (1) above, means the court by which he was so remanded, or any magistrates' court having jurisdiction in the place where he is for the time being;

(b) in relation to a person remanded to local authority accommodation under subsection (1A) above, means the court by which he was so remanded;

'requesting territory' means the territory to which a person's extradition is sought in extradition proceedings;

'secure accommodation' means accommodation which is provided in a children's home in respect of which a person is registered under Part II of the Care Standards Act 2000 for the purpose of restricting liberty, and is approved for that purpose by the Secretary of State or the National Assembly for Wales;

'sexual offence' means an offence specified in Part 2 of Sch 15 to the Criminal Justice Act 2003;

'violent offence' means murder or an offence specified in Part 1 of Sch 15 to the Criminal Justice Act 2003;

'young person' means a person who has attained the age of fourteen years and is under the age of seventeen years;

but, for the purposes of the definition of 'secure accommodation', 'local authority accommodation' includes any accommodation falling within s61(2) of the Criminal Justice Act 1991.

(13) In this section –

(a) any reference to a person who is being looked after by a local authority shall be construed in accordance with section 22 of the Children Act 1989;

(b) any reference to consultation shall be construed as a reference to such consultation (if any) as is reasonably practicable in all the circumstances of the case; and

(c) any reference, in relation to a person charged with or convicted of a violent or sexual offence, to protecting the public from serious harm from him shall be construed as a reference to protecting members of the public from death or serious personal injury, whether physical or psychological, occasioned by further such offences committed by him.

(14) This section has effect subject to –

(a) ...

(b) section 128(7) of that Act (remands to the custody of a constable for periods of not more than three days),

but section 128(7) shall have effect in relation to a child or young person as if for the reference to three clear days there were substituted a reference to twenty-four hours.

ACPO Youth offender case disposal gravity factor system[1]

Introduction

This youth offender case disposal gravity factor system has been drawn up by the Association of Chief Police Officers in consultation with the Crown Prosecution Service, the Home Office and the Youth Justice Board. For further information please contact:

PS Ian Carter
PEPYS Programme Manager
Essex Police Headquarters
PO Box 2, Springfield
Chelmsford CM2 6DA

Tel: 01245 491491
E-mail: ian.carter538@essex.pnn.police.uk

The key factors which will be relevant in deciding whether to charge, warn or reprimand a young person for an offence are: (a) *the young person's offending history*, and (b) *the seriousness of the offence*. If the young offender has previously been convicted of any offence (except where the only sentence was an Absolute or Conditonal Discharge), **or** received a warning within the previous two years, these gravity factors are irrelevant since the young offender **cannot** be reprimanded or warned. The seriousness of any offence relates both to the *nature of the offence and to the circumstances which surround it*. These issues are considered in more detail below. A further factor to be considered is whether or not it is *in the public interest* for the young offender to be prosecuted. This issue is examined further in the main body of the Final Warning Scheme Guidance.

The tables below classify most common offences on a scale of 1 (low gravity) up to 4 (high gravity) based on the seriousness of the individual offence. The classifications in the tables are designed to assist in decision-making, but they cannot be regarded as a definitive guide, and must be considered alongside all the other issues outlined below. Factors which can make an offence more serious are shown as aggravating (+) while mitigating factors, making an offence less serious, are shown as (–). Some factors apply to all offences, including excluded offences in exceptional circumstances, and are listed as 'General Factors' while others are only applicable to specific offences and are listed as 'Offence Specific Gravity Factors'.

It is most important that the appropriate offence is determined according to the evidence, and that this is done before any consideration of the gravity factors. Equally, if having applied all the criteria, the police decision-maker is considering a reprimand or warning, care must be taken to ensure the offender stands reported or bailed for the appropriate offence and that there is no upgrading or down-grading simply to circumvent the criteria.

Having decided the appropriate offence, the gravity score can only be up-graded or downgraded by one point irrespective of the number of factors present. However,

---

1 Annex D to Home Office Circular 14/2006, May 2006. This circular can be downloaded from www.knowledgenetwork.gov.uk.

the mere presence of a (+) or (−) factor does not always mean an offence gravity score will be changed. It signifies a specific issue that **must** be considered by a decision-maker, together with all the other matters and, if significant, can change the decision that would otherwise have been made. As a result it could be the deciding factor for a particular decision or have no bearing on the decision. It is important for decision makers to ensure that both the 'offence specific gravity factors' and the 'general factors for all offences' are considered for each offence for which a decision is made. This will ensure that the seriousness of the offence, the particular circumstances of it, and the offender's current and previous behaviour are all considered. In every case the consideration given to aggravating and mitigating factors **must** be noted within the decision recorded.

Offences not shown in the matrix

Not all offences are included within this document. Any offences that are not shown should be dealt with in accordance with the general principles of this document.

Victims

One important factor will be the impact of the offence on the victim. Wherever possible, the victim should be contacted before a decision is made, to establish their view about the offence, the nature and extent of any harm or loss and its significance relative to the victim's circumstances. The victim's view about the offence may have a bearing on how serious the offence is judged to be but cannot be regarded as conclusive.

Racially and Religiously aggravated offences

Another important aggravating factor will be where an offence has a racial motivation. The 1998 Act and Anti-terrorism, Crime and Security Act 2001 introduced a range of new offences, based on existing offences, which incorporate this aggravating factor as part of the offence itself. Guidance on Racially and Religiously Aggravated Offences, part of the Crime & Disorder Act series, is available from the Home Office. The new offences are not included specifically in the matrix because the process of determining the gravity of the offence itself requires that where the victim's race is a motivation, consideration **must** be given to raising the gravity score of the offence. For example, the Act introduces a new offence of racially aggravated ABH (OAP Act 1861 s47). ABH attracts a gravity score of 3 in the matrix. Where the offence is racially aggravated ABH consideration **must** be given to raising this to 4.

Values of Property

Some of the criteria include a consideration of monetary value relevant to offences. Flexibility should be demonstrated by police decision-makers in comparing these values to those recorded against the relevant incident. Estimates of the value of property and of damage are often unreliable and tend to be subjective.

Traffic related offences

Where a young person commits a minor road traffic offence a fixed penalty notice remains an appropriate response for 16 and 17 year olds. If a young person receives such a penalty this has no bearing on the capacity of the police to issue reprimands or warnings for any further offences nor does it count as a conviction. Where a traffic offence is dealt with at court and results in a conviction this will, as with any other conviction, preclude the administration of a reprimand or warning for a further offence. Where offenders guilty of road traffic offences are dealt with by means of a caution, in the case of young offenders, this should result in a reprimand, warning or charge as appropriate.

Children and young people involved in prostitution

The final warning scheme replaces all cautioning for young people, which means that the prostitute's cautions will no longer be available as a disposal for prostitutes under the age of 18.

Young persons under the age of 18 who come to notice as being involved in prostitution should be dealt with in accordance with the joint Home Office/Department of Health guidance on the issue. That guidance emphasises that males and females under 18 are primarily victims of abuse who do not consent freely to prostitution. As such, they should if at all possible be diverted away from prostitution without recourse to the criminal justice system. However, the guidance makes it clear that in exceptional cases, where diversion has repeatedly failed, the police may, after consultation with others in the multi-agency group, take criminal action against a person under the age of 18 for loitering, soliciting or importuning. Where the offence is admitted, the young person can be dealt with under the final warning scheme. The guidance also sets out the approach to take where the person under 18 does not admit the offence.

Breaches of anti-social behaviour orders

Where an anti-social behaviour order (ASBO) has been obtained for a juvenile any breach of that ASBO should be dealt with in line with normal procedures for dealing with juvenile offenders. The police, in consultation with the youth offending team, should make an assessment of both the seriousness of the breach and of the young person's offending history. Where the breach of an ASBO is effectively a first criminal offence by the juvenile then a final warning may be appropriate, provided the breach was not a flagrant one. Where the breach was flagrant, then the expectation would be to charge, unless there were some very unusual circumstances.

Using the ACPO gravity factors

The following pages show various tables that can be applied to the gravity factor system; the first page deals with offences that would usually be excluded from the options of reprimand or warning, though in exceptional circumstances the general factors may be so significant that they could influence a reduction in gravity; the second and third pages list a number of general factors that might aggravate or mitigate the commission of any type of offence, including excluded offences in exceptional circumstances; and the remaining pages show lists of offences together with their standard gravity scores and those offence specific gravity factors that are considered appropriate to aggravate or mitigate each type of offence, according to the particular circumstances surrounding it. However, it should be remembered throughout the process that each case must be considered on its own merits.

The Criminal Justice Act 2003 passed the responsibility for making charging decisions from the police to the CPS in all indictable only, either way or summary offences, except those cases specified in the Director's Guidance, which the police may continue to charge. The police may still take the decision to issue a reprimand or final warning in all summary and either way offences without reference to the CPS where the police consider that the youth is eligible for diversion.

NB All indictable only offences must be referred to the CPS to decide whether to charge or divert, as only the CPS can make this decision.

The final gravity score

The presumptions applicable to the final gravity score reached, when all the relevant factors have been applied to the circumstances of a particular offence, are listed in the following table. This must be used in conjunction with the legislation in relation to the offender's qualification for reprimand, warning or charge. Where this assessment leads the police officer to consider a warning or charge there is also the option to ask the youth offending team to undertake a prior assessment of the young offender to inform their decision-making process.

Final score	Action
4	Normally result in charge.
3	Normally warn for a first offence. If offender does not qualify for a warning then charge. Only in exceptional circumstances should a reprimand be given. Decision-maker needs to justify reprimand.
2	Normally reprimand for a first offence. If offender does not qualify for a reprimand but qualifies for a warning then give warning. If offender does not qualify for a warning then charge.
1	Always the minimum response applicable to the individual offender, ie, reprimand, warning or charge.

Discretion does exist to deviate from the normal response, as indicated above, but only in exceptional circumstances, and such action would need to be justified by the decision maker. It would be impossible to articulate those circumstances which could be deemed to be exceptional, but police decision-makers will be aware that even the most serious of offences could amount to technical offences, the circumstances of which might appropriately attract a reprimand or warning. It would often be inappropriate to charge in such cases.

An 'informal warning', which falls outside the parameters of the table above, should only be given in exceptional circumstances where a minimal response is appropriate and usually when anti-social behaviour falls short of a substantive criminal offence. It may be administered instantly by the officer in the case, or by letter if the decision is made by a police decision-maker, when the case against the young person is unlikely to be proceeded with in the Youth Court.

'No Further Action' also has not been included in the above table as it is not so much a method of disposal for an admitted case of a young offender, as an acknowledgement that no action is appropriate or warranted in a particular case. No substantive offence can be mitigated down to warrant no further action, using the gravity factor decision process alone.

Recording the final gravity score

Where an offence attracts a reprimand or a warning, the final gravity score attributed to the offence should be clearly indicated on the record that is passed to the Youth Offending Team.

Monitoring use of the ACPO gravity factors

It is important that police apply the gravity factors accurately and consistently when undertaking gravity assessments. We recommend that Chief Officers put in place procedures to monitor how their staff administers the gravity assessment tool.

List of excluded offences

Abduction – girl under 16 years

Arson – with intent to endanger life / reckless whether life endangered

Assault – GBH/wounding with intent

Assault by penetration

Bail personation

Blackmail

Burglary – aggravated

Burglary with intent to commit indictable only offence

Causing/inciting person to engage in sexual activity without consent but with penetration

Child destruction

Corrosive fluid etc. throw with intent to maim etc.

Criminal damage – with intent to endanger life/ reckless as to whether life endangered

Escape – from lawful custody

Explosive substances offences (most)

False imprisonment

Firearm – possession with intent to endanger life/injure property

Firearm – possession while committing offence or with intent to commit offence or use to resist arrest

Infanticide

Kidnap

Murder / Manslaughter

Paying for sexual services of child under 13 with penetration

Perjury

Pervert course of justice, inc. conspiracy/attempt

Poison – administer/cause to be administered noxious substances with intent to injure etc.

Prison – escape/aid/assist

Rape

Riot

Robbery & assault with intent to rob

Sexual activity with person with mental disorder with penetration

Suicide/attempted – aid/abet/counsel

Trespass with intent to commit sexual offence

Traffic:

• death by dangerous driving

• death by careless driving aggravated by drugs or drink

• refusing to provide specimen of breath/blood/urine at police station

• excess alcohol/driving when unfit through drink/drugs

• drunk in charge

• driving whilst disqualified

• speeding (above fixed penalty speed)

• wanton and furious driving

General factors for consideration

The circumstances surrounding the offence should always be taken into account in determining the most appropriate response. There are a number of general factors that can affect the decision about how to proceed. These are set out in the next two tables.

Important: only one reprimand may be given. Where an offender has already received a reprimand, the minimum response will be a warning. Only one warning may normally be given. A second warning is only available where the previous offence was committed more that 2 years ago, and the offence is minor. Where an offender has already been warned, a further offence should normally result in a charge.

General factors for all offences

(+)	(−)
Conviction is likely to result in significant sentence.	Conviction is likely to result in unusually small or nominal penalty.
Weapon used or violence threatened during commission of offence.	Prosecution is likely to have bad effect on victim's physical or mental health.
Offence against public servant (eg, police, nurse, council employee, etc).	Offender supplied information which reduced risk, loss or harm to others.
Offender abused a position of trust – eg, banker, baby-sitter, shop assistant.	Offender was influenced by others more criminally sophisticated.
Offender was ringleader/organiser.	Genuine mistake or misunderstanding.
Evidence of premeditation.	Vulnerability of the offender.
Offender was part of an organised team or offence was committed by a group.	Provocation from victim or victim's group and offender reacted impulsively.
Victim was vulnerable, deliberately put in considerable fear or suffered personal attack, damage, disturbance, or domestic violence.	The offence is minor and offender has put right harm or loss caused; has expressed regret; offered reparation or compensation.
Offence motivated by discrimination against victim's racial or ethnic origin, religious beliefs, gender, political views or sexual preference.	Offender is or was at time of offence suffering from significant mental or physical ill-health and offence is not likely to be repeated.
There are grounds for believing the offence is likely to be repeated or continued – eg, by a history of recurring conduct.	The offence is so old that the relevance of any response is minimised, ie, there has been a long delay between the offence occurring and the point of decision making – Unless the offence is serious; the offender contributed to the delay; the offence only recently came to light; or the complexity of the offence has contributed to long investigation.
Evidence of exploitation.	
The offence, though minor, is prevalent in the local area – as identified in the local crime audit, specified in the youth justice plan or specifically agreed with CPS to warrant more serious response.	
Offence committed with intent to commit a sexual offence	

General factors for traffic offences

(+)	(−)
Serious injury caused to public or significant damage caused.	Genuine oversight, technically of the offence or emergency circumstances.
Multiple offenders involved in similar offences at same time/location.	No danger caused to public.
	Lack of knowledge.
Potential risk to public or resultant danger.	

Offence specific gravity factors for all offences

Offence	Gravity Score	Aggravating/Mitigating Factors +	−
ABDUCTION			
Abduction of girl under 16 Years	4	Defer decision to CPS	
Kidnap	4	Defer decision to CPS	
False imprisonment	4	Defer decision to CPS	
ANIMALS			
Causing unnecessary suffering by doing any act (Protection of Animals Act 1911)	3	• serious injury	• minor injury
Causing unnecessary suffering by omitting to do any act (1911 Act)	2	• not following instructions	• instructions not given
Cruelly ill-treat etc (1911 Act)	3	• premeditated instigator	• reckless participant
Permitting ill-treatment (1911 Act)	2		
Abandonment (Abandonment of Animals Act 1961)	2	• animal dies	• animal survives
Dog worrying livestock	2		• no apparent injury
Poaching offences	2	• organised/ sophistication • commercial purpose	
Dangerous dog (order to be kept under control or destroyed)	4		• dog destroyed
Abandoning, or allowing to stray, a fighting dog (Dangerous Dogs Act 1991 s1.2(e))	4		• dog destroyed
Possession without exemption of a pit bull terrier, Japanese tosa or other designated fighting dog (Dangerous Dogs Act 1991 s1.3)	4		• dog destroyed
Owner or person in charge allowing dog to be dangerously out of control in a public place injuring any person (Dangerous Dogs Act 1991 s3.1)	3	• serious injury • no effort to control	• minor injury • dog destroyed • beyond physical limitation of owner/ person in charge • first time in charge
Owner or person in charge allowing dog to be dangerously out of control in a public place, no injury being caused (Dangerous Dogs Act 1991 s3.1)	3	• person placed in fear • intent/disregard	• no injury/fear • dog destroyed • circumstances beyond the control of the offender

Offence specific gravity factors for all offences *continued*

Offence	Gravity Score	Aggravating/Mitigating Factors	
		+	−
ANIMALS *continued*			
Owner or person in charge allowing dog to enter a non-public place, and injure any person (Dangerous Dogs Act 1991 s3.3)	3	• serious injury	• minor injury • dog destroyed
Owner or person in charge allowing dog to enter a non-public place, causing reasonable apprehension that it would injure a person (Dangerous Dogs Act 1991 s3.3)	3	• intent/disregard	• dog destroyed • circumstances beyond the control of the offender
Allowing a fighting dog to be in a public place without a muzzle or a lead (Dangerous Dogs Act 1991 s1.2(d))	4	• fear/injury caused	• escaped despite precautions • dog destroyed
ANTI-SOCIAL BEHAVIOUR			
Breach of ASBO	3	• Flagrant breach	• Unaware of consequence of breach
Breach of ISO	3	• Flagrant breach	• Unaware of consequence of breach
Failing to disperse	2	• Flagrant breach	
ASSAULTS			
Threats to kill (OAP Act 1861 s16)	3	• calculated	• threat made in heat of the moment – no likelihood of violence now existing
Poison – administer/cause to be administered noxious substance with intent to injure, etc.	4	Defer decision to CPS	
Corrosive fluid, etc – throw with intent to maim, etc.	4	Defer decision to CPS	
GBH/wounding with intent (OAP Act 1861 s18)	4	Defer decision to CPS	
GBH/wounding (OAP Act 1861 s20)	4	• Weapon used • More than one blow • Unprovoked attack • Premeditation • Group action • Domestic violence	• Impulsive action • Provocation • Nature of the injury (especially where superficial wound)

Offence specific gravity factors for all offences *continued*

Offence	Gravity Score	Aggravating/Mitigating Factors +	−
ASSAULTS *continued*			
ABH (OAP Act 1861 s47)	3	• weapon used • more than one blow • attacked while victim 'vulnerable/ defenceless', eg, 'on floor' • unprovoked attack • nature of the injury (especially where serious/ disfiguring injury) • premeditation • domestic violence • group action	• Impulsive action • Provocation • Minor injury
Assault on police (Police Act 1996 s51)	3	• sustained assault • attempt to prevent arrest of another • premeditation • any injuries caused • group action	
Common assault (Criminal Justice Act 1988 s39)	2	• significant injury caused • deliberate aggression without provocation • vulnerable victim • weapon used • premeditation • domestic violence • group action	• trivial nature of action • impulsive action • injury very minor
BURGLARY			
Aggravated burglary	4	Defer decision to CPS	
Burglary with intent to inflict GBH	4		

Offence specific gravity factors for all offences *continued*

Offence	Gravity Score	Aggravating/Mitigating Factors	
		+	−
BURGLARY *continued*			
Burglary with intent to steal/ criminal damage	3	• night-time • occupier present • deliberately frightening occupants	• vacant premises • low value • coercion from others in group on reluctant offender
Burglary dwelling	4	• soiling/ ransacking/ damage	
Burglary non-dwelling	3	• professional operation • group offence • 'ram-raiding' • unrecoverable property of considerable value	
CRIMINAL DAMAGE			
Criminal damage	2	• damage deliberate rather than reckless • potential of greater danger • group offence • damage £500+ approx.	• damage £100 or less
Arson (where life not endangered)	3	• damage deliberate • potential of greater danger • group offence • damage £500+ approx.	• damage £100 or less
Criminal damage (including arson) with intent to endanger life or reckless as to whether life is endangered	4	Defer decision to CPS	
Threat to destroy property of another	2	• intent to cause fear • potential value of damage £500+ approx.	• potential value of damage £100 or less
Possession of articles with intent to commit criminal damage	2	• evidence of intent to commit serious criminal damage • potential value of damage £500+ approx.	• potential value of damage £100 or less

Offence specific gravity factors for all offences *continued*

Offence	Gravity Score	Aggravating/Mitigating Factors +	−
CROSSBOWS			
Purchase/hire of crossbow or part by person under 17 (Crossbows Act 1987 s2)	2	• supply by dealer • aware it was an offence • evidence of firing	
Possession of crossbow or part by person under 17 (Crossbows Act 1987 s3)	2	• aware it was an offence • evidence of discharge in public place	
CRUELTY			
Cruelty/ill treatment to a child in a manner likely to cause unnecessary suffering or injury	3	• persistent neglect over long period • sadistic violence • repeated violence • substantial injury • premeditation	
DEATHS			
Suicide/attempted suicide – aid/abet/counsel	4	Defer decision to CPS	
Child destruction	4	Defer decision to CPS	
Infanticide	4	Defer decision to CPS	
Familial homicide	4	Defer decision to CPS	
Murder/manslaughter	4	Defer decision to CPS	
DRUGS			
Class 'A' drug Supply/possession with intent to supply	4		
Class 'B' or 'C' drug Supply/possession with intent to supply	4		• group of people pooling resources to buy a supply to share between them • no profit made
Class 'A' drug Possession	3	• in prison establishment • large quantity	• small quantity consistent with personal use
Class 'B' or 'C' drug Possession	2	• in prison establishment • large quantity	• small quantity consistent with personal use
Class 'A' drug Production	4	• commercial cultivation • large quantity	• small quantity consistent with personal use

Offence specific gravity factors for all offences *continued*

Offence	Gravity Score	Aggravating/Mitigating Factors +	−
DRUGS *continued*			
Class 'B' or 'C' drug Production/cultivation	4		• small quantity consistent with personal use
Permit use of premises for smoking cannabis or cannabis resin	2	• on commercial basis • evidence of widespread use	• vulnerable offender
DRUNKENNESS			
Drunk and disorderly	1	• risk of escalation • busy public place • offensive language or behaviour • threatening	• only witnessed by a police officer and little inconvenience to public • non-threatening
Drunk and incapable	1	• serious alcohol problem	
FALSE MESSAGES			
Bomb hoax (Criminal Law Act 1977 s51)	3	• 'copy-cat' scenario • existing climate of fear • caused dangerous or large-scale evacuation, ie, hospital, large sporting event • serious financial loss	• obvious to recipient that a hoax
Sending malicious communication (Malicious Communication Act 1988 s1)	3	• persistency	• obvious to recipient that a hoax
False alarms to emergency services (Telecommunications Act 1984 s43) (Also specific offence of false fire alarm under Fire Services Act 1947 s31)	2	• persistency	• obvious to recipient that a hoax
	2	• persistency	• obvious to recipient that a hoax
Other false emergency calls (Telecommunications Act 1984 s43)	2	• persistency	• obvious to recipient that a hoax
Improper use of telecom systems (Telecommunications Act 1984 s43)	3	• persistency • sexual and/or sadistic in nature	• obvious to recipient that a hoax

Offence specific gravity factors for all offences *continued*

Offence	Gravity Score	Aggravating/Mitigating Factors + −
FIREARMS		
Possession of firearm with intent to endanger life/injure property (Firearms Act 1968 s16)	4	Defer decision to CPS
Possession of firearms while committing offence or with intent to commit offence (Firearms Act 1968 ss17 and 18)	4	Defer decision to CPS
Carrying in public place (Firearms Act 1968 s19)		• type of weapon • discharge of weapon
Loaded firearm	3	
Unloaded air weapon/imitation firearm	2	
Trespass in building with loaded firearm (Firearms Act 1968 s20)	3	• type of weapon • discharge of weapon
Person under 17 purchasing firearm or ammunition (Firearms Act 1968 s22)	2	• type of weapon
Person under 17 having air weapon in public place (Firearms Act 1968 s22)	1	• impact on the public • aware it was an offence • evidence of firing
Supply (including sale) firearm or ammunition to persons under 17 (Firearms Act 1968 s24)	2	• supply by firearms dealer
Possession of firearm/shotgun without certificate (ss1.1 and 2.1) a) no certificate ever held b) following non-renewal	 3 2	• any form of usage or possession in public • type/construction of weapons, eg, sawn-off, prohibited, etc. • history of slow renewal • deliberate supply of false information
Making false statements to procure grant/renewal/variation of firearm/shotgun certificate (Firearms Act 1968 ss26.5 and 29.3)	3	• previous conviction(s) omitted which would affect decision to grant/renew/vary certificate • deliberate avoidance of renewal procedure

Offence specific gravity factors for all offences *continued*

Offence	Gravity Score	Aggravating/Mitigating Factors +	−
FIREARMS *continued*			
Failure to comply with condition of certificate relating to security of weapons (Firearms Act 1968 ss1.2 and 2.2)	2	• degree of carelessness/ insecurity • previous history of insecurity • certificate held for period of time – therefore knew of the requirement	
FOOTBALL GROUNDS			
Throwing a missile in ground (Football (Offences) Act 1991 s2)	2	• likelihood of injury • incitement factors	• no injury or minor injuries
Taking part in racial or indecent chanting (Football (Offences) Act 1991 s3)	3	• intent to incite others to stir up racial hatred • risk of escalation	• isolated incident
Going into the playing area or adjacent area without lawful authority or excuse (Football (Offences) Act 1991 s4)	2	• risk of escalation	• no threatening circumstances
Breach of Football Banning Order (Football Spectators Act 1989 s14A or 14B)	3		• unaware that order was in force
FORGERY			
Making a false document (Forgery and Counterfeiting Act 1981 s1)	2	• nature of documents & potential consequences • organised team • sophistication	• poverty/personal need • coercion from others
Using a false document (Forgery and Counterfeiting Act 1981 s3)	2	• nature of documents & potential consequences • organised team • sophistication	• poverty/personal need • coercion from others
Possessing a false document with intent (Forgery and Counterfeiting Act 1981 s5)	2	• nature of documents & potential consequences • organised team • sophistication	• poverty/personal need • coercion from others
Forgery of documents, etc. (Road Traffic Act 1988)	2	• nature of documents & potential consequences • organised team • sophistication	• poverty/personal need • coercion from others

Offence specific gravity factors for all offences *continued*

Offence	Gravity Score	Aggravating/Mitigating Factors +	−
INTERFERENCE WITH THE COURSE OF JUSTICE			
Conspiracy/attempt to pervert the course of justice	4	Defer decision to CPS	
Perjury	4	Defer decision to CPS	
Bail personation	4	Defer decision to CPS	
Escape from lawful custody	4	Defer decision to CPS	
Prison – escape/aid/assist	4	Defer decision to CPS	
MISCELLANEOUS			
Most non-recordable offences	1		
Breach of bye-laws	1		• not a local resident
OBSTRUCTION			
Obstruct police (Police Act 1964 s51)	1	• attempt to prevent arrest of another • premeditated • group action • violence used or threatened	
Wilful obstruction of highway	2	• close to traffic hazard, eg, school	• brief period only • no considerable problems caused to other road users and/or pedestrians
OFFENSIVE WEAPONS			
Possession of offensive weapon	3	• method of use • concern caused to member(s) of the public • degree of danger	
Possession of sharp pointed blade	2	• method of use • concern caused to member(s) of public	• genuine oversight in retaining blade after a lawful possession
PUBLIC ORDER			
Riot (s1)	4	Defer decision to CPS	
Violent disorder (s2)	3	• planned/ premeditated • use of weapons • busy public place • large group • people put in fear • damage caused	

Offence specific gravity factors for all offences *continued*

Offence	Gravity Score	Aggravating/Mitigating Factors +	−
PUBLIC ORDER *continued*			
Affray (s3)	3	• use of weapons • busy public place • group action • people put in fear • damage caused	
Threatening abusive or insulting words or behaviour intended to cause fear of violence or to provoke violence (s4)	2	• risk of escalation • use of weapons • busy public place • group action • people put in fear	• no risk of escalation
Intentional causing harassment, alarm or distress through threatening abusive or insulting words, behaviour or display (s4A)	3	• racial overtones • risk of escalation • group action	• no risk of escalation
Threatening abusive or insulting words or behaviour likely to cause harassment, alarm or distress (s5)	2	• risk of escalation • group action	• no risk of escalation • isolated incident
ROAD TRAFFIC			
Causing death by dangerous driving (Road Traffic Act 1988 s1)	4	Defer decision to CPS	
Causing death by careless driving under the influence of drink or drugs (Road Traffic Act 1988 s3)	4	Defer decision to CPS	
Driving whilst disqualified	4		
Excess alcohol/driving when unfit through drink/drugs	4		
Refusing to provide specimen of breath/blood/urine at police station	4		
Drunk in charge	4		
Driving after false declaration as to physical fitness/failing to notify disability and refusal or revocation of licence (Sections 92–94 Road Traffic Act 1988)	4		• Voluntary surrender of licence

Offence specific gravity factors for all offences *continued*

Offence	Gravity Score	Aggravating/Mitigating Factors +	–
ROAD TRAFFIC continued			
Dangerous driving (Road Traffic Act 1988 s2)	4	• avoiding detection or apprehension • competitive driving, racing, showing off • disregard of warnings, eg, from passengers or others in vicinity • evidence alcohol/drugs • excessive speed • prolonged, persistent, deliberate bad driving • serious risk	• continuing for only a short period • contributed to by action of another
Failing to stop after accident/failing to report accident	3	• blatant disregard of need • serious injury & failure to remain at scene • serious injury and/or serious damage • evidence of drinking	• no intent to evade liability for the offence • genuine belief that relevant person aware • negligible damage
Careless driving (Road Traffic Act 1988 s3) Inconsiderate driving (Road Traffic Act 1988 s3)	3 2	• major error of judgement • excessive speed • driving with disregard for road safety taking account of road, weather and/or traffic conditions • re-test may be appropriate – Road Traffic (Offences) Act 1988 s36 • disability – RTOA 1988 s22 • deliberate act of selfishness, impatience or aggressiveness causing inconvenience	• minor error of judgement • defect in road surface/signing, etc. • momentary lapse • adverse weather conditions • both (or more) drivers may have been at fault

Offence specific gravity factors for all offences *continued*

Offence	Gravity Score	Aggravating/Mitigating Factors +	−
ROAD TRAFFIC continued			
a) vehicle left in dangerous position	2	• potential or actual danger intended	
b) tampering with vehicle (RTA 1988 s25)	3	• danger of serious injury to other road users	
c) causing danger to other road users (RTA 1988 s22(a))	3		
Failure to provide roadside test	2		
Speeding (above fixed penalty speed)	4		
Wanton and furious driving/ riding	4	Defer decision to CPS	
ROAD TRAFFIC DOCUMENTS			
Driving other than in accordance with driving licence, ie,		• blatant disregard of need	
no 'L' plates	2		
'L' driver unaccompanied	2		
'L' driver carrying passengers	2		
No driving licence	3		
Drive vehicle subject to prohibition notice (Road Traffic Act 1988 s71(1))	4		• not aware of notice
No insurance	3	• deliberate offence • offence involving TWOC or other offence giving rise to danger	• genuine mistake/ technicality • duty to provide insurance resting with another, eg, parent, company, hirer, etc.
No test certificate	2	• blatant disregard of need	• genuine oversight
Fraudulent use of excise licence	2		• both vehicles owned by offender
Failure to notify change of ownership	2	• blatant disregard of need	• genuine oversight
Construction and use offences	3	• blatant disregard of need • seriousness of defect(s)	• genuine oversight • minor defect(s)
Motorway offences	3	• blatant disregard of regulations • serious risk to offender or other road user	• genuine mistake

Offence specific gravity factors for all offences *continued*

Offence	Gravity Score	Aggravating/Mitigating Factors	
		+	−
SEXUAL OFFENCES			
Rape (s1)	4	Defer decision to CPS	
Assault by Penetration (s2)	4	Defer decision to CPS	
Sexual Assault (s3)	3	• Force used • Elderly / younger victim • Group action	
Causing Person to Engage in Sexual Activity without Consent (s4)			
With Penetration	4	Defer decision to CPS	
Without Penetration	3	• Force used • Elderly / younger victim • Group action	
Rape of Child Under 13 (s5)	4	Defer decision to CPS	
Assault of Child Under 13 by Penetration (s6)	4	Defer decision to CPS	
Sexual Assault of Child Under 13 (s7)	3	• Facilitated by drugs/ alcohol • Force used • Group action	• Offender and victim of similar age and no element of coercion or corruption present
Causing/Inciting Child Under 13 to Engage in Sexual Activity without Consent (s8)			
With Penetration	4	Defer decision to CPS	
Without Penetration	3	• Facilitated by drugs/ alcohol • Force used • Group action	
Sexual Activity with Child (s13)		• Facilitated by drugs/ alcohol • Force used • Group action	• Offender and victim of similar age and no element of coercion or corruption present
Victim under 13	3		
Victim under 16	2		
Causing/Inciting Child to Engage in Sexual Activity (s13)		• Facilitated by drugs/ alcohol • Force used • Group action	
Victim under 13	3		
Victim under 16	2		

Offence specific gravity factors for all offences *continued*

Offence	Gravity Score	Aggravating/Mitigating Factors +	−
SEXUAL OFFENCES continued			
Engaging in Sexual Activity in Presence of Child (s13)		• Facilitated by drugs/ alcohol	• Offender and victim of similar age and no element of coercion or corruption present
Victim under 13	3	• Force used	
Victim under 16	2	• Group action	
Causing Child to Watch Sexual Act (s13)		• Facilitated by drugs/ alcohol	• Offender and victim of similar age and no element of coercion or corruption presen
Victim under 13	3	• Force used	
Victim under 16	2	• Group action	
Sexual Activity with Child Family Member (s25)	3	• Victim did not wholly consent • Element of coercion • Victim Under 13	• Offender & victim are similar in age • Both parties over age of consent and no element of coercion/ seduction
Inciting Child Family Member to Engage in Sexual Activity (s26)	2	• Victim did not wholly consent • Element of coercion • Victim Under 13	• Offender & victim are similar in age • Both parties over age of consent and no element of coercion/ seduction
Sex with Adult Relative with Penetration and with or without Consent (s64 & 65)		• Facilitated by drugs/ alcohol • Force used • Element of coercion • Group action	
Sexual Activity with Person with Mental Disorder (s30)			
With Penetration	4	Defer decision to CPS	
Without Penetration	3	• Facilitated by drugs/ alcohol • Force used • Group action	• Offender & victim are similar in age • Both parties over age of consent and no element of coercion/ seduction • Offender has mental disorder

Offence specific gravity factors for all offences *continued*

Offence	Gravity Score	Aggravating/Mitigating Factors +	−
SEXUAL OFFENCES continued			
Causing/Inciting Person with Mental Disorder to Engage in Sexual Activity without Consent (s31)			
With Penetration	4	Defer decision to CPS	
Without Penetration	3	• Facilitated by drugs/ alcohol • Force used • Group action	• Offender & victim are similar in age • Both parties over age of consent and no element of coercion/ seduction • Offender has mental disorder
Engaging in Sexual Activity in Presence of Person with Mental Disorder (s32)	3	• Facilitated by drugs/ alcohol • Force used • Group action	• Offender and victim of similar age and no element of coercion or corruption present • Offender has mental disorder
Causing Person with Mental Disorder to Watch Sexual Act (s33)	3	• Facilitated by drugs/ alcohol • Force used • Group action	• Offender and victim of similar age and no element of coercion or corruption present • Offender has mental disorder
Paying for Sexual Services of Child (sec. 47) with Penetration			
Victim under 13	4		
Victim under 16	3		
Victim under 18	2		
Causing/Inciting Child Prostitution/Pornography (s48)	3	• Victim under 13	
Controlling Child Involved in Prostitution/Pornography (s49)	3	• Victim under 13	
Arranging/Facilitation Child Prostitution/Pornography (s50)	3	• Victim under 13	
Administering Substance with Intent to Commit Sexual Offence (s61)	3		

Offence specific gravity factors for all offences *continued*

Offence	Gravity Score	Aggravating/Mitigating Factors +	−
SEXUAL OFFENCES continued			
Commit Offence with Intent to Commit Sexual Offence (s62)		Refer to offence committed and see General Factors for All Offences	
For Kidnapping/False Imprisonment offences only	4		
Trespass with Intent to Commit Sexual Offence (s63)	4		
Exposure (s66)	2	• Victim put in fear • Repeat performances	
Voyeurism (s67)	2	• Victim distressed • Victim observed in person • Repeat performances	
Sexual Activity in Public Lavatory (s71)	2	• Genuine chance of public witnessing the offence • Youth victim	• Consenting victim but age of legal consent
Common prostitute loitering for prostitution	2		
Before any formal action is considered, the assumption that a child prostitute is a victim must first be acted on by referral to the multi-agency group. Only when advised by them can formal action be considered			
'Kerb Crawling'	2	• Affects residential areas	
SPORTING EVENTS			
Intoxicating liquor in possession on a specified vehicle (ss1.3 and 1A.3)	2	• group involvement • large quantity	• small quantity
Drunk in a specified vehicle (ss1.4 and 1A.4)	2	• group involvement • risk of escalation • threatening	• non-threatening
Intoxicating liquor/article in possession whilst entering or inside (viewing area) sports ground (s2.1)	2	• group involvement • risk of escalation	
Entering or being in a sports ground whilst drunk (s2.2)	2	• group involvement • risk of escalation • threatening	• non-threatening
THEFT			
Robbery/assault with intent to rob	4	Defer decision to CPS	

Offence specific gravity factors for all offences *continued*

Offence	Gravity Score	Aggravating/Mitigating Factors +	–
THEFT continued			
Theft – up to £100 in value – over £100 (approx.)	2 3	• planned • sophistication • organised team • adult involving children • significant related damage • unrecoverable property of considerable value • value £200+ (approx.)	• theft for reasons of poverty/ personal need • coercion from others in group on reluctant offender
Going equipped to steal	2		
Handling stolen property	3	• property stolen to order • professional receiver • youth coercing children • property of high value	• very low value • receiving under pressure from another
Abstracting electricity	2	• special equipment • high usage • prolonged period	• poverty/personal need • coercion by others
Obtaining property by deception (Theft Act 1968 s15)	2	• sophistication • two or more involved • committed over lengthy period • unrecoverable property of considerable value • value £200+ (approx.)	• poverty/personal need • coercion by others in group on reluctant offender • value £50 or less
Obtaining services by deception (Theft Act 1968 s1)	2	• sophistication • organised team • unrecoverable property of considerable value • value £200+ (approx.)	• poverty/personal need • coercion by others in group on reluctant offender • value £50 or less

Offence specific gravity factors for all offences *continued*

Offence	Gravity Score	Aggravating/Mitigating Factors +	−
THEFT continued			
Evasion of liability by deception (Theft Act 1968 s2)	2	• sophistication • organised team • unrecoverable property of considerable value • value £200+ (approx.)	• poverty/personal need • coercion by others in group on reluctant offender • value £50 or less
False accounting	2	• sophistication • value £200+ (approx.)	• value £50 or less
Blackmail	4	Defer decision to CPS	
Taking vehicle without consent	2	• premeditated • group action • related damage	• taken from family member • the taking is a technical offence
Aggravated vehicle-taking where owing to the driving of the vehicle, an accident occurred causing injury to any person	4		• the taking is a technical offence • injured is member of driver's family
Aggravated vehicle-taking where: a) damage to any property other than the vehicle b) damage was caused to the vehicle c) the vehicle was driven dangerously on a road or other public place (Aggravated Vehicle-taking Act 1992 s1)	3	• Avoiding detection or apprehension • competitive driving: racing, showing off • disregard for warnings, eg, from passengers or other in vicinity • excessive speed • evidence of alcohol or drugs • group action • premeditated • serious risk	• the taking is a technical offence • damage to own family property • minor damage
Tampering with motor vehicle (RTA 1988 s25)	2	• potential or actual damage intended	
Interference with vehicle (Criminal Attempts Act 1981 s9)	2	• damage to vehicle	
Making off without payment (Theft Act 1978 s3)	2	• deliberate plan • two or more involved • large amount involved	• small amount involved

Offence specific gravity factors for all offences *continued*

Offence	Gravity Score	Aggravating/Mitigating Factors +	−
WASTING POLICE TIME			
Wasting police time	2	• detention of innocent person • substantial time wasted	• early retraction and remorse • innocent prank

Grave crimes

Detention under section 91(3) of the Powers of Criminal Courts (Sentencing) Act 2000 is available for the following offences:

- Abduction of a woman by force or for the sake of her property (Sexual Offences Act 1956 s17 – 14 years)
- Aggravated burglary (Theft Act 1968 s10 – life)
- Aggravated vehicle-taking involving accident which caused the death of any person (Theft Act 1968 s12A(4) – 14 years for offences committed on or after 27 February 2004)
- Aiding suicide (Suicide Act 1961 s2 – 14 years)
- Arson (Criminal Damage Act 1971 s1 – life)
- Arranging commission of a child sex offence (Sexual Offences Act 2003 s14 – 14 years)
- Assault by penetration (Sexual Offences Act 2003 s2 – life)
- Assault of a child under 13 by penetration (Sexual Offences Act 2003 s6 – life)
- Assault with intent to rob (Theft Act 1968 s8 – life)
- Attempted murder (Criminal Attempts Act 1981 s4(1) – life)
- Attempting to strangle with intent to endanger life (Offences Against the Person Act 1861 s21 – life)
- Blackmail (Theft Act 1968 s21 – 14 years)
- Buggery with a person under the age of 16 or with an animal (Sexual Offences Act 1956 s12 – life)
- Burglary of dwelling (Theft Act 1968 s9(3)(a) – 14 years) *nb. does not include non-dwelling burglaries*
- Causing death by aggravated vehicle–taking (Theft Act 1968 s12A(5) – 14 years, only for offences committed on or after 27 February 2004)
- Causing death by dangerous driving (Road Traffic Act 1988 s1 – 14 years for offences committed on or after 27 February 2004/10 years, for offences committed before 27 February 2004 and only in relation to offenders who have attained 14 years)
- Causing death by careless driving while under the influence of alcohol or drugs (Road Traffic Act 1988 s3 – 14 years for offences committed on or after 27 February 2004/10 years, for offences committed before 27 February 2004 and only in relation to offenders who have attained 14 years)
- Causing child under 13 to engage in sexual activity (Sexual Offences Act 2003 s8 – 14 years/life if subs (2) applies)
- Causing person with a mental disorder impeding choice to engage in sexual activity (Sexual Offences Act 2003 s31– 14 years/life if subs (3) applies)
- Causing a person with a mental disorder to engage in or agree to engage in sexual activity by inducement, threat or deception (Sexual Offences Act 2003 s35 – 14 years/life if subsection (2) applies)
- Child destruction (s1 Infant Life (Preservation) Act 1929 – life)

- Child prostitution or pornography
  - Paying for sexual services of a child (Sexual Offences Act 2003 s47 – 14 years if child under 14/life if child under 13)
  - causing or inciting child prostitution or pornography (Sexual Offences Act 2003 s48 – 14 years)
  - Controlling a child prostitute or a child involved in pornography (Sexual Offences Act 2003 s49– 14 years)
  - Arranging or facilitating child prostitution or pornography (Sexual Offences Act 2003 s50 – 14 years)
- Child sex offences (Sexual Offences Act 2003 s13 – 5 years)
- Criminal damage with intent to endanger life (Criminal Damage Act 1971 s1(2) – life)
- Demanding money with menaces (Theft Act 1968 s21– 14 years)
- Destroying property with intent to endanger life (Criminal Damage Act 1971 s1– life)
- Drugs
  - production (Misuse of Drugs Act 1971 s4(2): class A – life; class B – 14 years)
  - supplying/offering to supply/being concerned in the supply (Misuse of Drugs Act 1971 s4(3): class A – life; class B and C – 14 years)
  - possession with intent to supply (Misuse of Drugs Act 1971 s5(3): class A – life; class B and C – 14 years)
  - cultivation of cannabis (Misuse of Drugs Act 1971 s6(2) – 14 years)
- Endangering safety of aircraft (Aviation Security Act 1982 s3 – life)
- Endangering safety of railway passengers (Offences Against the Person Act 1961 s32 – life)
- Explosives
  - causing explosion likely to endanger life (Explosive Substances Act 1883 s1 – life)
  - attempting to cause explosion (Explosive Substances Act 1883 s2 – life)
  - possession of explosive substance with intent (Explosive Substances Act 1883 s2– life)
  - making or possessing explosive substance (Explosive Substances Act 1883 s4 – 14 years)
- Facilitating commission of a child sex offence (Sexual Offences Act 2003 s14 – 14 years)
- False imprisonment (common law)
- Female genital mutilation (Female Genital Mutilation Act 2003 ss1 to 3 – 14 years)
- Firearms
  - possession of prohibited weapon (Firearms Act 1968 s5(1)(a), (ab), (aba), (ac), (ad), (af) or (c) or (1A)(a) – only for offenders who have attained 16 by the date of offence and are subject to the minimum mandatory sentence under Firearms Act 1968 s51A)
  - possession with intent to endanger life (Firearms Act 1968 s16 – life)
  - using a firearm with intent to resist arrest (Firearms Act 1968 s17(1) – life)
  - possession of a firearm at time of commission of offence or arrest for scheduled offence (Firearms Act 1968 s17(2) – 14 years)
  - possession with intent to commit an indictable offence or to resist arrest (Firearms Act 1968 s18 – 14 years)
- GBH with intent (Offences Against the Person Act 1861 s18 – life)

- Genocide (International Criminal Court Act 2001 s51 – 30 years)
- Handling stolen goods (Theft Act 1968 s22 –14 years)
- Hijacking (Aviation Security Act 1982 s1 – life)
- Hostage-taking (Taking of Hostages Act 1982 s1 – life)
- Impeding person endeavouring to save himself or another from shipwreck (Offences Against the Person Act 1861 s17 – life)
- Incest by man with girl under 13 (Sexual Offences Act 1956 s10 – life
- Inciting a child under 13 to engage in sexual activity (Sexual Offences Act 2003 s8 – 14 years/life if subsection (2) applies)
- Inciting a person with a mental disorder impeding choice to engage in sexual activity (Sexual Offences Act 2003 s31 – 14 years/life if subsection (3) applies)
- Indecent assault upon a female (Sexual Offences Act 1956 s14 – 10 years)
- Indecent assault upon a male (Sexual Offences Act 1956 s15 – 10 years)
- Inducement, threat or deception to procure sexual activity with a person with a mental disorder (Sexual Offences Act 2003 s34 – 14 years/life if subsection (2) applies)
- Infanticide (Infanticide Act 1938 s1 – life)
- Kidnapping (common law)
- Manslaughter (Offences Against the Person Act 1981 s5 – life)
- Perverting the course of justice (common law)
- Placing object on railway with intent to obstruct or overthrow any engine (Malicious Damage Act 1861 s35 – life)
- Racially–aggravated criminal damage (Crime and Disorder Act 1998 s30)
- Rape (Sexual Offences Act 1956 s1– life)
- Rape (Sexual Offences Act 2003 s1– life)
- Rape of a child under 13 (Sexual Offences Act 2003 s5 – life)
- Robbery (Theft Act 1968 s8 – life)
- Sexual activity with a child family member (Sexual Offences Act 2003 s25 – 5 years)
- Sexual activity with a person with a mental disorder impeding choice (Sexual Offences Act 2003 s30– 14 years/life, if subsection (3) applies)
- Sexual assault (Sexual Offences Act 2003 s3– 10 years)
- Sexual assault of a child under 13 (Sexual Offences Act 2003 s7 – 14 years)
- Soliciting to murder (Offences Against the Person Act 1861 s4 – life)
- Throwing corrosive liquid with intent to endanger life (Offences Against the Person Act 1861 s29– life)
- Throwing object with intent to endanger rail passenger (Offences Against the Person Act 1861 s33– life)
- Torture (Criminal Justice Act 1988 s134 – life)
- Trafficking for sexual exploitation (Sexual Offences Act 2003 ss57 to 59 – 14 years)
- Unlawful sexual intercourse with a girl under the age of 13 (Sexual Offences Act 1956 s5 – life)
- Using chloroform to commit indictable offence (Offences Against the Person Act 1861 s22 – life)
- Wounding with intent (Offences Against the Person Act 1861 s18 – life)

Note an attempt or conspiracy to commit any of the above offences will also be a grave crime (Criminal Attempts Act 1981 s1 and Criminal Law Act 1977 s1 respectively).

Dangerous offenders – specified offences

For the purposes of the Criminal Justice Act 2003 s224 and Sch 15 the following offences are specified offences. Those marked with an asterisk are also serious offences.

Specified violent offences

1 Manslaughter.*

2 Kidnapping.*

3 False imprisonment.*

4 An offence under section 4 of the Offences against the Person Act 1861 (soliciting murder).*

5 An offence under section 16 of that Act (threats to kill).*

6 An offence under section 18 of that Act (wounding with intent to cause grievous bodily harm).*

7 An offence under section 20 of that Act (malicious wounding).

8 An offence under section 21 of that Act (attempting to choke, suffocate or strangle in order to commit or assist in committing an indictable offence).*

9 An offence under section 22 of that Act (using chloroform, etc. to commit or assist in the committing of any indictable offence).*

10 An offence under section 23 of that Act (maliciously administering poison etc. so as to endanger life or inflict grievous bodily harm).*

11 An offence under section 27 of that Act (abandoning children).

12 An offence under section 28 of that Act (causing bodily injury by explosives).*

13 An offence under section 29 of that Act (using explosives etc. with intent to do grievous bodily harm).*

14 An offence under section 30 of that Act (placing explosives with intent to do bodily injury).*

15 An offence under section 31 of that Act (setting spring guns etc. with intent to do grievous bodily harm).

16 An offence under section 32 of that Act (endangering the safety of railway passengers).*

17 An offence under section 35 of that Act (injuring persons by furious driving).

18 An offence under section 37 of that Act (assaulting officer preserving wreck).

19 An offence under section 38 of that Act (assault with intent to resist arrest).

20 An offence under section 47 of that Act (assault occasioning actual bodily harm).

21 An offence under section 2 of the Explosive Substances Act 1883 (causing explosion likely to endanger life or property).*

22 An offence under section 3 of that Act (attempt to cause explosion, or making or keeping explosive with intent to endanger life or property).*

23 An offence under section 1 of the Infant Life (Preservation) Act 1929 (child destruction).*

24 An offence under section 1 of the Children and Young Persons Act 1933 (cruelty to children).*

25 An offence under section 1 of the Infanticide Act 1938 (infanticide).*

26 An offence under section 16 of the Firearms Act 1968 (possession of firearm with intent to endanger life).*

27 An offence under section 16A of that Act (possession of firearm with intent to cause fear of violence).*

28 An offence under section 17(1) of that Act (use of firearm to resist arrest).*

29 An offence under section 17(2) of that Act (possession of firearm at time of committing or being arrested for offence specified in Schedule 1 to that Act).*

30 An offence under section 18 of that Act (carrying a firearm with criminal intent).*

31 An offence under section 8 of the Theft Act 1968 (robbery or assault with intent to rob).*

32 An offence under section 9 of that Act of burglary with intent to –
(a) inflict grievous bodily harm on a person;* or
(b) do unlawful damage to a building or anything in it.*

33 An offence under section 10 of that Act (aggravated burglary).*

34 An offence under section 12A of that Act (aggravated vehicle-taking) involving an accident which caused the death of any person.*

35 An offence of arson under section 1 of the Criminal Damage Act 1971.*

36 An offence under section 1(2) of that Act (destroying or damaging property with intent to endanger life).*

37 An offence under section 1 of the Taking of Hostages Act 1982 (hostage-taking).*

38 An offence under section 1 of the Aviation Security Act 1982 (hijacking).*

39 An offence under section 2 of that Act (destroying, damaging or endangering safety of aircraft).*

40 An offence under section 3 of that Act (other acts endangering or likely to endanger safety of aircraft).*

41 An offence under section 4 of that Act (offences in relation to certain dangerous articles).

42 An offence under section 127 of the Mental Health Act 1983 (ill-treatment of patients).

43 An offence under section 1 of the Prohibition of Female Circumcision Act 1985 (prohibition of female circumcision).

44 An offence under section 1 of the Public Order Act 1986 (riot).*

45 An offence under section 2 of that Act (violent disorder).

46 An offence under section 3 of that Act (affray).

47 An offence under section 134 of the Criminal Justice Act 1988 (c. 33) (torture).*

48 An offence under section 1 of the Road Traffic Act 1988 (c. 52) (causing death by dangerous driving).*

49 An offence under section 3A of that Act (causing death by careless driving when under influence of drink or drugs).*

50 An offence under section 1 of the Aviation and Maritime Security Act 1990 (endangering safety at aerodromes).*

51 An offence under section 9 of that Act (hijacking of ships).*

52 An offence under section 10 of that Act (seizing or exercising control of fixed platforms).*

53 An offence under section 11 of that Act (destroying fixed platforms or endangering their safety).*

54 An offence under section 12 of that Act (other acts endangering or likely to endanger safe navigation).*

55 An offence under section 13 of that Act (offences involving threats).*

56 An offence under Part II of the Channel Tunnel (Security) Order 1994 (SI 1994 No 570) (offences relating to Channel Tunnel trains and the tunnel system).

57 An offence under section 4 of the Protection from Harassment Act 1997 (putting people in fear of violence).

58 An offence under section 29 of the Crime and Disorder Act 1998 (racially or religiously aggravated assaults).

59 An offence falling within section 31(1)(a) or (b) of that Act (racially or religiously aggravated offences under section 4 or 4A of the Public Order Act 1986.

60 An offence under section 51 or 52 of the International Criminal Court Act 2001 (genocide, crimes against humanity, war crimes and related offences), other than one involving murder.*

60A An offence under section 5 of the Domestic Violence, Crime and Victims Act 2004 (causing or allowing the death of a child or vulnerable adult).

61 An offence under section 1 of the Female Genital Mutilation Act 2003 (female genital mutilation).*

62 An offence under section 2 of that Act (assisting a girl to mutilate her own genitalia).*

63 An offence under section 3 of that Act (assisting a non-UK person to mutilate overseas a girl's genitalia).*

64 An offence of:
   (a) aiding, abetting, counselling, procuring or inciting the commission of an offence specified in this Part of this appendix,
   (b) conspiring to commit an offence so specified, or
   (c) attempting to commit an offence so specified.

65 An attempt to commit murder or a conspiracy to commit murder.*

Specified sexual offences

66 An offence under section 1 of the Sexual Offences Act 1956 (rape).*

67 An offence under section 2 of that Act (procurement of woman by threats).

68 An offence under section 3 of that Act (procurement of woman by false pretences).

69 An offence under section 4 of that Act (administering drugs to obtain or facilitate intercourse).

70 An offence under section 5 of that Act (intercourse with girl under thirteen).*

71 An offence under section 6 of that Act (intercourse with girl under 16).

72 An offence under section 7 of that Act (intercourse with a defective).

73 An offence under section 9 of that Act (procurement of a defective).

74 An offence under section 10 of that Act (incest by a man).

75 An offence under section 11 of that Act (incest by a woman).

76 An offence under section 14 of that Act (indecent assault on a woman).*

77 An offence under section 15 of that Act (indecent assault on a man).*

78 An offence under section 16 of that Act (assault with intent to commit buggery).*

79 An offence under section 17 of that Act (abduction of woman by force or for the sake of her property).*

80 An offence under section 19 of that Act (abduction of unmarried girl under eighteen from parent or guardian).

81 An offence under section 20 of that Act (abduction of unmarried girl under sixteen from parent or guardian).

82 An offence under section 21 of that Act (abduction of defective from parent or guardian).

83 An offence under section 22 of that Act (causing prostitution of women).

84 An offence under section 23 of that Act (procuration of girl under twenty-one).

85 An offence under section 24 of that Act (detention of woman in brothel).

86 An offence under section 25 of that Act (permitting girl under thirteen to use premises for intercourse).*

87 An offence under section 26 of that Act (permitting girl under sixteen to use premises for intercourse).

88 An offence under section 27 of that Act (permitting defective to use premises for intercourse).

89 An offence under section 28 of that Act (causing or encouraging the prostitution of, intercourse with or indecent assault on girl under sixteen).

90 An offence under section 29 of that Act (causing or encouraging prostitution of defective).

91 An offence under section 32 of that Act (soliciting by men).

92 An offence under section 33 of that Act (keeping a brothel).

93 An offence under section 128 of the Mental Health Act 1959 (sexual intercourse with patients).

94 An offence under section 1 of the Indecency with Children Act 1960 (indecent conduct towards young child).

95 An offence under section 4 of the Sexual Offences Act 1967 (procuring others to commit homosexual acts).

96 An offence under section 5 of that Act (living on earnings of male prostitution).

97 An offence under section 9 of the Theft Act 1968 of burglary with intent to commit rape.*

98 An offence under section 54 of the Criminal Law Act 1977 (inciting girl under sixteen to have incestuous sexual intercourse).

99 An offence under section 1 of the Protection of Children Act 1978 (indecent photographs of children).*

100 An offence under section 170 of the Customs and Excise Management Act 1979 (penalty for fraudulent evasion of duty etc.) in relation to goods prohibited to be imported under section 42 of the Customs Consolidation Act 1876 (indecent or obscene articles).

101 An offence under section 160 of the Criminal Justice Act 1988 (possession of indecent photograph of a child).

102 An offence under section 1 of the Sexual Offences Act 2003 (rape).*

103 An offence under section 2 of that Act (assault by penetration).*

104 An offence under section 3 of that Act (sexual assault).*

105 An offence under section 4 of that Act (causing a person to engage in sexual activity without consent).*

106 An offence under section 5 of that Act (rape of a child under 13).*

107 An offence under section 6 of that Act (assault of a child under 13 by penetration).*
108 An offence under section 7 of that Act (sexual assault of a child under 13).*

109 An offence under section 8 of that Act (causing or inciting a child under 13 to engage in sexual activity).*

110 Not applicable.

111 Not applicable.

112 Not applicable.

113 Not applicable.

114 An offence under section 13 of that Act (child sex offences committed by children or young persons).

115 An offence under section 14 of that Act (arranging or facilitating commission of a child sex offence).*

116 Not applicable.

117 Not applicable.

118 Not applicable.

119 Not applicable.

120 Not applicable.

121 An offence under section 25 of that Act (sexual activity with a child family member).

122 An offence under section 26 of that Act (inciting a child family member to engage in sexual activity).

123 An offence under section 30 of that Act (sexual activity with a person with a mental disorder impeding choice).*

124 An offence under section 31 of that Act (causing or inciting a person with a mental disorder impeding choice to engage in sexual activity).*

125 An offence under section 32 of that Act (engaging in sexual activity in the presence of a person with a mental disorder impeding choice).*

126 An offence under section 33 of that Act (causing a person with a mental disorder impeding choice to watch a sexual act).*

127 An offence under section 34 of that Act (inducement, threat or deception to procure sexual activity with a person with a mental disorder).*

128 An offence under section 35 of that Act (causing a person with a mental disorder to engage in or agree to engage in sexual activity by inducement, threat or deception).*

129 An offence under section 36 of that Act (engaging in sexual activity in the presence, procured by inducement, threat or deception, of a person with a mental disorder).*

130 An offence under section 37 of that Act (causing a person with a mental disorder to watch a sexual act by inducement, threat or deception).*

131 An offence under section 38 of that Act (care workers: sexual activity with a person with a mental disorder).*

132 An offence under section 39 of that Act (care workers: causing or inciting sexual activity).*

133 An offence under section 40 of that Act (care workers: sexual activity in the presence of a person with a mental disorder).

134 An offence under section 41 of that Act (care workers: causing a person with a mental disorder to watch a sexual act).

135 An offence under section 47 of that Act (paying for sexual services of a child).*

136 An offence under section 48 of that Act (causing or inciting child prostitution or pornography).*

137 An offence under section 49 of that Act (controlling a child prostitute or a child involved in pornography).*

138 An offence under section 50 of that Act (arranging or facilitating child prostitution or pornography).*

139 An offence under section 52 of that Act (causing or inciting prostitution for gain).

140 An offence under section 53 of that Act (controlling prostitution for gain).

141 An offence under section 57 of that Act (trafficking into the UK for sexual exploitation).*

142 An offence under section 58 of that Act (trafficking within the UK for sexual exploitation).*

143 An offence under section 59 of that Act (trafficking out of the UK for sexual exploitation).*

144 An offence under section 61 of that Act (administering a substance with intent).*

145 An offence under section 62 of that Act (committing an offence with intent to commit a sexual offence).*

146 An offence under section 63 of that Act (trespass with intent to commit a sexual offence).*

147 An offence under section 64 of that Act (sex with an adult relative: penetration).

148 An offence under section 65 of that Act (sex with an adult relative: consenting to penetration).

149 An offence under section 66 of that Act (exposure).

150 An offence under section 67 of that Act (voyeurism).

151 An offence under section 69 of that Act (intercourse with an animal).

152 An offence under section 70 of that Act (sexual penetration of a corpse).

153 An offence of:
   (a) aiding, abetting, counselling, procuring or inciting the commission of an offence specified in this part of this appendix;
   (b) conspiring to commit an offence so specified;
   (c) attempting to commit an offence so specified.

Trigger offences for drug testing

1 Offences under the following provisions of the Theft Act 1968:

section 1 (theft)
section 8 (robbery)
section 9 (burglary)
section 10 (aggravated burglary)
section 12 (taking a motor vehicle or other conveyance without authority)
section 12A (aggravated vehicle-taking)
section 15 (obtaining property by deception)
section 22 (handling stolen goods)
section 25 (going equipped for stealing etc.)

2 Offences under the following provisions of the Misuse of Drugs Act 1971, if committed in respect of heroin or cocaine:

section 4 (restriction on production and supply of controlled drugs)
section 5(2) (possession of a controlled drug)
section 5(3) (possession of a controlled drug with intent to supply)

3 An offence under the Criminal Attempts Act 1981 s1(1) if committed in respect of an offence under any of the following provisions of the Theft Act 1968:

section 1 (theft)
section 8 (robbery)
section 9 (burglary)
section 15 (obtaining property by deception)
section 22 (handling stolen goods)

4 Offences under the following provisions of the Vagrancy Act 1824:

section 3 (begging)
section 4 (persistent begging)

Registration as a sex offender – applicable offences

Where an offender was under 18 years at the time of the offence, registration under Sexual Offences Act 2003 Pt 2 and Sch 3 is required following conviction for the following offences:

Automatic registration

- Rape (Sexual Offences Act 2003 s1)
- Assault by penetration (Sexual Offences Act 2003 s2)
- Causing sexual activity without consent (Sexual Offences Act 2003 s4)
- Rape of child under 13 (Sexual Offences Act 2003 s5)
- Assault of child under 13 by penetration (Sexual Offences Act 2003 s6)
- Causing or inciting a child under 13 to engage in sexual activity (Sexual Offences Act 2003 s8)
- Offences against persons with a mental disorder (Sexual Offences Act 2003 ss30 –37)
- Administering a substance with intent (Sexual Offences Act 2003 s61)

Registration only required if custodial sentence of 12 months or more imposed

- Indecent photographs of children under 16 (Protection of Children Act 1978 s1)
- Importing indecent photographs of children under 16 (Customs and Excise Management Act 1979 s170 and Customs Consolidation Act 1876 s42)
- Possession of indecent photographs of children under 16 (Criminal Justice Act 1988 s160)
- Sexual assault (Sexual Offences Act 2003 s3)
- Sexual assault of a child under 13 (Sexual Offences Act 2003 s7)
- Child sex offences committed by children or young persons (Sexual Offences Act 2003 s13)
- Arranging or facilitating the commission of a child sex offence (Sexual Offences Act 2003 s14)
- Familial child sex offences (Sexual Offences Act 2003 ss25-26)
- Care worker offences (Sexual Offences Act 2003 ss38–41)
- Paying for the sexual services of a child (where the victim was under 16) (Sexual Offences Act 2003 s47)
- Committing an offence with intent to commit a sexual offence (Sexual Offences Act 2003 s62)
- Trespassing with intent to commit a sexual offence (Sexual Offences Act 2003 s63)
- Sex with an adult relative (Sexual Offences Act 2003 ss64–65)

- Exposure (Sexual Offences Act 2003 s66)
- Voyeurism (Sexual Offences Act 2003 s67)
- Intercourse with an animal (Sexual Offences Act 2003 s70)
- Sexual penetration of a corpse (Sexual Offences Act 2003 s71)

Offences against children (disqualification orders)

The following offences are defined as offences against children by Criminal Justice and Court Services Act 2000 Sch 4:

1 **The offences mentioned in Criminal Justice and Court Services Act 2000 s26(1)(a) are:**
   (a) an offence under section 1 of the Children and Young Persons Act 1933 (cruelty to children),
   (b) an offence under section 1 of the Infanticide Act 1938 (infanticide),
   (c) an offence under section 5 of the Sexual Offences Act 1956 (intercourse with a girl under 13),
   (d) an offence under section 6 of that Act (intercourse with a girl under 16),
   (e) an offence under section 19 or 20 of that Act (abduction of girl under 18 or 16),
   (f) an offence under section 25 or 26 of that Act (permitting girl under 13, or between 13 and 16, to use premises for intercourse),
   (g) an offence under section 28 of that Act (causing or encouraging prostitution of, intercourse with or indecent assault on, girl under 16),
   (h) an offence under section 1 of the Indecency with Children Act 1960 (indecent conduct towards young child),
   (i) an offence under section 54 of the Criminal Law Act 1977 (inciting girl under sixteen to incest),
   (j) an offence under section 1 of the Protection of Children Act 1978 (indecent photographs of children),
   (k) an offence under section 1 of the Child Abduction Act 1984 (abduction of child by parent),
   (l) an offence under section 160 of the Criminal Justice Act 1988 (possession of indecent photograph of child),
   (m) an offence under any of sections 5 to 26 and 47 to 50 of the Sexual Offences Act 2003 (offences against children).

2 **The offences mentioned in Criminal Justice and Court Services Act 2000 s26(1)(b) are:**
   (a) murder,
   (b) manslaughter,
   (c) kidnapping,
   (d) false imprisonment,
   (e) an offence under section 18 or 20 of the Offences against the Person Act 1861 (wounding and causing grievous bodily harm),
   (f) an offence under section 47 of that Act (assault occasioning actual bodily harm),
   (g) an offence under section 1 of the Sexual Offences Act 1956 (rape),
   (h) an offence under section 2 or 3 of that Act (procurement of woman by threats or false pretences),
   (i) an offence under section 4 of that Act (administering drugs to obtain or facilitate intercourse),

793

(j) an offence under section 14 or 15 of that Act (indecent assault),

(k) an offence under section 16 of that Act (assault with intent to commit buggery),

(l) an offence under section 17 of that Act (abduction of woman by force or for the sake of her property),

(m) an offence under section 24 of that Act (detention of woman in brothel or other premises),

(n) an offence under any of sections 1 to 4, 30 to 41, 52, 53, 57 to 61, 66 and 67 of the Sexual Offences Act 2003.

3 A person falls within this paragraph if –

(a) he commits an offence under section 16 of the Offences against the Person Act 1861 (threats to kill) by making a threat to kill a child,

(b) he commits an offence under section 7 of the Sexual Offences Act 1956 (intercourse with defective) by having sexual intercourse with a child,

(c) he commits an offence under section 9 of that Act (procurement of defective) by procuring a child to have sexual intercourse,

(d) he commits an offence under section 10 of that Act (incest by a man) by having sexual intercourse with a child,

(e) she commits an offence under section 11 of that Act (incest by a woman) by allowing a child to have sexual intercourse with her,

(f) he commits an offence under section 12 of that Act by committing buggery with a child under the age of 16,

(g) he commits an offence under section 13 of that Act by committing an act of gross indecency with a child,

(h) he commits an offence under section 21 of that Act (abduction of defective from parent or guardian) by taking a child out of the possession of her parent or guardian,

(i) he commits an offence under section 22 of that Act (causing prostitution of women) in relation to a child,

(j) he commits an offence under section 23 of that Act (procuration of girl under 21) by procuring a child to have sexual intercourse with a third person,

(k) he commits an offence under section 27 of that Act (permitting defective to use premises for intercourse) by inducing or suffering a child to resort to or be on premises for the purpose of having sexual intercourse,

(l) he commits an offence under section 29 of that Act (causing or encouraging prostitution of defective) by causing or encouraging the prostitution of a child,

(m) he commits an offence under section 30 of that Act (man living on earnings of prostitution) in a case where the prostitute is a child,

(n) she commits an offence under section 31 of that Act (woman exercising control over prostitute) in a case where the prostitute is a child,

(o) he commits an offence under section 128 of the Mental Health Act 1959 (sexual intercourse with patients) by having sexual intercourse with a child,

(p) he commits an offence under section 4 of the Sexual Offences Act 1967 (procuring others to commit homosexual acts) by-

(i) procuring a child to commit an act of buggery with any person, or

(ii) procuring any person to commit an act of buggery with a child,

(q) he commits an offence under section 5 of that Act (living on earnings of male prostitution) by living wholly or in part on the earnings of prostitution of a child,

(r) he commits an offence under section 9(1)(a) of the Theft Act 1968 (burglary), by entering a building or part of a building with intent to rape a child,

(s) he commits an offence under section 4(3) of the Misuse of Drugs Act 1971 by

(i) supplying or offering to supply a Class A drug to a child,

(ii) being concerned in the supplying of such a drug to a child, or

(iii) being concerned in the making to a child of an offer to supply such a drug,

(sa) he commits an offence under section 62 or 63 of the Sexual Offences Act 2003 (committing an offence or trespassing with intent to commit a sexual offence) in a case where the intended offence was an offence against a child,

(t) he commits an offence of-

(i) aiding, abetting, counselling, procuring or inciting the commission of an offence against a child, or

(ii) conspiring or attempting to commit such an offence.

Robbery Definitive Guideline: Sentencing Guidelines Council[1]

Contents

A Statutory provision

Section 8(1) Theft Act 1968 provides:

A person is guilty of robbery if he steals, and immediately before or at the time of doing so, and in order to do so, he uses force on any person or puts or seeks to put any person in fear of being then and there subjected to force.

B Forms of robbery and structure of the Guideline

For the purposes of this guideline, five categories of robbery have been identified and established from sentencing ranges and previous guidance. They are:

1. Street robbery or 'mugging';
2. Robberies of small businesses;
3. Less sophisticated commercial robberies;
4. Violent personal robberies in the home;
5. Professionally planned commercial robberies.

The guideline is divided into two parts.

Part 1

This part covers categories 1–3 above.

For each of the three categories, three levels of seriousness have been identified based on the extent of force used or threatened.

For each level of seriousness a sentencing range and a starting point within that range have been identified.

Adult and youth offenders are distinguished and the guideline provides for them as separate groups.

---

1   Issued July 2006.

Part 2

No guideline is provided for categories 4 and 5. Violent personal robberies are often accompanied by other serious offences which affect sentencing decisions. For professionally planned commercial robberies, existing case authority is still valid and this is summarised in Part 2.

ROBBERY

C Part 1

Street robbery or 'mugging'

Street robberies will usually involve some physical force (or threat) to steal modest sums, although in some cases there is significant intimidation or violence. The victim may or may not be physically injured.

Robberies of small businesses

This category covers robberies of businesses such as a small shop or post office, petrol station or public transport/taxi facility which may well lack the physical and electronic security devices available to banks or building societies and larger businesses. The less sophisticated robberies are typically committed by a single offender using a real or imitation weapon to threaten the victim(s).

Less sophisticated commercial robberies

This category covers a wide range of locations, extent of planning and degree of violence including less sophisticated bank robberies or where larger commercial establishments are the target but without detailed planning or high levels of organisation.

D Assessing seriousness

The offence of robbery will usually merit a custodial sentence but exceptional circumstances may justify a non-custodial penalty for an adult and, more frequently, for a young offender.

The factors to be taken into account in assessing seriousness are:

- It is the element of violence that is the most serious part of the offence of robbery, but it is not the only determinative factor.
- The relative seriousness of each offence depends on factors such as the degree of injury to the victim or the nature and duration of threats.
- The degree of force used is important in determining the seriousness of the offence but the degree of fear which was experienced by the victim is a relevant consideration.
- Use of a weapon or presence of a weapon even if not used.

(i) Levels of seriousness

Three levels of seriousness are identified by reference to the features or type of activity that characterise an offence at each level and the degree of force or threat present. The levels apply to all three categories of robbery but will be very rare for robberies of small businesses or less sophisticated commercial robberies to have the features of the lowest level of seriousness.

Level 1 – threat and/or use of minimal force

The offence includes the threat or use of force and removal of property such as snatching from a person's grasp causing bruising/pain and discomfort.

The relative seriousness of a level 1 offence depends on:

a) the nature and duration of any force, threat or intimidation;
b) the extent of injury (if any) to the victim;

c) the value of the property taken;
d) the number and degree of aggravating factors

Level 2 – use of weapon to threaten and/or use of significant force
A weapon is produced and used to threaten, and/or force is used which results in injury to the victim.

The relative seriousness of a level 2 offence depends on:
a) the nature and duration of the threat or intimidation;
b) the extent of injury (if any) to the victim;
c) the nature of the weapon used, whether it was real and, if it was a real firearm, whether it was loaded;
d) the value of the property taken;
e) the number and degree of aggravating factors.

Level 3 – use of weapon and serious injury caused
The victim is caused serious physical injury, such as a broken limb, stab wound or internal injury, by the use of significant force and/or use of a weapon. Offences at this level are often accompanied by the presence of additional aggravating factors such as a degree of planning or the targeting of large sums of money or valuable goods.

The relative seriousness of a level 3 offence depends on:
a) the extent of the injury to the victim;
b) the nature of the weapon used;
c) the value of the property taken;
d) the number and degree of aggravating factors.

(ii) Aggravating and mitigating factors
The presence of one or more aggravating features will indicate a more severe sentence within the suggested range. If the aggravating feature(s) are exceptionally serious, the case may move to the next level of seriousness.

Aggravating factors particularly relevant to robbery
(a) Degree of force or violence
• Use of a particular degree of force is more serious than the threat (which is not carried into effect) to use that same degree of force.
• Depending on the facts, however, a threat to use a high degree of force might properly be regarded as more serious than actual use of a lesser degree of force.

(b) Use of a weapon
• Possession of a weapon during the course of an offence will be an aggravating factor, even if it is not used, because it indicated planning.
• Possession of a firearm which is loaded is more serious than possession of a firearm which is unloaded.
• Whether the weapon is real or imitation is not a major factor in determining sentence because the amount of fear created in the victim is likely to be the same.
• In cases of robbery in which a firearm is carried by the offender, a separate offence of possession of a firearm may be charged. In such circumstances, sentencers should consider, where appropriate, the use of consecutive sentencing which properly reflect the totality of the offending.

(c) Vulnerability of the victim
• Targeting the elderly, the young, those with disabilities and persons performing a service to the public, especially outside normal working hours, will aggravate an offence.

(d) Number involved in the offence and roles of offenders
• Group offending will aggravate an offence because the level of intimidation and fear caused to the victim is likely to be greater.

• It may also indicate planning or 'gang' activity.
• The precise role of each offender will be important. Being the ringleader in a group is an aggravating factor. However, an offender may have played a peripheral role in the offence and, rather than having planned to take part, may have become involved spontaneously through the influence of others (see Mitigating factors below).

(e) Value of items taken
• Property value may be more important in planned/sophisticated robberies.
• The value of the property capable of being taken should be taken into account as well as the amount/value of the property actually taken.

(f) Offence committed at night/in hours of darkness
• A victim is more vulnerable while in darkness than during daylight, all other things being equal.
• The degree of fear experienced by the victim is likely to be greater if an offence is committed at night or during hours of darkness.

(g) Wearing of a disguise
• The wearing of a disguise in order to commit an offence of robbery usually indicates a degree of planning on the part of the offender.
• The deliberate selection of a particular type of disguise in advance of the offence, for example, a balaclava or a mask, will be more serious than the improvised use of items of clothing such as a hat or hood.

Mitigating factors particularly relevant to robbery
(a) Unplanned/opportunistic
• Many street robberies are unplanned or opportunistic by their nature so the extent of the mitigation in such cases may be limited.

(b) Peripheral involvement
• Where, as part of a group robbery, the offender has played a peripheral role in the offence this should be treated as a mitigating factor although it should be borne in mind that by participating as part of a group, even in a minor role, the offender is likely to have increased the degree of fear caused to the victim (see Aggravating factors above).

(c) Voluntary return of property taken
• The point at which the property is returned will be important and, in general, the earlier the property is returned the greater the degree of mitigation the offender should receive.

The court will also take account of the presence or absence of other factors including:
•   Personal mitigation
•   First offence of violence
•   Clear evidence of remorse
•   Ready co-operation with the police
•   Response to previous sentences

A list of the most important general aggravating and mitigating factors can be found in the Guideline *Overarching Principles: Seriousness*. These factors are reproduced at Annex A for ease of reference.

Young Offenders
• Young offenders may have characteristics relevant to their offending behaviour which are different from adult offenders. Also, by statute, the youth justice system

has the principal aim of preventing offending by children and young persons.[2] Because of this, there may be factors which are of greater significance in cases involving young offenders including

- Age of the offender
- Immaturity of the offender
- Group pressure

Sentencers should recognise the varying significance of these factors for different ages.

(iii) Reduction in sentence for guilty plea

Having taking account of aggravating and mitigating factors the court should consider whether the sentence should be reduced to take account of a guilty plea and by how much, in accordance with the Guideline *Reduction in Sentence for a Guilty Plea.*

E Public Protection Sentences – dangerous offenders

Robbery is a serious offence for the purposes of section 225 of the Criminal Justice Act 2003 and sentencers should consider whether a life sentence for public protection should be imposed.

F Ancillary orders

In all cases, courts should consider making the following orders:

Restitution Order[3] – requiring the return of property.

Compensation Order[4] – for injury, loss or damage suffered.

Where a non-custodial sentence is imposed, courts may also consider making:

Anti-social behaviour order[5] – to protect the public from behaviour causing harassment, alarm or distress. This order may be particularly appropriate where the offence of robbery forms part of a pattern of behaviour but such an order may be unnecessary if it will simply prohibit what is already criminal conduct. It may be used to prevent some offenders associating with other offenders with whom offences of robbery have been committed.

G Factors to take into consideration – adult offenders

1. Robbery is a serious offence for the purposes of section 225 of the Criminal Justice Act 2003 and sentencers should consider whether a life sentence or sentence for public protection should be imposed. **The following guidelines apply to offenders who have <u>not</u> been assessed as dangerous.**

2. The sentencing ranges and presumptive starting points apply to all three categories of robbery detailed above:
   - Street robbery or 'mugging'
   - Robberies of small businesses
   - Less sophisticated commercial robberies

3. The 'starting points' are based upon a first-time offender who pleaded not guilty.

4. A reduction to the appropriate sentence, taking account of seriousness and aggravating and mitigating factors, will need to be made if an offender has pleaded guilty. The effect of applying the reduction may be that the sentence imposed for an offence at one level of seriousness may fall within the range suggested for the next lowest level of seriousness.

---

2 Crime and Disorder Act 1998 s37.
3 Powers of Criminal Courts (Sentencing) Act 2000 ss148–149.
4 Ibid, s130.
5 Crime and Disorder Act 1998 s1 as amended.

5. The relative seriousness of each offence will be determined by the following factors:
   • Degree of force and/or nature and duration of threats
   • Degree of injury to the victim
   • Degree of fear experienced by the victim
   • Value of property taken

6. Use of a particular degree of force is more serious than the threat (which is not carried into effect) to use that same degree of force. Depending on the facts, however, a threat to use a high degree of force might properly be regarded as more serious than actual use of a lesser degree of force.

7. If a weapon is involved in the use or threat of force, the offence will be more serious. Possession of a weapon during the course of an offence will be an aggravating factor, even if it is not used, because it indicates planning. If the offence involves a real firearm it will be more serious if that firearm is loaded. Whether the weapon is real or imitation is not a major factor in determining sentence because the amount of fear created in the victim is likely to be the same.

8. The value of the property capable of being taken as well as the actual amount taken is important.

9. The presence of one or more aggravating features will indicate a more severe sentence within the suggested range and, if the aggravating feature(s) are exceptionally serious, the case will move up to the next level.

10. In all cases, courts should consider making a restitution order and/or a compensation order. Where a non-custodial sentence is imposed, the court may also consider making an anti-social behaviour order.

11. Passing the custody threshold does not mean that a custodial sentence should be deemed inevitable.

ROBBERY
Street robbery or 'mugging'
Robberies of small businesses
Less sophisticated commercial robberies

Robbery is a serious offence for the purposes of sections 225 and 227
Criminal Justice Act 2003

Maximum Penalty: Life imprisonment

ADULT OFFENDERS

Type/nature of activity	Starting point	Sentencing Range
The offence includes the threat or use of minimal force and removal of property.	12 months custody	Up to 3 years custody
A weapon is produced and used to threaten, and/or force is used which results in injury to the victim.	4 years custody	2–7 years custody
The victim is caused serious physical injury by the use of significant force and/or use of a weapon.	8 years custody	7–12 years custody

Additional aggravating factors	Additional mitigating factors
1. More than one offender involved.	1. Unplanned/opportunistic.
2. Being the ringleader of a group of offenders.	2. Peripheral involvement.
3. Restraint, detention or additional degradation, of the victim.	3. Voluntary return of property taken.
4. Offence was pre-planned.	4. Clear evidence of remorse.
5. Wearing a disguise.	5. Ready co-operation with the police.
6. Offence committed at night.	
7. Vulnerable victim targeted.	
8. Targeting of large sums of money or valuable goods	
9. Possession of a weapon that was not used	

H Factors to take into consideration – young offenders

1. A youth court cannot impose a custodial sentence on an offender aged 10 or 11. If the offender is aged 12, 13 or 14, a detention and training order can only be imposed by a youth court in the case of persistent young offenders. In the Crown Court, however, long-term detention in accordance with the Powers of Criminal Courts (Sentencing) Act 2000 can be ordered on any young offender without the requirement of persistence. The Crown Court may also impose an extended sentence, detention for public protection or detention for life where the young offender meets the criteria for being a 'dangerous offender'. **The following guidelines apply to offenders who have <u>not</u> been assessed as dangerous.**

2. If a youth court is considering sending a case to the Crown Court, the court must be of the view that it is such a serious case that detention above two years is required, or that the appropriate sentence is a custodial sentence approaching the two-year limit which is normally applicable to older offenders.[6]

3. The sentencing ranges and presumptive starting points apply to all three categories of robbery detailed above:
   - **Street robbery or 'mugging'**
   - **Robberies of small businesses**
   - **Less sophisticated commercial robberies**

4. The 'starting points' are based upon a first-time offender, aged 17 years old, who pleaded not guilty. For younger offenders sentencers should consider whether a lower starting point is justified in recognition of the offender's age or immaturity.

5. Young offenders may have characteristics relevant to their offending behaviour which are different from adult offenders. Also, by statute, the youth justice system has the principal aim of preventing offending by children and young persons.[7] Because of this, there may be factors which are of greater significance in cases involving young offenders. Sentencers should recognise the varying significance of such factors for different ages.

6. A reduction to the appropriate sentence, taking account of seriousness, and aggravating and mitigating factors, will need to be made if an offender has pleaded guilty. The effect of applying the reduction may be that the sentence imposed for an offence at one level of seriousness may fall within the range suggested for the next lowest level of seriousness.

6 *W v Southampton Youth Court, K v Wirral Borough Magistrates' Court* [2003] 1 Cr App R (S) 87.
7 Crime and Disorder Act 1998 s37.

7. The relative seriousness of each offence will be determined by the following factors:
   • Degree of force and/or nature and duration of threats
   • Degree of injury to the victim
   • Degree of fear experienced by the victim
   • Value of property taken

8. Use of a particular degree of force is more serious than the threat (which is not carried into effect) to use that same degree of force. Depending on the facts, however, a threat to use a high degree of force might properly be regarded as more serious than actual use of a lesser degree of force.

9. If a weapon is involved in the use or threat of force, the offence will be more serious. Possession of a weapon during the course of an offence will be an aggravating factor, even if it is not used, because it indicates planning. If the offence involves a real firearm it will be more serious if that firearm is loaded. Whether the weapon is real or imitation is not a major factor in determining sentence because the amount of fear created in the victim is likely to be the same.

10. The value of the property *capable of being taken* as well as the actual amount taken is important.

11. The presence of one or more aggravating features will indicate a more severe sentence within the suggested range and, if the aggravating feature(s) are exceptionally serious, the case will move up to the next level.

12. In all cases, courts should consider making a restitution order and/or a compensation order. Where a non-custodial sentence is imposed, the court may also consider making an anti-social behaviour order.

13. Courts are required by section 44(1) of the Children and Young Persons Act 1933 to have regard to the welfare of the child, and under section 37 of the Crime and Disorder Act 1998 to have regard to the overall aim of the youth justice system of preventing re-offending.

14. Passing the custody threshold does not mean that a custodial sentence should be deemed inevitable.[8]

15. Where there is evidence that the offence has been committed to fund a drug habit and that treatment for this could help tackle the offender's offending behaviour, sentencers should consider a drug treatment requirement as part of a supervision order or action plan order.

Street robbery or 'mugging'
Robberies of small businesses
Less sophisticated commercial robberies

Robbery is a serious offence for the purposes of sections 226 and 228
Criminal Justice Act 2003

Maximum Penalty: Life imprisonment

YOUNG OFFENDERS*

Type/nature of activity	Starting point	Sentencing Range
The offence includes the threat or use of minimum force and the removal of property.	Community Order	Community Order – 12 months detention and training order

8 Guideline *Overarching Principles: Seriousness*, para 1.32.

Type/nature of activity	Starting point	Sentencing Range
A weapon is produced and used to threaten, and/or force is used which results in injury to the victim.	3 years detention	1–6 years detention
The victim is caused serious physical injury the use of significant force and/or by use of a weapon.	7 years detention	6–10 years detention

Additional aggravating factors	Additional mitigating factors
1. More than one offender involved.	1. Unplanned/opportunistic.
2. Being the ringleader of a group of offenders.	2. Peripheral involvement.
3. Restraint, detention or additional degradation of the victim.	3. Voluntary return of property taken.
4. Offence was pre-planned.	4. Clear evidence of remorse.
5. Wearing a disguise	5. Ready co-operation with the police.
6. Offence committed at night.	6. Age of the offender.
7. Vulnerable victim targeted.	7. Immaturity of the offender.
8. Targeting large sums of money or valuable goods.	8. Peer group pressure.
9. Possession of a weapon that was not used.	

- *The 'starting points' are based upon a first-time offender aged 17 years old who pleaded not guilty. For younger offenders, sentencers should consider whether a lower starting point is justified in recognition of the offender's age or immaturity.*

Part 2

Relevant guidance from the Court of Appeal (which is summarised below, for ease of reference) should apply to cases falling within the two final categories of robbery.

Violent personal robberies in the home

The sentencing range for robbery in the home involving physical violence is 13-16 years for a first time offender pleading not guilty. In this type of case, the starting point reflects the high level of violence, although it is clear that longer terms will be appropriate where extreme violence is used.[9]

This category overlaps with some cases of aggravated burglary (an offence which also carries a maximum sentence of life imprisonment) where comparable sentences are passed.

Consideration will need to be given as to whether the offender is a 'dangerous offender' for the purposes of the Criminal Justice Act 2003.

Professionally planned commercial robberies

The leading Court of Appeal decision on sentencing for robbery is the 1975 case of Turner. [10] This focuses on serious commercial robberies at the upper end of

9 *O'Driscoll* (1986) 8 Cr App R (S) 121.
10 (1975) 61 Cr App R 89.

the sentencing range but just below the top level - planned profession robberies of banks and security vehicles, involving firearms and high-value theft, but without the additional elements that characterise the most serious cases. The Court of Appeal said it had 'come to the conclusion that the normal sentence for anyone taking part in a bank robbery or in the hold-up of a security or a Post Office van should be 15 years if firearms were carried and no serious injury done.

The Court also said that 18 years should be about the maximum for crimes which are not 'wholly abnormal' (such as the Great Train Robbery).[11]

In cases involving the most serious commercial robberies the Court has imposed 20-30 years (15–20 years after a plea of guilty).

Consideration will need to be given as to whether the offender is a 'dangerous offender' for the purposes of the Criminal Justice Act 2003.

Annex A

Extracts from Guideline *Overarching Principles: Seriousness*

This is a general list which is included for ease of reference. Not every factor will apply to an offence of robbery.

(i) Aggravating factors

1.22 Factors indicating higher culpability:

- Offence committed whilst on bail for other offences
- Failure to respond to previous sentences
- Offence was racially or religiously aggravated
- Offence motivated by, or demonstrating, hostility to the victim based on his or her sexual orientation (or presumed sexual orientation)
- Offence motivated by, or demonstrating, hostility based on the victim's disability (or presumed disability)
- Previous conviction(s), particularly where a pattern of repeat offending is disclosed
- Planning of an offence
- An intention to commit more serious harm than actually resulted from the offence
- Offenders operating in groups or gangs
- 'Professional' offending
- Commission of the offence for financial gain (where this is not inherent in the offence itself)
- High level of profit from the offence
- An attempt to conceal or dispose of evidence
- Failure to respond to warnings or concerns expressed by others about the offender's behaviour
- Offence committed whilst on licence
- Offence motivated by hostility towards a minority group, or a member/members of it
- Deliberate targeting of vulnerable victim(s)
- Commission of an offence while under the influence of alcohol or drugs
- Use of a weapon to frighten or injure victim
- Deliberate and gratuitous violence or damage to property, over and above what is needed to carry out the offence

11 *Wilson and others* (1964) 48 Cr App R 329.

- Abuse of power
- Abuse of a position of trust

1.23 Factors indicating a more than usually serious degree of harm:

- Multiple victims
- An especially serious physical or psychological effect on the victim, even if unintended
- A sustained assault or repeated assaults on the same victim
- Victim is particularly vulnerable
- Location of the offence (for example, in an isolated place)
- Offence is committed against those working in the public sector or providing a service to the public
- Presence of others, eg relatives, especially children or partner of the victim
- Additional degradation of the victim (eg taking photographs of a victim as part of a sexual offence)
- In property offences, high value (including sentimental value) of property to the victim, or substantial consequential loss (eg where the theft of equipment causes serious disruption to a victim's life or business)

(ii) Mitigating factors

1.24 Some factors may indicate that an offender's culpability is unusually low, or that the harm caused by an offence is less than usually serious.

1.25 Factors indicating significantly lower culpability:

- A greater degree of provocation than normally expected
- Mental illness or disability
- Youth or age, where it affects the responsibility of the individual defendant
- The fact that the offender played only a minor role in the offence

(iii) Personal mitigation

1.26 Section 166(1) Criminal Justice Act 2003 makes provision for a sentencer to take account of any matters that 'in the opinion of the court, are relevant in mitigation of sentence'.

1.27 When the court has formed an initial assessment of the seriousness of the offence, then it should consider any offender mitigation. The issue of remorse should be taken into account at this point along with other mitigating features such as admissions to the police in interview.

Extracted from Guideline, *Overarching Principles: Seriousness*, Sentencing Guidelines Council, December 2004

Pilot areas

Action plan order – drug treatment and testing requirement

Local justice areas of Bradford, Calderdale, Keighley, Manchester, Newham and that part of Teesside local justice area that is coterminous with the borough of Middlesbrough.

Criminal Justice Act 2003 (Commencement No 6 and Transitional Provisions) Order 2004 SI No 3033.

Curfew order (removal of three-month maximum for 10- to 15-year olds)

Local authority areas of:

Birmingham City Council;

Bolton Metropolitan Borough Council;

Bridgend County Borough Council;

Calderdale Metropolitan Borough Council;

Cardiff County Council;

City and County of Swansea Council;

Coventry City Council;

Leeds City Council;

Liverpool City Council;

London Boroughs of Barking and Dagenham, Bexley, Bromley, Croydon, Greenwich, Havering, Lewisham, Merton, Redbridge, Richmond-upon-Thames, Southwark, Sutton and Waltham Forest;

Merthyr Tydfil County Borough Council;

Neath Port Talbot County Borough Council;

Nottingham City Council;

Oldham Metropolitan Borough Council;

Rhonda Cynon Taf County Borough Council;

Royal borough of Kingston-upon-Thames;

Solihull Metropolitan Borough Council;

Stockport Metropolitan Borough Council;

Thameside Metropolitan Borough Council; and

Vale of Glamorgan Council.

Anti-social Behaviour Act 2003 (Commencement No 4) Order 2004 SI No 2168.

Exclusion order

Hampshire/Wessex YOT area, Greater Manchester and West Midlands.

Drug testing (pre-sentence)

No pilot areas at time of writing.

Supervision order

(i) Drug treatment and testing requirement

Local justice areas of Bradford, Calderdale, Keighley, Manchester, Newham and that part of Teesside local justice area that is coterminous with the borough of Middlesbrough.

Criminal Justice Act 2003 (Commencement No 6 and Transitional Provisions) Order 2004 SI No 3033.

(ii) Foster parent residence requirement

Hampshire and Staffordshire.

(iii) Intensive supervision and surveillance programmes (12-month duration)

Local authority areas of:

Birmingham City Council;

Bolton Metropolitan Borough Council;

Bridgend County Borough Council;

Calderdale Metropolitan Borough Council;

Cardiff County Council;

City and County of Swansea Council;

Coventry City Council;

Leeds City Council;

Liverpool City Council;

London Boroughs of Barking and Dagenham, Bexley, Bromley, Croydon, Greenwich, Havering, Lewisham, Merton, Redbridge, Richmond-upon-Thames, Southwark, Sutton and Waltham Forest;

Merthyr Tydfil County Borough Council;

Neath Port Talbot County Borough Council;

Nottingham City Council;

Oldham Metropolitan Borough Council;

Rhonda Cynon Taf County Borough Council;

Royal borough of Kingston-upon-Thames;

Solihull Metropolitan Borough Council;

Stockport Metropolitan Borough Council;

Thameside Metropolitan Borough Council; and

Vale of Glamorgan Council.

Anti-social Behaviour Act 2003 (Commencement No 4) Order 2004 SI No 2168.

Mode of trial – law on full implementation of Criminal Justice Act 2003, Sch 3

Introduction

A13.1 This appendix sets out the law on determining the appropriate court for trial of a youth defendant on full implementation of the provisions of the Criminal Justice Act 2003, Schedule 3. The relevant parts of the statutes are reproduced at the end of this appendix.

A13.2 The most important changes are the introduction of a plea before venue in certain circumstances for the child or young person and the abolition of committal proceedings in all cases for both the adult and youth defendants. Where appropriate, there will be a plea before venue procedure for the child or young person in the youth court and in the adult magistrates' court. The decision on mode of trial that will follow a not guilty indication may now be referred to as the allocation decision. The changes are intended to reduce the number of children and young persons being tried in the Crown Court.[1] It is not clear, however, whether the amendments will have the intended effect.

A13.3 The abolition of committal proceedings means that where a court decides that trial is to take place in the Crown Court, the case is sent immediately and all subsequent hearings will take place in the Crown Court. In the case of a youth defendant this will also mean that a preliminary hearing will normally take place before the plea and case management hearing in the Crown Court.

Presumption of summary trial

A13.4 The Magistrates' Courts Act 1980 s24(1) provides:

> **24**(1) Where a person under the age of 18 years appears or is brought before a magistrates' court on an information charging him with an indictable offence he shall, subject to sections 51 and 51A of the Crime and Disorder Act 1998 and to sections 24A and 24B below, be tried summarily.[2]

A13.5 The Crime and Disorder Act 1998 s51 and s51A[3] relate to the sending of cases for both youth and adult defendants to the Crown Court without the need for committal proceedings. The Magistrates' Courts Act 1980 s24A to s24D introduce a plea before venue procedure for children and young persons.[4]

A13.6 The general rule remains that a defendant under the age of 18 should be tried summarily unless s/he:
- is charged with a homicide offence;
- is charged with possession of a firearm;
- may need to be sentenced under the dangerousness provisions;
- is charged with a serious or complex fraud or a case involving children;
- is charged with a grave crime and a longer than usual sentence may be necessary;

---

1 Criminal Justice Act 2003, Explanatory Notes.
2 Inserted by Criminal Justice Act 2003, Sch 3 para 9.
3 Ibid, Sch 3 para 18
4 Ibid, Sch 3 para 10.

- is jointly charged with an adult and it is necessary in the interests of justice to send them both for trial.

Each of these exceptions is examined below.

Homicide

A13.7 A child or young person charged with an offence of homicide must be tried in the Crown Court. There will be no mode of trial hearing.

Definition

A13.8 There is no complete statutory definition of 'homicide', but it is likely to include:
- murder,
- attempted murder,[5]
- manslaughter,
- infanticide.

A13.9 Causing or allowing the death of a child or vulnerable adult under Domestic Violence, Crime and Victims Act 2004, s5 is specifically defined as an offence of homicide.[6]

A13.10 It is not clear whether homicide extends to causing death by dangerous driving, causing death by careless driving whilst under the influence of drink or drugs or causing death by aggravated vehicle taking. However, all of these offences are now 'grave crimes' as they carry a maximum sentence of 14 years imprisonment in the case of an adult. The penalties were increased by Criminal Justice Act 2003, s285.

Sending for trial

A13.11 There is no mode of trial hearing and the case will be sent to the Crown Court forthwith.[7]

Related offences

A13.12 Any indictable offences with which the defendant is also charged, and which could be joined on the same indictment may be sent for trial at the same time.[8] Any summary matters charged can also be sent to the Crown Court if they are related to other indictable matters charged and are punishable by imprisonment or involve obligatory or discretionary disqualification from driving.[9] The plea before venue provisions may apply to these matters (see paras A13.57–A13.61 below).[10]

Firearms possession

Criteria

A13.13 A young person must be tried at the Crown Court if:
- s/he is charged with an offence under s5(1)(a), (ab), (aba), (ac), (ad), (ae),(af) or (c) of the Firearms Act 1968 (prohibited weapons) or s/he is charged with an offence under s5(1A)(a) of the Firearms Act 1968; and
- the offence was committed on or after 22 January 2004; and
- at the time of the offence s/he was aged 16 or over.[11]

Sending for trial

A13.14 The young people who meet these criteria will be subject to a sentence of detention

---

5 By virtue of Criminal Attempts Act 1981 s2(2)(c).
6 Domestic Violence, Crime and Victims Act 2004 s6(5).
7 Crime and Disorder Act 1998 s51A(2),(3)(a) and (12) and Magistrates' Courts Act 1980 s24A(1)(a).
8 Crime and Disorder Act 1998 s51A(4)(a).
9 Ibid, s51A(4)(b) and(9).
10 Magistrates' Courts Act 1980 s24A(1)(b); Crime and Disorder Act 1998 s51A(4) and (5).
11 Firearms Act 1968 s51A, inserted by Criminal Justice Act 2003, s287.

of a minimum of three years. There is no mode of trial hearing and the case will be sent forthwith to the Crown Court.[12]

Related offences

A13.15 Any indictable offences with which the defendant is also charged, and which could be joined on the same indictment may be sent for trial at the same time.[13] Any summary matters charged can also be sent to the Crown Court if they are related to other indictable matters charged and are punishable by imprisonment or involve obligatory or discretionary disqualification from driving.[14] The plea before venue provisions may apply to these matters (see paras A13.57–A13.61 below).[15]

Dangerous offenders

A13.16 The youth court shall send forthwith a child or young person for trial at the Crown Court if:
- the offence was committed on or after 4 April 2005; and
- the offence is a specified offence; and
- it appears to the court that if s/he is found guilty of the offence charged the criteria for the imposition of detention for life, detention for public protection or extended detention would be met.[16]

A13.17 To impose detention for public protection or extended detention the court must consider there is a 'significant risk to members of the public of serious harm occasioned by the commission by the offender of further specified offences'.[17]

A13.18 Before addressing a court considering these provisions at the mode of trial stage, the legal representative is advised to familiarise him/herself with the legal provisions to be considered on sentence so as to be in a position to assist the court as to their likely relevance, or otherwise. These sentencing provisions are considered in detail in Chapter 24.

Criteria
'Specified offence'

A13.19 A violent or sexual offence listed in the Criminal Justice Act 2003 Schedule 15 (see appendix 6).

'Serious offence'

A13.20 A specified offence which is punishable in the case of an adult with life imprisonment or imprisonment for 10 years or more.[18]

There are a number of offences that are specified offences which are not grave crimes eg affray, assault occasioning actual bodily harm, racially aggravated public order offences, wounding/grievous bodily harm contrary to the Offences Against the Persons Act 1861 s20.

'Serious harm'

A13.21 Serious harm is defined as 'death or serious personal injury, whether physical or psychological'.[19]

'Significant risk'

A13.22 This term is not defined by statute. The 'significant risk' relates to the risk of serious

---

12 Crime and Disorder Act 1998 s51A(2),(3)(a) and(12) and Magistrates' Courts Act 1980 s24A(1)(a).
13 Crime and Disorder Act 1998 s51A(4)(a).
14 Ibid, s51A(4)(b) and(9).
15 Magistrates' Courts Act 1980 s24A(1)(b) and Crime and Disorder Act 1998 s51A(4) and (5).
16 Criminal Justice Act 2003 ss226 and 228 and Crime and Disorder Act 1998 s51A(2) and(3)(d).
17 Criminal Justice Act 2003 ss226(1) and 228(1).
18 Ibid, s224(2).
19 Ibid, s224(3).

harm and the risk of re-offending.[20] It is submitted that the court's attention may need to be drawn to this element of the provisions. It will be a matter for the judgment of the sentencing court once it is in possession of all the relevant information about the offence and the offender.

No statutory presumption

A13.23 It is important to distinguish the provisions relating to adult dangerous offenders from those relating to children and young persons. The statutory presumption of risk which applies to adult offenders with relevant previous convictions, does not apply to children or young persons.[21]

The assessment of dangerousness

A13.24 The court:
- must take into account all such information as is available to it about the nature and circumstances of the offence;
- may take into account any information which is before it about any pattern of behaviour of which the offence forms part; and
- may take into account any information about the offender which is before it.[22]

Applying the provisions

A13.25 The Crime and Disorder Act 1998, s51A(2) and (3)(d) (sending for sentence under the 'dangerousness' provisions) were in force before the amendment of the Magistrates' Courts Act 1980, s24[23] and made no mention of section 24. The sections are now explicitly subject to each other.[24]

A13.26 The unequivocal terms of section 51A(2) mean that the court must send a defendant straight to the Crown Court if, at any stage prior to conviction, it is of the view that a sentence under the dangerousness provisions may be imposed on the defendant.

A13.27 In considering the relationship between the provisions as now enacted it is submitted that the guidance in *R(CPS) v South East Surrey Youth Court*[25] remains of relevance. In that case Rose LJ expressed considerable sympathy with those in the youth court who have to deal with the 'labyrinthine' and 'manifestly inconsistent' provisions as then enacted. The court sought to give guidance as to how the provisions should be approached. In the view of the authors the provisions remain labyrinthine after full implementation.

A13.28 In *R(CPS) v South East Surrey Youth Court*[26] Rose LJ stated that the youth court should bear in mind:
- the policy of the legislature is that those who are under 18 should, wherever possible, be tried in a youth court, which is best designed for their specific needs;
- the guidance given by the Court of Appeal (Criminal Division) in the judgement of *R v Lang and others*[27], particularly in relation to non-serious specified offences;
- the need in relation to those under 18, to be particularly rigorous before concluding that there is a significant risk of serious harm by the commission of further offences: such a conclusion is unlikely to appropriate in the absence of a pre-sentence report following assessment by a youth offending team;
- in most cases where a non-serious specified offence is charged an assessment of dangerousness will not be appropriate until after conviction, when, if the dangerousness criteria are met, the defendant can be committed to the Crown Court for sentence.[28]

20 *R v Lang and others* [2005] EWCA Crim 2864. See paras 24.117 – 24.142.
21 Criminal Justice Act 2003 s229(3).
22 Ibid, s229(2).
23 Amended by Criminal Justice Act 2003 Sch 3 para 9.
24 Magistrates' Courts Act 1980 s24(1) and Crime and Disorder Act 1998 s51A(1).
25 [2005] EWHC 2929.
26 Ibid.
27 [2005] EWCA Crim 2864, paras 24.117 – 24.142.
28 *CPS v South East Surrey Youth Court* [2005] EWHC 2929 para 17.

A13.29 In practical terms, where the issue of dangerousness is raised initially, either by the prosecution or the court, the clear guidance is that the court should consider summary trial wherever possible. For non-serious specified offences the court should, in most cases, take the view that it does not have sufficient information to make a decision as to dangerousness at this stage, reserving its position in relation to a possible committal for sentence on a plea or finding of guilt.[29] At this later stage the court will have far more information, including a pre-sentence report, available to it in order to make an assessment of the possibility of the need for the imposition of a sentence under the dangerous offender provisions.

A13.30   The *South East Surrey* case concerned an example of a non-serious specified offence. In the view of the authors the same considerations will arise with many serious specified offences. At an early stage in the proceedings the court will have limited information available in relation to the risks posed by the defendant in the future, in relation to the risk of offending and the risk of serious harm to the public from further offending. The court will, having taken a plea, be in a position to consider its sentencing powers in relation to grave crimes.[30] If the court decided to retain the matter for trial or sentence (depending on the plea), the court would retain the ability to send the defendant to the Crown Court for consideration of a sentence under the 'dangerousness' provisions once a pre-sentence report was available to assist the court in the assessment of those risks. It would only be in the most obvious of cases that a defendant would be sent to the Crown Court, under the provisions of the Crime and Disorder Act 1998 s51A(3)(d), before a plea is taken.

Co-defendants

A13.31 The decision regarding dangerousness is taken separately for each defendant. Where one defendant is to be sent to the Crown Court in accordance with these provisions, there is no provision for the sending at the same time of a youth co-defendant who is not deemed dangerous.

Related offences

A13.32 Indictable and summary matters which are related to the matter being sent to the Crown Court can be sent for trial at the same time.[31] Summary-only matters can be sent if they are punishable by imprisonment or involve obligatory or discretionary disqualification from driving.[32] The plea before venue provisions may apply to these matters (see paras A13.57–A13.61 below).[33]

Preparing for the dangerousness argument
The court

A13.33 It is important that the defence lawyer is ready to deal with this issue whether or not s/he has notice that it is to be raised by the prosecution or the court. When considering the issue of dangerousness in an early stage of the proceeding the court will have available some details of the allegation and the young offender's previous convictions. Full details of the offence itself and of the offences which led to the earlier convictions (if any) are unlikely to be available. It may be necessary for a defence lawyer to look at further details of previous convictions, which may be contained in previous files for the same defendant, in order to address the court on the issue of whether the defendant should be treated as a dangerous offender. The lawyer will need to consider sentencing guidelines (if any) for the substantive offence and the factors to be considered in the court's assessment of the offence and the offender. At the early stage of the proceedings the most effective argument may be that there is as yet insufficient information available to enable the court to make the appropriate decision as to whether a longer than usual sentence should be available on the sentencing of the particular offender.

29 Powers of the Criminal Courts (Sentencing) Act 2000 s3C.
30 See para A13.49 below.
31 Crime and Disorder Act s51A(4).
32 Ibid, s51A(9).
33 Magistrates' Courts Act 1980, s24A(1)(b) and Crime and Disorder Act 1998 s51A(4) and (5).

The client

A13.34 The process of the court's decision-making on this issue may be alarming for the client and any family member attending court with him/her. During the course of the hearing they will hear the prosecution evidence at its highest and the use of the term 'dangerous' may seem to be emotive. It is important that the defence lawyer takes time to explain to the client, as far as possible, the nature of this part of the proceedings, using language appropriate to his/her age and understanding.

Notice given to the court under s51B – cases involving serious fraud

A13.35 This provision requires that the case be sent forthwith to the Crown Court.[34] As cases are no longer to be delayed by committal proceedings it is difficult to envisage the circumstances in which this procedure will be used.

A13.36 　The notice may be served where the designated authority is of the opinion that the evidence of the offence charged:
- is sufficient for the person charged to be put on trial for the offence; and
- reveals a fraud of such seriousness or complexity that it is appropriate that the management of the case should without delay be taken over by the Crown Court.[35]

Who can serve notice?

A13.37 The 'designated authorities' empowered to serve notice are:
- the Director of Public Prosecutions;
- the Director of the Serious Fraud Office;
- the Commissioners of the Inland Revenue;
- the Commissioners of Customs and Excise; or
- the Secretary of State.[36]

The notice

A13.39 The notice must specify the proposed place of trial.[37] It must be served upon the magistrates' court before any summary trial begins. The decision to serve a notice shall not be subject to appeal or liable to be questioned in any court.[38]

Effect of notice

A13.40 The effect of such a notice is that the functions of the magistrates' court cease in relation to the case, except for determining whether the defendant is on bail or in custody until the first Crown Court hearing and administrative matters such as extending any representation order.[39]

Notice given to the court under s51C – cases involving children

A13.41 This provision requires that the case be sent forthwith to the Crown Court.[40] It is almost identical to the provision which it replaces.[41] As cases are no longer to be delayed by committal proceedings it is difficult to envisage the circumstances in which this procedure will be used.

　The notice will be served with the purpose of avoiding any prejudice to the wel-

34 Crime and Disorder Act 1998 s51A(2) and (3)(c).
35 Ibid, s51B(1) and (5).
36 Ibid, s51B(9).
37 Ibid, s51B(3).
38 Ibid, s51B(8).
39 Ibid, s51B(6).
40 Ibid, s51A(2) and (3)(c).
41 'Transfer' provisions of the Criminal Justice Act 1991 s53.

fare of a child witness and to ensure that the case is taken over and proceeded with by the Crown Court without delay.[42]

Which offences?

A13.42   The notice may be served in relation to the following offences:
- an offence which involves an assault on, or injury or a threat of injury to a person;
- an offence under Children and Young Persons Act 1933 s1 (cruelty to persons under 16);
- an offence under the Sexual Offences Act 1956, the Protection of Children Act 1978 or the Sexual Offences Act 2003;
- an offence of kidnapping or false imprisonment, or an offence under the Child Abduction Act 1984 ss1 or 2;
- an offence which consists of attempting or conspiring to commit, or of aiding, abetting, counselling, procuring or inciting the commission of, an offence listed above.[43]

Service of the notice

A13.43   To initiate the sending for trial procedure, the Director of Public Prosecutions must serve a notice upon the relevant youth court or adult magistrates' court, certifying that s/he is of the opinion:
- that the evidence of the offence would be sufficient for the person charged to be put on trial for the offence;
- that a child would be called as a witness at the trial; and
- that, for the purposes of avoiding any prejudice to the welfare of the child, the case should be taken over and proceeded with without delay by the Crown Court.[44]

A13.44   That opinion must be certified by the Director of Public Prosecutions (or by an officer exercising this function on his/her behalf) in the notice.[45] In practice the notice is likely to be certified by a prosecutor with delegated authority to act on behalf of the Director.

Definition of child

A13.45   Child is defined as follows:
- A person who is under the age of 17 years;
- Any person of whom a video-recording[46] was made when he was under the age of 17 years with a view to its admission as evidence in chief in the trial referred to.[47]

The notice

A13.46   The notice must be served upon the magistrates' court before any summary trial begins.[48] The decision to serve a notice shall not be subject to appeal or liable to be questioned in any court.[49]

Effect of notice

A13.47   The effect of such a notice is that the functions of the magistrates' court cease in relation to the case, except for determining whether the defendant is on bail or in custody until the first Crown Court hearing and administrative matters such as extending any representation order.[50]

---

42 Crime and Disorder Act 1998 s51C(1)(c).
43 Ibid, s51C(3).
44 Ibid, s51C(1).
45 Ibid, s51C(2) and (5).
46 As defined in the Youth Justice and Criminal Evidence Act 1999 s63(1).
47 Crime and Disorder Act 1998 s51C(7).
48 Ibid, s51C(4) and s51B(5).
49 Ibid, s51C(6).
50 Ibid, s51C(4) and s51B(6).

A13.48 Table A: Sending for trial without plea before venue: Crime and Disorder Act 1998 s51A

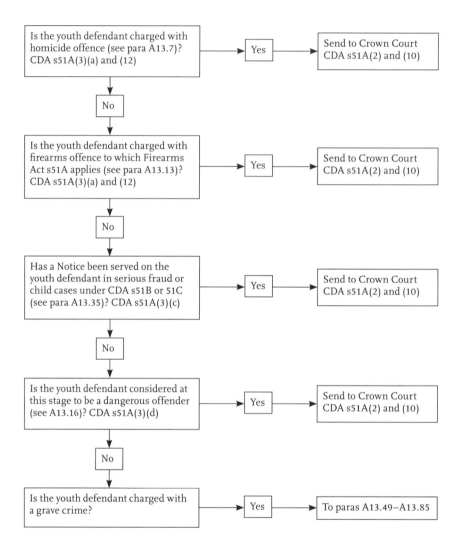

Grave crimes

A13.49   The plea before venue procedure will be familiar to practitioners in the adult magistrates' court. Its introduction for grave crimes in the youth court means that the court will only send cases for trial to the Crown Court where a not guilty plea or no plea has been indicated. The court will decide whether, if the defendant is convicted at trial, the youth court would have adequate sentencing powers.

A13.50   If the court retains the case at this stage it will lose the power to send the case to the Crown Court for sentence in the event of a conviction. The court will still be able to send the defendant to the Crown Court for sentence under the Powers of Criminal Courts (Sentencing) Act 2000 s3C if it appears to the court that the criteria for sentencing as a dangerous offender would be met.

A13.51   If the defendant pleads guilty the court will decide whether it has sufficient power to sentence. The defendant can be committed to the Crown Court for sentence under the new committal for sentence provisions of the Powers of Criminal Courts (Sentencing) Act 2000 s3B.

A13.52   The decision-making process is summarised in Table B below.

Definition

A13.53   A 'grave crime' is defined by the Powers of Criminal Courts (Sentencing) Act 2000 s91. The definition includes:
- an offence punishable in the case of an adult with imprisonment for 14 years or more;
- firearms possession (see above);
- various sexual offences

Offences punishable with 14 years or more

A13.54   The definition would include robbery, residential burglary and handling stolen goods. It does not include non-residential burglary (maximum penalty 10 years) or theft (maximum penalty 7 years). A full list of offences which are grave crimes is produced in appendix 6.

Sexual offences specifically defined as grave crimes

A13.55   The following sexual offences may be treated as grave crimes notwithstanding the fact that the maximum sentence is less than 14 years:
- sexual assault contrary to the Sexual Offences Act 2003 s3;
- child sex offences committed by children and young persons contrary to the Sexual Offences Act 2003 s13;
- sexual activity with a child family member contrary to Sexual Offences Act 2003 s25; and
- inciting a child family member to engage in sexual activity contrary to the Sexual Offences Act 2003 s26.

Fatal driving offences

A13.56   The Criminal Justice Act 2003 s285 increased to 14 years the maximum penalty for the following offences:
- causing death by dangerous driving contrary to the Road Traffic Act 1988 s1;
- causing death by careless driving whilst under influence of drink or drugs contrary to Road Traffic Act 1988 s3A;
- aggravated vehicle-taking resulting in death contrary to the Theft Act 1968 s12A(4).

Plea before venue

A13.57   When a child or young person is charged with a grave crime, the court must carry out a plea before venue procedure before a mode of trial hearing.[51]

---

51 Magistrates Courts Act 1980 s24A to 24D.

Procedure

A13.58   The court must read the written charge to the defendant in his/her presence and explain in ordinary language that, if an indication of a guilty plea is made, the indication will be taken as a guilty plea and the court will then go on to determine whether the case should be sent to the Crown Court for sentence under the Powers of the Criminal Courts (Sentencing) Act 2000 s3B.[52]

- *Indicating a guilty plea.* If the young person indicates that s/he intends to plead guilty the court will regard this as the entering of a guilty plea and will proceed to sentence. The magistrates will have the power to commit the young person to the Crown Court for sentence under the Powers of the Criminal Courts (Sentencing) Act 2000 s3B if the court is of the view that it should be possible to sentence the child or young person to detention under the Powers of Criminal Courts (Sentencing) Act 2000 s91.[53]

- *Not guilty/no plea indication.* If the child or young person indicates a not guilty plea or gives no indication as to the intended plea, the consideration of the appropriate place for trial will proceed in the usual way (see below). Where the child or young person enters a guilty plea at a later stage there is no longer a power to commit for sentence under section 3B.[54]

A13.59   A single justice can conduct the plea before venue procedure.[55] The court may adjourn the proceedings at any time, and on doing so on any occasion when the accused is present may remand the accused.[56] This may be of assistance to the defence lawyer where there is insufficient information available to enable the lawyer to advise the young client about the evidence and his/her plea. This would, for example, allow for service of further relevant evidence or consideration of video or audio evidence.[57]

Related offences

A13.60   Indictable and summary matters which are related to the matter being sent to the Crown Court can be sent for trial at the same time.[58] Summary only matters can be sent if they are punishable by imprisonment or involve obligatory or discretionary disqualification from driving.[59] Before making the decision whether to send such matters to the Crown Court, an indication of plea(s) should be sought.[60] This will enable the court to decide whether such matters should also be sent to the Crown Court or whether they can appropriately be dealt with in the youth court.

Absence of the defendant

A13.61   If the defendant is legally represented and the court considers that by reason of the defendant's disorderly conduct it is not practicable for the proceedings to be conducted in his presence, the court can deal with plea before venue in the absence of the defendant. The representative will be asked to indicate a plea.[61] Only the indication of a guilty plea will be taken as the entering of a plea.[62]

---

52 Magistrates' Courts Act 1980 s24A(3), (4) and (5). Powers to commit for sentence are inserted by Criminal Justice Act 2003 Sch 3 paragraph 23. See chapter 19.
53 The court will be able to send the defendant to the Crown Court for sentence under the provisions of Powers of Criminal Courts (Sentencing) Act 2000, s3C if it appears to the court that the criteria for sentencing as a dangerous offender would be met.
54 Ibid, s3B(1). The ability to commit for sentence under the dangerousness provisions remains.
55 Magistrates' Courts Act 1980 s24D.
56 Ibid, s24C(1).
57 See below.
58 Ibid, s51A(4).
59 Ibid, s51A(9).
60 Magistrates' Courts Act 1980 s24A(1)(b) and Crime and Disorder Act 1998 s51A(4) and (5).
61 Magistrates' Courts Act 1980 s24B.
62 Ibid, s24B(2)(c) and (4).

Criteria for mode of trial decision

A13.62   Where a youth court decides to deal with a young offender, on conviction the maximum penalty is a 2 year detention and training order. For younger offenders there may be no custodial powers in the event of conviction.[63] The decision being made at this stage involves considering whether an offence may require a greater punishment than the youth court has available. Once the youth court has agreed to deal with a case under these provisions there is no power to commit the child or young person to the Crown Court for sentence, save under the dangerousness provisions discussed above.

A13.63   In recent years there have been a number of decisions in the Administrative Court regarding mode of trial decisions in the youth court.[64] In an attempt to provide straightforward guidance to magistrates considering the question of jurisdiction under s24(1)(a) Leveson J in *R (on the application of H,O and A) v Southampton Youth Court*[65] summarised the principles derived from these cases as follows:

1.   The general policy of the legislature is that those who are under 18 years of age and in particular children of under 15 years of age should, wherever possible, be tried in the youth court. It is that court which is best designed to meet their specific needs. A trial in the Crown Court with the inevitably greater formality and greatly increased number of people involved (including a jury and the public) should be reserved for the most serious cases.

2.   It is a further policy of the legislature that, generally speaking, first-time offenders aged 12 to 14 and all offenders under 12 should not be detained in custody and decisions as to jurisdiction should have regard to the fact that the exceptional power to detain for grave offences should not be used to water down the general principle. Those under 15 will rarely attract a period of detention and, even more rarely, those who are under 12.

3.   In each case the court should ask itself whether there is a real prospect, having regard to his or her age, that this defendant whose case they are considering might require a sentence of, or in excess of, two years or, alternatively, whether although the sentence might be less than two years, there is some unusual feature of the case which justifies declining jurisdiction, bearing in mind that the absence of a power to impose a detention and training order because the defendant is under 15 is not an unusual feature.'

A13.64   This guidance has been adopted and repeated in subsequent cases where it has been contended that magistrates' have failed to properly exercise their discretion in relation to jurisdiction.[66]

A13.65   Further specific guidance is available in relation to younger defendants:

'... the fact that an offender does not qualify for a detention and training order because he is only 14 and not a persistent offender is not an exceptional circumstance to justify passing a sentence of less than 2 years under section 91 of the 2000 Act.'[67]

Factors to be taken into consideration

A13.66   The Criminal Justice Act 2003 introduced a statutory regime to assist the courts in assessing the seriousness of an offence. In the future the Sentencing Guidelines Council will produce guidance on the allocation of cases in the youth court. Certain

---

63   See chapter 19.
64   See, among others, *R (on the application of D) v Manchester City Youth Court* [2001] EWHC 860 (Admin); [2002] 1 Cr App R (S) 373; (2001) 166 JP 15, *R (on the application of W) v Thetford Youth Justices* [2002] EWHC 1252 (Admin), *R (on the application of W) v Southampton Youth Court* [2002] EWHC 1640 (Admin), and *R (on the application of C) v Balham Youth Court* [2003] EWHC 1332 (Admin); [2004] 1 Cr App R 22; (2003) 167 JP 525; [2003] Crim LR 636.
65   [2004] EWHC 2912 Admin.
66   *CPS v South East Surrey Youth Court* [2005] EWHC 2929, *R (On the application of W,S and B) v Brent, Enfield and Richmond Youth Courts* [2006] EWHC 95 (Admin).
67   *R (C) v Balham Youth Court*, [2003] EWHC 1332 Admin.

principles may also be extracted from the occasions when the higher courts have considered the question of determining mode of trial in the youth court.

Facts of allegation

A13.67   It is not appropriate for the court to consider evidence (even by being invited to read prosecution witness statements) to determine seriousness.[68] The facts of the case as alleged, which must be assumed to be true unless manifestly not, should be accurately put before the court. For that reason, the summary of the facts must be scrupulously fair and balanced.[69] In offences involving discrimination on the basis of disability or sexual orientation, or involving racial or religious aggravation these must be regarded as an aggravating factor in sentencing.[70]

A13.68   The Criminal Justice Act 2003 sets out some of the aggravating factors to be taken into account on sentence.[71] The Sentencing Guidelines Council guidance on *Overarching Principles: Seriousness* (December 2004) will be relevant to assist the court in considering the aggravating and mitigating factors to be taken in assessing the seriousness of the offence by reference the culpability of the defendant and the harm caused.[72]

Age of the defendant

A13.69   When considering the likely sentence the court must have regard to the offender before them and the discount that a sentencing court would allow to the appropriate sentence for an adult to take account of the age of the defendant.

Defendant's previous criminal convictions

A13.70   When dealing with a child or young person the court may take into account previous convictions.[73] The court must, in considering the seriousness of an offence, consider previous convictions as an aggravating factor.[74] The defendant's previous record should be accurately described.[75]

Relevant mitigation

A13.71   The court should take into account any undisputed facts put forward as mitigation, such as the good character of the accused.[76]

Age of witnesses

A13.72   This consideration will only be relevant on the entering of a not guilty plea or no indication. Although in general a court would take into account the age of the witnesses and the desirability of disposing of the case expeditiously, such considerations could not outweigh the decision as to the proper penalty.

Welfare of defendant

A13.73   The question of whether the court should have regard to the suitability of the Crown Court as a venue for the trial of a child or young person was discussed in *R v Devizes Youth Court ex p A*[77] where it was held that the court had no discretion once it formed the view that it ought to be possible to sentence the offender pursuant to section 91. The case must then go to the Crown Court. In the opinion of the authors

68 *R v South Hackney Juvenile Court ex p RB and CB (Minors)* (1984) 77 Cr App R 294, QBD.
69 *R (on the application of W,S and B) v Brent, Enfield and Richmond Youth Courts* [2006] EWHC 95 (Admin).
70 Criminal Justice Act 2003 ss145 and 146.
71 Ibid, s143.
72 Ibid, ss143 and 144. The guideline can be obtained from the Sentencing Guidelines Council website. See appendix 14 for contact details.
73 *R (T) v Medway Magistrates' Court* [2003] EWHC 2279 (Admin) – reversing *R v Hammersmith Juvenile Court ex p O (a Minor)* (1986) 151 JP 740, QBD.
74 Criminal Justice Act 2003 s143.
75 *R (on the application of W, S and B) v Brent, Enfield and Richmond Youth Courts* [2006] EWHC 95 (Admin).
76 *R (C and D) v Sheffield Youth Court* [2003] EWHC 35 (Admin).
77 (2000) 164 JP 330.

there may be circumstances which affect the courts' view of the suitable venue for trial now that the issues of effective participation are more widely recognised.[78]

Aggregating seriousness of more than one offence

A13.74 Where not guilty pleas have been entered to more than one charge, the courts' opinion on the adequacy of its sentencing powers is to be formed on the combination of the offence and any offences associated with it.[79]

Guidance relating to specific offences
Sentencing Guidelines Council

A13.75 Guidelines on the allocation of cases and sentencing are issued by the Sentencing Guidelines Council.[80] It is the duty of every court to have regard to those guidelines.[81] At the time of writing there are no guidelines specifically addressing the question of mode of trial in the youth court. The Council will produce sentencing guidelines on various specific offences.[82] For the first time the guidelines give specific sentencing advice in relation to children and young persons. The Definitive Guideline on robbery is reproduced at Appendix 11.

Sentencing Advisory Panel

A13.76 The panel continues to advise the Sentencing Guidelines Council and can make proposals to it.[83] There are conflicting decisions as to whether a court can consider published advice of the panel where it is relevant to sentencing but has not yet been adopted by the Sentencing Guidelines Council. Where there is no guidance from the Sentencing Guidelines Council it may be permissible and helpful for the court to consider any relevant publication of the Sentencing Advisory Panel. In *R (DPP) v Camberwell Youth Court*[84] Kennedy LJ said that:

> '... although the Sentencing Advisory Panel's advice has no legal force, as it is yet to be acted upon, it is helpful as an indication of a considered response to a sentencing problem. In short, providing that the court recognises that the advice does not carry legal force, it is legitimate and helpful to consider such a publication.'

A13.77 This was followed in *R (on the application of W,S and B) v Brent, Enfield and Richmond Youth Courts*[85] where the court held that a youth court could consider the published advice on sentencing for robbery, allowing it to retain jurisdiction where a previous Court of Appeal guideline case advised a substantial custodial sentence.[86] However in *R v Doidge*[87] the Court of Appeal indicated that it was only the final guidelines of the Council to which the courts had to have regard.

Specific cases

A13.78 The court may take account of guidance on the sentencing of specific types of offences where a court has expressly stated that it is giving guidance of general application, but such cases must be treated with caution as the facts and circumstances of offences vary infinitely.[88] The Sentencing Guidelines Council website is linked to a helpful Court of Appeal Compendium of relevant cases.

---

78 See chapter 10.
79 Powers of the Criminal Courts (Sentencing) Act 2000 s3B as inserted by Criminal Justice Act 2003 Sch 3 para 23.
80 Criminal Justice Act 2003 ss167–173.
81 Ibid, s172.
82 Both definitive and draft guidelines may be viewed on the Sentencing Guidelines Council website. See Appendix 14 for contact details.
83 Ibid, s171.
84 [2005] 1 Cr App R 26.
85 [2006] EWHC 95 (Admin).
86 *Attorney General's References Nos 4 and 7 of 2002* [2002] EWCA Crim 127, known as *Lobban and Sawyers*.
87 (2005) *Times* 10 March.
88 *R v Lyon* [2005] EWCA Crim 1365.

Burglary (residential)

A13.79 The statutory minimum sentence of three years imprisonment for a third offence of residential burglary does not apply to defendants under 18 years of age.[89] However in the case of *R v McInerney*[90] the Lord Chief Justice gave the following guidance endorsing the Sentencing Advisory Panel[91] advice:

> '49. As to Juvenile offenders, the Panel stated its advice in the following terms:
>
> > "36. Exceptionally, since domestic burglary is one of the offences which may attract a sentence of long-term detention under s.91 of the Powers of Criminal Courts (Sentencing) Act 2000, a young offender may be committed by the youth court for trial in the Crown Court with a view to such a sentence being passed. A sentence of long-term detention is available in respect of any offender aged 10 to 17 inclusive who is convicted of domestic burglary.
> >
> > 37. Where an offender who is now aged 18 or over has two qualifying previous convictions for domestic burglary as a juvenile, a third alleged domestic burglary must be tried in the Crown Court, and the presumptive minimum sentence is a custodial sentence of three years. Although section 111 does not apply until the offender has attained the age of 18, would seem to follow that for an offender who is under 18 but is charged with a third domestic burglary, a custodial sentence in excess of 24 months (the maximum term available for a detention and training order) will be the likely sentence and so the youth court should generally commit the case to Crown Court for trial with a view to sentence under section 91."
>
> 50. We generally endorse this approach subject to reiterating more strongly in relation to juveniles what we have already said. The Youth Justice Board is spearheading effective punishment in the community and it is important that, where appropriate, juvenile offenders are dealt with in Youth Court and not the Crown Court.'

Robbery

A13.79A The Sentencing Guidelines Council has issued a guideline on the offence of robbery.[92] The guideline recognises that robbery may take a number of different forms. In particular the guidance on street robbery and the factors to be taken into account for young defendants will be of assistance to the defence representative.

Rape

A13.80 In the case of *R v Billam*[93], subsequently approved in *R v Fareham Youth Court ex p M (a minor)*[94] rape was said to be an offence which it would not be appropriate to deal with in the youth court. However, at the time of these decisions there was a statutory presumption that males under the age of 14 years were not capable of committing this offence. The abolition of the presumption has altered the courts' view.[95] In *R (on the application of W, S and B) v Brent, Enfield and Richmond Youth Courts*[96] at paragraph 44 of her judgment Smith J states:

> 'I would like to add that it was drawn to our attention that a footnote to Section 24 of the Magistrates' Courts Act 1980 in Stones Justices Manual, the dicta of the court in *R v Billam* [1986] 1 All ER 985 to the effect that a Youth Court should *never* accept jurisdiction in the case of a minor charged with rape ... I doubt that there should be such a hard and fast rule in the case of a child aged 12. We were reminded that, at the time of *Billam*, the offence of rape could be committed only by a male of 14 years or over. At that time a boy of 12 or 13

---

89 Powers of the Criminal Courts (Sentencing) Act 2000 s111.
90 [2002] EWCA Crim 3003.
91 Sentencing Advisory Panel, April 2002. Contact details in appendix 14.
92 July 2006. Available at www.sentencing-guidelines.gov.uk. The Guideline is reproduced at appendix 11 above.
93 [1986] 1 WLR 349.
94 (1998) 163 JP 812.
95 See para 6.10.
96 [2006] EWHC 95 (Admin).

could not be charged with rape. It appears to me that now that a boy of 12 or 13 can be charged with rape, there may- well be some cases in which it will not be appropriate to commit such a defendant to the Crown Court. I suggest perhaps that the rule set out in *Billam* and noted in Stone Justices' Manual could now properly be modified so as to indicate that in the case of very young defendants it may be appropriate to accept jurisdiction.'

Procedure

A13.81 A mode of trial hearing may be conducted be one justice.[97] Although the detailed procedural requirements contained in the Magistrates' Courts Act 1980 ss18-23 do not apply, it is submitted that as far as possible they should be followed in the interests of fairness to the defendant. Firstly, the prosecutor should present the facts dispassionately. S/he should then make representations as to the court's decision regarding jurisdiction, but care should be taken not to invite the court to accept jurisdiction when it would be inappropriate to do so. The defence lawyer should then be given the opportunity of making representations. It is important that the lawyer has had sufficient opportunity to consider the prosecution evidence in order to fully address the court and deal with points raised by the prosecutor, particularly where the prosecution statements differ from the police summary.

Preparing for the grave crime decision
The court

A13.82 It is essential that the defence lawyer is in a position to assist the court in its consideration of likely sentence and on the factors which will be taken into account. The lawyer will need to consider:
- prosecution disclosure
- previous convictions
- guidelines on sentencing
- relevant law on the nature of the decision being taken by the court.

A13.83 The defence lawyer should not hesitate to request an adjournment if he/she is not in a position to adequately deal with the issues to be raised. In *R (on the application of H,O and A) v Southampton Youth Court* the mode of trial decision was taken prior to the service of video-taped evidence of child witnesses. In the subsequent judicial review of the youth court's decision Leveson J stated:

> '... the very least one would expect is that each solicitor would have taken careful instructions before permitting the court to embark upon the grave crimes procedure. It is said that there is increasing pressure on advocates to make early decisions and rapidly progress all cases, especially those involving serious charges and young people and, rightly or wrongly, the solicitors did not ask for an adjournment, did not obtain further disclosure and did not consider the case in full prior to this hearing. Suffice it to say, it was for the defence representatives to ensure that they knew enough about the case to make an informed judgment about the submissions to be made.'[98]

The client

A13.84 The court's decision on jurisdiction is a complex one and it is therefore important that the defence lawyer takes time to explain to the client, as far as possible, the nature of this part of the proceedings, using language appropriate to his/her age and understanding.

Is the Crown Court a better trial venue?

A13.85 Where a choice is available, the Crown Court has traditionally been regarded by defence lawyers as the court of preference for the trial of adults. The Crown Court is seen as having a statistically higher acquittal rate, although this may be due to a number of factors. In the opinion of the authors this view is not always applicable to

---

97 Crime and Disorder Act 1998 s51A(11) as inserted by Criminal Justice Act 2003 Sch 3 para 18.
98 [2004] EWHC 2912 Admin at [10].

children and young people who may be better dealt with in the more informal atmosphere of the youth court. There has been suggestion that young people are not always sympathetically received by juries or judges. The defence lawyer needs to assist his/her client in understanding and participating in the proceedings and it is submitted that the Crown Court is a more difficult environment for this to take place.[99]

The adult magistrates' court

A13.86   The introduction of the amendments to the Crime and Disorder Act 1998 and the Magistrates' Courts Act 1980 mean that for the first time youth defendants appearing in the adult court are subject to their own plea before venue procedure. This change also has repercussions for the adult defendant. Committal proceedings are abolished both for adult and youth defendants and in future any case sent to the Crown Court will be sent for trial in a similar manner to that previously only used for indictable-only offences.

A13.87   The mode of trial for a youth defendant in the adult court has previously been determined by the mode of trial decision in relation to the adult co-defendant and the court's view of the interests of justice. This position will still remain in some circumstances but in many cases the adult court will need to undertake a decision previously considered almost exclusively in the youth court namely the likely sentence which might be imposed on the youth defendant if convicted.

A13.88   A right to request a sentencing indication during the mode of trial hearing is introduced.[100] It should be noted that this only applies to adult defendants.

A13.89   The provisions of the Crime and Disorder Act 1998 ss50A, 51 and 51A do not clearly set out an order in which the various decisions as to mode of trial should take place. In some circumstances the decision for the adult will follow the decision which has been taken for the child or young person. In other circumstances the decision for the adult will come first. In the view of the authors, the lack of clarity as to the structure of decision–making is likely to cause difficulties for the adult magistrates' court. It is also likely that the adult court will be considering issues relating to the likely sentence for a child and young person without necessarily being familiar with the specific and complex provisions relating to them.

Exceptions to the presumption of summary trial

A13.90   The general rule remains that a defendant under the age of 18 should be tried summarily unless any of the statutory exceptions apply. These are dealt with at para A13.6. Some of the statutory exceptions do not involve the plea before venue procedure. The court will only consider the interests of justice test once it is satisfied that none of the other exceptions apply.

Plea before venue

A13.91   The plea before venue procedure for a youth defendant in the adult court will arise:
- where the charge is a grave crime;
- where the court is to decide if it is in the interests of justice to send the defendant to the Crown Court with an adult;
- where the court is to decide whether any related indictable or summary matters should also be sent to the Crown Court.

The court will be deciding whether the case should be tried in the magistrates' court or the Crown Court. This decision is referred to as the 'relevant determination' in the amended Magistrates' Courts Act 1980.[101] Where such determination would arise the plea before venue procedure is to take place prior to that determination.[102]

99 See chapter 10.
100 Magistrates' Courts Act 1980 s20(3) as substituted by Criminal Justice Act 2003 Sch 3 para 6.
101 Magistrates' Courts Act 1980 s24A(1)(b).
102 Ibid, s24A(2).

Table B: Youth defendant plea before venue procedure under Magistrates' Courts Act 1980 s24A

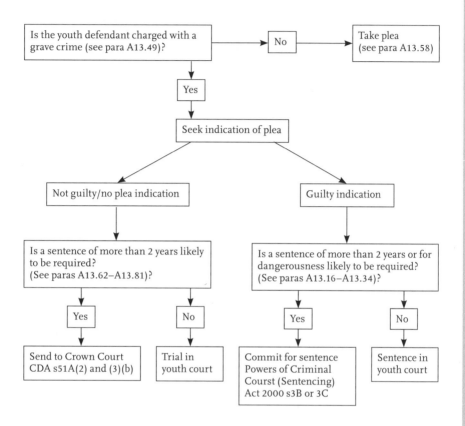

Procedural considerations

A13.92 The court must read the written charge to the defendant in his/her presence and explain in ordinary language that if a plea of guilty is entered the court will then go on to determine whether the case should be sent to the Crown Court for sentence under the Powers of the Criminal Courts (Sentencing) Act 2000 s3B where appropriate.[103]

A13.93   A single justice may conduct the plea before venue procedure.[104] The court may adjourn the proceedings at any time, and on doing so on any occasion when the accused is present may remand him/her.[105] This may be of assistance to the defence lawyer where there is insufficient information available to enable the lawyer to fully consider the way in which the court is to be addressed on the decision as to mode of trial. An adjournment would, for example, allow for service of further relevant evidence or consideration of video or audio evidence.

Related matters

A13.94 Indictable and/or summary matters which are related to the matter being sent to the Crown Court can be sent for trial at the same time.[106] Summary-only matters can be sent if they are punishable by imprisonment or involve obligatory or discretionary disqualification from driving.[107] Before making the decision whether to send such matters to the Crown Court, the plea before venue procedure will apply.[108] This will enable the court to decide whether such matters should also be sent to the Crown Court or whether they can appropriately be dealt with in the youth court.

Absence of the defendant

A13.95 If the defendant is legally represented and the court considers that by reason of the defendant's disorderly conduct it is not practicable for the proceedings to be conducted in his presence, the court can deal with plea before venue in the absence of the defendant. The representative will be asked to indicate a plea.[109] Only the indication of a guilty plea will be taken as the entering of a plea.[110]

Interests of justice test

A13.96 This decision will be taken for indictable matters after the court has gone through a plea before venue procedure and only when it has determined that the matter with which the youth defendant is charged could be dealt with summarily. In all other circumstances the court will not need to apply this test.

Procedure

A13.97 When deciding whether it is in the interests of justice to send a child or young person for trial along with an adult, the magistrates must act judicially[111] and the court should invite separate representations from the prosecutor and the defence lawyer representing the child or young person.

Criteria

A13.98 In considering whether it is in the interests of justice to send a defendant under the age of 18 years to the Crown Court alongside an adult defendant the court must have regard to any allocation guidelines issued by the Sentencing Guidelines

---

103 Ibid, s24A(3), (4) and (5). Powers to commit for sentence are inserted by Criminal Justice Act 2003 Sch 3 para 23. See chapter 19/24.
104 Magistrates' Courts Act 1980 s24D.
105 Magistrates' Courts Act 1980 s24C as inserted by Criminal Justice Act 2003 Sch 3 para 10.
106 Crime and Disorder Act 1998 s51A(4) and s51(8)(a).
107 Ibid, s51A(9) and s51(8)(b).
108 Magistrates' Courts Act 1980 s24A(1)(b) and Crime and Disorder Act 1998 s51A(4) and (5).
109 Ibid, s24B.
110 Ibid, s24B(2)(c) and (4).
111 *R v Newham JJ ex p Knight* [1976] Crim LR 323, QBD.

Council.[112] The *National Allocation Guidelines 2006*[113] state that any presumption that a joint trial would be preferable must be balanced with the general presumption that young people should be tried in the youth court. Examples of the factors to be considered include:

- the young age of the defendant, especially where the age gap between the adult and the youth is substantial;
- the immaturity and intellect of the youth;
- the relative culpability of the youth compared with the adult and whether or not the role played by the youth was minor;
- lack of previous convictions on the part of the youth compared with the adult;
- whether or not the trial of the youth and the adult can be severed without inconvenience to witnesses or injustice to the case as a whole.

The court will need to balance these factors with the desire to avoid witnesses having to give evidence twice and the possible risk of disparity in sentence if a conviction results.

Role of the defence lawyer

A13.99 The defence lawyer needs to be prepared to address the court in relation to these factors. S/he will need to consider the issues raised in Chapter 10, the guidance in relation to mode of trial in the youth court and to address the court as to the more appropriate venue for trial of a child or young person. It is of note that the *Consolidated Criminal Practice Direction* Part IV.39 urges judges in the Crown Court to consider severing young defendants from adults at an early stage in the proceedings.[114] The adult court may not be familiar with these issues and the defence lawyer should be ready to deal with this in some depth in order to assist the court in exercising its discretion.

Adult facing indictable-only matter

A13.100 The adult will be sent for trial to the Crown Court without a plea being taken as there are no plea before venue provisions for adults facing these matters. The court will send the adult to the Crown Court under the Crime and Disorder Act 1998 s51(1).[115]

A13.101 The child or young person jointly charged with the adult is subject to a separate decision on mode of trial which involves the consideration of section 51A and, in some circumstances, section 51. The process is summarised below:

A13.102 **Table C: Procedural decision for youth**

- Is the youth defendant:
    - charged with homicide offence (see para A13.7)?
    - charged with firearms offence (see para A13.13)?
    - had Notice served in serious fraud or child witness case (see para A13.5)?
    - likely to be sentenced as a dangerous offender (see para A13.16)?

  YES, send to Crown Court: CDA s51A(2),(3)(a),(c) or (d) and (10).

- **NO**, are any of the offences grave crimes?

  If yes, plea before venue procedure applies.

  If not guilty and court does not send for trial under s51A(3)(b), court considers interests of justice test. See para A13.96 below.

- If not grave crime, plea before venue procedure applies.

  If not guilty court considers interests of justice test.

---

112 Criminal Justice Act 2003 s172(b).
113 At the time of writing these guidelines were still in draft form.
114 See para 10.5.
115 Crime and Disorder Act 1998, s51(2)(a).

Order of decision-making

A13.103 The Crime and Disorder Act 1998 s51A(10)(a) states that where the child or young person is charged with an offence which satisfies any of the conditions of section 51A(3) the offence should be sent to the Crown Court under section 51A(2) and not under any other provisions of sections 51 or 51A. Therefore the court must consider whether any of the conditions of section 51A(3) apply to the youth defendant before going on to consider the youth in relation to the adult defendant. If the court decides that any of the conditions apply it must send the youth defendant to the Crown Court under section 51A. The position of the adult will not be relevant at that stage. This would result in the adult and youth defendants being sent to the Crown Court but under different sections.

A13.104   However, if none of the conditions apply, the court will need to go on to consider the interests of justice test. The Crime and Disorder Act 1998, s51(7) provides that the child or young person shall be sent to the Crown Court if:
- the child or young person appears on the same or subsequent occasion as an adult; and
- the child or young person is charged jointly with the adult with an indictable offence or a related indictable offence; and
- the adult is sent for trial;[116] and
- the court considers that it is necessary in the interests of justice to do so.

Plea before venue

A13.105 The taking of a plea and the subsequent decision as to where the case is to be heard may arise where grave crimes or other indictable offences are charged.

Grave crime

A13.106 Where the child or young person is charged with a grave crime, the court will seek an indication of the intended plea. The procedure that follows depends on that indication:
- *Guilty plea indicated.* If the young person indicates that s/he intends to plead guilty the court will regard this as the entering of a guilty plea and will proceed to sentence. The magistrates will have the power to commit the young person to the Crown Court for sentence under the Powers of the Criminal Courts (Sentencing) Act 2000 s3B if the court is of the view that it should be possible to sentence the child or young person to detention under the Powers of Criminal Courts (Sentencing) Act 2000 s91.[117] The court will be able to send the defendant to the Crown Court for sentence under the provisions of Powers of Criminal Courts (Sentencing) Act 2000 s3C if it appears to the court that the criteria for sentencing as a dangerous offender would be met.[118] Otherwise the sentencing will take place in the adult court if the case may be disposed of by way of a discharge, financial order or a parental bindover.[119] If this is not appropriate s/he should be remitted to the youth court for sentence.
- *Not guilty/no plea indication.* If the child or young person indicates a not guilty plea or gives no indication as to the intended plea, the consideration of the appropriate place for trial will proceed in the usual way as set out in paras A13.49–A13.85 above. If the court decides to deal with the case summarily it would lose the power to commit the young defendant for sentence on conviction, unless at that time the court felt that a sentence under the dangerousness provisions should be available to the sentencing court.[120] Where the child or young person enters a guilty plea at a later stage there is no longer a power to commit for sentence under section 3B.[121] If the court decides that it would have

---

116 Sent under s51(1),(3) or(5).
117 Introduced by Criminal Justice Act 2003, Sch 3 para 23.
118 See paras 24.117–24.142.
119 Powers of Criminal Courts (Sentencing) Act 2000 s8.
120 Ibid, s3C.
121 Ibid, s3B(1).

Table D: Adult charged with either-way offence gives not guilty or no plea indication

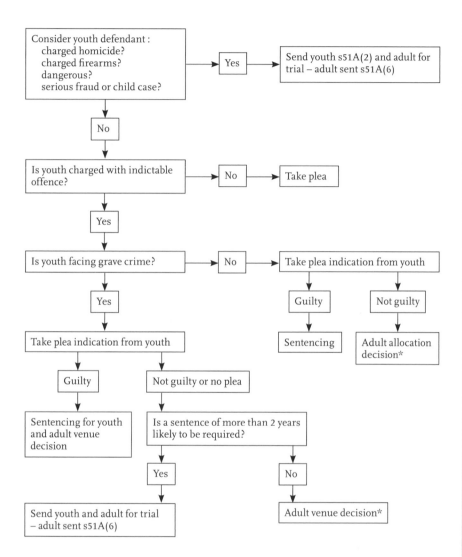

* If court decides Crown Court trial or adult elects, court must decide if in INTERESTS OF JUSTICE to also send youth for trial under section 51(7).

Table E: Adult charged with either-way offence pleads guilty

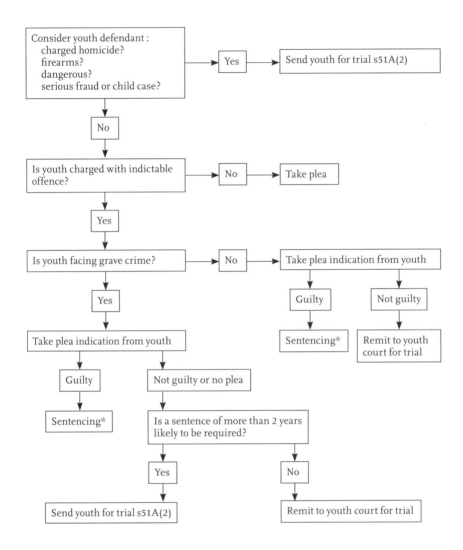

* Youth can be sentenced in Crown Court if dangerousness provisons apply – Powers of the
  Criminal Courts (Sentencing) Act 2000 s3C.

Adult can be sentenced in the magistrates' court or committed to the Crown Court for
sentence under Powers of the Criminal Courts (Sentencing) Act 2000 s3A.

sufficient power to deal with the youth defendant on conviction it will go on to consider whether it is in the interests of justice to send the youth defendant for trial with the adult in the Crown Court.[122] See paras A13.96–A13.99 below.

Other indictable offences

A13.107 • *Guilty plea indicated.* The sentencing will take place in the adult court if the case may be disposed of by way of a discharge, financial order or a parental bindover.[123] Otherwise s/he should be remitted to the youth court for sentence, unless the dangerous offender provisions apply.
   • *Not guilty plea indicated.* The court must apply the interests of justice test to decide whether the child or young person should stand trial in the Crown Court alongside the adult.

Adult facing either-way offence

A13.108 Offences which are triable either-way in the case of an adult may be specified offences and/or grave crimes for a child or young person. The order of consideration for either-way matters in the case of an adult is set out in the Crime and Disorder Act 1998 s50A.

A13.109   First, the adult will be asked to give an indication of plea.[124] The decision-making process that follows depends on the indication given by the adult.

Adult gives not guilty/no plea indication

A13.110 The procedure is outlined in the table below.

Adult indicates guilty plea

A13.111 The procedure is outlined in the table below:

What about the adult?

A13.112 Where a court sends a child or young person to the Crown Court for trial under section 51A(2) or (4) and an adult appears on the same occasion charged jointly with an either-way offence, or a related either-way offence, s/he shall be sent to the Crown Court forthwith.[125] There is no equivalent to the interests of justice test. If the adult's appearance at court is subsequent to the appearance of the co-defendant the court has a discretion whether to send the adult.[126] However, if the adult is charged with an offence to which sections 51B or 51C apply (notice cases involving serious fraud or children cases) the case must be sent under that provision.[127]

Section 51 or 51A – does it matter?

A13.113 When a case is sent to the Crown Court the court must serve a notice on the defendant and the Crown Court. The notice must specify the offence or offences sent for trial and the place at which trial is to take place. Where more than one offence is sent the notice must specify the subsection under which each offence is sent.[128] If sending takes place under the wrong provision it may be invalid.

---

122 Crime and Disorder Act 1998 s51(7).
123 Powers of Criminal Courts (Sentencing) Act 2000 s8.
124 Save for the situation set out in Crime and Disorder Act 1998 s 50A(3)(a)(i).
125 Crime and Disorder Act 1998 s51A(6).
126 Ibid, s51A(6) and s51(12)(b).
127 Ibid, s51(12)(a) and s51(2)(c)
128 Crime and Disorder Act 1998 s51D inserted by Criminal Justice Act 2003 Sch 3 para 18.

Extracts from legislation

Mode of trial – law on full implementation of Criminal Justice Act 2003 Sch 3

Magistrates' Courts Act 1980

Summary trial of information against child or young person for indictable offence

24 (1) Where a person under the age of 18 years appears or is brought before a magistrates' court on an information charging him with an indictable offence he shall, subject to sections 51 and 51A of the Crime and Disorder Act 1998 and to sections 24A and 24B below, be tried summarily.

(2) [*Repealed.*]

(3) If on trying a person summarily in pursuance of subsection (1) above the court finds him guilty, it may impose a fine of an amount not exceeding £1,000 or may exercise the same powers as it could have exercised if he had been found guilty of an offence for which, but for section 89(1) of the said Act of 2000, it could have sentence him to imprisonment for a term not exceeding -

(a) the maximum term of imprisonment for the offence on conviction on indictment; or

(b) six months,

whichever is the less.

(4) In relation to a person under the age of 14 subsection (3) above shall have effect as if for the words '£1,000' there were substituted the words '£250'.

Child or young person to indicate intention as to plea in certain cases

24A(1) This section applies where –

(a) a person under the age of 18 years appears or is brought before a magistrates' court on an information charging him with an offence other than one falling within section 51A(12) of the Crime and Disorder Act 1998 ('the 1998 Act'); and

(b) but for the application of the following provisions of this section, the court would be required at that stage, by virtue of section 51(7) or (8) or 51A(3)(b), (4) or (5) of the 1998 Act to determine, in relation to the offence, whether to send the person to the Crown Court for trial (or to determine any matter, the effect of which would be to determine whether he is sent to the Crown Court for trial).

(2) Where this section applies, the court shall, before proceeding to make any such determination as is referred to in subsection (1)(b) above (the 'relevant determination'), follow the procedure set out in this section.

(3) Everything that the court is required to do under the following provisions of this section must be done with the accused person in court.

(4) The court shall cause the charge to be written down, if this has not already been done, and to be read to the accused.

(5) The court shall then explain to the accused in ordinary language that he may indicate whether (if the offence were to proceed to trial) he would plead guilty or not guilty, and that if he indicates that he would plead guilty –

(a) the court must proceed as mentioned in subsection (7) below; and

(b) (in cases where the offence is one mentioned in section 91(1) of the Powers of Criminal Courts (Sentencing) Act 2000) he may be sent to the Crown Court for sentencing under section 3B or (if applicable) 3C of that Act if the court is of such opinion as is mentioned in subsection (2) of the applicable section.

(6) The court shall then ask the accused whether (if the offence were to proceed to trial) he would plead guilty or not guilty.

(7) If the accused indicates that he would plead guilty, the court shall proceed as if-

  (a) the proceedings constituted from the beginning the summary trial of the information; and

  (b) section 9(1) above was complied with and he pleaded guilty under it,

  and, accordingly, the court shall not (and shall not be required to) proceed to make the relevant determination or to proceed further under section 51 or (as the case may be) section 51A of the 1998 Act in relation to the offence.

(8) If the accused indicates that he would plead not guilty, the court shall proceed to make the relevant determination and this section shall cease to apply.

(9) If the accused in fact fails to indicate how he would plead, for the purposes of this section he shall be taken to indicate that he would plead not guilty.

(10) Subject to subsection (7) above, the following shall not for any purpose be taken to constitute the taking of a plea-

  (a) asking the accused under this section whether (if the offence were to proceed to trial) he would plead guilty or not guilty;

  (b) an indication by the accused under this section of how he would plead.

Intention as to plea by child or young person: absence of accused

24B(1) This section shall have effect where –

  (a) a person under the age of 18 years appears or is brought before a magistrates' court on an information charging him with an offence other than one falling within section 51A(12) of the Crime and Disorder Act 1998;

  (b) but for the application of the following provisions of this section, the court would be required at that stage to make one of the determinations referred to in paragraph (b) of section 24A(1) above ('the relevant determination');

  (c) the accused is represented by a legal representative;

  (d) the court considers that by reason of the accused's disorderly conduct before the court it is not practicable for proceedings under section 24A above to be conducted in his presence; and

  (e) the court considers that it should proceed in the absence of the accused.

(2) In such a case-

  (a) the court shall cause the charge to be written down, if this has not already been done, and to be read to the representative;

  (b) the court shall ask the representative whether (if the offence were to proceed to trial) the accused would plead guilty or not guilty;

  (c) if the representative indicates that the accused would plead guilty the court shall proceed as if the proceedings constituted from the beginning the summary trial of the information, and as if section 9(1) above was complied with and the accused pleaded guilty under it;

  (d) if the representative indicates that the accused would plead not guilty the court shall proceed to make the relevant determination and this section shall cease to apply.

(3) If the representative in fact fails to indicate how the accused would plead, for the purposes of this section he shall be taken to indicate that the accused would plead not guilty.

(4) Subject to subsection (2)(c) above, the following shall not for any purpose be taken to constitute the taking of a plea –

  (a) asking the representative under this section whether (if the offence were to proceed to trial) the accused would plead guilty or not guilty;

  (b) an indication by the representative under this section of how the accused would plead.

Intention as to plea by child or young person: adjournment

24C(1) A magistrates' court proceeding under section 24A or 24B above may adjourn the proceedings at any time, and on doing so on any occasion when the accused is present may remand the accused.

(2) Where the court remands the accused, the time fixed for the resumption of proceedings shall be that at which he is required to appear or be brought before the court in pursuance of the remand or would be required to be brought before the court but for section 128(3A) below.

Functions under sections 24A to 24C capable of exercise by single justice

24D(1) The functions of a magistrates' court under sections 24A to 24C above may be discharged by a single justice.

(2) Subsection (1) above shall not be taken as authorising –

(a) the summary trial of an information (other than a summary trial by virtue of section 24A(7) or 24B(2)(c) above); or

(b) the imposition of a sentence,

by a magistrates' court composed of fewer than two justices.

Crime and Disorder Act 1998

Order of consideration for either-way offences

50A (1) Where an adult appears or is brought before a magistrates' court charged with an either-way offence (the 'relevant offence'), the court shall proceed in the manner described in this section.

(2) If notice is given in respect of the relevant offence under section 51B or 51C below, the court shall deal with the offence as provided in section 51 below.

(3) Otherwise –

(a) if the adult (or another adult with whom the adult is charged jointly with the relevant offence) is or has been sent to the Crown Court for trial for an offence under section 51(2)(a) or 51(2)(c) below-

(i) the court shall first consider the relevant offence under subsection (3), (4), (5) or, as the case may be, (6) of section 51 below and, where applicable, deal with it under that subsection;

(ii) if the adult is not sent to the Crown Court for trial for the relevant offence by virtue of sub-paragraph (i) above, the court shall then proceed to deal with the relevant offence in accordance with sections 17A to 23 of the 1980 Act;

(b) in all other cases –

(i) the court shall first consider the relevant offence under sections 17A to 20 (excluding subsections (8) and (9) of section 20) of the 1980 Act;

(ii) if, by virtue of sub-paragraph (i) above, the court would be required to proceed in relation to the offence as mentioned in section 17A(6), 17B(2)(c) or 20(7) of that Act (indication of guilty plea), it shall proceed as so required (and, accordingly, shall not consider the offence under section 51 or 51A below);

(iii) if sub-paragraph (ii) above does not apply-

(a) the court shall consider the relevant offence under sections 51 and 51A below and, where applicable, deal with it under the relevant section;

(b) if the adult is not sent to the Crown Court for trial for the relevant offence by virtue of paragraph (a) of this sub-paragraph, the court shall then proceed to deal with the relevant offence as contemplated by section 20(9) or, as the case may be, section 21 of the 1980 Act.

(4) Subsection (3) above is subject to any requirement to proceed as mentioned in subsections (2) or (6)(a) of section 22 of the 1980 Act (certain offences where value involved is small).

(5) Nothing in this section shall prevent the court from committing the adult to the Crown Court for sentence pursuant to any enactment, if he is convicted of the relevant offence.

Sending cases to the Crown Court: adults

51 (1) Where an adult appears or is brought before a magistrates' court ('the court') charged with an offence and any of the conditions mentioned in subsection (2) below is satisfied, the court shall send him forthwith to the Crown Court for trial for the offence.

(2) Those conditions are –
    (a) that the offence is an offence triable only on indictment other than one in respect of which notice has been given under section 51B or 51C below;
    (b) that the offence is an either-way offence and the court is required under section 20(9)(b), 21, 23(4)(b) or (5) or 25(2D) of the Magistrates' Courts Act 1980 to proceed in relation to the offence in accordance with subsection (1) above;
    (c) that notice is given to the court under section 51B or 51C below in respect of the offence.

(3) Where the court sends an adult for trial under subsection (1) above, it shall at the same time send him to the Crown Court for trial for any either-way or summary offence with which he is charged and which –
    (a) (if it is an either-way offence) appears to the court to be related to the offence mentioned in subsection (1) above; or
    (b) (if it is a summary offence) appears to the court to be related to the offence mentioned in subsection (1) above or to the either-way offence, and which fulfils the requisite condition (as defined in subsection (11) below).

(4) Where an adult who has been sent for trial under subsection (1) above subsequently appears or is brought before a magistrates' court charged with an either-way or summary offence which –
    (a) appears to the court to be related to the offence mentioned in subsection (1) above; and
    (b) (in the case of a summary offence) fulfils the requisite condition,
the court may send him forthwith to the Crown Court for trial for the either-way or summary offence.

(5) Where –
    (a) the court sends an adult ('A') for trial under subsection (1) or (3) above;
    (b) another adult appears or is brought before the court on the same or a subsequent occasion charged jointly with A with an either-way offence; and
    (c) that offence appears to the court to be related to an offence for which A was sent for trial under subsection (1) or (3) above,
the court shall where it is the same occasion, and may where it is a subsequent occasion, send the other adult forthwith to the Crown Court for trial for the either-way offence.

(6) Where the court sends an adult for trial under subsection (5) above, it shall at the same time send him to the Crown Court for trial for any either-way or summary offence with which he is charged and which-
    (a) (if it is an either-way offence) appears to the court to be related to the offence for which he is sent for trial; and
    (b) (if it is a summary offence) appears to the court to be related to the offence for which he is sent for trial or to the either-way offence, and which fulfils the requisite condition.

(7) Where –
    (a) the court sends an adult ('A') for trial under subsection (1), (3) or (5) above; and
    (b) a child or young person appears or is brought before the court on the same or a subsequent occasion charged jointly with A with an indictable offence for

which A is sent for trial under subsection (1), (3) or (5) above, or an indictable offence which appears to the court to be related to that offence,

the court shall, if it considers it necessary in the interests of justice to do so, send the child or young person forthwith to the Crown Court for trial for the indictable offence.

(8) Where the court sends a child or young person for trial under subsection (7) above, it may at the same time send him to the Crown Court for trial for any indictable or summary offence with which he is charged and which-

    (a) (if it is an indictable offence) appears to the court to be related to the offence for which he is sent for trial; and

    (b) (if it is a summary offence) appears to the court to be related to the offence for which he is sent for trial or to the indictable offence, and which fulfils the requisite condition.

(9) Subsections (7) and (8) above are subject to sections 24A and 24B of the Magistrates' Courts Act 1980 (which provide for certain cases involving children and young persons to be tried summarily).

(10) The trial of the information charging any summary offence for which a person is sent for trial under this section shall be treated as if the court had adjourned it under section 10 of the 1980 Act and had not fixed the time and place for its resumption.

(11) A summary offence fulfils the requisite condition if it is punishable with imprisonment or involves obligatory or discretionary disqualification from driving.

(12) In the case of an adult charged with an offence-

    (a) if the offence satisfies paragraph (c) of subsection (2) above, the offence shall be dealt with under subsection (1) above and not under any other provision of this section or section 51A below;

    (b) subject to paragraph (a) above, if the offence is one in respect of which the court is required to, or would decide to, send the adult to the Crown Court under-

        (i) subsection (5) above; or

        (ii) subsection (6) of section 51A below,

    the offence shall be dealt with under that subsection and not under any other provision of this section or section 51A below.

(13) The functions of a magistrates' court under this section, and its related functions under section 51D below, may be discharged by a single justice.

Sending cases to the Crown Court: children and young persons

51A(1) This section is subject to sections 24A and 24B of the Magistrates' Courts Act 1980 (which provide for certain offences involving children or young persons to be tried summarily).

(2) Where a child or young person appears or is brought before a magistrates' court ('the court') charged with an offence and any of the conditions mentioned in subsection (3) below is satisfied, the court shall send him forthwith to the Crown Court for trial for the offence.

(3) Those conditions are-

    (a) that the offence falls within subsection (12) below;

    (b) that the offence is such as is mentioned in subsection (1) of section 91 of the Powers of Criminal Courts (Sentencing) Act 2000 (other than one mentioned in paragraph (d) below in relation to which it appears to the court as mentioned there) and the court considers that if he is found guilty of the offence it ought to be possible to sentence him in pursuance of subsection (3) of that section;

    (c) that notice is given to the court under section 51B or 51C below in respect of the offence;

    (d) that the offence is a specified offence (within the meaning of section 224 of the Criminal Justice Act 2003) and it appears to the court that if he is found guilty of the offence the criteria for the imposition of a sentence under section 226(3) or 228(2) of that Act would be met.

(4) Where the court sends a child or young person for trial under subsection (2) above, it may at the same time send him to the Crown Court for trial for any indictable or summary offence with which he is charged and which-

   (a) (if it is an indictable offence) appears to the court to be related to the offence mentioned in subsection (2) above; or

   (b) (if it is a summary offence) appears to the court to be related to the offence mentioned in subsection (2) above or to the indictable offence, and which fulfils the requisite condition (as defined in subsection (9) below).

(5) Where a child or young person who has been sent for trial under subsection (2) above subsequently appears or is brought before a magistrates' court charged with an indictable or summary offence which-

   (a) appears to the court to be related to the offence mentioned in subsection (2) above; and

   (b) (in the case of a summary offence) fulfils the requisite condition,

the court may send him forthwith to the Crown Court for trial for the indictable or summary offence.

(6) Where –

   (a) the court sends a child or young person ('C') for trial under subsection (2) or (4) above; and

   (b) an adult appears or is brought before the court on the same or a subsequent occasion charged jointly with C with an either-way offence for which C is sent for trial under subsection (2) or (4) above, or an either-way offence which appears to the court to be related to that offence,

the court shall where it is the same occasion, and may where it is a subsequent occasion, send the adult forthwith to the Crown Court for trial for the either-way offence.

(7) Where the court sends an adult for trial under subsection (6) above, it shall at the same time send him to the Crown Court for trial for any either-way or summary offence with which he is charged and which-

   (a) (if it is an either-way offence) appears to the court to be related to the offence for which he was sent for trial; and

   (b) (if it is a summary offence) appears to the court to be related to the offence for which he was sent for trial or to the either-way offence, and which fulfils the requisite condition.

(8) The trial of the information charging any summary offence for which a person is sent for trial under this section shall be treated as if the court had adjourned it under section 10 of the 1980 Act and had not fixed the time and place for its resumption.

(9) A summary offence fulfils the requisite condition if it is punishable with imprisonment or involves obligatory or discretionary disqualification from driving.

(10) In the case of a child or young person charged with an offence-

   (a) if the offence satisfies any of the conditions in subsection (3) above, the offence shall be dealt with under subsection (2) above and not under any other provision of this section or section 51 above;

   (b) subject to paragraph (a) above, if the offence is one in respect of which the requirements of subsection (7) of section 51 above for sending the child or young person to the Crown Court are satisfied, the offence shall be dealt with under that subsection and not under any other provision of this section or section 51 above.

(11) The functions of a magistrates' court under this section, and its related functions under section 51D below, may be discharged by a single justice.

(12) An offence falls within this subsection if-

   (a) it is an offence of homicide; or

   (b) each of the requirements of section 51A(1) of the Firearms Act 1968 would be satisfied with respect to –

(i) the offence; and

(ii) the person charged with it,

if he were convicted of the offence.

Notices in serious or complex fraud cases

51B(1) A notice may be given by a designated authority under this section in respect of an indictable offence if the authority is of the opinion that the evidence of the offence charged –

(a) is sufficient for the person charged to be put on trial for the offence; and

(b) reveals a case of fraud of such seriousness or complexity that it is appropriate that the management of the case should without delay be taken over by the Crown Court.

(2) That opinion must be certified by the designated authority in the notice.

(3) The notice must also specify the proposed place of trial, and in selecting that place the designated authority must have regard to the same matters as are specified in paragraphs (a) to (c) of section 51D(4) below.

(4) A notice under this section must be given to the magistrates' court at which the person charged appears or before which he is brought.

(5) Such a notice must be given to the magistrates' court before any summary trial begins.

(6) The effect of such a notice is that the functions of the magistrates' court cease in relation to the case, except-

(a) for the purposes of section 51D below;

(b) as provided by paragraph 2 of Schedule 3 to the Access to Justice Act 1999; and

(c) as provided by section 52 below.

(7) The functions of a designated authority under this section may be exercised by an officer of the authority acting on behalf of the authority.

(8) A decision to give a notice under this section shall not be subject to appeal or liable to be questioned in any court (whether a magistrates' court or not).

(9) In this section 'designated authority' means-

(a) the Director of Public Prosecutions;

(b) the Director of the Serious Fraud Office;

(c) the Commissioners of the Inland Revenue;

(d) the Commissioners of Customs and Excise; or

(e) the Secretary of State.

Notices in certain cases involving children

51C(1) A notice may be given by the Director of Public Prosecutions under this section in respect of an offence falling within subsection (3) below if he is of the opinion –

(a) that the evidence of the offence would be sufficient for the person charged to be put on trial for the offence;

(b) that a child would be called as a witness at the trial; and

(c) that, for the purpose of avoiding any prejudice to the welfare of the child, the case should be taken over and proceeded with without delay by the Crown Court.

(2) That opinion must be certified by the Director of Public Prosecutions in the notice.

(3) This subsection applies to an offence –

(a) which involves an assault on, or injury or a threat of injury to, a person;

(b) under section 1 of the Children and Young Persons Act 1933 (cruelty to persons under 16);

(c) under the Sexual Offences Act 1956, the Protection of Children Act 1978 or the Sexual Offences Act 2003;

(d) of kidnapping or false imprisonment, or an offence under section 1 or 2 of the Child Abduction Act 1984;

(e) which consists of attempting or conspiring to commit, or of aiding, abetting, counselling, procuring or inciting the commission of, an offence falling within paragraph (a), (b), (c) or (d) above.

(4) Subsections (4), (5) and (6) of section 51B above apply for the purposes of this section as they apply for the purposes of that.

(5) The functions of the Director of Public Prosecutions under this section may be exercised by an officer acting on behalf of the Director.

(6) A decision to give a notice under this section shall not be subject to appeal or liable to be questioned in any court (whether a magistrates' court or not).

(7) In this section 'child' means –

(a) a person who is under the age of 17; or

(b) any person of whom a video recording (as defined in section 63(1) of the Youth Justice and Criminal Evidence Act 1999) was made when he was under the age of 17 with a view to its admission as his evidence in chief in the trial referred to in subsection (1) above.

Notice of offence and place of trial

51D(1) The court shall specify in a notice –

(a) the offence or offences for which a person is sent for trial under section 51 or 51A above; and

(b) the place at which he is to be tried (which, if a notice has been given under section 51B above, must be the place specified in that notice).

(2) A copy of the notice shall be served on the accused and given to the Crown Court sitting at that place.

(3) In a case where a person is sent for trial under section 51 or 51A above for more than one offence, the court shall specify in that notice, for each offence –

(a) the subsection under which the person is so sent; and

(b) if applicable, the offence to which that offence appears to the court to be related.

(4) Where the court selects the place of trial for the purposes of subsection (1) above, it shall have regard to –

(a) the convenience of the defence, the prosecution and the witnesses;

(b) the desirability of expediting the trial; and

(c) any direction given by or on behalf of the Lord Chief Justice with the concurrence of the Lord Chancellor under section 75(1) of the Supreme Court Act 1981.

Interpretation of sections 50A to 51D

51E   For the purposes of sections 50A to 51D above –

(a) 'adult' means a person aged 18 or over, and references to an adult include a corporation;

(b) 'either-way offence' means an offence triable either way;

(c) an either-way offence is related to an indictable offence if the charge for the either-way offence could be joined in the same indictment as the charge for the indictable offence;

(d) a summary offence is related to an indictable offence if it arises out of circumstances which are the same as or connected with those giving rise to the indictable offence.'

Provisions supplementing section 51

52 (1) Subject to section 4 of the Bail Act 1976, section 41 of the 1980 Act, regulations under section 22 of the 1985 Act and section 25 of the 1994 Act, the court may send a person for trial under section 51 above –

(a) in custody, that is to say, by committing him to custody there to be safely kept until delivered in due course of law; or

(b) on bail in accordance with the Bail Act 1976, that is to say, by directing him to appear before the Crown Court for trial.

(2) Where –

(a) the person's release on bail under subsection (1)(b) above is conditional on his providing one or more sureties; and

(b) in accordance with subsection (3) of section 8 of the Bail Act 1976, the court fixes the amount in which a surety is to be bound with a view to his entering into his recognisance subsequently in accordance with subsections (4) and (5) or (6) of that section,

the court shall in the meantime make an order such as is mentioned in subsection (1)(a) above.

Powers of Criminal Courts (Sentencing) Act 2000

Committal for sentence on indication of guilty plea by child or young person

3B(1) This section applies where –

(a) a person aged under 18 appears or is brought before a magistrates' court ('the court') on an information charging him with an offence mentioned in subsection (1) of section 91 below ('the offence');

(b) he or his representative indicates under section 24A or (as the case may be) 24B of the Magistrates' Courts Act 1980 (child or young person to indicate intention as to plea in certain cases) that he would plead guilty if the offence were to proceed to trial; and

(c) proceeding as if section 9(1) of that Act were complied with and he pleaded guilty under it, the court convicts him of the offence.

(2) If the court is of the opinion that –

(a) the offence; or

(b) the combination of the offence and one or more offences associated with it,

was such that the Crown Court should, in the court's opinion, have power to deal with the offender as if the provisions of section 91(3) below applied, the court may commit him in custody or on bail to the Crown Court for sentence in accordance with section 5A(1) below.

(3) Where the court commits a person under subsection (2) above, section 6 below (which enables a magistrates' court, where it commits a person under this section in respect of an offence, also to commit him to the Crown Court to be dealt with in respect of certain other offences) shall apply accordingly.

Committal for sentence of dangerous young offenders

3C(1) This section applies where on the summary trial of a specified offence a person aged under 18 is convicted of the offence.

(2) If, in relation to the offence, it appears to the court that the criteria for the imposition of a sentence under section 226(3) or 228(2) of the Criminal Justice Act 2003 would be met, the court must commit the offender in custody or on bail to the Crown Court for sentence in accordance with section 5A(1) below.

(3) Where the court commits a person under subsection (2) above, section 6 below (which enables a magistrates' court, where it commits a person under this section in respect of an offence, also to commit him to the Crown Court to be dealt with in respect of certain other offences) shall apply accordingly.

(4) Nothing in this section shall prevent the court from committing a specified offence to the Crown Court for sentence under section 3B above if the provisions of that section are satisfied.

(5) In this section, references to a specified offence are to a specified offence within the meaning of section 224 of the Criminal Justice Act 2003.

Committal for sentence on indication of guilty plea by child or young person with related offences

4A(1) This section applies where –

    (a) a person aged under 18 appears or brought before a magistrates' court ('the court') on an information charging him with an offence mentioned in subsection (1) of section 91 below ('the offence');

    (b) he or his representative indicates under section 24A or (as the case may be) 24B of the Magistrates' Courts Act 1980 (child or young person to indicate intention as to plea in certain cases) that he would plead guilty if the offence were to proceed to trial; and

    (c) proceeding as if section 9(1) of that Act were complied with and he pleaded guilty under it, the court convicts him of the offence.

  (2) If the court has sent the offender to the Crown Court for trial for one or more related offences, that is to say one or more offences which, in its opinion, are related to the offence, it may commit him in custody or on bail to the Crown Court to be dealt with in respect of the offence in accordance with section 5A(1) below.

  (3) If the power conferred by subsection (2) above is not exercisable but the court is still to determine to, or to determine whether to, send the offender to the Crown Court for trial under section 51 or 51A of the Crime and Disorder Act 1998 for one or more related offences –

    (a) it shall adjourn the proceedings relating to the offence until after it has made those determinations; and

    (b) if it sends the offender to the Crown Court for trial for one or more related offences, it may then exercise that power.

  (4) Where the court –

    (a) under subsection (2) above commits the offender to the Crown Court to be dealt with in respect of the offence; and

    (b) does not state that, in its opinion, it also has power so to commit him under section 3B(2) or, as the case may be, section 3C(2) above,

  section 5A(1) below shall not apply unless he is convicted before the Crown Court of one or more of the related offences.

  (5) Where section 5A(1) below does not apply, the Crown Court may deal with the offender in respect of the offence in any way in which the magistrates' court could deal with him if it had just convicted him of the offence.

  (6) Where the court commits a person under subsection (2) above, section 6 below (which enables a magistrates' court, where it commits a person under this section in respect of an offence, also to commit him to the Crown Court to be dealt with in respect of certain other offences) shall apply accordingly.

  (7) Section 4(7) above applies for the purposes of this section as it applies for the purposes of that section.

Power of Crown Court on committal for sentence under sections 3B, 3C and 4A

5A(1) Where an offender is committed by a magistrates' court for sentence under section 3B, 3C or 4A above, the Crown Court shall inquire into the circumstances of the case and may deal with the offender in any way in which it could deal with him if he had just been convicted of the offence on indictment before the court.

  (2) In relation to committals under section 4A above, subsection (1) above has effect subject to section 4A(4) and (5) above.

Committal for sentence in certain cases where offender committed in respect of another offence

6 (1) This section applies where a magistrates' court ('the committing court') commits a person in custody or on bail to the Crown Court under any enactment mentioned in subsection (4) below to be sentenced or otherwise dealt with in respect of an offence ('the relevant offence').

(2) Where this section applies and the relevant offence is an indictable offence, the committing court may also commit the offender, in custody or on bail as the case may require, to the Crown Court to be dealt with in respect of any other offence whatsoever in respect of which the committing court has power to deal with him (being an offence of which he has been convicted by that or any other court).

(3) Where this section applies and the relevant offence is a summary offence, the committing court may commit the offender, in custody or on bail as the case may require, to the Crown Court to be dealt with in respect of –

(a) any other offence of which the committing court has convicted him, being either-

   (i) an offence punishable with imprisonment; or

   (ii) an offence in respect of which the committing court has a power or duty to order him to be disqualified under section 34, 35 or 36 of the Road Traffic Offenders Act 1988 (disqualification for certain motoring offences); or

(b) any suspended sentence in respect of which the committing court has under section 120(1) below power to deal with him.

(4) The enactments referred to in subsection (1) above are –

(a) the Vagrancy Act 1824 (incorrigible rogues);

(b) sections 3 to 4A above (committal for sentence for offences triable either way);

(c) section 13(5) below (conditionally discharged person convicted of further offence);

(d) section 116(3)(b) below (offender convicted of offence committed during currency of original sentence); and

(e) section 120(2) below (offender convicted during operational period of suspended sentence).

Power of Crown Court on committal for sentence under section 6.

7 (1) Where under section 6 above a magistrates' court commits a person to be dealt with by the Crown Court in respect of an offence, the Crown Court may after inquiring into the circumstances of the case deal with him in any way in which the magistrates' court could deal with him if it had just convicted him of the offence.

(2) Subsection (1) above does not apply where under section 6 above a magistrates' court commits a person to be dealt with by the Crown Court in respect of a suspended sentence, but in such a case the powers under section 119 below (power of court to deal with suspended sentence) shall be exercisable by the Crown Court.

(3) Without prejudice to subsections (1) and (2) above, where under section 6 above or any enactment mentioned in subsection (4) of that section a magistrates' court commits a person to be dealt with by the Crown Court, any duty or power which, apart from this subsection, would fall to be discharged or exercised by the magistrates' court shall not be discharged or exercised by that court but shall instead be discharged or may instead be exercised by the Crown Court.

(4) Where under section 6 above a magistrates' court commits a person to be dealt with by the Crown Court in respect of an offence triable only on indictment in the case of an adult (being an offence which was tried summarily because of the offender's being under 18 years of age), the Crown Court's powers under subsection (1) above in respect of the offender after he attains the age of 18 shall be powers to do either or both of the following –

(a) to impose a fine not exceeding £5,000;

(b) to deal with the offender in respect of the offence in any way in which the magistrates' court could deal with him if it had just convicted him of an offence punishable with imprisonment for a term not exceeding six months.

Offenders under 18 convicted of certain serious offences: power to detain for specified period

91 (1) Subsection (3) below applies where a person aged under 18 is convicted on indictment of –

(a) an offence punishable in the case of a person aged 21 or over with imprisonment for 14 years or more, not being an offence the sentence for which is fixed by law; or

(b) an offence under section 3 of the Sexual Offences Act 2003 (in this section, 'the 2003 Act') (sexual assault); or

(c) an offence under section 13 of the 2003 Act (child sex offences committed by children or young persons); or

(d) an offence under section 25 of the 2003 Act (sexual activity with a child family member); or

(e) an offence under section 26 of the 2003 Act (inciting a child family member to engage in sexual activity).

(1A) Subsection (3) also applies where-

(a) a person aged under 18 is convicted on indictment of an offence –

(i)   under subsection (1)(a), (ab), (aba), (ac), (ad), (ae)< (af) or (c) of section 5 of the Firearms Act 1968 (prohibited weapons), or

(ii) under subsection (1A)(a) of that section,

(b) the offence was committed after the commencement of section 51A of that Act and at at iem when he was aged 16 or over, and

(c) the court is of the opinion mentioned in section 51A(2) of that Act (exceptional circumstances which justify its not imposing required custodial sentence).

(2) [*Repealed.*]

(3) If the court is of the opinion that neither a community sentence nor a detention and training order is suitable, the court may sentence the offender to be detained for such period, not exceeding the maximum term of imprisonment with which the offence is punishable in the case of a person aged 21 or over, as may be specified in the sentence.

(4) Subsection (3) above is subject to (in particular) section 152 and 153 of the Criminal Justice Act 2003.

(5) Where subsection (2) of section 51A of the Firearms Act 1968 requires the imposition of a sentence of detention under this section for a term of at least the required minimum term (within the meaning of that section), the court shall sentence the offender to be detained for such period, of at least that term but not exceeding the maximum term of imprisonment with which the offence is punishable in the case of a person aged 18 or over, as may be specified in the sentence.

Useful contacts

Advisory Centre on Education
1C Aberdeen Studios
22 Highbury Grove
London N5 2DQ

Tel: 020 7704 3370
General Advice line: *Freephone 0808 800 5793* (open 2.00pm to 5.00pm Mon to Fri)
Fax: 020 7354 9069
E-mail: enquiries@ace-ed.org.uk
Website: www.ace-ed.org.uk

Association of Chief Police Officers (ACPO)
25 Victoria Street
London SW1H 0EX

Tel: 020 7227 3434
Fax: 020 72273400
E-mail: info@acpo.pnn.police.uk
Website: www.acpo.police.uk

The website has copies of guidance issued to police officers.

Bar Council and Bar Standards Board
289–293 High Holborn
London WC1V 7HZ

Tel (Bar Council): 020 7242 0082
Tel (Bar Standards Board): 020 7611 1444
Fax: 020 7831 9217
Website: www.barcouncil.org.uk

British and Irish Legal Information Institute
Website: www.bailii.org

The website provides free access to transcripts of judgments of the House of
Lords, Court of Appeal and High Court from 1996 onwards.

Child Rights Information Network
Child Rights Information Network (CRIN)
c/o Save the Children
1 St John's Lane
London EC1M 4AR

Tel: 020 7012 6865
Fax: 020 7012 6952
E-mail: info@crin.org
Website: www.crin.org

Children's Commissioner for England
Office of the Children's Commissioner
1 London Bridge
London SE1 9BG

Tel: 0844 8009113
E-mail: support@childrenscommissioner.org
Website: www.everychildmatters.gov.uk

Children's Commisioner for Wales
Oystermouth House
Charter Court
Phoenix Way
Llansamlet
Swansea SA7 9FS

Tel: 01792 765600
Fax: 01792 765601
E-Mail: post@childcomwales.org.uk
Website: www.childcom.org.uk

Penrhos Manor
Oak Drive
Colwyn Bay
Conwy LL29 7YW

Tel: 01492 523333
Fax: 01492 523336
E-mail: post@childcomwales.org.uk
Website: www.childcom.org.uk

Children's Legal Centre
University of Essex
Wivenhoe Park
Colchester
Essex CO4 3SQ

Tel: 01206 872 466
Education Law advice line: 0845 456 6811
Fax: 01206 874 026
E-mail: clc@essex.ac.uk
Website: www.childrenslegalcentre.com

Publishes information leaflets, handbooks and a monthly bulletin covering all aspects of law and policy affecting children and young people in England and Wales.

Children's Rights Alliance
94 White Lion Street
London N1 9PF

Tel: 020 7278 8222
Fax: 020 7278 9552
E-mail: info@crae.org.uk
Website: www.crae.org.uk

Court Service
Customer Service Unit
5th Floor
Clive House
Petty France
London SW1H 9HD

Tel: 020 7189 2000 / 0845 456 8770
Fax: 020 7189 2732
E-mail: customerservicecshq@hmcourts-service.gsi.gov.uk
Website: www.hmcourts-service.gov.uk

Crimeline
Website: www.crimeline.info

A free weekly email update. It covers all aspects of the criminal justice system, but issues relating to youth justice are well covered. As well as giving information about implementation of new legislation it provides a summary of new cases with, in many cases, links to the official transcript.

Crown Prosecution Service
CPS Correspondence Unit
50 Ludgate Hill
London EC4M 7EX

Tel: 020 7796 8500
E-mail: enquiries@cps.gsi.gov.uk
Website: www.cps.gov.uk

The Code for Prosecutors as well as the CPS Legal Guidance may be accessed on the website. For legal guidance: www.cps.gov.uk/legal/index.html.

Department for Constitutional Affairs
Selborne House
54 Victoria Street
London SW1E 6QW
Tel: 020 7210 8500
E-mail: general.queries@dca.gsi.gov.uk
Website: www.dca.gov.uk

See www.dca.gov.uk/criminal/procrules_fin/index.htm for the Criminal Procedure Rules and the Consolidated Criminal Practice Direction.

Department for Education and Skills
Sanctuary Buildings
Great Smith Street
London SW1P 3BT

Tel: 0870 000 2288.
Fax: 01928 794248
E-mail: info@dfes.gsi.gov.uk
Website: www.dfes.gov.uk

The website has guidance on children's services and the operation of the Children Act 1989 issued since June 2003.

Department of Health
Richmond House
79 Whitehall
London SW1A 2NS

Tel 020 7210 4850
E-mail: dhmail@dh.gsi.gov.uk
Website: www.doh.gov.uk

The website has guidance on the operation of the Children Act 1989 issued since June 2003.

European Court of Human Rights
Council of Europe
67075 Strasbourg-Cedex
France

Tel: +33(0)3 88 41 20 18
Fax: +33(0)3 88 41 27 30
Website: www.echr.coe.int

The website contains a database of the court's decisions since 1960.

Home Office
2 Marsham Street
London SW1P 4DF

Tel: 020 7035 4848
Website: www.homeoffice.gov.uk

Policy questions regarding the youth justice system should be directed to the Youth Justice and Children Unit (formerly the Juvenile Offenders Unit).

Copies of Home Office Circulars may be found at www.circulars.homeoffice.gov.uk

Copies of the PACE Codes of Practice and operational guidance to police officers may be found at www.police.homeoffice.gov.uk

Information about anti-social behaviour orders may be found at www. crimereduction.gov.uk

The Home Office oversees the work of HM Chief Inspector of Prisons and HM Inspector of Probation. Copies of reports on young offender institutions and youth offending teams may be found on www.inspectorates.homeoffice.gov.uk

Statistical bulletins and research studies published by the Research, Development and Statistics directorate may be found at www.homeoffice.gov.uk/rds

House of Lords
Website (for judgments): www.publications.parliament.uk/pa/ld/ldjudgmt.htm

The website contains copies of all judgments of the Judicial Committee of the House of Lords since 1996.

Howard League for Penal Reform
The Howard League for Penal Reform
1 Ardleigh Road
London N1 4HS

Tel: 020 7249 7373
Fax:020 7249 7788

E-mail: info@howardleague.org
Website: www.howardleague.org.uk

The Howard League operates an advice line for young people in custody. The freephone number is 0808 801 0308, available Tuesday and Wednesday 11am to 5pm and Thursday 11am to 7pm.

Information Commissioner's Office
Wycliffe House
Water Lane
Wilmslow
Cheshire SK9 5AF

Tel: 01625545745
Fax: 01625 524510
E-mail: mail@ico.gsi.gov.uk
Website: www.ico.gov.uk

Judicial Studies Board
Millbank Tower
Millbank
London SW1P 4QU

Tel: 020 7217 4708
Fax: 020 7217 4779
E-mail: jsb.web@jsb.gsi.gov.uk
Website: www.jsboard.co.uk

A copy of the Youth Court Bench Book may be downloaded from the website.

Law Society
113 Chancery Lane
London WC2A 1PL

Tel: 020 7242 1222
E-mail: info.services@lawsociety.org.uk
Website: www.lawsociety.org.uk

The Guide to the Professional Conduct of Solicitors is available at www.guide.lawsociety.org.uk

Professional Ethics may be contacted on 0870 606 2577.

Legal Action Group
242 Pentonville Road
London N1 9UN

Tel: 020 7833 2931
Fax: 020 7837 6094
E-mail: lag@lag.org.uk
Website: www.lag.org.uk

Legal Services Commission
85 Gray's Inn Road
London WC1X 8TX

For regional offices see www.legalservices.gov.uk/about us/regions/regions.asp

Website: www.legalservices.gov.uk

Local Government Ombudsman for England
There are three Local Government Ombudsmen in England. Each of them deals with complaints from different parts of the country:

London boroughs north of the River Thames (including Richmond but not including Harrow or Tower Hamlets), Essex, Kent, Surrey, Suffolk, East and West Sussex, Berkshire, Buckinghamshire, Hertfordshire and the City of Coventry:

Local Government Ombudsman
10th Floor
Millbank Tower
Millbank
London SW1P 4QP

Tel: 020 7217 4620
Fax: 020 7217 4621

London Borough of Tower Hamlets, City of Birmingham, Solihull MBC, Cheshire, Derbyshire, Nottinghamshire, Lincolnshire, Warwickshire and the North of England (except the cities of Lancaster, Manchester and York:

Local Government Ombudsman
Beverley House
17 Shipton Road
York YO30 5FZ

Tel: 01904 380200
Fax: 01904 380269

London boroughs south of the River Thames (except Richmond) and Harrow; the cities of Lancaster, Manchester and York; and the rest of England:

Local Government Ombudsman
The Oaks No 2
Westwood Way
Westwood Business Park
Coventry CV4 8JB

Tel: 024 7682 0000
Fax: 024 7682 0001

For more information about making a complaint see www.lgo.org.uk/complain.htm.

Nacro
London office:
NACRO Youth Crime Section
169 Clapham Road
London SW9 0PU

Tel: 020 7582 6500
Fax: 020 7735 4666

Manchester office:
NACRO Youth Crime Section
First Floor, Princess House
105–107 Princess Street
Manchester M1 6DD

Tel: 0161 236 5271
Fax: 0161 236 5618

Website: www.nacro.org.uk

National Association of Youth Justice (NAYJ)
Website: www.nayj.org.uk

Established in 1994, the Association aims to promote the rights of, and justice for, children in trouble. The Association publishes a newsletter and the journal *Youth Justice* (jointly with Russell House Publishing) and organises training courses and an annual conference.

Membership is open to anyone involved or interested in the youth justice process.

For membership details download an application form from the website or contact:

Ken Hunnybun
Membership Secretary
NAYJ
4 Spring Close
Ratby
Leicester LE6 0XD

Tel: 0116 238 8354

NSPCC
Weston House,
42 Curtain Road
London EC2A 3NH

Tel: 020 7825 2500
Fax: 020 7825 2525
Website: www.nspcc.org.uk

NSPCC publications may be purchased via the website.

Office for Public Service Information
Website: www.opsi.gov.uk

The website has copies of all UK Acts of Parliament since 1988 and all statutory instruments since 1987, in their original form, ie not amended.

Parole Board
Grenadier House
99–105 Horseferry Road
London SW1P 2DD

Tel: 0870 420 3505
Fax: 020 7217 0118
E-Mail: info@paroleboard.gov.uk
Website: www.paroleboard.gov.uk

Prison and Probation Ombudsman
Ashley House
2 Monck Street
London SW1P 2BQ

Tel: 020 7035 2876 or 0845-010 7938
Fax: 020 7035 2860
Website: www.ppo.gov.uk

Prison Service Headquarters
Cleland House
Page Street
London SW1P 4LN

Tel: 020 7210 3000
Website: www.hmprisonservice.gov.uk

The website contains the up-to-date text of the Young Offender Rules as well as copies of relevant Prison Service Orders. There is also useful information about each institution including details of how to travel to the institution and visiting hours.

Decisions regarding licence recall are dealt with by the Release and Recall Section.

Head of Section (containing the Public Protection Team and Oral Hearings and Review Team) is based at:

Abell House
John Islip Street
London SW1P 4LH

Other recall casework teams are based at:

7th Floor
Amp House
Croydon CR0 2LX

Sentencing Guidelines Council
Sentencing Guidelines Secretariat
85 Buckingham Gate
London SW1E 6PD

Tel: 020 7411 5551
Fax: 020 7411 5571
E-mail: info@sentencing-guidelines.gsi.gov.uk
Website: www.sentencing-guidelines.gov.uk

The website has copies of all the definitive sentencing guidelines issued by the Council as well as a very useful digest of sentencing authorities derived from previous decisions of the Court of Appeal.

Welsh Assembly Government
Cathays Park
Cardiff CF10 3NQ

Tel: 0845 010 3300
Website: http://new.wales.gov.uk

The Welsh Assembly Government is the devolved government for Wales. Led by the First Minister, it is responsible for many issues, including health, education and children's services.

Legislation and guidance issued by the Welsh Assembly may be accessed via the website

Witness Service
Website: www.victimsupport.org/vs_england_wales/services/witness_services.
php

A national service provided by Victim Support which is available not just to the victims of crime but also to all witnesses whether prosecution or defence. The website has useful information and information leaflets for young witnesses which may be downloaded.

For contact details of local witness services go to: www.victimsupport.org/vs_england_wales/contacts/index.php

Young Minds
102 Clerkenwell Road
London EC1M 5SA

Tel: 020 7336 8445
Fax: 020 7336 8446
E-mail: info@youngminds.org.uk
Website: www.youngminds.org.uk

Works to promote the mental health of children and young people.

Youth Justice Board of England and Wales
11 Carteret Street
London SW1H 9DL

Tel: 020 7271 3033
Fax: 020 7271 3030
E-mail: enquiries@yjb.gov.uk
Website: www.youth-justice-board.gov.uk

Placements Clearinghouse: 0845 363 6363
E-mail: placements@yjb.gov.uk

Youth offending teams
Contact details for youth offending teams in England and Wales may be found at www.youth-justice-board.gov.uk/YouthJusticeBoard/YouthOffendingTeams/contactdetails.htm

Index